tongues of
Angels

tongues of
Men

tongues of

Angels

tongues of

Men

A BOOK OF SERMONS

Edited by

John F. Thornton and

Katharine Washburn

DOUBLEDAY

New York   London

Toronto   Sydney   Auckland

PUBLISHED BY DOUBLEDAY
a division of Random House, Inc.
1540 Broadway, New York, New York 10036

DOUBLEDAY and the portrayal of an anchor with a dolphin are trademarks
of Doubleday, a division of Random House, Inc.

Library of Congress Cataloging-in-Publication Data
Tongues of angels, tongues of men / edited by John F. Thornton
and Katharine Washburn. — 1st ed.
p.   cm.
Includes bibliographical references and indexes.
1. Sermons, Judaeo-Christian.   I. Thornton, John F., 1942–   .
II. Washburn, Katharine.
BV4241.T65   1998
252—DC21   98-27567
                                                   CIP

ISBN 0-385-48892-0

Book design by Donna Sinisgalli

To Myles M. Bourke, exemplar of *ars praedicandi*

JFT

To my children

KW

When Pulpits Did Like Beacons Flame

—A Dose for Chamberlain (1660)

Contents

III. "Great Was the Company of the Preachers"
The Medieval Pulpit

IV. "Behold I Will Make My Words in Thy Mouth Fire, and This People Wood, and It Shall Devour Them."
Rebirth, Reform, and Counter Reform

V. "When Pulpits Did Like Beacons Flame"
The Seventeenth Century

VIII. "The Bringing of Truth Through Personality"
The Nineteenth Century

IX. "Woe Is Unto Me If I Preach Not the Gospel"
The Twentieth Century

X. "Who Will Go for Us?"
Living Preachers

Though I speak with the tongues of men and of angels, and
have not charity, I am become as sounding brass, or a tinkling cymbal.

—1 Corinthians 13:1 (King James Version, 1611)

Introduction

"In the beginning was the Word, and the Word was with God. . . ." This book hopes to tell by example the story of how the Word has reached the ears of mankind for the past two millennia. It is a story more than it is a history because we are not historians and because, even if we were, the history of how the Word has been preached has been so multifarious and vast and far-flung that to our knowledge no historian has ever stepped forward claiming to have produced a complete and definitive account.[1]

We will, then, try to tell the story in another way—through the actual words of some of the world's greatest preachers. The thunder of those words, their reverberation in the spaces in which they were uttered, their unedited, *ex tempore* quality, the emotions, the thoughts, the compunction they evoked in their listeners, the mood of their bygone era or culture—these, sadly, we cannot supply. Instead we will try to do what Cortez and his men did in Keats's sonnet written on his astonishment at first reading Homer, when we, too, felt "like some watcher of the skies / When a new planet swims into his ken"—we will try to share with you our wild surmise at what we found on looking into the vast, beautiful ocean of sermon literature.

The Psalmist sang, "The Lord gave the word: Great was the company of the preachers." And indeed, when examined across the expanse of twenty centuries, the company of the preachers seems nearly numberless. Why is

---

[1] Although a good start is being made by Hughes Oliphant Old in the first two volumes of his series, *The Reading and Preaching of the Scriptures in the Worship of the Christian Church.* Vol. 1: *The Biblical Period;* Vol. 2: *The Patristic Age* (Grand Rapids, Mich.: William B. Eerdmans, 1998). In Vol. 1 he nonetheless demurs, "I really have to confess that writing the definitive history of preaching is quite beyond me. . . ."

it, we asked ourselves, that no standard collection of at least a representative handful of the greatest sermons ever preached is easily available to the common reader? Without it, anyone seriously interested in exploring this wide and deep reservoir of spiritual refreshment would be forced, as we were, to delve into the thousands upon thousands of fugitive and nearly inaccessible volumes of the collected—or, just as often, the uncollected and untranslated—works of preachers past and present—one sermon, one pamphlet, one (prospectively) good, bad, or indifferent preacher at a time. There are no road signs pointing directly to those sermons still alive and full of meaning for today—or pointing a warning away from those so timebound and dry as to have lost any power they may once have possessed. Our goal was to cram this one book to the muzzle with the best, the strongest, and the most readable sermons we could find, absent a lifetime in which to find them.

You have the results in your hands. It is not the first work of its kind, but it can safely be said that its predecessors are hoary with age and not much seen anymore around the home or on the library bookshelf. The works and lives and critical studies of preachers, Christian and Jewish, from which it has been compiled represent a staggering mountain of publication. The idea that two interested amateurs might scale it, two years after determining to make the ascent, no longer seems to us laughable or wildly overambitious but is now a completed endeavor.

What must be said is that the contents of this book could easily be repeated three or four times over with either the same or a completely different cast of preachers of equal fame and sermons of equal merit. We have included as much as the price of a book of reasonable length in a bookshop permitted. About what was left out, more below.

What Is Preaching?

Consider the English Congregationalist preacher John Henry Jowett (1864–1923), who asked, rhetorically, "The preacher, what is he?" and answered: herald, evangelist, logician, conversationalist. Some have found an invocation by the preacher in the prophetic mode, in the Lord's message to Isaiah after his lips were touched by a burning coal from the altar: "Go, and tell this people." In more recent times, among the most frequently mentioned definitions of "preaching" is that of Phillips Brooks, Episcopal bishop of Boston toward the end of the last century: "the communication of truth by man to men. It has two essential elements, truth and personality. . . . preaching is the bringing of truth through personality."[2]

A later preacher of renown, the American Harry Emerson Fosdick (1878–1969), touched on these key elements in an article he wrote in *Harper's* magazine in July 1928, "What Is the Matter with Preaching?":

> Every sermon should have for its main business the solving of some problem—a vital, important problem, puzzling minds, burdening consciences, distracting lives—and any sermon which thus does tackle a real problem, throw even a little light on it and help some individuals practically to find their way through it cannot be altogether uninteresting.

And this is his prayer for all preachers: "Whoever stands in a pulpit, bless Thou his spirit and touch his lips with a coal from off the altar that he may speak Thine everlasting Gospel, carrying the truth far into the hearts and consciences of those who hear."

From the Roman Catholic tradition, the Archbishop of Paris, Jean-Marie Cardinal Lustiger (see his sermon on St. Thérèse of Lisieux, p. 761), has commented:

> The homily is an integral part of the proclamation of the Gospel. For this reason, it is always given by an ordained minister (a priest or a bishop), and preferably it is given by the same priest who celebrates the Eucharist. The homily is neither a catechistic lesson nor an expression of the minister's personal views about life—nor is it a test of eloquence. It is a strict and unequivocal *mission:* the priest has the task of making meaningful to the particular group of people before him the Word of Christ that he has just proclaimed.
>
> The act of faith required of the people who listen to the homily is just as necessary as that required of the priest who is fulfilling his mis-

---

[2]Phillips Brooks, *On Preaching* (London: SPCK, 1965), p. 5. First given as a lecture series at Yale University in 1877.

sion. Remember the admonishment of Jesus after one of his sermons in parable: "Let everyone heed what he hears!" (Matt. 13:9.)[3]

The Right Reverend Paul Moore, Jr., Episcopal bishop, who retired in 1989 from the pulpit of New York City's Cathedral of St. John the Divine, notes, "The teaching you get in seminary is about the three-point sermon, and 'Make sure you base it on the liturgical context.' Some of our clergy *read* their sermons. It drives me wild. Preaching is not teaching, it's not lecturing. It's preaching. I think you should communicate as much as possible with your whole being. It's more like acting. And if you get Laurence Olivier up there, banging it out, it's something else." (*New York Times,* Jan. 14, 1998.)

So much self-help literature and advice of every sort is usually traceable, without much difficulty, to a handful of sources or even a single source. With preaching, this assumption, after skimming back through century after century of repetitive advice, takes us directly to the final part of a most interesting treatise by Augustine of Hippo entitled *On Christian Teaching (De Doctrina Christiana,* Book Four), completed about A.D. 427. It is considered the first extended and consistent look at the subject of who the preacher is and how he ought to go about his business.

Having trained to be a rhetorician, which was in fact his vocation in Carthage, Rome, and Milan until he was ordained at the age of thirty-seven, Augustine naturally began by considering the preacher as a special type of orator. Rhetoricians of the fourth century A.D. were already heirs to a confluence of Greek and Roman tradition at least a millennium in the making. Rhetoric, then, was for him no simple term dismissively descriptive of an overblown style of public speaking best forgotten; it was a living tradition, not only the ground on which rested public life—law, politics, philosophical debate—but the crucial means by which all effective human communication is most appropriately expressed. Augustine had read and memorized many of the works of the great writers on rhetoric in the Latin tradition, such as Cicero (106–43 B.C.) and Quintilian (ca. 35/40–ca. A.D. 100). So he began with the basic notion of the orator handed down from Cato (234–149 B.C.) as "a good man, skilled in speaking."

[3]Cardinal Jean-Marie Lustiger, *The Mass,* tr. by Rebecca Howell Balinski (San Francisco: Harper & Row, 1987), pp. 43–44.

For Augustine's purpose—part of which was to defend Christian preachers and what they had to say as being every bit as worthy of respect as the speech of their pagan fellows—each element in this definition could be retained and expanded in terms of Christian belief, i.e., "good," "man" (because the Church permitted only male bishops or those appointed by them to preach at a liturgy), "skilled," and "speaking." Around these basics he wove *On Christian Teaching,* a lovely tapestry on the art of preaching that circulated widely after his death. It appeared at the court of Charlemagne, and continued on into the Middle Ages and the writings of Cassiodorus, Abelard, Aquinas, and Erasmus, among many others. Though obscure to most modern readers in comparison with his *Confessions* or *The City of God,* in the Renaissance it was the first of Augustine's writings to be printed with movable type. And in the explosion of competitive preaching that came with the Reformation, Book Four by itself became the contemporary equivalent of a best-seller.

Here is a composite portrait of Augustine's preacher and what he does. He must first be a man of good character and a man of prayer before he is a man of words. He "must pray that God will place a good sermon on [his] lips." He must be a wise man and wisely choose his texts from Scripture; if he speaks with wisdom, eloquence will accompany his words, that is, his words will be suited to his audience, and—obeying the classical rules of rhetoric and grammar—thus render his audience favorable to his words, interested in his message, and receptive to its meaning. In describing the relationship of message to rhetoric, Augustine compares it to the master who goes forth from his home, followed by his ever-present slave, who never needs to be told he must follow along discreetly.

When a preacher speaks thus, he will bring heartfelt emotion to his words, and they will be holy, good, true, and just. Augustine also notes that a "crowd that is eager to learn tends to show by its movements whether it has understood. Until it does show this, the topic must be rolled around in a variety of different ways, . . ." which may account for the great length of many sermons, ancient or modern. If the hearers understand and are persuaded by the sermon, take delight in it, and obey its direction, their minds will be moved to good actions, and the preacher's goal will be accomplished.

The model of Augustine's preacher may be found in Mark: "Do not worry about what to say or how to say it; for you will be given words to speak when the time comes. For it is not you who speak, but the Spirit of your Father who speaks within you." (13:11.) Even so, Augustine notes that a wicked or insincere preacher can still deliver a good sermon if God's words are rightly explained (though it will do himself no good), and he is the first commentator to record—and deem acceptable—the practice of delivering someone else's sermon: "There are indeed some people who can give a good speech but not compose one. If they borrow from others something composed with eloquence and wisdom and commit it to memory and then bring that to their audience, they are not doing anything wrong, provided that they adhere to this role."

Of the types and classes of sermons, many accounts have been given. Over the centuries endless lists of sermon types have been compiled and refined. The great German preacher Friedrich Schleiermacher (1768–1834) left us ten volumes of his own sermons, among which one scholar identified the following: pastoral, ordinary, occasional, festal, confirmation, baptismal, funeral, burial, confessional, parenetic (moral exhortation), family life, national, expository, candidate, etc. To these might be added missionary, exegetical, prophetic, catechetical, Lenten, Easter, Christmas, university, controversial, children's, memorial, conversionist (e.g., in the thirteenth century Albigensian heretics were made to listen to such sermons and had their ears checked beforehand against cotton wads inserted to keep them out), Reformation, penitential, exhortational, eulogistic, wedding, dedication, jubilee, and dozens of other categories assigned by scholars and clergy. There is even a historical term for a short, informal sermonette, the *fervorino*.

In the pages of this book you will find a goodly selection of examples of these basic staples of preaching.

A Selective but Plausible History of Preaching

Our intention in compiling this book was emphatically not—and we repeat, for all edgy critics poised at this page—*not* to provide a full history of homiletics through examples. Nor did we ever intend to include only sermons of historical or theological or even sentimental importance (though a few do make their appearance, e.g., St. Francis's sermon to the birds, which did not appear until a century after his death in the collection called *The Little Flowers of St. Francis of Assisi*); nor even to identify what a putative consensus of practicing preachers, scholars, rhetoricians, and other experts might over time have concluded were the best preachers and their best sermons.

Our reasons for our approach are, first, that we wanted to offer the interested reader a chance to encounter the preaching on equal terms, that is, not to be obliged first to become for the nonce a theologian, a scholar of sectarian controversy, or a church historian. We wanted the reader to experience the fresh, new taste of these time-honored words. We felt that if *we* liked each sermon we chose the reader might well, too. So some idiosyncrasy entered in. And so, because the book has not been prepared for a final examination by a board of major-seminary homiletics-department chairmen, we hope this nonetheless represents a net benefit for the common reader.

Nor did we determine we were under any obligation to offer the one sermon the reader may ever have heard of by any given preacher under consideration; e.g., Jonathan Edwards's "Sinners in the Hands of an Angry God" springs immediately to mind (included). Or Billy Graham on John 3:16, the verse so favored for homemade signs brought to sports stadiums (not included).

THE FIRST SERMON

The Sermon on the Mount, three chapters of the gospel of Matthew, with which this collection opens, takes fifteen minutes, more or less, to deliver in English. Its hallowed place in Scripture was recognized from the earliest times. Its beauty and concision have made it the keystone of the Christian faith and way of life, and commentaries on it could easily comprise a lifetime's reading all by themselves. For most of us, if we thought about it, it doubtless stands as the paradigm of the sermon, indeed as the Sermon of Sermons. Yet one writer, the late Japanese novelist and Christian convert Shusako Endo, in *A Life of Jesus* (1973), found it to be the exact moment of Jesus' failure in his earthly ministry, at least in the ears of his contemporary auditors:

A commotion stirred through the crowd. They never dreamed that Jesus would react to their shouted expectations with an amazing answer like this. The rabbinical Judaism on which they had been raised was by no means in total disregard of the notion of love, but the rabbis had not inculcated this ideal of love as the value par excellence to ignite their religious fervor. There had been no thought of exalting to such an extreme the value of those who are poor in spirit, and meek, or who mourn and are pure in heart. What on earth was Jesus attempting to imply in words like these? . . .

It shook the crowd. Now they had their unequivocal answer from Jesus—flat refusal. The crowd had expected no such response to their nationalistic clamor. They sat there disillusioned. There was simply no reconciling the image of Jesus, on which they had centered their dreams, and the reality of Jesus when he delivered to them his own call for action. Jesus turned down the popular demand in words which have since become famous. People got to their feet and began to move down the hill. . . .[4]

Regardless of its original effectiveness, the Sermon on the Mount should not be regarded as Jesus' first sermon. To examine that, we must look at the beginning of his ministry:

And he came to Nazareth, where he had been brought up: and, as his custom was, he went into the synagogue on the sabbath day, and stood up for to read. And there was delivered unto him the book of the prophet Isaiah. And when he had opened the book, he found the place where it was written, "The spirit of the Lord is upon me, because he hath anointed me to preach the gospel to the poor; he hath sent me to heal the broken-hearted, to preach deliverance to the captive, and recovering of sight to the blind, to set at liberty them that are bruised, to preach the acceptable year of the Lord." And he closed the book and he gave it again to the minister, and sat down. And the eyes of all them that were in the synagogue were fastened on him. And he began to say unto them, "This day is this Scripture fulfilled in your ears." (Luke 4:16–21.)

[4] Tr. by Richard A. Schuchert, S.J. (New York: Paulist Press, 1978), pp. 67–68.

Here we have ground zero of Christian preaching, the moment when the Jewish tradition out of which it grew is now transformed through the person of Jesus. The occasion of the Sabbath day, the attendance at a liturgy in the town synagogue, the appointment to read, the standing up, the giving by the attendant of the scroll of a book of the Bible, the reading aloud of a passage from it to the congregation, and finally the sitting down to give a spontaneous talk about its meaning—each of these elements came to form the tradition of preaching that has survived with so little change that they might amount to instructions for a Christian service anywhere in the world on any Sunday.

THE JEWISH ORIGIN OF PREACHING
AND THE JEWISH SERMON

For the ultimate origin of these elements, however, we must go back six centuries earlier to the period after the destruction of the Temple—and the possibility for worship there—and the Babylonian Exile that followed, to the Book of Nehemiah. There the task of reconstituting the religious life of the Israelites, who had now been allowed to return to Jerusalem, is described as falling to Ezra:

> And all the people gathered themselves together as one man into the street that was before the water gate; and they spake unto Ezra the scribe to bring the book of the law of Moses, which the Lord had commanded to Israel. And Ezra the priest brought the law before the congregation both of men and women, and all that could hear with understanding, upon the first day of the seventh month. And he read therein . . . from the morning until midday, before the men and the women, and those that could understand; and the ears of all the people were attentive unto the book of the law. And Ezra the scribe stood upon a pulpit of wood, which they had made for the purpose; . . . And Ezra opened the book in the sight of all the people, for he was above all the people; and when he opened it, all the people stood up; and Ezra blessed the Lord the great God. And all the people answered, Amen, Amen, with lifting up their hands: and they bowed their heads, and worshipped the Lord with their faces to the ground . . . and the Levites caused the people to understand the law: and the people stood

in their place. So they read in the book in the law of God distinctly, and gave the sense, and caused them to understand the reading. (8:1–8.)

Though there is some dispute among scholars about the precise origin of the synagogue service, who could doubt that here we have the prototype of the liturgy in which we glimpse Jesus participating in Nazareth? The Jewish tradition of teaching from set passages of the Torah and the prophets—the Midrash—would take its own course of development over the centuries. But it is fascinating to think of the first pulpit being erected and the first homily being delivered from it two and a half millennia ago.

The oratory of Moses in Exodus, as well as the speeches of the Old Testament prophets, can certainly be read as early and powerful examples of sermons. We decided, however, that their availability, for the general reader who has read the Hebrew Bible, made their inclusion superfluous in this collection. There is, nonetheless, an early model for the sermon in the Jewish tradition, beginning with the Levites' (i.e., the descendants of the tribe of Levi, appointed assistants to priests in the Temple) explication of the Torah at a public assembly.

The sermon, in Hebrew, is called *derashah*, coming from the word for preacher, *darshan*. After the exiles' return from Babylonia in the fifth century B.C., the study of the Torah became a national object of dedication and a radiant source of spiritual illumination for the Jewish people. As glimpsed above, the prophet Ezra, arriving with the blessing and mission of the philo-Semitic Persian king Cyrus, was given power to reestablish the Jewish state; Ezra's reading, beginning at daybreak, of the Torah scroll democratized the holy document and ushered in the tradition of the public sermon. In the beginning, its rituals were simple. With the unrolling of the book, in scroll form, Ezra the scribe pronounced a blessing on a large assembly in the main square of Jerusalem and gave a public reading of the Torah from dawn until noon. In the first century B.C., Philo of Alexandria observed that the sermon, delivered in Greek, in the Egyptian capital under the Ptolemys, had become a cornerstone of Sabbath worship.

By that time the Jewish state had come to an end. In A.D. 70 the last remnants of the Jewish state collapsed with the destruction of the Temple during the Roman emperor Titus's war and the fall of the fortress of Masada at the Dead Sea, where an army of zealots manned a siege that ended in mass suicide. Thereafter, the history of the Jewish sermon is fused with the history of the Jews in the Diaspora. Out of dispersal and persecution came the most important books of rabbinic Judaism, including the tradition of homilies called *midrashim:* playful versions of biblical stories, fables, fairy tales, and folk tales whose mixture of symbolism, intellectual mischief, and moral seriousness have shaped the literature of Europe and America for two millennia.

The Judaeo-Christian tradition of the sermon has its deepest roots in the emphasis placed on preaching after the extinction of the Temple cult on Mount Zion. Both Jesus of Nazareth and St. Paul of Tarsus are seen in the rabbinic tradition as popular itinerant preachers, much like the mendicant friars of the Middle Ages. But there were two distinct practitioners of the Jewish sermon, each with different skills and each serving different requirements of the community. The rabbi himself was not expected to preach but simply to clarify questions of ritual and to interpret Jewish law as it applied to daily life. His colleagues were the *darshan,* himself a rabbi learned in Torah and in Talmudic hermeneutics, with a powerful base in scholarship, and the *maggid.* When the *darshan* preached (always in Hebrew), the sermons were close readings of biblical texts. He was a paid functionary in the community and spoke on Sabbath afternoons in the synagogue. The collective reputation of *darshans* frequently upheld the highest claims of scholarship, but along with this dazzling display of learning came a decay into an occasionally sterile pedantry and an arid casuistry, qualifying them for the sort of indictments made of medieval scholastics for supposedly counting how many angels could dance on the head of a pin.

The wandering *maggidim* preached in a style during the Middle Ages and the early Renaissance which depended on the sophistication and culture of their audience. In Spain, Provence, and Renaissance Italy, the sermons of the *maggidim* occupied an intellectual high ground; in the world of Yiddish-speaking Jewry in Central and Eastern Europe, perceived as a cultural backwater inhabited by peasants and small merchants, the sermon was shaped by its ethical content, its moralistic fervor, and, like a musical note from faraway Western Europe, a cascade of allusions to the Bible and to the rabbinical authorities. The Yiddish vernacular language made the sermon intelligible to its hearers in Germany and the Polish provinces. In these small ghetto communities of the Jewish *shtetl,* the roving *maggid* spoke during the midafternoon in the synagogue, his sermon having little connection with the prayer service. These were sermons designed for a Jewish market town in Eastern Europe, the origin in the eighteenth century of the popular pietistic and mystical movement of the Hasidim. The charismatic rabbis known as *zaddikim* were its ecstatic advocates, the intellectual progeny of Israel Baal Shem (ca. 1700–60), whose surviving heirs, after the Holocaust, have found still another homeland, long after the virtual extinction of the Jewish communities of Russia and Poland.

In Italy and medieval Spain the sermon was delivered from a raised platform in the synagogue, during the morning of the Sabbath or a holy day, just after the reading of the Torah. These orations had, in their world, a prestige close to that John Donne enjoyed in early seventeenth-century London. The great French essayist Montaigne has testified to their eloquence and grandeur.

Our collection does not follow the Jewish tradition much past the eighteenth century and gives only a small sample of its power to comfort, exhort, and laugh at the folly and imaginative wisdom of a world waiting for the Messiah. There were, in fact, two schools of *maggidim,* the larger referred to as the "awakeners," or "terror *maggidim.*" Their fulminations were directed toward the miserable sinners in the ghetto audiences of the Slavic countries where they journeyed on foot, wagon, and horseback. These firebrands—familiar to us from their counterparts in the ages of Knox, Calvin, and Wesley—had colleagues known as the "gentle *maggidim,*" the earthy, folkloric, and tolerant preachers whose understanding of human frailty was coupled with an inexhaustible sense of humor, a taste for irony, and a wit that survived centuries of persecution and despair.

A sense of impending disaster no doubt shaped this double tradition, one which this book can only lightly represent. In the nineteenth century the new Reform movement in Germany took the sermon down still another road, one compounded of the political, moral, and cultural hopefulness of Zionism. The Jewish Reform movement's founders made the Lutheran tradition of the sermon an integral part of the worship service. In modern Orthodox and Conservative synagogues in Europe and America, the discussion of *halakhic,* or legal, material remained essential to the sermon. At the same time, the role of social critic, invented and developed by

speakers in the Jewish pulpit from the prophets on through the tragic witnesses to the suffering of the Diaspora, came into its own in the social flux
of twentieth-century America. An assimilating drive led to a greater influence from the Protestant sermon in both the carpentry and the tone of the
sermon in the contemporary synagogue. But the binding force between the
Christian sermon and the Jewish, whether delivered in Yiddish in Brooklyn,
in Hebrew in contemporary Jerusalem, or in literary English in late twentieth-century London, must lie in the great weight given to passages from
Scripture and in the emphasis, in both traditions, on the memory of the sacred text.

THE APOSTOLIC ERA

It is likely, although the gospels record no literal examples of preaching, that
Jesus first sent his apostles to speak at synagogue services in the small towns
of Judea. And it is clear in the Acts of the Apostles that after his death his
followers took their mission to the synagogues of the Jewish communities
from Jerusalem to Antioch to Rome itself. The brief talks that are recounted
from their travels are probably a composite residue of many actual examples of the first Christian sermons.

From the period between the death of the last apostles and disciples
who knew Jesus and the early Church Fathers of the late second century, no
real sermons have come down to us. This is probably because the Church,
in its pioneering and experimenting phase, had not yet evolved to self-
conscious acts of historical record-keeping. The earliest preaching, therefore, was of a simple sort, mostly consisting of paraphrases or basic
explanations of Scripture passages read before the breaking of the bread and
delivered as extemporaneous and heartfelt reactions to the readings. A description survives from the mid-second century in the writing of Justin
Martyr: "On the day called Sunday there was a meeting in one place . . .
and the memoirs of the apostles or the writings of the prophets are read as
long as time permits. When the reader has finished, the president in a discourse urges and invites us to the imitation of these noble things." And, like
Jesus in Nazareth, the bishop was usually seated on his chair when he spoke.

It is when we reach the figure of Origen (184–254) of the Egyptian
Christian community at Alexandria that we encounter the first series of preserved homilies. He was nearly fifty before he was ordained a priest, though

his preaching had begun much earlier. Of course, at that time and for centuries to come, only a bishop could preach in his own diocese without permission; all others—even a bishop visiting a diocese not his own—had to be given license to preach. And bishops, thus charged to preach, were in fact strongly exhorted to do so as often as they could. Origen left behind two hundred homilies, and his series on the gospel of Luke is the first such example of its kind.

It is worth noting something about the form of the sermon. For our purpose, the term is interchangeable with "homily," though there are many subtle historical distinctions to be made for the curious, e.g., the former can be considered a more expansive, often prophetic form of speech, the latter, more typically linked to the interpretation of a set passage—or, in a series, a set book—of Scripture, or *pericope,* to give it its technical name (pron. pear·ik´·oh·pee´) read as part of a liturgy. By this time the twofold form of the Christian liturgy had become clearly established: the liturgy of the Word and the liturgy of the Eucharist. Those who had not received baptism as adults (infant baptism was as yet unknown) were called the catechumens and were permitted to hear the homily preached but could not remain for the celebration of the Eucharist.

THE GOLDEN AGE OF PATRISTIC PREACHING

After Origen a great, glorious delta of preaching by the Fathers of the Church began to spread out east and west far into the early Middle Ages. It divided into the Greek Fathers—especially three from Cappadocia (modern eastern Turkey), the brothers Basil the Great and Gregory of Nyssa, and Gregory of Nazianzus—and the Latin Fathers, such as Zeno of Verona, Ambrose of Milan, and Jerome, whose Latin Vulgate Bible translation would provide the texts for Western preaching through the Renaissance to the Reformation.

Standing tallest in this mountain range of discourse were the twin peaks of John Chrysostom, fourth-century Patriarch of Constantinople, and his contemporary Augustine, bishop of Hippo in North Africa. Each had his own style of preaching, to be sure, but both hewed to the biblical text read out at the liturgy on any given day and both provided clear, pastoral instruction to their congregations. Augustine once even joked about having unexpectedly to preach on an unprepared topic when the lector read the wrong passage from Scripture! He preached on it nonetheless. Chrysostom, whom Pope Pius X designated the patronal saint of all preachers, has left many side comments in sermons admonishing his hearers to stop breaking in with applause—an early expression of audience participation that would emerge again with the evangelical preaching of Methodism fourteen centuries later.

Thus, against this backdrop of a waxing Church and a waning Roman Empire now split politically in two, the work of these early Fathers, along with such others as Leo the Great (d. 461), Caesarius of Arles (d. 542), and Gregory the Great (d. 604), began to accumulate into a significant body of sermon literature. The endless raging of theological heresy and dispute that had provoked so much careful and aggressive pulpit teaching of basic doctrine had proved a boon for preaching and provided a basis for the next notable period.

THE MIDDLE AGES

With the rise of monasticism, first among Egyptian and Jewish converts to Christianity and later spreading throughout the eastern Mediterranean and thence to Europe by the seventh century, monasteries had begun to represent both stability and a focal point for Christians living in a far-flung empire that had lost its center. Through the institution of the papacy, the Church provided some of the missing continuity. Pope Gregory the Great had established the order of the mass as the basic form of worship and gave strong prominence to preaching, being himself a notable pulpit figure. Nonetheless, the tradition of strong, original preaching so characteristic of the Fathers now began to dry up. In its place arose the common practice of reading past sermons instead of preaching new ones. A type of collection known as the *homiliarium* became the increasingly popular way to give encouragement and instruction, as the old vigor and practice of Greco-Roman public rhetoric waned in dying cities overrun by new groups of invaders with names like Vandals, Goths, Franks, and so on. These sermon books were gathered out of the sermons and writings of the Fathers, in the West especially from Augustine, and copies and still more copies were made. For a clergy without formal training (remember that the seminary as an institution for the preparation of the religious would not emerge until the Counter Reformation of the late sixteenth century), such compilations were a real benefit, if not a godsend.

Among others, they were prepared by such medieval figures as the Venerable Bede and at the command of no less a personage than Charlemagne (742?–814) himself. Priests who had a difficult enough time translating the Scripture readings into the vernacular tongues of Europe (Anglo-Saxon, German, Italian, Gaelic, etc.) now had real help with sermons similarly translated and ready made. The great monasteries had undergone various subdivisions and reforms over the centuries but had always remained guardians of the settled practices of the Church's worship. Within their precincts attention was generally paid to the liturgical year, not only Sunday after Sunday, but on the great feast days and especially at Christmas and Easter, with their respective periods of preparation, Advent and Lent. The intensified call to the Christian to engage in prayer, fasting, and almsgiving also brought with it a marked increase in the frequency and intensity of preaching that exhorted one and all to repentance and preparation of the soul.

Throughout this period, despite the decline of original preaching, the popularity of preachers, many of them itinerant, was consistently high. An entry in the *Catholic Encyclopedia* (1910) noted, "so popular was preaching, and so deep the interest taken in it, that preachers commonly found it necessary to travel by night, lest their departure should be prevented." It has been estimated that nearly 100,000 sermons have survived from the late Middle Ages alone. Concurrent with the reality that the pulpit was the central means of public communication was an interest in the method of giving a successful sermon. Manuals on the art of preaching, the *ars praedicandi,* abounded at this time. Their emphasis on allegorical interpretation had its correlative in the explosion of figurative sculpture, stained glass, and manuscript decoration that perhaps tried to tell without words to unlettered hearers what was not being revealed from the pulpit.

THE CRUSADES, THE UNIVERSITIES, AND MENDICANT PREACHERS

Our preaching focus has been on medieval Europe, watching it decentralize and lose some of its sophistication and power in the turmoil that attended the end of the Roman Empire. Meanwhile, the rise of Islam, and the threat it presented to secular and religious powers, brought about a unique period of preaching fervor when Pope Urban II traveled to France late in the summer of 1095. There, at the Council of Clermont, on a platform outside the city gate, he appealed for help for the Eastern Christians:

> . . . the Turks were advancing into the heart of Christian lands, mal-treating the inhabitants and desecrating their shrines. . . . [The Pope] stressed the special holiness of Jerusalem and described the sufferings of the pilgrims that journeyed there. Having painted the sombre pic-ture, he made his great appeal. Let western Christendom march to the rescue of the East. Rich and poor alike should go. They should leave off slaying each other and fight instead a righteous war, doing the work of God; and God would lead them. For those who died in battle there would be absolution and the remission of sins. Life was miserable and evil here, with men wearing themselves out to the ruin of their bod-ies and their souls. Here they were poor and unhappy, there they would be joyful and prosperous and true friends of God. There must be no delay. . . .
>
> Urban spoke with fervour and with all the art of a great orator. The response was immediate and tremendous. Cries of "Deus le volt!"— "God wills it!"—interrupted the speech.[5]

Coincidental with the early Crusades was the flowering of monastic reform. If the hundreds of primarily Benedictine monasteries dotting the hills and valleys of Europe represented the spiritual center of Europe dur-ing the early Middle Ages, there was a positive outburst of monastic reform and new foundation beginning in the eleventh century and finding its great-est champion in the twelfth century in Bernard of Clairvaux, the most no-table preacher of his age. In addition to preaching against the Albigensian heresy in Languedoc and preaching the Second Crusade, which was a fail-ure, Bernard alone founded some seventy-five monasteries during his life-time and at his death in 1153 left behind an unfinished sermon series on the Song of Songs, a favorite medieval text because it is so unusually rich in pos-sibility for allegorical interpretation. (See an example from it on page 158.)

However, the apogee of the new monastic movement, once reached, still fell short of the need of the ordinary folk for solid, regular preaching

[5]Steven Runciman, *The First Crusade* (Cambridge University Press, 1951, 1980), pp. 61–62.

on Church doctrine, moral counsel, and gospel proclamation. The overall awakening of commerce, communication, and general movement through-out Europe at this time threw into relief the cloistered, interior-looking dimension of monastic life. Moreover, the general level of ignorance and apathy shown by local clergy with respect to preaching, with some notable exceptions, filled the air with a demand for reform. Thus were born the mendicant orders.

It is not to be thought that itinerant preaching had no prior existence. Indeed its history stretched back to the gospel itself when Jesus sent his disciples out to evangelize the countryside (e.g., "Behold, I send you forth as sheep in the midst of wolves." Matt. 10:16). But the effectiveness, the authority, and the character of these wandering preachers had become questionable by the beginning of the thirteenth century, when two remarkable men appeared—Francis of Assisi (b. 1181/82) and Dominic de Guzman (b. 1170). Each would found a religious order devoted to preaching. But no longer would their members be stable like the monks of old but rather mendicant (literally, "begging") and mobile. These new Franciscans, Dominicans, Augustinians, and Carmelites would be known as friars and would be sent to all the cities and towns of Europe, where the greatest number of those in need of repentance could readily be reached with their preaching. The charisma, the fervor, the exemplary virtue shown in the lives of these early mendicants induced wave after wave of new vocations and the multiplication of preachers. Though their motivating ideals of radical poverty and renunciation of the world proved hard to maintain, their inspiration carried the growth of the orders along for many generations.

The friars fanned out to preach in churches and cathedrals and often, because of the crowds, outdoors. St. Francis's first biographer, Thomas of Celano, tells us that his preaching was very simple, accomplished not by compounding subtle theological distinctions but by speaking directly and fervently, "as if he had made his whole body a tongue." Another friar, Hugh of Digne, whose voice was described as like a trumpet, was so moving that when he spoke his listeners shook like rushes in the water; still another, Berthold of Regensburg (b. 1210), speaking in the German vernacular, preached to large open-air congregations from an improvised pulpit, which flew a little flag so anyone could determine the wind's direction and take his or her seat for the preaching accordingly. Such sermons were often filled with colorful folk stories and accounts of miracles and marvels of all sorts. They were designed to hold the attention of their mostly illiterate hearers. But this is not to say that erudite Latin sermons were not also commonly preached in monasteries, cathedrals, and at the new universities.

Together with the need for more preachers was the necessity to educate them to their task. The rise of the universities of Europe also began in the twelfth and thirteenth centuries. Growing out of monastery schools devoted to teaching scriptural exegesis and to codifying and administering Church law, their theological interests were explosively supplemented by the arrival of new Latin translations, via the Crusades and Arabic, of the complete works of Aristotle, thereby bringing new tools for studying and analyzing doctrine and its application. The friars thronged the classes available at the Universities of Paris, Bologna, and elsewhere to hear the teaching of Peter Abelard, Albert the Great, or Thomas Aquinas, among many others.

The excitement and newness of this Aristotle-based "scholastic" philosophy would eventually give way to rigid, prescribed ways of thinking, and the enthusiasm of the friars, to tyranny and oppression. The Crusades, successful beyond all reasonable expectation at first, eventually devolved into searches for adversaries and miscreants closer to home, producing the Inquisition, over which for the most part the friars were given charge. Ever reforming, ever in need of reform, each of the Church's signal successes seemed to hold the seeds of decay; yet each period of decay also seemed to hold the seeds of new growth.

By the end of the Middle Ages, if preaching in Europe was now more widespread, frequent, and available, it was also delivered through the means of an institution that increasingly had come to be seen as disordered, avaricious, invasive, and resistant to sensible change. Symptoms of its problems were the appearance of individuals and movements that challenged—directly by openly denying or, indirectly, by simply ignoring—the doctrine or authority of the Church. Considering all this, however, it is well to remember something we have no modern concept of or feel for—daily life as citizens in a theocratic world.

In such a world, where popes could often bend kings and emperors to their will, where public order was sustained and maintained by a civil order inextricably bound up with an ecclesiastical order, and where the assumption of universal assent to Christianity in all its doctrines and practices was a given, tolerance was neither an objective nor even a fully formed idea:

> . . . we cannot properly conceive of a State which gives corporate recognition to a revealed religion, which takes it for granted that there are Three Persons in one Godhead as it takes it for granted that two and two makes four. We do not realize how intimately, in such a community, the interests of religion are bound up with those of public morality and of social order; how natural (and, we may add, how just) is the suspicion that a secret sect which attacks the truth of revealed theology attacks also the moral presuppositions of the whole community.[6]

THE REFORMATION

Though the word was not used to designate it at the time, the Reformation—and the sometimes mirror-image reaction to it, the Catholic Reformation, or Counter Reformation—functions usefully as the right term for purposes of this rapid account of the sixteenth and seventeenth centuries of preaching history. (Even today in Germany, the cradle of the Reformation, the adjective used for "Protestant" is "Evangelical.")

If we have thus far visited the Apostolic, the Patristic, and the Mendicant eras of preaching, we now come to a period unsurpassed in Church history for the all-encompassing variety, intensity, and life-or-death consequences of its preaching. It began with foreshadowing figures of dissent like John Wyclif in England, Savonarola, the Dominican puritan of Florence, and Jan Hus of Bohemia, and by the opening of the sixteenth century, the tension in the pulpit was palpable. Despite the growth of new forms of devotion epitomized by Thomas à Kempis (d. 1471) in his *The Imitation of Christ,* and despite the excitement of a new humanistic scholarship sown across Europe by the cosmopolite Desiderius Erasmus of Rotterdam (d. 1536), the Church was on a collision course with history.

[6]Ronald Knox, from the Introduction to A. L. Maycock, *The Inquisition: From Its Establishment to the Great Schism* (New York and London: Harper & Brothers, 1927), p. xiii.

A liberal by our standards, in his own day Erasmus believed, as did the majority of churchmen, that reform from within was still possible. Taking up "the apostolate of the pen," he worked intently to make it a reality. One of his treatises, a manual for preachers entitled *Ecclesiastes,* stated his belief that "If elephants can be trained to dance, lions to play, and leopards to hunt, surely preachers can be taught to preach." In 1516 he published his landmark edition of the New Testament in Greek. Replying in 1519 to a criticism of it, he wrote, "My New Testament has been out now for three years. Where are the heresies, schisms, tempests, tumults, brawls, hurricanes, devastations, shipwrecks, floods, general disasters, and anything worse you can think of?" Two years earlier an Augustinian hermit named Martin Luther had nailed ninety-five pieces of his mind to the door of his parish church in Wittenberg. The shipwreck had already begun.

Wittenberg, Zurich, Geneva, and Canterbury. Luther, Ulrich Zwingli, John Calvin, Henry VIII. A fifth site and a fifth protagonist of the Reformation might be named: Mainz and Johannes Gutenberg:

> By the end of the fifteenth century printing presses existed in over two hundred cities and towns. An estimated six million books had been printed and half of the thirty thousand titles were on religious subjects. More books were printed in the forty years between 1460 and 1500 than had been produced by scribes and monks throughout the entire Middle Ages. Religious books continued to dominate the presses through the first decade of the Reformation. . . .[7]

It took three hundred sheepskins to make a manuscript Bible. With the invention of movable type and the equally important invention of a way to make cheap paper, the preaching of a pulpit in a parish church in Constance could be heard again in Scotland, a debate over doctrine in Worms could be analyzed in Rome. Though only an estimated three or four percent of Europe's peoples could read, the war of the pamphlets had begun. And most of the pamphlets were sermons or commentary on them. Soon they would lead to real wars and an era of persecution and bloodshed over

[7]Steven Ozment, *The Age of Reform, 1250–1550: An Intellectual and Religious History of Late Medieval and Reformation Europe* (New Haven, Conn.: Yale University Press, 1980), pp. 199–201.

new religio-political realities that would be prolonged for a century and a half.

At the center of the hurricane was the pulpit. From it was proclaimed the Word. Never before had preaching of the gospel taken on so deep and sacramental a form as it did during the Reformation. As the old monasteries closed, as the altars were stripped, as the saints' images were stolen or burned, as the vessels and the vestments of the mass disappeared, as the meaning of the Eucharist was questioned on every side, the pulpit seemed only to grow in strength and importance with every ritual doubted or discarded.

There is an anonymous old satirical woodcut whose meaning saves us at least a thousand words of explanation by attempting to show the difference between Calvin and the Pope. Flanking a large set of scales in the foreground are, on one side, a bank of bishops, cardinals, and priests, and, on the other, a bank of sober Genevans all in modest black. On one scale stands a monk together with the heavy keys of Peter and the triple-tiered crown of the Pope. Another monk is pulling hard on the same side to offset the irresistible weight resting on the ground in the opposite scale: a single copy of the Bible.

Critical to the Reformation and its urge to rid Christianity of the superstitions and sometimes absurd rules and pietistic practices accreted over the centuries was the primacy of Scripture—and the Church Fathers—first read aloud and then given intense exegesis. For Luther, religion was "nothing if Christ is not preached." From 1509 until the week he died in 1546, he preached continuously, occasionally four new sermons on a single Sunday, leaving us some two thousand examples. He always searched his text for the *Herzpunkt,* or heart of the matter, and his forceful, direct use of the vernacular set the tone for much Protestant preaching in generations to come. He put into practice his belief that "the ears alone are the organ of the Christian man."

John Calvin preached some three hundred sermons a year, and more than a thousand can still be read. In contrast to the traditional Catholic liturgical practice of reading and preaching on Scripture selections formally assigned to each Sunday and feast day, his liberating devotion to the Bible resulted in the preaching of long series on individual books of the Bible, verse after verse—a teaching method the Church Fathers before him had used. Similarly, Ulrich Zwingli, a Swiss priest and Bible scholar, would preach the entire gospel of Matthew, opening the Greek text before him in the pulpit. The reaction of one of his hearers, a young humanist named Thomas Platter, has been described as follows:

> So great was [Platter's] ardor for ancient tongues that he supported himself through manual labor by day and at night studied with sand in his mouth, that the gritting against his teeth might keep him awake. This lad, so passionately eager to master the wisdom of the ages, when he heard from the pulpit the complete, unadulterated Word of God, for so many centuries withheld from the people, declared that he felt as if he were being pulled up by the hair of his head. The news of the discovery of America had produced no such excitement.[8]

A favorite contrast found in the woodcuts that often decorated the pamphlets and books of these polemical times showed two pulpits: in one, the Word of God was preached; in the other, the mere word of the Pope.

PAUL'S CROSS

The old quip that the Church of England was founded on the testicles of Henry VIII has more than an iota of truth. The truth in the jest is that in contrast to the clearly discernible new sects of Christianity springing up in specific regions of Europe, England's religious scene—from Henry's self-appointment as head of a national church in 1534 until the formal recognition of greater religious tolerance with the Glorious Revolution of 1688–89—might be likened less to the interesting panorama of a Renaissance tapestry than to some riotous Jackson Pollock action painting. Writing of Thomas More, C. S. Lewis called his era a "coarse and courageous century."

Perhaps a way to capture a feel for what was going on is to take a compressed look at the one place that became the epicenter of English public religious life and politics for two centuries: the outdoor pulpit in St. Paul's

---

[8]Roland H. Bainton, *The Reformation of the Sixteenth Century,* enlarged ed. (Boston: Beacon Press, 1952, 1985), p. 83.

churchyard in London, known as Paul's Cross. Though Christianity has had its famous pulpits from Constantinople to the Ebenezer Baptist Church in Atlanta, none has been host to a greater variety of preachers, politicians in prophets' robes, royals and commoners, compromisers and crackpots, eloquence and bombast, love and hatred.

A public place for sermons and secular proclamations for several centuries even before the church was built, Paul's Cross by the sixteenth century had become a crossroads in every sense. No matter what the weather, political, theo- or meteorological, appointed preachers were summoned by episcopal and royal authority to Paul's Cross to proclaim the gospel every Sunday until it was finally shut down under Oliver Cromwell in the 1640s. Standing in the open air, in a raised, covered pulpit with a cross on top and the customary hourglass at his side, each preacher talked for his allotted hour or two to the most varied crowd imaginable—ranging from monarchs, august clergy, and nobility in special open-air stalls to the lord mayor and his aldermen, to commoners and even pets and livestock tethered at the perimeters. Men and women sat on wooden benches or stood in separate sections. It resembled not a little the Elizabethan and Jacobean theater scene in Shakespeare's day (although the crowds at Paul's Cross far outdrew any contemporary theater production). And no matter whether the old Catholicism or the new forms of Protestantism were ascendant, the relentless parade of preachers never failed to fill the air. A short list would include: Thomas Cranmer, Hugh Latimer, Nicholas Ridley, John Foxe, Henry Smith, John Donne, and William Laud. These few represent a far larger pool of preachers drawn from the ranks of Church of England hierarchy, the universities of Oxford and Cambridge, chaplains to royalty, vicars of outlying parishes, and so on.

In the words of the Victorian Thomas Carlyle, "Paul's Cross [was] a kind of *Times Newspaper,* but edited partly by Heaven itself . . . a most important entity." Like some combination of a buzzing hive and a national loudspeaker system, we assemble from the annual records of its personnel and events a rich babble of voices, ideas, gossip, hobbyhorses, party-line politics, self-promotion, apologetics, recantation, and occasionally rising above the din: thoughtful, useful, powerful eloquence and preaching of the Word. Below are some excerpts taken from an annual "Register of Sermons Preached at Paul's Cross, 1534–1642," noting also the monarch under

whom the sermon was preached. In the aggregate they provide a glimpse of
the English Reformation figuring itself out as it went along while gradually
becoming a powerful state church:

HENRY VIII

1534 (Jan. 15)   The customary prayer for the Pope was
omitted. . . .

1536 (Feb. 6)   Thomas Cranmer, Archbishop of Canterbury. A defence of the royal supremacy, with a proof that the
Pope is Antichrist. . . .

1536 (Mar. 12)   Hugh Latimer, Bishop of Worcester. . . . He declared also that one might "eat fleshe and whit mete
in Lent, so that it be don without hurtying of weke
consciences. . . ."

1538 (Dec. 22)   John Harrydaunce, a Whitechapel bricklayer, who
had been preaching to large audiences from a tub in
his garden, bore a faggot [i.e., was there to repent]
with two other persons, one of them a priest. . . .

1545 (Feb. 8)   A priest of Kent did penance for counterfeiting the
blood of Christ at mass, by "cutting of hys fynger and
[making] it to blede on the host." For his penance he
wore a "broad stole of linen cloath, couloured with
drops like bloud."

1546 (Sept. 26)   Heretical books were burned in the sermon time,
including Tyndale's Testament and Coverdale's Bible
[i.e., forbidden vernacular translations].

EDWARD VI

1547 (Nov. 27)   William Barlow, Bishop of St. David's. He showed
and broke two images, one of the Virgin . . . and a
picture of the Resurrection "made with [de]vices,
which putt out his legges of sepulchre and blessed
with his hand, and turned his head."

1549 (May 12)   An Anabaptist, a butcher, dwelling by Old Fish
Street, bore a faggot.

1550 (Mar. 30)   A sermon of thanksgiving for peace with France, at-

tended by the Lord Mayor and the aldermen in their
scarlet.

MARY I

1553 (Oct. 22)   Hugh Weston, Dean of Westminster. He announced
a disputation between the men of the old faith and
the Protestants at Convocation. . . . "He named the
Lord's table an oyster-board. . . ."

1554 (Apr. 8)   Dr. Henry Pendleton, chaplain. . . . A cat made like
a priest ready to say mass, with a shaven crown,
which was hung on the cross in Cheapside, was exhibited at the Cross. A reward of 20 nobles was offered for the apprehension of the guilty person, but
"none could or would earn it."

1554 (Nov. 4)   Nicholas Harpsfield, Archdeacon of Canterbury.
Five priests who were content to put away their
wives . . . did penance in sheets, with tapers, and
rods with which the preacher struck them as he
"showyd their oppynyons."

ELIZABETH I

1560 (Mar. 17)   John Veron, vicar of St. Martin's in Ludgate. "After
the sermon done they songe all, old and yong, a
salme in myter, the tune of Genevay ways."

1564 (Jan. 26)   Thomas Cole, Archdeacon of Essex. He rejoiced at
the end of the plague, which he attributed to Romish
superstition among the citizens. The Roman faith, he
said, stood upon four "rotyn postis": images, purgatory, the mass, transubstantiation. . . .

1579 (May 10)   John Stockwood, Master of the Tunbridge Grammar
School . . . extolled the virtue and absolute necessity of preaching, exhorted his audience to attend
church instead of filthy plays, which usurp the time
of sermons, and declared for the plain style in
preaching, without rhetorical tricks and extensive
quotation from the Fathers. . . .

1583 (ca. Feb.?)	John Aylmer, Bishop of London. A sermon denouncing Richard Harvey's "An Astrologicall Discourse upon the great and notable Conjunction of the Two Superiour Planets, Saturne & Jupiter, which shall happen the 28. day of April, 1583." . . .
1588 (Aug. 20)	Alexander Nowell, Dean of St. Paul's. A sermon of thanksgiving for the victory over the Armada.
1601 (Feb. 22)	The preacher spoke from written instructions supplied by Bancroft, which the bishop had first submitted to Cecil for approval. . . .
1602 (Dec. 19)	"One with a long browne beard, a hanging looke, a gloting eye, and a tossing learing jesture." He preached upon the favorite theme of false prophets, and "his whole sermon was a strong continued invective against the papistes and jesuites. . . ."

JAMES I

1604 (Oct. 7)	Richard Jefferay [Geoffrey], of Magdalen College, Oxford. A denunciation of the sins of England and especially London, worse, he said than any he saw in his travels abroad. . . .
1605 (Nov. 10)	William Barlow, Bishop of Rochester. On the Powder Plot, "this late Tragi-comicall treason."
1607 (Aug. 5)	John Milward, chaplain to the King. After an eloquent exordium upon the troubles of man—"his entrance is blindnesse, his birth a crying, his progresse labour, and his end dolour"—he . . . reviewed the other deliverances of the sovereign from treasons, especially "that Salt-Peter Treason, or Peters salt Treason of Rome." . . .
1607 (Nov. 1)	Samuel Collins, Rector of Fen Ditton, Cambridgeshire . . . "an admirable and biting wit." A full-scale attack on the whole puritan position. . . .
1607 (Nov. 5)	Martin Fotherby, Archdeacon of Canterbury. . . . The sermon on the anniversary of the Powder Plot. A contemplation of England's blessings: "the dewe of

Gods blessing hath onely fallen on our land, when all our neighbour countries have been destitute of it." . . .

1612 (Feb. 9) One Ratcliffe, of Brasenose College, Oxford. The occasion of the penance of Moll Cutpurse, the Roaring Girl, for wearing men's apparel. She was drunk, the preacher did "extreem badly," her confederates picked pockets during the service, and the whole affair was anything but edifying.

1612 (Aug. 2) Thomas Draxe, Vicar of Dovercourt-cum-Harwich, Essex. Of the resurrection of the body, with a refutation of Aristotle and the Sadducees. . . . The resurrection of the body excludes the blessed angels, devils and reprobates, all beings of equivocal and mixed generation, as "Mules, Wolfe-dogs, Wolfe-bitches, and all monstrous creatures," all creatures bred of putrefaction, as "frogs, flies, wormes, moules, mise, crickets, bats, barnacles," the ocean ("there shall be no more sea"), and hence all creatures therein, all cities, buildings, monuments, inventions and devices of man.

1613 (Jan. 3) Thomas Sutton, Fellow of Queen's College, Oxford. . . . He reproved ignorance, swearing, and lying, before the hourglass caught up with him.

1619 (Apr. 11) John King, Bishop of London. A sermon of thanksgiving for the recovery of the King from his serious illness. . . . "All the people of the earth may stand upon the shore of my text [Isa. 38:17], and see the face of their fraile & inconstant condition."

1620 (Mar. 26) John King, Bishop of London. Upon a text set by the King, "a voyce from earth that is next to heaven," he preached upon the repair, long overdue, of the cathedral. . . .

1622 (Sept. 15) John Donne, Dean of St. Paul's. A defence of the King's orders concerning preaching, and of his "constancie in the true reformed religion. . . ."

CHARLES I

1629 (Nov. 22)	John Donne, Dean of St. Paul's. An exhortation to good works, opposing the Protestant to the Catholic doctrine of works. Good works, he said, constitute the reclamation from offence in Christ (Matt. 11:6), and offence may arise from a propensity to misinterpret the words and actions of others. . . .
1637 (Jan. 8)	[Obadiah?] Whitbie, perhaps the Rector of St. Nicholas Olaves. . . . A sermon preached on the cessation of the plague, with a sharp reproof of those who would lead true Christians into schism. . . .
1641 (Oct. 10)	Thomas Cheshire, curate at Yarmouth, "an orthodox minister." He brooded sadly over the fantastic and irregular sectaries then flourishing. "Coblers and Weavers, and Feltmongers . . . take upon them to interpret Gods Word." . . . "not many daies since, comming in Saint Sepulchres Church . . . I saw a woman dandling and dancing her child upon the Lords Holy Table; when she was gone, I . . . saw a greate deale of water upon the Table; I verely think they were not teares of devotion, it was well it was not worse."

The foregoing* is one means of traversing the briar patches of the Reformation. We can see, by the time of the Glorious Revolution of 1688, as the smoke and fire of controversy began to clear away, when the wars of religion had ebbed, and all the martyred bodies had been taken away for a decent burial, England—and Europe and, increasingly, America—had a new religious landscape. There were also new names to describe the Christian denominations born of this turmoil: Anabaptists, Anglicans, Baptists, Calvinists, Congregationalists, Diggers, Huguenots, Hutterites, Lutherans, Mennonites, Presbyterians, Puritans, Quakers, among many others. And preaching had taken on the central task of supporting religious belief.

*Adapted from Millar MacLure, The Paul's Cross Sermons, 1534–1642, Toronto: University of Toronto Press, 1958.

THE CATHOLIC REFORMATION AND THE PURITANS

It can readily be discerned from the excerpted pulpit topics of Paul's Cross that Catholics and Puritans had become nearly equal threats to the Establishment and equal objects of its scorn and wrath. If the Church of England needed its bishops and its monarchs in order to survive and preserve civil order, it felt threatened in bipolar fashion: from the top down by Rome and a wildly demonized Pope and from the bottom up by the Puritan phobia toward hierarchy.

Though it is only lightly covered in this book, Roman Catholic Europe, caught off guard by Martin Luther & Co., soon began to make its own the old Erasmian agenda of reform from within. By the early sixteenth century the papacy had already reestablished itself in Rome with authority and a better bank account after a century of exile in Avignon (1309–77). From the eighteen-year Council of Trent (1545–63) came welcome fresh air from the inner precincts of the papacy. New religious orders and movements came into being—along with saints to lead them—with explicit instructions to provide better religious teaching, better preaching, and better communication. Notable among them were Philip Neri of Rome and his Oratorians (whose spiritual descendants would include John Henry Newman in Victorian England), Francis de Sales, Charles Borromeo, Teresa of Avila and John of the Cross, Vincent de Paul, and of course Ignatius of Loyola and his Jesuits. Their mother church, the Gesu, built in Rome at this time, took its shape from the new Protestant pulpit-centered architecture, the so-called auditory churches, that permitted the greatest possibility for hearing the Word proclaimed. And in France, under Louis XIV, some of the most eloquent preaching ever heard would come from the lips of Bishops Jacques Bénigne Bossuet (1627–1704) and François de Salignac de La Mothe Fénelon (1651–1715).

The antiauthoritarian impulses set in motion by the Reformation continued all through the second half of the sixteenth and the seventeenth centuries. Their most successful expression may be found in the various new dissenting and nonconforming religious cults. Offspring of the Swiss Reformation and relying for faith on the Bible and the person of the preacher, they began to make fresh contributions to the broadening stream of proclamation. They were often kept from preaching in Church of England pulpits, but they found a clever means to do so through what was called the lec-

tureship. By paying an outside preacher to come to a church with a dissenting congregation, though the bishop might deny him the normal means of
giving a sermon, these "lecturers" got their message across in the extra-
liturgical setting of a public lecture. (This form of sermon has its earlier
analogues in the so-called conference in which an abbot spoke to his monks
and in the Renaissance catechetical lectures of the Jesuits.) Their restlessness with the efforts from above to impose a status quo eventually induced
many dissenting groups to emigrate to the New World, a pattern begun
with the Cromwellian colonization of Ireland.

GOD SETTLES IN NEW ENGLAND

Whether they were called Pilgrims in Plymouth, Massachusetts, Puritans in
the Massachusetts Bay Colony, or Baptists in Roger Williams's new city of
Providence (or, for that matter, Dutch Reformed on Manhattan Island), the
earliest North Europeans in the New World clearly saw themselves doubly
reincarnated as the Israelites wandering from Egypt in the desert and as the
primitive Christians suffering Roman persecution. They were "dedicated to
the destruction of an entire world view, a whole system of values and meaning woven from Roman liturgical forms and pagan religious traditions. . . ."[9] Ironically, Puritan asceticism had much in common with
monastic reform of earlier centuries, although its contempt for rituals of
the past and its emphasis on the individual family as paradigm and on the
value of worldly endeavor as a means of attracting divine approval marked
clear differences. Stretching and even severing their tenuous connections
with the Church of England, they blazed new paths in the wilderness.

To take the example of Boston, its settlement began in April 1630
when four ships embarked from England after their passengers heard a stirring farewell sermon by John Cotton (who indeed would later join them).
En route aboard the *Arbella,* their leader, John Winthrop, preached them a
document he had composed, "A Model of Christian Charity" (see page
356), outlining a community that would place itself in the providential hand
of God in order to build "a city on a hill." In little more than a decade another twenty thousand sympathetic souls would arrive, and the building of

---

[9]Charles E. Hambrick-Stowe, *The Practice of Piety. Puritan Devotional Discipline in Seventeenth-Century New England* (Chapel Hill: University of North Carolina Press, 1982), p. 27.

church after church—and pulpit after pulpit within—all over the landscape ensured that God's Word would always guide the mission. And the legacy of that first sermon can still be heard in a thousand American pulpits every Sunday.

The story of the preachers of New England through the seventeenth and into the eighteenth centuries is chiaroscuro, to be sure. The perceived presence of Satan—in the stoic faces of Native Americans, in the dark forests beyond the coastland, and in the souls of community members who deviated from unyielding norms—would induce such phenomena as might bring a blush to the cheek of Dostoyevsky's Grand Inquisitor. Still, in a recapitulation of the twelfth-century Renaissance, they also brought forth universities (Harvard and Yale), excellent preaching (Increase Mather, his son, Cotton, and Jonathan Edwards), and new spiritual movements (the Great Awakening of the 1730s and the Second Awakening at the end of the eighteenth century). And as in the Reformation, in the vanguard of the printed word, sermon pamphlets led the way.

JOHN WESLEY AND GEORGE WHITEFIELD

In England, by the early eighteenth century, the pulpit, which in the Reformation, as one commentator put it, had been "vigorously, sometimes dangerously, alive . . . drenched in blood and bigotry, superstition and intolerance,"[10] had, by the time of the now-constitutional monarchs, the Hanoverian Georges, become a far tamer reflection of a more ordered, Enlightened age. It was an age that gave us the poorhouse, the Sunday school, and Methodism.

John Wesley (1703–91), the son of a clergyman and himself a lifelong Anglican priest, showed even as a student at Oxford an ardent devotion to the spread of the gospel. What began there as a "Holy Club" of fellow students later became one of the world's great evangelical movements. Wesley manifested a fervor for preaching in the manner of the early Christian preachers who seemed to be sent directly by the Holy Spirit from community to community. He moved about constantly all his life to preach wherever the opportunity presented itself. Though in the early years he was

---

[10]John Chandos, ed., *In God's Name: Examples of Preaching in England from the Act of Supremacy to the Act of Uniformity, 1534–1662* (Indianapolis, Ind.: Bobbs-Merrill Co., 1971), p. xvii.

rejected as often as he was permitted to speak, during the second half of the eighteenth century his trademark outdoor sermons commonly reached tens of thousands of listeners at a time and were given with almost superhuman frequency. By the time he died, he had covered a quarter of a million miles—in England and in America—and had preached for half a century as many as four sermons a day calling for moral reform and holding out the promise of personal salvation. Moreover, his genius for creating fellowship and structure wherever he preached, typically among the poor, eventually produced a powerful new denomination, once weakening ties with the Church of England were finally severed.

Wesley and his brother Charles had briefly visited the colony of Georgia in 1736 and preached with success, but two years later it was the person of George Whitefield (1714–70), a friend from the Holy Club days, who would take up their initiative and through sheer eloquence become the first national celebrity preacher in the New World. England's then greatest actor, David Garrick, appraised Whitefield's oratorical powers by noting that he would gladly give a hundred guineas to be able to pronounce just one "O!" as Whitefield did. After personally pacing off the perimeter of the crowd that came to hear him in Philadelphia—and estimating it at thirty thousand souls—Benjamin Franklin offered to be his publisher. When he finally returned to England, he gave a farewell sermon on Boston Common to a similar throng, his unamplified voice apparently carrying to the farthest ear. By a rough guess, he probably preached close to twenty thousand sermons in his lifetime; mere dozens were preserved, perhaps a historical comment on their reliance for effect on Whitefield's personal charisma.

It is in Whitefield that we see the beginning of a pattern in American preaching that continues to this day. By his circuit riding, by his dramatic and emotional style, by having no stable congregation to call his own, by seeking on-the-spot conversion as his goal, and by leaving very little in the way of infrastructure in his wake, he made possible a nineteenth century that would be filled with *ad hoc* evangelism, revivalism, camp meetings, Chatauquas, and sudden, fevered personal testimony. In our own century, with newly invented means of amplification and broadcasting, George Whitefield's offspring would include Billy Sunday, Aimee Semple McPherson, Father Coughlin, Billy Graham, and Robert Schuller, among hosts of others. "How American it seems in retrospect, this confessional impulse, the assertion of self, the insistence on justification," writes novelist Robert Stone.[11] Whitefield's emotional preaching style and approach would also be found transformed but clearly evident in the emerging black churches in America, so largely grown from Methodist and Baptist roots.

THE NINETEENTH AND EARLY TWENTIETH CENTURIES

The nineteenth century in Protestant England and America produced two diverging streams—or better, rivers, even lakes and oceans—of preaching: high and low. At the high end, we find such divergent preachers as John Henry Newman, the most famous Protestant convert to Catholicism of the century, John Keble, founder of the Oxford Movement, Ralph Waldo Emerson, with his difficult, intellectual style, or Phillips Brooks, bestriding his Trinity Church pulpit in Boston like a Colossus; in Europe, such disparate preachers as Friedrich Schleiermacher, at another Trinity Church, this one in Berlin, or the anguished ironist Søren Kierkegaard blending deeply intellectual thinking with religious reflection.

In contrast to what we might call the mainline Protestant style, we find the increasingly familiar fundamentalist style of preaching that has inaccurately come to stand in the popular mind for preaching in general. Primarily descended in America through Methodist and Baptist lines, this simplified approach would increasingly depend on shouting, repetition, emotional manipulation, calls for audience participation, musical accompaniment, a colorful *mise-en-scène,* and sometimes a fretful pacing about instead of delivery from the pulpit—all aimed at heightening the emotions to precipitate conversions among the congregation. The Bible text, the pericope, used for such preaching was more often than not chosen subjectively by the preacher with little or no relation to any liturgical context or the cycle of a church year; in fact, aside from announcements and hymn singing, often the sermon *was* the liturgy. What a postmodern critic might call the "deconstruction" of preaching had begun.

Of course, the advantages of such preaching were obvious. It could be

[11]"American Apostle," a review of Alfred Kazin's *God and the American Writer* in the *New York Review of Books,* Mar. 26, 1998, p. 26. Kazin's point is that three centuries of American writers have been preoccupied with notions of Calvinist theology.

set up anywhere—on the prairie, in a stadium, a theater or a tent, indoors or out. Its message suited all comers. Its prophetic tone was full of promise, often for worldly success. And when everyone woke up the next day, the preacher was usually gone to set up in the next town or city down the line. (Today he or she is gone at the flip of a TV remote control.) The peculiarly American search for religious freedom had produced the colorful figure of the Preacher, but somewhere along the way it may have discarded the Church.

In place of the more traditional catechetical and exegetical sermons of Catholicism, Lutheranism, and Episcopalianism, set in a liturgy and Scripture-based, the freedom seized on by the evangelical churches in America often took on social issues for substantive preaching. By the middle of the nineteenth century, slavery was the first great object of reforming pulpit zeal (e.g., Henry Ward Beecher); over the next century everything from Darwinism, temperance, life insurance, the gold standard, bobbed hair, anti-Semitism, Communism, materialism, rock 'n' roll, civil rights, homosexuality, secular humanism, and "family values" would follow in due course. Whether such free-wheeling speechifying always deserved the name of preaching is another matter.

TWENTIETH-CENTURY GERMANY

Along with the Reformation, the people of modern Germany inherited a centuries-old anti-Semitism, a belief that Judaism was of only biblical or historical interest and that otherwise it was a "fossil" religion and accordingly either to be scorned or suppressed in an enlightened time such as our own. Once the National Socialist Party came to power under Hitler in 1933, it soon became apparent that Judaism and its adherents were marked for some inevitably dark and inescapable fate. What was not so clear at first was that the Protestant and Roman Catholic churches would also soon find themselves sliding to the brink of disaster.

While in retrospect there is no question that the mass of German clergy and people of all denominations—with the possible exception of the marginal Jehovah's Witnesses—gave ample evidence of their indifference to, apathy over, acquiescence in, and resignation to the shocking state policy against the Jews and Judaism during the period 1933–45 (even after deportation and evidence of atrocities became known to many during the early years of the Second World War), it was nonetheless a handful of out-standing church members whose speech and actions give us reason not simply to blot out the whole period with the blackest of inks.

Even though a policeman might typically be sitting directly beneath the pulpit taking careful notes that could lead to a death warrant, some German ministers nonetheless determined to speak truth to power. Martyred theologian Dietrich Bonhoeffer (1906–45) and pastor Martin Niemöller (1892–1984) of the Confessing Church were not the only ones to place their lives and freedom on the scales to counterbalance the nihilistic weight of Nazi state obsession. Because of their witness, a bright, if thin, thread of powerful gospel proclamation managed to run through the ghastly tapestry of murder and horror woven during those years.

THE PREACHER AS GLOBAL FIGURE

If the Victorian era marked the high-water mark of printed sermon literature, the twentieth century soon made its own contribution to the immense, branching streams of preaching. New media and means of communication seemed to fix the pulpit in time and space and make it begin to feel confining and old-fashioned. The public-address system, the outdoor stadium and the indoor auditorium, radio and television transmission, and eventually fiber-optic and digital communication—all have extended the reach of the preacher beyond the boundaries of sanctuary and nave to potential global simultaneity.

Of all those who have seized on the worldwide possibilities now opened for preaching and witnessing to the Word, no one has done so with more vigor and success than Pope John Paul II. He is the first pope to visit every continent and preach to almost every nation and people on earth. His message of peace and brotherhood has been heard through every known means of communication, from primitive drums to web sites. Yet one does well to remember that, when he speaks, he stands on the shoulders of his saintly predecessor, John XXIII, summoner of the Second Vatican Council (1962–65).

Without a generation of clerical and lay commitment to renewal, to education, to ecumenism, and to a general increase of its missionary spirit (including focus on Scripture-based preaching), the Church of Rome would likely never have had the courage to elevate an obscure anti-Communist Polish archbishop to the chair of Peter. The innate conservatism and exclusiveness of the institutional Church, its preference for secrecy and rigidity over openness and debate, would probably never have bowed to any command but one from the stout, cheerful peasant Pope John. His legacy lives on in the hope of his flock that, no matter how difficult things get, the potential for positive outcomes must not be forgotten.

THE BLACK CHURCH IN AMERICA

No account of the history of preaching could end without a look at one of its most unique traditions: the black church. If we measure its trajectory from the seventeenth-century practice of Christian baptism of newly landed slaves (concomitant with denial of any further access to Christian life) to the person of our near contemporary, Martin Luther King, Jr., we have also described an arc of more than three centuries of remarkable preaching.

It was not until the beginning of the eighteenth century that white clergy made concerted missionizing efforts among the black slaves in America. Stripped of their African gods, their culture, their kin and mores, these mostly young males began to find a new basis for social cohesion in the limited teaching they were given by various Episcopalian, Quaker, Presbyterian, and Catholic clergy. The Lord's Prayer, the Ten Commandments, and assorted Bible stories constituted their repertoire of Christianity. Naturally, slaves were forbidden to learn to read lest it produce yearnings unwanted by their owners.

By the end of the eighteenth century America had fallen under the spell of Methodist and Baptist evangelizers, whose circuit riding and fiery preaching made new efforts to reach out to the poor, the marginalized, and the ignorant, which included blacks enslaved in the South and freed in the North. The imposition of segregation within churches in the North and the growing permission granted by owners to their slaves to have their own church services eventually led to the emergence of preachers as the first professional class among blacks in America. Rarely permitted any significant education, they were instead called by their communities to minister, and they grew in stature and importance as the new "invisible institution" in their charge took shape.

The irresistible combination of gospel preaching on themes such as the Israelites gaining their freedom from bondage in Egypt, and the singing of so-called Negro spirituals at their services, did much to make an often unbearable life in the New World tolerable. The isolation, the loneliness, and the brevity of that life were powerful incentives for all to forge close bonds with the church, bonds strongly reinforced by preaching.

After Emancipation and the end of the Civil War, the black church began to function ever more powerfully as the provider of education, job opportunity, status, moral standards, and, at some level, virtually every element of daily life from social activities to burial services. With the addition of white philanthropy, new colleges, vocational schools, and seminaries sprang up to spur the addition of professional members to the community.

By the First World War the black population had begun a profound shift in location to the cities of the Northern, Middle Atlantic, and Midwestern states. They took their churches with them, both the more formal and prosperous American Methodist Episcopal (A.M.E.) Church as well as the numerous evangelical storefront operations—analogous to the small-town churches of the South—that provided fellowship and comfort in harsh urban settings to those given little or no assistance to rise in their surrounding white context.

The image of the strong, autocratic shepherd in complete control of his flock certainly fit such ambiguous figures as Father Divine and Daddy Grace, both celebrity preachers who attained national audiences through their evangelizing, beginning in the pit of the Great Depression in such black urban centers as Chicago and Harlem. And among those who stayed behind in the South, powerful, authentic speakers like Martin Luther "Daddy" King, Sr., in Atlanta's Ebenezer Baptist Church served as a reminder of how successful the notion of a nation within a nation could be for its thousands of congregants. It was there in the 1930s and 1940s that he "learned that when the preacher assumes his proper place in the hierarchy above the people and beneath the cross—and says what God wants him to say—the entire organism hums with celestial power. The people had better pay attention."[12] Such churches across the South and elsewhere did much to

---

[12]Richard Lischer, *The Preacher King: Martin Luther King, Jr. and the Word That Moved America* (New York: Oxford University Press, 1995), p. 22.

assuage the sore testing of black Americans that was being done in the world at large by Jim Crow laws, segregated schools, job discrimination, civil-rights violations, and the generally vigilant policing of the established frontiers between white and black life at every level of existence. But it couldn't last.

MARTIN LUTHER KING, JR.

His story now has the character of a myth, much larger than any real man's life, and it has become the repository of the hopes and fears of us all. Some salient details of his historical life are given elsewhere in this book (see page 637) as a preface to one of his own favorite sermons. He said of himself, "In the inner recesses of my heart, I am fundamentally . . . a Baptist preacher." It is curious how the national curating of his memory thirty years after his assassination (he would only be sixty-nine at this writing) is so devoid of his preaching. Dutifully each year, on the January national holiday or in April on his death anniversary, the local television news anchors of every station in the land run a ten-second film clip of his "I Have a Dream" speech at the Lincoln Memorial. They usually begin talking over it after three or four seconds, saying something about how his dream lives on, perhaps in a local high school pageant or at a rally in a nearby housing project.

Such tributes, so cut and dried, wedged in the news between the latest political scandal and the weather forecast, don't exactly convey how the sound of his voice made the hairs on our necks stand up and our eyes well with tears as, for a moment, he preached to us and we believed the truth that blacks and whites alike in this country did not have to bear the insoluble dilemma of race forever. He preached to us that the love of our enemies was possible and that the never-failing love of Jesus for each of us was a reality. In the prophetic insistence of his preaching, hope was born and spirits were renewed. For all his self-doubt and melancholy, he never wavered in his belief that the Word of God, once cast on the waters, would return. In him we finally have within living memory the embodiment of what true preaching is: we find the passion of Paul; the piercing insight of Augustine; the poetry of Bernard of Clairvaux; the moral clarity of his namesake, Martin Luther; the unyielding perseverance of John Wesley; the gentleness of John Henry Newman; and the enlarged vision of Phillips

Brooks, whom he admired. (Ironically, some of King's best preaching is still available to us because it was taped as part of surveillance by Southern police and FBI observers. Cf. German preachers under Nazism, noted on p. 36.)

An Apologia for Our Sermon Selection

Like sculptors, we began with an armature, that is, a generalized hypothesis about what sermons and homilies are and in what historical eras they would probably abound. As with most hypotheses, our initial assumptions were only partly right. The written remains of the spoken word have not always faithfully recorded the turning points and intense periods in history when preaching was widespread. To give just a few examples, virtually no actual sermons survive after St. Paul in the first century until the Church Father Origen in the third. Again, by the fourth century, once extemporaneous preaching was established as a regular occurrence after the Scripture readings in the liturgy, preserved examples do not abound. The Fathers of the Latin sermon in the West and the Greek homily in the East—St. Augustine and St. John Chrysostom—left, through their stenographers, a rich store of sermons on all occasions; even so, at a time when Christianity had more or less triumphed all around the Mediterranean basin, between them just these two men account for more than *half* of all the preaching saved from the Patristic era.

In the Middle Ages, when the renaissance of the twelfth century produced the preeminent preaching orders, the Franciscans and the Dominicans, no sermons survive directly from the mouths of either Francis of Assisi or Dominic. And in the sixteenth century, when the Catholic Reformation got under way, the stirring pulpit voice of St. Ignatius of Loyola is silent. Many other such lamentable lacunae could be cited.

At the outset, determining whom to include was our goal. At the end, deciding who could not be included became an overriding and often painful issue. There are ninety sermons here; at least twice that number would have been desirable to have in the mix. In fact, space permitting, this book might happily have been ten thousand pages long and yet only begun to include all the highlights of its subject. It is, therefore, of necessity an abstract of abstracts. The net could easily have broken with the catch. So we took to heart an old Korean proverb, "Behind the mountains there are more mountains."

To consider a single subject for sermons: Mary, the Mother of God. Some 90,000 books and other printed materials on the topic reside in the library at Ohio's University of Dayton, the world's largest (and perhaps unlikeliest) such repository. Our needs on Mary encompassed one or perhaps two sermons. How to find them, cull them, read some of them, and make a selection? It wasn't always easy. (We didn't go to Dayton.)

Speaking of Mary inevitably brought us to consider women preachers. The exclusion of women from the pulpit, with scattered exceptions— Quakers and Moravians come to mind—until late in our own century may represent a scandal of history, but it does not leave the researcher much to go on. We do not regard this intractable reality as matter for apology, any more than a historian of child rearing should have to apologize for the absence over endless centuries of fathers from the nursery. *Pace* Dr. Johnson's shopworn witticism, the subject of women preachers is not to be wondered at but rather is fully deserving of its own collection, which we fervently hope will now appear.

Although solid bibliographies on women and preaching have appeared in recent years, along with a handful of anthologies of contemporary women preachers, the typical rarity and/or antiquity of the materials to be tracked down suggest to the determined anthologist a long and diligent search—with a generous allotment of time—to locate the best selections. As the place of women in the church and synagogue comes more and more to be central, as more denominations permit the ordination of women,[13] and as their contributions at all levels come to be recognized as equal, they deserve better than to be marginalized or patronized. (Notwithstanding the foregoing, because we liked it, we have included an example from Hildegard of Bingen because, as a medieval German abbess, though not entitled

---

[13]"Though no exact statistics are available, there are probably fewer women serving parishes today than there were at the turn of the century, though the number with some theological education is larger because for many years the major Protestant seminaries have admitted women without protest. But to have a theological degree does not ensure that one will preach, or be ordained, or even enter a religious vocation as a profession." Georgia Harkness, *Women in Church and Society* (Nashville, Tenn.: Abingdon Press, 1972), quoted in *And Blessed Is She: Sermons by Women,* David Albert Farmer and Edwina Hunter, eds. (New York: Harper & Row, 1990), p. 14.

to preach at a liturgy, she would probably have spoken to or read her writings to her own nuns in a setting very like that in which a sermon would be heard.)[14]

The constraints of time permitted a few desired preachers to elude our grasp, for example, Lewis Carroll, whose Oxford admirers were known to take copious notes on his preaching; Robert Livingstone, missionary extraordinary who died in Africa of a fever and whose lifeless form was discovered kneeling beside his bed; Thomas Merton, whose writings are voluminous and whose merely *posthumous* bibliography, which continues growing to this day, would be the envy of many a productive living writer. There were also historic occasions—e.g., a sermon on Hiroshima, a sermon on the first lunar landing—too numerous to list, for which many a good sermon has doubtless been preached but was not uncovered by us.

More important, whole time periods, religious subcultures, and continents, hypothetically abundant sources of good preaching, could not possibly be in the book. Just a partial list would have to include almost the whole of the Eastern and Russian Orthodox traditions; the sermons of Latin and Central and Caribbean America—and Canada; then there are Scandinavia and Scotland; and finally, the preachers of Asia and—with the exceptions of St. Augustine, Origen, and Archbishop Desmond Tutu—Africa. From the great roll of saints and martyrs Catholic, Protestant, and Jewish, notable figures in religious orders, denominations great and small, we could give places to only a few. The absence of missionaries here can only be excused by broadly defining preaching in every age as essentially a missionary activity.

No attempt was made to look at the "spiritual" writing or speaking of secular figures as sermons, e.g., a quasi-religious fireside chat on the radio by President Roosevelt during World War II. Nor did we go in search of sermonlike examples from religions other than Christianity and Judaism, in which the sermon form first arose, e.g., a talk by Mahatma Gandhi or Mohammed. Beautiful examples of religious and spiritual speaking occur in

---

[14]See also an important new essay collection, *Women Preachers and Prophets Through Two Millennia of Christianity*, Beverly Mayne Kienzle and Pamela J. Walker, eds. (Berkeley and Los Angeles: University of California Press, 1998): "Yet, although exemplary women have received increased scholarly attention in the last ten to fifteen years, their preaching and sermons generally have not been the focus of research," p. xvi.

every culture, religion, and era. Our task was to fill a modest book, not empty the ocean into a teacup. So let us not repine over what is not here but rejoice in the riches that are.

Preparing the Texts

Early in the process of searching out the sermons for this project, several realities became apparent: older sermons are, more often than not, very long by today's impatient standards. However, impatience with preaching is nothing new, *vide* Mark Twain's remark that "very few sinners have been saved after the first fifteen minutes of a sermon." Or that of Caesarius, the sixth-century bishop of Arles in the then Roman province of Gaul, who on occasion ordered his church doors barred to prevent early departures.

Humor and impatience to one side, the increasingly common contemporary approach to present older, often difficult or complex texts is to look for sound bites and short passages that will serve an *ad hoc* purpose. Collections of golden nuggets have their place and their beauties, to be sure, but we have, wherever exceeding length has not prevented us, instead tried to include whole or only moderately abridged sermons. Some of our preachers were tireless. John Chrysostom, the patron saint of all preachers, comes to mind. During Lent he often preached twice daily, that is, two complete sermons of several hours' total duration. And Cotton Mather's father, Increase, did the same in the morning and afternoon in Boston's Old North Church, while his son dutifully, simultaneously transcribed his seventeenth-century English into Latin! Perhaps in our own day only the Jesuit-educated Communist Fidel Castro is capable of such oratorical endurance.

We took these sermons from a wide variety of sources, some recently translated in crisp new scholarly editions; some in dilapidated Victorian bindings with no helpful annotation or introduction; still others in poor translations or with Elizabethan orthography and punctuation. To create as consistent and readable an appearance as possible for the book as a whole, we undertook editorial steps, case by case, that we do not believe have done any violence to an original text but rather come under the broad heading of "silent emendation." No "translation" has been made of any source written originally in older forms of English, however odd the words of a John

Donne or a Lancelot Andrewes might initially strike a modern reader. Spelling has, however, been modernized to reduce distraction.

Quotations from the Bible appear in virtually every sermon. The biblical translation used in the original source from which we took the sermon has been retained, though it may not always be clearly identified. In some cases a translator of a sermon may simply have translated a Scripture passage along with everything else, not bothering to take the English from a standard Bible translation matching the one the author used. For example, St. Augustine, who had little Greek and no Hebrew or Aramaic, had only St. Jerome's Latin Vulgate Bible available.

Footnotes appear on the pages of religious texts like lichen on a damp wall. The vast majority of them are devoted to scholarly housekeeping that could only impede and distract a general reader, so wherever possible we have deleted them. If here and there an allusion is not explained or a cross-reference is not made, we apologize but ask the reader to consider the greater good of fluency.

Nonetheless, many of the footnotes are Scripture citations, and those we have usually incorporated into the text in parentheses where they occur. It is a remarkable—and wonderful—phenomenon how like breathing in and out the citation of Scripture is in all preaching. Equally interesting is how the frequency of citation tends to decline over the centuries, from almost every other phrase in the Church Fathers' sermons to barely a moderate sprinkling in our own day. The decline of Bible memorization in semi-literate cultures along with the decline of private and family Bible reading may be the culprits. The practice in monasteries from the early Middle Ages of reciting the whole Psalter in communal liturgies once every two weeks as well as hearing nearly the entire Bible read once a year was a noble practice now greatly decayed.

Many sermons come with titles ready made. A recent December newspaper advertisement for holiday preaching listed an offering entitled "A New You This Christmas." Many of the sermons in this book were similarly given their original titles; others simply took their numerical place in line in a sermon series and have no formal title; still others have their *pericope,* or scriptural theme text, as a heading.

Before each sermon is a headnote. In them our aim is minimally to prepare the reader for what is to come. In some, historical background is called for; in others, it may be called for but is not readily available. We want the reader to taste and see how good are the strangeness, the surprise, and yet the universality of these words from times long past. As Hilaire Belloc has written, "Anyone, however ignorant, can discover what is repulsive and absurd in standards different from their own; and one's learning, no matter how detailed, is wasted if one gets no further than that. The whole art of [writing] history consists in eliminating that shock of noncomprehension and in making the reader feel as the men of the past felt."

When these sermons raise questions of dogma, doctrine, theology, and sectarian controversy, we take a neutral stance. If an offending idea appears on the page, let the reader make of it what he or she would have in any case, whether we chose to add some editorial demurral or not.

Preaching Today and Tomorrow

Despite some stirring examples included in these pages, it is hard to deny that the preaching tradition today is weakened in circumstance and ineffectual in practice. Despite the immense, ongoing output of pulpit oratory all over the world, to anticipate a comeback for the influence of the sermon any time soon represents the triumph of hope over experience. Why should this be so? The conjectures that follow are not meant to be exhaustive, only to provide some cumulative sense of how the sermon has come to exist in our time.

Looking back over the long centuries discussed above, it is clear that something basic happened at the Reformation. It saw the onset of new forms of government in Europe that in time would no longer place Christianity at their center. Add to that the momentous change implied by the new ways of disseminating information from the printing press, and you have the early diminishing of the pulpit as the fountain and origin of most of society's publicly expressed ideas. Thus, while preaching temporarily moved to the heart of everyone's concern in the sixteenth century, it was simultaneously being devalued by parallel secular movements. Two centuries of division, war, and bitter religious antagonism ensured that, when the archipelago of recognizable modern nation states surfaced and dried during the late seventeenth and eighteenth centuries, they would be governed by practical men of state, not theocrats. Priorities of eternity took a back seat.

The European Enlightenment after the mid-eighteenth century produced Voltaire and Rousseau and Hume; it also gave birth to an intense, Romantic cultural period that upended all notions of a chain of Being with God at one end. Instead, Promethean man at the other end, relying on his own inner resources, would henceforth take on the future. The fires of preaching were banked, and preachers retreated to a new role of aiding the state in maintaining domestic social control and good citizenship. The notion of anyone being invested with some divine, prophetic authority to speak to all had by the Victorian age begun to look suspicious to many, faintly ridiculous to others, and dangerous to some, especially scientists like Sigmund Freud or Thomas Huxley and social engineers like Karl Marx.

As we entered the twentieth century, the competitive means of spreading information—religious and otherwise—began to multiply with quantum force: the urbanization and literacy of the populace, the newspaper, the magazine, the public library, the telephone, the radio, television, the overwhelming Orwellian world of public advertising, the computer, the Internet. A new world of communications duly spawned a new world of communicators and schools to teach how best to train them in its most effective techniques. The training of ministers and priests in homiletics took notice of them, too.

The expectation of the present generation of young adults when confronted by, say, a sermon delivered by Ralph Waldo Emerson would in all likelihood be completely confounded. The dense scriptural quotation, the biblical and historical allusion, the extended argument of heads and subheads, and the overall complex ratiocination—never mind the time-consuming length—would doubtless have them nervously eyeing their watches or sinking into slumber.

The accumulation of distraction in our culture is not a recent phenomenon. Consider an extraordinary painting made by the eccentric Belgian James Ensor in 1888, entitled *The Entry of Christ into Brussels*. It is a huge canvas, some eight by twelve feet in dimension and—foreground, middle ground, background—crammed with thousands of individual figures, all parading into the city and carrying political and civic banners, playing musical instruments, wearing carnival masks, showing off their coarse, irreducible personal or civic identities in the tradition of Bosch, Breughel, or Hogarth. In the center, the tiny figure of Jesus extends his hand in blessing, but literally no one seems to notice. It is an emblem of a world to come, the world we now inhabit.

The twentieth century has seen the hollowing out of the pulpit by indifference, by mockery and cynicism that give us the adjective "preachy" and the verb "sermonize," by the competing faiths of reason and unreason, by so many superseding "isms" that want to make the Word into mere words, by a disordered fear of personal commitment to belief, by a nervous diffidence over the power of ritual, by sheer impatience, and by the failure of the preacher to preach—or by preaching that abuses the very office of preaching.

Too many concessions have now been made to the world outside the church and synagogue doors, so that even if God did make an entry into Brussels—or New York or London or Geneva—this afternoon, He would first have to find His way through the parking lots and the food courts and the megachurch vestibules to get to the pulpit. The decline of preaching is no surprise. It happened because live public speech is no longer fostered, because so-called communication skills are prized above permitting the Word to flow through the heart and mind. The call to God's community is not to be confined to a sound bite or an infomercial. It may take different forms, but it is always clear, and it is always compelling.

The foregoing notwithstanding, as the lawyers say, as long as and wherever there are men and women who want to hear the Word of God, there will be preachers who will preach it to them. If preaching and the figure of the preacher have diminished in authority in our complex culture, it may be because they are too eager to please, too quick to assimilate to the larger culture around them by borrowing the latest communication techniques from television, advertising, and politics. Savonarola was not burned alive in medieval Florence because he made his audiences feel good. He moved them because he made his hearers look at their lives, feel compunction for their vanity, feel God's infinite mercy despite it, and take willed action to change their lives.

In the First Book of Kings we meet the ninth-century B.C. prophet Elijah, called to his office during the reign of Ahab. Who could imagine more difficult circumstances? He complained to the people, "I, even I only, remain a prophet of the Lord; but Ba'al's prophets are four hundred and fifty men." Then, when he had definitively demonstrated God's power working through him, and all the prophets of Ba'al were slain, he found himself still persecuted by Jezebel, wife of Ahab, whose god, Ba'al, had first distracted the Israelites and to whom she remained loyal. Fleeing to a cave in Mount Horeb, he waited for instructions:

> And behold, the Lord passed by, and a great and strong wind rent the mountains, and brake in pieces the rock before the Lord; but the Lord was not in the wind: and after the wind an earthquake; but the Lord was not in the earthquake; and after the earthquake a fire; but the Lord was not in the fire: and after the fire a still small voice. And it was so, when Elijah heard it, that he wrapped his face in his mantle, and went out, and stood in the entering in of the cave. (19:11–13.)

The responsibility for hearing the still small voice is ours alone.

Let us conclude with a thought or two on the pleasures of reading sermons, which, like oratory in general, are precursors of the essay. Sermons in volume form were once arrayed in the bookcase next to the family Bible as staples of lay reading. In the late fifteenth and the sixteenth centuries in Europe, they formed the backbone of the exploding new printing industry. And there was a time from which we are not long removed when auditors traveled great, arduous distances to hear a preacher, and when newspapers such as the *New York Times* regularly printed précis of the Sunday sermons preached in the major city churches.

Our hope is that through the portal of this volume many new readers will discover some of the finest and least-known English prose ever written, prose that easily takes its place beside anything they may have encountered before; that others will want to seek out the remaining sermons of individual preachers in English or in translation (try John Henry Newman or the incomparable Augustine); and that a positive reception of this effort may succeed in turning the tiny trickle of contemporary sermon publication into at least a babbling brook. The current unavailability of the sermons of many, many first-rate preachers past and present is, if not a shame, certainly a sad reality. By doing this minimalist archaeological work and revealing the richness of possibility that now lies open to explore, we rest provisionally content.

It is our further hope that reading these sermons will delight and move you—whatever your religion or lack thereof and whatever expectation you have of them—as you begin to turn the pages. However, as you read them, it might be worth calling to your attention a practice nearly as old as the oldest sermons in the book. It is known as *lectio divina,* "spiritual reading," a method for experiencing a sacred text so as to derive its highest benefit: the cure of the soul. Though it was already familiarly referred to as a practice in the sixth-century monastic *Rule of St. Benedict, lectio divina* in essence calls for the reader to read slowly and carefully in stages designed not merely to gather the sense or store the information, as we might read a report or even a novel.

Instead, the idea is, first, carefully to read a passage, a line, a phrase, even just a word until it yields its meaning; next, to meditate on that meaning in one's own circumstances; then to experience the spiritual good the words bring to one's life; finally, to let the process result in good actions. As reading for a fast-paced, active modern life, sermons will never compete with television advertising or newspaper headlines (though, as we have seen, there was a time when they would have won such a competition hands down!). Yet in their way they may still offer us moderns a means of attaining a state of reflective tranquillity so clearly desirable to offset the slings and arrows of everyday life. It is well to recall the caution of St. Vincent de Paul (ca. 1580–1660), "He who is in a hurry delays the things of God." To go apart, however briefly, from what one medieval writer called "the shipwreck of the world" and, through such reading, come upon a transforming insight for one's life from the silence of centuries past is a joy we wish all who read TONGUES OF ANGELS, TONGUES OF MEN.

JOHN F. THORNTON
New York City
Spring 1999

"Are Not My Words
as a Fire? Saith the
Lord, and as a
Hammer That Breaketh
the Rock in Pieces?"

The Apostolic Era

Jesus of Nazareth

4 B.C.—ca. A.D. 32

As the poet Gerard Manley Hopkins would put it eighteen centuries later, "Nowhere in literature is there anything to match the Sermon on the Mount: if there is let men bring it forward." Its grandeur and its epitomization of an entire faith are astonishing, yet this Sermon is in some ways an anomalous inspiration for the very sermon form.

In Matthew's version (there is another to be found in Luke 6:17–49) Jesus speaks outdoors, apparently to his disciples, even though multitudes surround them; he is not speaking while conducting any religious ceremony but is rather teaching these twelve men who have given up their former lives and have now become his followers.

That this teaching will lead to the cross is hinted at when he speaks to them directly in the last of the eight Beatitudes: "Blessed are ye, when men shall revile you, and persecute you, and shall say all manner of evil against you falsely, for my sake." (5:11.)

Of the new ways in which they were being taught to stand in relation to God, perhaps none is so startling as the command to "love your enemies," meaning we are no longer to have enemies and indeed are to give love in return for any hatred we may receive. The reaction of his listeners to this radical injunction—and to the rest of his teaching—was astonishment. But it was the astonishment of those whose minds had been opened to a new reality by the uncanny authority (see 7:29) with which he taught.

This sermon of sermons, never after surpassed, remains for men and women of faith a standard by which all religious speech may be measured.

The Sermon on the Mount

Matthew 5–8:1 (King James Version)

And seeing the multitudes, he went up into a mountain: and when he was set, his disciples came unto him: and he opened his mouth, and taught them, saying,

Blessed are the poor in spirit: for theirs is the kingdom of heaven.
Blessed are they that mourn: for they shall be comforted.
Blessed are the meek: for they shall inherit the earth.
Blessed are they which do hunger and thirst after righteousness: for they shall be filled.
Blessed are the merciful: for they shall obtain mercy.
Blessed are the pure in heart: for they shall see God.
Blessed are the peacemakers: for they shall be called the children of God.
Blessed are they which are persecuted for righteousness' sake: for theirs is the kingdom of heaven.

Blessed are ye, when men shall revile you, and persecute you, and shall say all manner of evil against you falsely, for my sake. Rejoice, and be exceeding glad: for great is your reward in heaven: for so persecuted they the prophets which were before you.

Ye are the salt of the earth: but if the salt have lost his savour, wherewith shall it be salted? it is thenceforth good for nothing, but to be cast out, and to be trodden under foot of men.

Ye are the light of the world. A city that is set on an hill cannot be hid. Neither do men light a candle, and put it under a bushel, but on a candlestick; and it giveth light unto all that are in the house. Let your light so shine before men, that they may see your good works, and glorify your Father which is in heaven.

Think not that I am come to destroy the law, or the prophets: I am not come to destroy, but to fulfil. For verily I say unto you, Till heaven and earth pass, one jot or one tittle shall in no wise pass from the law, till all be fulfilled. Whosoever therefore shall break one of these least commandments, and shall teach men so, he shall be called the least in the kingdom of heaven: but whosoever shall do and teach them, the same shall be called great in the kingdom of heaven. For I say unto you, That except your righteousness shall exceed the righteousness of the scribes and Pharisees, ye shall in no case enter into the kingdom of heaven.

Ye have heard that it was said by them of old time, Thou shalt not kill; and whosoever shall kill shall be in danger of the judgment: But I say unto you, That whosoever is angry with his brother without a cause shall be in danger of the judgment: and whosoever shall say to his brother, Raca [Fool], shall be in danger of the council: but whosoever shall say, Thou fool, shall be in danger of hell fire. Therefore if thou bring thy gift to the altar, and there rememberest that thy brother hath aught against thee; leave there thy gift before the altar, and go thy way; first be reconciled to thy brother, and then come and offer thy gift. Agree with thine adversary quickly, whiles thou art in the way with him; lest at any time the adversary deliver thee to the judge, and the judge deliver thee to the officer, and thou be cast into prison. Verily I say unto thee, Thou shalt by no means come out thence, till thou hast paid the uttermost farthing.

Ye have heard that it was said by them of old time, Thou shalt not commit adultery: but I say unto you, That whosoever looketh on a woman to lust after her hath committed adultery with her already in his heart. And if thy right eye offend thee, pluck it out, and cast it from thee: for it is profitable for thee that one of thy members should perish, and not that thy whole body should be cast into hell. And if thy right hand offend thee, cut it off, and cast it from thee: for it is profitable for thee that one of thy members should perish, and not that thy whole body should be cast into hell.

It hath been said, Whosoever shall put away his wife, let him give her a writing of divorcement: but I say unto you, That whosoever shall put away his wife, saving for the cause of fornication, causeth her to commit adultery: and whosoever shall marry her that is divorced committeth adultery.

Again, ye have heard that it hath been said by them of old time, Thou shalt not forswear thyself, but shalt perform unto the Lord thine oaths: but I say unto you, Swear not at all; neither by heaven; for it is God's throne: nor by the earth; for it is his footstool: neither by Jerusalem; for it is the city of the great King. Neither shalt thou swear by thy head, because thou canst not make one hair white or black. But let your communication be, Yea, yea; Nay, nay: for whatsoever is more than these cometh of evil.

Ye have heard that it hath been said, An eye for an eye, and a tooth for a tooth: but I say unto you, That ye resist not evil: but whosoever shall smite thee on thy right cheek, turn to him the other also. And if any man will sue thee at the law, and take away thy coat, let him have thy cloak also. And whosoever shall compel thee to go a mile, go with him twain. Give to him that asketh thee, and from him that would borrow of thee turn not thou away.

Ye have heard that it hath been said, Thou shalt love thy neighbour, and hate thine enemy. But I say unto you, Love your enemies, bless them that curse you, do good to them that hate you, and pray for them which despitefully use you, and persecute you; that ye may be the children of your Father which is in heaven: for he maketh his sun to rise on the evil and on the good, and sendeth rain on the just and on the unjust. For if ye love them which love you, what reward have ye? do not even the publicans the same? And if ye salute your brethren only, what do ye more than others? do not even the publicans so? Be ye therefore perfect, even as your Father which is in heaven is perfect.

Take heed that ye do not your alms before men, to be seen of them: otherwise ye have no reward of your Father which is in heaven.

Therefore when thou doest thine alms, do not sound a trumpet before thee, as the hypocrites do in the synagogues and in the streets, that they may have glory of men. Verily I say unto you, They have their reward. But when thou doest alms, let not thy left hand know what thy right hand doeth: That thine alms may be in secret: and thy Father which seeth in secret himself shall reward thee openly.

And when thou prayest, thou shalt not be as the hypocrites are: for they love to pray standing in the synagogues and in the corners of the streets, that they may be seen of men. Verily I say unto you, They have their reward. But thou, when thou prayest, enter into thy closet, and when thou hast shut thy door, pray to thy Father which is in secret; and thy Father which seeth in secret shall reward thee openly.

But when ye pray, use not vain repetitions, as the heathen do: for they think that they shall be heard for their much speaking. Be not ye therefore like unto them: for your Father knoweth what things ye have need of, before ye ask him. After this manner therefore pray ye:

> Our Father which art in heaven,
> Hallowed be thy name.
> Thy kingdom come.
> Thy will be done
> in earth, as it is in heaven.
> Give us this day our daily bread.
> And forgive us our debts,
> as we forgive our debtors.
> And lead us not into temptation,
> but deliver us from evil:
> For thine is the kingdom, and the
> power, and the glory, for ever.
> Amen.

For if ye forgive men their trespasses, your heavenly Father will also forgive you: But if ye forgive not men their trespasses, neither will your Father forgive your trespasses.

Moreover when ye fast, be not, as the hypocrites, of a sad countenance: for they disfigure their faces, that they may appear unto men to fast. Verily I say unto you, They have their reward. But thou, when thou fastest, anoint thine head, and wash thy face; that thou appear not unto men to fast, but unto thy Father which is in secret: and thy Father, which seeth in secret, shall reward thee openly.

Lay not up for yourselves treasures upon earth, where moth and rust doth corrupt, and where thieves break through and steal: but lay up for yourselves treasures in heaven, where neither moth nor rust doth corrupt, and where thieves do not break through nor steal: for where your treasure is, there will your heart be also.

The light of the body is the eye: if therefore thine eye be single, thy whole body shall be full of light. But if thine eye be evil, thy whole body shall be full of darkness. If therefore the light that is in thee be darkness, how great is that darkness!

No man can serve two masters: for either he will hate the one, and love the other; or else he will hold to the one, and despise the other. Ye cannot serve God and mammon.

Therefore I say unto you, Take no thought for your life, what ye shall eat, or what ye shall drink; nor yet for your body, what ye shall put on. Is not the life more than meat, and the body than raiment? Behold the fowls of the air: for they sow not, neither do they reap, nor gather into barns; yet your heavenly Father feedeth them. Are ye not much better than they? Which of you by taking thought can add one cubit unto his stature? And why take ye thought for raiment? Consider the lilies of the field, how they grow: they toil not, neither do they spin: and yet I say unto you, That even Solomon in all his glory was not arrayed like one of these. Wherefore, if God so clothe the grass of the field, which today is, and tomorrow is cast into the oven, shall he not much more clothe you, O ye of little faith? Therefore take no thought, saying, What shall we eat? or, What shall we drink? or, Wherewithal shall we be clothed? (For after all these things do the Gentiles seek:) for your heavenly Father knoweth that ye have need of all these things. But seek ye first the kingdom of God, and his righteousness; and all these things shall be added unto you.

Take therefore no thought for the morrow: for the morrow shall take thought for the things of itself. Sufficient unto the day is the evil thereof.

Judge not, that ye be not judged. For with what judgment ye judge, ye shall be judged: and with what measure ye mete, it shall be measured to you again. And why beholdest thou the mote that is in thy brother's eye, but considerest not the beam that is in thine own eye? Or how wilt thou say to thy brother, Let me pull out the mote out of thine eye; and, behold, a beam is in thine own eye? Thou hypocrite, first cast out the beam out of thine own eye; and then shalt thou see clearly to cast out the mote out of thy brother's eye.

Give not that which is holy unto the dogs, neither cast ye your pearls before swine, lest they trample them under their feet, and turn again and rend you.

Ask, and it shall be given you; seek, and ye shall find; knock, and it shall be opened unto you: For every one that asketh receiveth; and he that seeketh findeth; and to him that knocketh it shall be opened. Or what man is there of you, whom if his son ask bread, will he give him a stone? Or if he ask a fish, will he give him a serpent? If ye then, being evil, know how to give good gifts unto your children, how much more shall your Father which is in heaven give good things to them that ask him? Therefore all things whatsoever ye would that men should do to you, do ye even so to them: for this is the law and the prophets.

Enter ye in at the strait gate: for wide is the gate, and broad is the way, that leadeth to destruction, and many there be which go in thereat: because strait is the gate, and narrow is the way, which leadeth unto life, and few there be that find it.

Beware of false prophets, which come to you in sheep's clothing, but inwardly they are ravening wolves. Ye shall know them by their fruits. Do men gather grapes of thorns, or figs of thistles? Even so every good tree bringeth forth good fruit; but a corrupt tree bringeth forth evil fruit. A good tree cannot bring forth evil fruit, neither can a corrupt tree bring forth good fruit. Every tree that bringeth not forth good fruit is hewn down, and cast into the fire. Wherefore by their fruits ye shall know them.

Not every one that saith unto me, Lord, Lord, shall enter into the kingdom of heaven; but he that doeth the will of my Father which is in heaven. Many will say to me in that day, Lord, Lord, have we not prophesied in thy name? and in thy name have cast out devils? and in thy name done many wonderful works? And then will I profess unto them, I never knew you: depart from me, ye that work iniquity.

Therefore whosoever heareth these sayings of mine, and doeth them, I will liken him unto a wise man, which built his house upon a rock: and the rain descended, and the floods came, and the winds blew, and beat upon that house; and it fell not: for it was founded upon a rock. And every one that heareth these sayings of mine, and doeth them not, shall be likened unto a foolish man, which built his house upon the sand: and the rain descended, and the floods came, and the winds blew, and beat upon that house; and it fell: and great was the fall of it.

. . .

And it came to pass, when Jesus had ended these sayings, the people were astonished at his doctrine: for he taught them as one having authority, and not as the scribes.

When he was come down from the mountain, great multitudes followed him.

St. Peter

d. A.D. 67

One of the twelve disciples of Jesus Christ, and first bishop of Rome, St. Peter's missionary activities are chronicled in the Acts of the Apostles. In Christian churches the feast of Pentecost on the seventh Sunday after Easter recalls the rush of a great wind from heaven into the house where the apostles sat after the ascension of Christ, and the appearance of "cloven tongues" of fire over their heads. According to the opening of Chapter 2 of the Acts, those present were filled with the Holy Spirit and granted the "gift of tongues," a miraculous capacity for polyglot speech and instant understanding of the languages of other nations. Miracle or parable of the spread of Christianity throughout the known world, the event is celebrated today in Pentecostal churches as a commission to express the uninhibited love of the Holy Spirit through *glossolalia,* an incomprehensible and ecstatic flow of speech. The skeptical witnesses to the original event mocked the participants, calling them "full of new wine."

Peter's response refutes their charge of drunkenness and verbal intoxication. He preached to the men of Judea with the same blunt voice with which the gospels credit this simple, rocklike, yet impulsive man, although wonders, signs, and the workings of God on the Last Day are part of his testimony. In Christian legend, the saint is the patron of fishermen; in Church history, the fisher of souls and keeper of the keys and the sword of the new heaven and new earth his sermon promises. On this occasion, the eloquence of the unlikely disciple whom Christ made head of the early Church can be read as the New Testament's most persuasive evidence of the gift of tongues and as an important proclamation of early Christian eschatology: Peter's sermon demands not only otherworldliness but a response to the commandment of love.

The Pentecost Sermon

Acts 2:14–39 (King James Version)

Ye men of Judaea, and all ye that dwell in Jerusalem, be this known unto you, and hearken to my words; for these are not drunken, as ye suppose, seeing it is but the third hour of the day. But this is that which was spoken by the prophet Joel:

> And it shall come to pass in the last days, saith God, I will pour out of my Spirit upon all flesh; and your sons and your daughters shall prophesy, and your young men shall see visions, and your old men shall dream dreams; and on my servants and on my handmaidens I will pour out in those days of my Spirit; and they shall prophesy. And I will shew wonders in heaven above, and signs in the earth beneath; blood, and fire, and vapor of smoke. The sun shall be turned into darkness, and the moon into blood, before that great and notable day of the Lord come; and it shall come to pass, that whosoever shall call on the name of the Lord shall be saved.

Ye men of Israel, hear these words: Jesus of Nazareth, a man approved of God among you by miracles and wonders and signs, which God did by him in the midst of you, as ye yourselves also know—him, being delivered by the determinate counsel and foreknowledge of God, ye have taken, and by wicked hands have crucified and slain, whom God hath raised up, having loosed the pains of death, because it was not possible that he should be holden of it. For David speaketh concerning him:

I foresaw the Lord always before my face, for he is on my right hand, that I should not be moved. Therefore did my heart rejoice, and my tongue was glad; moreover also my flesh shall rest in hope; because thou wilt not leave my soul in hell, neither wilt thou suffer thine Holy One to see corruption. Thou hast made known to me the ways of life; thou shalt make me full of joy with thy countenance.

Men and brethren, let me freely speak unto you of the patriarch David, that he is both dead and buried, and his sepulchre is with us unto this day. Therefore, being a prophet, and knowing that God had sworn with an oath to him, that of the fruit of his loins, according to the flesh, he would raise up Christ to sit on his throne; he, seeing this before, spake of the resurrection of Christ, that his soul was not left in hell, neither his flesh did see corruption. This Jesus hath God raised up, whereof we all are witnesses. Therefore, being by the right hand of God exalted, and having received of the Father the promise of the Holy Ghost, he hath shed forth this, which ye now see and hear. For David is not ascended into the heavens; but he saith himself,

The Lord said unto my Lord, Sit thou on my right hand until I make thy foes thy footstool.

Therefore, let all the house of Israel know assuredly, that God hath made that same Jesus, whom ye have crucified, both Lord and Christ.

Repent, and be baptised every one of you in the name of Jesus Christ for the remission of sins, and ye shall receive the gift of the Holy Ghost. For the promise is unto you, and to your children, and to all that are afar off, even as many as the Lord our God shall call.

St. Paul

d. A.D. 64

*P*aul, born Saul of Tarsus, the most famous convert (and earliest persecutor) in the history of early Christianity, was the great apostle to the Gentiles, a traveling missionary whose journeys met with hardship, persecution, and a final martyrdom in Rome. He was released for missionary service with Barnabas, as one of two of the most gifted and outstanding men in the Church. Their itinerary took them through the Greek archipelago where they encountered sorcerers, skeptics, and shipwreck. In Antioch, Paul visited the synagogue, where he connected the narrative of the life and death of Jesus Christ to the history of the House of David; there, he began to unfold the uniquely Pauline vision of Christian freedom and spoke throughout the ancient world in the language he prescribed in his First Epistle to the Corinthians:

> "Though I speak with the tongues of men and of angels, and have not charity, I am become as sounding brass, or a tinkling cymbal. And though I have the gift of prophecy, and understand all mysteries, and all knowledge, and though I have all faith, so that I could remove mountains, and have not charity, I am nothing." (1 Cor. 13:1–2.)

Expelled from Antioch, Paul continued to endure persecution and stoning, like the first martyr, Stephen, whose death at the hands of a mob he himself had witnessed in Damascus. After many perils, he arrived in Athens. There, this fiercest of the early evangelists met his most formidable opponents. In a dialectical engagement with the Epicurean and Stoic philosophers of pagan antiquity, Paul threw down his most powerful challenge to the altars of the classical world. That sermon from Acts was preached to refute the spiritual autonomy of the Stoic thinkers with the message of Christ's gift of deliverance from the self.

Standing on the hill known as the Areopagus (Hill of Mars), Paul delivered his speech to an audience in the rock-cut seats on the northeastern slope of the high place where the oldest council of the city held its meetings, a practice begun long before the Roman conquest of Greece. The "devotions" Paul refers to are images; the reference to the altar of the "Unknown God" comes from a tale in Diogenes Laertius which states that the Athenians during a plague sent for one Epimenides, a wise man from Crete, who advised them to make sacrifice at various spots to "whatever God might be concerned," and that, to commemorate the occasion, altars to nameless gods were set up all over the city.

Paul is the great model of a missionary, endeavoring constantly to establish common ground with his audience, brilliantly alluding both to the Epicurean doctrine that God needs nothing from men and to the Stoic belief that God is the source of all life. Against the Greek claim to racial superiority over non-Greeks ("barbarians"), the fearless Paul asserts the unity of all mankind. In his reference to living and moving in God, St. Paul's syncretic genius alludes once more to the Cretan elder, to Zeus's son, the pagan half human, half bull, Minos, and the Zeus of the Stoic poets. At the same time, he emphasizes the personality of the divine, in contrast to a materialistic pantheon, "graven by art and man's device." He appeals as well to the Greek notion of the immortality of the soul, while introducing the idea of the resurrection of the dead.

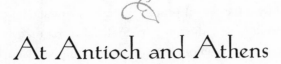

At Antioch and Athens

Acts 13:16–41; 17:22–31 (King James Version)

Then Paul stood up, and beckoning with his hand said,

Men of Israel, and ye that fear God, give audience. The God of this people of Israel chose our fathers, and exalted the people when they dwelt as strangers in the land of Egypt, and with a high arm brought he them out of it. And about the time of forty years suffered he their manners in the wilderness. And when he had destroyed seven nations in the land of Canaan, he divided their land to them by lot. And after that he gave unto them judges about the space of four hundred and fifty years, until Samuel the prophet. And afterward they desired a king: and God gave unto them Saul the son of Kish, a man of the tribe of Benjamin, by the space of forty years. And when he had removed him, he raised up unto them David to be their king; to whom also he gave testimony, and said, I have found David the son of Jesse, a man after mine own heart, which shall fulfil all my will. Of this man's seed hath God, according to his promise, raised unto Israel a Saviour, Jesus: when John had first preached before his coming the baptism of repentance to all the people of Israel. And as John fulfilled his course, he said, Whom think ye that I am? I am not he. But, behold, there cometh one after me, whose shoes of his feet I am not worthy to loose.

Men and brethren, children of the stock of Abraham, and whosoever among you feareth God, to you is the word of this salvation sent. For they that dwell at Jerusalem, and their rulers, because they knew him not, nor yet the voices of the prophets which are read every sabbath day, they have fulfilled them in condemning him. And though they found no cause of death in him, yet desired they Pilate that he should be slain. And when they had fulfilled all that was written of him, they took him down from the tree, and laid him in a sepulchre. But God raised him from the dead: and he was seen many days of them which came up with him from Galilee to Jerusalem, who are his witnesses unto the people. And we declare unto you glad tidings, how that the promise which was made unto the fathers, God hath fulfilled the same unto us their children, in that he hath raised up Jesus again; as it is also written in the second psalm, Thou art my Son, this day have I begotten thee.

And as concerning that he raised him up from the dead, now no more to return to corruption, he said on this wise, I will give you the sure mercies of David.

Wherefore he saith also in another psalm, Thou shalt not suffer thine Holy One to see corruption.

For David, after he had served his own generation by the will of God, fell on sleep, and was laid unto his fathers, and saw corruption: but he, whom God raised again, saw no corruption. Be it known unto you there-

fore, men and brethren, that through this man is preached unto you the forgiveness of sins: and by him all that believe are justified from all things, from
which ye could not be justified by the law of Moses. Beware therefore, lest
that come upon you, which is spoken of in the prophets;

Behold, ye despisers, and wonder, and perish: for I work a work in
your days, a work which ye shall in no wise believe, though a man declare
it unto you. . . .

Then Paul stood in the midst of Mars' hill, and said, Ye men of Athens,
I perceive that in all things ye are too superstitious. For as I passed by, and
beheld your devotions, I found an altar with this inscription, To the Unknown God. Whom therefore ye ignorantly worship, him declare I unto
you. God that made the world and all things therein, seeing that he is Lord
of heaven and earth, dwelleth not in temples made with hands; neither is
worshipped with men's hands, as though he needed any thing, seeing he
giveth to all life, and breath, and all things; and hath made of one blood all
nations of men for to dwell on all the face of the earth, and hath determined
the times before appointed, and the bounds of their habitation; that they
should seek the Lord, if haply they might feel after him, and find him,
though he be not far from every one of us: for in him we live, and move,
and have our being; as certain also of your own poets have said, For we are
also his offspring.

Forasmuch then as we are the offspring of God, we ought not to think
that the Godhead is like unto gold, or silver, or stone, graven by art and
man's device.

And the times of this ignorance God winked at; but now commandeth
all men every where to repent: because he hath appointed a day, in the
which he will judge the world in righteousness by that man whom he hath
ordained; whereof he hath given assurance unto all men, in that he hath
raised him from the dead.

Clement of Rome

d. A.D. 97

*V*arious editors have described this speech by Clement, and its exposition of Isaiah's text, as not only an anonymous document, but possibly the oldest surviving sermon manuscript, a relic from the early Church at the beginning of the second century. Whatever its attribution, it has a secure place in the development of orthodox Christian doctrine, announcing a uniquely Christian historiography in which the God of both the New and the Old Testaments are one and the same. In this sermon, the history of salvation becomes part of the inner history of the world and an early Christian theory of revelation, while man and his destiny become the center of the universe. If the author was indeed Clement of Rome, he is the Pope who became the second successor, after Linus, to St. Peter.

The imagery employed by this elusive and perhaps anonymous figure (often confused with the later Clement of Alexandria, whose Christianity was steeped in Hellenism) reflects the persecution of the Christians under the Emperors Nero and Vespasian. Its author calls on the flock to remember that they shall be as "lambs in the midst of wolves," and, in his vision of Christ and the Church, suggests the struggle between paganism and Christianity in the amphitheater as well as in the forum where the revelation of the new Church first was forged in "a furnace of fire."

Christ and the Church

We ought to think highly of Christ. Brethren, it is fitting that you should think of Jesus Christ as of God—as the Judge of the living and the dead. And it does not become us to think lightly of our salvation; for if we think little of Him, we shall also hope but to obtain little *from* Him. And those of us who hear carelessly of these things, as if they were of small importance, commit sin, not knowing whence we have been called, and by whom, and to what place, and how much Jesus Christ submitted to suffer for our sakes. What return, then, shall we make to Him? or what fruit that shall be worthy of that which He has given to us? For, indeed, how great are the benefits which we owe to Him! He has graciously given us light; as a Father, He has called us sons; He has saved us when we were ready to perish. What praise, then, shall we give to Him, or what return shall we make for the things which we have received? We were deficient in understanding, worshiping stones and wood, and gold, and silver, and brass, the works of men's hands; and our whole life was nothing else than death. Involved in blindness, and with such darkness before our eyes, we have received sight, and through His will have laid aside that cloud by which we were enveloped. For He had compassion on us, and mercifully saved us, observing the many errors in which we were entangled, as well as the destruction to which we were exposed, and that we had no hope of salvation except it came to us from Him. For He called us when we were not, and willed that out of nothing we should attain a real existence.

True confession of Christ. Let us, then, not only call Him Lord, for that will not save us. For He saith, "Not everyone that saith to Me, Lord, Lord, shall be saved, but he that worketh righteousness." Wherefore, brethren, let us confess Him by our works, by loving one another, by not committing adultery, or speaking evil of one another, or cherishing envy; but being continent, compassionate, and good. We ought also to sympathize with one another, and not be avaricious. By such works let us confess Him, and not by those that are of an opposite kind. And it is not fitting that we should fear men, but rather God. For this reason, if we should do such wicked things, the Lord hath said, "Even though ye were gathered together to Me in My very bosom, yet if ye were not to keep My commandments, I would cast you off, and say unto you, Depart from Me; I know not whence ye are, ye workers of iniquity."

This world should be despised. Wherefore, brethren, leaving willingly our sojourn in this present world, let us do the will of Him that called us, and not fear to depart out of this world. For the Lord saith, "Ye shall be as lambs in the midst of wolves." And Peter answered and said unto Him, "What, then, if the wolves shall tear in pieces the lambs?" Jesus said unto Peter, "The lambs have no cause after they are dead to fear the wolves; and in like manner, fear not ye them that kill you, and can do nothing more unto you; but fear Him who, after you are dead, has power over both soul and body to cast them into hell-fire." And consider, brethren, that the sojourning in the flesh in this world is but brief and transient, but the promise of Christ is great and wonderful, even the rest of the kingdom to come, and of life everlasting. By what course of conduct, then, shall we attain these things, but by leading a holy and righteous life, and by deeming these worldly things as not belonging to us, and not fixing our desires upon them? For if we desire to possess them, we fall away from the path of righteousness.

The present and future worlds are enemies to each other. Now the Lord declares, "No servant can serve two masters." If we desire, then, to serve both God and mammon, it will be unprofitable for us. "For what will it profit if a man gain the whole world, and lose his own soul?" This world and the next are two enemies. The one urges to adultery and corruption, avarice and deceit; the other bids farewell to these things. We cannot therefore be the friends of both; and it behoves us, by renouncing the one, to make sure of the other. Let us reckon that it is better to hate the things present, since they are trifling, and transient, and corruptible; and to love those which are to come, as being good and incorruptible. For if we do the will of Christ, we shall find rest; otherwise, nothing shall deliver us from eternal punishment, if we disobey His commandments. For thus also saith the Scripture in Ezekiel, "If Noah, Job, and Daniel should rise up, they should not deliver their children in captivity." Now, if men so eminently righteous are not able by their righteousness to deliver their children, how can we hope to enter into the royal residence of God unless we keep our baptism holy and undefiled? Or who shall be our advocate, unless we be found possessed of works of holiness and righteousness?

We must strive in order to be crowned. Wherefore, then, my brethren, let us struggle with all earnestness, knowing that the contest is in our case close at hand, and that many undertake long voyages to strive for a corruptible reward; yet all are not crowned, but those only that have labored hard and striven gloriously. Let us therefore so strive, that we may all be crowned. Let us run the straight course, even the race that is incorruptible; and let us in great numbers set out for it, and strive that we may be crowned. And should we not all be able to obtain the crown, let us at least come near to it. We must remember that he who strives in the corruptible contest, if he be found acting unfairly, is taken away and scourged, and cast forth from the lists. What then think ye? For of those who do not preserve the seal unbroken, the Scripture saith, "Their worm shall not die, and their fire shall not be quenched, and they shall be a spectacle to all flesh."

The necessity of repentance while we are on earth. As long, therefore, as we are upon earth, let us practice repentance, for we are as clay in the hand of the artificer. For as the potter, if he make a vessel, and it be distorted or broken in his hands, fashions it over again; but if he have before this cast it into the furnace of fire, can no longer find any help for it; so let us also, while we are in this world, repent with our whole heart of the evil deeds we have done in the flesh, that we may be saved by the Lord, while we have yet an opportunity of repentance. For after we have gone out of the world, no further power of confessing or repenting will there belong to us. Wherefore, brethren, by doing the will of the Father, and keeping the flesh holy, and observing the commandments of the Lord, we shall obtain eternal life. For the Lord saith in the Gospel, "If ye have not kept that which was small, who will commit to you the great? For I say unto you, that he that is faithful in that which is least, is faithful also in much." This, then, is what He means: "Keep the flesh holy and the seal undefiled, that ye may receive eternal life."

We shall be judged in the flesh. And let no one of you say that this very flesh shall not be judged, nor rise again. Consider ye in what state ye were saved, in what ye received sight, if not while ye were in this flesh. We must therefore preserve the flesh as the temple of God. For as ye were called in the flesh, ye shall also come to be judged in the flesh. As Christ the Lord who saved us, though He was first a Spirit, became flesh, and thus called us, so shall we also receive the reward in this flesh. Let us therefore love one another, that we may all attain to the kingdom of God. While we have an opportunity of being healed, let us yield ourselves to God that healeth us, and give to Him a recompense. Of what sort? Repentance out of a sincere heart; for He knows all things beforehand, and is acquainted with what is in our hearts. Let us therefore give Him praise, not with the mouth only, but also with the heart, that He may accept us as sons. For the Lord has said, "Those are My brethren who do the will of My Father."

Vice is to be forsaken, and virtue followed. Wherefore, my brethren, let us do the will of the Father who called us, that we may live; and let us earnestly follow after virtue, but forsake every wicked tendency which would lead us into transgression; and flee from ungodliness, lest evils overtake us. For if we are diligent in doing good, peace will follow us. On this account, such men cannot find it, *i.e.*, peace, as are influenced by human terrors, and prefer rather present enjoyment to the promise which shall afterward be fulfilled. For they know not what torment present enjoyment incurs, or what felicity is involved in the future promise. And if, indeed they themselves only did such things, it would be the more tolerable; but now they persist in imbuing innocent souls with their pernicious doctrines, not knowing that they shall receive a double condemnation, both they and those that hear them.

We ought to serve God, trusting in His promises. Let us therefore serve God with a pure heart, and we shall be righteous; but if we do not serve Him, because we believe not the promise of God, we shall be miserable. For the prophetic word also declares, "Wretched are those of a double mind, and who doubt in their heart, who say, All these things have we heard even in the times of our fathers; but though we have waited day by day, we have seen none of them accomplished. Ye fools! compare yourselves to a tree; take, for instance, the vine. First of all it sheds its leaves, then the bud appear; after that the sour grape, and then the fully ripened fruit. So, likewise, my people have borne disturbances and afflictions, but afterward shall they receive their good things." Wherefore, my brethren, let us not be of a double mind, but let us hope and endure, that we also may obtain the reward. For He is faithful who has promised that He will bestow on every one a reward according to his works. If, therefore, we shall do righteousness in the sight of God, we shall enter into His kingdom, and shall receive the promises, "which ear hath not heard, nor eye seen, neither have entered into the heart of man."

We are constantly to look for the kingdom of God. Let us expect, therefore, hour by hour, the kingdom of God in love and righteousness, since we know not the day of the appearing of God. For the Lord Himself, being asked by one when His kingdom would come, replied, "When two shall be one, and that which is without as that which is within, and the male with the female, neither male nor female." Now, two are one when we speak the truth one to another, and there is unfeignedly one soul in two bodies. And "that which is without as that which is within" meaneth this: He calls the soul "that which is within," and the body "that which is without." As, then, thy body is visible to sight, so also let thy soul be manifest by good works. And "the male with the female, neither male nor female," this meaneth, that a brother seeing a sister should think nothing about her as of a female, nor she think anything about him as of a male. If ye do these things, saith He, the kingdom of my Father shall come.

The living Church is the Body of Christ. Wherefore, brethren, if we do the will of God our Father, we shall be of the first Church, that is, spiritual, that hath been created before the sun and moon; but if we do not the will of the Lord, we shall be of the Scripture that saith, "My house was made a den of robbers." So then let us choose to be of the Church of life, that we may be saved. I do not, however, suppose ye are ignorant that the living Church is the body of Christ; for the Scripture saith, "God made man, male and female." The male is Christ, the female is the Church. And the Books and the Apostles plainly declare that the Church is not of the present, but from the beginning. For she was spiritual, as our Jesus also was, but was manifested in the last days that He might save us. Now the Church, being spiritual, was manifested in the flesh of Christ, thus signifying to us that, if any of us keep her in the flesh and do not corrupt her, he shall receive her again in the Holy Spirit: for this flesh is the copy of the spirit. No one then who corrupts the copy shall partake of the original. This then is what He meaneth, "Keep the flesh, that ye may partake of the spirit." But if we say that the flesh is the Church and the spirit Christ, then he that hath shamefully used the flesh hath shamefully used the Church. Such a one then shall not partake of the spirit, which is Christ. Such life and incorruption this flesh can partake of, when the Holy Spirit is joined to it. No one can utter or speak "what the Lord hath prepared" for His elect.

Faith and love the proper return to God. Now I do not think I have given you any light counsel concerning self-control, which if anyone do he will not repent of it, but will save both himself and me who counseled him. For it is no light reward to turn again a wandering and perishing soul that it may be saved. For this is the recompense we have to return to God who created us, if he that speaketh and heareth both speaketh and heareth with faith and love. Let us therefore abide in the things which we believed, righteous and holy, that with boldness we may ask of God who saith, "While thou art yet speaking, I will say, Lo, I am here." For this saying is the sign of a great promise; for the Lord saith of Himself that He is more ready to give than he that asketh to ask. Being therefore partakers of so great kindness, let us not be envious of one another in the obtaining of so many good things. For as great as is the pleasure which these sayings have for them that have done them, so great is the condemnation they have for them that have been disobedient.

The excellence of almsgiving. Wherefore, brethren, having received no small occasion for repentance, while we have the opportunity, let us turn unto God that called us, while we still have Him as One that receiveth us. For if we renounce these enjoyments and conquer our soul in not doing these its evil desires, we shall partake of the mercy of Jesus. But ye know that the day of judgment even now "cometh as a burning oven," and some "of the heavens shall melt," and all the earth shall be as lead melting on the fire, and then the hidden and open works of men shall appear. Almsgiving therefore is a good thing, as repentance from sin; fasting is better than prayer, but almsgiving than both; "but love covereth a multitude of sins." But prayer out of a good conscience delivereth from death. Blessed is everyone that is found full of these; for almsgiving lighteneth the burden of sin.

The danger of impenitence. Let us therefore repent from the whole heart, that no one of us perish by the way. For if we have commandments that we should also practice this, to draw away men from idols and instruct them, how much more ought a soul already knowing God not to perish! Let us therefore assist one another that we may also lead up those weak as to what is good, in order that all may be saved; and let us convert and admonish one another. And let us not think to give heed and believe now only, while we are admonished by the presbyters, but also when we have returned home, remembering the commandments of the Lord; and let us not be dragged away by worldly lusts, but coming more frequently let us attempt to make advances in the commandments of the Lord, that all being of the same mind we may be gathered together unto life. For the Lord said, "I come to gather together all the nations, tribes, and tongues." This He speaketh of the day of His appearing, when He shall come and redeem us, each one according to his works. And the unbelievers "shall see His glory," and strength; and they shall think it strange when they see the sovereignty of the world in Jesus, saying, Woe unto us, Thou wast He, and we did not know and did not believe, and we did not obey the presbyters when they declared unto us concerning our salvation. And "their worm dieth not, and their fire is not quenched, and they shall be for a spectacle unto all flesh." He speaketh of that day of judgment, when they shall see those among us that have been ungodly and acted deceitfully with the commandments of Jesus Christ. But the righteous who have done well and endured torments and hated the enjoyments of the soul, when they shall behold those that have gone astray and denied Jesus through their words or through their works, how that they are punished with grievous torments in an unquenchable fire, shall be giving glory to God, saying, There will be hope for him that hath served God with his whole heart.

The Preacher confesseth his own sinfulness. Let us also become of the number of them that give thanks, that have served God, and not of the ungodly that are judged. For I myself also, being an utter sinner, and not yet escaped from temptation, but still being in the midst of the engines of the devil, give diligence to follow after righteousness, that I may have strength to come even near it, fearing the judgment to come.

He justifieth his exhortation. Wherefore, brethren and sisters, after the God of truth hath been heard, I read to you an entreaty that ye may give heed to the things that are written, in order that ye may save both yourselves and him that readeth among you. For as a reward I ask of you that ye repent with the whole heart, thus giving to yourselves salvation and life. For by doing this we shall set a goal for all the young who are minded to labor on behalf of piety and the goodness of God. And let us not, unwise ones that we are, be affronted and sore displeased, whenever someone admonisheth and turneth us from iniquity unto righteousness. For sometimes while we are practicing evil things we do not perceive it on account of the double-mindedness and unbelief that is in our breasts, and we are "darkened in our understanding" by our vain lusts. Let us then practice righteousness that we may be saved unto the end. Blessed are they that obey these ordinances. Even if for a little time they suffer evil in the world, they shall enjoy the immortal fruit of the resurrection. Let not then the godly man be grieved, if he be wretched in the times that now are; a blessed time waits for him. He, living again above with the fathers, shall be joyful for an eternity without grief.

Concluding word of consolation. Doxology. But neither let it trouble your understanding, that we see the unrighteous having riches and the servants of God straitened. Let us therefore, brethren and sisters, be believing; we are striving in the contest of the living God, we are exercised by the present life, in order that we may be crowned by that to come. No one of the righteous received fruit speedily, but awaiteth it. For if God gave shortly the recompense of the righteous, straightway we would be exercising ourselves in business, not in godliness; for we would seem to be righteous, while pursuing not what is godly but what is gainful. And on this account Divine judgment surprised a spirit that was not righteous, and loaded it with chains.

To the only God invisible, the Father of truth, who sent forth to us the Savior and Prince of incorruption, through whom also He manifested to us the truth and the heavenly life, to Him be the glory for ever and ever. Amen.

PART II

"And They Went Forth and Preached Everywhere"

The Church Fathers

Origen

ca. 185–253

*I*n the third-century Church, Origen is said by a twentieth-century editor to have stood out "like an oak on the prairie," introducing themes and issues which are still among the most vexed and disturbing in the history of Christian thought. Thanks to Eusebius's *Ecclesiastical History,* written to include events as late as the year 324, we know something of this great Alexandrian's life, the martyr's son's zeal for martyrdom, his application to the study of the Scriptures, and his loathing, in the cauldron of Hellenistic learning which the capital represented, of unorthodoxy, heresy, and deviation from the ascetic life he embraced with exceptional fervor. According to Eusebius, he underwent castration, taking literally the precepts of Matthew 19:12 concerning eunuchs and the kingdom of heaven, but contemporary scholars dismiss the story as evidence of the Church historian's own tendency to a florid and orientalized narrative. But Eusebius exaggerated neither the vastness of his learning nor his prodigious literary production—estimated at somewhere between two and six thousand items.

He introduced Neoplatonic elements into Christian philosophy, giving the early Church a strong transfusion of mysticism, the power of belief over matter, and a theory of earthly beauty as an image of absolute beauty. However, the Bible itself, and the authority of the Scripture, was the other intellectual sphere Origen inhabited, after, according to hagiographic legend, this teacher and scholar sold his secular library for a secure income of four obols a day. His immersion in Scripture produced the homiletic outpourings on Genesis and other books of the Hebrew Bible, which remain vital to the curricula of both Jewish and Christian seminaries to this day. In the liturgical cycle of Bible readings still maintained in contemporary synagogues,

Genesis is introduced long after the Wisdom books and the Prophetic books.

Origen's quest for martyrdom was nearly fulfilled during the persecutions of either Decius or Valerian when he refused to offer sacrifice to the gods during a revival of ancient paganism. He was imprisoned, released, and died not long after.

Exodus Homily 3

*On that which is written: "I am feeble in speech
and slow in tongue" (Exod. 4:10)*

While Moses was in Egypt and "was educated in all the wisdom of the Egyptians," he was not "feeble in speech" nor "slow in tongue" nor did he profess to be ineloquent (cf. Acts 7:22; Exod. 4:10). For, so far as concerned the Egyptians, his speech was sonorous and his eloquence incomparable. But when he began to hear the voice of God and recognize divine communications, then he perceived his own voice to be meager and feeble and he understands his own tongue to be slow and impeded. When he began to recognize that true Word which "was in the beginning with God" (John 1:1), then he announces that he is mute. But let us use an analogy that what we are saying may be more easily understood. If a rational man be compared to the dumb animals, although he may be ignorant and unlearned, he will appear eloquent in comparison to those who are devoid of both reason and speech. But if he be compared to learned and eloquent men who are most excellent in all wisdom, he will appear ineloquent and dumb. But if someone should contemplate the divine Word himself and look at the divine wisdom itself, however learned and wise he be, he will confess that he is a dumb animal in comparison with God to a much greater extent than the cattle are in comparison with us. The blessed David was doubtless contemplating this and weighing himself in the balance of the divine wisdom when he said, "I became like a beast of burden before you." (Ps. 72:22.) It is in this sense, therefore, that Moses also, the greatest of the prophets, says to God in the present text that he is "feeble in speech" and "slow in tongue" and that he is not eloquent. (Exod. 4:10.) For all men, in comparison to the divine Word must be considered not only ineloquent, but also dumb.

(2) Divine dignity, therefore, recompenses him because he advanced into self-understanding where lies the greatest portion of wisdom. Hear how rich and magnificent were his gifts. "I," the text says, "will open your mouth and instruct you what you must say." (Exod. 4:12.) Blessed are those whose mouth God opens that they might speak. God opens the prophets' mouth and fills it with his eloquence, just as he says in the present text: "I will open your mouth and instruct you what you must say." (Exod. 4:12.) But God also says through David, "Open your mouth wide and I will fill it." (Ps. 80:11.) Paul likewise says, "That speech might be given to me in the opening of my mouth." (Eph. 6:19.) God, therefore, opens the mouth of those who speak the words of God.

I fear, however, that, on the contrary, there are some whose mouth the devil opens. For it is certain that the devil has opened the mouth of the man who speaks falsehood to speak falsehood. The devil has opened the mouth of the man who speaks false testimony. He has opened the mouth of those who bring forth scurrility, foulness, and other things of this kind from their mouth. I fear that also the devil opens the mouth "of the whisperers and dis-paragers" (cf. Rom. 1:29–30), and also of those who "bring forth idle words for which an account must be given in the day of judgment" (cf. Matt. 12:36). Now indeed who doubts that the devil opens the mouth of those who "speak iniquity against the Most High" (Ps. 72:8), "who deny that my Lord Jesus Christ has come in the flesh" (cf. 2 John 7), or "who blaspheme the Holy Spirit" for whom "there will be forgiveness neither in the present nor in the future age" (cf. Luke 12:10; Matt. 12:32)?

Do you wish that I show you from the Scriptures how the devil opens the mouth of men of this kind who speak against Christ? Note what has been written about Judas, how it is reported that "Satan entered him" (John 13:27), and that "the devil put it in his heart to betray Him" (cf. John 13:2). He, therefore, having received the money, opened his mouth that "he might confer with the leaders and the Pharisees, how he might betray him" (cf. Luke 22:4). Whence it seems to me to be no small gift to perceive the mouth which the devil opens. Such a mouth and words are not discerned without the gift of the Holy Spirit. Therefore, in the distributions of spiritual gifts, it is also added that "discernment of spirits" is given to certain people (cf. 1 Cor. 12:10). It is a spiritual gift, therefore, by which the spirit is discerned, as the Apostle says elsewhere, "Test the spirits, if they are from God" (cf. 1 John 4:1).

But as God opens the mouth of the saints, so, I think, God also may open the ears of the saints to hear the divine words. For thus Isaias the prophet says: "The Lord will open my ear that I may know when the word must be spoken" (cf. Isa. 50:4–5). So also the Lord opens eyes, as "the Lord opened Agar's eyes and she saw a well of living water." (Gen. 21:19.) But also Eliseus the prophet says: " 'Open, O Lord, the eyes of the servant that he may see that there are more with us than with the enemy.' And the Lord opened the eyes of the servant and behold, the whole mountain was full of horses and chariots and heavenly helpers." (4 Kings 6:16–17.) For "the angel of the Lord encircles those who fear him and will deliver them." (Ps. 33:8.)

As we said, therefore, God opens the mouth, the ears and the eyes, that we may either speak, or discern or hear what words are of God. But I also take this which the prophet says to be meaningful: "The instruction of the Lord has opened my ear." (Isa. 50:5.) This, I take it, pertains to us, that is commonly to the whole Church of God. For if we live in the instruction of the Lord, "the instruction of the Lord" opens our "ear" also. But the ear which is opened by the instruction of the Lord is not always opened, but is sometimes opened, sometimes closed. Hear the lawgiver saying, "Do not receive a vain report." (Exod. 23:1.) If ever, therefore, vain things are said, if ever things are brought forth which are empty, improper, shameful, profane, wicked, he who knows "the instruction of the Lord," closes his ears and turns away from listening and says: "I, however, as one deaf, did not hear, and I was as one dumb who has not opened his mouth." (Ps. 37:14.) But if what is said is useful for the soul, if it is a word from God, if it teaches morals, if it invites virtues, if it restrains vices, the ears ought to stand open to teachings of this kind, and not only the ears, but also the heart and mind and every entrance of the soul should be thrown open to such a report.

The Law, nevertheless, has used great moderation in stating the precept, "You shall not receive a vain report." (Exod. 23:1.) It did not say, "You shall not hear a vain report," but "You shall not receive such." We frequently hear vain words. What Marcion says is vain. What Valentinus says is vain. All who speak against the creator God speak vain words. Nevertheless, we frequently listen to those words so that we can respond to them lest they secretly snatch away by their embellished speech some of the simple who are also our brothers. Therefore, we hear these words, but we do not receive them. For they are spoken by that mouth which the devil has opened. And, therefore, we should pray that the Lord may think it proper to open our mouth that we might be able to refute those who contradict us and to close the mouth which the devil opens. We have said these things about the statement: "I will open your mouth and instruct you what you must say." (Exod. 4:12.)

It is promised not only to Moses, however, that his mouth will be opened by the Lord, but also to Aaron. For it is said of him also, "I will open your mouth and his mouth, and I will instruct you what you shall do." (Exod. 4:15.) For Aaron also "went to meet" Moses and he departed from Egypt. Where, however, did he go to meet him; to what sort of place? For it is of interest where he whose mouth is to be opened by God "meets" Moses. "He went to meet him," it says, "on the mountain of God." (Exod. 4:27.) Do you see that his mouth is opened deservedly who can "go to meet" Moses "on the mountain of God"? Peter, James, and John ascended the mountain of God that they might be worthy to see Jesus transfigured and that they might see Moses and Elias with him in glory. And you, therefore, unless you ascend the "mountain of God" and "go to meet" Moses there, that is unless you ascend the lofty understanding of the Law, unless you mount up to the peak of spiritual understanding, your mouth has not been opened by the Lord. If you stand in the lowly place of the letter and connect the text of the story with Jewish narratives, you have not gone to meet Moses "on the mountain of God," nor has God "opened your mouth" nor "instructed you in what you must say" (cf. Exod. 4:12). Unless, therefore, "Aaron had gone to meet Moses on the mountain" (Exod. 4:27), unless he had seen his sublime and elevated mind, unless he had perceived his lofty understanding, never would Moses have spoken the words of God to him nor delivered to him the power of signs and wonders nor have decreed him a participant in such a great mystery.

(3) But since it would take too long to speak about the individual

things one after another, let us see what "Moses and Aaron" said "when they went in" to Pharaoh. "Thus says the Lord, 'Send my people out that they may serve me in the wilderness.' " (Exod. 5:1.) Moses does not wish the people to serve God while they are in Egypt, but to go out into the desert and serve the Lord there. This means, without doubt, that as long as anyone remains in the gloomy activities of the world and lives in the darkness of daily business he cannot "serve the Lord," for he is not able "to serve two Lords." He cannot "serve the Lord and mammon" (cf. Luke 16:13; Matt. 6:24). Therefore, we must go forth from Egypt. We must leave the world behind if we wish "to serve the Lord." I mean, however, that we must leave the world behind not in space, but in the soul; not by setting out on a journey, but by advancing in faith. Hear John saying these same things: "Little children, do not love the world nor those things which are in the world, since everything which is in the world is the desire of the flesh and the desire of the eyes." (1 John 2:15–16.)

And what, however, does Moses say? Let us see how or to what extent he orders us to set out from Egypt. "We will go," he says, "a journey of three days into the wilderness and there we will sacrifice to the Lord our God." (Exod. 3:18.) What is the "journey of three days" which we are to go, that going out from Egypt we can arrive at the place in which we ought to sacrifice? I understand "way" to refer to him who said, "I am the way, the truth, and the life." (John 14:6.) We are to go this way for three days. For he who "has confessed with his mouth the Lord Jesus and believed in his heart that God raised him from the dead" on the third day, "will be saved" (cf. Rom. 10:9). This, therefore, is "the way of three days" by which one arrives at the place in which the "sacrifice of praise" (cf. Ps. 49:14) is sacrificed and offered to the Lord. What we have said pertains to the mystical meaning.

But if we also require a place for the moral meaning which is very useful for us, we travel a "journey of three days" from Egypt if we thus preserve ourselves from all filth of soul, body, and spirit, that, as the Apostle said, "our spirit and soul and body may be kept whole in the day of Jesus Christ." (1 Thess. 5:23.) We travel a "journey of three days" from Egypt if, ceasing from worldly things we turn our rational, natural, moral wisdom to the divine laws. We travel a "journey of three days" from Egypt if, purifying our words, deeds, or thoughts—for these are the three things by which men can sin—we would be made "pure in heart" so that we could "see God" (cf. Matt. 5:8).

Do you wish to see, however, that this is what the Holy Spirit indicates in the Scriptures? When this Pharaoh, who is the prince of Egypt, sees that he is strongly pressed to send the people of God out, he wishes to effect by this inferior place that "they not go farther away," that they not travel the full three days. He says, "Go not far away." (Exod. 8:24.) He does not wish the people of God to be far from himself. He wishes them to sin, if not in deed, certainly in word: to fail, if not in word, certainly in thought. He does not want them to travel a full three days from himself. He wishes to have one day at least in us as his own. In some he has two days, in others he possesses the full three days. But blessed are those who withdraw a whole three days from him and he possesses no day in them as his own.

Do not suppose, therefore, that Moses led the people out of Egypt only at that time. Even now Moses, whom we have with us—"for we have Moses and the prophets" (cf. Luke 16:29)—that is, the Law of God, wishes to lead you out of Egypt. If you would hear it, it wishes to make you "far" from Pharaoh. If only you would hear the Law of God and understand it spiritually, it desires to deliver you from the work of mud and chaff. It does not wish you to remain in the activities of the flesh and darkness, but to go out to the wilderness, to come to the place free from the confusions and disturbances of the world, to come to the rest of silence. For "words of wisdom are learned in silence and rest" (cf. Eccles. 9:17). When you come to this place of rest, therefore, you will be able "to sacrifice to the Lord" there. You will be able to know the Law of God and the virtue of the divine voice there. For that reason, therefore, Moses desires to bring you out of the midst of vacillating daily business and from the midst of noisy people. For that reason he desires you to depart from Egypt, that is from the darkness of ignorance that you might hear the Law of God and receive the light of knowledge.

But Pharaoh resists. "The ruler of this darkness" (cf. Eph. 6:12) does not wish you to relax; he does not wish you to be dragged away from his darkness and to be led to the light of knowledge. And hear what he says, "Who is he whose voice I shall heed? I do not know the Lord, and I will not send Israel out." (Exod. 5:2.) Do you hear what "the prince of this world" responds (cf. John 16:11)? He says he does not know God. Do you see what crude pride does? Pride controls him as long as "he does not share in human sufferings and is not scourged with men" (cf. Ps. 72:5). A little later you will see how much he advances by scourgings, how much better he is made having been chastised. He who now says, "I do not know the Lord" (Exod. 5:2), will say later, when he shall have felt the force of the whip, "Pray to the Lord for me." (Exod. 8:8.) And not only this, but he will also admit with his own magicians as witnesses that "it is the finger of God" (cf. Exod. 8:19) in the power of the signs. Let no one, therefore, be so ignorant of divine discipline that he thinks the divine scourgings to be destruction or believes the chastenings of the Lord to be penal annihilation. Behold even Pharaoh, a most hard man; nevertheless, he profits when he has been scourged. He does not know the Lord before the scourgings; after being scourged he asks that Moses pray to the Lord for him. He has advanced by punishments to recognize why he deserves punishment. Therefore, he said, "I do not know the Lord and I am not sending Israel out." (Exod. 5:2.) But notice how, having been scourged, he corrects this statement in the Gospels. For it is written that the demons cried out to the Lord and said, "Why have you come to torment us before the time? We know who you are. You are the Son of the living God" (cf. Matt. 8:29; Mark 1:24; Luke 4:34; Matt. 16:16). When they have experienced torments they know the Lord. Before the scourgings he says: "I do not know the Lord and I am not sending Israel out." (Exod. 5:2.) But he will send Israel out and not only will he send them out, but he himself will urge them to depart. For there is no "fellowship between light and darkness," no "sharing between faith and unbelief" (cf. 2 Cor. 6:14–15).

But what does he add further to his responses? "Why," he says, "O Moses and Aaron do you turn my people aside from their work? Each of you go off to your work." (Exod. 5:4.) While the people are with him and work in "mud" and "brick," while they are occupied in "chaff," he does not think them perverted, but to be traveling the right way. But if the people say, I wish to go "a way of three days" and "serve the Lord" (cf. Exod. 3:18), he says they are perverted by Moses and Aaron.

This indeed "was said to the ancients" (cf. Matt. 5:24). But even today, if Moses and Aaron, that is the prophetic and priestly word, stir a soul to the service of God, invite it to depart from the world, to renounce all things which it possesses, to give attention to the divine Law and to follow the word of God, immediately you will hear it said by those who are of one mind with Pharaoh and his friends: "See how men are seduced and perverted. Like youths, they do not work, they do not serve as soldiers, they do not do anything which profits them. They abandon necessary and useful things and follow silliness and leisure. Is this what serving God means? They do not wish to work and they seek opportunities for idle leisure." These were Pharaoh's words at that time, and now his friends and close associates say these things.

Pharaoh does not limit himself to words; scourgings also follow. He orders that the Hebrew scribes be beaten, that chaff not be given, that work be exacted. This is what the fathers endured. The people of God who are in the Church also often suffer in a manner similar to them. For you will find, if you consider those who have delivered themselves anew "to the prince of this world" (cf. John 16:11), that they act with prosperous results, that all things, as they themselves think, turn out favorably for them. Often, however, not even these small and lowly things of human sustenance prosper for the servants of God. I consider such things to be the chaff which is handed out by Pharaoh. It often turns out, therefore, that those who fear God lack even this sustenance which is cheap and similar to chaff. They also often endure the persecutions of tyrants and bear tortures and fierce torments so that some, wearied, say to Pharaoh, "Why do you afflict your people?" (cf. Exod. 5:22). For some, overcome by the scourgings, fall away from the faith and confess that they are the people of Pharaoh. "For not all who are of Israel are Israelites; nor because they are seed are they all also sons." (Rom. 9:6–7.) Those, therefore, who are doubtful and wearied by the tribulations also speak against Moses and Aaron and say, "From the day which you went in to Pharaoh and went out, you made our odor detestable before him" (cf. Exod. 5:23, 21). They speak the truth, although perhaps they do not know what they say, just as Caiphas, when he said, "It is expedient for you that one die for the people," was speaking the truth, but did not know what he was saying. (John 11:50.) For, as the Apostle says, "We are a good odor of Christ," but he adds, "To some an odor of life to life, but to others an odor of death to death." (2 Cor. 2:15–16.) So also the prophetic word is "a sweet odor" to those who believe, but to the doubting and unbelieving and those who confess that they are Pharaoh's people, it becomes a detestable odor.

But Moses himself also says to the Lord, "Ever since I have spoken with Pharaoh, he has afflicted your people" (cf. Exod. 5:23). It is certain that before the word of God is heard, before the divine preaching is known, there is no trouble, there is no temptation, because war does not begin unless the trumpet sounds. But where the trumpet of preaching gives the signal for war, there affliction follows; there every troublesome fight arises. The people of God are afflicted from the moment that Moses and Aaron began to speak to Pharaoh. From the moment the word of God has been brought into your soul a struggle is necessarily stirred up within you between virtues and vices. Before the word which reproves comes, the vices within you continue in peaceful existence, but when the word of God begins to make a division between each, then a great disturbance arises and war without treaty is born. "For when can there be agreement between justice and injustice," immodesty and moderation, a lie and the truth (cf. 2 Cor. 6:14)? And, therefore, let us not be greatly disturbed if our "odor" seems detestable to Pharaoh, for virtue is an abomination to vices.

Nay rather as it says later that Moses stood "before Pharaoh," let us also stand "against Pharaoh" and let us neither bow nor bend, but let us stand "having girded our loins with the truth and having shod our feet with the preparation of the Gospel of peace." (Eph. 6:14–15.) For thus the Apostle exhorts us saying, "Stand, therefore, and do not again submit to the yoke of slavery." (Gal. 5:1.) And again he says, "In which we stand, and we glory in the hope of the glory of God" (cf. Rom. 5:2). We stand confidently, however, if we pray to the Lord that "he set our feet upon the rock" (cf. Ps. 39:3), lest that happen to us which the same prophet says: "But my feet were nearly shaken, and my steps nearly slackened." (Ps. 72:2.) Therefore, let us stand "before Pharaoh," that is, let us resist him in the struggle as also the apostle Peter says, "Whom resist ye strong in the faith." (1 Pet. 5:9.) But Paul also says no less: "Stand in the faith and act like a man." (1 Cor. 16:13.) For if we stand strongly, that also which Paul prays for the disciples consequently happens. "God will swiftly grind Satan under your feet." (Rom. 16:20.) For the longer we stand firmly and staunchly the weaker and feebler Pharaoh will be. If, however, we begin to be either feeble or doubtful, he will become stronger and firmer against us. And truly that of which Moses gave a figure is fulfilled in us. For when Moses "lifted his hands" Amalec was conquered. But if "he cast" them "down" as though weary and put down weak arms, "Amalec would become strong" (cf. Exod. 17:11). So, therefore, let us also lift our arms in the power of the cross of Christ and "let us raise holy hands" in prayer "in every place without anger and dispute" (cf. 2 Tim. 2:8) that we might deserve the Lord's help. For the apostle James also urges this same thing, saying, "Resist the devil and he will flee from you." (James 4:7.) Therefore, let us go in full confidence that not only "may he flee from us," but also "Satan may be ground under our feet," as also Pharaoh was drowned in the sea and destroyed in the deep abyss. If, however, we withdraw from the Egypt of vices we will pass over the floods of the world as on a solid road through Jesus Christ our Lord, "to whom belong glory and sovereignty forever and ever. Amen" (cf. 1 Pet. 4:11).

St. John Chrysostom

350–407

*H*ere is a description by John himself—John with the Golden Mouth—of his audience: "Your frequent visits, your unvarying attention, and the fact that you even push and shove one another in order to come as near as possible to the pulpit (where my voice may be heard better, and that it does not even discourage you when someone treads on your feet in the crowd and you endure to the end until this spiritual drama is finished), your loud applause and everything else, proves sufficiently what zeal animates you, and how gladly you listen to the sermon." Except for the lavish personages of the Emperor's court and the stenographers who took down his Greek words, the picture is complete.

John Chrysostom in the East and his Latin-speaking contemporary Augustine (354–430) in the West were the twin fountains of inspiration for Christian preachers, not only in the fast-spreading Church of their day, but for centuries to come. By the sixth century, collections of John's sermons circulated throughout the Roman Empire.

It all began in Antioch in ancient Syria, some two hundred and fifty miles from Jerusalem and some twelve hundred miles from Rome, which Paul the Apostle had first evangelized three centuries earlier, and it was at Antioch that the followers of Christ were first called Christians. John was the son of a military official, but under the tutelage of his mother, Anthusa, he chose a clerical vocation. After the customary education in Greek classics and especially training in rhetoric, he received baptism at the not uncommon age of twenty into a Church that had not long before been given official status by the Roman emperor Constantine. After his mother's death, John became first a monk and then a hermit in the Desert Father tradition. Poor health from the strain of his austere life brought him back to Antioch. There he rose from reader to deacon to ordination as priest in 386.

Recognition of his oratorical skills came early when his bishop, Flavian, to whom the duty of preaching would normally be strictly reserved, assigned the task to John. His fame spread far and wide until attendance at his sermons nearly superseded his fellow citizens' addiction to the theater and the racecourse. In 398, on the death of Nectarius, the Patriarch of Constantinople, John was suddenly kidnapped—for fear Antioch would never surrender him—and was quickly consecrated successor to the see of Constantinople. His inability to adapt to the complex politics and luxurious excesses of the court (remember, this is how the term "Byzantine" arose!) and his frequent public admonishments of the Empress Eudoxia herself finally resulted in his banishment. He died in faraway Pontus, in modern northern Turkey, which borders the Black Sea. Little more than a generation later his bones were brought back to Constantinople, and his name was inscribed and revered with those of the other early saints of the Church.

John left us a dozen sermon series, virtually all of them expositions of one or another particular book of the Bible. Each begins with the reading of a passage (called the *pericope,* which literally means "cutout") followed by detailed explication of its layered meanings. John believed that the preacher's work was to teach and to inspire the people, combining his own powers of classical eloquence with the cooperation of the Holy Spirit. The result, as he once put it, "happened then as it does with a burning fire. In the beginning the fire is but small: but if it seizes on wood, it leaps up to a greater height . . . as the sermon grew longer and laid hold of the material, and the wood of instruction came to it in ever increasing quantity, then your anxiety to hear what I had to say grew and grew and produced louder applause."

While a superficial look at the text for the sermon that follows might provoke dismay in some modern readers, it is fitting testimony to John's powers to see what deep truths he has extracted from a few verses of Paul's Epistle to the Ephesians.

❧

Homily 20

Wives, be in subjection unto your own husbands, as unto the Lord. For the husband is the head of the wife, as Christ also is the head of the Church: being Himself the Saviour of the body. But as the Church is subject to Christ, so let the wives also be to their husbands in everything.

—EPHESIANS 5:22–24

A certain wise man, setting down a number of things in the rank of blessings, set down this also in the rank of a blessing, "A wife agreeing with her husband." (Ecclus. 25:1.) And elsewhere again he sets it down among blessings, that a woman should dwell in harmony with her husband. (Ecclus. 40:23.) And indeed from the beginning, God appears to have made special provision for this union; and discoursing of the twain as one, He said thus, "Male and female created He them" (Gen. 1:27); and again, "There is neither male nor female." (Gal. 3:28.) For there is no relationship between man and man so close as that between man and wife, if they be joined together as they should be. And therefore a certain blessed man too, when he would express surpassing love, and was mourning for one that was dear to him, and of one soul with him, did not mention father, nor mother, nor child, nor brother, nor friend, but what? "Thy love to me was wonderful," saith he, "passing the love of women." (2 Sam. 1:26.) For indeed, in very deed, this love is more despotic than any despotism: for others indeed may be strong, but this passion is not only strong, but unfading. For there is a certain love deeply seated in our nature, which imperceptibly to ourselves knits together these bodies of ours. Thus even from the very beginning woman sprang from man, and afterward from man and woman sprang both man and woman. Perceivest thou the close bond and connection? . . .

Hence Christ said, "He which made them from the beginning, made them male and female." (Matt. 19:4.)

For great evils are hence produced, and great benefits, both to families and to states. For there is nothing which so welds our life together as the love of man and wife. For this many will lay aside even their arms, for this they will give up life itself. And Paul would never without a reason and without an object have spent so much pains on this subject, as when he says here, "Wives, be in subjection unto your own husbands, as unto the Lord." And why so? Because when they are in harmony, the children are well brought up, and the domestics are in good order, and neighbors, and friends, and relations enjoy the fragrance. But if it be otherwise, all is turned upside down, and thrown into confusion. And just as when the generals of an army are at peace one with another, all things are in due subordination, whereas on the other hand, if they are at variance, everything is turned upside down; so, I say, is it also here. Wherefore, saith he, "Wives, be in subjection unto your own husbands, as unto the Lord." . . .

Let us take as our fundamental position then, that the husband occupies the place of the "head," and the wife the place of the "body."

Ver. 23, 24. Then, he proceeds with arguments and says that "the husband is the head of the wife, as Christ also is the head of the Church, being Himself the Savior of the body. But as the Church is subject to Christ, so let the wives be to their husbands in everything."

Then after saying, "The husband is the head of the wife, as Christ also is of the Church," he further adds, "and He is the Savior of the body." For in-

deed the head is the saving health of the body. He had already laid down beforehand for man and wife, the ground and provision of their love, assigning to each their proper place, to the one that of authority and forethought,
to the other that of submission. As then "the Church," that is, both husbands
and wives, "is subject unto Christ, so also ye wives submit yourselves to
your husbands, as unto God."

Ver. 25. "Husbands, love your wives, even as Christ also loved the
Church."

Thou hast heard how great the submission; thou hast extolled and
marveled at Paul, how, like an admirable and spiritual man, he welds together our whole life. Thou didst well. But now hear what he also requires
at thy hands; for again he employs the same example.

"Husbands," saith he, "love your wives, even as Christ also loved the
Church."

Thou hast seen the measure of obedience, hear also the measure of
love. Wouldest thou have thy wife obedient unto thee, as the Church is to
Christ? Take then thyself the same provident care for her, as Christ takes for
the Church. Yea, even if it shall be needful for thee to give thy life for her,
yea, and to be cut into pieces ten thousand times, yea, and to endure and
undergo any suffering whatever,—refuse it not. Though thou shouldest undergo all this, yet wilt thou not, no, not even then, have done anything like
Christ. For thou indeed art doing it for one to whom thou art already knit;
but He for one who turned her back on Him and hated Him. In the same
way then as He laid at His feet her who turned her back on Him, who hated,
and spurned, and disdained Him, not by menaces, nor by violence, nor by
terror, nor by anything else of the kind, but by his unwearied affection; so
also do thou behave thyself toward thy wife. Yea, though thou see her looking down upon thee, and disdaining, and scorning thee, yet by thy great
thoughtfulness for her, by affection, by kindness, thou wilt be able to lay her
at thy feet. For there is nothing more powerful to sway than these bonds,
and especially for husband and wife. A servant, indeed, one will be able,
perhaps, to bind down by fear; nay not even him, for he will soon start away
and be gone. But the partner of one's life, the mother of one's children, the
foundation of one's every joy, one ought never to chain down by fear and
menaces, but with love and good temper. For what sort of union is that,

where the wife trembles at her husband? And what sort of pleasure will the husband himself enjoy, if he dwells with his wife as with a slave, and not as with a free woman? Yea, though thou shouldest suffer anything on her account, do not upbraid her; for neither did Christ do this. . . .

Ver. 28. "Even so ought husbands to love their own wives," saith he, "as their own bodies."

What, again, means this? To how much greater a similitude, and stronger example has he come; and not only so, but also to one how much nearer and clearer, and to a fresh obligation. For that other one was of no very constraining force, for He was Christ, and was God, and gave Himself. He now manages his argument on a different ground, saying, "so ought men"; because the thing is not a favor, but a debt. Then, "as their own bodies." And why?

Ver. 29. "For no man ever hated his own flesh, but nourisheth and cherisheth it."

That is, tends it with exceeding care. And how is she his flesh? Hearken; "This now is bone of my bones," saith Adam, "and flesh of my flesh." (Gen. 2:23.) For she is made of matter taken from us. And not only so, but also, "they shall be," saith God, "one flesh." (Gen. 2:24.)

"Even as Christ also the Church." Here he returns to the former example.

Ver. 30. "Because we are members of His body, of His flesh and of His bones."

Ver. 31. "For this cause shall a man leave his father and mother, and shall cleave to his wife, and the twain shall become one flesh."

Behold again a third ground of obligation; for he shows that a man leaving them that begat him, and from whom he was born, is knit to his wife; and that then the one flesh is, father, and mother, and the child, from the substance of the two commingled. For indeed by the commingling of their seeds is the child produced, so that the three are one flesh. Thus then are we in relation to Christ; we become one flesh by participation, and we much more than the child. And why and how so? Because so it has been from the beginning.

Tell me not that such and such things are so. Seest thou not that we have in our own flesh itself many defects? For one man, for instance, is lame, another has his feet distorted, another his hands withered, another some other member weak; and yet nevertheless he does not grieve at it, nor cut it off, but oftentimes prefers it even to the other. Naturally enough; for it is part of himself. As great love as each entertains toward himself, so great he would have us entertain toward a wife. Not because we partake of the same nature; no, this ground of duty toward a wife is far greater than that; it is that there are not two bodies but one; he the head, she the body. And how saith he elsewhere, "and the Head of Christ is God"? (1 Cor. 11:3.) This I too say, that as we are one body, so also are Christ and the Father One. And thus then is the Father also found to be our Head. He sets down two examples, that of the natural body and that of Christ's body. And hence he further adds,

Ver. 32. "This is great mystery: but I speak in regard of Christ and of the Church."

Why does he call it a great mystery? That it was something great and wonderful, the blessed Moses, or rather God, intimated. For the present, however, saith he, I speak regarding Christ, that having left the Father, He came down, and came to the Bride, and became one Spirit. "For he that is joined unto the Lord is one Spirit." (1 Cor. 6:17.) And well saith he, "it is a great mystery." And then as though he were saying, "But still nevertheless the allegory does not destroy affection," he adds,

Ver. 33. "Nevertheless do ye also severally love each one his own wife even as himself; and let the wife see that she fear her husband."

For indeed, in very deed, a mystery it is, yea, a great mystery, that a man should leave him that gave him being, him that begat him, and that brought him up, and her that travailed with him and had sorrow, those that have bestowed upon him so many and great benefits, those with whom he has been in familiar intercourse, and be joined to one who was never even seen by him and who has nothing in common with him, and should honor her before all others. A mystery it is indeed. And yet are parents not distressed when these events take place, but rather, when they do not take place; and are delighted when their wealth is spent and lavished upon it.— A great mystery indeed! and one that contains some hidden wisdom. Such Moses prophetically showed it to be from the very first; such now also Paul proclaims it, where he saith, "concerning Christ and the Church."

However not for the husband's sake alone it is thus said, but for the wife's sake also, that "he cherish her as his own flesh, as Christ also the

Church," and, "that the wife fear her husband." He is no longer setting down the duties of love only, but what? "That she fear her husband." The wife is a second authority; let not her then demand equality, for she is under the head; nor let him despise her as being in subjection, for she is the body; and if the head despise the body, it will itself also perish. But let him bring in love on his part as a counterpoise to obedience on her part. For example, let the hands and the feet, and all the rest of the members be given up for service to the head, but let the head provide for the body, seeing it contains every sense in itself. Nothing can be better than this union. . . .

Supply her with everything. Do everything and endure trouble for her sake. Necessity is laid upon thee.

Here he does not think it right to introduce his counsel, as he in many cases does, with examples from them that are without. That of Christ, so great and forcible, were alone enough; and more especially as regards the argument of subjection. "A man shall leave," he saith, "his father and mother." Behold, this then is from without. But he does not say, and "shall dwell with," but "shall cleave unto," thus showing the closeness of the union, and the fervent love. Nay, he is not content with this, but further by what he adds, he explains the subjection in such a way as that the twain appear no longer twain. He does not say, "one spirit," he does not say, "one soul" (for that is manifest, and is possible to any one), but so as to be "one flesh." She is a second authority, possessing indeed an authority, and a considerable equality of dignity; but at the same time the husband has somewhat of superiority. In this consists most chiefly the well-being of the house. For he took that former argument, the example of Christ, to show that we ought not only to love, but also to govern; "that she may be," saith he, "holy and without blemish." But the word "flesh" has reference to love—and the word "shall cleave" has in like manner reference to love. For if thou shalt make her "holy and without blemish," everything else will follow. Seek the things which are of God, and those which are of man will follow readily enough. Govern thy wife, and thus will the whole house be in harmony. Hear what Paul saith. "And if they would learn any thing, let them ask their own husbands at home." (1 Cor. 14:35.) If we thus regulate our own houses, we shall be also fit for the management of the Church. For indeed a house is a little

Church. Thus it is possible for us by becoming good husbands and wives, to surpass all others.

. . . How then art thou to show that affection? By saying, "when it was in my power to take many to wife, both with better fortunes, and of noble family, I did not so choose, but I was enamored of thee, and thy beautiful life, thy modesty, thy gentleness, and soberness of mind." Then immediately from these beginnings open the way to your discourse on true wisdom, and with some circumlocution make a protest against riches. For if you direct your argument at once against riches, you will bear too heavily upon her; but if you do it by taking an occasion, you will succeed entirely. For you will appear to be doing it in the way of an apology, not as a morose sort of person, and ungracious, and overnice about trifles. But when you take occasion from what relates to herself, she will be even pleased. You will say then, (for I must now take up the discourse again,) that "whereas I might have married a rich woman, and with good fortune, I could not endure it. And why so? Not capriciously, and without reason; but I was taught well and truly, that money is no real possession, but a most despicable thing, a thing which moreover belongs as well to thieves, and to harlots, and to grave-robbers. So I gave up these things, and went on till I fell in with the excellence of thy soul, which I value above all gold. For a young damsel who is discreet and ingenuous, and whose heart is set on piety, is worth the whole world. For these reasons then, I courted thee, and I love thee, and prefer thee to my own soul. For the present life is nothing. And I pray, and beseech, and do all I can, that we may be counted worthy so to live this present life, as that we may be able also there in the world to come to be united to one another in perfect security. For our time here is brief and fleeting. But if we shall be counted worthy by having pleased God to so exchange this life for that one, then shall we ever be both with Christ and with each other, with more abundant pleasure. I value thy affection above all things, and nothing is so bitter or so painful to me, as ever to be at variance with thee. Yes, though it should be my lot to lose my all, and to become poorer than Irus [the well-known beggar of Ithaca, the home of Ulysses], and undergo the extremest hazards, and suffer any pain whatsoever, all will be tolerable and endurable, so long as thy feelings are true toward me. And then will my children be most dear to me, whilst thou art affectionately disposed toward me. But thou must do these duties too." Then mingle also with your discourse the Apostle's words, that "thus God would have our affections blended together; for listen to the Scripture, which saith, 'For this cause shall a man leave his father and mother, and cleave to his wife.' . . ."

Let your prayers be common. Let each go to Church; and let the husband ask his wife at home, and she again ask her husband, the account of the things which were said and read there. If any poverty should overtake you, cite the case of those holy men, Paul and Peter, who were more honored than any kings or rich men; and yet how they spent their lives, in hunger and in thirst. Teach her that there is nothing in life that is to be feared, save only offending against God. If any marry thus, with these views, he will be but little inferior to monks; the married but little below the unmarried.

. . . And again, never call her simply by her name, but with terms of endearment, with honor, with much love. Honor her, and she will not need honor from others; she will not want the glory that comes from others, if she enjoys that which comes from thee. Prefer her before all, on every account, both for her beauty and her discernment, and praise her. Thou wilt thus persuade her to give heed to none that are without, but to scorn all the world except thyself. Teach her the fear of God, and all good things will flow from this as from a fountain, and the house will be full of ten thousand blessings. If we seek the things that are incorruptible, these corruptible things will follow. "For," saith He, "seek first His kingdom, and all these things shall be added unto you." (Matt. 6:33.) What sort of persons, think you, must the children of such parents be? What the servants of such masters? What all others who come near them? Will not they too eventually be loaded with blessings out of number? For generally the servants also have their characters formed after their master's, and are fashioned after their humors, love the same objects, which they have been taught to love, speak the same language, and engage with them in the same pursuits. If thus we regulate ourselves, and attentively study the Scriptures, in most things we shall derive instruction from them. And thus shall be able to please God, and to pass through the whole of the present life virtuously, and to attain those blessings which are promised to those that love Him, of which God grant that we may all be counted worthy, through the grace and lov-

ingkindness of our Lord Jesus Christ, with Whom, together with the Holy
Ghost, be unto the Father, glory, power, and honor, now, and ever, through
all ages. Amen.

St. Basil the Great

330–379

The great historian of the late Roman Empire Edward Gibbon's
hostility to the triumph of Christianity over paganism did not
color his judgment of the imperious bishop of Caesarea in the fourth century: Gibbon wrote that "his [Basil's] zeal for orthodoxy did not blind him
to what was good in an opponent; and for the sake of peace and charity he
was content to waive the use of orthodox terminology when it could be
surrendered without a sacrifice of truth." The evidence of this lively and
generous spirit in an age riven by disputes over the Arian heresy and the
reformation of the monastic orders of the East is preserved in three hundred letters, revealing a playful and tender optimism coupled with the classical and theological learning acquired in Constantinople and, later,
Athens.

A great teacher and a great ascetic, Basil bridges in his Lenten sermons
and theological writings one of the great divides in the Patristic authority of
his day, a split between a complete rejection and an enthusiastic acceptance
of the classical heritage and literature of pagan antiquity. The spirit of his
writing and his instruction is one of compromise, a desire to keep numerous traits of the pagan world alive in the new Christian society, while purg-
ing away the spirit of paganism. His homily "On the Creation of Crawling
Creatures" is striking in its use of the narrative of Genesis 1, the resource-
ful dependence on Aristotle's taxonomy of the parts of animals, and the very

modern idea of the progression of all life from the sea. Like the fifth-century B.C. Greek poet Pindar, whose First Olympian Ode begins with the statement that "Water is preeminent," St. Basil seems to find in the oceans both a metaphor for the infinity of God's grace and a sign of the boundaries the Divine has set on all His created things.

❧

Homily 7
On the Creation of Crawling Creatures

Let the waters bring forth crawling creatures.

—GENESIS 1:20

Then God said, "Let the waters bring forth crawling creatures" of different kinds "that have life, and winged creatures" of different kinds "that fly below the firmament of the heavens." (Gen. 1:20.) After the creation of the lights, then the waters were filled with living creatures, so that this portion of the world also was adorned. The earth had received its ornamentation from its own plants; the heavens had received the flowers of stars and had been adorned with two great lights as if with the radiance of twin eyes. It remained for the waters, too, to be given their proper ornament. The command came. Immediately rivers were productive and marshy lakes were fruitful of species proper and natural to each; the sea was in travail with all kinds of swimming creatures, and not even the water which remained in the slime and ponds was idle or without its contribution in creation. For, clearly, frogs and mosquitoes and gnats were generated from them. Things still seen, even at the present time, are a proof of what is past. Thus all water was in eager haste to fulfill the command of its Creator, and the great and ineffable power of God immediately produced an efficacious and active life in creatures of which one would not even be able to enumerate the species, as soon as the capacity for propagating living creatures came to the waters through His command. "Let the waters bring forth crawling creatures that have life." Now, for the first time an animal was created which possessed life and sensation. Plants and trees, even if they are said to live because they share the power of nourishing themselves and of growing, yet are not animals nor are they animate. For this reason, "Let the earth bring forth crawling creatures."

Every creature able to swim, whether it swims at the surface of the water or cuts through its depths, is of the nature of crawling creatures, since it makes its way through a body of water. Even though some of the aquatic animals have feet and are able to walk (especially the amphibians, which are many, for instance, seals, crocodiles, hippopotamuses, frogs, and crabs), yet the ability to swim is antecedent. Therefore, "Let the waters bring forth crawling creatures." In these few words what species has been omitted? What has not been embraced by the command of the Creator? Have not the vivipara, such as seals and dolphins and rays and those like them that are called cartilaginous? Are not the ovipara included, which are, roughly speaking, all the different kinds of fishes? Are not those which are scaly and those which are horny scaled, those which have fins and those which do not? The words of the command were few, rather, there was no word, but only the force and impetus of the will; yet, the variety of meaning in the command is as great as the various species and families of fishes. To mention all these accurately is like counting the waves of the sea or trying to measure the water of the sea in the hollow of the hand.

"Let the waters bring forth crawling creatures." Among them are animals of the open sea, those frequenting the shores, those of the deep sea, those which cling to rocks, those which travel in shoals, those which live solitary, the sea monsters, the enormous, and the tiniest fish. By the same power and by an equal command, in fact, both the large and the small were given existence. "Let the waters bring forth." He showed you the natural kinship of the swimming creatures with water, and therefore, when the fish are removed from the water for a short time, they perish. They do not even have organs for breathing, so as to draw in this air; but, water is for the swimming species what air is for land animals. And the cause is evident. We have lungs, internal organs of loose texture and many passages, which receive air by the dilation of the chest, fan away our inner heat, and refresh us; but, for them the dilation and folding of the gills, which receive the water and eject it, fulfill the purpose of breathing organs. Fish have a peculiar state, a characteristic nature, a distinct nourishment, a specific mode of life. For this reason none of the water animals is able to be tamed, nor does it endure at all the touch of the human hand.

"Let the waters bring forth crawling creatures of different kinds that have life." (Gen. 1:20.) God orders the firstlings of each kind to be brought forth, seeds, as it were, for nature; and their numbers are controlled by successive progeny, whenever they must increase and become numerous. Of one kind are those which are called testaceans, such as mussels, scallops, sea snails, conchs, and numberless varieties of bivalves. Again, another kind besides these are the fish named crustaceans: crayfish, crabs, and all similar to them. Still another kind are the so-called soft fish, whose flesh is tender and loose: polyps, cuttlefish, and those like them. And among these, again, there are innumerable varieties. In fact, there are weevers, and lampreys, and eels, which are produced in the muddy rivers and swamps, and which resemble in their nature venomous animals more than fish. Another class is that of ovipara, and another, that of vivipara. The sharks and the dogfish and, in general, the cartilaginous fish are vivipara. And of the cetaceans the majority are vivipara, as dolphins and seals; these are said to readmit and hide in their belly the cubs, while still young, whenever they have for some reason or other been startled. "Let the waters bring forth the different kinds." The cetacean is one kind, and the tiny fish is another. Again, among the fish numberless varieties are distinguished according to species. Since their peculiar names and different food and form and size and qualities of flesh, all differ with the greatest variations from each other, the fish are placed in various classes. Now, what men who watch for tunneys are able to enumerate for us the varieties of its species? And yet, they say that they report even the number of fish in the great schools. Who of those who have grown old around the shores and beaches is able to acquaint us accurately with the history of all fishes?

The fishermen in the Indian Ocean know some kinds; those in the Egyptian Gulf, others; islanders, others; and Mauretanians, still others. That first command and that ineffable power produced all things, both small and great alike. Many are the differences of their modes of life; many also are the varieties in the method of perpetuation of the species. The majority of the fishes do not hatch out the young as the birds do, nor do they fix nests or nourish the young with their own labors; but the water, taking up the egg when it has been laid, brings forth the living creature. And the method of perpetuation for each species is invariable and is without mixture with any other nature. There are not such unions as produce mules on land or such as of some birds which debase their species. None of the fishes is halfway equipped with teeth, as among us the ox and the sheep are; indeed, none of them ruminates, except only, as some historians write, the parrot-wrasse. But, all the species are furnished with serried and very sharp pointed teeth, in order that the food may not slip through in the long-continued chewing; for, unless it is quickly cut up and swallowed, it is likely to be carried away by the water in the process of being ground.

Different foods are assigned for different fish according to their species. Some feed on slime, others on seaweeds, and others are content with the plants that grow in the water. The majority of fish eat one another, and the smaller among them are food for the larger. If it ever happens that the victor over a smaller becomes the prey of another, they are both carried into the one stomach of the last. Now, what else do we men do in the oppression of our inferiors? How does he differ from that last fish, who with a greedy love of riches swallows up the weak in the folds of his insatiable avarice? That man held the possessions of the poor man; you, seizing him, made him a part of your abundance. You have clearly shown yourself more unjust than the unjust man and more grasping than the greedy man. Beware, lest the same end as that of the fish awaits you—somewhere a fish-hook, or a snare, or a net. Surely, if we have committed many unjust deeds, we shall not escape the final retribution.

Since you have already perceived much wickedness and plotting in weak animals, I want you to avoid imitating the evildoers. The crab longs for the flesh of the oyster; but, because of the shell of the oyster, it is a prey hard for him to conquer. Nature has fastened the tender flesh in an unbroken enclosure. Therefore, the oyster is called "sherd-hide." Since the two enveloping shells, fitted exactly to each other, enclose the oyster, the claws of the crab are necessarily of no avail. What does he do, then? When he sees it pleasantly warming itself in spots sheltered from the wind and opening its valves to the rays of the sun, then, stealthily inserting a small pebble, he prevents it from closing and is found to gain through inventiveness what he fell short of by strength. This is the wickedness of the creatures endowed with neither reason nor voice. Now, I want you, although emulating the crabs' acquisitiveness and their inventiveness, to abstain from injury to your neighbors. He who approaches his brother with deceit, who adds to the troubles of his neighbors, and who delights in others' misfortunes, is like the crab. Avoid the imitation of those who by their conduct convict themselves. Be satisfied with your own possessions. Poverty with an honest sufficiency is preferred by the wise to all pleasure.

Let me pass over the deceitfulness and trickery of the octopus, which assumes on every occasion the color of the rock to which it fastens itself. As a result, many of the fish swimming unwarily fall upon the octopus as upon a rock, I suppose, and become an easy prey for the cunning fellow. Such in character are those men who always fawn upon the ruling powers and adapt themselves to the needs of every occasion, not continuing always in the same principles, but easily changing into different persons, who honor self-control with the chaste, but incontinence with the incontinent, and alter their opinions to please everyone. It is not easy to avoid nor to guard against harm from them because the evil they have fostered in themselves is hidden under a pretext of profound friendship. Such characters the Lord calls ravenous wolves which show themselves in sheep's clothing (cf. Matt. 7:15). Avoid inconstancy and fickleness, pursue truth, sincerity, simplicity. The serpent is subtle, and for that reason has been condemned to crawl. The just man is without pretense, such as was Jacob (cf. Gen. 25:27). Therefore, "The Lord maketh men of one manner to dwell in a house" (cf. Ps. 67:7). So in this great sea, which stretcheth wide its arms: "there are creeping things without number: Creatures little and great" (cf. Ps. 103:25). Nevertheless, there is a certain wisdom among them and an orderly arrangement. Not only are we able to bring charges against the fish, but there is also something worthy of imitation in them. How is it that all of the different species of fishes, having been allotted a place suitable for them, do not intrude upon one another, but stay within their own bounds? No surveyor apportioned the dwellings among them; they were not surrounded with walls nor divided by boundaries; but what was useful for each was definitely and spontaneously settled. This bay gives sustenance to certain kinds of fish and that one, to other kinds; and those that teem here are scarce elsewhere. No mountain extending upward with sharp peaks separates them; no river cuts off the means of crossing; but there is a certain law of nature which allots the habitat to each kind equally and justly according to its need.

We, however, are not such. Why? Because we pass beyond the ancient bounds which our fathers set (cf. Prov. 22:28). We cut off a part of the land amiss; we join house to house and field to field, so that we may take something of our neighbor's. The cetaceans know the habitats assigned them by nature. They have taken the sea beyond the inhabited regions, that part free from islands, in which there is no continent confronting them on the opposite side, because, since neither desire of inquiry nor any necessity persuades the sailors to venture on it, it is not navigated. The cetaceans which occupy that sea, in size like the mightiest mountains, as they who have seen them say, remain within their own boundaries and do not injure the islands nor the seaboard cities. So then, each kind abides in the parts of the sea assigned to it, as if in certain cities or villages or ancient countries.

However, some of the fish also are migratory and, as if dispatched by a common council to foreign lands, set out all together at one preconcerted signal. When the appointed time for breeding arrives, being roused by the common law of nature, they migrate from the different bays, hastening toward the North Sea. And at the time of the journey up you may see the fish united and flowing like a stream through the Propontis into the Euxine Sea. Who is it who sets them in motion? What is the command of the King? What lists, set up in the market place, show the appointed time? Who are the guides? You see that the divine plan fulfills all things and extends even to the smallest. A fish does not oppose the law of God, but we men do not endure the precepts of salvation. Do not despise the fish because they are absolutely unable to speak or to reason, but fear lest you may be even more unreasonable than they by resisting the command of the Creator. Listen to the fish, who through their actions all but utter this word: "We set out on this long journey for the perpetuation of our species." They do not have reason of their own, but they have the law of nature strongly established and showing what must be done. Let us proceed to the North Sea, they say. That water is sweeter than that of the rest of the sea, because the sun, tarrying there only a short time, does not draw out all the freshness from it with its rays. And the sea animals rejoice in the sweet waters. For this reason they frequently swim up the rivers and go far from the sea. Therefore, they prefer the Euxine Sea to the rest of the bays as a suitable place for breeding and rearing the young. But, when their purpose has been satisfactorily accomplished, again, in a body they all turn back homeward. Let us hear from these silent animals what the reason is. The North Sea, they say, is very shallow and, lying exposed to the violence of the winds, has few beaches and shelters. The winds, therefore, easily upturn it from the bottom so as to stir even the deep sand with the waves. Moreover, it is also cold in the winter season since it is filled by many great rivers. For this reason, having taken advantage of it to a certain measure in the summer, in the winter they hasten again to the warmth in the depths and to the sunny regions and, fleeing the stormy arctic parts, they come for haven into less agitated bays.

I have seen these wonders myself and I have admired the wisdom of God in all things. If the unreasoning animals are able to contrive and look out for their own preservation, and if a fish knows what it should choose and what avoid, what shall we say who have been honored with reason, taught by the law, encouraged by the promises, made wise by the Spirit, and who have then handled our own affairs more unreasonably than the fish? Even though they know how to have some foresight for the future, yet we, through hopelessness for the future, waste our lives in brutish pleasure. A fish traverses so many seas to find some advantage; what do you say who pass your life in idleness? And idleness is the beginning of evildoing. Let no one allege ignorance. Natural reason which teaches us an attraction for the good and an aversion for the harmful is implanted in us. I do not reject examples drawn from the sea, since these lie before us for examination. I have heard from one of the dwellers along the seacoast that the sea urchin, a quite small and contemptible creature, often forecasts calm or rough waters to the sailors. Whenever it foresees a disturbance from the winds, going under a strong pebble, it tosses about safely, clinging to this as to an anchor, prevented by the weight from being easily dragged away by the waves. When the sailors see this sign, they know that a violent windstorm is expected. No astrologer, no Chaldean, estimating the disturbances of the air by the rising of the stars, taught these things to the sea urchin, but the Lord of the sea and of the winds placed in the small animal a clear sign of His own wisdom. There is nothing unpremeditated, nothing neglected by God. His unsleeping eye beholds all things (cf. Prov. 15:3). He is present to all, providing means of preservation for each. If God has not put the sea urchin outside of His watchful care, does He not have regard for your affairs?

"Husbands, love your wives" (Eph. 5:25), even though external to each other, you came together into the union of marriage. May the bond of nature, may the yoke imposed by the blessing make as one those who were divided. A viper, the cruelest of reptiles, comes for marriage with the sea lamprey and, having announced its presence by hissing, summons it forth from the depths for the nuptial embrace. And the lamprey hearkens and is united with the venomous animal. What do my words mean? That, even if the husband is rough, even if he is fierce in his manners, the wife must endure and for no cause whatsoever permit herself to break the union. Is he a brawler? Nevertheless, he is your husband. Is he a drunkard? Nevertheless, he is united to you by Nature. Is he savage and ill-tempered? Nevertheless, he is your member and the most honored of your members.

But, let the husband also listen to proper advice for himself. The viper, through respect for his marriage, disgorges his venom. Will you not put aside the roughness and cruelty of your soul through reverence for the union? Or, perhaps, the example of the viper will be useful for us in other ways also, because the union of the viper and the sea lamprey is an adulterous violation of nature. Therefore, let those who are plotting against other men's marriages learn what sort of reptile they resemble. The edification of the Church in every way is my one aim. Let the passions of the incontinent be restrained and trained by these examples from the land and sea.

The weakness of my body and the lateness of the hour compel me to stop here, although I would be able to add much deserving of admiration about the things produced in the sea for my attentive audience. About the sea itself; how the water crystallizes into salt; how the very precious stone, the coral, is a plant in the sea but, when it is exposed to the air, it is changed into a hard stone; how it is that nature encloses the costly pearl in the most insignificant animal, the oyster. These stones, which the treasuries of kings covet, are scattered around the shores and beaches and sharp rocks, enclosed in the shells of the oysters. How do the sea pens produce their golden byssus, which no dyer up to this time has imitated? How is it that the shellfish bestow on kings the purple robes which surpass even the flowers of the meadow in beauty of color?

"Let the waters bring forth." And what, that is necessary, has not been made? What precious object is there that has not been given for our life? Some things for the service of men; others for their contemplation of the marvel of creation; and some terrible things, taking to task our idleness. "God created the great sea monsters." (Gen. 1:21.) And not because they are larger than the shrimp and herring, are they called great, but, because with their immense bodies they are like huge mountains. Indeed, they frequently look like islands when they swim upon the surface of the water. These sea monsters, because they are so large, do not stay around the coasts and beaches, but inhabit the sea called the Atlantic. Such are the animals which have been created for our fear and consternation. And, if you hear that the very small fish, the remora, stops the greatest boat as it is being borne along by a fair wind with sails spread, so that it keeps the ship immovable for a very long time, as if firmly rooted in the sea itself, would you not possess in this little fish also the same proof of the power of the Creator? Not only the swordfish, the sawfish, the dogfish, the whales, and the hammer-headed sharks are to be feared; but the spike of the sting ray, even when it is dead, and the sea hare, too, are not less fearful, since they bring swift and inevitable death. Thus, the Creator wants you to be kept awake by all things, in order that, through hope in God, you may escape the harm that comes from them.

But, let us come up from the depths and take refuge on the land. For, somehow, the wonders of creation, coming upon us one after another in continuous and quick succession like waves, have submerged our discourse. And yet, I would not be surprised if our spirit, though meeting up with greater wonders on land, would again, like Jonah, slip away to the sea. It seems to me that my sermon, lighting upon the numberless marvels, has forgotten its proper measure and has had the same experience as sailors on the sea, who judging their progress from no fixed point, are ignorant frequently of the distance they have sailed. Truly, this seems to have happened in our case, that, as our discourse moved quickly through creation, we did not perceive the great multitude of creatures mentioned. But, even though this august assembly is pleased to listen and the narration of the wonders of the Master is sweet to the ears of His servants, let us bring our talk to anchor here and await the day for the explanation of the facts omitted. Let us rise and give thanks for what has been said; let us ask for the completion of the omissions.

While partaking of your food, may you discuss at table the stories which my words reviewed for you early in the morning and throughout the evening; and, falling asleep while engaged in thoughts of these things, may you enjoy the pleasure of the day, even while sleeping, so that it may be possible for you to say, "I sleep and my heart watcheth" (Cant. 5:2), since it has meditated night and day on the law of the Lord, to whom be glory and power forever. Amen.

St. Ambrose

340?–397

*O*nce Christianity had spread to the capital cities of the Roman Empire, its ranks began to include many of the latter's officials and functionaries. Often their administrative and legal experience made them especially attractive for service to the Church. Ambrose of Milan was one such figure. He was born at Trier, now in northwestern Germany, the son of a Roman official for the prefecture of the province of Gaul, which at that time encompassed a territory stretching from Spain to modern-day Germany. His family were Christians; in fact, his older sister, Marcellina, had professed at a young age to remain a virgin, a practice not uncommon among the pious.

Arriving at the city of Milan, Ambrose, by then himself a provincial ruler, had been sent to preserve civil order, which was threatened by the death of the city's Arian bishop, Auxentius. Ongoing strife between the orthodox Christians and the Arian Christians had begun to verge on open fighting. At an assembly in the church, his biographer, one Paulinus, tells us, "as he was speaking to the throng, the voice of a small child all at once made itself heard among the people: 'Ambrose for bishop!' At the sound of this voice the whole tone of the gathering changed, and they acclaimed Ambrose as their bishop. So it was that those who had previously been violently divided, because the Catholics and the Arians each wanted to best the other and to have a bishop ordained for themselves, suddenly agreed, with remarkable and unbelievable harmony, on this one man." Clearly he was someone to be reckoned with.

Ambrose had not yet even been baptized. Within a week of his acclamation, he had gone through all the steps leading up to and including formal consecration as bishop. He seemed born to the task that awaited him. Whether it was speaking out against heresy, drawing firm lines between the respective authority of God and Caesar, counseling his flock (St. Augustine was Ambrose's most famous convert), or writing beautiful hymns, his range of talents and his energy were enormous. In an age of constant political violence and bloody religious contests, he was a bulwark of unshakable strength and steadiness.

In the selection that follows, the first part of a nine-sermon series on the Hexameron, or first Six Days of Creation, preached during Holy Week sometime between 386 and 390, he shows clearly the richness of his Greek philosophical training, the extent of his knowledge of natural phenomena, and of course, his close reading of Scripture. He also drew on a text on Genesis composed by another Eastern Church Father, Basil the Great (330–97), bishop of Caesarea.

ᴄ℥

On the First Day of Creation

"In the beginning," he said. What a good arrangement that he should first assert what these men are accustomed to deny, that they may realize, too, that there was a beginning to the world, lest men be of the opinion that the world was without a beginning. For this reason David, too, in speaking of "heaven, earth, and sea," says: "Thou hast made all things in wisdom."

(Ps. 103:24.) He [Moses] gave, therefore, a beginning to the world; he gave also to the creature infirmity, lest we believe him to be without a beginning, uncreated, and still partaking in the divine essence. And fittingly he added: "He created, lest it be thought there was a delay in creation." Furthermore, men would see also how incomparable the Creator was who completed such a great work in the briefest moment of His creative act, so much so that the effect of His will anticipated the perception of time. No one saw Him in the act of creation; they saw only the created work before them. Where, therefore, was there a delay, since you may read: "For He spoke and they were made; He commanded and they were created"? (Pss. 32:9; 148:5.) He who in a momentary exercise of His will completed such a majestic work employed no art or skill so that those things which were not were so quickly brought into existence; the will did not outrun the creation nor the creation, the will.

You admire the work, you seek for a Creator who granted a beginning to such a great work, who so speedily made it? He [Moses] gives us the information immediately, saying that "God created heaven and earth." You have the name of the Creator; you ought not to have any doubts. He it is in whose name Melchisedech blessed Abraham, the forefather of many peoples, saying: "Blessed be Abram by the most high God, creator of heaven and earth." (Gen. 14:19.) And Abraham believed God and said: "I raise my hand to the Lord God most high, creator of heaven and earth." (Gen. 14:22.) You see that this was not an invention made by man, but an announcement made by God. For God is Melchisedech, that is, "He is king of peace and justice, having neither the beginning of days nor end of life." (Heb. 7:2, 3.) No wonder, therefore, that God, who is without end, gave a beginning to all things, so that what was not began to exist. No wonder that God, who contains all things in His power and incomprehensible majesty, created the things that are visible, since He also created those things that are not visible. Who would assert that the visible is more significant than the invisible, "for the things that are seen are temporal, but the things that are not seen are eternal"? (2 Cor. 4:18.) Who can doubt that God, who spoke by the Prophets, created these things, saying: "Who hath measured the waters in the hollow of his hand and weighed the heavens with his palm? Who hath poised with three fingers the bulk of the earth and weighed the mountains in scales and the hills in a balance? Who hath understood the sense of the Lord? Or who hath been his counsellor; or who hath taught him?" (Isa. 40:12, 13.) Of Him we also read elsewhere: "For he holds the circuit of the earth and made the earth as nothing." (Isa. 40:22, 23.) And Jeremias says: "The gods that have not made heaven and earth will perish from the earth and from among those places that are under heaven. He that made the earth by his power and prepared the world by his wisdom and stretched out the heavens at his knowledge and a multitude of waters in the heaven." And he added: "Man is become a fool for knowledge." (Jer. 10:11–14.) How can one who pursues the corruptible things of the world and thinks that from these things he can comprehend the truth of divine nature not become a fool as he makes use of the artifices of sophistry?

Since, therefore, so many oracles are heard in which God gives testimony that He made the world, do not then believe that it was without a beginning because the world is said to be, as it were, a sphere in which there would appear to be no beginning. And when it thunders, everything is stirred around about us as if in a whirling movement, so that one cannot easily comprehend either where the vortex begins or where it ends. The reason is this: To perceive by one's senses the beginning of a circle is considered to be impossible. You cannot discover the beginning of a sphere or from what point the round disk of the moon begins or where it ends in its monthly wanings. Not even if you do not understand it yourself does this phenomenon cease to begin or in any way to come to an end. If you were to draw a circle with ink or pencil or with a compass, you could not easily detect with your eyes or mentally recall after an interval of time the point where you began or where you completed your circle. Yet you are conscious that you made a beginning and also came to an end. The reason is this: What has escaped the senses has not caused the truth to be undermined.

Again, what has a beginning also has an end; it is obvious that which has an end also has a beginning. The Savior Himself tells us in the Gospel that there is to be an end of the world, saying: "For this world as we see it is passing away"; and "Heaven and earth will pass away, but my words will not pass away"; and further on: "Behold I am with you all days, even unto the consummation of the world." (1 Cor. 7:31; Matt. 24:35; 28:20.)

How, then, can philosophers maintain that the world is co-eternal with God and make the created equal with the Creator of all things? How can they hold that the material body of the world should be linked with the invisible and unapproachable divine nature?—so much the more, since, according to their own teachings, they cannot deny that an object whose parts are subject to corruption and mutability must as a whole be subject to the same influences which its own separate parts undergo.

Therefore, He who uttered these words, "In the beginning God created heaven and earth," teaches us that there is a beginning. The term "beginning" has reference either to time or to number or to foundation. We see that this is true in the construction of a house: the foundation is the beginning. We know, too, from the authority of Scripture that one can speak of a beginning of a conversion or of a falling away. (Wisd. 14:12–14.) The beginning of a work of art lies in the craft itself, which is the source of the individual skills of a series of craftsmen. There is also a beginning to good works. This consists in a most commendable purpose or end, as, for example, acts of charity have their source in deeds which are done to do honor to God, for we are especially urged to come to the aid of our fellow men. The term "beginning" is applied also to the power of God. It is concerned with the category of time when we deal with the question of the time when God made heaven and earth, that is, at the commencement of the world, when it began to come into being, in the words of Wisdom: "When he prepared the heaven I was present." (Prov. 8:27.) If we apply the term to number, then it is right that you understand that at first He created heaven and earth; next, hills, regions, and the boundaries of the inhabitable world. Or we may understand that before He created the rest of visible creatures, day, night, fruit-bearing trees, and the various kinds of animals He created heaven and earth. But, if you apply the term to foundation, you will see, if you read the words of Wisdom, that the beginning is the foundation: "When he made the foundations of the earth, I was with him forming all things." (Prov. 8:29, 30.)

There is also the beginning of good instruction, as it is said: "The fear of the Lord is the beginning of wisdom" (Prov. 1:7), since he who fears the Lord departs from error and directs his ways to the path of virtue. Except a man fear the Lord, he is unable to renounce sin.

In like manner, also, we can understand this statement: "This month shall be to you the beginning of months" (Exod. 12:2), although that statement is to be interpreted merely of time, because there is reference to the Pasch of the Lord, which is celebrated at the beginning of spring. Therefore, He created heaven and earth at the time when the months began, from which time it is fitting that the world took its rise. Then there was the mild temperature of spring, a season suitable for all things.

Consequently, the year, too, has the stamp of a world coming to birth, as the splendor of the springtime shines forth all the more clearly because of the winter's ice and darkness now past. The shape of the circles of years to come has been given form by the first dawn of the world. Based on that precedent, the succession of years would tend to arise, and at the commencement of each year new seedlings would be produced, as the Lord God has said: "Let the earth bring forth the green herb and such as may seed, and the fruit tree, yielding fruit after its kind. And immediately the earth produced the green herb and the fruit-bearing tree." (Gen. 1:11.) By this very fact both the constant mildness of divine Providence and the speed in which the earth germinates favor for us the hypothesis of a vernal period. For, although it was in the power of God to ordain creation at any time whatsoever and for earthly nature to obey, so that amid winter's ice and frost earth might bear and produce fruits under the fostering hand of His celestial power, He refrained. It was not in His eternal plan that the land held fast in the rigid bonds of frost should suddenly be released to bear fruits and that blooming plants should mingle with frosts unsightly.

Wherefore, in order to show that the creation of the world took place in the spring, Scripture says: "This month shall be to you the beginning of months, it is for you the first in the months of the year" (Exod. 12:2), calling the first month the springtime. It was fitting that the beginning of the year be the beginning of generation and that generation itself be fostered by the gentler breezes. The tender germs of matter would be unable to endure exposure to the bitter cold of winter or to the torrid heat of summer.

At the same time, one may note, since it belongs here by right, that the entrance into this generation and into this way of life seems to have occurred at the time when the regular transition from this generation to re-generation takes place.

The sons of Israel left Egypt in the season of spring and passed through the sea, being baptized in the cloud and in the sea, as the Apostle said (cf. 1 Cor. 10:1). At that time each year the Pasch of Jesus Christ is celebrated, that is to say, the passing over from vices to virtues, from the desires of the flesh to grace and sobriety of mind, from the unleavened bread of malice and wickedness to truth and sincerity (cf. 1 Cor. 5:8). Accordingly, the regenerated are thus addressed: "This month shall be to you the beginning of months; it is for you the first in the months of the year."

The person who is baptized leaves behind and abandons in a spiritual sense that prince of the world, Pharaoh, when he says: "I renounce thee, devil, both thy works and thy power." (John 14:30.) No longer will he serve him, either by the earthly passions of his body or by the errors of a corrupt mind. On this occasion every evil deed of his sinks to the bottom like lead. Protected as he is by good works on his right and his left, he endeavors to cross over the waters of this life with step untainted.

Scripture also says in the book called Numbers: "Amalec, the beginning of nations, whose seed will be destroyed." (Num. 24:20.) And, of course, Amalec is not the first of all nations. Amalec, in fact, is interpreted to mean the king of the wicked and by the wicked it is intended to mean the Gentiles. There is no reason why we should not accept him as one whose seed shall perish. His seed are the wicked and the unfaithful, to whom the Lord says: "You are the voice of your father the devil" (cf. John 8:44).

A beginning in a mystical sense is denoted by the statement: "I am the first and last, the beginning and the end." (Rev. 1:8.) The words of the Gospel are significant in this connection, especially wherein the Lord, when asked who He was, replied: "I am the beginning, I who speak with you." (John 8:25.) In truth, He who is the beginning of all things by virtue of His divinity is also the end, because there is no one after Him. According to the Gospel, the beginning of the ways of God is in His work, so that the race of men might learn by Him to follow the ways of the Lord and to perform the works of God (cf. Prov. 8:22).

Therefore, in this beginning, that is, in Christ, God created heaven and earth, because "All things were made through him and without him was made nothing that was made." (John 1:3.) Again: "In him all things hold together and he is the firstborn of every creature." (Col. 1:15.) Moreover, He was before every creature because He is holy. The firstborn indeed are holy, as "the firstborn of Israel" (Exod. 4:22), not in the sense of being before all, but because the firstborn are holier than the rest. The Lord is holy above all creatures for the very reason that He assumed a body. He alone is without sin and without vanity, while all "creation was made subject to vanity." (Rom. 8:20.)

St. Augustine of Hippo

354–430

The written literature of Greek and Roman antiquity extends easily for half a dozen centuries in either direction from the birth of Jesus. Varied as its subjects and authors were, there is none whose intellectual range was broader and none about whose life we know more than Aurelius Augustinus. As the ripples of his thought spread outward in the centuries after his death, this greatest of the Church Fathers has often been depicted with the miter and crozier of his office. Yet at age nineteen, already having fathered a child by his concubine and more than a casual student of Manichean heresy, the forecast would have been for a most unlikely bishop and pillar of Catholic orthodoxy.

It is interesting to recall that Augustine was an African, born in a farming community that was part of the vast and prosperous granary of North Africa that supplied imperial Rome with its daily bread. At the same time, the port city of Carthage and environs was no provincial backwater. The currency of the Latin language and the Roman way of life, the

influence of Greek culture, art, and philosophy, the new and far from settled overlay of Christianity, and the lively comings and goings of merchants
and travelers of many nations—all made an early cosmopolitan of Augustine.

His education was deeply imbued with the classics, and his first
career was that of rhetorician. In an illiterate age, the ability to deliver
polished public speech was of far greater advantage than any gift for literary flourishes. Augustine traveled to Milan with his devout mother, Mon-
ica, to earn a living as a teacher. There he encountered the writings of
Plotinus, the interpreter of Plato, as they were gradually being trans-
muted into a Christian synthesis by disciples such as Porphyry and, more
importantly, Ambrose, the bishop of Milan. It was in a garden in that city
that one of the world's most commemorated conversions occurred when
Augustine heard a voice telling him to pick up a book of the epistles of
St. Paul and read whatever his eye should first light on. It was the passage "not in reveling and drunkenness, not in debauchery and licentiousness, not in quarreling and jealousy. But put on the Lord Jesus Christ,
and make no provision for the flesh, to gratify its desires." (Rom.
13:13–14.)

From that moment, Augustine became an indefatigable worker in the
vineyard of the Holy Spirit. He was first baptized by Ambrose, and then in
391 ordained a presbyter, or priest, shortly after his return to North Africa,
by the bishop of Hippo Regius (the modern Algerian port city of Annaba),
whom he would succeed five years later. It was in the early years of his bish-
opric that he composed his masterpiece, *The Confessions,* rightly termed the
first true autobiography in literature.

As a preacher, Augustine is nonpareil. It is no exaggeration to say that
until the appearance of Bernard of Clairvaux, with the twelfth-century revival of learning in Europe, virtually all sermons of the late Roman Empire
and the Middle Ages are directly traceable to one of the nearly six hundred
examples he left behind. Faithfully transcribed by contemporary stenographers, they are often as fresh, as lively, as witty, as profound and stirring
today as when they first drew the applause and cheering of their listeners in
the churches of fourth-century Carthage or Hippo.

Because he is truly the *fons et origo* of all Christian preaching in the
West, two—rather than a single example—of his sermons follow. (It

seemed the least we could do to thank him.) The first is an early sermon preached on Easter to those who had been baptized only the previous night and who had prepared intensively for their initiation over the forty days of Lent and, typically, the many months and even years of instruction that went before. The second is late—"an old man's sermon," as he puts it—on a text from 1 Corinthians 13, which contains the phrase adapted for the title of this book.

To the Newly Baptized—on the Eucharist

What you see here on the Lord's table, my dear brethren, is bread and wine. But once the word is pronounced over them, this bread and this wine become the body and the blood of the divine Word. He is the very Lord who "in the beginning was the Word, and the Word was with God, and the Word was God." (John 1:1.) Owing to His mercy, the Lord did not disdain the nature created by Him in His own image, but, as you know, "the Word was made flesh and dwelt among us." (John 1:14.) The same Word assumed human nature; in other words, He took a human soul and body, became man, yet ever remained God. And since the Word suffered on our behalf, He left us His body and blood in this sacrament, in which He also included us. For we, too, have been incorporated into His body, and through His mercy we are the very thing that we receive.

Bear in mind what this creature, wheat, was formerly when it still grew in the field; how the earth caused it to germinate, how the rains nurtured it, how it ripened in kernels; and how afterward the laborers carried it to the threshing floor, treaded it, winnowed it, stored it in the granary, brought it out again to be milled, then added water to it and baked it, until at last it emerged as bread. Bear in mind what happened in your own case, imagining a time when you did not yet exist, but then you were created and brought to the threshing floor of the Lord, threshed by hardworking oxen, that is to say, by the heralds of the Gospel. The period of your probation as catechumens was the time when you were being stored in the granary. Then came the day when you handed in your names, and the milling process began by means of the fasts and the exorcisms to which you were subjected.

Afterward you came to the font, were immersed in the water, and kneaded into one dough. Finally you were baked in the fire of the Holy Spirit, and became the bread of the Lord.

Now ponder on what you have received. And as it dawns on you what unity there is in the sacrament which has been instituted, be impressed with the unity that ought to prevail among yourselves, causing you to love one another, to remain steadfast in one faith, in one hope, and in mutual charity. Heretics, when they receive this sacrament, bear witness against themselves, for they promote discord, whereas this bread signifies concord. So, too, the wine made from many grapes is now one liquid, one sweet liquid in the chalice after being crushed in the wine press. In Christ's name you also, as it were, have come to be present in the chalice of the Lord, through your fasts and good works, through your humility and contrition. There you are on the altar, there you are in the chalice. In this sacrament you are united with us—we are joined together, we drink together, because we share life together.

Shortly you are to hear for the second time what you already heard last night. But today you are going to receive an explanation of the words you heard and the responses you made—or perhaps you remained silent while the others made the responses. At any rate, you were made aware last night of the responses you are to make today.

Following the greeting, "The Lord be with you," which you know so well, you heard the words, "Lift up your heart." Now the whole life of true Christians is a matter of lifting up the heart. To lift up the heart is a duty of Christians who are such in very fact and not in name alone. To lift up the heart—what does this mean? It means that you must trust in God, not in yourself since God is so superior to you. When you trust in yourself, your heart stays fettered to the earth, not fixed on God. So when you hear the priest say, "Lift up your heart," you respond, "We have lifted it up to the Lord." See to it, then, that your response rings true, since it is God Himself who takes cognizance of your words. Let there be truth in what you say, lest your conscience deny what your tongue professes. And since it is by God's grace, not by your own resources, that you are enabled to lift your heart heavenward, the dialogue proceeds, after you have averred that your heart is lifted up to the Lord, with the words of the priest, "Let us give thanks to the Lord our God." Why should we give thanks? Because our heart has ascended on high, and yet, had He not raised it up, we should still be wallowing in the earth.

Now this is what happens in the sacred prayers you are about to hear. As soon as the word is spoken, the elements become the body and blood of Christ. For take away the word, and there is simply bread and wine. But add the word, and it is altogether something else. What else is it? The body of Christ and the blood of Christ. Take away the word, and it is only bread and wine. Add the word, and it becomes a sacrament. Thereupon you say *Amen*. To say *Amen* is to subscribe to what has taken place. *Amen* in Latin signifies, "So be it."

Then the Lord's Prayer is said, the prayer that was handed over to you and that you in turn gave back.* Why is this prayer said before one receives the body and blood of Christ? Because it may have happened, through human frailty, that our mind conceived an improper thought, or that our tongue let slip an unseemly word, or that our eyes gazed on an indecent object, or that our ears listened avidly to evil speech. Now if anything of the like was committed through worldly temptation and human frailty, then all is blotted out by the Lord's Prayer, namely, when one says, "Forgive us our trespasses." And thus we can approach the sacrament in the assurance that we do not eat and drink to our condemnation.

This is followed by the words, "Peace be to you." What a lofty sign is the kiss of peace! Let this kiss be given so as to foster mutual love. Be not a Judas. Judas, the traitor, kissed Christ with his mouth, although there was treachery in his heart. If it happens that a person is unfriendly to you, and you cannot win him over, then you must bear with him. Your heart must not repay his evil with evil. If he hates you, you must love him nevertheless, for then you can feel free to give him the kiss of peace.

You have heard only a few things, but they are great. Do not regard them of little worth. For the present you ought not to be burdened with more, so that you may easily retain what has just been explained to you.

---

*These words are a reference to the practice of "handing over" formally the Lord's Prayer to the candidates for baptism, and their own formal recitation of the same at a later date in the course of the rites of initiation.

On Charity

All the varied plenty and wide-ranging teaching of the divine scriptures is grasped, my brothers and sisters, and kept without any difficulty by the person whose heart is full of charity. It's what the apostle says: *Now the fullness of the law is charity* (Rom. 13:10); and in another place, *Now the end of the commandment is charity from a pure heart, and a good conscience, and unfeigned faith* (1 Tim. 1:5). But what can the end of the commandment be, but the fulfillment of the commandment? And what is the fulfillment of the commandment but the fullness of the law? So what he said there, *the fullness of the law is charity,* is what he also said here, *the end of the commandment is charity.*

Nor can there be the slightest doubt that the temple of God is the person in whom charity is dwelling. John too, you see, says, *God is charity.* (1 John 4:8.16.) Now when the apostles said these things and urged upon us the absolute primacy of charity, they could only be belching forth what they had themselves eaten. The Lord himself, in fact, feeding them on the word of truth, the word of charity, which he is himself, the living bread which came down from heaven, said, *A new commandment I give you, that you should love one another.* And again, *By this shall everybody know that you are my disciples, if you love one another.* (John 13:34–35.)

He came, you see, to put an end to the corruption of the flesh by the mockery he endured on the cross, and to unfasten the old chain of our death by the newness of his death; and so he made the new man with a new commandment. It was, after all, an old matter, stale news, that man should die. To prevent this prevailing over man forever, a new thing was done, that God should die. But because he died in the flesh, not in his divinity, through the everlasting life of his divinity he did not permit the destruction of the flesh to be everlasting. And so, as the apostle says, *He died on account of our transgressions, he rose again on account of our justification.* (Rom. 4:25.) So because he has brought the newness of life into action against the oldness of death, he himself sets a new commandment against the old sin. Any of you, then, who wish to extinguish the old sin, douse cupidity with the new commandment, and embrace charity. Just as cupidity, you see, is the root of all evil, so in the same way is charity the root of all good things.

Charity is in secure possession of the whole length and breadth of the divine utterances, the charity with which we love God and neighbor. After all, the one and only heavenly master teaches us, *You shall love the Lord your God with your whole heart and your whole soul and your whole mind; and you shall love your neighbor as yourself. On these two commandments depend the whole law and the prophets.* (Matt. 22:37, 39–40.) So if there's no time or leisure to pore over all the sacred pages, to leaf through all the volumes of the words they contain, to penetrate all the secrets of the scriptures, hold on to charity, on which they all depend. In this way you will hold on to what you have learned there; you will also get hold of what you haven't yet learned. I mean, if you know charity, you know something from which that also depends which perhaps you don't yet know; and in whatever you do understand in the scriptures, charity is revealed; while in the parts you don't understand, charity is concealed. And so it is that those who keep a grip on charity in their behavior, have a grasp both of what is revealed and of what is concealed in the divine writings.

Therefore, brothers and sisters, pursue after charity, the sweet and salutary bond of our minds, without which the rich man is poor, and with which the poor man is rich. This it is that endures in adversity, is moderate in prosperity; brave under harsh sufferings, cheerful in good works; utterly reliable in temptation, utterly openhanded in hospitality; as happy as can be among true brothers and sisters, as patient as you can get among the false one's. Acceptable in Abel through his sacrifice, safe in Noah through the flood, absolutely faithful in the wanderings of Abraham, as meek as meek can be in Moses amid insults, so mild and gentle in David's trials and tribulations. In the three young men it innocently awaits the kindly fires; in the Maccabees it bravely endures the ferocious fires. Chaste in Susanna toward her husband, in Anna after her husband, in Mary apart from her husband. Free in Paul for rebuking, humble in Peter for listening and yielding. Human in Christians for confessing, divine in Christ for pardoning.

But what can I say in praise of charity that surpasses in grandeur what the Lord thunders forth through the mouth of his apostle, as he *shows us a more excellent way,* and says, *If I speak with the tongues of men and of angels, but do not have charity, I have become booming bronze, or a clashing cymbal. And if I*

have prophecy, and know all sacraments, and have all knowledge, and if I have all
faith, such that I transfer mountains, but do not have charity, I am nothing. And if I
give away all my property, and if I distribute all that is mine to the poor, and if I
hand over my body so that I burn, but do not have charity, it profits me nothing. Char-
ity is magnanimous, charity is kind. Charity is not jealous, does not act boastfully, is
not conceited, does not behave shamelessly, does not seek its own advantage, is not ir-
ritable, does not think evil, does not rejoice over iniquity, but rejoices together with
the truth. It tolerates all things, believes all things, hopes all things, endures all
things. Charity never falls away. (1 Cor. 12:31–13:8.)

What a great thing this charity is! The soul of the scriptures, the force
of prophecy, the saving power of the sacraments, the fruit of faith, the
wealth of the poor, the life of the dying. What could be more magnanimous
than to die for the godless, what more kindly than to love one's enemies? It
is the one thing that is not cast down by another's good fortune, because it
is not jealous. It is the one thing that its own good fortune does not puff up,
because it is not conceited. It is the one thing that is not pricked by a bad
conscience, because it does not act boastfully. It is steady and unshaken amid
reproaches, it is well disposed in the face of hatred; calm in the face of
anger, innocent in the midst of intrigues, groaning in the midst of iniquity,
breathing again in the presence of truth. What could be braver than charity,
not for paying back insults, but for not caring about them? What could be
more faithful, not for vanity, but for eternity?

You see, the reason it endures all things in the present life, is that it believes all things about the future life; and it endures everything that is inflicted on it here, because it hopes for everything that is promised it there.
Rightly does it never fall away. So pursue after charity, and by thinking holy
thoughts about it bring forth the fruits of justice. And whatever you can find
in the praises of charity that is grander than what I have been able to say, let
it appear in your behavior. It is right, after all, that an old man's sermon
should be not only weighty, but brief.

St. Gregory the Great

540–604

A recent resurgence of interest in the ancient system of liturgical music known as plainsong, or "Gregorian chant," carries an echo of the name of the Pope who compiled its monophonic free rhythms and limited scale in the *Antiphonarium*. The music was sung partly by a choir, partly by soloists; the soloist and choir singing responsorial chants, the half choruses singing antiphonally. The texts consisted mostly of psalms and established a basis for the mass and for the offices (services of the hours) of the Roman Catholic Church. Tradition, at any rate, assigns him this great accomplishment, and he was clearly a dazzling prodigy, conspicuous even in the ranks of the Latin Patristic writers.

Pope Gregory I was a zealous propagator of Christian reform in the monastic disciples, and the author of pastoral letters, homilies, and a tract on the spiritual education of the clergy which Alfred I of England translated from Latin into Old English. His messianic concern with the conversion of the remote British Isles has provided a famous anecdote, from the eve of his dispatching St. Augustine of Canterbury with forty monks to convert the Anglo-Saxon heathen: On seeing Anglo-Saxon boys offered for sale in the Roman slave market, St. Gregory is said to have remarked: *"Non Angli, sed Angeli.* [Not Angles, but angels.]" His papacy in the Dark Ages included a stubborn dedication to the conversion, also, of the Jews and the introduction of picture books for illiterates to replace the reading of the Bible at a time when learning was, save for its preservation in a small class of scribes and clerics, in almost total eclipse.

Whatever St. Gregory's contribution to musical liturgy may have been, legend or fact, his homilies have a rhythmic cadencing closely allied to the musical: his imagery here of the sea creature, or crocodile, symbolizing the devil, is as pictorial as the colored illustrations he commissioned when the art of letters was in decline. The *pericope* (extract from Scripture), designed to be read on the Thursday after Easter, takes wing once more from Gregory's learned exegesis. The term "mercy seat," to which he refers, is mysterious; it may allude to the place above the Ark of the Covenant which contained the two tablets of the law.

ᴄᴇ

Homily 25

But Mary stood outside the sepulchre weeping. And as she wept she stooped down and looked into the sepulchre. She saw two angels in white, sitting, one at the head and one at the feet where the body of Jesus had been laid. And they said to her, "Woman, why are you weeping?" And she said to them, "Because they have taken away my Lord, and I do not know where they have put him." When she had said this, she turned round and saw Jesus standing, and she did not know that it was Jesus. Jesus said to her, "Woman, why are you weeping? Whom do you seek?" She thought that it was the gardener, and said to him, "Sir, if you have taken him away, tell me where they have put him and I will take him away." Jesus said to her, Mary. She turned and said to him, Rabboni, which is to say, Master. Jesus said to her, "Do not touch me, for I am not yet ascended to my Father. But go to my brothers and say to them, I ascend to my Father and your Father and to my God and your God." Mary Magdalene came and made known to his disciples, I have seen the Lord, and that he said these things to me.

—JOHN 20:11–18

Mary Magdalene, *who had been a sinner in the city* (Luke 7:37), loved the Truth, and so washed away with her tears the stains of wickedness. Thus was fulfilled the voice of the Truth who said: *Her many sins have been forgiven her, because she loved much.* (Luke 7:47.) She whose sins had kept her cold afterward burned irresistibly by loving. After she came to the sepulchre and failed to find the body of the Lord there, she believed that it had been taken away and reported this to the disciples. (John 20:1–2.) They came, and saw, and they believed that it was as the woman had said. (John 20:3–8.) And immediately it is written of them, *And so the disciples went back to the place where they had been* (John 20:10); and then: *But Mary stood outside the sepulchre weeping.*

We must consider in this the woman's state of mind, that a great force of love inflamed her. When even the disciples departed from the sepulchre, she did not depart. She sought for him whom she had not found, weeping as she searched; being inflamed with the fire of her love, she burned with desire for him who she believed had been taken away. So it happened that she who stayed behind to seek him was the only one who saw him. Surely the essence of every good work is perseverance, and Truth has told us that *the person who perseveres to the end is the one who will be saved* (Matt. 24:13); and the Law commands that the tail of the victim is to be offered in sacrifice. (Lev. 3:9.) Now the tail is the end of a body, and that person makes a perfect offering who carries out the sacrifice of a good work to its due completion. Joseph is described as the only one of his brothers to have a tunic reaching to the ankles. (Gen. 37:3.) A tunic reaching to the ankles is a good work reaching completion.

But Mary, *while she was weeping, stooped down and looked into the sepulchre.* It is true that she had already seen that the sepulchre was empty, and had already reported that the Lord had been taken away. Why did she stoop down again, why did she again long to see? It is not enough for a lover to have looked once, because the force of love intensifies the effort of the search. She sought a first time and found nothing; she persevered in seeking, and so it happened that she found him. It came about that her unfulfilled desires increased, and as they increased they took possession of what they had found.

This is the reason the Church says of this person, her own spouse, in the Song of Songs: *Upon my bed during the night I sought him whom my soul loves; I sought him and did not find him. I will rise and go about the city, through its squares and streets; I will seek him whom my soul loves.* (Cant. 3:1–2.) In her failure to find him she redoubled her efforts saying, *I sought him and did not find him* (Cant. 3:2), but since discovery is not long delayed if the search is not abandoned, *The watchmen who guard the city found me, "Have you seen him whom my soul loved?" Scarcely had I passed them by when I found him whom my soul loves.* (Cant. 3:4.)

We seek the one we love upon our beds when we sigh with longing for our Redeemer during our short period of rest during the present life. We seek him during the night, because even though our hearts are already watchful for him, our eyes are still darkened. But it remains for the person who does not find the one he loves to rise and go about the city, that is, he must travel about the holy Church of the elect with an inquiring heart; he must seek her through its streets and squares, making his way, that is, through narrow and broad places, on the watch to make inquiries if any traces of her can be found in them, because there are some, even of those leading worldly lives, who have something worth imitating of virtue in their actions. The watchmen who guard the city find us as we search, because the holy Fathers who guard the Church's orthodoxy come to meet our good efforts, to teach us, by their words of their writings. Scarcely have we passed them by when we find him whom we love. Although in his humility our Redeemer was a human being in the midst of human beings, in his divinity he was above human beings. Therefore once the watchmen have been passed by, the beloved is found, because when we consider that the prophets and the apostles are lower than he, we realize that he who is God by nature is above human beings. We first seek the one we cannot find so that when later on we find him we may hold on to him more intimately.

Holy desires, as I've told you before, increase by delay in their fulfillment; if delay causes them to fail, they were not desires. Anyone who has been able to reach out for the Truth has been on fire with this love. For this reason David said: *My soul has thirsted for the living God; when shall I come and appear before the face of God?* (Ps. 42:2.) And he counseled us, saying: *Seek his face continually.* (Ps. 105:4.) And for this reason the prophet said: *My soul has desired you in the night, and with my spirit within my breast I will watch for you in the morning* (Isa. 26:9); and again the Church says to him in the Song of Songs: *I have been wounded with love* (Cant. 2:5).

It is right that the soul after bearing in its heart a wound of love brought on by its burning desire, should reach out for healing at the sight of the doctor. And so, again, it says: *My soul melted when he spoke.* (Cant. 5:6.) The heart of a person who does not seek the face of his creator is hardened by his wickedness, because in itself it remains cold. But if it now begins to burn with the desire of following him whom it loves, it runs since the fire of love has melted it. Its desire makes it anxious. Everything that used to please it in the world seems worthless; it finds nothing agreeable outside of its creator; things that once delighted the heart afterward become grievously oppressive. Nothing brings it consolation in its sadness as long as the one it desires is not beheld. The heart sorrows. Light itself is loathsome. Scorching fire burns away the rust of sin in the heart. The soul is inflamed as if it were gold, because gold loses its beauty through use but fire restores its brightness. So Mary loved, who turned a second time to the sepulchre she had already looked into. Let us see the result of her search, which had been redoubled by the power of love.

She saw two angels in white sitting, one at the head and one at the feet where the body of Jesus had been laid. Why were two angels seen in the place of the Lord's body, one sitting at the head and the other at the feet? In Latin, the word "angel" means "messenger." From his passion the message was to go out that he who was God before all ages is a human person at their end. An angel is sitting at his head, so to speak, when the Apostle preaches, *In the beginning was the Word, and the Word was with God, and the Word was God* (John 1:1); and an angel is sitting at his feet when he says that *the Word became flesh and dwelt among us.* (John 1:14.) We can also recognize the two testaments in the two angels, one earlier, and the other later. These angels are brought together at the place of the Lord's body, because while both testaments proclaim equally the message that the Lord became a man and died and rose, the earlier testament sits at his head, so to speak, and the later at his feet.

The two cherubim which covered the mercy seat beheld one another with their countenances turned toward it. (Exod. 25:18–20.) The word "cherubim" means fullness of knowledge. What do the two cherubim signify but the two testaments? And what does the mercy seat prefigure but the Lord become a man? John says of him: *For he is the expiation* for our sins. (1 John 2:2.) When the Old Testament declares of the Lord that something was to be done, which the New Testament proclaims has been done, it is as

if the two cherubim are beholding one another while they turn their countenances toward the mercy seat. When they see the Lord become man
placed between them, they do not disagree about what they see, but are of
one heart in describing the mystery of his dispensation.

The angels asked Mary, saying: *"Woman, why are you weeping?" And she
said to them: "Because they have taken away my Lord, and I do not know where they
have put him."* The sacred message which stirs up tears of love in us provides
consolation for these tears when it promises us the sight of our Redeemer.
But we should note that, in the historical sense, the woman did not say,
"They have taken away the body of my Lord," but, *"They have taken away my
Lord."* It is customary in the sacred writings that the whole is sometimes indicated by a part and the part sometimes by a whole. The part indicates a
whole when it is written of Jacob's sons that he went down into Egypt with
seventy souls (Gen. 46:27): the soul did not go down into Egypt apart from
their bodies, but the soul signified the entire human being, since the whole
is expressed by a part. The Lord's body alone had lain in the sepulchre; Mary
was not seeking the body, but the Lord who had been taken away, indicating the part by the whole.

*When she had said this, she turned round and saw Jesus standing, and she did
not know that it was Jesus.* Mary, who was still in doubt about the Lord's resurrection, turned around to see Jesus. By this doubt she had turned her
back to the face of the Lord, whom she did not believe had risen. Because
she loved, and doubted, she saw and did not recognize him. Her love revealed him to her, and her doubt prevented her from knowing him. What
follows indicates her continued lack of recognition:

He said to her: "Woman, why are you weeping? Whom do you seek?" He asked
the reason for her sorrow to increase her desire, so that when he asked
whom she was seeking she might feel a more vehement love for him.

*She thought that it was the gardener, and said to him: "Sir, if you have taken
him away, tell me where you have put him, and I will take him away."* Perhaps this
woman was not as mistaken as she appeared to be when she believed that
Jesus was a gardener. Was he not spiritually a gardener for her, when he
planted the fruitful seeds of virtue in her heart by the force of his love? But
why did she say to the one she saw and believed to be the gardener, when
she had not yet told him whom she was seeking, *"Sir, if you have taken him*

away"? She had not yet said who it was who made her weep from desire, or mentioned him of whom she spoke. But the force of love customarily brings it about that a heart believes everyone else is aware of the one of whom it is always thinking. It is understandable that the woman did not say whom she was seeking, and yet said, *"If you have taken him away."* She did not believe that the one for whom she herself so constantly wept in her desire was unknown to the other.

Jesus said to her:"Mary." After he had called her by the common name of "woman," he called her by her own name, as if to say, "Recognize him who recognizes you." To a perfect man also it was said, *I know you by name* (Exod. 33:12), because "man" is the common appellation of us all, but Moses was his own name. He was rightly told that he was known by name, as if the Lord was saying to him openly: "I do not know you in a general way as I know others, but particularly." And so because Mary was called by name, she acknowledged her Creator, and called him at once *"rabboni,"* that is, *"teacher."* He was both the one she was outwardly seeking and the one who was teaching her inwardly to seek him.

Now the evangelist does not add what the woman did, but he implies it by what she heard. He said to her: *"Do not touch me, for I have not yet ascended to my Father."* These words show us that Mary wished to embrace the feet of him she recognized. Her teacher did not tell her, *"Do not touch me,"* because the Lord refused the touch of women after his resurrection. It is said of the two women at his sepulchre, *They drew near and took hold of his feet.* (Matt. 28:9.)

The reason he wasn't to be touched was added in the following words: *"For I have not yet ascended to my Father."* In our hearts, Jesus ascends to the Father when he is to be the Father's equal. In the heart of one who does not believe that he is equal to the Father, the Lord has still not ascended to his Father. That one truly touches Jesus who believes that he is coeternal with the Father. In Paul's heart Jesus had already ascended to the Father, when he said: *Though he was in the form of God, he did not think that the fact of his being equal to God was robbery.* (Phil. 2:6.) John also touched our Redeemer with the hand of faith when he said: *In the beginning was the Word, and the Word was with God, and the Word was God* (John 1:1); *all things were made through him* (John 1:3). And so that person touches the Lord who believes that he is equal to the Father in substance from eternity.

But someone may wonder how the Son can be the Father's equal. In this matter human nature is unable to comprehend what fills it with wonder. Nevertheless he can believe this, since he knows other things because of the wonder they bring about in him. There is at hand an answer to the question that he may come to briefly on his own. It is clear that the Lord himself created the mother in whose virgin womb he was created as a human being. Why then should we wonder if he is equal to the Father, when he existed before his mother? We have also learned from Paul that *Christ is the power and wisdom of God.* (1 Cor. 1:24.) Therefore anyone who considers the Son less than the Father particularly diminishes him when he professes that his wisdom is unequal to the Father's. What powerful person would take it calmly if someone should say to him, "Indeed you are important, but your wisdom is less than you are"? The Lord himself said: *The Father and I are one* (John 10:30); and again: *The Father is greater than I* (John 14:28). It is also written that he was subject to his parents. (Luke 2:51.) Why should we wonder if he declared that in his human nature he was less than the Father in heaven, when because of it he was subject even to his parents on earth?

In this human nature he now says to Mary: *"Go to my brothers and say to them, 'I ascend to my Father and your Father, to my God and your God.' "* Since he said "my" and "your," why didn't he use the general word "our"? But in speaking thus distinctly he indicated that he has the same Father who is such by nature, *"and your Father,"* who is such by grace; *"to my God,"* because I descended, *"and to your God,"* because you have ascended. Because I too am a human being he is my God; because you have been freed from error he is your God. He is my Father and God in a distinctive way, because he begot me as God before the ages but created me as a human being at the end of the ages.

Mary Magdalene came and made known to his disciples, "I have seen the Lord, and he said these things to me." See, how the sin of the human race was removed where it began. In paradise a woman was the cause of death for a man (Gen. 3:6); coming from the sepulchre a woman proclaimed life to men. Mary related the words of the one who restored her to life; Eve had related the words of the serpent who brought death. It is as if the Lord was telling the human race, not by words but by actions, "Receive the draught of life from the hand of the one who offered you the drink of death."

I have completed this concise explanation of the Gospel lesson. Now with the assistance of this same Lord of whom I have been speaking let us reflect on the glory of his resurrection and the depth of his kindness. He willed to rise quickly from death lest our souls remain for a long time in the death of unbelief. Hence it was aptly said by the psalmist: *He drank from the stream on his journey; therefore he lifted up his head.* (Ps. 110:7.) The stream of death had been flowing in the human race from the very beginning of the world. The Lord drank from this stream on his journey, because he tasted death in his passing; and therefore he lifted up his head, because by rising he lifted up above the angels what by dying he laid in the sepulchre. He overthrew the ancient enemy forever by allowing his persecutors' hands to prevail over his body for a brief time.

The Lord revealed this clearly to blessed Job when he said: *Will you catch leviathan* with a fishhook? (Job 41:1.) Leviathan, which means "their increment," designates that fish-like destroyer of the human race which, when he promised to bestow divinity upon human beings, took away their immortality. He was the cause, in the first human being, of the sin of collusion; when by his evil persuasive powers he increases many times over the sins of those who come after, he heaps up punishment for them without end. On a fishhook, the food is evident, the barb is concealed. The all-powerful Father caught this fish-like creature by means of a fishhook, because he sent his only-begotten Son, who had become a human being, to his death. The Son had both a visible body which could suffer, and an invisible nature which could not. When, through the actions of his persecutors the serpent bit the food of his body, the barb of his divine nature pierced him. Earlier, indeed, he had recognized that he was God by his miracles, but he fell to doubting when he saw that he was capable of suffering. It is, then, as if the fishhook got caught in his throat as he was swallowing. The food of the Lord's body, which the destroyer craved, was visible on it; at the time of his passion his divine nature, which the destroyer would do away with, lay hidden. He was caught by the fishhook of the Lord's incarnation because while he was craving the food of his body, he was pierced by the barb of his divine nature. There was in the Lord a human nature which would lead the destroyer to him, and there was a divine nature which would pierce him; there was in him the obvious weakness which would entice him, and there was the hidden power which would pierce the throat of the one who seized him. Therefore was the destroyer caught by a fishhook, because the cause of his destruction was where he bit. And he lost the mortal human beings whom he rightfully held because he dared to crave the death of one who was immortal, over whom he had no claim.

Thus it is that this Mary, of whom I was speaking, was alive, because he who owed nothing to death died on behalf of the human race; thus it is that we ourselves daily return to life after we sin, because our Creator, who was sinless, came down to suffer our punishment. See how the ancient enemy lost those spoils he had taken from the human race, how he destroyed the victory he had won by deception. Daily do sinners return to life, daily are they snatched from his throat by our Redeemer's hand.

How fitting are these further words of our Lord to blessed Job: *Who will pierce its jaw with a band?* (Job 41:2.) A band constricts by its binding force. What does the band signify then but the divine mercy which embraces us. It pierces the jaw of leviathan when it shows that we still have the remedy of repentance after we have committed what is forbidden. The Lord pierces the jaw of leviathan with a band because he so counteracts the cunning of our ancient enemy with the indescribable power of his mercy, that sometimes our enemy even loses those he has already caught. It's as if they fall out of its mouth, when they return to a state of innocence after having sinned. Who would escape its jaw having once been seized, if it were not pierced? Did it not hold Peter in its mouth when he made his denial? (Matt. 26:70.) Did it not hold David in its mouth when it pulled him down into such a great whirlpool of dissipation? (2 Sam. 11:14.) But when both returned to life by repentance, it is as if leviathan lost them in some way by the breaching of its jaw. And so these men, who returned by repentance after having committed such great wickedness were rescued from its mouth by the breaching of its jaw.

Is there any human being who escapes leviathan's mouth so that he avoids all forbidden actions? By this we recognize what great debtors we are to the Redeemer of the human race, who not only forbade us to enter leviathan's mouth, but also allowed us to return from its mouth. He did not take away the sinner's hope, but he pierced its jaw to give a way of escape, so that a person who was heedlessly unwilling to guard against being bitten in the first place might at least get away afterwards. Divine Medicine meets us at every turn: it gave us human beings commandments so that we might not sin, and gave us sinners a remedy to keep us from despair. Hence we must take every precaution against being seized by leviathan's mouth when we take pleasure in sin. But then, if any of us is seized, let him not despair, because if he has perfect sorrow for his sin, he finds a breach in its jaw through which he may escape.

This very Mary of whom I have been speaking, is here as a witness of the divine mercy. When the Pharisee wanted to stifle the spring of her devotion he said: *If this man were a prophet, he would surely know who and what sort of woman this is who is touching him, that she is a sinner.* (Luke 7:39.) But she had abandoned her wicked ways, and she washed away the stains of heart and body with her tears, and touched the feet of her Redeemer. She sat at the feet of Jesus, and listened to the words of his mouth. She had clung to him when he was alive, and she sought him when he was dead. She found alive the one she had sought when he was dead; and she found such a position of grace with him that it was she who brought the message to his apostles, who were themselves his messengers.

What ought we to see in this, my friends, except the boundless mercy of our Creator. He has put before us, as if for signs and examples of repentance, those he brought to life through repentance after a fall. I look at Peter, at the thief, at Zaccheus, at Mary and I see in them nothing else but examples put before our eyes of hope and repentance. Perhaps someone has fallen away from the faith: let him look on Peter, who wept bitterly for his fainthearted denial. (Matt. 26:75.) Perhaps someone else has been enflamed with malice and cruelty against his neighbor: let him look on the thief, who even at the moment of death attained the reward of life by repenting. (Luke 23:43.) Perhaps another, enflamed by avarice, has plundered a stranger's goods: let him look at Zaccheus, who if he had stolen anything from anyone restored it fourfold. (Luke 19:8.) Perhaps another yet, being enkindled with the fire of lust, has lost the purity of his body: let him look on Mary, who purged away the love of her body by the fire of divine love. (Luke 7:47.)

See how almighty God puts before our eyes at every turn those whom we ought to imitate; he provides at every turn examples of his mercy. Let us find evils distasteful, even if we have experienced them. Almighty God freely forgets that we have been guilty; he is ready to count our repentance as innocence. If we have become dirtied after the water of salvation, let us be born again from our tears. Accordingly we must listen to the voice of our first pastor: *Like newborn children, desire milk.* (1 Pet. 2:2.) Return, little children, to the bosom of your mother, the eternal wisdom. Drink from the bountiful breasts of the loving kindness of God. Weep for your past misdeeds; shun those that avoid what lies ahead. Our Redeemer will solace our fleeting sorrows with eternal joy, he who lives and reigns with the Father in the unity of the Holy Spirit, God for ever and ever. Amen.

PART III

"Great Was the
Company of the Preachers"

The Medieval Pulpit

St. Patrick

373–463

St. Patrick, the patron saint of Ireland, was born into mixed parentage in Britain, probably the offspring of a Roman father and a British mother. We know from tradition, and from this confessional and epistolary sermon, probably read aloud in churches and parishes all over Ireland, that he was captured in a raid by Picts and Scots around A.D. 389 and sold as a slave to a chieftain in Antrim. After years of bondage he was released to study in Gaul under St. Martin of Tours and felt a supernatural call to return and preach throughout heathen Ireland where he established his evangelical mission.

Patrick's original name was "Sucat," in the language of Britain; his role in captivity was to tend sheep. As in the tradition of the Old Testament, tenders of sheep often became visionaries and leaders of religion; the adult Patrick became a pastor of the Celtic flock, and his statement of the Creed in this autobiographical confession became a powerful prose statement, rendering the same passionate conviction as the anonymous hymn, sometimes attributed to Patrick himself, known as "The Deer's Cry," or "Patrick's Breastplate." Among the legends converging on St. Patrick, we have the story of the hymn's composition: Patrick is said to have sung it while the saint and his followers were transformed, under pursuit, into a herd of deer. This tale is suggestive of the harmonious relation of Irish Christianity and the natural world of the Druid priesthood which it overlaid.

In the hymn, the saint's canticle, sung during the legendary flight, closes with a famous incantation:

> Christ to shield me today
> Against poison, against burning,

Against drowning, against wounding,
So that there may come to me abundance of reward.
Christ with me, Christ before me, Christ behind me,
Christ in me, Christ beneath me, Christ above me,
Christ on my right, Christ on my left,
Christ when I lie down, Christ when I sit down, Christ when I
    arise,
Christ in the heart of every man who thinks of me,
Christ in the mouth of every one who speaks of me,
Christ in every eye that sees me,
Christ in every ear that hears me.

I arise today
Through a mighty strength, the invocation of the Trinity,
Through belief in the threeness,
Through confession of the oneness
Of the Creator of Creation.

This invocation of early Christianity's belief in the Trinity, while standing "at the very edge of the earth," is the summation not only of Patrick's
poem but of his sermon as well.

A Slave in Ireland

I, Patrick, a sinner, am the most unlearned and the lowest of all the
faithful, utterly despised by many. My father was Calpornius, a deacon, and
my grandfather Potitus, a priest. I was brought up near the town of Ban-
naven Tiburnia. At the age of sixteen, before I knew God, I was taken captive and shipped to Ireland, along with thousands of others.

When I arrived in Ireland I was sent to tend sheep. I used to pray many
times each day; and, as I prayed, I felt God's love fill my heart and
strengthen my faith. Soon I was saying up to a hundred prayers each day, and
almost as many at night. I had to stay all night in the forests and on the

mountains, looking after the sheep, and I would wake to pray before dawn in all weathers, snow, frost and rain; I felt no fear, nor did I feel sleepy, because the Spirit was so fervent within me.

It was there one night, while I was asleep, that I heard a voice speaking to me: "You do well to fast and pray, for soon you shall be returning to your home country." And shortly afterward I heard another voice: "See, your ship is ready." The ship was not near, but was two hundred miles away in a place where I knew nobody and had never visited. I immediately fled from the man who had enslaved me for six years, and in the strength of God traveled to the coast. During the whole journey I met no dangers whatever.

On the day that I arrived the ship was ready to set sail, and I insisted that I come aboard. But the captain became angry, saying, "You are wasting your time asking to come with us." When I heard this I left the ship to go back to the hut where I was staying, and began to pray. But before I had finished my prayer, I heard one of the crew shouting loudly after me: "Come quickly!" When I got back to the ship they said to me, "Come aboard—we'll take you on trust, treating you as a friend." I refused to be too intimate with them, for fear of God; but I was happy to befriend them, in the hope of bringing them to faith in Jesus Christ. We set sail at once.

After three days at sea, we reached land. For the next month we traveled on foot through a vast region where no one lived; eventually our food ran out, and we became extremely hungry. One of my companions said: "Tell us, Christian, you say that your God is great and all-powerful, so why can you not pray for us, and save us from starving?" I replied, "Turn with all your heart to the Lord my God, to whom nothing is impossible, and today he will provide abundant food." And that is precisely what happened: a herd of pigs appeared before us, and we killed enough of them to satisfy our hunger. After this my companions gave thanks to God, and I gained respect in their eyes.

The Call of Ireland

At last I reached my home, and spent the next few years with my family. They begged that now, after suffering so many hardships, I should never leave them again. But one night in a dream I saw a man coming from Ireland, whose name was Victoricus, carrying countless letters. He gave one of them to me, and I read the heading: "The Voice of the Irish." And as I looked at these words, I heard a voice coming from the Forest of Foclut in the far west of Ireland, calling me: "We implore you, young man, to return and walk among us." My heart seemed to be breaking and I could read no more.

During another night I heard a voice—I do not know whether it was within me or beside me, God only knows—whose words I could not understand, except the final sentence: "He who lay down his life for you, it is he that speaks within you." And I awoke full of joy. And sometime later I saw him praying within me: I was, as it were, inside my own body and I could hear his voice. He was praying most powerfully. I was dumbfounded, wondering who it could be praying within me; but at the end of the prayer he said that he was the Spirit. And then I awoke, remembering the apostle's words: "The Spirit helps us in our weakness; for we do not know how to pray as we ought, but the Spirit himself intercedes for us with sighs too deep for words."

Finally I knew I must go to Ireland. But I did not give way to the Spirit's promptings until I was utterly exhausted. The Lord thus broke down my stubbornness, and molded me according to his will, making me fit to do work which once had been far beyond me. I could now dedicate myself to the salvation of others, whereas once I had been indifferent even to my own salvation.

Missionary Labors

It would be tedious to relate all my labors in detail, or even in part; what matters is that God often forgave my stupidity and carelessness, and took pity upon me thousands and thousands of times. There were many who tried to prevent my mission, saying behind my back: "What is this fellow up to, talking to God's enemies?" They were not being malicious, but were unhappy that a man so uneducated as I am should conduct such a mission. But, though I am untalented, I have done my best always to be honest and sincere, with Christians and heathen alike.

I have baptized many thousands of people, but never asked as much as a halfpenny in return. Despite being such an unexceptional person myself, I have trained and ordained priests throughout the country; but I have never asked even the price of a shoe as reward. Instead, I have spent whatever money I possessed for the benefit of the common people.

I have traveled in the remotest regions of the country, where no Christian has ever been before, and there I have baptized and confirmed people, and ordained priests; and I have done so with a joyful heart and tireless spirit. I have given presents to kings and persuaded them to release slaves; and I have inspired the sons of kings to travel with me on my missions. I and my companions have at times been arrested and put in irons, and our captors have been eager to kill us; yet the Lord has always set us free.

But I now see that in this present world I am exalted above my true merit, and I am more privileged than I deserve. I am more suited to poverty and adversity than to riches and luxury—for the Lord Christ was poor for our sakes. Yet in truth I have no wealth of my own, and every day I expect to be killed, betrayed or reduced to slavery. I am frightened of none of these things, because my heart is set on the riches of heaven.

I now commend my soul to God, for whom, despite my obscurity, I have served as ambassador—indeed, in choosing me for this noble task, he has shown that he is no respecter of persons, because I am the least of his servants. May God never separate me from his people on this island, which stands at the very edge of the earth. And may God always make me a faithful witness to him, until he calls me to heaven.

PATRICK'S CREED

There is no other God except God the Father; nor was there ever in times past, nor will there ever be in the future. He is the beginning of all things, and himself has no beginning. He possesses all things, but is possessed by none.

His Son Jesus Christ has been with the Father before the beginning; and through him all things were created, both spiritual and material. He became man, and conquered death; and was taken back into heaven to the Father.

The Father has given to his Son power over all things in heaven and on earth, and under the earth, that every tongue should confess that Jesus Christ is Lord.

He has poured upon us his Spirit, so that our spirits are overflowing. Through his Spirit we receive the promise of eternal life. And in his Spirit we are taught to trust and obey the Father, and, with Christ, become his sons and daughters.

Caesarius of Arles

469/70–542

Though the image of Arles in the modern mind is heavily filtered through the late paintings of Van Gogh, it was one of the chief cities of ancient Gaul. When Caesarius, who was a member of one of the region's old aristocratic families, became its bishop, this walled city ranked just after Rome as a center of Western Christianity. Caesarius had previously trained for the clerical life as a monk at the island monastery of Lérins on the coast of Provence. It was the first great Western monastery, founded from the fourth-century Desert Father tradition of Egypt and Sinai.

In the period after Augustine (d. 430) and the Church Fathers, preaching began to decline as Europe was overrun by successive waves of new peoples with new names like Vandals, Franks, and Goths. The lighthouse centers of Christianity were becoming more dispersed, and given the Church rule that only bishops had the right to preach, the people found themselves less frequently evangelized.

It was to this need that Caesarius devoted himself. Not just content to exhort his fellow bishops to preach more ardently and often, he urged ordinary priests and deacons to take copies of his sermons and others—notably Augustine's—and read them to the (largely illiterate) people if a bishop were not available. He challenged one and all with the words of the apostle Paul: "Woe to me if I do not spread the gospel." (1 Cor. 9:16.)

The results of all his exhorting—some 250 surviving sermons—have been identified, codified, and published only in the twentieth century. They reflect Caesarius's strong emphasis on pastoral care and for the most part concentrate on strengthening the moral fiber. And they are unusually short, most being delivered in a quarter of an hour. The example here is a call to arms at the approach of Lent.

On the Beginning of Lent

Behold, dearest brethren, through the mercy of God the season of Lent is approaching. Therefore I beseech you, beloved, with God's help let us celebrate these days, salutary for bodies and healing for the soul, in so holy and spiritual a manner that the observance of a holy Lent may lead to progress for us and not judgment. For if we lead a careless life, involving ourselves in too many occupations, refusing to observe chastity, not applying ourselves to fasting and vigils and prayers, neither reading Sacred Scripture ourselves nor willingly listening to others read it, the very remedies are changed into wounds for us. As a result of this we shall have judgment, where we could have had a remedy.

For this reason I exhort you, dearest brethren, to rise rather early for the vigils, and above all to come to terce, sext and nones. Let no one withdraw himself from the holy office unless either infirmity or public service or at least great necessity keeps him occupied. Let it not be enough for you that you hear the divine lessons in church, but read them yourselves at home or look for someone else to read them and willingly listen to them when they do. Remember the thought of our Lord, brethren, when He says: "If he were to gain the whole world and destroy himself in the process, what can a man offer in exchange for his very self?" (Matt. 16:26.) Above all keep in mind and always fear greatly what is written: "The burdens of the world have made them miserable." Therefore busy yourself in your home in such a way that you do not neglect your soul. Finally, if you cannot do more, at least labor as much on behalf of your soul as you desire to labor for the sake of your body.

For this reason, dearest brethren, "Have no love for the world, nor the things the world affords" (1 John 2:15), because "the world with its seductions is passing away" (1 John 2:17). What, then, remains in a man except what each one has stored up in the treasury of his conscience for the salvation of his soul by reading or prayer or the performance of good works? For miserable pleasure, still more wretched lust and dissipation, through a passing sweetness prepare eternal bitterness; but abstinence, vigils, prayer, and fasting lead to the delights of paradise through the briefest hardships. The truth does not lie when He says in the Gospel: "Strait and narrow is the road that leads to life, and how few there are who find it!" (Matt. 7:14.) Not for long is there rejoicing on the broad way, and not for long is there labor on the strait and narrow road. After brief sadness those who travel the latter receive eternal life, while those who travel the former, after short joy, suffer endless punishment.

For this reason, dearest brethren, by fasting, reading, and prayer in these forty days we ought to store up for our souls provisions, as it were, for the whole year. Although through the mercy of God you frequently and devoutly hear the divine lessons throughout the entire year, still during these days we ought to rest from the winds and the sea of this world by taking refuge, as it were, in the haven of Lent, and in the quiet of silence to receive the divine lessons in the receptacle of our heart. Devoting ourselves to God out of love for eternal life, during these days let us with all solicitude strive to repair and compose in the little ship of our soul whatever throughout the year has been broken or destroyed or damaged or ruined by many storms, that is, by the waves of sins. And since it is necessary for us to endure the storms and tempests of this world while we are still in this frail body, as often as the enemy wills to lead us astray by means of the roughest storms or to deceive us by the most voluptuous pleasures, with God's help may he always find us prepared against him.

Therefore I beseech you again and again. During these holy days of

Lent if you cannot cut off the occupations of this world, at least strive to curtail them in part. By fleeing from this world, through an expedient loss and a most glorious gain you may take away from earthly occupations a few hours in which you can devote yourselves to God. For this world either laughs at us or is laughed at by us; either we yield to it and are despised, or we despise it in order to obtain eternal rewards. Thus you either reject and despise the world, or you yield to it and are pursued or even trampled upon by it. But it is better for you to despise the world and by trampling upon it to make a step for yourself whereby you may ascend on high. If in accord with your usual practice you both willingly heed and strive faithfully to fulfill, dearest brethren, the truths which we are suggesting for the salvation of all by presuming upon your obedience, you will celebrate Easter with joy and will happily come to eternal life. May He Himself deign to grant this, who together with the Father and the Holy Spirit lives and reigns for ever and ever. Amen.

The Venerable Bede

671–735

In one of the most numinous moments in Old English literature, Bede, in his *Ecclesiastical History,* describes a seventh-century conversion. In this famous passage a pagan chieftain, rising in assembly after hearing the Christian missionary Paulinus, testifies to the divine inspiration of the occasion. From his rebuke to the pagan priest who is his adversary comes this celebrated utterance from the threshold world of seventh-century Britain:

> "The present life of man, O king, seems to me, in comparison of that which is unknown to us, like to the swift flight of a sparrow through

the room wherein you sit at supper in winter, with your commanders and ministers, and a good fire in the midst, whilst the storms of rain and snow prevail abroad; the sparrow, I say, flying in at one door, and immediately out at another, whilst he is within, is safe from the wintry storm; but after a short space of fair weather, he immediately vanishes out of your sight, into the dark winter from which he had emerged. So this life of man appears for a short space, but of what went before what is to follow, we are utterly ignorant. If, therefore, this new doctrine contains something more certain, it seems justly to deserve to be followed."

One of the greatest scholars of his time, Bede ("Baeda" in Anglo-Saxon) spent most of his life at the monastery of Jarrow in Northumbria, immersed in Greek and Latin texts while demonstrating a true wisdom closely linked to his piety and simplicity. It was the Venerable Bede's good fortune to live in the brief light of Northumbrian Christianity before its extinction by Viking raids, escaping the destruction that was to come while living a life of prayer and scholarship. His gentleness and serenity of spirit survive not just in his monumental testimony to the moral purpose of history, but in this quiet and exquisite sermon which corresponds to the parables of Jesus Christ.

The speech of Bede's pagan convert in the *Ecclesiastical History* is deservedly famous for its eloquence and the poignancy of its image of the transiency of human life; Bede's sermon on mercy and justice is no less evocative of a brief and contemplative moment in the history of a religion under siege and imperiled by the violent invasions which burned the monasteries of the north but spared this text and Bede's individual and remarkable voice.

The Meeting of Mercy and Justice

Mercy and truth are met together.

—PSALM 85:10

There was a certain Father of a family, a powerful King, who had four daughters, of whom one was called Mercy; the second, Truth; the third, Justice; the fourth, Peace; of whom it is said, "Mercy and Truth are met together; Justice and Peace have kissed each other." He had also a certain most wise Son, to whom no one could be compared in wisdom. He had, also, a certain servant, whom he had exalted and enriched with great honor; for he had made him after his own likeness and similitude, and that without any preceding merit on the servant's part. But the lord, as is the custom with such wise masters, wished prudently to explore, and to become acquainted with, the character and the faith of his servant, whether he were trustworthy toward himself or not: so he gave him an easy commandment, and said, "If you do what I tell you, I will exalt you to further honors; if not, you shall perish miserably."

The servant heard the commandment, and without any delay, went and broke it. Why need I say more? Why need I delay you by my words and by my tears? This proud servant, stiff-necked, full of contumely, and puffed up with conceit, sought an excuse for his transgression, and retorted the whole fault on his Lord. For when he said, "The woman whom thou gavest to be with me, she deceived me," he threw all the fault on his Maker. His Lord, more angry for such contumelious conduct, than for the transgression of his command, called four most cruel executioners, and commanded one of them to cast him into prison, another to behead him, the third to strangle him, and the fourth to afflict him with grievous torments. By and by, when occasion offers, I will give you the right name of these tormentors.

These torturers, then, studying how they might carry out their own cruelty, took the wretched man and began to afflict him with all manner of punishments. But one of the daughters of the King, by name Mercy, when she had heard of this punishment of the servant, ran hastily to the prison, and looking in and seeing the man given over to the tormentors, could not help having compassion upon him, for it is the property of Mercy to have mercy. She tore her garments and struck her hands together, and let her hair fall loose about her neck, and crying and shrieking, ran to her father, and kneeling before his feet began to say with an earnest and sorrowful voice: "My beloved father, am not I thy daughter Mercy? and art not thou called merciful? If thou art merciful, have mercy upon thy servant; and if thou wilt not have mercy upon him, thou canst not be called merciful; and if thou art not merciful, thou canst not have me, Mercy, for thy daughter." While she was thus arguing with her father, her sister Truth came up, and demanded why it was that Mercy was weeping. "Your sister Mercy," replied the father, "wishes me to have pity upon that proud transgressor whose punishment I have appointed." Truth, when she heard this, was excessively angry, and looking sternly at her father, "Am not I," said she, "thy daughter Truth? art not thou called true? Is it not true that thou didst fix a punishment for him, and threaten him with death by torments? If thou art true, thou wilt follow that which is true; if thou dost not follow it, thou canst not be true; if thou art not true, thou canst not have me, Truth, for thy daughter." Here, you see, "Mercy and Truth are met together." The third sister, namely, Justice, hearing this strife, contention, quarreling, and pleading, and summoned by the outcry, began to inquire the cause from Truth. And Truth, who could only speak that which was true, said, "This sister of ours, Mercy, if she ought to be called a sister who does not agree with us, desires that our father should have pity on that proud transgressor." Then Justice, with an angry countenance, and meditating on a grief which she had not expected, said to her father, "Am not I thy daughter Justice? art thou not called just? If thou art just, thou wilt exercise justice on the transgressor; if thou dost not exercise that justice, thou canst not be just; if thou art not just, thou canst not have me, Justice, for thy daughter." So here were Truth and Justice on the one side, and Mercy on the other. Peace fled into a far distant country. For where there is strife and contention, there is no peace; and by how much greater the contention, by so much further Peace is driven away.

Peace, therefore, being lost, and his three daughters in warm discussion, the King found it an extremely difficult matter to determine what he should do, or to which side he should lean. For, if he gave ear to Mercy, he would offend Truth and Justice; if he gave ear to Truth and Justice, he could not have Mercy for his daughter; and yet it was necessary that he should be both merciful and just, and peaceful and true. There was great need then of good advice. The Father therefore called his wise Son, and consulted him about the affair. Said the Son, "Give me, my Father, this present business to manage, and I will both punish the transgressor for thee, and will bring back to thee in peace thy four daughters." "These are great promises," replied the Father, "if the deed only agrees with the word, if thou canst do that which thou sayest, I will act as thou shalt exhort me."

Having therefore received the royal mandate, the Son took his sister Mercy along with him, and "leaping upon the mountains, passing over the hills," came to the prison, and "looking through the windows, looking through the lattice," he beheld the imprisoned servant, shut out from the present life, devoured of affliction, and "from the sole of the foot even to the crown there was no soundness in him." He saw him in the power of death, because through him death entered into the world. He saw him devoured, because, when a man is once dead, he is eaten of worms. And because I now have an opportunity of telling you, you shall hear the names of the four tormentors. The first, who put him in prison, is the Prison of the present life, of which it is said, "Woe is me that I am constrained to dwell in Mesech"; the second, who tormented him, is the Misery of the World, which besets us with all kind of pain and wretchedness; the third, who was putting him to death, is Death, which destroys and slays all; the fourth, who was devouring him, is the Worm. . . . Therefore the Son, beholding his servant given over to these four tormentors, could not but have mercy upon him, because Mercy was his companion, and bursting into the prison of death, "conquered death, bound the strong man, took his goods," and distributed the spoils. And "ascending up on high, led captivity captive and gave gifts for men," and brought back the servant into his Country, crowned with double honor, and endued with a garment of immortality. When Mercy beheld this, she had no grounds for complaint. Truth found no cause of discontent, because her Father was found true. The servant had paid all his penalties. Justice in like manner complained not, because justice had been executed on the transgressor; and thus "he who had been lost was found." Peace, therefore, when she saw her sisters at concord, came back and united them. And now, behold "Mercy and Truth are met together, Justice and Peace have kissed each other." Thus, therefore, by the Mediator of men and angels, man was purified and reconciled, and the hundredth sheep was brought back to the fold of God. To which fold Jesus Christ bring us, to Whom is honor and power everlasting. Amen.

Anonymous

ca. 1000

The dazzling "word-hoard" of Anglo-Saxon literature and the homiletic rhetoric, designed to explicate Scripture in expository prose, of the British Isles in the late tenth century converge in this great eschatological sermon from the Vercelli manuscript. The Vercelli Book, deposited in a monastery in northern Italy along the pilgrim route to Rome for those who traveled by the great St. Bernard Pass, is a manuscript collection of prose sermons and religious poems which probably made its way from England at some time not long after the year 1000. The multi-sourced Anglo-Saxon Chronicle gives us a good register of its contemporary context, recording severe famine, sightings of "a cloud red as blood . . . with the appearance of fire," pestilence, and fierce invasions, burnings, and pillagings by Norse pirates. In the year 995 the "long haired-star" called "comet" appeared, a sign from heaven of doom and destruction.

    The eschatological tradition deals with "last things," doomsday, final judgment and the afterlife, visions of the Second Coming, and a penitential terror evoked by a universal response to the arrival of the millennium in the Anglo-Saxon kingdom where heathenism had yielded to a powerful Christian Church. The signs of the Second Coming—the extinction of sun, moon, and stars, the burning of the planet, and the appearance of a cross in the empty heavens—gain force through the alliterative verse inserted into the prose text. Consolation, for terrors present and to come, arrives late in this anonymous sermon through the reminder to the hearer, who might have been either a member of an all-male cloistered audience or a woman in a mixed congregation in a parish church, that the tumultuous and imperiled "middle-earth" which they occupy through invasion and plague and "the bitter day" has nonetheless been redeemed by Jesus Christ.

The middle-earth to which these preachers allude may recall, for modern readers, Tolkien's hobbits. What is meant, as another homily explains, is the place of humans: higher than hell-dwellers, lower than heaven-dwellers, wiser than cattle, lower than angels.

Homily 2
The End of the World

Dearly beloved, the great action of doomsday will be very fearful and dreadful to all creatures. On that day the resounding flames will burn up the blood-mingled earth, and will burn up those who now are here engaged in great boasting and in the useless sight of gold and of silver and of finecloth and of ill-gotten property. But we now have most likely trusted rashly in that; namely, that He will not come to us. And on that day will depart the light of the sun and the light of the moon and the light of all the stars. And on that day the rood of the Lord will be flowing with blood among the clouds. And on that day the countenance of the Lord will be very fearful and dreadful, and in that appearance which He was in when the Jews struck Him and hanged Him and spat on Him with their spittle. On that day the sinful ones will lament and weep because they earlier would not amend their sins, but they, sorrowful, will wander about and fall in torment. On that day will be blowing those trumpets from the four corners of this middle-earth. And then will all arise; whatsoever the earth swallowed up and fire burned and the sea sank and wild animals devoured and birds bore away, all that will arise on that day. On that day our Lord will come in His majestic, great glory and show His face and His body. Then the wound will be seen by the sinful ones, and He will be seen whole by the trustworthy ones. And then the Jews may see that which they earlier killed and hanged. And the Righteous Judge then will judge each of all men according to his own works. Lo, then, it will seem to the sinful, that nothing is so hot or so cold, so hard or so soft, so dear or so hated, so that it then may remove him from the love of the Lord and separate him from His will. And, now, we will not wish to work His will, now that we easily may.

Lo, indeed, that is beyond all measure for to see, reflect on; namely, that the wretched, sinful ones must, sorrowful, grieve as a result of the visage of Our Lord, and as a result of His saints, and as a result of the glory of the kingdom of heaven; and then they will depart into the torment of eternal hell. Alas, lo, minds are wretchedly darkened, that they must ever allow that death-bearing devil to deceive them by useless cunning to the extent that they perform sin and not work the will of that one who created them on earth, and endowed them with life with His spirit, and gave them eternal life. Lo, indeed, men will not entirely fear how the devil will impute to them all those wicked deeds which here are performed before the multitude of the great judgment. Lo, indeed, men will not fear that great devil Anti-Christ with his hell torments, and with his reproaches, and with his grievous tortures, which will be given to them as a reward for their sins. Lo, indeed, we will not fear the future terror of doomsday, which is the day of miseries, and the day of hardships, and the day of sadness, and the day of cries, and the day of lamentation, and the day of suffering and the day of sorrow, and the dark day. On that day shall be manifested to us

    the open heaven   and might of angels
    and destruction of all creatures   and ruin of the earth,
    the hardships of the faithless   and fall of stars,
    uproar of the thunder-road   and the dark storm,
    the light of the sky   and the blast of flames,

the creation of those groaning   and the strife of those spirits
and the grim vision   and the godly might
and the hot shower   and mirth of hell-dwellers
and bursting of mountains   and the song of trumpets,
and the broad burning   and the bitter day
and the great pestilence   and the sins of men
and the painful sorrow   and the separation of souls
and the death-bearing dragon   and the destruction of devils
and the narrow pit   and the swarthy death
and the burning abyss   and the bloody stream
and the great fear of fiends   and the fiery rain
and groaning of heathens   and the fall of armies
multitude of heaven-inhabitants   and the might of their lord
and that great council   and the fearful army
and the harsh rod   and the right judgment
the shame of sins   and the accusations of fiends
and the pale countenance   and trembling word,
the fearful cry   and the weeping of the people
and the shamed army   and the sinful throng
the groaning abyss   and the devouring hell
and the horror of the serpents.

And then shall be manifested to each of us such fear. There the sinful then
might wish that they were never brought forth by their fathers and mothers, or the sinful might wish each of them to be as dumb beasts. Lo, that
then was dearer to them than all middle-earth with treasures, which heaven
vaulted over. Indeed, we do not fear that which we daily see before our
eyes; now we do not believe others; namely, that those nearest to us will
die. A hateful bed will be prepared in the cold earth, and then, in that, the
bodies will decay. And that transitory body will rot there to foulness and as
food for corpse-biting worms.

Lo, that, then, will be there a painful sorrow and a miserable separation of the body and the soul, if then that miserable inner evil, which is the
accursed soul, who for having neglected the commands of God will be here
condemned, with the result that it then after the separation must slide into

eternal hell-torments, and there live with devils in crime and sin, in torment and sorrow, in woe and worms, among the dead and devils, in burning and bitterness, in foulness and in all those tortures which the devils prepared from the beginning, which they created for themselves, and which they themselves deserved.

But let us be mindful of the need of our souls, and let us work good on that day, that we carry out good deeds. And let us forsake crime and sin and pride and envy and empty boasting and unrighteousness and adultery, breaking prescribed fasts, and drunkenness, and folly, and heretical deceits, avarice, and gluttony, lying and hypocrisy, slander and deceit, enmities, wickednesses, and miserliness, and all the customs which the devils in themselves created. And let us love our Lord with all mind and might, with all our heart and soul, with all truthfulness and wisdom. And let us love those nearest to us just as ourselves. And let us be merciful to poor men and foreigners and the sick, so that our Lord will honor us through that mercy. And still whosoever of us sins against another in word or in deed, let him gently refrain, lest God with anger punish him for that, as He himself said, "Forgive and ye shall be forgiven." (Luke 6:37.) May we suffer all for the love of our Lord, so that for the hardships here in the world one will grant us that.

Lo, we have need that we remember how much He suffered for us, after He took on a human body for the eternal salvation of mankind, and through that saved us from the devil's slavery, and gave us a return to that eternal life, which we before forfeited, if we wish to earn it as the wise one said, "The Lord will save and keep those in the kingdom of heavens, who here in this world are humble to God and to men."

Lo, we hear that they shall be blessed and rich before God, who in this world are humble and kind. Lo, we can then by that know and understand that they shall be wretched and accursed before God who here in this world are proud and envious. That is of all sins the most loathsome and displeasing to God, because mankind first through that envy was plunged into hell; and again, through mercy and humility, they were released from the devil's thralldom.

Lo, behold, we have need that we open our ears and our hearts to those gospel teachings which people often before us discuss and our teachers command and declare. Lo, we now in vain arrogance adorn ourselves with gold and with gems, and we rejoice and we are cheerful; thus, we may think that we shall never leave it, and much too seldom do we remember our Lord and our soul's need, though we shall be in eternity after this life with soul and with body in whatever state we here now earn. Let us have genuine sorrow for our sins, though it happens that each of us against another may sin in word and in deed. This then shall be the best remedy, because that man is never so exceedingly sinful that help may not ever be granted him.

Let us now, therefore, hasten to God before death seizes us since he quickly approaches. And may we be wise and true and merciful and generous and just and eager to give alms and clean-hearted and beneficent and God-fearing and teachable and steady in service and obedient to God and to our lords and patient to the will of God. And He then will grant us that eternally as a reward, that which was intended for us in the beginning. Let us now hasten to that, the while that we may control our ways. There they never separate from the beloved nor join with the hated, nor does day ever come after day, nor night after night. But there shall be eternal light and bliss and eternal glory and eternal joy with our Lord, Redeemer of middle-earth. That is even the same God who lives and rules with the Father and with the Son and with the Holy Ghost, who is glory and honor through the world of all worlds ever without end. Amen.

St. Bernard of Clairvaux

1090–1153

ernard was destined for the Church by a mother with ambitions for his ecclesiastical eminence, although his own bent was for

personal piety and asceticism. Moving from a languishing order of Cistercian monks to a new monastery in a rough and inhospitable valley, he became its abbot at the age of twenty-four and transformed the place.
Renamed Clara Vallis (Clairvaux), its reputation for industry and holiness
caused his order to expand in influence while Bernard himself became one
of the great preachers of the medieval Church. Crowds of pilgrims made
their way to the monastery; many sought his powers of healing and his
brand of lively and personal mysticism.

His mystical vision stresses God's grace and the preeminence of faith
over reason, in the Augustinian contemplative tradition. The "Cistercian
Program" which St. Bernard designed and expounded informed medieval
poetry from the troubadours of southern France through Dante. In
Bernard's unfolding of the progression of carnal love to the spiritual, the literary converges with the moral and human. Denouncing the pure impulse
after knowledge for its own sake as heathenish, drawing on the language of
the Psalms and the Song of Songs (or Canticle of Canticles) for some of his
most radiant sermons, Bernard's contemplative mission found powerful expression in the pulpit where he, paradoxically, summoned people to the
Second Crusade and secured the official condemnation of Peter Abelard. He
was canonized twenty years after his death; in his life, and in his monastic
reforms, he sought the last of twelve stages of humility in which the individual disappears in the eternal and divine essence "as the drop of water in
a cask of wine."

Various Meanings of the Kiss

During my frequent ponderings on the burning desire with which the
patriarchs longed for the incarnation of Christ, I am stung with sorrow and
shame. Even now I can scarcely restrain my tears, so filled with shame am I
by the lukewarmness, the frigid unconcern of these miserable times. For
which of us does the consummation of that event fill with as much joy as the
mere promise of it inflamed the desires of the holy men of pre-christian
times? Very soon now there will be great rejoicing as we celebrate the feast
of Christ's birth. But how I wish it were inspired by his birth! All the more

therefore do I pray that the intense longing of those men of old, their heart-felt expectation, may be enkindled in me by these words: "Let him kiss me with the kiss of his mouth." (Cant. 1:2.) Many an upright man in those far-off times sensed within himself how profuse the graciousness that would be poured upon those lips. (Ps. 44:3.) And intense desire springing from that perception (Isa. 26:8) impelled him to utter: "Let him kiss me with the kiss of his mouth," hoping with every fiber of his being that he might not be deprived of a share in a pleasure so great.

The conscientious man of those days might repeat to himself: "Of what use to me the wordy effusions of the prophets? Rather let him who is the most handsome of the sons of men (Ps. 44:3), let him kiss me with the kiss of his mouth. No longer am I satisfied to listen to Moses, for he is a slow speaker and not able to speak well. (Exod. 4:10.) Isaiah is 'a man of unclean lips' (Isa. 6:5), Jeremiah does not know how to speak, he is a child (John 1:6); not one of the prophets makes an impact on me with his words. But he, the one whom they proclaim, let him speak to me, 'let him kiss me with the kiss of his mouth.' I have no desire that he should approach me in their person, or address me with their words, for they are 'a watery darkness, a dense cloud' (Ps. 17:12); rather in his own person 'let him kiss me with the kiss of his mouth'; let him whose presence is full of love, from whom exquisite doctrines flow in streams, let him become 'a spring inside me, welling up to eternal life (John 4:14). Shall I not receive a richer infusion of grace from him whom the Father has anointed with the oil of gladness above all his rivals (Ps. 44:8), provided that he will bestow on me the kiss of his mouth? For his living, active word (Heb. 4:12) is to me a kiss, not indeed an adhering of the lips that can sometimes belie a union of hearts, but an unreserved infusion of joys, a revealing of mysteries, a marvelous and indistinguishable mingling of the divine light with the enlightened mind, which, joined in truth to God, is one spirit with him. (1 Cor. 6:17.) With good reason then I avoid trucking with visions and dreams; I want no part with parables and figures of speech; even the very beauty of the angels can only leave me wearied. For my Jesus utterly surpasses these in his majesty and splendor. (Ps. 44:5.) Therefore I ask of him what I ask of neither man nor angel: that he kiss me with the kiss of his mouth.

II. "Note how I do not presume that it is with his mouth I shall be kissed, for that constitutes the unique felicity and singular privilege of the human nature he assumed. No, in the consciousness of my lowliness I ask to be kissed with the kiss of his mouth, an experience shared by all who are in a position to say: 'Indeed from his fullness we have, all of us, received.' " (John 1:16.)

I must ask you to try to give your whole attention here. The mouth that kisses signifies the Word who assumes human nature; the nature assumed receives the kiss; the kiss however, that takes its being both from the giver and the receiver, is a person that is formed by both, none other than "the one mediator between God and mankind, himself a man, Christ Jesus." (1 Tim. 2:5.) It is for this reason that none of the saints dared say: "let him kiss me with his mouth," but rather, "with the kiss of his mouth." In this way they paid tribute to that prerogative of Christ, on whom uniquely and in one sole instance the mouth of the Word was pressed, that moment when the fullness of the divinity yielded itself to him (Col. 2:9) as the life of his body. A fertile kiss therefore, a marvel of stupendous self-abasement that is not a mere pressing of mouth upon mouth; it is the uniting of God with man. Normally the touch of lip on lip is the sign of the loving embrace of hearts, but this conjoining of natures brings together the human and divine, shows God reconciling "to himself all things, whether on earth or in heaven." (Col. 1:20.) "For he is the peace between us, and has made the two into one." (Eph. 2:14.) This was the kiss for which just men yearned under the old dispensation, foreseeing as they did that in him they would "find happiness and a crown of rejoicing" (Ecclus. 15:6), because in him were hidden "all the jewels of wisdom and knowledge" (Col. 2:3). Hence their longing to taste that fullness of his. (John 1:16.)

You seem to be in agreement with this explanation, but I should like you to listen to another.

III. Even the holy men who lived before the coming of Christ understood that God had in mind plans of peace for the human race. (Jer. 29:11.) "Surely the Lord God does nothing without revealing his secret to his servants, the prophets." (Amos 3:7.) What he did reveal however was obscure to many. (Luke 18:34.) For in those days faith was a rare thing on the earth, and hope but a faint impulse in the heart even of many of those who looked forward to the deliverance of Israel. (Luke 2:38.) Those indeed who foreknew also proclaimed that Christ would come as man, and with him, peace. One of them actually said: "He himself will be peace in our land when he comes." (Mic. 5:5.) Enlightened from above they confidently spread abroad the message that through him men would be restored to the favor of God. John, the forerunner of the Lord, recognizing the fulfillment of that prophecy in his own time, declared: "Grace and truth have come through Jesus Christ." (John 1:17.) In our time every christian can discover by experience that this is true.

In those far-off days however, while the prophets continued to foretell the covenant, and its author continued to delay his coming (Matt. 25:5), the faith of the people never ceased to waver because there was no one who could redeem or save. (Ps. 7:13.) Hence men grumbled at the postponements of the coming of this Prince of Peace (Isa. 9:6) so often proclaimed by the mouth of his holy prophets from ancient times. (Luke 1:70.) As doubts about the fulfillment of the prophecies began to recur, all the more eagerly did they make demands for the kiss, the sign of the promised reconcilement. It was as if a voice from among the people would challenge the prophets of peace: "How much longer are you going to keep us in suspense? (John 10:24.) You are always foretelling a peace that is never realized; you promise a world of good but trouble on trouble comes. (Jer. 14:19.) At various times in the past and in various different ways (Heb. 1:1) this same hope was fostered by angels among our ancestors, who in turn have passed the tidings on to us. (Ps. 43:2). 'Peace! Peace!' they say, 'but there is no peace.' (Jer. 6:14.) If God desires to convince me of that benevolent will of his, so often vouched for by the prophets but not yet revealed by the event, then let him kiss me with the kiss of his mouth, and so by this token of peace make my peace secure. For how shall I any longer put my trust in mere words? It is necessary now that words be vindicated by action. If those men are God's envoys let him prove the truth of their words by his own advent, so often the keynote of their predictions, because unless he comes they can do nothing. (John 15:5.) He sent his servant bearing a staff, but neither voice nor life is forthcoming. (2 Kings 4:26–31.) I do not rise up, I am not awakened, I am not shaken out of the dust (Isa. 52:2), nor do I breathe in hope, if the Prophet himself does not come down and kiss me with the kiss of his mouth."

Here we must add that he who professes to be our mediator with God is God's own Son, and he is God. But what is man that he should take notice of him, the son of man that he should be concerned about him? (Ps. 143:3.) Where shall such as I am find the confidence, the daring, to entrust myself to him who is so majestic? How shall I, mere dust and ashes, presume that God takes an interest in me? (Ecclus. 10:9.) He is entirely taken up with loving his Father, he has no need of me nor of what I possess. (Ps. 15:2.) How then shall I find assurance that if he is my mediator he will never fail me? If it be really true, as you prophets have said, that God has determined to show mercy, to reveal himself in a more favorable light (Ps. 76:8), let him establish a covenant of peace, (Ecclus. 45:30), an everlasting covenant with me (Isa. 61:8) by the kiss of his mouth. If he will not revoke his given word (Ps. 88:35), let him empty himself (Phil. 2:7), let him humble himself, let him bend to me and kiss me with the kiss of his mouth. If the mediator is to be acceptable to both parties, equally dependable in the eyes of both, then let him who is God's Son become man, let him become the Son of Man, and fill me with assurance by this kiss of his mouth. When I come to recognize that he is truly mine, then I shall feel secure in welcoming the Son of God as mediator. Not even a shadow of mistrust can then exist, for after all he is my brother, and my own flesh. (Gen. 37:27.) It is impossible that I should be spurned by him who is bone from my bones, and flesh from my flesh. (Gen. 2:23.)

We should by now have come to understand how the discontent of our ancestors displayed a need for this sacrosanct kiss, that is, the mystery of the incarnate Word, for faith, hard-pressed throughout the ages with trouble upon trouble, was ever on the point of failing, and a fickle people, yielding to discouragement, murmured against the promises of God. Is this a mere improvisation on my part? I suggest that you will find it to be the teaching of the Scriptures: for instance, consider the burden of complaint and murmuring in those words: "Order on order, order on order, rule on rule, rule on rule, a little here, a little there." (Isa. 28:10.) Or those prayerful exclamations, troubled yet loyal: "Give those who wait for you their reward, and let your prophets be proved worthy of belief." (Ecclus. 36:18.) Again: "Bring about what has been prophesied in your name." (Ecclus. 36:17.) There too you will find those soothing promises, full of consolation: "Behold the Lord will appear and he will not lie. If he seems slow, wait for him, for he will surely come and he will not delay." (Heb. 2:3.) Likewise: "His time is close at hand when he will come and his days will not be prolonged." (Isa. 14:1.) Speaking in the name of him who is promised the prophet announces: "Behold I am coming towards you like a river of peace, and like a stream in spate with the glory of the nations." (Isa. 66:12.) In all these statements there is evidence both of the urgency of the preachers and of the distrust of those who listened to them. The people murmured, their faith wavered, and in the words of Isaiah: "the ambassadors of peace weep bitterly." (Isa. 33:7.) Therefore because Christ was late in coming (Matt. 25:5), and the whole human race in danger of being lost in despair, so convinced was it that human weakness was an object of contempt with no hope of the reconciliation with God through a grace so frequently promised, those good men whose faith remained strong eagerly longed for the more powerful assurance that only his human presence could convey. They prayed intensely for a sign that the covenant was about to be restored for the sake of a spiritless, faithless people.

O root of Jesse, that stands as a signal to the peoples (Isa. 11:10), how many prophets and kings wanted to see what you see, and never saw it! (Luke 10:24.)

IV. Happy above them all is Simeon, by God's mercy still bearing fruit in old age! (Ps. 91:14.) He rejoiced to think that he would see the long-desired sign. He saw it and was glad (John 8:56); and having received the kiss of peace he is allowed to go in peace, but not before he had told his audience that Jesus was born to be a sign that would be rejected (Luke 2:25–34). Time proved how true this was. No sooner had the sign of peace arisen than it was opposed, by those, that is, who hated peace (Ps. 119:7); for his peace is with men of goodwill (Luke 2:14), but for the evil-minded he is "a stone to stumble over, a rock to bring men down" (1 Pet. 2:8). Herod accordingly was perturbed, and so was the whole of Jerusalem. (Matt. 2:3.) Christ "came to his own domain, and his own people did not accept him." (John 1:11.) Those shepherds, however, who kept watch over their flocks by night (Luke 2:8–20), were fortunate for they were gladdened by a vision of this sign. Even in those early days he was hiding these things from the learned and the clever, and revealing them to mere children. (Matt. 11:25; Luke 10:21.) Herod, as you know, desired to see him (Luke 23:8), but because his motive was not genuine he did not succeed. The sign of peace was given only to men of goodwill, hence to Herod and others like him was given the sign of the prophet Jonah. (Matt. 12:19.) The angel said to the shepherds: "Here is a sign for you" (Luke 2:12), you who are humble, obedient, not given to haughtiness (Rom. 12:16), faithful to prayer and meditating day and night on God's law (Ps. 1:2). "This is a sign for you," he said. What sign? The sign promised by the angels, sought after by the people, foretold by the prophets; this is the sign that the Lord Jesus has now brought into existence and revealed to you, a sign by which the incredulous are made believers, the dispirited are made hopeful and the fervent achieve security. This therefore is the sign for you. But as a sign what does it signify? It reveals mercy, grace, peace, the peace that has no end. (Isa. 9:7.) And finally, the sign is this: "You will find a baby, wrapped in swaddling clothes and lying in a manger." (Luke 2:12.) God himself, however, is in this baby, reconciling the world to himself. (2 Cor. 5:19.) He will be put to death for your sins and raised to life to justify you (Rom. 4:25), so that made righteous by faith you may be at peace with God (Rom. 5:1). This was the sign of peace that the Prophet once urged King Achez to ask of the Lord his God, "either from the depths of Sheol or from the heights above." (Isa. 7:11.) But the ungodly king refused. His wretched state blinded him to the belief that in this sign the highest things above would be joined to the lowest things below in peace. This was achieved when Christ, descending into Sheol, saluted its dwellers with a holy kiss (1 Cor. 16:20), the pledge of peace, and then going up to heaven, enabled the spirits there to share in the same pledge in joy without end.

I must end this sermon. But let me sum up briefly the points we have raised. It would seem that this holy kiss was of necessity bestowed on the world for two reasons. Without it the faith of those who wavered would not have been strengthened, nor the desires of the fervent appeased. Moreover, this kiss is no other than the Mediator between God and man, himself a man, Christ Jesus (1 Tim. 2:5), who with the Father and Holy Spirit lives and reigns as God for ever and ever. Amen.

Hildegard of Bingen

1098–1179

*T*he mystic, prophet, and political reformer Hildegard of Bingen preached in public while founding two convents, composing music, and writing one of the first known morality plays. She was, as abbess and founder of a Benedictine community of women in twelfth-century Germany, a daring speaker in monastic orders and public places, and a brilliant administrator of the nunneries she had founded over considerable opposition. Frederick Barbarossa was crowned Holy Roman Emperor in 1167; disapproving of her patron's role in the schismatic contest with the Pope, she sent him unsolicited letters of advice and strong rebuke. Her reputation in the late twentieth century has blossomed in a series of performances of her liturgical music, made one of her abbeys a site for pilgrims, and earned her a German postage stamp honoring the eight-hundredth anniversary of her death. She was a contemporary of Peter Abelard's great lover, Héloïse, but where only Abelard's voice remains from their union of passion and learning, Hildegard's polymathic accomplishment still speaks through her surviving literary and homiletic work.

The daughter of a noble family in the Rhineland, Hildegard was enrolled early in the elite order of Benedictine monasticism. To her contemporaries, she was a Sibylline figure, a prophetess of the Apocalypse, and a woman whose enigmatic writings seemed lit by a fiery prescience, predictive of the German Reformation which later heralded her indictment of the worldly princes and corrupt clerics of the mid-twelfth century.

Her biographers have remarked on her visionary proclivities and her encounter with "the living Light," but secular historians have been engaged as well by her alignment with the prophets of the Old Testament and her sonorously articulated terror of history as a force which might serve as God's scourge on His faithless and unrepentant people.

The German pulpit, for centuries after Hildegard's death, was particularly mesmerized by the threat of Satan, the principle of the Evil One, and the cosmic history of Lucifer's assault on virtue. Her visionary language, her (occasional) displacement of devilry and wickedness onto the heretics and ordinary mortals who depart from her canonical view of Christianity at the time, can be read, like Martin Luther's later fulminations, in a somewhat sinister vein. And, like Luther's use of the demonizing imagery of plague, sulphur, and excrement, her lexicon and her frame of reference are often disturbing. But the imaginative and thematic use of the Devil, the marketplace, and the merchandise of Vanity Fair, which she proposes in this text, underscores her longing for social order and her quest for social justice. *Vision Seven*, near its close, invokes the wisdom of Solomon and the words of Proverbs 13: on the pursuit of evil and the requital to the just for their longing for divine truth.

CS

Vision Seven
The Devil

Then I saw a burning light, as large and as high as a mountain, divided at its summit as if into many tongues. And there stood in the presence of this light a multitude of white-clad people, before whom what seemed like a screen of translucent crystal had been placed, reaching from their breasts to their feet. And before that multitude, as if in a road, there lay on its back a monster shaped like a worm, wondrously large and long, which aroused an indescribable sense of horror and rage. On its left stood a kind of marketplace, which displayed human wealth and worldly delights and various sorts of merchandise; and some people were running through it very fast and not buying anything, while others were walking slowly and stopping both to sell and to buy. Now that worm was black and bristly, covered with ulcers and pustules, and it was divided into five sections from the head down through the belly to its feet, like stripes. One was green, one white, one red, one yellow and one black; and they were full of deadly poison. But its head had been so crushed that the left side of its jawbone was dislocated. Its eyes were bloody on the surface and burning within; its ears were round and bristly; its nose and mouth were those of a viper, its hands human, its feet a viper's feet, and its tail short and horrible. And around its neck a chain was riveted, which also bound its hands and feet; and this chain was firmly fastened to a rock in the abyss, confining it so that it could not move about as its wicked will desired. Many flames came forth from its mouth, dividing into four parts: One part ascended to the clouds, another breathed forth among secular people, another among spiritual people, and the last descended into the abyss.

And the flame that sought the clouds was opposing the people who wanted to get to Heaven. And I saw three groups of these. One was close to the clouds, one in the middle space between the clouds and the earth, and one moved along near the earth; and all were shouting repeatedly, "Let us get to Heaven!" But they were whirled hither and thither by that flame; some did not waver, some barely kept their balance, and some fell to the earth but then rose again and started toward Heaven. The flame that breathed forth among secular people burned some of them so that they were hideously blackened, and others it transfixed so that it could move them anywhere it wanted. Some escaped from the flame and moved toward those who sought Heaven, reiterating shouts of "O you faithful, give us help!" But others remained transfixed. Meanwhile, the flame that breathed forth among spiritual people concealed them in obscurity; but I saw them in six categories. For some of them were cruelly injured by the flame's fury; but when it could not injure one of them, it burningly breathed on them the deadly poison that flowed from the worm's head to its feet, either green or white or red or yellow or black. But the flame that sought the abyss contained in itself diverse torments for those who had worshiped Satan in place of God, not washed by the font of baptism or knowing the light of truth and faith.

And I saw sharp arrows whistling loudly from its mouth, and black smoke exhaling from its breast, and a burning fluid boiling up from its loins, and a hot whirlwind blowing from its navel, and the uncleanness of frogs issuing from its bowels; all of which affected human beings with grave disquiet. And the hideous and foul-smelling vapor that came out of it infected many people with its own perversity. But behold, a great multitude of people came, shining brightly; they forcefully trod the worm underfoot and severely tormented it, but could not be *injured by its flames or its poison.* And I heard again the voice from Heaven, saying to me:

1. GOD STRENGTHENS THE FAITHFUL SO THAT THE DEVIL CANNOT CONQUER THEM

God, Who disposes all things justly and rightly, calls His faithful people to the glory of the celestial inheritance; but the ancient deceiver lurks in ambush and tries to hinder them by using all his wicked arts against them. But he is conquered by them and is confounded as his presumption deserves, for they possess the celestial country, and he suffers the horrors of Hell.

Therefore, *you see a burning light, as large and as high as a mountain, divided at its summit as if into many tongues.* This is the justice of God, which burns in the faith of believers, displaying the greatness of His power, sanctity and glory, and wonderfully declaring in that glory the diverse gifts of the Holy Spirit.

2. THE MULTITUDE OF THE FAITHFUL AND THE DIVINE LAW DISPLAYED BEFORE THEM

And there stand in the presence of this light a multitude of white-clad people, a cohort of people in the presence of God's justice, shining with faith and well and honorably constituted in good works. *Before them what seems like a screen of translucent crystal has been placed, reaching from their breasts to their feet;* for, from their decision to do good actions to their completion, they have before their eyes the strong and splendid sight of the divine law. And thus they are so strengthened in these actions that no cunning or deception of false persuasion can conquer them.

3. THE DECEPTIONS OF THE DEVIL LIE IN THE PATH HUMANS TAKE IN THIS WORLD

And before that multitude, as if in a road, there lies on its back a monster shaped like a worm, wondrously large and long. This means that the ancient serpent is wellknown to humanity in the course of the pilgrimage of the good and the bad through the world, not in that visible form but in its inner meaning. Its mouth is gaping upward in order to pull down by deception those who are tending toward the celestial regions; but it is lying down, because the Son of God destroyed so much of its strength that it cannot stand up. *And it arouses an indescribable sense of horror and rage;* for the mental capacity of mortal humans is insufficient to understand the manifold variations of its poisonous fury and malicious exertions.

4. THE DEVIL OFFERS FRAUDULENT RICHES AND DELIGHTS, AND SOME BUY THEM

On its left stands a kind of marketplace, which displays human wealth and worldly delights and various sorts of merchandise. For the left hand of the destroyer signifies death, and there is seen a marketplace composed of Death's evil works: pride and vainglory in corruptible riches, licentiousness and lust for transitory pleasures, and trafficking in all kinds of earthly desires. Thus those who would be terrified by the horror of the Devil if they met it openly are deceived by these things; they are lightly offered persuasions to vice as a merchant displays his diverse wares to people, and delighted by the display so that they buy what is offered. So the Devil offers humanity his lying arts; and those who desire them buy them. How? They throw away a good conscience as if selling it, and they collect deadly wounds in their souls as if buying them.

5. THE STRONG RESIST THE DEVIL'S OFFERS, THE APATHETIC CONSENT TO THEM

And some people are running through it very fast and not buying anything; they know God, and so they carry the treasure of good will and the sweet spices of virtue and eagerly accumulate more of them, and quickly pass by the pleasures of the world and the filth of the Devil, obeying God's commands and despising the sweetness of their flesh. *But others are walking slowly and stopping both to sell and to buy;* they are slow to do good works and apathetic of heart, and so they smother their own desire for Heaven as if selling it, and nurture the pleasures of their flesh as if buying them.

Therefore, the former will receive the reward of good works, and the latter will suffer the punishment of iniquity, as Ezekiel shows, saying:

6. WORDS OF EZEKIEL ON THIS SUBJECT

"The justice of the just shall be upon him, and the wickedness of the wicked shall be upon him." (Ezek. 18:20.) What does this mean? The shining works of the pure person bathe him in sanctity and surround him like a thousand eyes that see into the heights and the depths; as the Holy Spirit inspires him, they bear him aloft to great honor and leave his wrong desires behind for dead, as a bird is borne aloft in the air by its wings whenever it pleases. But the person who faithlessly follows the wickedness of the savage viper who hisses at Heaven, covering the pearl with mud and raging at the Most Beautiful among all the beautiful, is degraded by its snakelike poison; he is cut off from the noble work of God's hands, from all honor and from the beatitude of the celestial vision, and exiled from the Living Fruit and the root of the Just Tree.

7. THE DEVIL LABORS TO DECEIVE THE FIVE SENSES OF HUMANITY

But you see that *that worm is black and bristly, covered with ulcers and pustules.* This shows that the ancient serpent is full of the darkness of black betrayal, and the bristles of concealed deception, and the ulcers of impure pollution, and the pustules of repressed fury. *And it is divided into five sections from the head down through the belly to its feet, like stripes;* for from the time of his first deception when he tried to put himself forward until the final time when his madness will end, he does not cease to inspire the five human senses with the desire for vices. Simulating a deceitful rectitude, he draws people to the downward slopes of his unclean arts. *One is green, one white, one red, one yellow, and one black; and they are full of deadly poison.* The green indicates worldly melancholy; the white, improper irreverence; the red, deceptive glory; the yellow, biting envy; and the black, shameful deceit, with all other perversities that bring death to the souls of those who consent to them.

8. THE DEVIL'S PRIDE WAS OVERTHROWN BY THE INCARNATION

But its head has been so crushed that the left side of its jawbone is dislocated. This means that his pride was so overthrown by the Son of God that even the enmity of Death is already destroyed and cannot exert its full strength of bitterness.

9. WHAT THE EYES AND EARS AND NOSTRILS
   OF THE SERPENT SIGNIFY

Its eyes are bloody on the surface and burning within; because his wicked intent outwardly inflicts harm on human bodies and inwardly drives a fiery dart into their souls. *Its ears are round and bristly;* for the bristles of his arts pierce a person all around, so that if he finds anything that is his in that person, he may quickly throw him down. *Its nose and mouth are those of a viper;* for he shows people unbridled and vile behavior, through which, transfixing them with many vices, he may cruelly slay them.

10. ITS HANDS AND FEET AND TAIL AND WHAT THEY SIGNIFY

Its hands are human, for he practices his arts in human deeds; *its feet a viper's feet,* because he ceaselessly ambushes people when they are journeying and inflicts devilish lacerations on them; *and its tail short and horrible,* for it signifies his power in the short but most evil time of the son of perdition, whose desire to run wild exceeds his power to do it.

11. THE MIGHT OF GOD HAS BROKEN THE DEVIL'S
   STRENGTH TO DO WHAT HE WANTS

And around its neck a chain is riveted, which also binds its hands and feet; which is to say that the strength of the Devil was so broken and crushed by the power of Almighty God that he cannot freely work his evil and accost humans in the way. *And this chain is firmly fastened to a rock in the abyss, confining it so that it cannot move about as its wicked will desires;* for the power of God abides unfailingly and immovably for eternity, and by saying souls oppresses the Devil so forcibly that he is not able by inner or outer means to take away redemption from the faithful, or keep them from that place of joy from which he perversely exiled himself.

12. THE DEVIL SENDS HIS FIRE TO LEAD ASTRAY ALL KINDS
   OF PEOPLE ON EARTH

Many flames come forth from its mouth, dividing into four parts. This means that in his rapacious voracity he sends forth in cruel flames the terrible and manifold evil of his wicked counsels; he breathes it into all four corners of the world, that the people there may follow him.

One part ascends to the clouds; for the sharpness of the Devil's breath drags down those who with all their mind's longing seek Heaven. *Another breathes forth among secular people;* for its many forms deceive those who live among earthly affairs. *And another among spiritual people;* for its pretence infects those who labor in spiritual disciplines. *And the last descends into the abyss;* for its persuasions put the faithless who consent to it into the torments of Hell. For they have walked the way of falsity and deception and left the way of rectitude, and they have not shown the reverence due to the true God, as David testifies, saying:

13. WORDS OF DAVID

"Destruction and unhappiness in their ways, and the way of peace they have not known; there is no fear of God before their eyes." (Ps. 13:5.) What does this mean?

People who expel God from their hearts by their wicked and damnable deeds are overwhelmed by His innocent and mighty works, which arise in the pure living Fountain, as a great rain submerges an object so that it is no longer visible. And so they are not formidable in the sight of God, for misery is in their ways wherever they go, and most unhappy companionship, and the food of death. How? They taste and eat what is evil. Hence in their deeds they do not know the way that ascends in the sunlight, and do not taste in honor or in love the sweetness of God; they cast away their fear of Him as if it were fear of another person, desiring neither to see Him nor to look Him in the face.

14. THE DEVIL ASSAILS SPIRITUAL AND SECULAR PEOPLE IN MANY WAYS

Hence you also see that *the flame that seeks the clouds is opposing the people who want to get to Heaven.* For when that wicked flame feels that the minds of the faithful are tending upward, it rages against them most cruelly with its arts, so that they may not come to the celestial places to which they aspire.

15. THE THREE GROUPS OF THESE PEOPLE

And you see three groups of these; for they do not cease to worship the true and ineffable Trinity, although greatly fatigued by their struggles. *One is close to the clouds;* these are fighting most strongly against the Devil and raising their thoughts from earthly deeds to heavenly things as a cloud floats above the earth. *And one is in the middle space between the clouds and the earth.* These people control themselves moderately well, but their whole mind is not set on heavenly things nor their whole desire on earthly ones; they take a middle way, seeking inner qualities but not refusing outer ones. *And one moves along near the earth;* for these people have not perfectly renounced the transitory but cling a little to passing things, and so have great labor and suffer much fatigue. But, with the help of Heaven, they are all victors; for *all are shouting repeatedly, "Let us get to Heaven!"* And so the former and the latter people, with sighs of desire, exhort themselves to move toward the secret places of Heaven, even though tired out by the arts of the ancient serpent. *But they are whirled hither and thither by that flame,* being driven to various actions by the wind of the Devil's temptation. *Some do not waver,* for they are exceedingly strong fighters and manfully defend themselves from these illusions. *Some barely keep their balance,* for they keep their feet in the path of rectitude and persevere in God's commandments, but are worn out by their labors and can scarcely conquer the Devil's arts; and *some fall to the earth but then rise again and start toward Heaven,* for they fall into different ways of vice but are then raised up by penitence and place their hope in God and good works.

16. THE TEMPTATIONS OF SECULAR PEOPLE

Now *the flame that breathes forth among secular people burns some of them so that they are hideously blackened.* This is to say that the flame of evil deception aims itself at those who pursue worldly affairs and subjects some of them to its perversity; it stains them with dark and iniquitous vices, so that they despise the brightness of the true faith. Thus they slay themselves by a bitter death, and fall to the ground and there do evil deeds. *And others it transfixes so that it can move them anywhere it wants;* for it dominates them by its wickedness and bends them to all the vices of its own depravity, seducing them into the embrace of worldly pleasure, so that according to their desires they have different ways in their speech, hair, clothing, gait and other such things. Therefore they become confused and neglect the justice of God, breaking the law and failing to circumcise their minds; they seek excess in lust and do not observe the times of the Law God constituted for them. And as the sea is stirred into turbulence by the wind, they are stirred into diverse vices by the breath of the ancient dragon. *Some of these escape from the flame and move toward those who seek Heaven, reiterating shouts of "O you faithful, give us help!"* For they withdraw themselves from shameful and harmful companionship and imitate those who fix their mind on celestial things, desiring with heart and voice their solicitude and help. *But others remain transfixed,* continuing to be ensnared in evil actions by their various vices.

17. THE SIX WAYS OF TEMPTATION OF THE SPIRITUAL

But the flame that breathes forth among spiritual people conceals them in obscurity. This means that the breath of the Devil's persuasion, when it flames toward those who should be assenting totally to the Spirit, beclouds them with the perversity of its vices, so that they long for the flesh more than for the Spirit.

And you see them in six categories; for the ancient enemy strives to pervert both their five exterior senses and the sixth inner one, the devotion of the heart. *Some of them are cruelly injured by the flame's fury;* for the Devil unlooses his arts on them and inspires them with carnal desires and pleasures, and so enkindles them to lust and unclean pollution. *But when it cannot injure one of them, it burningly breathes on them the deadly poison that flows from the worm's head to its feet, either green or white or red or yellow or black.* How? When they refuse the delights of pollution, he pours into them the sprouting green of mundane sadness, so oppressing them that they have no strength for spiritual or worldly matters; or he sends against them the empty whiteness of vicious irreverence, so that they do not hide their shame before God or Man; or he displays to them the bright red of earthly glory, giving them bitterness and anxiety of heart; or he puts into them the dull yellow of contempt for their neighbor, and thus they become whisperers and hypocrites; or he imposes on them the horrid blackness of feigned justice, through which their hearts are wretchedly darkened.

All these are deadly plagues; they have proceeded from the destroyer from the beginning of his time of deception, and will do so until the end of time, when his madness will end in the world. And through them he injures and burns people up with vices.

18. CONCERNING THE UNBAPTIZED

But the flame that seeks the abyss contains in itself diverse torments for those who have worshipped Satan in place of God, not washed by the font of baptism or knowing the light of truth and faith. This is to say that the fire that accompanies perdition inflicts dire and bitter torments on those souls who were not washed clean in the font of salvation and did not see the brightness of the celestial inheritance or the faith instituted by the Church, and who continue to venerate the lurker in ambush who tries to kill human souls, rather than the One Who granted humanity life and salvation.

19. WHAT IS MEANT BY HIS MOUTH'S ARROWS, BREAST'S SMOKE AND LOINS' FLUID

And you see sharp arrows whistling loudly from its mouth; these are the terrible and evil thrusts of the Devil's rage, which issue forth in madness and iniquity; *and black smoke exhaling from its breast,* which is the outpouring of his malicious impulses of hideous wrath and envy; *and a burning fluid boiling up from its loins,* which is the effusion of his uncleanness in ardent lust.

20. WHAT IS MEANT BY HIS NAVEL'S WHIRLWIND AND BOWELS' UNCLEANNESS OF FROGS

And a hot whirlwind is blowing from its navel, which is the suffocating wind of fornication that proceeds from his voracity to dominate; *and the uncleanness of frogs issuing from its bowels,* which is the fetid excrement of his obduracy in desperation and his perverse concentration on it. For the ancient waylayer hopes to subjugate those who follow him completely to his will. *And all of these things affect human beings with grave disquiet;* for such perversities bring those who fix their hope in the earthly and not the heavenly, and so most miserably become involved with them, into extreme ruin.

21. THE DEVIL MAKES THE FOOLISH BELIEVE WHAT HE FALSELY SHOWS THEM

And the hideous and foul-smelling vapor that comes out of it infects many people with its own perversity. This means that the black wrong of a fetid conscience proceeds from the Devil and disturbs the foolish with wicked unbelief. How?

From the time of the beheading of John the Baptist, who declared that the Son of God is the One Who heals the wounds of sin, most evil error arose, whereby the Devil seduces different people by different false images; so that they think that what he shows them, each according to his understanding, is true. And many are deceived thus, because their faith is constantly weak and wavering.

But you, O My children, if you wish to live justly and devoutly, fly from this most wicked error, lest death catch you in your unbelief.

22. HERETICS WHO WORSHIP THE DEVIL FOR GOD MUST BE AVOIDED AND EXCOMMUNICATED

And fly from those who linger in caves and are cloistered supporters of the Devil. Woe to them, woe to them who remain thus! They are the Devil's very viscera, and the advance guard of the son of perdition.

Therefore, O you My beloved children, avoid them with all devotion and with all the strength of your souls and bodies. For the ancient serpent feeds and clothes them by his arts, and they worship him as God and trust in his false deceptions. They are wicked murderers, killing those who join them in simplicity before they can turn back from their error; and they are wicked fornicators upon themselves, destroying their semen in an act of murder and offering it to the Devil. And they also invade My Church with their schisms in the fulness of vice; in their shameful plots they wickedly scoff at baptism, and the sacrament of My Son's body and blood, and the other institutions of the Church. Because they are afraid of My people, they do not openly resist these institutions of Mine, but in their hearts and their deeds they hold them as nothing. By devilish illusion, they pretend to have sanctity; but they are deceived by the Devil, for if he were to show himself to them openly they would understand him and flee him. By his arts he shows them things he pretends are good and holy, and thus deludes them. O woe to those who perservere in this death!

But because the Devil knows he has only a short time for his error, he is now hastening to perfect infidelity in his members: you, you evil deceivers, who labor to subvert the Catholic faith. You are wavering and soft, and thus cannot avoid the poisonous arrows of human corruption, which you employ as you wish against the Law. And after you pour out your lust in the poisonous seed of fornication, you pretend to pray and falsely assume an air of sanctity, which is more unworthy in My eyes than the stinking mire.

And thus for certain the punishment of all the schisms shall fall upon you: The one that arose in Horeb when the Jewish people made a graven image and played before it in devilish mockery, as some wantonly do to this very day; and the one about Baal, in which many perished; and the one about fornications, where the Midianites did shameful deeds; and all the others. For you have part in all of them by your evil actions; but you are worse than the earlier people, because you perceive the true law of God but stubbornly abandon it.

But, O you who desire to be saved and have received baptism and form the holy mountain of God, resist Satan, and do not descend from the height of your salvation.

23. GOD'S GRACE FORSAKES HIS DESPISERS BUT MERCIFULLY HELPS HIS SEEKERS

The Devil ceaselessly sets his snares against a person who is so hard-hearted as to despise God's help in resisting him; for then he sees a blackness of iniquity rising up in that person, bringing such bitterness into his whole body that its strength dries up. Hence, when a person begins to contemplate his evil and so crushes himself in despair, deeming it impossible for him to avoid evil and do good, the Devil sees this and says, "Behold a person who is like us, denying his God and turning to follow us. Let us hasten and run swiftly to him, urging him by our arts so that he cannot escape us. For to leave God and follow us is what he wants."

But a person who is assailed by these evils through the Devil's agency, and polluted by murder, adultery, voracity, drunkenness and excess of all vices, will fall into death if he continues in them impenitent; while one who resists the Devil and withdraws repenting from these vices will rise again to life. For if a person follows the longing of his flesh and neglects the good desires of his spirit, the Maker of this globe says of him, "He despises Me and sinfully loves his flesh, and rejects the knowledge that he should turn away from perdition. And therefore he must be cast out." But if a person loves the virtuous ardor of his spirit and rejects the pleasure of his flesh, the Creator of the world says of him, "He looks toward Me and does not nourish his body on filth, and desires the knowledge of how to avoid death. And therefore help will be given him." How? As Solomon says, in accordance with My will:

24. WORDS OF SOLOMON

"Evil pursues sinners; and to the just good shall be repaid." (Prov. 13:21.) What does this mean? Those who fall into error and slide into ruin are invaded on all sides by deadly sickness; and so they do not wisely regard what is true, but carelessly abandon it. And, because they reject God and choose the Devil, they are not worthy to look at God or take any pleasure in God or other people, and the evil they do brings them much adversity. But in good people, right sense and just thoughts erect a tall building; they receive in their bosom the inheritance of the Father, for they long for the celestial light. For they are not among the deceivers in the derisive marketplace, where this or that is sold without regard for its value, but in God they possess that which is true.

25. TRUE WORSHIPERS OF GOD CRUSH THE ANCIENT SERPENT

But you see that *a great multitude of people come, shining brightly; they forcefully tread the worm underfoot and severely torment it.* This is to say that those who are born into human misery, but who constitute the faithful army of believers, hasten to attain their desire for Heaven by the faith of baptism and blessed virtues, which are beautiful adornments; and by their deeds they cast down the ancient seducer. They are virgins, martyrs and all other kinds of worshippers of God, who in full knowledge tread worldly things underfoot and desire the heavenly; and they surround the Devil and crush him with force, weakening him with dire suffering. But *they cannot be injured by its flames or its poison;* for they are protected by God with such strength and constancy that neither the open flame nor the hidden persuasion of the Devil's wickedness can touch them. For they forsake all vain fictions, and with great strength in virtue hold fast to sanctity.

But let the one who sees with watchful eyes and hears with attentive ears welcome with a kiss My mystical words, which proceed from Me Who am life. Amen.

St. Francis of Assisi

1182–1226

*S*t. Francis, known as *Il Poverello,* the "little poor man," emerged on the stage of a world we can scarcely imagine today. The physical uncertainty, indeed the violence, of everyday life; the division of society into noble haves and peasant have-nots; the ignorance and illiteracy, the superstition and the isolation in which most people, including their contentious clergy, lived—it all seems buried in the remoteness of the misty hills and ravines of thirteenth-century Umbria. Yet his message of love for the least of God's creatures, his witness through a life of radical poverty, and his mission to teach God's Word continue to challenge and renew the world eight hundred years later.

The son of a prosperous cloth merchant, Francis lived half his forty-four years not much distinguished from his peers until his conversion, so famously depicted by Giotto. The flooding of his consciousness with God's love and grace enabled this charismatic, expressive, but disorganized and eccentric man to launch one of Christianity's greatest movements.

From the beginning, preaching was central to what it means to be a Franciscan, and in the story that follows, from the *Fioretti,* or "little flowers," first compiled in Latin from various sources about a century after his death, we see—in the literal and enormously charming story of St. Francis preaching to the birds on a text from Matthew's Sermon on the Mount—the underlying nature of his mission to spread the gospel to the four corners of the earth.

℃ℰ

St. Francis Preaches to the Birds

St. Francis, humble servant of God, a short time after his conversion, having gathered together many companions and received them into the Order, fell into great perplexity and doubt touching what it behooved him to do—whether to be wholly intent on prayer, or sometimes to preach. And greatly he desired to know the will of God touching these things. But since the holy humility wherewith he was filled suffered him not to lean over-much on his own judgment, nor on his own prayers, he thought to seek the divine will through the prayers of others. Wherefore he called Friar Masseo to him and spoke to him thus, "Go to Sister Clare and bid her from me that she and some of the most spiritual of her companions pray devoutly unto God, that He may be pleased to reveal to me which is the more excellent way: whether to give myself up to preaching or wholly to prayer; then go to Friar Silvester and bid him do the like."

Now he had been in the world and was that same Friar Silvester that beheld a cross of gold issue from the mouth of St. Francis, the length whereof was high as heaven, and the breadth whereof reached to the utter-most parts of the earth. And this Friar Silvester was a man of such great devotion and holiness that whatsoever he asked of God he obtained, and the same was granted to him; and ofttimes he spoke with God, wherefore great was the devotion of St. Francis to him. Friar Masseo went forth and gave his message first to St. Clare, as St. Francis had commanded, and then to Friar Silvester, who no sooner had heard the command than he straightway be-took himself to prayer, and when he had received the divine answer, he returned to Friar Masseo and spoke these words, "Thus saith the Lord God, 'Go to Friar Francis and say unto him that God hath not called him to this state for himself alone, but that he may bring forth fruit of souls and that many through him may be saved.' "

Friar Masseo, having received this answer, returned to Sister Clare to learn what answer she had obtained of God; and she answered that she and her companions had received the selfsame response from God that Friar Silvester had. And Friar Masseo returned with this answer to St. Francis, who greeted him with greatest charity, washing his feet and setting meat before him. And St. Francis called Friar Masseo, after he had eaten, into the wood, and there knelt down before him, drew back his cowl, and making a cross with his arms, asked of him, "What doth my Lord Jesus Christ command?" Friar Masseo answers, "Thus to Friar Silvester and thus to Sister Clare and her sisterhood hath Christ answered and revealed His will: that thou go forth to preach throughout the world, for He hath not chosen thee for thyself alone, but also for the salvation of others." Then St. Francis, when he had heard these words and learned thereby the will of Christ, rose up and said with great fervour, "Let us then go forth in God's name." And with him he took Friar Masseo and Friar Agnolo, holy men both, and setting forth with great fervour of spirit and taking heed neither of road nor path, they came to a city called Saburniano.

And St. Francis began to preach, first commanding the swallows to keep silence until his sermon were ended; and the swallows obeying him, he preached with such zeal that all the men and women of that city desired in their devotion to follow after him and forsake the city. But St. Francis suffered them not, saying, "Be not in haste to depart, for I will ordain what ye shall do for the salvation of your souls." And then he thought about the third Order which he established for the universal salvation of all people. And so, leaving them much comforted and well disposed to penitence, he departed thence and came to a place between Cannara and Bevagna. And journeying on in that same fervor of spirit, he lifted up his eyes and beheld some trees by the wayside whereon were an infinite multitude of birds; so that he marveled and said to his companions, "Tarry here for me by the way, and I will go and preach to my little sisters the birds."

And he entered into the field and began to preach to the birds that were on the ground; and soon those that were on the trees flew down to hear him, and all stood still while St. Francis made an end of his sermon; and even then they departed not until he had given them his blessing. And according as Friar Masseo and Friar James of Massa thereafter related, St. Francis went among them, touching them with the hem of his garment, and not one stirred. And the substance of the sermon St. Francis preached was this,

My little sisters the birds, much are ye beholden to God your Creator, and always and in every place ye ought to praise Him for that He hath given you a double and a triple vesture; He hath given you freedom to go into every place, and also did preserve the seed of you in the ark of Noah, in order that your kind might not perish from the earth. Again, ye are beholden to Him for the element of air which He hath appointed for you; moreover, ye sow not, neither do ye reap, and God feedeth you and giveth you the rivers and the fountains for your drink; He giveth you the mountains and the valleys for your refuge, and the tall trees wherein to build your nests, and forasmuch as ye can neither spin nor sew God clotheth you, you and your children: wherefore your Creator loveth you much, since He hath dealt so bounteously with you; and therefore beware, little sisters mine, of the sin of ingratitude, but ever strive to praise God.

While St. Francis was uttering these words, all those birds began to open their beaks, and stretch their necks, and spread their wings, and reverently to bow their heads to the ground, showing by their gestures and songs that the holy father's words gave them greatest joy: and St. Francis was glad and rejoiced with them, and marveled much at so great a multitude of birds and at their manifold loveliness, and at their attention and familiarity; for which things he devoutly praised the Creator in them. Finally, his sermon ended, St. Francis made the sign of holy cross over them and gave them leave to depart; and all those birds soared up into the air in one flock with wondrous songs, and then divided themselves into four parts after the form of the cross St. Francis had made over them; and one part flew toward the east; another toward the west; the third toward the south, and the fourth toward the north. And each flock sped forth singing wonderously, betokening thereby that even as St. Francis, standard-bearer of the cross of Christ, had preached to them and had made the sign of the cross over them, according to which they had divided themselves, singing, among the four quarters of the world, so the preaching of Christ's cross, renewed by St. Francis, was, through him and his friars, to be borne throughout the whole world; and these friars possessing nothing of their own in this world, after the manner of birds, committed their lives wholly to the providence of God.

St. Thomas Aquinas
1225–1274

G. K. Chesterton wrote, "You can make a sketch of St. Francis: you could only make a plan of St. Thomas, like the plan of a labyrinthine city." If Thomas were alive today, what would he be? Wall Street's most powerful lawyer? Silicon Valley's most successful entrepreneur? Washington's top political analyst? In the thirteenth century, when the best minds of Europe were trained to take their part in a God-centered world, Thomas became a Master of Theology.

Thomas was born a Sicilian in a noble family with a castle in the town of Aquino. As a son and the youngest child, by custom he was offered at the age of five to a local Benedictine monastery. There he studied until his early teens, when he was sent to Naples to prepare for advanced training in theology; he spent those years poring over the works of Boethius, Euclid, and Ptolemy. The works of his great master Aristotle were just then becoming available in Latin translations.

The then new and rapidly expanding mendicant orders were the most galvanizing social forces of the day; at nineteen Thomas became a member of the Dominican Order of Friars (from the French *frères*), the order entrusted by the Pope with the Inquisition. He was sent by his superiors to Paris to complete his studies, drawing on the great ordering of knowledge and learning which contributed to the rise of the medieval universities in his day. (Oxford University was founded during his lifetime, as were the national colleges of the University of Paris.) His mentor in Paris was the brilliant German Dominican Albertus Magnus, whom he followed to Cologne to found a center of study there. In Cologne, his fellow students nicknamed him "the dumb ox," referring probably both to his natural reticence and his heavyset physique. Albert's rejoinder to the taunt was that "the bellowing of that ox will resound throughout the whole world."

And Thomas's renown resounded indeed, for his lectures in Paris on the interpretation of the Scripture and his consummate synthesis of Aristotelian and Christian thought. His masterworks include the staggeringly rich *Summa Theologiae,* which became the cornerstone for the interpretation of Roman Catholic doctrine. Author of a number of beautiful hymns, the Angelic Doctor (a title conferred along with his canonization in 1323) was an extraordinary preacher as well. The sermons resonate with his pedagogic passion for instructing a congregation on the threshold of the high Middle Ages, setting in place rational structures of belief where simple faith and, earlier, medieval superstition had once reigned. The educated faith of the Thomists became a solid dogmatic shield against the cultural clashes of the European religious revolt to come.

This sermon on the final phrase of the Apostles' Creed was part of a series preached during Lent to the thronging public and clergy of Naples. Though he spoke in the Neapolitan vernacular, his longtime private secretary recorded his words in Latin. The text is suffused with Thomas's great clarity, his magisterial thoroughness and uncanny focus on the heart of the matter—all consistent with the thanks he once gave to God because "I have understood every page I ever read."

⚬

On the Apostles' Creed

He descended into hell.

As we say, the death of Christ lies in the separation of the soul from the body, just as in the death of other human beings. But, the divinity was so indissolubly united to the humanity of Christ that, although body and soul were separated from each other, nonetheless the very divinity was always perfectly present both to the soul and the body. Therefore, the Son of God was both in the tomb with the body and descended into hell with the soul. And thus the holy apostles said: "he descended into hell."

There are four reasons why Christ as a soul descended into hell. (1) To shoulder the full punishment of sin, and so expiate all of its guilt. The punishment of sin for humanity, however, was not only the death of the body, but also involved the soul, because sin also belonged to the soul. And thus before the coming of Christ, the soul after death descended into hell. In order that Christ completely shoulder the entire punishment due to sinners, he wished not only to die, but also to descend into hell as a soul. Thus we read: "I am labeled with those going down into the depths." (Ps. 87:5.)

Nonetheless, Christ descended into hell in one way, and the fathers of old in another. The ancient fathers were conducted and detained there from necessity, and as if violently, whereas Christ went down in power and on his own initiative. And therefore the Psalm above continues: "I am made like a man without help, yet free among the dead." (Ps. 87:5–6.) The others who were dead were there as slaves but Christ was there as a free man.

(2) So that he would completely rescue all good people of past generations and his own friends who died in his lifetime. Christ indeed had his own friends not only in the upper world, but also in the underworld. People were friends of Christ in the world insofar as they had charity. In the underworld, however, there were many people, such as Abraham, Isaac, Jacob, and David, and other just and virtuous men, who departed with charity and with faith in the One who was to come. And therefore just as Christ visited his own friends in this world and rescued them through his own death, so he wanted to visit his own who were in hell, and to rescue them by descending to them: "I will penetrate the deepest parts of the earth, and I will look upon all those who have died, and I will enlighten all those hoping in God" and so forth. (Ecclus. 24:45.)

(3) That he might completely triumph over the devil. Consider that someone perfectly triumphs over another when they not only conquer them in the open field but also snatch from them the heart of their own kingdom and their home. Christ, however, triumphed over the devil on the cross and he conquered him, whence he says "Now is the judgment of the world, now is the judgment of the prince of this world," that is, the devil, "and he will be tossed out," from the world. (John 12:31.) Therefore, in order to triumph completely, Christ wanted also to capture the heart of the devil's kingdom, and to bind him in his own house, which was hell. Christ thus went down there and plundered all his goods; he bound the devil and stripped from him his own spoils: "Undoing the principalities and powers, he disgraced [them] with ease" and so forth. (Col. 2:15.)

Similarly, since Christ already had reigned sovereign in heaven and on earth, he wished also to assume possession over hell, as Paul says: "In the name of Jesus every knee should bend of those in heaven, and on earth, and in hell" and so forth. (Phil. 2:10.) And in the last chapter of Mark we read: "and these signs will follow those who believe. In my name they will cast out demons." (Mark 16:17.)

(4) That he might free the saints who were in hell. Just as Christ wished to suffer death that he might free from death those living, so he wished to descend into hell that he might free from hell the saints who were there: "As for you, in the blood of the covenant, I will set free your captives from the dry depths." (Zech. 9:11.) And in Hosea: "From the hand of death I will free them, from death I will redeem them. I will be your death, O death! I will be your sting, O hell!" and so forth. (Hos. 13:14.) Although Christ completely destroyed death, nonetheless he did not all together destroy hell. Rather, Christ stung hell, because he did not free everyone from hell, but only those who were without mortal sin, that is, without original sin (from which they are cleansed as individuals by circumcision) and without actual [mortal] sin. These souls were there on account of the original sin of Adam, from which they could not be freed by nature but only by Christ. But he sent away those who were there in mortal sin and children who were not baptized. Therefore it is said: "I will be your sting" and so forth.

It is clear therefore that Christ did descend into hell and why he did so.

From these considerations we can draw four conclusions for our own instruction. (1) Firm hope in God. No matter how anyone may be in affliction, they should not despair nor lose trust in the assistance of God. Nothing can be found so dire as being in hell. If Christ freed those who were in hell, everyone ought to trust greatly, if they are a friend of God, that they will be freed by God no matter what may be the tribulation: "She," that is, wisdom, "did not abandon the just man when he was sold, but she went down with him into the pit and freed him from sinners." (Wisd. 10:13.) And because God helps especially God's servants, anyone who serves God should be quite secure: "Anyone who fears God will not be alarmed, and will not panic, because God is their hope." (Ecclus. 34:16.)

(2) We should become afraid of hell and drive away presumption. Although Christ suffered for sinners and did descend into hell, he nonetheless

did not free everyone, but only those who were without mortal sin. As it is said: but those who died in mortal sin he sent away. Therefore, no one who dies in mortal sin should hope for pardon, but should expect to be in hell just as long as the saints are in paradise, that is to say, forever: "And those on Christ's left hand will go into eternal torment, the just, however, into everlasting life" and so forth. (Matt. 25:46.)

(3) We should become careful. Christ descended as a soul into hell for our salvation, and hence we ought frequently to descend there by considering eternal punishment: "I said: in the middle of my days I will go to the gates of hell" and so forth. (Isa. 38:10.) Whoever frequently goes down to hell in thought during this life, will not go down there easily in death, because the consideration of hell draws one away from sin. We see how people in this world protect themselves against earthly pain from evildoers; how much more ought they to protect themselves against the pain of hell, which is greater in duration as well as in bitterness: "And in all you do, remember the end of your days, and for eternity you will not sin" and so forth. (Ecclus. 7:40.)

(4) We are shown an example of love. Christ descended into hell in order to free those who were there. Consequently, we ought to go down to that place, that we might come to the aid of our own friends who are there, for they are not able to do anything. Therefore we should support those who are in purgatory. The man who would not come to the aid of his friend who was in prison would be thoroughly callous. How much more unfeeling the man who does not come to the aid of a friend who is in purgatory. "Have pity on me, have pity on me at least you, my friends, because the hand of God has pressed upon me" and so forth. (Job 19:21.) And in Ecclesiasticus we read: "From the dead you will not withdraw grace." (Ecclus. 7:37.) And in Maccabees: "Therefore it is a holy and beneficial thought to pray for the dead, that they might be absolved from their sins" and so forth. (2 Macc. 12:46.)

We come to their assistance principally in three ways, as Augustine says: through masses, through almsgiving, and through prayers. Gregory adds a fourth way, through fasting. We should not wonder, because even in the world one friend can make satisfaction for another. We should understand the same thing about those in purgatory.

Let us pray to the Lord.

Eternal Life

Eternal life. Amen.

Fittingly, with the end of all our desires, that is to say, with eternal life, an end is given to those matters to be believed in the Symbol [the creed]. Thus we read: "eternal life. Amen." This stands against those who say the soul perishes with the body. If that were true, a human being would be in the same condition as brute animals. Against these objectors the Psalm argues: "A human being does not understand when he is held in honor; he is to be compared with the dumb beasts of the field, and he makes himself like them" and so forth. (Ps. 48:21.) The human soul in its immortality resembles God, whereas in its sensibility it resembles the animals. Therefore, when anyone believes that the soul dies with the body, they fall away from the likeness to God and are compared to the animals. In opposition Wisdom says: "And they did not know the mysteries of God, nor did they hope for a reward for justice, nor did they weigh the high state of holy souls" and so forth. (Wisd. 2:22.)

In this article the first thing that should be considered is life eternal. In this regard we should know that eternal life first of all consists in this, that a human being is intimately espoused to God. Indeed, God is the reward and end of all our labors: "I, the Lord, am your reward." (Exod. 2:9.)

This union, however, consists in perfect vision of God: "Now we see through a mirror in symbols, but then we shall see face to face" and so forth. (1 Cor. 13:12.) This union consists in a most intense love, for the more one knows, the more one loves. And this union consists in supreme worship. Augustine writes: "We will see, and we will love, and we will praise" and so forth. And, "the Lord will console Zion, and all her ruins; he will make her desert like a garden of the Lord. Joy and celebration will be found within her, and thanksgiving and the sound of praise" and so forth. (Isa. 51:3.)

In eternal life there is full and perfect satiation of desire. Each and every blessed one will have there fulfilled his or her own desires and hopes. The reason is that nothing in this life can fill our desire, nor any creature ever satiate the desire of a human being. God alone, who surpasses infinity, satisfies. And thus it is that humankind will not be at rest except in God. Augustine says: "You have made us, O Lord, for yourself" and so forth. Wherefore, in our fatherland the saints perfectly possess God, since God himself is our reward. So obviously God will satisfy our desire. The glory of God will surpass all that went before, and therefore the Lord says, "Well done, good and faithful servant, because you have been faithful over a few things, I will place you over many things; enter into the joy of your Lord." (Matt. 25:21.) Thus David said: "But I will appear in your sight in justice; I will be satisfied when your glory appears" and so forth. (Ps. 16:15.) And it is said, "Who fulfills with good things one's desire" and so forth. (Ps. 102:5.)

Whatever is desirable will be all there superabundantly. If delights are yearned for, there will be supreme and fully perfect delight, because they come from God who is the highest good: "Then you will abound in the delights of the Almighty, and you will lift up your face to God." (Job 22:26.)

If honors are yearned for, every honor will be there. People desire vehemently to be kings, if they are lay people, and to be bishops, if they are clerics. And there in heaven this will be: "And you have made us into priests and into a kingdom for our God, and we will reign over the earth." (Rev. 5:10.) And "Behold how they are counted among the sons of God" and so forth. (Wisd. 5:5.)

If knowledge is yearned for, it will there be most perfect, because we will know there the nature of everything, all truth, and whatsoever we wish to know. And whatever we want to have, we shall there have it as part of life eternal: "All good things have come to me along with her" and so forth. (Wisd. 7:11.) And, "What the wicked fears will come over him; the wishes of the just will be granted." (Prov. 10:24.)

In life eternal there is security most perfect. In this world there is no complete security, because the more one has and the more one stands out, so much the more does one fear and still lack many things. But, in eternal life there will be no sadness, no labor, no fear of loss. "But whoever listens to me will rest without terror, and will enjoy abundance, with the fear of evils taken away" and so forth. (Prov. 1:33.)

In heaven there will be every kind of sharing of all goods, which society is supremely delightful to good people. There all goods will be shared with all good people, and each one there will love the other as oneself. Thus they will rejoice over the good of another as over their own good. Given this, insofar as the joy and felicity of anyone is increased, so the joy of all is increased: "Like all those rejoicing, our dwelling is in you" and so forth. (Ps. 86:7.)

Those who will be in eternal life will have all this. The wicked, however, who are in eternal death, will have no less sorrow or pain than the blessed have joy and glory. Their pain will be exaggerated, first of all by separation from God and all good things. And this is the pain of loss, which is greater than the pain of the senses: "Cast the useless servant outside into outer darkness; there one will weep and gnash one's teeth" and so forth. (Matt. 25:30.) In this life the wicked have interior darkness, that is to say, sinfulness, but then in eternal death they will have exterior darkness.

Their pain will be exaggerated from remorse of conscience: "You have done these things and I have been silent. You estimated wickedly that I was like you. I will confront you and I will lay a charge against you." (Ps. 49:21.) And, "Speaking among themselves in repentance, and groaning in the stress of their spirit" and so forth. (Wisd. 5:3.) Nevertheless, this penitence will be useless, for it is not on account of hatred of evil, but of fear of pain.

Their pain will be exaggerated from the immensity of pain that is of the senses, that is to say, of the fire of hell which is excruciating to soul and body, and which is the most bitter of pains (as the blessed saints do say). Indeed, they will be always dying but never dead, and this hell is called eternal death: "Like sheep are put in the underworld, death will pasture them." (Ps. 48:15.)

Their pain will be exaggerated from despair, for if hope of freedom from pain were to be given to them, their pain would be mitigated. When all hope is withdrawn from them, however, then the pain is rendered most intense. And "And they will go forth and look upon the body of those men who plotted against me; their worm will not die, and their fire will not be extinguished, and they will be so unto the satiation of the sight of all flesh" and so forth. (Isa. 66:24.)

Therefore, the difference between living a good life and an evil life is clear, for good works lead up to life, but evil works draw down to death. For this reason humanity ought frequently to recollect itself, because from this it will be spurred on to good and drawn back from evil. Thus, at the end of all of the articles of the creed eternal life is placed conspicuously, so that it may be impressed in memory always and ever more.

In summary, we should know that according to some commentators there are twelve articles [in the Apostles' Creed]; six about the divinity, that is to say, that there is essentially one God. Thus we say (1) "I believe in one God"; (2) three in persons, and thus we say "Father and Son and Holy Spirit"; (3) creator of all things, and thus we say "creator of heaven and earth"; (4) from God is all grace and the forgiveness of sins; (5) God will raise up our bodies, and (6) God will give to the blessed eternal life.

Similarly, there are six articles of the creed about the humanity of Christ: namely, (1) conceived and born, (2) suffered and died, (3) descended into hell, (4) rose on the third day, (5) ascended into heaven, and (6) will come again to judge, and so forth.

Let us pray to the Lord, and so forth.

Meister Johannes Eckhart

1260–1327

One of the founders and the greatest exponent of German mysticism, Eckhart enjoyed the early favor of Pope Boniface VIII, who conferred on him as a Dominican the title *Meister* ("Master") and the later hostility of the bishop of Cologne, who forced him to recant many of his views. This masterful preacher remains controversial, a Western mystic who is now regarded as a conduit to the great mystical traditions of Asia.

Johannes Eckhart was born a century after the poetic reign of the early German minnesingers. (Love, or *Minne,* was a central theme.) Poets like Walter von der Vogelweide and Wolfram von Eschenbach had used Middle High German in the service of lyric poetry and to discourse on courtly love, religion, and politics. (Something of that difficult fusion survives in Wagner's opera *Tannhäuser,* in which the union of the spiritual and the worldly is technically replicated in a nineteenth-century musical drama.) Borrowing from that linguistic and literary tradition, the Dominican monk

Eckhart used its secularized vocabulary of love between men and women and recharged it with an older expression of the love between man and God.

He preached in both German and Latin, playing in this text on the language of the scholastic philosophers such as his predecessor Thomas Aquinas, specifically on the homonym of the Latin word *mundus* (for "the world" and "the soul"). He also treats one of the standard topics in his vernacular sermons: the birth of the Word and the Father in the soul of the just man. His linguistic and theological genius do not always translate, in either of his tongues, into ease of accessibility, but his oratory about the interplay between the mystery of God and the soul leaves modern readers dazzled, if perplexed.

The Feast of the Holy Trinity

1. "ALL THINGS ARE FROM HIM, AND THROUGH HIM, AND IN HIM" (ROM. 11:36)

Note that when it says "all things are through him," the sense of "through him" is that he is in all things. Everything through which anything exists is certainly in him in a general way. For example, the whiteness through which anything is white is surely in it, for nothing is white by a whiteness that is in something else. The Apostle wants to say and teach that all things are in God, God is in all and all in him.

Secondly, note that he does not say or add "all things are" for his sake. First, because God and hence the divine man does not act for the sake of a why or wherefore. Secondly, because all things do what they do in God from him and through him, but God himself does all things in himself. "In him" is not "for the sake of." Thirdly, because that person really works for the sake of God who works from God, through God, and in God, just as the just man does just things or works justly, but not for the sake of justice insofar as "for the sake of" is distinguished from "of," "through," and "in." Therefore, all things are "from him, through him, and in him." What is written in Proverbs, "The Lord has done all things for his own sake" (Prov.

16:4), is explained from what has been said. He says, "for his very own sake," not for the sake of anything else, according to the text in Genesis, "I have sworn through my very own self." (Gen. 22:16.)

Note that these three terms (from, through, and in) seem to be not only appropriated, but proper to the divine Persons. Second, note that they are the same, as will appear below; and third, note that universally, even in creatures, that "from which" any single thing is, is the same as that "through" and "in" which it is. Fourth, note that the term "from" is properly not the efficient cause, but rather the idea of the efficient cause.

"All things are from him, through him, and in him"—"from him," the Father, "through him," the Son, "in him," the Holy Spirit. Concerning the term "in him," first remark that all things are in the Holy Spirit in such a way that what is not in him must be nothing. He says, "All things are in him." What is not among all things, but is outside all things, must be nothing. Whoever says "all" excludes nothing, but "All things are in him." This is what John 1 says, "without him" (that is, not in him), "what was made is nothing." (John 1:3.)

On the second point, note that "All things are in him" in such a way that if there is anything not in the Holy Spirit, the Holy Spirit is not God. Just as if anything were white outside of or without whiteness, whiteness would not be whiteness, because all that is white is so by means of whiteness, so too what is not in existence, but is outside of or without existence, is nothing. How might there be or might something be that is beyond existence, or without existence, or not in existence? Existence is from God alone, and he alone is existence: "I am who am," and "He who is sent me." (Exod. 3:14.) If there were anything outside him or not in him, he would not be existence and consequently not God. This is why John 1 says again, "All things were made through him." (John 1:3.)

Third, "All things are in him" in such a way that the Father would not be in the Son nor the Son in the Father, if the Father were not one and the same as the Holy Spirit, or the Son the same as the Holy Spirit. It is contrary to the property of the Father, that is, to the constitutive relation which is Paternity, to exist in another or in something else. Paternity alone is the "from which"—"From which all fatherhood in heaven and on earth is named." (Eph. 3:15.) "From which," because nothing in any way possesses or is named "fatherhood" without the "from which." But if this is in another or in something else, then as such it is no longer the Father, but as such is what the Holy Spirit is. "I am in the Father and the Father is in me," and "The Father and I are one." (John 14:11; 10:30.) This is why the church prays:

> Now [come] to us, Holy Spirit,
> One with the Father and the Son.

"Existence in" in no way pertains to the Son by reason of his personal property, but only "existence from," or out of another. The Holy Spirit who is the "bond" (this is his personal property, the "bond") possesses "[existence] in which," and thus all other things "are in him."

Fourth. "All things are in" the Holy Spirit in such a way that God is not in us nor are we in God unless in the Holy Spirit. "Existence in" does not belong to or agree with the Father or the Son, both because it does not fit the personal property of either, and also because it is special to the personal property of the Holy Spirit and thus agrees with it alone. If it were to fit either the Father or the Son, the Father would now be the Holy Spirit, and so would the Son. Hence 1 John 4: "God is love." I say, "God," the Holy Spirit, "is love," according to Augustine, and thus, "he who remains in love," that is, in the Holy Spirit, "remains in God, and God in him." (1 John 4:16.) Romans 5: "God's love is poured out in our hearts through the Holy Spirit" (Rom. 5:5); and John 14: "If anyone loves me, my Father will love him," and what follows, "we will come to him and make our abode with him" (John 14:23). Hence, the Father and the Son love us by the Holy Spirit, and we ought to love God in the Holy Spirit.

Fifthly, "All things are in him" in such a way that nothing is in the Father, nothing in the Son, except because the Father and the Son are what the Holy Spirit is. Just as the Father is not in another or in something else, and nothing else is in the Father, so too there is nothing in the Son as Son except insofar as it is what the Holy Spirit is.

"All things are in him." "All things" has three references. "All things in him," therefore, are [those of] nature, grace, and glory. Again, "all things," because of

> The triple fabric of the world . . .
> The three-fold fabric of things
> Of heaven, of earth, and of below.

Indeed, even "Hell and destruction are before God." (Prov. 15:11.) In another sense, "all things," because things substantial, accidental, and artificial. And another sense: "all things," because the whole existence of what is uncreatable, what is creatable and what is makable. "All things," even those made by art, "are through him, and without him," not in him, "nothing was made." (John 1:3.) Concerning these three Acts 17 says, "In him we live and move and have our being." (Acts 17:28.) Further, "All things are in him," namely, the work of creation, of distinction, and of adornment.

Here note that when we say that all things are in God that means that just as he is indistinct in his nature and nevertheless most distinct from all things, so in him all things in a most distinct way are also at the same time indistinct. The first reason is because man in God is God. Therefore, just as God is indistinct and completely distinct from a lion, so too man in God is indistinct and completely distinct from a lion, and likewise with other things. Second, because everything that is in something else is in it according to the nature of that in which it is. Third, because just as God is totally indistinct in himself according to his nature in that he is truly and most properly one and completely distinct from other things, so too man in God is indistinct from everything which is in God ("All things are in him"), and at the same time completely distinct from everything else. Fourth, according to what has been said note that all things are in God as spirit without position and without boundary. Further, just as God is ineffable and incomprehensible, so all things are in him in an ineffable way. Again, every effect is always in the cause in a causal way and not otherwise.

2. THE TRINITY. "ALL THINGS ARE FROM HIM, THROUGH HIM, AND IN HIM" (ROM. 11:36)

This text is commonly explained in terms of the Trinity. Say then that "all things" are "from" the maker, "through" the form, and "in" the end. Therefore, God is the "from whom" of all, that is, the maker of all; the "through whom" of all, that is, the form of all or what forms all; and the "in whom" of all, because he is the end of all things. In this connection note that many have a crude and false picture here, first, because they imagine that action, form, and end are taken away from created things by this. Second, they think that the maker, the form, and the end in creatures along with God are two makers or efficient causes, two forms, two ends. That is crude, first, because no being can be counted alongside God. Existence and being, existence and nothing, and also a form and what it informs make up no number. Existence is more intimate than any form and is not a source of number. Second, because every being, every maker, every form, every end that is conceived of outside or beyond existence or that is numbered along with existence is nothing—it is neither a being, nor a maker, nor a form, nor an end. This is because existence, that is, God, is within every being, every form and end, and conversely every being, form, and end is in existence itself. Indeed, every maker works through its existence, form informs through its existence, and every end moves through its existence—through nothing else! And where one acts for the sake of the other, in both cases there is still only one. Furthermore, every number or duality takes one thing outside or alongside another; but every maker, form, and end outside of existence is taken as nothing. Therefore, there are not two efficient causes, two forms, two ends.

In summary, note that everything that is said or written about the Holy Trinity is in no way really so or true. First, this follows from the nature of the distinction of terms, especially between the distinct and the indistinct, between temporal and eternal things, between the sensible and the intellectual heaven, between the material body and the spiritual body. Second, that since God is inexpressible in and of his nature, what we say he is, surely is not in him. Hence the Psalm text "Every man is a liar." (Ps. 115:11.) It is true, of course, that there is something in God corresponding to the Trinity we speak of and to other similar things. Third, it follows because every name or in general everything that denotes a number or makes a number come to mind or be conceived is far from God. According to Boethius, "That is truly one in which there is no number," not even in conception.

In this matter two remarks. First, the terms good, true, truth, goodness, and the like, are not properly spoken of God because they add something and cause a number in thought, concept, or idea. Second, this is why Mary Magdalene, who sought the One (that is, God), grieved so much when she saw the number two, that is, the two angels (cf. John 20:11–13).

Thomas à Kempis

1379–1471

In George Eliot's classic novel *The Mill on the Floss* (1860), her intelligent and frustrated heroine, Maggie Tulliver, spends her brief provincial life immersed in the power of imagination, self-examining scrupulousness, and formative books. Thomas à Kempis's *The Imitation of Christ,* in Eliot's fiction, shaped the nobility of Maggie's mind and her poignant and self-renunciatory death.

This Augustinian monk (born Thomas Hammerken von Kempen to poor parents in a small town near Cologne) wrote one of the most celebrated works of Christian spirituality. In it he traced, in Latin prose, four stages of the soul's progress toward Christian perfection. The book was translated into English in the middle of the fifteenth century, despite its attribution at the time to a fashionable French theologian. The dispute over the origins of Thomas à Kempis's work, uneasily aware of its emotional and spiritual genius, resembles the "authorship" controversy over the identity of Shakespeare, although the quality of mind and thought in his well-attested sermons, their simplicity and sincerity, are surely sufficient evidence of the unique signature for that famous book. The theme of "taking up the cross" of Jesus Christ is even more congruent with the message of *The Imitation of Christ* as it is mirrored in his religious teaching.

Thomas à Kempis preached this sermon in a remote German hamlet, far from cathedral towns and widely frequented pulpits, and far from wars and rumors of wars shortly to come. The Protestant heroine Maggie Tulliver

could read his work without a shadow of sectarian unease, just as the
Calvinist Scot John Knox could translate the universal language of a
Catholic monk during one of the bloodiest periods of the Reformation.

ᴄᵬ

Taking Up the Cross

But God forbid that I should glory, save in the Cross of
Christ Jesus.

—GALATIANS 6:14

Beloved brethren, blessed Paul, the excellent beholder of heavenly secrets, sets forth to us in the aforesaid words, that the Cross is the right way
of living well; is the best teaching how to suffer adversity; is the firmest lad-
der whereby we may ascend to heaven by its most unconquered sign. It is
this which leads its lovers into the country of eternal light, of eternal peace,
of eternal blessedness, which the world cannot give, nor the Devil take
away. Human frailty abhors the suffering of poverty, contempt, vileness,
hunger, labor, pain, necessity, derision, which all are so often its lot, and
which weigh down and disturb men. But all these things joined together
form by their manifold sufferings a salutary Cross, God so ordering this dispensation for us; and to the true bearers of the Cross they open the gate of
the celestial kingdom. To them that fight, they prepare the palm of life; to
them that conquer, they give the diadem of eternal glory.

O truly blessed Cross of Christ, which didst bear the King of
Heaven, and which didst bring to the whole world the joy of salvation! By
thee the devils are put to flight; the weak are cured; the timid are strengthened; the sinful are cleansed; the idle are excited; the proud are humbled;
the hard-hearted are touched; and the devout are bedewed with tears.
Blessed are they who daily call to mind the Passion of Christ, and desire to
carry their own cross after Christ. Good and religious brethren, who are
enrolled under obedience, have, in the daily affliction of their body, and in
the resignation of their own will, a cross which, in its outward aspect is
heavy and bitter, but which is internally full of sweetness, because of the
hope of eternal salvation, and the affluence of Divine comfort which is

promised to those that are broken in heart: which, if they do not feel at once, or perceive to be bestowed upon them by slow degrees, nevertheless they ought to expect it with patience, and to resign themselves to the Divine Will. For He Himself best knows the time of showing mercy, and the method of assisting the afflicted, as the physician is best acquainted with the art of curing, and the master of the ship with the craft of steering. Those that have taken up the Cross in their hearts, have great confidence and cause of glorying, in the Cross of Jesus Christ, because they confide not, nor trust that they shall be saved in their own merits and works, but through the mercy of God, and the merits of Christ Jesus, crucified for our sins, in Whom they believe faithfully; Whom with their heart they love,— with their mouth they confess, praise, preach, honor, and extol. God is wont to prove His familiar friends by the holy Cross, whether they love Him truly or in pretence, and whether they can perfectly observe His commandments.

Principally, however, they are proved by tolerance of injuries, and the removal of internal consolations; by the death of friends, and by the loss of property; by pains in the head, and injuries in the limbs; by abstinence from food, and roughness of garments; by the hardness of their bed, and the coldness of their feet; by the long watches of the night, and the labors of the day; by the silence of the mouth, and the reproofs of superiors; by worms that gnaw, and tongues that detract. In their sufferings, however, they are consoled by the devout meditation of the Lord's Passion, as many devout persons know very well in their own hearts. It is theirs to taste the hidden honey from the rock, and the oil of mercy that drops from the blessed wood of the holy Cross; whose taste is most delicious; whose odor is most sweet; whose touch is most healthy; whose fruit is most happy. O most truly worthy and precious Tree of life, planted in the midst of the Church for the medicine of the soul! O Jesus of Nazareth, Thou That wast crucified for us! Thou loosenest the bands of sinners; freest the souls of saints; humblest the necks of the haughty; breakest down the power of the wicked; comfortest the faithful; puttest to flight the unbelievers; deliverest the pious; punishest the hardened; overthrowest the adversaries. Thou raisest up them that are fallen; Thou settest at liberty them that are oppressed; Thou smitest them that do hurt; Thou defendest them that are innocent; Thou lovest them that are true; Thou hatest them that are false; Thou despisest the carnal; Thou hast regard to the spiritual; Thou receivest them that come to Thee; Thou hidest them that take refuge in Thee. Them that call upon Thee, Thou hearest; them that visit Thee, Thou rejoicest; them that seek Thee, Thou helpest; them that cry to Thee, Thou strengthenest. Thou honorest them that honor Thee; Thou praisest them that praise Thee; Thou lovest them that love Thee; Thou glorifiest them that adore Thee; Thou blessest them that bless Thee; Thou exaltest them that exalt Thee. On them that look to Thee Thou lookest; them that kiss Thee, Thou kissest; them that embrace Thee, Thou embracest; them that follow Thee, Thou leadest to heaven.

O religious brother, why art thou sorrowful, and why dost thou complain of the weight of thy cross, in long vigils; in many fasts; in labor and silence; in obedience and strict discipline? which things were instituted at the inspiration of God, by holy fathers for thy profit, and the salvation of thy soul; in order that by them thou mightest walk securely and prudently, who canst not govern thyself well and virtuously. Dost thou think that without the Cross and without grief thou canst enter into the kingdom of heaven, when Christ neither could nor would, nor did any of His most beloved friends and saints gain from Him such a privilege? For he Himself said, "Ought not Christ to suffer, and so enter into His glory?" Thou art altogether mistaken in thy thought: thou attendest not to the footsteps of Christ shown to thee; for He, by the Cross, passed from this world to His Heavenly Father. Ask whom thou wilt of the victors and citizens of the celestial kingdom how he came to possess forever this glory of God. Was it not by the Cross and by suffering? Well then, brethren, take up the sweet and light yoke of the Lord; embrace with all affection the holy Cross,—it flowers with all virtues; it is full of celestial unction,—to the end that it may lead you without mistake, with the hope of glory, to life eternal.

What will ye more? This is the way, and there is none other; the right way, the holy way, the perfect way, the way of Christ, the way of the just, the way of the elect that shall be saved. Walk in it, persevere in it, endure in it, live in it, die in it, breathe forth your spirits in it. The Cross of Christ conquers all the machinations of the devil; the Cross draws to itself the hearts of all the faithful; the Cross destroys all things evil, and confers on us all things good, through Jesus Christ, Who hung and died upon it. There is no armor so strong, no arrow so sharp and so terrible, against the power and cruelty of the devil, none which he so fears as the sign of the Cross, in which he brought to pass that the Son of God should be suspended and slain, Who was innocent and pure from all spot. O truly blessed Cross of Christ, most worthy of all honor, to be embraced with all love; that causest those who love thee to bear their burdens with ease, that consolest the sorrowful in enduring reproaches; that teachest the penitent how to obtain pardon for every offense. This is very honorable to the holy Angels; most lovely to men, most terrible to devils; despised by the proud, acceptable to the humble; rough to the carnal, sweet to the spiritual; insipid to the foolish, delicious to the devout; affable to the poor, companionable to the stranger; friendly to the afflicted, consolatory to the sick, comfortable to the dying. Lay up, therefore, all the sacred Wounds of Jesus, in the recesses of your heart; they have a savor beyond all spices to the devout soul that is in affliction, and that seeks not consolation from men.

Follow Christ, Who leads by His Passion and His Cross to eternal rest and light; because if ye are now His companions in tribulation, ye will shortly sit down with Him at the heavenly table in perpetual exultation. Plant in the garden of your memory, the tree of the holy Cross; it produces a very efficacious medicine against all the suggestions of the devil. Of this most noble and fertile tree, the root is humility and poverty; the bark, labour and penitence; the branches, mercy and justice; the leaves, true honor and modesty; the scent, sobriety and abstinence; the beauty, chastity and obedience; the splendor, right faith and firm hope; the strength, magnanimity and patience; the length, long-suffering and perseverance; the breadth, benignity and concord; the height, charity and wisdom; the sweetness, love and joy; the fruit, salvation and life eternal. Well, then, and worthily, sings the Church of the Holy Cross,

> Faithful Cross, above all other
> One and only noble tree;
> None in foliage, none in blossom
> None in fruit thy peers may be!

There was no such plant to be found in the gardens of Solomon, no herb so salutary for the curing of all diseases, as the tree of the Holy Cross, which bears its spices of divine virtue, for the obtaining of human salvation. This is that most fruitful tree, blessed above all the trees of Paradise;

stretching forth its lovely branches, adorned with green leaves, extended with rich fruit through the world; by its altitude, touching heaven; by its profundity, penetrating hell; by its extent, surrounding mountains and hills; by its magnitude, filling the round world; by its fortitude, conquering wicked kings and the persecutors of the faith; by its mercy, attracting the weak; by its suavity, healing sinners. This is the glorious palm, that is rightly called Christiferous, carried on the shoulders of Jesus, set up on the mountain of Calvary; condemned by the Jews, set at naught by the Gentiles, reviled by the wicked, lamented by the faithful, implored by the pious.

Blessed is the man, faithful is that servant, who perpetually carries the Sacred Wounds of Jesus in his heart; and, if adversity meets him, receives it as from the Hand of God, and piously endures it, that he may at least in some degree become conformed to the Crucified. For he is worthy to be visited and consoled by Christ, who studies fully to conform himself in life and in death to His Passion. This is the way of the Holy Cross, this is the doctrine of the Savior, this is the wisdom of saints, this is the rule of monks, this the life of the good, this the lection of clerks, this the meditation of the devout; to imitate Christ humbly, to suffer evil for Christ, to choose the bitter instead of the sweet; to despise honors, to bear contempt with equanimity, to abstain from evil delights; to fly the occasions of vice, to avoid dissipation; to lament for our own sins and for those of others, to pray for the troubled and the tempted, to render thanks for benefactors, to make supplication for adversaries that they may be converted; to rejoice with them that are in prosperity, to grieve with them that suffer injury, to succor the indigent; not to seek high things, to choose that which is humble, to love that which is simple; to cut off superfluities, to be contented with a little, to labor for virtues, to struggle every day against vices; to subdue the flesh by fasting, to strengthen the spirit by prayer and by reading, to refuse human praise; to seek solitude, to love silence, to be at leisure for God; to sigh for things celestial, to despise from the heart all that is earthly, to think that nothing save God can bring comfort. He that does this, may say with blessed Paul the Apostle, "To me to live is Christ, and to die is gain." And again: "God forbid that I should glory, save in the Cross of our Lord Jesus Christ, by which the world is crucified unto me, and I unto the world." O religious monk and follower of the stricter life, depart not from the Cross which thou hast taken up; but bear it and carry it with thee even to death; and thou shalt find eternal rest, and celestial glory and honor. When any tribulation meets thee, it is Christ Who lays His Cross upon thee, and shows thee the way by which thou must go to the heavenly kingdom. But if any one boasts himself and hopes in the glories and in the honors of this world, he is truly deceived, and he will carry with him nothing at all of that which he has been accustomed to love in the world. But he who boasts himself in Christ, and despises all things for the sake of Christ, he shall be consoled by Christ in the present life, and in the life to come shall be filled with celestial blessings, and shall felicitously rejoice with Christ and with all saints, world without end. Which Jesus Christ vouchsafe to grant us, Who for us suffered and died upon the Cross; to Whom be praise and glory, to ages of ages. Amen.

Jacob Anatoli

ca. 1250

*I*n southern France, during the late twelfth and thirteenth centuries, Jewish preachers like Jacob ben Abba Mari Anatoli participated in a transformation of Jewish intellectual life. A contemporary of the troubadour poets of Provence, Anatoli married the daughter of the translator of Maimonides' *Guide for the Perplexed* and himself rendered a number of Arabic works on logic and astronomy into Hebrew. One of his patrons for the project was the Emperor Frederick II, whom Anatoli called "our lord the great king, the Emperor Frederick II in gratitude for the stimulation and patronage of his court at Naples."

Jacob Anatoli preached to a hostile congregation, his sermons forming a cultural avant-garde for the day, as he cited Aristotle, used philosophical material, and gave allegorical interpretations of Bible stories. In his preface to the first five books of the medieval corpus (in Arabic) of Aristotle's *Organon,* he remarked that his motive for the translation was grounded in his belief that, "without knowledge of [Aristotelian] logic, we Jews are unable to stand up against the clever scholars of the other nations who polemicize against us."

It appears that Anatoli's synagogue preaching was radical for its day; in his sermons, like this one on a group of verses from the Book of Proverbs (22:28–23:12), Anatoli expresses a profound conviction about the value of education and the transmission of culture during the beginning of a dark time for the Jews in Europe. In 1229 the Inquisition in Toulouse forbade the reading of the Bible by all laymen, and in 1240 the Talmud, declared a forbidden work, was put on trial in Paris, judged guilty of blasphemy, and publicly burned. (Anatoli's preaching was perhaps informed by a historical memory of a more tolerant age in Arab Andalusia.) Despite his critique of Christian teachings, the tone of his sermons is one of respect, and the Christian scholastic Duns Scotus is referred to, in Anatoli's idealized vision of the pulpit as a courtroom where fine rhetoric, piety, and civil debate reigned, as "my learned colleague." Typically, he ends here with a benediction from the morning liturgy and an expression of hope for the enlightenment of mind and heart.

&

On Proverbs

See a man skilled at his work—he shall stand before kings, he shall not stand before obscure men.

—PROVERBS 22:29

Solomon's subject in this verse, and in the verses preceding and following it, is the supreme vocation: study of the Torah, philosophical wisdom, and the pursuit of prophecy. We already know that *skilled scribe* (Ps. 45:2; Ezra 7:6) refers to the master scholar, whose philosophical task is similar to that of a scribe diligently engaged in writing. That is why this verse was interpreted homiletically to refer to Moses our teacher. Since he was the supreme prophet, it is appropriate to call him a *man skilled at his work,* for he attained the perfection of prophecy more than anyone else because of his diligence in learning from everyone.

This is the definition of a wise man, according to the rabbis: "Who is wise? He who learns from everyone," as the Bible says, *From all my teachers I have gained insight, for Your decrees are my study.* (Ps. 119:99.) Their proof from this verse shows that they understood it to mean not that the speaker was praising himself for having greater wisdom and insight than his teachers, but that he learned and acquired wisdom from everyone he found capable of teaching him, even if that person was not of his faith, which can be a cause of hatred. But since he relies upon the Torah and applies himself to know it fully, learning from an adherent of a different religion can bring nothing but great benefit. This is the meaning of *for Your decrees are my study.*

This same idea is the subject of the preceding verse, which says, *Your commandment enables me to gain wisdom from my enemies, for it always stands by me.* (Ps. 119:98.) Because he relies and depends upon the Torah, because the commandments are an enduring support, it will benefit him to learn from everyone. This is the desired diligence with regard to wisdom: to seek it from everyone, whether esteemed or scorned, whether a believer or a heretic. An intelligent person who finds a nut breaks it open, eats the kernel, and throws away the shell. That is what Moses our teacher did when he was raised as a son by the king's daughter. Many sages were there, as was common in the courts of ancient kings, and Moses learned as a youth from every sage he encountered, both those from his own people and those from other nations. Because he excelled all others in his diligence, he achieved a status attained by no one else, either before or since.

The verse from Proverbs indicates that we should not scorn prophecy or philosophy because we see the prophet or the philosopher surrounded by inferior, unenlightened neighbors. This shows not that he lacks stature, but rather that they lack discernment. Let us recall that Moses our teacher arose powerfully against Pharaoh in response to God's instruction to lead the multitudes of the slaves out of the land. Earlier he had killed the Egyptian because he [Moses] could not endure injustice, even though the Egyptian was one of the nobles and Moses himself had an honored position in the royal palace, having been raised by the king's daughter, who loved him like a son. He was undoubtedly also wise, as his later life proves, for prophecy belongs only to one who is wise, strong, and wealthy.

Yet despite all this honor, one inferior Israelite, whom Moses tried to prevent from committing a crime, spoke to him in an insulting and threatening manner, saying *Who made you chief and ruler over us? Do you mean to kill me as you killed the Egyptian?* (Exod. 2:14.) Moses could not stand up to him, and because of this criminal he fled from his own people. But eventually, he *stood before kings* (Prov. 22:29): before a king of flesh and blood, and before the King of kings of kings, the Holy One, blessed be He.

The same verse (Prov. 22:29) can be interpreted in a different way. This is that the *ḥashukim* ("obscure men") refers to a people walking in *ḥoshek* ("darkness")—the ignorant—and *kings* refers to the philosophers, who understand the secrets of the Torah and therefore have diadems and crowns, as Solomon said, *She will crown you with a glorious diadem* (Prov. 4:9), and *Through me kings reign and rulers decree just laws* (Prov. 8:15).

Because the Torah is perfect, making the ignorant wise, and because it is necessary for everyone, since human wisdom cannot endure without religious awe and ethical discipline, Solomon warned all philosophers not to rely so much on their own wisdom that they make light of the Torah's teachings. That is why he said, *Do not remove the ancient boundary stone that your ancestors set up.* (Prov. 22:28.) He called the Torah an *ancient boundary stone* because it is the primal and eternal set of limits. And he said *your ancestors,* in the plural, because Aaron was also God's prophet. God did not transmit everything exclusively to Moses. Rather, Moses was in the position of God and Aaron of a prophet, as the Bible says, *I set you in God's place to Pharaoh; and your brother Aaron shall be your prophet.* (Exod. 7:1.)

This was because Moses our teacher was slow of speech and tongue (Exod. 4:10). Even though God worked many great and wondrous deeds through Moses, it was not God's will to remove his speech impediment by a miracle. Because of Moses' superiority over other great men, God wanted to make him somewhat lower than the angels, so that, remembering his affliction, he would recognize his human nature. This was His purpose in saying, *Who gives a person speech? Who makes a person dumb?* (Exod. 4:11.) In other words, it was God's will that Moses was slow of speech. If this were not the meaning of the verse, it would not have been a sufficient answer to Moses.

Another reason was so that Moses' perfection would not be diminished and his reception of divine inspiration interrupted. A person who causes divine inspiration to flow over others has no opportunity to draw it to himself, as the rabbis said with regard to physical matters: "While it is involved in discharging, it does not absorb." Therefore it was God's will that Aaron be his prophet, and that both of them be *ancestors*. It is possible that *your ancestors* refers to Abraham, Isaac, Jacob, Moses, and Aaron, and that *a man skilled* refers to Moses alone, for he was the most skilled, the one who *stood before kings,* not the others, as the Bible says, *But by My name YHWH I did not make Myself known to them.* (Exod. 6:2.) The meaning of this has already been explained.

After mentioning diligence in the mastery of philosophical wisdom, Solomon indicated to the student the proper method of study, saying, *When you sit down to dine with a ruler, consider well who is before you; thrust a knife into your gullet if you have a large appetite.* (Prov. 23:1–2.) The rabbis interpreted these verses as applying to a student sitting before his master, saying, "If you know that your master is capable of answering the question sensibly, you may ask it; if not, try to understand on your own; if not, *thrust a knife into your gullet; if you have a large appetite,* leave." They meant by this statement that students must not accept anything from their teacher unless the teacher explains the reason for it. This is good, appropriate advice for the student who has already worked hard and achieved something in a particular discipline, but for the beginner in that discipline it is not so.

Since the verse says *When you sit down to eat,* it seems to apply to beginners in their studies, warning them about what is necessary and appropriate. They should concentrate solely on what they hear from their teacher, thinking about it and attempting to grasp it fully. They should not allow their minds to become agitated, and they should not ask about other things, even if related to the matter at hand. This will spoil their learning; they will be so engrossed in questioning that they will not grasp properly what they have heard, and they will force their teacher to explain things out of place. The teacher must simplify for his students at the beginning, and the students must take in the material little by little, in the proper order, whether learning from a teacher or reading from a book. In this way they will master the discipline they study.

They will not do so if they act like a glutton invited to dinner. When the host cuts a slice from one side [of the roast], the glutton says, "Cut me a piece from the other side," or "Cut me a different slice." This is not good manners for one who is invited to dine. A person of refinement should graciously accept what is served. This is what Solomon meant when he said, *Thrust a* sakkin (lit., "knife") *into your gullet.* I believe that the word *sakkin* here refers not to the implement that cuts, but rather to the piece of food cut by it, which is called by the name of the implement, just as this implement is also called *ma'akelet,* because of the *okel,* or food, that it cuts. This is not so strange in our language. We find *This is the finger of God* (Exod. 8:15) referring to that which was done by means of His "finger." We also have the word *hand* used for that which is done by means of the hand. Just as a person of refinement who is invited to dine should control his appetite and eat the portion given to him, so the discerning student should accept information from his teacher in the proper order.

This applies if the teacher is known to be a true philosopher, and expert in the various disciplines of logic, which lead to truth. Referring to the student of such a teacher, Solomon said, *One who is sparing with words becomes knowledgeable, one who is reticent gains discernment. Even a fool who keeps silent is deemed wise; intelligent, if he seals his lips.* (Prov. 17:27–28.) This is a great and beneficial rule for all students: that they make their ear a hopper, never departing either in word or thought from concentrating on what the teacher says, in the precise order of presentation.

To warn against the opposite of this quality, Solomon said, *He who isolates himself seeks his own desires, and disdains all sound wisdom.* (Prov. 18:1.) This refers to the seeker, that is, the student, for both in our language and in Arabic the student is also called *seeker.* Solomon said that when the seeker isolates himself by moving from one subject to another, and *disdains all sound wisdom,* that is to say, when he mixes into everything and gets entangled there, his seeking is motivated by naked desire, not by good intentions. His purpose is to show off his knowledge of many subjects by speaking a little about one after another. Therefore Solomon said in the following verse, *A fool does not desire understanding, but only to air his thoughts.* (Prov. 18:2.)

After this, he went on to warn students not to choose as their teacher someone who speaks at great length and argues with sophistries that are false and deceiving, namely, by stating premises constructed in a sophistical way. Wisdom cannot be attained in this manner. This is what he meant when he said, *Do not crave for his dainties* (Prov. 23:3), for that food will not satiate those who eat it. Whoever stuffs his belly with it will starve his soul, for they are words filled with vanity and emptiness, *counterfeit food* (Prov. 23:3).

He may have based this metaphor on the playful prank of young boys, who sometimes put coarse bran or sand inside fine, white dough, completely concealing it. Someone who sees how beautiful it looks may want very much to taste it, but when he chews it his mouth will be filled with gravel. This is like the verse, *Bread gained by fraud may be tasty to a man, but later his mouth will be filled with gravel.* (Prov. 20:17.) He also spoke elsewhere about such teachers, who boast about their wisdom by setting up extensive premises at the beginning of their lecture, in the manner of the Mutakallimun, who are mentioned in Maimonides' *Guide.*

Concerning this kind of teacher, Solomon said, *Like clouds, wind—but no rain—is one who boasts of gifts not given.* (Prov. 25:14.) He raises clouds in the proper manner as if to reveal true secrets, and creates much wind by discussing the many false premises presented to the students. But in the end his words do not help in the attainment of truth, which is called *rain,* the goal that is sought. They are no more than clouds and wind.

This is a most corrupt method of teaching, for it leads to an unfortunate result. When the premises from which syllogisms are constructed to produce true conclusions are discovered to be false, the truth derived from these premises will be suspect. It would have been better not to have investigated such matters rationally at all. Solomon alluded to this when he said, *Those who spurn gifts will live long* (Prov. 15:27), for it is better not to accept premises established in an illogical way, but rather to rely upon tradition concerning what is found in the Torah and the other books of prophecy, even though this is not knowledge derived by logical demonstration.

Such knowledge is without doubt like rain, as is seen in the statement of the prophet Hosea, *Let us pursue knowledge of the Lord and we shall attain it. His appearance is as sure as the daybreak; He will come to us like rain, like latter rain that refreshes the earth.* (Hos. 6:3.) Moses, the supreme prophet, alluded to this same matter when he said, *My speech shall distill as the dew* (Deut. 32:2), teaching that his speech was not obviously and notably beneficial like the rain. That is why there is no explicit mention of rain during the revelation at Sinai, only darkness, cloud, and thick fog (Deut. 4:11).

In fact, there *was* a little rain in the cloud and the fog, proportionate to the capacity of those who received the revelation. Little could be apprehended by all, and few could apprehend very much. Consequently, there was no general rainfall. This is what Deborah said: *O Lord, when You came forth from Seir, advanced from the country of Edom, the earth trembled, the heavens dripped, yes, the clouds dripped water.* (Judg. 5:4.) This verse teaches that no more than a few drops of rain were there.

Similarly, the psalmist said, *The earth trembled, the sky dripped, because of God, even Sinai,* and then, *With bountiful rain You quenched our thirst.* (Ps. 68:9, 10.) Maimonides alluded to this in the ninth chapter of part 3 of the *Guide:* "It was misty, cloudy, and a little rainy." It is better to live by means of that little rain than to toil after vanity, surrounded by wind and clouds that have no rain at all. Solomon referred to this when he said *clouds and wind* (Prov. 25:14). An intelligent person should strive to acquire knowledge of God, as the prophet said, *Let us pursue knowledge of the Lord and we shall attain it [His appearance is as sure as daybreak, and He will come to us like rain].* (Hos. 6:3.) The three things mentioned in this verse should be carefully examined, namely, *pursue,* which implies movement, then *daybreak,* which is the first rays of light, and then *rain.*

It makes most sense to me that *pursue* alludes to the propaedeutic disciplines, which provide the path for the pursuit of wisdom; the first rays of light allude to the natural sciences, and *rain* to the metaphysical sciences, which truly quench the thirst. It may be that the prophet hinted at this in the previous verse, *In two days He will make us whole again, on the third day He will raise us up, and we shall live in His presence.* (Hos. 6:2.) These are diverse paths, mastered one after the other. All of them together bring life from God, but the third brings perpetual life in God's presence. This is like the rain that comes from Him after proper searching, not superficial reading or inferior searching, of the Torah. Solomon warned against this when he said, *Do not crave for his dainties.* (Prov. 23:3.)

He then warned students not to disregard the precise formulation of what they learn from their teacher. This applies even to students who are extremely bright and think that they need not worry if they forget something the teacher says, since their own sharp minds will enable them to learn the subject by reviewing it themselves. Such an approach makes students too weary to attain true wealth and leads to a waste of time. Had they concerned themselves properly with the formulation of what they learned, they would not have needed to make such an effort [to review], and they would have had free time to study whatever they wanted. Solomon hinted at this when he said, *Do not toil to gain wealth, have the sense to desist. You see it, then it is gone; it grows wings and flies away, like an eagle, heavenward.* (Prov. 23:4–5.)

He went on to warn students further that they should not sit before a teacher, even one with a reputation for wisdom, if that teacher, jealous of his own disciples, withholds food and imagines that he will lose what he teaches to others. One who is stingy in this way makes his students idle and wastes their time with trivial tasks, causing them to flit from one subject to another without attaining wisdom. His own wisdom will progressively diminish, just as he imagined it would if he had taught his students properly. That would have been good for him, for his wisdom would have increased day by day. The rabbis compared this to small trees that kindle large trees. But this is not what he imagines. He thinks of it as students snatching his daily bread from him, leaving him to die of hunger. He therefore guards his wisdom as a miser guards his money, keeping what is good from those entitled to it—and thereby robbing it. One should not take up lodging with a miser, for the lodger will be dissatisfied. At the same time, the miser will act as if he is sorely aggrieved at the loss of his food, or he will die as Nabal died when the servants of David came to him. Similarly, no student should sit before such a teacher.

With this in mind, Solomon said, *Do not eat of a stingy man's food, do not crave for his dainties. He is like one keeping accounts; "Eat and drink" he says to you, but he does not really mean it.* (Prov. 23:6–7.) This shows that you will derive no benefit from a relationship with such a person. You will harm him just as he imagines you will. By pointing this out to the student, Solomon has affirmed that the teacher should not guard his wisdom as a miser would.

He then proceeds to assert that the teacher should rather guard his wisdom like a benefactor, who dispenses wealth justly, giving to those who deserve the gift and withholding from those who do not. Such benefactors do not give equally to all. Those who give generously to evil people, frequenters of prostitutes, drunkards, and idlers are not called benefactors but squanderers and wasters of money. Their influence upon the drunkard or the lecher is actually detrimental. A benefactor should therefore withhold money from such people.

Similarly, a teacher should not teach a student of unfit character, for that violates wisdom and gives it a bad reputation. The results are bad for the student, who rises to a level where he does not belong and then plummets downward. Concerning this matter, Solomon said, *The morsel you eat you will vomit; you will waste your courteous words. Do not speak to a dullard, for he will disdain your sensible words.* (Prov. 23:8–9.) One of the philosophers once said on this subject, "Do not transmit wisdom to one who is unworthy, lest you violate wisdom, and do not withhold wisdom from those who are deserving, lest you violate them."

Similarly, all philosophers who attain some philosophical insight that is not written should write it down, lest they rob those of their generation or any posterity who are worthy of it. That is why the ancients took the trouble to write books. At the same time, they should write in such a way that not everyone will apprehend what is meant in their book, lest the ignorant pervert the author's fine thoughts and show contempt for the reasoning in his words. Deep truths are not fitted to the whole people. If a matter is made explicit in a book, many people will be led to discuss what they do not understand, and they will speak rebelliously about God. The prophet or sage who has written so explicitly awakens the "sleeping dog."

Solomon alluded to this when he said, *A passerby who gets embroiled in someone else's quarrel is like one who seizes a dog by the ears.* (Prov. 26:17.) Explicit explanation of esoteric matters is *someone else's quarrel.* Silence is preferable, for the masses are troubled by ontological problems. This is as he said in subsequent verses, *For lack of wood a fire goes out; without a querulous person, contention is stilled.* (Prov. 26:20.) Regarding those who speak at length explicitly about profound matters, he said, *Charcoal for embers and wood for a fire and a contentious person for kindling strife.* (Prov. 26:21.)

Truly, this is the reason why the content of the Bible is so difficult. This is why they wrote elliptically and enigmatically, so that great scholars disagree about the meaning. Even conflicting interpretations are the words of the living God. Let no one who has aspired to perfection through philosophy fail to show respect for a single one of their words that are known by tradition, or draw heretical conclusions, or mock them, for their authors are not alive to inform us of the true meaning of what they said. This is a great sin; one who does so perverts the Torah and rebels against God.

The rabbis warned against criticizing a leading scholar in any generation, saying, "You must not argue against the lion after his death." It is all the more necessary to be careful with regard to the words of the Prophets and the Writings, and even more so with regard to the Torah. This is what

Solomon warned at the conclusion of the section when he said, *Do not remove ancient boundary stones; do not encroach upon the fields of orphans, for they have a mighty kinsman, who will surely take up their cause with you.* (Prov. 23:10–11.)

He called the sacred writings *fields of orphans* because the authors, who are the "parents," have died. As these authors are known for their wisdom or prophecy, every intelligent person should judge the content of their books favorably. All their words should be accepted as an enduring tradition, just as Solomon said: *Apply your mind to discipline, and your ears to wise sayings.* (Prov. 23:12.) May God in His mercy enable our minds to understand and to discern, to heed and to perform in love all the words of instruction in His Torah.

PART IV

"Behold I Will Make My Words in Thy Mouth Fire, and This People Wood, and It Shall Devour Them."

Rebirth, Reform, and Counter Reform

Fra Girolamo Savonarola

1452–1498

Savonarola in fifteenth-century Florence lit a furnace of passionate repentance and amendment of sin. His extraordinary eloquence, thereafter without comparison until the time of Luther, stoked "the bonfire of the vanities" associated with his reform of the moral corruption of church and state. A monk of the Dominican Order of Preachers, who held immense political and spiritual power over the city considered the cradle of the Renaissance, Savonarola attracted vast crowds to his sermons, inciting the citizens of Florence to appease their terror in the aftermath of the recent plague by casting dice, gaming tables, and books by Boccaccio and the heathen Plato onto a pyramid of vanities erected for burning in the Piazza della Signoria on the last day of the carnival before Lent in 1497. The great bonfire's doomed worldly goods and pagan frivolities included women's jewelry and perfumes, lutes, songbooks, and false hair, as well as paintings of nudes.

Savonarola's very nature seemed, according to the historian Jacob Burkhardt, "made of fire." The conflagration he ignited would eventually engulf the preacher of divine wrath himself in the vengeful wrath of the papacy he charged with simony. After Savonarola's excommunication in 1497, he was tried for heresy the next year, tortured, hanged, and burned at the stake.

A sense of imminent calamity in Savonarola's world was signaled in 1484, an *annus mirabilis,* or "extraordinary year," foreseen by astrologers and others as heralding the coming of the Antichrist and a new purification of the Church. Wars and plagues, past and future, were immediate to the itinerant preachers who prophesied a long chain of earthly disasters and a sulphurous vision of the Apocalypse. But Savonarola, who believed his calling to be the result of divine illumination, and that the preacher, in the great hierarchy of spirits, occupied a place next to that of the angels, was also "the preacher of the despairing." He addressed many of his ferocious attacks against the iniquities of the tax system and its injustice to the poor. In this sermon on the feast of the Ascension, Savonarola alludes to the humility of the biblical Balaam's ass, hurls fewer thunderbolts of rhetoric than in many of his sermons, and offers his audience a small glimpse of the redemption he hoped for Florence as the scene, one day, of the kingdom of God upon Tuscan soil.

Balaam's Ass

And Balaam rose up in the morning and saddled his ass, and went with the princes of Moab. And God's anger was kindled because he went: and the angel of the Lord stood in the way for an adversary against him. Now he was riding upon his ass, and his two servants were with him. And the ass saw the angel of the Lord standing in the way, and his sword drawn in his hand: and the ass turned aside out of the way, and went into the field: and Balaam smote the ass, to turn her into the way. But the angel of the Lord stood in a path of the vineyards, a wall being on this side, and a wall on that side. And when the ass saw the angel of the Lord, she thrust herself unto the wall, and crushed Balaam's foot against the wall, and he smote her again. And the angel of the Lord went further, and stood in a narrow place, where was no way to turn either to the right hand or to the left. And when the ass saw the angel of the Lord, she fell down under Balaam: and Balaam's anger was kindled, and he smote the ass with a staff. And the Lord opened the mouth of the ass, and she said unto Balaam, What have I done unto thee, that thou hast smitten me these three times? And Balaam said unto the ass, Because thou hast mocked me: I would there were a sword in mine hand, for now would I kill thee. And the ass said unto Balaam, Am not I thine ass, upon which thou hast ridden ever since I was thine unto

this day? was I ever wont to do so unto thee? And he said, Nay.
Then the Lord opened the eyes of Balaam, and he saw the angel
of the Lord standing in the way, and his sword drawn in his hand:
and he bowed down his head, and fell flat on his face. And the
angel of the Lord said unto him, Wherefore hast thou smitten
thine ass these three times? behold, I went out to withstand thee,
because thy way is perverse before me: And the ass saw me, and
turned from me these three times: unless she had turned from me,
surely now also I had slain thee, and saved her alive.

—NUMBERS 22:21–33

In everything am I oppressed; even the spiritual power is against me
with Peter's mighty key. Narrow is my path and full of trouble; like Balaam's
ass, I must throw myself on the ground and cry: "See, here I am; I am ready
to die for the truth." But when Balaam beat his fallen beast, it said to him:
"What have I done to thee?" So I say to you: "Come here and tell me: what
have I done to you? Why do you beat me? I have spoken the truth to you; I
have warned you to choose a virtuous life; I have led many souls to Christ."
But you answer: "Thou hast spoken evil of us, therefore, thou shouldst suffer the stripes thou deservest." But I named no one, I only blamed your vices
in general. If you have sinned, be angry with yourselves, not with me. I
name none of you, but if the sins I have mentioned are without question
yours, then they and not I make you known. As the smitten beast asked Balaam, so I ask you: "Tell me, am I not your ass? and do you not know that I
have been obedient to you up to this very moment, that I have even done
what my superiors have commanded, and have always behaved myself
peaceably?" You know this, and because I am now so entirely different, you
may well believe that a great cause drives me to it. Many knew me as I was
at first; if I remained so I could have had as much honor as I wanted. I lived
six years among you, and now I speak otherwise, nevertheless I announce
to you the truth that is well known. You see in what sorrows and what opposition I must now live, and I can say with Jeremiah: "O, my mother, that
thou hast borne me a man of strife and contention to the whole earth!" But
where is a father or a mother that can say I have led their son into sin; one
that can say I have ruined her husband or his wife? Everybody knows my

manner of life, therefore it is right for you to believe that I speak the truth which everybody knows. You think that it is impossible for a man to do what the faith I have preached tells him to do: with God it would be easy for you.

The ass alone saw the angel, the others did not; so open your eyes. Thank God, many have them open. You have seen many learned men whom you thought wise, and they have withstood our cause: now they believe; many noted masters who were hard and proud against us: now humility casts them down. You have also seen many women turn from their vanity to simplicity; vicious youths who are now improved and conduct themselves in a new way. Many, indeed, have received this doctrine with humility. That doctrine has stood firm, no matter how attacked with the intention of showing that it was a doctrine opposed to Christ. God does that to manifest His wisdom, to show how it finally overcomes all other wisdom. And He is willing that His servants be spoken against that they may show their patience and humility, and for the sake of His love not be afraid of martyrdom.

O ye men and women, I bid you to this truth; let those who are in captivity contradict you as much as they will, God will come and oppose their pride. Ye proud, however, if you do not turn about and become better, then will the sword and the pestilence fall upon you; with famine and war will Italy be turned upside down. I foretell you this because I am sure of it: if I were not, I would not mention it. Open your eyes as Balaam opened his eyes when the angel said to him: "Had it not been for thine ass, I would have slain thee." So I say to you, ye captives: Had it not been for the good and their preaching, it would have been woe unto you. Balaam said: "If this way is not good, I will return." You say likewise, you would turn back to God, if your way is not good. And to the angel you say as Balaam said: "What wilt thou that we should do?" The angel answers thee as he answered Balaam: "Thou shalt not curse this people, but shalt say what I put in thy mouth." But in thy mouth he puts the warning that thou shouldst do good, convince one another of the divine truth, and bear evil manfully. For it is the life of a Christian to do good and to bear wrong and to continue steadfast unto death, and this is the Gospel, which we, according to the text of the Gospel for today, shall preach in all the world.

What wilt thou have of us, brother? you ask. I desire that you serve Christ with zeal and not with sloth and indifference. I desire that you do not mourn, but in thankfulness raise your hands to heaven, whenever your brother or your son enters the service of Christ. The time is come when Christ will work not only in you but through you and in others; whoever hears, let him say: "Come brother. Let one draw the other. Turn about, thou who thinkest that thou art of a superior mind and therefore canst not accept the faith." If I could only explain this whole Gospel to thee word for word, I would then scourge thy forehead and prove to thee that the faith could not be false and that Christ is thy God who is enthroned in heaven, and waits for thee. Or dost thou believe? Where are thy works? Why dost thou delay about them?

Hear this: There was once a monk who spoke to a distinguished man about the faith, and got him to answer why he did not believe. He answered thus: "You yourself do not believe, for if you believed you would show other works." Therefore, to you also I say: If you believe, where are your works? Your faith is something everyone knows, for everyone knows that Christ was put to death by the Jews, and that everywhere men pray to Him. The whole world knows that His glory has not been spread by force and weapons, but by poor fishermen. O wise man, do you think the poor fishermen were not clever enough for this? Where they worked, there they made hearts better; where they could not work, there men remained bad; and therefore was the faith true and from God. The signs which the Lord had promised followed their teaching: in His name they drove out the devil; they spoke in new tongues; if they drank any deadly drink, they received therefrom no harm. Even if these wonders had not occurred, there would have been the wonder of wonders, that poor fishermen without any miracle could accomplish so great a work as the faith. It came from God, and so is Christ true and Christ is thy God, who is in heaven and awaits thee.

You say you believe the Gospel, but you do not believe me. But the purer anything is, so much the nearer it stands to its end and purpose. The Christian life purifies the heart, and places it very near to the truth. To the Christian life will I lead you, if you would have the knowledge of the truth. If I had wished to deceive you, why should I have given you as the chief of my gifts the means of discovering my fraud? I would be verily a fool to try to impose upon you with a falsehood which you would soon detect; only because I offered you the truth, did I call you. Come here, I fear you not; the closer you examine, the clearer the truth will become to you.

There are some, however, who are ashamed of the cross of Jesus

Christ, and say: If we should believe that, we should be despised every-where, especially by the wisest. But if you would know the truth, look only on the lives of those who would have to cry woe on their unbelief if they should be measured by deeds. If you are ashamed of the cross, the Lord was not ashamed to bear that cross for you, and to die on that cross for you. Be not ashamed of His service and of the defense of the truth. Look at the ser-vants of the devil, who are not ashamed in the open places, in the palaces, and everywhere to speak evil and to revile us. Bear then a little shame only for your Lord; for whoever follows Him will, according to our gospel, in His name drive out the devil; that is, he will drive out his sins, and lead a virtuous life; he will drive out serpents; he will throw out the lazy who come into the houses, and say evil things under the pretense of righteous-ness, and so are like poisonous serpents. You will see how children can with-stand them with the truth of God, and drive them away. If a believer drinks anything deadly it will not hurt him: this deadly drink is the false doctrines of the lazy, from whom, as you contend with them, a little comes also to you. But he who stands unharmed in the faith, cries to you: See that you do good; seek God's glory, not your own. He that does that is of the truth, and remains unharmed. The Lord says further of the faithful: They shall lay their hands on the sick and shall heal them. The hands are the works, and the good lay such hands on the weak that they may support them when they totter. Do I not teach you according to the Gospel? Why do you hesitate and go not into the service of the Lord? Do you ask me still what you ought to do? I will, in conclusion, tell you.

Look to Christ and you will find that all He says concerns faith. Ask the apostle; he speaks of nothing else than of faith. If you have the ground of all, if you have faith, you will always do what is good. Without faith man always falls into sin. You must seek faith in order to be good, or else your faith will become false. Christ commanded His disciples to preach the Gospel to all the world, and your wise men call a man a little world, a mi-crocosm. So then preach to yourself, O man, woman, and child. Three parts the world has in you also. Preach first of all to your knowledge, and say to it: If you draw near this truth, you will have much faith; wherefore do you hesitate to use it? To your will, say: Thou seest that everything passes away; therefore love not the world, love Christ. Thereupon turn to the second part of your world, and say to it: Be thankful, O my memory, for the mercies God has shown thee, that thou thinkest not of the things of this world but of the mercy of thy creation, and thy redemption through the blood of the Son of God. Then go to the third part, to thy imagination, and proclaim to it: Set nothing before my eyes but my death, bring nothing before me but the Crucified, embrace Him, fly to Him. Then go through all the cities of thy world and preach to them.

First say to thine eyes: Look not on vanity. To thy ears say: Listen not to the words of the lazy, but only to the words of Jesus. To thy tongue say: Speak no more evil. For thy tongue is as a great rock that rolls from the summit of a mountain, and at first falls slowly, then ever faster and more furiously. It begins with gentle murmuring, then it utters small sins, and then greater, until it finally breaks forth in open blasphemy. To thy palate say: It is necessary that we do a little penance. In all thy senses be clean, and turn to the Lord, for He it is who will give you correction and purity. To thy hands say: Do good and give alms; and let thy feet go in the good way.

Our reformation has begun in the Spirit of God, if you take it to heart that each one has to preach to himself. Then will we in the name of Jesus drive out the devils of temptation. Yes, call upon Jesus as often as temptation approaches: call upon Him a hundred times and believe firmly, and the temptation will depart. Then will we speak with new tongues; we will speak with God. We shall drive away serpents; the enticement of the senses are these serpents. If we drink anything deadly it will not hurt us; if anger and lust arise in us, at the name of Jesus they will have to give way. We shall lay our hands upon the sick and heal them; with good deeds shall we strengthen the weak soul. If thou feelest thy weakness, flee to God, and He will strengthen; therefore He is thy only refuge. He is thy Savior and thy Lord, who went into the heavens to prepare a place for thee, and to wait thee there. What do you intend to do? Go and follow Jesus, who is praised from everlasting to everlasting. Amen.

St. John Fisher

1469–1535

When John Fisher, the bishop of Rochester, was sent to the Tower for refusing to swear to the Act of Succession, under which Henry VIII established supremacy over the Church of Rome, Pope Paul III did nothing to improve his chances for survival by sending him a cardinal's hat. Fisher lived in a tempestuous time, as a courtier and sympathizer of the aristocratic ideal who remained fervent in his support of the Old Religion during its rough transformation, under Henry VIII, to the Church of England. A founder of a college at Cambridge University and an early patron of Erasmus, whom he invited to lecture there on Greek, he wrote three treatises on the Lutheran Reformation before his own arrest and execution by beheading. Christendom throughout Europe was outraged by his fate; Fisher was not canonized until the 1930s, a decade in Europe in which the need for saints, martyrs, and spokesmen may have seemed more urgent than ever. A preacher who believed in both the dignity of constituted authority and the resistance of principle to its transgressions, his invocation here of lions, tigers, and bears and the treachery of the world must have evoked, to his audience during the Tudor reign, something of the commerce with king and court which cost him his life.

His adherence to the old creed is matched by a passion, originality, and independence which contribute to his particular talent for English prose and the ability of a poet to capture the imagery of the external world by fusing the Anglo-Saxon word with classical synonyms. Fisher's scholarship and his graceful prose became, as one of his editors has remarked, part of the art which made his preaching a cornerstone in shaping the eloquence of the English pulpit.

Dependence upon Divine Mercy

That man were put in great peril and jeopardy that should hang over a very deep pit holden up by a weak and slender cord or line, in whose bottom should be most *woode* and cruel beasts of every kind, abiding with great desire his falling down, for that intent when he shall fall down anon to devour him, which line or cord that he hangeth by should be holden up and stayed only by the hands of that man, to whom by his manifold ungentleness he hath ordered and made himself as a very enemy. Likewise, dear friends, consider in yourself. If now under me were such a very deep pit, wherein might be lions, tigers, and bears gaping with open mouth to destroy and devour me at my falling down, and that there be nothing whereby I might be holden up and succoured, but a broken bucket or pail which should hang by a small cord, stayed and holden up only by the hands of him to whom I have behaved myself as an enemy and adversary by great and grievous injuries and wrongs done unto him. Would ye not think me in perilous conditions? yes, without fail. Truly all we be in like manner. For under us is the horrible and fearful pit of hell, where the black devils in the likeness of ramping and cruel beasts doth abide desirously our falling down to them. The lion, the tiger, the bear, or any other wild beast never layeth so busily await for his prey, when he is hungry, as doth these great and horrible hell hounds, the devils, for us. Of whom may be heard the saying of Moses: *Dentes bestiarum immittam in eos cum furore trahentium atque serpentum.* I shall send down among them wild beasts to gnaw their flesh, with the *woodness* of cruel birds and serpents drawing and tearing their bones. There is none of us living but that is holden up from falling down to hell in as feeble and frail vessel, hanging by a weak line as may be. I beseech you what vessel may be more *bruckle* and frail than is our body that daily needeth reparation. And if thou refresh it not, anon it perisheth and cometh to naught. An house made of clay, if it be not oft renewed and repaired with putting to of new clay shall at the last fall down. And much more this house made of flesh, this house of our soul, this vessel wherein our soul is holden up and borne about, but if it be refreshed by oft feeding and putting to of meat and drink, within the space of three days it shall waste and slip away. We be daily taught by experience how feeble and frail man's body is. Also beholding daily the goodly and strong bodies of young people, how soon they die by a short sickness. And therefore Solomon, in the book called Ecclesiastes, compareth the body of man to a pot that is *bruckle,* saying, *Memento creatoris tui in diebus juventutis tuæ, antequam conteratur hydria super fontem.* Have mind on thy Creator and Maker in the time of thy young age, or ever the pot be broken upon the fountain, that is to say, thy body, and thou peradventure fall into the well, that is to say into the deepness of hell. This pot, man's body, hangeth by a very weak cord, which the said Solomon in the same place calleth a cord or line made of silver. *Et antequam rumpatur funiculus argenteus.* Take heed, he saith, or ever the silver cord be broken. Truly this silver cord whereby our soul hangeth and is holden up in this pot, in this frail vessel our body, is the life of man. For as a little cord or line is made or woven of a few threads, so is the life of man knit together by four humors, that as long as they be knit together in a right order so long is man's life whole and sound. This cord also hangeth by the hand and power of God. For as Job saith, *Quoniam in illius manu est anima (id est vita) omnis viventis.* In this hand and power is the life of every living creature. And we by our unkindness done against His goodness have so greatly provoked Him to wrath that it is marvel this line to be so long holden up by His power and majesty, and if it be broken, this pot our body is broken, and the soul slippeth down into the pit of hell, there to be torn and all to rent of those most cruel hellhounds. O good Lord how fearful condition stand we in if we remember these jeopardies and perils, and if we do not remember them we may say, O marvelous blindness, ye our madness, never enough to be wailed and cried out upon. Heaven is above us, wherein Almighty God is resident and abiding, which giveth Himself to us as our Father, if we obey and do according unto His holy commandments. The deepness of hell is under us, greatly to be abhorred, full of devils. Our sins and wickedness be afore us. Behind us be the times and spaces that were offered to do satisfaction and penance, which we have negligently lost. On our right hand be all the benefits of our most good and meek lord, Almighty God, given unto us. And on our left hand be innumerable misfortunes that might have happed if that Almighty God had not defended us by his goodness and meekness. Within us is the most stinking abomination of our sin, whereby the image of Almighty God in us is very foul deformed, and by that we be made unto Him very enemies. By all these things before rehearsed we have provoked the dreadful majesty of Him unto so great wrath that we must needs fear, lest that He let fall this line our life from His hands, and the pot our body be broken, and we then fall down into the deep dungeon of hell. Therefore what shall we wretched sinners do, of whom may help and succor be had and obtained for us? By what manner sacrifice may the wrath and ire of so great a majesty be pacified and made easy? Truly the best remedy is to be swift in doing penance for our sins. He only may help them to that be penitent. By that only sacrifice His ire is mitigate and suaged chiefly. Our most gracious Lord Almighty God is merciful to them that be penitent. Therefore let us now ask His mercy with the penitent prophet David. Let us call and cry before the throne of His grace, saying, *Miserere mei Deus.* God have mercy on me.

Martin Luther

1483–1546

The Augustinian monk who taught biblical exegesis at Wittenberg, until his famous nailing of the Ninety-five Theses on the church door produced the foremost document of the Protestant Reformation, never ceased to conduct on the printed page his campaign for the revival of the primacy of faith over works. Banned by the papacy at the Diet of Worms in 1521, Luther left the monastic order, married, and committed himself and his life to forming the League of Protestantism. He then went on to produce an outpouring of hymns, which altered the relation of congregations to the church service, and a flow of so many polemical pamphlets and sermons as to make him the first religious heir to Johannes Gutenberg's invention of movable metal type. Gutenberg's Bible, an edition in 1456 of the Vulgate, in St. Jerome's late-fourth-century Latin translation, had additional significance in Luther's career when Martin Luther himself translated the

Old and New Testaments into German, a monumental literary and intellectual task, completed by 1534.

His stamina as preacher was equally formidable, sometimes, as his *Table Talk* admits, leading to four sermons in one day. The Weimar edition of his sermons runs to more than two thousand texts, although his editors have remarked that his treatises, much of his *Large Catechism,* and his *Articles* are themselves in essence all powerful sermons. Their formal structure, a legacy of his scholastic training, controls without extinguishing the force of his reforming fire and the tempestuousness of his personality. It is striking to notice the "objective" character of the preaching of this individual and rebel against the Church, and the way in which the simple biblical text becomes the living and inescapable Word of God through the very act of delivery in the pulpit.

This sermon on "The Raising of Lazarus" was probably recorded by a stenographer faithful to Luther's dynamic use of direct address. It reads as an imaginary dialogue between the preacher and his adversaries and reflects the brilliant dramatization of the issues of the theological battleground which Martin Luther's life and work engaged so tirelessly. Moreover, as it was for many of the great writers of the sixteenth century, Luther's German was stimulated by the possibilities of a freer, looser, and more vernacular paraphrase of the Bible. One commentator on the Lazarus sermon finds it a miniature treatise on salvation through the agency of the Divine, and an essential part of Luther's fierce debate on how God comes to us only in Christ, as the "door, anchor, and path," to Him, the way out of the tomb.

Sermon on the Raising of Lazarus, John 11:1–45

Preached on the Friday after Laetare, March 19, 1518

Then said Jesus unto them plainly, Lazarus is dead. And I am
glad for your sakes that I was not there, to the intent ye may believe; nevertheless, let us go unto him.

Dear Friends of Christ. I have told you the story of this Gospel in
order that you may picture in your hearts and remember well that Christ
our God, in all the Gospels, from beginning to end, and also all writings of
the prophets and apostles, desires of us nothing else but that we should have
a sure and confident heart and trust in him.

Augustine writes that we find in the Scriptures three dead persons
whom Christ restored to life. First, a twelve-year-old girl, when he was
alone in a house, behind closed doors, and in the presence only of the parents of the deceased girl and his intimate disciples (Matt. 9:18–26). Second,
the only son of a widow, who was being carried out through the gate in the
presence of all the people (Luke 7:11–17). Third, Lazarus, of whom this
Gospel tells us, is not raised by Christ privately in a house or at the gate, but
one who had been in the grave for four days and is raised in the presence of
many Jews and near Jerusalem.

According to Augustine's teaching, these three dead persons are to be
understood as three kinds of sinners. The first are those whose souls have
died. This is when temptation comes and conquers and captures the heart,
so that one consents to sin. Then follows a sense of pleasure and the evil poison begins to work its way in, kills the soul, and subjects it to the devil. This
is represented by the twelve-year-old girl. This kind rises up without too
much difficulty after a fall. With persons of this kind God deals in a very
tender way. He speaks to them secretly, sends inward instruction to their

hearts, which they alone hear and cannot evade, and prepares for them a rod of chastisement, which they must suffer to their grief.

The second dead person signifies those who have fallen into works, so that they have to be carried, since they cannot walk by themselves. These must take heed; otherwise, since one thing leads to another, they may, as St. Gregory says, be completely overborne by the weight of sins. It is the bier in which the dead person is carried.

Lazarus, finally, signifies those who are so entangled in sin that they go beyond all bounds; they drift into a habit (of sinning) which then becomes their very nature. They know nothing but sin; they stink and are buried in sin. It takes a lot of work (to save them). This is shown by the fact that in the case of the maiden Christ had only to take her by the hand and she immediately became alive (Matt. 9:25). The young man, however, sat upright, but not so easily as in the case of the maiden, for Luke writes that Christ first touched the bier and afterwards said, "Young man, I say to you, arise" (Luke 7:14). This had to be accomplished through a command. But in this story, Christ looked up to heaven and said, "Father, I thank thee that thou hast heard me," and then cried with a loud voice, "Lazarus, Lazarus, come out" (John 11:41, 43). And he came out, bound hand and foot, and his face also, and the apostles had to unbind him. This is the grave, the tomb: habituation in sin.

A question. If it is true that Lazarus and the other dead persons must be understood as signifying sin, how does this accord with the Gospel when the evangelist says in the speech of Martha, "Lord, he whom you love is ill" and "See how he loved him"? (John 11:3, 36). Is it not true that Christ does not love the sinner but rather the truth, as the Scriptures say, "You love righteousness and hate wickedness" (Ps. 45:7) and "In my sight the sinner is scorned"? (cf. Ps. 5:5). The answer is this: My dear man, (comfort yourself with this saying,) "I came not for the sake of the righteous, but to make righteous what is unrighteous and sinful and to lead the sinners to repentance" (cf. Matt. 9:13).

The whole human race was worthy of hatred, and yet Christ loved us. For if he had not loved us, he would not have descended from heaven. For the prophet says in the psalm: "There is none that does good," except one; "they have all become corrupt and sinners" (cf. Ps. 14:3) except Christ alone. So Christ loves the sinner at the command of the Father, who sent Him for our comfort. So the Father wills that we should look to Christ's humanity and love him in return, but yet in such a way as to remember that he did all this at the bidding of the Father's supreme good pleasure. Otherwise it is terrifying to think of Christ. For to the Father is ascribed power, to the Son, wisdom, and to the Holy Spirit goodness, which we can never attain and of which we must despair.

But when we know and consider that Christ came down from heaven and loved sinners in obedience to the Father, then there springs up in us a bold approach to and firm hope in Christ. We learn that Christ is the real epistle, the golden book, in which we read and learn how he always kept before him the will of the Father. So Christ is the "access to the Father" (Eph. 2:18) as St. Paul says. And John too bears witness that Christ said, "I am the way, and the truth, and the life" (John 14:6). "I am also the door" (John 10:7) and "no one comes to the Father, but by me" (John 14:6). Now we see that there is no shorter way to the Father except that we love Christ, hope and trust in him, boldly look to him for everything good, learn to know and praise him. For then it will be impossible that we should have a miserable, frightened, dejected conscience; in Christ it will be heartened and refreshed. But the Scriptures say concerning the sinners: "The wicked shall perish and be driven away like dust" (cf. Ps. 1:4, 6). Therefore the sinners flee and know not where to go; for when the conscience does not hope and trust in God it cowers and trembles before the purity and righteousness of God. It can have no sweet assurance; it flees and still has nowhere to go unless it finds and catches hold of Christ, the true door and anchor. Yes, this is the way that all Christians should learn. But we go plunging on, taking hold in our own name, with our understanding and reason, and do not see or ever take to heart how kindly, sweetly, and lovingly Christ has dealt with people. For the Father commanded him to do so. This tastes sweet to the faithful soul and it gives all the glory, praise, and honor to the Father through the Son, Christ Jesus. So God has nothing but the best and he offers it to us, weeds us, sustains us, and cares for us through his Son. That's the way our hearts are changed to follow Christ.

This is the way that Peter and Paul, the two leaders of the church, and all the other apostles taught with great diligence. Above all, they love the Father, as they declare in many passages: "Blessed be the Father, who has blessed us with every heavenly blessing through Jesus Christ" (Eph. 1:3). Therefore, let no one undertake to come to God except over this bridge.

This is the path that does not lead astray. Christ says, "Everything that my Father commands me I do" (John 14:31), and "I thank thee, dear Father, that thou hearest me always; but not for my sake, but for the sake of those who are standing down here, that they may believe that thou didst send me" (John 11:41–42). What he is saying is: If they see my love and my works, and that thou are effecting them, and that thou hast commanded me to do them, then they will be at one with thee and will know thee through me and my works; out of which then will grow thy love toward them, O Father. The reason why Christ loves sinners is that his Father commanded him to do so. For in Christ the Father pours himself out in his grace. And all this serves to the end that we freely hope in Christ and trust him unafraid.

Therefore, let the works go, no matter how great they may be, prayers, chants, yammering, and yapping; for it is certain that nobody will ever get to God through all these things. Besides, it is impossible. Rather the heart must have love for Christ, and through him, for the Father. It's all lost if the heart is not cleansed. It must all be left behind, and we must freely, boldly, and with sure confidence take the leap into God. That's what he wants of us.

But when we put forward our works, the devil will use them for his own end, and that's just what he does do with them. Let us therefore learn to know from the Gospel how kindly Christ deals with us; then we shall without a doubt love him and avoid sinning, and so see everything in a different light. See how kindly he draws our hearts to himself, this faithful God. He loves Lazarus, who was a sinner. He tolerates the timid faith of his disciples when they say, "Oh, Lord, don't go to Jerusalem, they will kill you" (John 11:8). All this he would have condemned, if he had wanted to deal harshly. "Ah," said his disciples further, "if Lazarus is sleeping, as you say, then it isn't necessary for you to go there" (John 11:12). And what about Mary and Martha? "Oh, Lord," they said, "if you had been here, our brother would not have died" (John 11:21). And also they were earthly, so that they were unable to refrain from weeping and the people had come to them to console them because of the death of their brother, as the evangelist describes so skillfully. From this we learn that they were all in unbelief and sin. And then we see how kindly the Lord deals with them, praying and weeping with them, and all this at the behest of his Father. This is the true guidebook, from which we learn the will of the eternal Father.

Take note, then, all you who have a timid conscience, that you will not
be saved by this or that work. For it will fare with you as with one who
works in a sandpit: the more sand he shovels out the more falls upon him.
That's why many have gone mad, as John Gerson says, so that they began to
imagine things, one that he was a worm, another that he was a mouse, and
so on. Just commit it to God and say: "Oh, my dear God, I have sinned, but
I confess it to thee, I pour it out to thee and pray thee for help; do thou help
me!" This is what God wants of us.

That's why I should like sermons about the saints to be more moderate in the sense that we would also tell how *they* fell, in accord with the
gospel, not the books of rhetoric. For there can be no doubt that they too
tripped and stumbled over great humps. They were of one flesh with us, one
faith, one baptism, one blood. But we have now set them so high above us
that we must despair of imitating them. Thus, for example, the gospel
speaks of Peter after his confession concerning Christ, when he said to him,
"You are the Christ, the Son of the living God" (Matt. 16:16). But soon afterwards he had to take these words: "Get behind me, Satan, you devil!"
(Matt. 16:23) whereas just a while before he had been told, "Blessed are
you, Simon Bar-Jona!" (Matt. 16:17). Just look; first he is blessed and holy,
and afterwards he topples into hell and is called a devil.

So it is: every one of us by himself is a devil, but in Christ we are holy.
So when we thus connect the saints with Christ, they are Christ's true
saints; but if we are not to despair, we must follow him.

This Gospel therefore expresses nothing but the sweetness of Christ
in his obedience to the Father and that he bestows nothing because of
merit. Therefore, when the devil assaults us with temptation, you say this:
"Ah, even though I have done nothing that is good, nevertheless I will not
despair, for He always dealt with men sweetly," and that is true. Only the
damned must remain until they have paid the last penny (Matt. 5:26). This
the Scriptures show again and again. In Ecclesiasticus (2:10) it is written,
"Who was ever forsaken by God?" Jerome says, "Cursed be he who holds
that Christ's power is flesh," and again, "Blessed be he who hopes in God."
And to Jeremiah God says, "Hear me, because you have hoped in me, I will
deliver you with power, and even though the city go down, I will preserve
you" (Jer. 39:16–18). From this we should learn how Christ loves us, even

though he might justly be angry, in order that we should also love our brethren. Look, this is the way God treats you! What are you going to do? You too must have a heart that is sweet toward him. Do this, then, forthwith! This I say in order that . . .

Hugh Latimer

1485–1555

The death of Hugh Latimer, by burning at the stake outside Balliol College, Oxford, made him one of the most celebrated martyrs in the history of religion. His last words on October 15, 1555, following a year of imprisonment in a common jail after the accession of Mary Tudor, were to his former colleague and fellow sufferer: "Be of good comfort, Master Ridley, and play the man. We shall this day light such a candle by God's grace in England, as I trust shall never be put out."

Preaching was the great vocation of Latimer's life. His father, as one sermon mentions, was a yeoman farmer who had "walked for a hundred sheep"; his mother "milked thirty kine." He shifted, with a conscience ever troubled by doubts and reservations about its results for English society, from the convictions of the Roman Catholic priesthood into the doctrines of the Reformation. Latimer was particularly opposed to Roman Catholic belief in the utility of pilgrimages, the intercession of the Blessed Virgin Mary and the saints, and prayers for the dead. (Lady Jane Grey was so schooled in the same Protestant aversion that her final words on the scaffold implored the watchers to pray for her only while she was "alive.") Henry VIII became his patron when Latimer supported his divorce from Catherine of Aragon; he became Anne Boleyn's chaplain, and when royal caprice and contentiousness with the reforms he advocated demoted him from favor, Hugh Latimer, bishop of Worcester, resigned. The bloody drama of the

Tudor dynasty finally involved its spiritual doyen when Edward VI's brief reign ended and Latimer, declining opportunities to escape to the Continent, was condemned, under Catholic Queen Mary, as a heretic.

The language of his sermons heralds a heroic age of the English language, sonorous and yet rippling with images of the homely and domestic. The record we have of his preaching is due to the tireless devotion of a Swiss servant who served as Latimer's scribe. Although he preached before kings and gentry, he was no docile court functionary, and his courageous plain speaking on the "rich citizens of London" must have troubled the audience on the wet winter day in 1548 when they heard the "Sermon of the Plow" in the "Shrouds," or covered indoor area of the crypt of the cathedral church of St. Paul's, London, used instead of the outdoor Paul's Cross pulpit when the weather was inclement.

Sermon of the Plow
January 18, 1548

Quaecumque scripta sunt ad nostram doctrinam scripta sunt.

—ROMANS 15:4

All things which are written are written for our erudition and knowledge. All things that are written in God's book, in the Bible book, in the book of the Holy Scripture, are written to be our doctrine.

. . . Now what shall we say of these rich citizens of London? what shall I say of them? Shall I call them proud men of London, malicious men of London, merciless men of London? No, no, I may not say so; they will be offended with me then. Yet must I speak. For is there not reigning in London as much pride, as much covetousness, as much cruelty, as much oppression, and as much superstition, as there was in Nebo? Yes, I think, and much more too. Therefore, I say, Repent, O London! repent, repent. Thou hearest thy faults told thee; amend them, amend them. I think, if Nebo had had the preaching that thou hast, they would have converted.

Oh London, London! repent, repent; for I think God is more displeased with London than ever he was with the city of Nebo. Repent, therefore; repent, London, and remember that the same God liveth now that punished Nebo, even the same God, and none other; and He will punish sin as well now as He did then: and He will punish the iniquity of London as well as He did them of Nebo. Amend, therefore. And you that are prelates, look well to your office; for right prelating is busy laboring, and not lording. Therefore preach and teach, and let your plow be going. Ye lords, I say, that live like loiterers, look well to your office—the plow is your office and charge. If you live idle and loiter, you do not your duty, you follow not your vocation; let your plow therefore be going, and not cease, that the ground may bring forth fruit.

But now methinks I hear one say unto me: "Wot ye what you say? Is it a work? Is it a labor? How then hath it happened that we have had for so many hundred years so many unpreaching prelates, lording loiterers, and idle ministers?" You would have me here to make answer, and to show the cause thereof. Nay, this land is not for me to plow, it is too stony, too thorny, too hard for me to plow. They have so many things that make for them, so many things to say for themselves, that it is not for my weak team to plow them. They have to say for themselves long customs, ceremonies, and authority, placing in Parliament, and many things more. And I fear this land is not yet ripe to be plowed; for, as the saying is, it lacketh weathering: it lacketh weathering, at least it is not for me to plow. For what shall I look for among thorns, but pricking and scratching? What among stones, but stumbling? What, I had almost said, among serpents, but stinging? But this much I dare say, that since lording and loitering hath come up, preaching hath come down, contrary to the apostles' time: for they preached and lorded not, and now they lord and preach not. For they that are lords will ill go to plow: it is no meet office for them; it is not seeming for their estate. Thus came up lording loiterers: thus crept in unpreaching prelates, and so have they long continued. For how many unlearned prelates have we now at this day! And no marvel; for if the plowmen that now are were made lords, they would give over plowing; they would leave off their labor, and fall to lording outright, and let the plow stand: and then both plows not walking, nothing should be in the commonweal but hunger. For ever since the prelates were made lords and nobles, their plow standeth, there is no work done, the people starve. They hawk, they hunt, they card, they dice, they pastime in their prelacies with gallant gentlemen, with their dancing minions, and with their fresh companions, so that plowing is set aside. And by the lording and loitering, preaching and plowing is clean gone. And thus, if the plowmen of the country were as negligent in their office as prelates are, we should not long live, for lack of sustenance. And as it is necessary to have this plowing for the sustentation of the body, so must we have also the other for the satisfaction of the soul, or else we can not live long spiritually. For as the body wastes and consumes away for lack of bodily meat, so the soul pines away for default of spiritual meat. But there are two kinds of enclosing, to hinder both these kinds of plowing; the one is an enclosing to hinder the bodily plowing, and the other to hinder the holy day plowing, the Church plowing.

But now for the fault of unpreaching prelates, methinks I could guess what might be said for excusing of them. They are so troubled with lordly living, they are so placed in palaces, couched in courts, ruffling in their rents, dancing in their dominions, burdened with embassages, pampering themselves like a monk that maketh his jubilee; and moiling in their gay manors and mansions, and so troubled with loitering in their lordships, that they can not attend it. They are otherwise occupied, some in the king's matters, some are embassadors, some of the privy council, some to furnish the court, some are lords of the Parliament, some are presidents, and some comptrollers of mints.

Well, well, is this their duty? Is this their office? Is this their calling? Should we have ministers of the Church to be comptrollers of the mints? Is this a meet office for a priest that hath cure of souls? Is this his charge?

The glory of God shall be spread abroad throughout all parts of the realm, if the prelates will diligently apply to their plow, and be preachers rather than lords. But our blanchers, who will be lords, and no laborers, when they are commanded to go and reside upon their cures, and preach in their benefices, they would say, Why? I have set a deputy there; I have a deputy that looks well to my flock, who shall discharge my duty. A deputy, quoth he, I looked for that word all this while. And what a deputy must he be, trow ye? Even one like himself; he must be a Canonist; that is to say, one that is brought up in the study of the Pope's laws and decrees; one that will set forth papistry as well as himself will do; and one that will maintain all superstition and idolatry; and one that will not at all, or else very weakly, resist the devil's plow; yea, happy it is if he take no part with the devil; and where he should be an enemy to him, it is well if he take not the devil's part against Christ. But in the mean time, the prelates take their pleasures. They are lords, and no laborers; but the devil is diligent at his plow. He is no unpreaching prelate; he is no lordly loiterer from his cure; but a busy plowman; he still applieth his business. Therefore, ye unpreaching prelates, learn of the devil; to be diligent in doing of your office, learn of the devil; and if you will not learn of God, nor good men, for shame learn of the devil; "I speak it for your shame"; if you will not learn of God, nor good men, to be diligent in your office, learn of the devil. Howbeit there is now very good hope that the king's majesty, being by the help of good governance of his most honorable counselors, trained and brought up in learning, and knowledge of God's word, will shortly provide a remedy, and set an order herein; which thing that it may so be, let us pray for him. Pray for him, good people; pray for him. You have great cause and need to pray for him.

CB

Duties and Respect of Judges

I will tell you my Lords Judges, if ye consider this matter well, ye should be more afraid of the poor widow, than of a nobleman with all the friends and power that he can make. But nowadays the Judges be afraid to hear a poor man against the rich, insomuch, they will either pronounce against him, or so drive off the poor man's suit, that he shall not be able to go through with it. The greatest man in a realm can not so hurt a Judge as the poor widow, such a shrewd turn she can do him. And with what armour I pray you? She can bring the Judge's skin over his ears, and never lay hands upon him. And how is that? *Lacrimae miserorum descendunt ad maxillas,* the tears of the poor fall down upon their cheeks, *et ascendunt ad cælum,* and go up to heaven, and cry for vengeance before God, the judge of widows, the father of the widows and orphans. Poor people be oppressed even by laws. *Væ iis qui condunt leges iniquas.* Woe worth to them that make evil laws. If woe be to them that make laws against the poor, what shall be to them that hinder and mar good laws? *Quid facietis in die ultionis?* What will ye do in the day of vengeance, when God will visit you? He saith, he will hear the tears of poor women when he goeth on visitation. For their sakes he will hurt the judge, be he never so high. *Deus transfert regna.* He will for widows' sakes change realms, bring them into subjection, pluck the judges' skins over their heads.

Cambyses was a great Emperor, such another as our master is; he had many Lord deputies, Lord presidents, and Lieutenants under him. It is a great while ago since I read the history. It chanced he had under him in one of his dominions a briber, a gift taker, a gratifier of rich men, he followed gifts, as fast as he that followed the pudding, a hand maker in his office, to make his son a great man, as the old saying is, Happy is the child whose father goeth to the Devil.

The cry of the poor widow came to the Emperor's ear, and caused him to flay the judge quick, and laid his skin in his chair of judgment, that all judges, that should give judgment afterward, should sit in the same skin. Surely it was a goodly sign, a goodly monument, the sign of the judge's skin: I pray God we may once see the sign of the skin in England. Ye will say peradventure that this is cruelly and uncharitably spoken: no, no, I do it charitably for a love I bear to my country. God saith, *Ego visitabo,* I will visit. God hath two visitations. The first is, when he revealeth his word by preachers and where the first is accepted, the second cometh not. The second visitation is vengeance. He went a visitation, when he brought the judge's skin over his ears. If his word be despised he cometh with his second visitation with vengeance.

Noah preached God's word an hundred years, and was laughed to scorn, and called an old doating fool. Because they would not accept this first visitation, God visited the second time: he poured down showers of rain till all the world was drowned.

Lot was a visitor of Sodom and Gomorrah, but because they regarded not his preaching, God visited them the second time, and brent them all up with brimstone saving Lot. Moses came first a visitation into Egypt with God's word, and because they would not hear him, God visited them again, and drowned them in the Red Sea. God likewise with his first visitation, visited the Israelites by his prophets, but because they would not hear his prophets, he visited them the second time, and dispersed them in Assyria and Babylon.

John Baptist likewise and our Savior Christ visited them afterwards declaring to them God's will, and because they despised these visitors, he destroyed Jerusalem by Titus and Vespasianus.

Germany was visited twenty years with God's word, but they did not earnestly embrace it, and in life follow it, but made a mingle-mangle and a hotchpotch of it, I can not tell what, partly popery, partly true religion mingled together. They say in my country, when they call their hogs to the swine trough, Come to thy mingle-mangle, come pyr, come pyr: even so they made mingle-mangle of it.

They could clatter and prate of the Gospel, but when all cometh to all, they joined popery so with it, that they marred all together, they scratched and scraped all the livings of the church, and under a color of religion turned it to their own proper gain and lucre. God, seeing that they would not come unto his word, now he visiteth them in the second time of his visitation with his wrath. For the taking away of God's word, is a manifest token of his wrath. We have now a first visitation in England: let us beware of the second. We have the ministration of his word, we are yet well, but the house is not clean swept yet.

God has sent us a noble King in this his visitation, let us not provoke him against us, let us beware, let us not displease him, let us not be unthankful, and unkind, let us beware of bywalking and contemning of God's word, let us pray diligently for our king, let us receive with all obedience and prayer, the word of God. A word or two more and I commit you to God. I will monish you of a thing. I hear say ye walk inordinately, ye talk unseemly other ways than it becometh Christian subjects. Ye take upon you to judge the judgments of judges. I will not make the king a Pope, for the Pope will have all things that he doth, taken for an Article of our faith. I will not say but that the king, and his council may err, the Parliament houses both the high and low may err. I pray daily that they may not err. It becometh us whatsoever they decree to stand unto it, and receive it obediently, as far-forth as it is not manifestly wicked, and directly against the word of God; it pertaineth unto us to think the best, though we cannot tender a cause for the doing of every thing. For *Caritas omnia credit, omnia sperat,* Charity doth believe and trust all things. We ought to expound to the best all things, although we cannot yield a reason.

Therefore I exhort you good people pronounce in good part all the facts and deeds of the magistrates and judges. Charity judgeth the best of all men, and specially of magistrates. St. Paul saith, *Nolite judicare ante tempus donec dominus advenerit,* Judge not before the time of the lord's coming. *Pravum cor hominis,* Man's heart is unsearchable, it is a ragged piece of work, no man knoweth his own heart, and therefore David prayeth and saith *Ab occultis meis munda me,* Deliver me from my unknown faults. I am a further offender than I can see. A man shall be blinded in love of himself, and not see so much in himself as in other men, let us not therefore judge judges. We are comptible to God, and so be they. Let them alone, they have their counts to make. If we have charity in us we shall do this. For *Caritas operatur,* Charity worketh. What worketh it? marry *Omnia credere, omnia sperare,* to accept all things in good part. *Nolite judicare ante tempus,* Judge not before the Lord's coming. In this we learn to know Antichrist, which doth elevate himself in the church, and judgeth at his pleasure before the time. His canonizations and judging of men before the Lord's judgment, be a manifest token of Antichrist. How can he know Saints? He knoweth not his own heart, and he can not know them by miracles. For some miracle workers shall go to the devil. I will tell you what I remembered yesternight in my bed. A marvelous tale to perceive how inscrutable a man's heart is. I was once at Oxford (for I had occasion to come that way, when I was in my office), they told me it was a gainer way, and a fairer way, and by that occasion I lay there a night. Being there I heard of an execution that was done upon one that suffered for treason. It was (as ye know) a dangerous world, for it might soon cost a man his life for a word's speaking. I cannot tell what the matter was, but the judge set it so out that the man was condemned. The twelve men came in, and said guilty, and upon that, he was judged to be hanged, drawn, and quartered. When the rope was about his neck, no man could persuade him that he was in any fault, and stood there a great while in the protestation of his innocency. They hanged him and cut him down somewhat too soon afore he was clean dead, then they drew him to the fire, and he revived, and then he coming to his remembrance confessed his fault, and said he was guilty. O a wonderful example! It may well be said, *pravum cor hominis et inscrutabile,* a crabbed piece of work and unsearchable. I will leave here, for I think you know what I mean well enough.

John Calvin

1 5 0 9 – 1 5 6 4

*T*he flippant "no pain, no gain" mantra of a generation of strivers in the physical-fitness gymnasiums and corporate corridors of America in the last two decades has an antecedent which might surprise the secular heirs of John Calvin's Protestant ethic: this French Protestant reformer derided the notion of "no toil, no pain, no trouble," and gave the rise of capitalism a theological base.

Calvin was born Jean Calvin in Paris and educated in the humanism of Plato, the Stoic philosophers, and, most significantly, St. Augustine. His radical Protestant views, delivered in an inaugural ceremony at the University of Paris, compelled him to leave the city in headlong flight for Geneva. (Ironically, the eighteenth-century Enlightenment philosopher Jean Jacques Rousseau left Geneva shaking his fist at what he considered Calvin's religious despotism in the theocratic city identified most closely with Calvin's pessimistic vision of Christian life and repression of pleasure and frivolity.) His influence was immense, making him the spiritual father of John Knox and the inspiration for the dogma of Scottish Presbyterianism; his views were uncompromising, offering men and women a doctrine of human depravity after the Fall, the absolute power of the Supreme Being, the futility of good works apart from grace, and the existence of the elect, divinely predestined to be saved.

Little wonder that the anxious burden of his message, its mix of resignation, hard work, and the rational organization of the individual's life, is associated by historians as well as religious figures with the rise of the Protestant ethic as a motivating force for the rise of capitalism. But the Calvinist discipline has had another effect, beyond its widespread sowing of the idea that hard work is an external emblem of inner faith. Calvin's message on suffering and persecution has sustained many generations of Protestants, during battles for survival of the Church, and as moral and psychological sustenance, when scattered overseas as colonials, afflicted by hostile governments, or sent to hardship posts where they preached the gospel in places of great discomfort and danger.

I Know My Redeemer Lives

My breath has been offensive to my wife, and so I have entreated her for the children of my loins. Even little children reject me, and when I rise, they taunt me. My friends have held me in abomination, and those whom I loved have turned against me. My bone clings to my skin and to my flesh, and I have escaped with the skin of my teeth. Have pity upon me, have pity upon me, you my friends; for the hand of God has struck me. Why do you persecute me like God, and are you not satisfied with my flesh? I desire that my statements should be written, that they should be registered in a book, with an iron pen in lead or in rock to eternity. I know that My Redeemer is living, and finally shall stand upon the earth.

—JOB 19:17—25

Inasmuch as God has joined men, in order that one may support the other, and that each one may try to help his neighbor, and, when we can do no better, that we may have pity and compassion one for another; if it happens that we are destitute of all help, that we are molested from all sides, and that no one shows humaneness toward us, but everyone is cruel toward us, this temptation is very hard. And that is why Job in this passage complains that there was neither wife, nor friends, nor domestic servants who pitied him, but that all the world rejected him. Now when we see this, we ought to apply it to ourselves; for God permits that men fail us, that everyone estrange himself from us, in order that we may run back so much sooner to Him. In fact, while we have some support from the world's side we shall not hope in God as we must; rather, we keep our attentions here below; for also our nature is entirely inclined that way, and we are too much given to it. So God sometimes, wishing to draw us to Himself, will cause us to be destitute of all human help. Or perhaps, it will be to humble us; for it seems to us that He surely ought to have regard for us, and that we are worthy of it; and everyone blinds himself with such presumption. Our Lord, then, sometimes wishes to instruct us in humility by this means; that everyone will hate us, that we shall be rejected by great and small. So then, we shall have to think that we are not such as we have supposed. But though that may be, if this comes, let us know that still we are not forsaken by God; for we see that Job still has recourse to Him, and that he is not disappointed in his attempt. God, then, extended to him His hand, although men had rejected him and surely supposed that there was no more hope for him; it is then that God considered to do him mercy. Let us confide, then, in this. Besides, may we be taught to do our duty toward those who are afflicted, following what I have said, that He has joined us together and united us in order that we may have a community; for men ought not to entirely separate themselves. It is true that our Lord has appointed the policy that each one shall have his house, that he shall have his household, his wife, his children, each one will be in his place; yet no one ought to except himself from the common life by saying, "I shall live to myself alone." This would be to live worse than as a brute beast. What then? Let us know that God has obligated us to one another in order to help us; and at least when we see someone in need, though we cannot do him the good that we may wish to, let us be humane toward him. If we do not do this much, let us note that in the person of Job the Holy Spirit here asks vengeance against us; for there is no doubt that Job (although he was agitated by great and excessive sufferings) was always governed by the Spirit of God, and especially with respect to the general principles, that is to say, with respect to the sentences which he uttered; as we have declared that they implied profitable doctrine. Let us note, then, that our Lord here declares that we are too cruel when we see a poor, afflicted man and we do not try to help him but rather we withdraw from him.

Let us also note that sometimes we can gather good doctrine even from things said incidentally in Holy Scripture: as here Job, speaking of his wife, says that *she could not bear his breath, although he entreated her for the sake of the children of his loins.* This shows that children ought to add to the love between the husband and the wife. For when God blesses a marriage with descendants, that ought to increase the mutual affection to live in greater concord. Pagans have known this well; but it is poorly observed by those who surely ought to see more clearly. And what condemnation will be for believers, who boast of having been taught in the Word of God, if they do not recognize that which nature has shown to the ignorant poor who are as it were blind! There are, then, pagans who have confessed that children were as it were earnests to better confirm the love between husband and the wife, to hold them in peace and union. Following this, Job says that he entreated his wife for the sake of the children which he had begotten by her. Now this did not move her at all. It shows, then, that it is a thing against nature, and that his wife showed herself to be like a savage beast in this situation. So let us note that those who cannot follow such an order are here rebuked in passing, as if the Holy Spirit had pronounced their sentence in explicit terms. Yet we see many who have no discretion, though God has done them the grace of giving them children. Here is a man who will have lived with his wife; it is true that marriage is already a thing so sacred that this word alone ought to well suffice, when it is said, "They will be two in one flesh," for the man to hold the union which he should have with his wife more precious than that which he will have with respect to father and mother; but when God yet adds as a superabundant confirmation of this grace, that the marriage produces children, if men and women are so brutal that they are not induced and incited by this to love each other still more, it is certain that their ingratitude is too base. Now (as we have already said) it is a thing very poorly practiced among Christians; but we must profit by this word, although it is here mentioned only incidentally.

Job, to add to the evil, says, *that friends, and the men of his counsel,* that is to say, those to whom he was accustomed to communicating all his secrets, *have turned against him,* or perhaps, have mocked him, that they no longer held him to be of any account; and that not only those who had some reputation or position despised him, but *the smallest,* the most ill-starred. He indicates, in summary, that he finds himself destitute of all help, seeing that his friends have failed him. Secondly, that he has been in such shame that the most despised of the world still have not deigned to consider him as of their rank. He surely had to say that his affliction was great, seeing that there was no one who recognized him as of the company of men; but that he was already more than exterminated. This, in summary, is what Job wished to say. Now (as we have already mentioned) God wished thus to train him, in order that he might be an example to us. If it happens, then, that those who are our nearest neighbors should be deadly enemies, and that they should persecute us, let us learn to run back to God, and to bear it patiently, seeing that it happened to Job before us. And let us remember even what is said of our Lord Jesus Christ, because He belongs to all the members of His Church, "He who ate bread at My table has lifted up his heel against me." (Ps. 41:9.) This must be fulfilled in all believers; and for this cause our Lord Jesus has shown us the way, in order that we may not be too much offended by being conformed to His image. We shall see, then, all the blows, that the children of God will be betrayed and persecuted by those in whom they had fully confided, and with whom they had had great intimacy. Well: this is a very hard thing, no one can deny it, and when we experience this evil, it is enough to make us lose courage; but since our God has declared to us that so it must be, and He has given us a witness to it in the person of His Only Son, let us overlook it and submit to this condition. This is still what we have to observe in this passage.

We come now to what Job adds. *"Pity me, pity me, you my friends; for the hand of God has touched me,"* he says. It is true, when we see that God punishes men, that we surely ought to glorify Him, saying, "Lord, Thou art just." But there was a special consideration in Job, who was not punished by God for faults that he had committed, it was for another purpose; and yet let us consider what would have been the case if he had been chastised according to what he deserved, yet when we shall see a poor evildoer whom God will have led to his condemnation, so we must be touched in ourselves, indeed, for two reasons. The one is, that when each one will look at himself, we shall find that God ought to punish us even more severely, when it should please Him to visit us according as we have deserved. Whosoever, then, will think of himself, will find himself blameworthy to be punished by God as grievously as those whom he sees hard pressed; and so we ought to regard them in pity and compassion. So, our vices and our iniquities ought to make us humble. There is a poor, miserable fellow; I see that God persecutes him: it is a horrible thing. But what of it? There is cause enough for which God could also punish me; I must, then, be humble, and I must look at myself in the person of this one. That is one item. And then, when we shall see a man who will have been afflicted as greatly as possible by the hand of God, may we know not only that he was created in the image of God, but also that he is neighbor to us, and as it were one with us; we are all of one nature, we have one flesh, we are mankind, that is to say, we came out of one same source. Since it is so, must we not think one of another, "Furthermore, I see a poor soul who is going to perish; ought I not to have compassion to relieve him, if it is in me?" And though I may not have the means, I ought to aspire to do it. These are (I say) the two reasons which ought to move us to pity when we see that God afflicts those who are worthy of it. When, then, we think of ourselves, it is certain that we must be very hard and stupid, or we shall have pitied those who are like us, as when we shall recognize, "Here is a man who is formed in the image of God, he is a soul which has been bought by the blood of the Son of God. If he perishes, ought we not to be touched by it?"

It is why Job says now, "*Pity me, my friends, since the hand of God has struck me.*" To understand this still better, we must take this sentence: "It is a horrible thing to fall into the hands of the Living God." (Heb. 10:31.) When, then, we see some punishment which God sends, we must be moved with fright, even though He spares us. I shall be at rest, and God seemingly will not touch me at all, but I shall see how He strikes one, how He afflicts another; is it not something to be astonished at? Must we wait for God to strike our heads with great blows? It would be too base. But when we see that He wishes to instruct us at the expense of others, we must consider the cause why He punishes men so, as Saint Paul shows us. (Eph. 5:6.) He does not say, "Fear ye, for the wrath of God will come upon you"; but he says, "My friends, you see how God punishes unbelievers, while He spares you; so you must know that it is for your instruction when He gives some sign of His wrath upon men." Let us note, then, this sentence of the Apostle, namely: It is a frightful thing to fall into the hands of God; and whenever He does some punishment, may we be moved. Now from this we shall be fully instructed to pity those who endure, by saying, "Alas! Here is a poor creature; if it were a mortal man who afflicted him, he could be given some alleviation; but God is against him; and ought we not to have pity as we see this?" If someone argues, "Is it not resisting God if we pity those who are chastised for their faults? Is it not as if we wished to set ourselves against the justice of God?" No; for we surely can have these two motives in us: (1) to approve the justice of God, giving Him glory and praise for what He does; and nevertheless (2) we allow ourselves to pity those who are punished, since we have deserved as much or more, since we ought to seek the salvation of all, whether those who are our near neighbors or whether there will be some bond that God will have placed between us; as we shall approve earthly justice, which is only as it were a little mirror of the justice of God, and yet we allow ourselves to pity an evildoer. When a criminal is punished, it is not said that he is wronged, nor that there was cruelty in the judge. It is said, then, that those who are constituted to enforce justice acquit themselves of their duty and that they offer a sacrifice acceptable to God when they cause a criminal to die; however we allow ourselves to pity a poor creature who suffers for his evil deeds; if we are not moved by it, there is no humaneness in us. If we recognize this in human justice which is only as it were a little spark from God; when we come nigh to the sovereign throne, I pray you, ought we not in the first place to glorify God in all that He does, knowing that He is just and equitable in everything and through everything? Nevertheless, this will not hinder us (as I have said) (1) from having compassion on those who endure, to care for them and to relieve them; and when we can do no better, (2) from desiring their salvation, praying God that in the end He may make their corrections profitable to draw them back to Himself, that He may not permit that they may remain hardened to chafe against His hand.

This is, I say, the basis upon which Job requests and exhorts his friends to pity him. He speaks especially to those who were closest to him; for although God has put some unity among men in general, that is to say, He has joined them all together (as we have said) and they ought not to separate themselves from each other; yet God obliges us doubly when we have either parenthood or some other bond, as we know that relatives ought to be incited to bear toward each other some more private friendship; for then God has put men, as one might put beasts under a yoke, saying after a fashion, "Brute beasts ought to teach us what we have to do." When two oxen are yoked together, if one wishes to be balky, they will torment each other; and if they do not agree to work together with one accord, then afterwards both to drink and to sleep, they will have to be there as their own tormentors. So it is with men when God draws some near to others in any manner whatever; it is as if He wishes to couple them under the same yoke to help and to support one another; and if they are balky, if they are worse than brute beasts, what condemnation do they deserve upon their heads? So then, let us note well, that according as God draws us together, and gives us means of communicating together, He obligates us to one another, for a friend will be so much more attached to his friend, although our charity must be general, and though we should love those whom God commends to us, and who might even be our deadly enemies; yet the husband will be more attached to his wife, the father to his children, the children to the father, the relatives also to one another; and in general we must recognize all the degrees of friendship which God has put in the world.

Now Job adds, *"Why do you persecute me like God?"* It surely seems that this sentence is not very reasonable here; for it is said (as we have already mentioned) that the just will wash his hands in the blood of the iniquitous. We ought, then, to rejoice when we see that God punishes the wicked; now Job states here that one ought not to persecute those whom God persecutes. But this question was already solved when we said that we can well agree with the justice of God; and yet we allow ourselves to pity those who endure, and to relieve them, if it is in our power; for at least we shall be moved to desire their salvation. It will be, then, a cruel thing when we shall persecute men like God. And why so? For when God afflicts sinners (I do not say the righteous like Job, but those who will have lived in evil, who will have been of a wicked life) it is not that we may raise our heads against them, and that we may molest them still further; but He wishes in the first place that each one of us may learn to condemn himself in the person of the other. I see that this one is now beaten by the rods of God. And why so? For his sins. Now is not God Judge of all the world? This includes me, then; for am I innocent? Alas! There are only too many faults, and only too base. This, then, is how in the person of another, one ought to condemn himself, whenever we contemplate in the other the chastisements which God sends; and then also God wishes to train us to pity and compassion. If we follow this order, we cannot go wrong; but if without regard to our faults we come to torment those who already have too much evil, is not this cruelty? We wish to usurp the office of God to be judges; and rather we ought to think of what is said, "We must all appear before the judgment-seat of God." It is true (as we have already said) that God must surely be glorified through all the punishments which He sends to men; but this is not to say that each one ought not to condemn himself, and to be held to some humaneness through this means; when we shall know that God must be the Judge of all. And that is why Job argues rightly with his friends that they persecute him like God. Let us note well, then, that if God displayed His vengeance upon those who have offended Him, it is not that He wishes to arm us to be inhumane, and to set us in fury against the poor patients who are entirely beaten down; but rather he wishes that we may have compassion on them.

Besides, Job here accuses his friends of cruelty, saying that they cannot be satisfied with his flesh. *"Why,"* he says, *"can you not be satisfied with my flesh?"* It is certain that this is a figure of speech which he uses; for when we are thus set (as they say) against our neighbors, it is as if we wished to eat them alive; and we also use these mannerisms of speech in our common language. So then, as a man will take pleasure in his meal, to eat, and to drink; also those who are cruel against their neighbors—it seems that they wish to make their repast, that they wish to eat and to gobble them alive. That, then, is why Job says, *"Why are you not satisfied with my flesh?"* For when we see that our neighbors have more and more evil, and still we are not satisfied, but we add to their evil, and still we are not satisfied, it is too great a cruelty, it is like eating them. This circumstance, then, is to be noted when Job says, "At least his friends ought to be satisfied to see him thus beaten down. What do you wish more? I am at the extremity, so that I can take no more." It is a natural thing, that when we shall have hated some person, and desired evil against him, and sought all the means to avenge ourselves; however if the worst possible affliction happens to him, then our rage is appeased. Now I do not say that this feeling ought here to be held as a virtue; for pagans, although they were wicked, though they supposed that vengeance was lawful for them, yet had the consideration to be appeased when they saw that their enemies were so molested that they need not inflict anything further with their hands. How so? Here is a man who will have done evil to someone; or perhaps, he who will be offended will wish to avenge himself, if it were possible to him. However, God goes before and sends some great calamity to the one who will have offended him; the man who previously was embittered, and asked only to ruin him whom he hated, will say now, "Indeed, and what more shall I do? He is so cast down that he is even to be pitied, he has had enough." This, then, is how the fire will be extinguished naturally, when we shall have been the most irritated man in the world against someone, if we see him in affliction. This (as I have said) is not virtue, and deserves to be counted neither as the service of God nor as charity. However, if it is a natural inclination, even among pagans, what about those today who are not satisfied when they see their enemies persecuted as much as possible, but they are insatiable and would still wish to have eaten them? And if it is condemnable when one is not satisfied with the afflictions that God sends upon enemies, how much more so will it be to act this way toward friends? So may those who are so cruel know that they are not worthy to be counted as of the number of men. Whoever, then, wishes to acquit himself of his duty, not only ought to be appeased by the evil and the affliction of his enemies; but he ought to be moved to pity; and instead of seeking vengeance, he ought rather to be ready to help them as much as he can; for there is no doubt when God sends some affliction to our enemies, and to those who have irritated us, that he wishes to soften the malice and the ill will which is in us, that He wishes to change that which causes us to be ill affected toward our neighbors. Now if God calls us to humaneness, and we go entirely the opposite way, is it not fighting against Him openly? Let us note well, then, when God afflicts those who have done us some wrong and injury, that it is to soften the spite that is in our hearts; and if we have previously been angered and piqued, or we have desired vengeance, that God wishes to moderate all these evil affections in us, and wishes to induce us to compassion and humaneness. This is what we have to note from this passage.

Now Job adds still new complaints of his miseries, saying *that his bone was attached to his skin, and that he has escaped with the skin of his teeth.* It is to better express the proposition that we already discussed: namely, that his friends surely ought to be satisfied, though they were like beasts seeking only to devour. And why? "For," says he, "you can see in what state I am. What do you ask more? Can anyone desire more evil to one person than God has sent to me?" Now when he says that his skin is attached to his bones, it is as if he said that he is all dried up, that he is like a corpse, that there is no longer juice or substance in him. When he says that he has escaped with the skin of his teeth, it is to indicate that there is no health in him except in his gums, or that his skin looks like his gums, for if vermin have spread in a body, the skin will no longer be dry; but it will look like the gums; that is to say, when the rot will spread, all will be eaten, bloody flesh will be seen, and there will come out half blood, half water, as from a wound, as we see that a wound looks like the gums. Here, then, is Job who declares that he was so disfigured that the appearance of a man was no longer recognized in him. Now when he came to this extremity, was it not reasonable that his friends should be satisfied? We are, then, here admonished to have more consideration for the afflictions of our friends than we do; and that when God will send them some calamities, we should pray to Him that He may give us grace to have our eyes more open to consider them, and to note them well, so that it may induce us to pity; that everyone may be employed in applying the remedy as much as he can, and that even at the end we should hope that when they are touched by the hand of God, He will show mercy toward them.

Now because Job was accused by his friends of having blasphemed against God, in that he justified himself against all reason, and in that he was blinded in his vices, not recognizing them; he says, *"I would that my statements were written, that they were engraved with an iron pen, that they were engraved in lead or in a stone to eternity,* and as a permanent memorial." Job, speaking thus, declares that he has not maintained his innocence in vain, and that he fears only what would be a reproach to him before God; for he knows that he has just cause to do it. This is, in summary, what he maintains. Now it is very certain with respect to the statements of Job, that some were excessive, there were many extravagant sentences; for he did not keep himself in bounds, and though he had a good and reasonable foundation, and though his case was approved by God, yet he pleaded it poorly (as we have previously declared) and there escaped from his mouth many words which were to be condemned. Why, then, does he now say that he would like his statements to be thus written? Is it not to bring double condemnation upon his head? Let us note that Job considered the principle, and that he was not bound by each word that he had pronounced; but he makes here these statements to defend his case. Now this defense was just; and although it was overly labored, and though he wandered from one side to the other, nevertheless he maintains rightly that he was not afflicted for his sins, and they must not think that he was the most wicked man in the world because God showed such severity against him. Job, then, proposed this rightly; yet he was still at fault, since he did not so recognize all his vices and he surely did not always consider himself guilty before God. By this we are admonished to speak very prudently. It is said in Psalm 39:2, "I resolved to keep my mouth closed, to bridle myself while the wicked have dominion and they hold sway; but in the end I could not contain myself." David knew well that when the children of God are tempted, seeing themselves oppressed by afflictions, while the wicked achieve their victories and have clear sailing, it is such a hard thing that it is very difficult for us to contain ourselves, that we should not murmur against God. For this cause he says, "I have resolved to hold myself as it were in check, I have put a sling over my lower jaw, I have barred my mouth, in order not to sound a word; but in the end all these checks were broken, all the resolution that I had made could not keep me from showing the desire that I had conceived within; and the fire in the end is lighted and broken out." By this David shows that it is a virtue very great and very rare, that we should be patient in silence and in restraining ourselves when wicked men press us, and above all when we see that the wicked have their mouths wide open to glorify themselves and to mock us. So, by joining this passage of David with the example of Job, we ought to be instructed to keep our mouths closed when God afflicts us. And why? For according as our passions are violent, although we may learn to speak in such simplicity as we ought, and to praise God, and to bless Him; still we cannot be so prudent or so moderate that nothing may escape us, that some froth may not come out, so that we shall always be guilty in our statements. So then, although we may not intend to blaspheme against God, or to say something which may not be to his honor, still it can only happen that we have been too bold in our speaking; as when Job asked that everything might be recorded, that all might be engraved as a memorial, that it should be put either in rock or in lead, in order that it could never be erased. Rather, let us be advised to pray to God that, with respect to the statements that we suppose are the cleanest, He may still pardon us our faults; for he who will be able to hold his tongue (says James 3:2) will have a rare virtue. For we are as ready to speak evil as can be, and when we suppose ourselves to have spoken perfectly uprightly, God will find that there will still be some excess. This, then, is what we have to note from this passage.

Now in the end Job adds, *that he knows that his Redeemer lives.* It is true that this could not be understood as fully then as now; so we must discuss the intention of Job in speaking thus. He intends, then, that he was not acting the part of a hypocrite by pleading his cause before men, and by justifying himself; he knew that he had to do with God. This is what we must know, for these sentences, if they were taken as out of their context, would not be to great edification, and we would not know what Job wished to say. Therefore let us remember what we have discussed. What does Job maintain? We know that men try as much as they can to excuse themselves, indeed, since they do not think of God; it is enough that the world is satisfied with them, and that they be considered gentlemen. This is the hypocrisy which engenders impudence. For if I do not know that God is my Judge, oh, I shall be satisfied that men applaud me, that they hold me in good reputation. And what have I gained? Nothing whatever. Is it not a great impudence, when, though my own conscience rebukes me, though I am convicted of having done evil, yet I put up a front and say, "Why am I accused? What have I done, Have I not a good case?" I shall make beautiful pretenses to cover my sin, and when I shall have so dazzled the eyes of men, behold, my case won. But it is what I have said, that hypocrisy engenders impudence, that is to say, that men are bold to maintain their case as good, since they have no regard for God.

Now Job, on the contrary, says, *"I know that my God is living, and that He shall stand in the end upon the dust."* As if he said, "I may be considered as a wicked and desperate man, as if I had blasphemed against God, trying to justify myself against him. No, not at all. I ask only to humble myself and to rest in His grace; however, I maintain my integrity against you, for I see that you proceed here only by slanderous words; I, then, defend myself in such a way that I regard God and have my eyes fixed on God." Now from this we can and ought to gather good instruction: namely, that we should not be as hypocrites, covering ourselves before men, making believe to maintain a good case, and showing ourselves to be gentlemen, while our conscience rebukes us. Let us learn, rather, to examine ourselves, to know our sins, and to humble ourselves before God; let us begin, I say, by saying, Now, how is it with me? It is true that I could easily excuse myself before men, but of what profit would it be to me before God? Would he accept me? No, not at all. According to this, then, let all of us, both great and small, come before this heavenly Judge, and let each one present himself there to ask forgiveness for his faults; and let us not doubt that when we come there sincerely, we are absolved by Him, not because we deserve it, but through His grace and mercy.

Now let us bow in humble reverence before the face of our God.

John Knox

1505–1572

*J*ohn Knox's preachings and his tracts belong to the school of fulmination: his objects of wrath in works like *Blasts of the Trumpet Against the Monstrous Regiment of Women* (an English critic has remarked that the title is the best part of the work) were various. They included Queen Elizabeth, Mary Queen of Scots (whom he called "Jezebel"), and the Roman Catholic Church in general.

Educated at Glasgow University, employed after some study of law as a notary, and called to the ministry of the Reformed Church, the Scots preacher met John Calvin in Geneva, where his contact with the French theologian intensified his own theory of predestination: salvation through grace at the expense of salvation through works. But where Calvin's Presbyterian reforms found utterance in a French prose of great precision and austerity, John Knox's sulphurous words still seem to scorch the page.

In British history, the closest parallel to Knox in self-confident faith and an untiring appetite for partisan conflict is Oliver Cromwell; the vehemence of Knox's language resembles the speech of an Old Testament prophet, not an evangelist of the New. A speaker at his graveside stated, "Here lies one who never feared the face of man." Knox's enemies had considerable and lingering reason to fear him and the power of his fierce and often pitiless tongue.

"O Lord Our God, Other Lords Besides Thee Have Ruled Us"

A Sermon preached on August 19, 1565

O Lord our God, other Lords besides thee have ruled us; but we will remember thee only, and thy Name.

The dead shall not live, neither shall the dead arise, because thou hast visited and scattered them, and destroyed all their memory.

Thou hast increased the nation, O Lord: thou hast increased the nation: thou art made glorious: thou hast enlarged all the coasts of the earth.

Lord, in trouble have they visited thee: they poured out a prayer when thy chastening was upon them.

Like as a woman with child, that draweth near to the travail, is in sorrow, and crieth in her pains, so have we been in thy sight, O Lord.

We have conceived, we have borne in pain, as thou we should have brought forth wind: there was no help in the earth, neither did the inhabitants of the world fall.

Thy dead men shall live, even with my body shall they rise.

Awake, and sing, ye that dwell in dust: for thy dew is as the dew of herbs, and the earth shall cast out the dead.

Come, my people: enter thou into thy chambers, and shut thy doors after thee: hide thyself for a very little while, until the indignation pass over.

For lo, the Lord cometh out of his place, to visit the iniquity of the inhabitants of the earth upon them: and the earth shall disclose her blood, and shall no more hide her slain.

—ISAIAH 26:13–21

As the cunning mariner, being master, having his ship tossed with vehement tempest, and winds contrarious, is compelled oft to traverse, least that either by too much resisting to the violence of the waves, his vessel might be overwhelmed; or by too much liberty granted, to be carried whither the fury of the tempest would, his ship should be driven upon the shore, and so make shipwreck. Even so doth our Prophet Isaiah, in this text, which presently ye have heard read; for he, foreseeing the great desolation that was decreed in the counsel of the Eternal, against Jerusalem and Judah; to wit, that the whole people that bear the name of God should be dispersed; that the holy city should be destroyed; the temple wherein was the Ark of the Covenant, and where God had promised to give his own presence, should be burnt with fire; the King taken; his sons in his own presence murdered; his own eyes immediately after to be put out; the nobility, some cruelly murdered, some shamefully led away captives; and finally, the whole seed of Abraham razed, as it were, from the face of the earth. The Prophet, I say, fearing these horrible calamities, doth, as it were, sometimes suffer himself, and the people committed to his charge, to be carried away with the violence of the tempest, without further resistance; than by pouring forth his and their dolorous complaint before the Majesty of God; as in the 13, 17, and 18 verse of this present text we may read. At other times he valiantly resisteth the desperate tempest, and pronounceth the fearful destruction of all such as trouble the Church of God; which he pronounceth, that God will multiply even in such time as when it appeareth utterly to be exterminate. But because there is no final rest to the whole body till that the head return to judgment, he calleth the afflicted to patience, and promiseth such a visitation, as whereby the wickedness of the wicked shall be disclosed, and finally recompenced in their own bosoms.

These are the chief points which, by the grace of God, we intend more largely at this present to entreat.

Vers. 13. *First, the Prophet sayeth, "O Lord our God, other Lords besides thee have ruled us."*

This, no doubt, is the beginning of this dolorous complaint, in the which he first complaineth of the unjust tyranny that the poor afflicted Israelites sustained during the time of their captivity. True it is, that the Prophet was gathered to his fathers in peace before that this extremity apprehended the people. For a hundred years after his decease, was not the people led away captive; yet, he, foreseeing the assurance of the calamity, did before hand indict unto them the complaint that after they should make.

But at the first sight it appeareth that the complaint hath small weight. For what new thing was it that other Lords than God in his own person ruled them, seeing that such had been their regiment from the beginning? For who knoweth not that Moses, Aaron, and Joshua, the Judges, Samuel, David, and other godly rulers, were men, and not God; and so other Lords than God ruled them in their greatest prosperity.

For the better understanding of this complaint, and of the mind of the Prophet, we must first observe from whence all authority and dominion floweth; and secondly, to what end powers are appointed of God: The which two points being discussed, we shall the better understand what Lords, and what authority rules beside God, and who are they in whom God and his merciful presence rules.

The first is resolved to us by the words of the Apostle, saying, "There is no power but of God." David bringeth in the eternal God speaking to Judges and rulers, saying, "I have said, ye are Gods, and the sons of the most highest." (Psalm 83.) And Solomon, in the person of God, affirmeth the same, saying, "By me kings reign, and princes discern the things that are just." Of which places it is evident, that it is neither birth, influence of stars, election of people, force of arms, nor, finally, whatsoever can be comprehended under the power of nature, that maketh the distinction betwixt the superior power and the inferior, or that doth establish the royal throne of kings; but it is the only and perfect ordinance of God, who willeth his power, terror, and Majesty in a part, to shine in the thrones of Kings, and in the faces of Judges, and that for the profit and comfort of man; so that whosoever would study to deface the order of regiment that God hath established, and by his holy word allowed, and bring in such a confusion as no difference should be between the upper powers and the subjects, doth nothing but evert and turn upside down the very throne of God, which he will to be fixed here upon earth, as in the end and cause of this ordinance more plainly shall appear; which is the second point we have to observe, for the better understanding of the Prophet's words and mind.

The end and cause then, why God printeth in the weak and feeble flesh of man this image of his own power and Majesty, is not to puff up flesh in opinion of itself; neither yet that the heart of him that is exalted above others shall be lifted up by presumption and pride, and so despise others; but that he shall consider that he is appointed Lieutenant to one, whose eyes continually watch upon him, to see and examine how he behaveth himself in his office. St. Paul in few words, declareth the end wherefore the sword is committed to the powers, saying, "It is to the punishment of the wicked doers, and unto the praise of such as do well." (Romans 13.)

Of which words, it is evident that the sword of God is not committed to the hand of man, to use as it pleaseth him, but only to punish vice and maintain virtue, that men may live in such society as before God is acceptable. And this is the very and only cause why God hath appointed powers in this earth. For such is the furious rage of man's corrupt nature, that unless severe punishment were appointed, and put in execution upon malefactors, better it were that man should live among brute and wild beasts than among men.

But at this present I dare not enter into the description of this common place; for so should I not satisfy the text, which, by God's grace, I purpose to absolve. This only by the way, I would that such as are placed in authority should consider whether they reign and rule by God, as that God ruleth them; or if they rule without, besides, and against God, of whom our Prophet doth here complain.

If any lust to take trial of this point, it is not hard; for Moses, in the election of Judges, and of a King, describeth not only what persons shall be chosen to that honor, but doth also give to him that is elected and chosen, the rule by the which he shall try himself, whether God reign in him or not, saying, "When he shall sit upon the throne of his kingdom, he shall write to himself an examplar of this law in a book, by the priests the Levites: It shall be with him, and he shall read therein all the days of his life, that he may learn to fear the Lord his God, and to keep all the words of this law, and these statutes, that he may do them; that his heart be not lifted up above his brethren, and that he turn not from the commandment, to the right hand or to the left."

The same is repeated to Joshua, in his inauguration to the regiment of the people, by God himself, saying, "Let not the book of this law depart from thy mouth; but meditate in it day and night, that thou may keep it, and do according to all that which is written in it; for then shall thy way be prosperous, and thou shalt do prudently." (Joshua 1.)

The first thing then that God craveth of him that is called to the honor of a King is, The knowledge of his will revealed in his word.

The second is, An upright and willing mind to put in execution such things as God commandeth in his law, without declining either to the right or left hand.

Kings then have not an absolute power in their regiment what pleaseth them; but their power is limited by God's word: so that if they strike where God commandeth not, they are but murderers; and if they spare when God commandeth to strike, they and their throne are criminal and guilty of the wickedness that aboundeth upon the face of the earth, for lack of punishment.

O! if kings and princes should consider what accompt shall be craved of them, as well of their ignorance and misknowledge of God's will, as for the neglecting of their office!

But now to return to the words of the Prophet. In the person of the whole people he doth complain unto God, that the Babylonians (whom he calleth "other Lords besides God," both because of their ignorance of God, and by reason of their cruelty and inhumanity), had long ruled over them in all rigor, without pity or compassion had upon the ancient men and famous matrons; for they being mortal enemies of the people of God, sought by all means to aggravate their yoke, yea, utterly to have exterminate the memory of them and of their religion from the face of the earth.

After the first part of this dolorous complaint, the Prophet declareth the protestation of the people, saying, "Nevertheless, only in thee shall we remember thy name" (others read it, *But we will remember thee only and thy name*); but in the Hebrew there is no conjunction copulative in that sentence. The mind of the Prophet is plain, to wit, that notwithstanding the long-sustained affliction, the people of God declined not to a false and vain religion, but remembered God, that sometime appeared to them in his merciful presence, which albeit then they saw not, yet would they still remember his Name; that is, they would call to mind the doctrine and promise which sometimes they heard, albeit in their prosperity they did sufficiently glorify God, who so mercifully ruled in the midst of them. . . .

Wouldest thou, O Scotland, have a King to reign over thee in justice, equity, and mercy? Subject thou thyself to the Lord thy God, obey his commandments, and magnify thou that word that calleth unto thee, "This is the way, walk into it" (Isaiah 30), and if thou wilt not, flatter not thyself—the same justice remaineth this day in God to punish thee, Scotland, and thee,

Edinburgh, in special, that before punished the land of Judea and the city of Jerusalem. "Every realm or nation," saith the prophet Jeremiah, "that likewise offendeth, shall be likewise punished." But if thou shalt see impiety placed in the seat of justice above thee, so that in the throne of God (as Solomon doth complain) reigneth nothing but fraud and violence, accuse thy own ingratitude and rebellion against God. For that is the only cause why God taketh away (as the same prophet in another place doth speak) "the strong man and the man of war, the judge and the prophet, the prudent and the aged, the captain and the honorable, the counselor and the cunning artificer." "And I will appoint, sayeth the Lord, children to be their princes, and babes shall rule over them. Children are extortioners of my people, and women have rule over them." (Isaiah 3.)

If these calamities, I say, apprehend us, so that we see nothing but the oppression of good men, and of all godliness, and wicked men without God to reign above us; let us accuse and condemn our selves as the only cause of our own miseries. For if we had heard the voice of the Lord our God, and given upright obedience unto the same, God should have blessed us, he should have multiplied our peace, and should have rewarded our obedience before the eyes of the world.

PART V

"When Pulpits Did
Like Beacons Flame"

The Seventeenth Century

Lancelot Andrewes

1555–1626

The famous line that opens T. S. Eliot's "Journey of the Magi," "A cold coming we had of it," is drawn from Sermon XV of Lancelot Andrewes's *Nativity Sermons*. In the full flush of his conversion to the Anglican Church, Eliot more than acknowledged his debt to the great divine of Jacobean England. In the twentieth-century poet's 1928 essay "For Lancelot Andrewes," Eliot ranks Andrewes's sermons, with their metaphysical wit, style, and playful display of wide learning, with the finest English prose of the day. Eliot found in Andrewes the spirited and assured voice of the "first great preacher of the English Catholic Church," cherishing his style for its structure, precision, and intensity. He so admired his religious passion that in comparing Andrewes to Donne he described John Donne as something of a "religious spellbinder, the Reverend Billy Sunday of his time." His reduction of Donne to a footstool for Andrewes must be taken as evidence of his enthusiasm for this dazzling scholastic rhetorician and preacher, at a court where the disputatious mode of theological and philosophical debate was a recreation of the highest order. Andrewes's contemporary audience loved to cross swords over epigrams, paradox, riddles, quotation matching, and punning conundrums. It is difficult to imagine a Lancelot Andrewes, first knight at the theological court of James I, without an abundance of courtiers whose own gifts were a suitable match for his high level.

Bishop Andrewes was a brilliant and precocious scholar, a lover of languages, and a lover of the natural world who delighted in long walks and observations of the countryside and its creatures; the swiftness and directness of his homeliest and even archaic metaphors owe something to his solitary strolls. We are not surprised then, in reading Andrewes, to find him declaring that "Christ is no Wild-Cat," to note a selective emphasis on the seasons of the wheeling calendar worthy of both great poets who were his contemporaries and the great poet of the twentieth century who, perhaps through perverse overstatement, brought him to our attention.

The incarnation of Jesus Christ was central to Andrewes's religious conviction and to his sermons. It informed their verbal exuberance in unfolding the great drama of how the Word ascended heavenward, just as the Son of God became man. Andrewes's celebrated Nativity Sermon XV was preached before the court of St. James's between 1605 and 1624. His text is the star of Bethlehem, the lodestar that draws us to it and shows us the Way. Early in the sermon he cites it as "the day-star of faith rising in our hearts." In reading this sermon with its intricate and not always easy play on Latin tenses and its wordplay on the Latin (*vidimus* refers to seeing; *venimus* to coming), and in grappling with its verbal pyrotechnics and antique allusions, it is helpful to remember that the very theme of Andrewes's message involves the difficulty of any route to the divine presence. In his vision, the epiphany was a hard-won experience, even for magi and kings.

A Cold Coming

Now when Jesus was born in Bethlehem of Judaea in the days of Herod the king, behold, there came wise men from the east to Jerusalem, Saying, Where is he that is born King of the Jews? for we have seen his star in the east, and are come to worship him.

—MATTHEW 2:1–2

Now, for *venimus*, their *coming* itself. And it follows well. For, it is not a *star* only, but a *Load-star:* And whither should *stella Ejus ducere*, but *ad Eum?* whither lead us, but to *Him*, whose the *star* is? to the *Stars Master*.

All this while we have been at *dicentes*, saying and seeing: Now we shall come to *Facientes*, see them do somewhat upon it. It is not *saying* or *seeing* will serve St. James: He will call, and be still calling for *Ostende mihi, show me* thy Faith by some Work. And, well may he be allowed to call for it, this

Day: It is the day of *Vidimus,* appearing, Being seen. You have seen His star: Let Him now see your star, another while. And so, they do. Make your faith to be seen: So it is: Their *Faith,* in the *steps* of their *Faith.* And, so was *Abraham's,* first, by *coming* forth of his country; As, these here do, and so *walk in the steps of the faith of Abraham;* do his first work.

It is not commanded, to stand *gazing into heaven* too long, Not *on Christ Himself ascending:* much less on His *star.* For, they sate not still gazing on the *star.* Their *Vidimus* begat *Venimus;* their *seeing* made them *come;* come a great journey. *Venimus* is soon said; but a *short word:* But, many a wide and weary step they made before they could come to say *Venimus,* Lo, here *we are come; Come,* and at our journeys end. To look a little on it. In this their *Coming,* we consider, 1. First, the *distance* of the Place they came from. It was not hard by, as the *shepherds* (but a step to *Bethlehem* over the fields:) This was riding many hundred miles, and cost them many a days journey. 2. Secondly, we consider the *way,* that they came: if it be *pleasant,* or plain and *easy:* For, if it be, it is so much the better. This was nothing *pleasant;* for through *deserts;* all the way waste and desolate. Nor (secondly) *easy* neither, For, over the rocks and crags of both *Arabies* (specially *Petraea)* their journey lay. 3. Yet if safe: But it was not; but exceeding dangerous, as lying through the midst of the *Black Tents of Kedar,* a Nation of *Thieves* and cutthroats; to pass over the *hills* of *Robbers;* Infamous then, and infamous to this day. No passing without great troops of convoy. 4. Last we consider the *time* of their *coming,* the season of the year. It was no *summer progress.* A cold *coming* they had of it, at this time of the year; just the worst time of the year, to take a journey, and specially a long journey in. The ways deep, the weather sharp, the days short, the sun farthest off in *solstitio brumali,* the very dead of *Winter, Venimus,* We are come, if that be one; *Venimus,* We are (now) come, come at this time, that (sure) is another.

And these difficulties they overcame, of a *wearisome, irksome, troublesome, dangerous, unseasonable* journey: And for all this, they came. And, came it cheerfully, and quickly; As appeareth by the speed they made. It was but *vidimus, venimus* with them; They *saw,* and they *came:* No sooner *saw,* but they set out presently. So, as upon the first appearing of the *star* (as it might be, last night) they knew it was *Balaam's star;* it called them away, they made ready straight to begin their journey this morning. A sign they were highly conceited of His *Birth,* believed some great matter of it, that they took all these pains, made all this haste, that they might be there to *worship Him,* with all the possible speed they could. Sorry for nothing so much, but that they could not be there soon enough, with the very first to do it even this *day,* the *day* of His *birth.* All considered, there is more in *venimus* than shows at the first sight. It was not for nothing, it was said (in the first verse) *Ecce venerunt;* their *coming* hath an *Ecce* on it: it well deserves it.

And we, what should we have done? Sure, these men of the *East,* shall *rise in judgment against the men of the West,* that is, us: and their *faith,* against ours, in this point. With them it was but *vidimus, venimus:* With us, it would have been but *veniemus* at most. Our fashion is, to see and see again, before we stir a foot: Specially, if it be to the worship of Christ. Come such a Journey, at such a time? No: but fairly have put it off till the spring of the year, till the days longer, and the ways fairer, and the weather warmer: till better traveling to Christ. Our *Epiphany* would sure have fallen in *Easter-week* at the soonest.

But then, for the *distance, desolateness, tediousness,* and the rest, any of them were enough to mar our *venimus* quite. It must be no great way (first) we must come: we love not that. Well fare the *Shepherds* yet, they came but hard by: Rather like them than the *Magi.* Nay, not like them neither. For, with us, the *nearer* (lightly) the *farthest off:* Our Proverb is (you know) *The nearer the Church, the farther from God.*

Nor, it must not be through a *Desert,* over no *Petrae.* If rugged or uneven the way; if the weather ill-disposed; If any never so little danger, it is enough to stay us. To *Christ* we cannot travel, but weather and way and all must be fair. If not, no journey but sit still and see further. As indeed, all our Religion is rather *vidimus,* a *Contemplation,* than *Venimus,* a *Motion,* or stirring to be ought.

But when we do it, we must be allowed leisure. Ever, *veniemus;* never *venimus:* Ever *coming;* never come. We love to make no very great haste. To other things perhaps: Not to *Adorare,* the Place of the worship of God. Why should we, *Christ,* is no Wild-Cat. What talk you of *twelve* days? And if it be *forty days* hence, ye shall be sure to find His mother and Him; She cannot be Churched till then: What needs such haste? The truth is, we conceit Him and His *Birth* but slenderly, and our haste is even thereafter. But, if we be at that point, we must be out of this *Venimus:* they like enough to leave us behind. Best, get us a new *Christ-masse* in *September:* we are not like to come to *Christ* at this *Feast*. Enough, for *venimus.*

John Donne
1 5 7 2 – 1 6 3 1

When John Donne spoke from the influential pulpit of St. Paul's Cathedral, where he was dean from 1621 until his death, he was unquestionably the most celebrated preacher in England. Crowds swarmed outside the doors of whatever chapel or cathedral from which Dr. Donne addressed the churchgoers. His parishioners included royalty, foreign eminences, and the commoners of London. Donne's broad audience was hungry for this poet's matchless prose and the "diamond dust of rhetorical brilliancies," which lit up not only the language of his sermonic style but the great body of verse that made him the first and greatest of the English metaphysical poets.

John Donne was born a Roman Catholic (his mother's family was related to Sir Thomas More), and his conversion to the Anglican Church remains as mysterious as the famous elopement and secret marriage that form part of the myth of his dissipated early life. Donne's enigmatic and high-spirited youth seems to have been a period of considerable learning, adventuring with Raleigh in the Azores, high living, and the essential gaiety of his faith in an age of ambiguity, paradox, and anxiety. Ordination came late in his career, after a long series of failures to open other conventional doors to secular advancement; the King finally prescribed holy orders as the route of last resort if Mr. Donne wished to obtain royal favor.

When high prestige and renown with King and congregation in Jacobean England came at last, it was through his startling success in the pulpit. John Donne delivered sermons that drew throngs of listeners through the charm and force of his complex personality and the lyrical and theatrical flights of a Baroque wit and imagination apprehensive of death but passionately wedded to the love of God. He had something of a cult following as a preacher in his day, eloquent, evangelical, and speaking with an hourglass before him in the pulpit to measure the length of his rhetoric as carefully as he composed his devotional poetry and his erotic verse analyzing the nature and psychology of human love.

The poetry was out of favor for several centuries after his death but was rediscovered in the twentieth. The hundred and sixty extant sermons are still a source of theological debate; their spiky modernism, their ecumenical zeal, and their subtle view of Christian life and the Christian approach to death are best rendered in his terrifying and rhapsodic sermon of 1630, included here. Donne, so ill and close to death that he appeared to many in the congregation as an almost spectral figure, spoke through tears. In what a contemporary called "a faint and hollow voice," he claimed a text that seemed prophetically chosen for what amounted to Dr. Donne's own funeral sermon. But the witness to his last sermon, Izaak Walton, still noted Donne's "joy that God had enabled him to perform this desired duty."

Death's Duel or, a Consolation to the Soul, against the Dying Life, and Living Death of the Body

*Delivered in a Sermon at Whitehall, before the Kings Majesty,
in the beginning of Lent (February 25), 1630. Being his last
Sermon, and called by his Majesties household
The Doctors Own Funeral Sermon*

…and unto God the Lord belong the issues of death.

—PSALM 68:20

Buildings stand by the benefit of their *foundations* that sustain and *support* them, and of their *buttresses* that comprehend and *embrace* them, and of their *contignations* that knit and *unite* them: the *foundations* suffer them not to *sink*, the *buttresses* suffer them not to *swerve*, and the *contignation* and knitting suffers them not to *cleave;* The body of our building is in the former part of this verse: It is this; he that *is our God* is the *God of salvation; ad salutes,* of salvations in the plural, so it is in the original; the *God* that gives us spiritual and temporal salvation too. But of this *building,* the *foundation,* the *buttresses,* the *contignations* are in this part of the *verse,* which constitutes *our text,* and in the three divers *acceptations* of the words among our expositors. *Unto God the Lord belong the issues from death.* For *first* the *foundation* of this *building,* (that our *God* is the *God of all salvations*) is laid in this; That *unto* this *God the Lord belong the issues of death,* that is, it is in his power to give us an *issue* and deliverance, even then when we are brought to the jaws and teeth of death, and to the lips of that whirlpool, the grave. And so in this acceptation of these words, and that upon which our *translation* lays hold, *The issues from death.* And then *secondly* the buttresses that comprehend and settle this building, That he that is *our God,* is the *God of* all *salvations,* are thus raised; *Unto God the Lord belong the issues of death,* that is, the disposition and *manner of our death:* what kind of *issue* and *transmigration* we shall have out of this world, whether prepared or sudden, whether violent or natural, whether in our perfect senses or shaken and disordered by sickness, there is no condemnation to be argued out of that, no Judgment to be made upon that, for how soever they die, *precious in his sight is the death of his saints,* and with him are *the issues of death,* the *ways* of our *departing* out of this *life* are in his *hands.* And so in this *sense* of the *words,* this *exitus mortis,* the *issue of death,* is *liberatio in morte, A deliverance in death;* Not that *God* will *deliver* us *from dying,* but that he will *have a care* of us in the *hour of death,* of what kind soever our passage be. And in this *sense* and acceptation of the *words,* the natural frame and contexture doth well and pregnantly administer unto us; and then *lastly* the *contignation* and knitting of this building, that he that is *our God* is the *God of all salvations,* consists in this, *Unto this God the Lord belong the issues of death,* that is, that this *God* the *Lord* having *united* and knit *both natures in one,* and being *God,* having also *come* into this *world,* in our *flesh,* he could have no other means to save us, he could have no other *issue* out of this world, nor *return* to his former *glory,* but by *death;* And so in this sense, this *exitus mortis,* this *issue of death,* is *liberatio per mortem,* a *deliverance by death,* by the death of this *God* our *Lord Christ Jesus.* And this is Saint *Augustines* acceptation of the words, and those many and great persons that have adhered to him. In all these three lines then, we shall look upon these words; *First,* as the *God* of *power,* the *Almighty Father* rescues his servants from the jaws of death: *And then* as the *God* of *mercy,* the glorious *Son* rescued us, by taking upon himself this *issue of death: And then* between these two, as the *God* of *comfort,* the *holy Ghost* rescues us from all discomfort by his blessed impressions beforehand, that what manner of death soever be ordained for us, yet this *exitus mortis* shall be *introitus in vitam,* our *issue in death* shall be an *entrance into everlasting life.* And these three considerations, our deliverance *à morte, in morte, per mortem, from death, in death, and by death,* will abundantly do all the offices of the *foundations,* of the *buttresses,* of the *contignation* of this our *building;* That he that is our *God,* is the *God of all salvations,* because *unto* this *God the Lord belong the issues of death.*

First, then, we consider this *exitus mortis,* to be *liberatio à morte,* that with *God* the *Lord* are the *issues of death,* and therefore in all our deaths, and deadly calamities of this life, we may justly *hope* of a good *issue* from him. And all our *periods* and *transitions* in this life, are so many passages *from death* to *death;* our very *birth* and entrance into this life, is *exitus à morte,* and *issue from death,* for in our Mothers *womb* we are *dead so,* as that we do *not know* we *live,* not so much as we do in our sleep, neither is there any *grave* so close, or so *putrid* a *prison,* as the *womb* would be unto us, if we stayed in it *beyond* our time, or died there *before* our time. In the *grave* the *worms* do not kill us, we *breed* and *feed,* and then *kill* those worms which we our selves produced. In the womb the dead *child* kills the *Mother* that conceived it, and is a murderer, nay a *parricide,* even after it is dead. And if we be not dead so in the *womb,* so as that being dead we kill her that gave us our first life, our life of *vegetation,* yet we are dead so, as *Davids Idols* are dead. In the *womb* we have *eyes and see not, ears and hear not;* There in the womb we are fitted for *works of darkness,* all the while deprived of light: And there in the *womb* we are taught *cruelty,* by being *fed with blood,* and may be *damned,* though we be *never born.* Of our very making in the *womb,* David says, *I am wonderfully and fearfully made,* and, *Such knowledge is too excellent for me,* for even that *is the Lords doing,* and it *is wonderful in our eyes; Ipse fecit nos,* it is *he that hath made us, and not we our selves* nor our parents neither; *Thy hands have made me and fashioned me round about,* saith *Job,* and (as the *original word is) thou hast taken pains about me,* and, *yet,* says he, *thou doest destroy me.* Though I be the *Masterpiece* of the greatest *Master (man* is so), yet if thou do no more for me, if thou leave me where thou madest me, destruction will follow, The *womb* which should be the *house of life,* becomes *death* it self, if *God* leave us there. That which God threatens so often, the *shutting of the womb,* is not so *heavy,* nor so discomfortable a *curse* in the *first,* as in the *latter* shutting, nor in the shutting of *barrenness,* as in the shutting of *weakness,* when *children are come to the birth,* and there is not *strength to bring forth.*

It is the *exaltation of misery,* to *fall* from a *near hope* of *happiness.* And in that vehement imprecation, the *Prophet* expresses the highest of *Gods* anger, *give them O Lord, what wilt thou give them?* give them a *miscarrying womb.* Therefore as soon as we are men (that is, *inanimated,* quickened in the *womb)* though we cannot our selves, our parents have reason to say in our behalf, *wretched man that he is, who shall deliver* him *from this body of death?* for even the *womb* is a *body of death,* if there be no deliverer. It must be he that said to *Jeremy,* Before *I formed thee I knew thee,* and *before thou camest out of the womb I sanctified thee.* We are not sure that there was no kind of ship nor boat to fish in, nor to pass by, till *God* prescribed *Noah* that absolute *form* of *the Ark.* That word which the *holy Ghost* by *Moses* useth for the *Ark*, is common to all kind of *boats, Thebah*, and is the same word that *Moses* useth for the *boat* that he was *exposed in*, That *his mother laid him in an ark of bulrushes*. But we are sure that *Eve* had no *Midwife* when she was *delivered* of *Cain*, therefore she might well say, *possedi virum à Domino, I have gotten a man from the Lord, wholly*, entirely from the Lord; It is the *Lord* that *enabled* me to *conceive*, The *Lord* that *infused a quickening soul* into that conception, the *Lord* that *brought into the world* that which himself *had quickened*, without all this might *Eve* say, My *body had been* but the *house of death*, and *Domini, Domini sunt exitus mortis*, to God the Lord belong the issues of death.

But then this *exitus à morte*, is but *introitus in mortem*, this *issue*, this deliverance *from* that *death*, the death of the *womb*, is an *entrance*, a delivering over to *another death*, the manifold deaths of this *world*. We have a winding sheet in our Mothers womb, which grows with us from our conception, and we come into the world, wound up in that *winding sheet*, for we come to *seek a grave;* And as prisoners discharged of actions may lie for fees, so when the *womb* hath discharged us, yet we are bound to it by *cords* of flesh by such a *string*, as that we cannot go thence, nor stay there; we celebrate our own funerals with cries, even at our birth; as though our *threescore and ten years life* were spent in our Mothers labor, and our circle made up in the first point thereof, we beg our *Baptism*, with another *Sacrament*, with *tears;* And we come into a world that lasts many ages, but we last not; *in domo Patris*, says our *Savior*, speaking of *heaven, multœ mansiones*, there *are many mansions*, divers and durable, so that if a man cannot possess a *martyrs* house, (he hath shed no blood for *Christ)* yet he may have a *Confessors*, he hath been ready to glorify *God* in the *shedding of his blood*. And if a woman cannot possess a *virgins* house (she hath embraced the *holy state of marriage)* yet she may have a *matrons* house, she hath brought forth and brought up *children in the fear of God. In domo patris, in my fathers house*, in heaven there *are many mansions;* but here upon earth the *son of man hath not where to lay his head*, says he himself. *Nonne terram dedit filiis hominum?* how then hath *God given this earth* to the *sons of men?* he hath *given* them *earth* for their *materials* to be made of earth, and he hath given them *earth* for their *grave* and sepulture, to *return* and resolve to *earth*, but not for their *possession: Here we have no continuing city*, nay no *cottage* that continues, nay no persons, no bodies that continue. Whatsoever moved Saint *Jerome* to call the journeys of the *Israelites,* in the *wilderness,* mansions; The *word* (the word is *Nasang)* signifies but a *journey,* but a peregrination. Even the *Israel of God* hath no mansions; but journeys, pilgrimages in this life. By that measure did *Jacob* measure his life to *Pharaoh; the days* of the years *of my pilgrimage.* And though the *Apostle* would not say *morimur,* that, whilest we *are in the body* we *are dead,* yet he says, *Peregrinamur,* whilest we are *in the body,* we are but in a *pilgrimage,* and we are *absent from the Lord;* he might have said *dead,* for this whole *world* is but a *universal churchyard,* but one *common grave,* and the life and motion that the greatest persons have in it, is but as the shaking of buried bodies in the grave, by an *earth-quake.* That which we call life, is but *Hebdomada mortium, a week of deaths,* seven days, seven periods of our life spent in dying, *a dying seven times over;* and there is an end. *Our birth dies* in *infancy,* and our *infancy* dies in *youth,* and *youth* and the rest die in *age,* and *age* also dies, and *determines all.* Nor do all these, youth out of infancy, or age out of youth arise so, as a *Phœnix* out of the *ashes* of another *Phœnix* formerly *dead,* but as a *wasp* or a *serpent* out of a *carrion,* or as a *Snake* out of *dung.* Our *youth* is *worse* than our *infancy,* and our *age worse* than our *youth.* Our *youth* is *hungry* and *thirsty,* after those *sins,* which our *infancy knew not;* And our *age* is *sorry* and *angry,* that it *cannot pursue* those *sins* which our *youth did;* and besides, all the way, so many deaths, that is, so many deadly calamities accompany every condition, and every period of this life, as that death it self would be an ease to them that suffer them: Upon this sense doth *Job* wish that *God had not given him* an *issue* from the *first death,* from the *womb, Wherefore hast thou brought me* forth *out of the womb? O that I had given up the Ghost, and no eye seen me! I should have been as though I had not been.* And not only the impatient *Israelites* in their murmuring *(would to God we had died by the hand of the Lord in the land of Egypt)* but *Eliah* himself, when he *fled* from *Jezebel,* and went for his life, as that text says, under the *Juniper tree,* requested that *he might die,* and said, *it is enough now, O Lord, take away my life.* So *Jonah* justifies his impatience, nay his anger toward *God* himself. *Now O Lord take, I beseech thee, my life from me, for it is better to die than to live.* And when *God* asked him, *doest thou well to be angry for this,* he replies, *I do well to be angry, even unto death.* How much worse a death than death, is this life, which so good men would so often change for death! But if my case be as Saint *Pauls* case, *quotidiè morior,* that *I die daily,* that something heavier than death falls upon me every day; If my case be *Davids* case, *tota die mortificamur; all the day long we are killed,* that not only every day, but every hour of the day something heavier than death falls upon me, though that be true of me, *Conceptus in peccatis, I was shapen in iniquity, and in sin did my mother conceive me* (there I died one death), though that be true of me *(Natus filius iræ) I was born* not only of the child of sin, but *the child of wrath,* of the wrath of *God* for sin, which is a heavier death; Yet *Domini Domini sunt exitus mortis,* with *God the Lord are the issues of death,* and after a *Job,* and a *Joseph,* and a *Jeremy,* and a *Daniel,* I cannot doubt of a deliverance. And if no other deliverance conduce more to his glory and my good, yet he hath the *keys of death,* and he can let me out at that door, that is, deliver me from the manifold deaths of this world, the *omni die* and the *tota die,* the *every days death* and *every hours death,* by that *one death,* the *final dissolution* of body and soul, the end of all. But then is that the end of all? Is that dissolution of body and soul, the last death that the body shall suffer? (for of spiritual death we speak not now) It is not. Though this be *exitus à morte,* It is *introitus in mortem;* though it be an *issue from* the manifold *deaths* of this *world,* yet it is an *entrance* into the *death of corruption* and *putrefaction* and *vermiculation* and *incineration,* and dispersion in and from the *grave,* in which every dead man dies over again. It was a *prerogative* peculiar to *Christ,* not to die this death, *not to see corruption:* what gave him this privilege? Not *Josephs* great proportion of *gums and spices,* that might have preserved his body from corruption and *incineration* longer than he needed it, longer than *three days,* but would not have done it for ever: what preserved him then? did his exemption and *freedom from original sin* preserve him from this corruption and *incineration?* 'tis true that original sin hath induced this corruption and *incineration* upon us; If we had not sinned in *Adam, mortality had not put on immortality,* (as the *Apostle* speaks) nor, *corruption had not put on incorruption,* but we had had our *transmigration* from this to the other world, without any *mortality,* and *corruption at all.* But yet since Christ took *sin* upon him, so far as made him *mortal,* he had it so far too, as might have made him see this corruption and *incineration,* though he had no *original sin* in himself, what preserved him then? Did the *hypostatical union* of both *natures, God* and *Man, preserve* him from this corruption and incineration? 'tis true that this was a most powerful *embalming,* to be embalmed with the *divine nature* it self, to be embalmed with *eternity,* was able to preserve him from corruption and *incineration* for ever. And he was embalmed so, embalmed with the *divine nature* it self, even in his *body* as well as in his *soul;* for the *Godhead,* the *divine nature* did not depart, but remained still *united* to his *dead body* in the *grave;* But yet for all this powerful *embalming,* this *hypostatical union* of both natures, we see *Christ* did *die;* and for all this *union* which made him *God* and *Man,* he became no man (for the *union* of the *body* and *soul* makes the man, and he whose soul and body are separated by *death* as long as that state lasts is properly no man). And therefore as in him the dissolution of *body* and *soul* was no *dissolution* of the *hypostatical union;* so is there nothing that constrains us to say, that though the *flesh* of *Christ* had *seen corruption* and *incineration* in the grave, this had been any *dissolution* of the *hypostatical union,* for the divine *nature,* the Godhead might have remained with all the *Elements* and *principles of Christs* body, as well as it did with the two *constitutive* parts of his *person,* his *body* and his *soul.* This *incorruption* then was not in *Josephs gums* and *spices,* nor was it in *Christs* innocence, and *exemption* from *original sin,* nor was it (that is, it is not necessary to say it was) in the *hypostatical union.* But this *incorruptibleness* of his *flesh* is most conveniently placed in that, *Non dabis, thou wilt not suffer thy holy one to see corruption.* We look no further for *causes* or *reasons* in the *mysteries of religion,* but to the *will* and pleasure of *God: Christ* himself limited his *inquisition* in that *ita est,* even *so Father, for so it seemeth good in thy sight. Christs* body did *not see corruption,* therefore, because *God* had *decreed* it should not. The humble soul (and only the humble soul is the religious soul) rests himself upon *Gods* purposes and the decrees of *God,* which he hath declared and manifested not such as are *conceived* and imagined in our selves, though upon some probability, some *verisimilitude.* So in our present case *Peter* proceeds in his *Sermon* at *Jerusalem,* and so *Paul* in *his* at *Antioch.* They preached *Christ* to have *been risen* without seeing *corruption* not only because *God* had *decreed* it, but because he had *manifested* that *decree* in his *Prophet.* Therefore doth Saint *Paul* cite by special number the *Second Psalm* for that *decree;* And therefore both Saint *Peter* and S. *Paul* cite for it that place in the 16. *Psalm,* for when *God* declares his *decree* and purpose in the express words of his *Prophet,* or when he declares it in the real execution of the decree, then he makes it ours, then he manifests it to us. And therefore as the *Mysteries* of our *Religion,* are *not* the *objects* of *our reason,* but *by faith we rest* on *Gods decree* and purpose, (It is so O *God,* because it is *thy will,* it should be so) so *Gods decrees* are ever to be considered in the *manifestation* thereof. All *manifestation* is either in

the *word* of *God,* or in the *execution* of the *decree;* And when these two concur and meet, it is the strongest *demonstration* that can be: when therefore
I find those *marks* of *adoption* and *spiritual filiation,* which are delivered in
the *word* of *God* to be upon me, when I find that real *execution* of his *good
purpose* upon me, as that *actually* I do *live* under the *obedience,* and under the
conditions which are *evidences* of *adoption* and *spiritual filiation;* Then so long
as I see these *marks* and live so; I may safely comfort my self in a *holy certi-
tude* and a *modest infallibility* of my *adoption. Christ* determines himself in
that, the purpose of *God* was manifest to him: S. *Peter* and S. *Paul* determine
themselves in those two ways of knowing the *purpose* of *God,* the *word* of
God before, the *execution* of the *decree* in the *fullness of time.* It was *prophesied
before,* say they, and it is *performed now, Christ is risen* without seeing corruption. Now this which is so singularly peculiar to him, that *his flesh should
not see corruption,* at his *second coming,* his coming to *Judgment,* shall extend
to all that are then alive, their flesh shall not *see corruption,* because as the
Apostle says, and says as *a secret,* as *a mystery; Behold I show you a mystery, we
shall not all sleep,* (that is, not continue in the state of the dead in the grave,)
but we shall all be changed in an instant, we shall have a *dissolution,* and in the
same instant a reintegration, a *recompacting* of *body* and *soul,* and that shall be
truly a death and truly a resurrection, but no sleeping in corruption; But
for us that die now and sleep in the state of the dead, we must all pass this
posthume death, this *death* after *death,* nay this death after burial, this *dissolution* after *dissolution,* this *death* of *corruption* and *putrefaction,* of *vermiculation* and *incineration,* of *dissolution* and *dispersion* in and *from* the *grave,* when
these bodies that have been the *children* of *royal parents,* and the *parents* of
royal children, must say with *Job, Corruption thou art my father,* and *to the Worm
thou art my mother and my sister. Miserable riddle,* when the *same worm* must be
my mother, and *my sister,* and *my self. Miserable incest,* when I must be *married*
to my *mother* and my *sister,* and be both *father* and *mother* to my own *mother*
and *sister, beget* and *bear* that *worm* which is all that *miserable penury;* when my
mouth shall be *filled* with *dust,* and the *worm* shall *feed,* and *feed sweetly* upon
me, when the *ambitious* man shall have *no satisfaction, if* the *poorest alive* tread
upon him, nor the *poorest* receive any *contentment* in being made *equal* to
Princes, for they *shall be equal* but *in dust.* One dies at his full strength, being
wholly at ease and in quiet, and another dies in the *bitterness of his soul,* and
never *eats* with *pleasure,* but they lie down *alike* in *the dust,* and the *worm cov-*

ers them; In *Job* and in *Esau*, it *covers them and is spread under them,* the worm
is spread *under thee,* and the *worm covers thee,* There's the *Mats* and the *Car-pets* that *lie under,* and there's the *State* and the *Canopy,* that *hangs over* the
greatest of the sons of men; Even those bodies that were *the temples of the
holy Ghost,* come to this *dilapidation,* to ruin, to rubbage, to dust, even the
Israel of the Lord, and *Jacob* himself hath no other specification, no other de-nomination, but that *vermis Jacob,* thou *worm of Jacob.* Truly the considera-tion of this *posthume death,* this death after burial, that after *God,* (with
whom are the *issues of death)* hath delivered me from the *death* of the *womb,*
by bringing me into the *world,* and from the manifold *deaths* of the *world,*
by laying me in the *grave,* I must die again in an *Incineration* of this *flesh,* and
in a dispersion of that dust. That that *Monarch,* who spread over many na-tions alive, must in his dust lie in a corner of that *sheet of lead,* and there,
but so long as that lead will last, and that private and *retired man,* that
thought himself his own forever, and never came forth, must in his dust of
the grave be published, and (such are the *revolutions* of the *graves)* be min-gled with the dust of every high way, and of every dunghill, and swallowed
in every puddle and pond: This is the most inglorious and contemptible *vil-ification,* the most deadly and peremptory *nullification* of man, that we can
consider; *God* seems to have carried the declaration of his *power* to a great
height, when he sets the *Prophet Ezekiel* in the *valley of dry bones,* and says,
Son of man can these bones live? as though it had been impossible, and yet they
did; The *Lord* laid *Sinews upon them, and flesh, and breathed into them,* and *they
did live:* But in that case there were *bones* to be *seen,* something visible, of
which it might be said, can this thing live? But in this death of *incineration,*
and dispersion of dust, we see *nothing* that we call *that mans;* If we say, can
this dust live? perchance it *cannot,* it may be the mere *dust* of the *earth,*
which never did live, never shall. It may be the dust of that mans *worm,*
which did live, but shall no more. It may be the dust of *another* man, that
concerns not him of whom it is asked. This death of *incineration* and dis-persion, is, to natural *reason,* the most *irrecoverable death* of all, and yet *Do-mini Domini sunt exitus mortis, unto God the Lord belong the issues of death,* and
by *recompacting* this *dust* into the *same body,* and *reinanimating* the *same body*
with the *same soul,* he shall in a blessed and glorious *resurrection* give me
such an *issue from* this *death,* as shall never pass into any other *death,* but es-tablish me into a life that shall last as long as the *Lord of life* himself.

And so have you that that belongs to the *first acceptation* of these words, *(unto God the Lord belong the issues of death)* That though from the *womb* to the *grave* and in the grave it self we pass from *death* to *death*, yet, as *Daniel* speaks, the *Lord our God is able to deliver us, and he will deliver us.*

And so we pass unto our *second accommodation* of *these words (unto God the Lord belong the issues of death)* That it *belongs* to *God*, and *not* to *man* to *pass a judgment* upon us at our death, or to conclude a dereliction on *Gods* part upon the manner thereof.

Those *indications* which the *Physicians* receive, and those *presagitions* which they give for *death* or *recovery* in the *patient*, they receive and they give out of the grounds and the *rules of their art:* But we have no such rule or art to give a *presagition* of *spiritual death* and damnation upon any such *indication* as we see in any *dying man;* we see often enough to be sorry, but not to despair; we may be deceived both ways; we use to comfort our self in the death of a *friend*, if it be testified that he went away like a *Lamb*, that is, without any *reluctation*. But, *God* knows, that (he) may be accompanied with a *dangerous damp* and *stupefaction*, and *insensibility* of his *present state.* Our blessed *Savior* suffered *coluctations* with *death*, and a *sadness even in his soul to death*, and an *agony* even to a *bloody sweat* in his *body*, and *expostulations* with *God*, and *exclamations* upon the cross. He was a *devout man*, who said upon his death bed, or dead turf (for he was a *Hermit) septuaginta annis Domino servivisti, et mori times? hast thou served a good Master threescore and ten years*, and *now art thou loath to go into his presence?* yet *Hilarion* was loath; *Barlaam* was a *devout* man (a *Hermit* too) that said that day he died *Cogita te hodie cœpisse servire Domino, et hodie finiturum. Consider this to be the first days service that ever thou didst thy Master*, to glorify him in a Christianly and a constant death, *and if thy first day* be *thy last day too, how soon dost thou come* to *receive thy wages?* yet *Barlaam* could have been content to have stayed longer for it: Make no *ill conclusions* upon any mans *loathness* to *die*, for the *mercies* of God work *momentarily* in minutes, and many times *insensibly* to by-standers or any other than the party departing. And then upon *violent deaths* inflicted, as upon malefactors, *Christ* himself hath forbidden us by his own death to make any *ill conclusion;* for his own *death* had those impressions in it; He was *reputed*, he was *executed* as a *malefactor*, and no doubt many of them who concurred to his death, did believe him to be so; Of *sudden death* there are scarce examples to be found in the *scriptures* upon *good men*, for *death* in *battle* cannot be called *sudden death;* But *God* governs not by *examples,* but by *rules,* and therefore make no *ill conclusion* upon *sudden death* nor upon *distempers* neither, though perchance accompanied with some *words of diffidence* and distrust in the *mercies of God:* The *tree lies as it falls* its true, but it is *not* the *last stroke* that *fells* the *tree,* nor the *last word* nor *gasp* that *qualifies* the *soul.* Still *pray* we for a *peaceable life* against *violent death,* and for *time* of *repentance* against *sudden death,* and for *sober* and *modest assurance* against *distempered* and *diffident death,* but never make *ill conclusions* upon persons overtaken with such deaths; *Domini Domini sunt exitus mortis, to God the Lord belong the issues of death.* And *he* received *Sampson,* who went out of this world in *such* a *manner* (consider it *actively,* consider it *passively* in his *own death,* and in those whom he *slew* with himself) as was subject to interpretation hard enough. Yet the *holy Ghost* hath moved *S. Paul* to celebrate *Sampson* in his *great Catalogue,* and so doth all the *Church:* Our *critical* day is *not* the *very day* of our *death:* but the whole course of our life. I thank him that *prays* for me when the *Bell tolls,* but I thank him much more that *Catechizes* me, or *preaches* to me, or *instructs me how to live. Fac hoc et vives, there's* my security, the mouth of the *Lord hath said it, do this and thou shalt live:* But *though I do it,* yet I *shall die too,* die a bodily, a natural death. But *God* never mentions, never seems to consider that death, the bodily, the natural death. *God* doth not say, live well and thou shalt die well, that is, an easy, a quiet death; But *live well here,* and thou shalt *live well for ever.* As the first part of a sentence pieces well with the last, and never respects, never harkens after the *parenthesis* that comes between, so doth a *good life* here flow into an *eternal life,* without any consideration, what *manner* of *death* we die: But whether the *gate* of *my prison* be *opened* with an *old key* (by a gentle and *preparing sickness), or* the gate be *hewn down* by a *violent death,* or the gate be *burned down* by a *raging* and *frantic fever, a gate into heaven* I *shall have,* for *from* the *Lord is the cause of my life,* and *with God the Lord* are the *issues of death.* And further we carry not this *second acceptation* of the *words,* as this *issue of death* is *liberatio in morte, God's care* that the *soul* be *safe,* what *agonies* soever the *body suffers* in the *hour* of *death.*

But pass to our *third part* and last part; as this *issue of death* is *liberatio per mortem,* a *deliverance by the death* of another, by the death of Christ. *Sufferentiam Job audiisti, et vidisti finem Domini,* says Saint *James* 5:11. *You have heard of the patience of Job,* says he, All this while you have done that, for in every man, calamitous, miserable man, a *Job* speaks; Now *see the end of the Lord*, saith that *Apostle*, which is not that end that the *Lord* proposed to himself *(salvation to us)* nor the end which he proposes to us *(conformity to him)* but *see the end of the Lord*, says he, The end, *that the Lord* himself *came to*, *Death* and a painful and a shameful death. But why did he die? and why die so? *Quia Domini Domini sunt exitus mortis* (as Saint *Augustine* interpreting this *text* answers that question) because *to* this *God our Lord belonged the issues of Death. Quid apertius diceretur?* says he there, what can be more obvious, more manifest than this sense of these words. In the former part of this verse, it is said; *He that is our God, is the God of salvation, Deus salvos faciendi,* so he reads it, the *God* that must save us. Who can that be, says he, but *Jesus?* for *therefore* that *name* was *given him*, because he was to *save us*. And to this *Jesus,* says he, this *Savior, belong the issues of death; Nec oportuit eum de hac vita alios exitus habere quam mortis.* Being come into this life in our mortal nature, *He could not go out of it* any other way *but by death. Ideo dictum,* says he, *therefore it is said,* To *God the Lord belong the issues of death; ut ostenderetur moriendo nos salvos facturum,* to *shew that his way to save us was to die.* And from this *text* doth Saint *Isodore* prove, that *Christ* was *truly Man* (which as many *sects* of *heretics denied,* as that he was *truly God)* because to him, though he were *Dominus Dominus* (as the *text* doubles it) *God* the *Lord,* yet to *him,* to *God the Lord belonged the issues of death, oportuit eum pati* more can not be said, than *Christ* himself says of himself; *These things Christ ought to suffer,* he had no other way but by death: So then *this part of* our *Sermon* must needs be a *passion Sermon;* since all his *life* was a *continual passion,* all *our Lent* may well be a *continual good Friday. Christs* painful life took off none of the pains of his death, he felt not the less then for having felt so much before. Nor will anything that shall be said before, lessen, but rather enlarge the devotion, to that which shall be said of his passion at the time of due *solemnization* thereof. *Christ* bled not a drop the less at the last, for having bled at his *Circumcision* before, nor will you shed a tear the less then, if you shed some now. And therefore be now content to consider with me how to *this God the Lord belonged the issues of death.* That *God,* this *Lord,* the *Lord of life could die,* is a strange contemplation; That the red *Sea* could be dry, That the *Sun* could *stand still,* That an *Oven* could be *seven times heat* and *not burn,* That *Lions* could be *hungry* and *not bite,* is strange, *miraculously strange,* but *supermiraculous* that *God could die;* but that *God would die* is an *exaltation* of that.

But even of that also it is a *superexaltation,* that *God should die, must die,* and *non exitus* (said S. *Augustine, God* the *Lord had no issue but by death,* and *opertuit pati* (says *Christ* himself, all this *Christ ought to suffer,* was bound to suffer; *Deus ultionum Deus* says *David, God* is the *God of revenges,* he would *not pass* over the *sin of man* unrevenged, unpunished. But then *Deus ultionum liberè egit* (says *that place)* The *God of revenges works freely,* he *punishes,* he *spares whom he will.* And would he *not spare himself?* he would not: *Dilectio fortis ut mors, love is strong as death,* stronger, it drew in death that naturally is not welcome *Si possible,* says *Christ, If it be possible, let this Cup pass* when his *love expressed in a former decree* with his *Father,* had *made it impossible.* Many *waters quench not love, Christ* tried many; He was *Baptized* out of his *love,* and his love determined not there. He *mingled blood* with *water* in his *agony* and that determined not his love; he *wept pure blood,* all his blood at all his eyes, at all his pores, in his *flagellation* and *thorns (to the Lord our God belonged the issues of blood)* and these *expressed,* but these did *not quench his love.* He *would not* spare, nay he *could not spare himself.* There was nothing more free, more voluntary, more spontaneous than the death of *Christ.* 'Tis true, *liberè egit,* he *died voluntarily,* but yet when we consider the *contract* that had passed between his *Father* and *him,* there was an *oportuit,* a kind of *necessity* upon him. All this *Christ ought to suffer.* And when shall we *date* this *obligation,* this *oportuit,* this *necessity?* when shall we say *that begun?* Certainly this *decree* by which *Christ was to suffer* all this, was an *eternal decree,* and was there any thing before that, that was eternal? *Infinite love, eternal love;* be pleased to follow this home, and to consider it seriously, that what liberty soever we can *conceive* in *Christ,* to die or not to die; this *necessity* of *dying,* this *decree* is as *eternal* as that *liberty;* yet how small a matter made he of this *necessity* and this *dying?* His *Father* calls it but a *bruise,* and but a *bruising of his heel (the serpent shall bruise his heel)* and yet that was that, the *serpent* should *practice* and *compass* his *death.* Himself calls it but a *Baptism,* as though he were to be the better for it. *I have a Baptism to be Baptized with,* and he was in apine till it was accomplished, and yet this *Baptism* was *his death.* The *holy Ghost* calls it *Joy* (for *the Joy which was set before him he endured the Cross)* which was not a *joy* of his reward after his passion, but a joy that filled him even in the midst of those torments, and arose from him; when *Christ* calls his *Calicem, a Cup,* and no worse *(can ye drink of my Cup)* he speaks not odiously, not with detestation of it: Indeed it was a *Cup, salus mundo, a health to all the world*. And *quid retribuam*, says *David, what shall I render to the Lord?* answer you with *David, accipiam Calicem,* I *will take the Cup of salvation,* take it, that *Cup* is *salvation,* his *passion,* if not into your *present imitation,* yet into your *present contemplation.* And behold how that *Lord* that was *God,* yet *could die, would die, must die,* for your *salvation.* That *Moses* and *Elias talked with Christ* in the *transfiguration,* both Saint *Matthew* and Saint *Mark* tell us, but what they talked of only S. *Luke, Dicebant excessum ejus,* says he, *they talked of his decease,* of *his death* which *was to be accomplished* at *Jerusalem,* The *word* is of his *Exodus,* the very word of our *text, exitus,* his *issue by death. Moses* who in his *Exodus* had *prefigured* this *issue of our Lord,* and in passing *Israel* out of *Egypt* through the *red Sea,* had foretold in that actual *prophecy, Christ passing* of *mankind through* the *sea* of his *blood.* And *Elias,* whose *Exodus* and *issue out of* this *world* was a *figure* of *Christs ascension* had no doubt a great satisfaction in *talking* with our *blessed Lord de excessu ejus,* of the *full consummation of all this* in *his death,* which was to be *accomplished* at *Jerusalem.* Our *meditation* of his *death* should be more *visceral* and affect us more because it is of a thing already done. The ancient *Romans* had a certain tenderness and detestation of the name of death, they could not name death, no, not in their wills. There they could not say *Si mori contigerit,* but *si quid humanitus contingat,* not if, or when I die, but when the course of nature is accomplished upon me. To us that speak daily of the *death of Christ,* (he was *crucified, dead* and *buried)* can the memory or the mention of our own *death* be irksome or bitter? There are in these latter times among us, that name death freely enough, and the death of *God,* but in *blasphemous oaths* and *execrations.* Miserable men, who shall therefore be said never to have named Jesus, because they have named him *too often.* And therefore hear *Jesus* say, *Nescivi vos, I never knew you,* because they made themselves *too familiar* with him. *Moses* and *Elias* talked with *Christ* of his *death,* only, in a *holy* and *joyful sense* of the *benefit* which *they* and *all* the world were to *receive by that. Discourses of Religion* should not be *out* of curiosity, but to *edification.* And then they talked with *Christ* of his *death* at that time, when he was in the greatest *height of glory* that ever he admitted in this world, that is, his *transfiguration.* And we are afraid to speak to the *great men* of this world of their *death,* but nourish in them a *vain imagination* of *immortality,* and *immutability.* But *bonum est nobis esse hic* (as Saint *Peter* said there) It *is good to dwell here,* in this *consideration* of his *death,* and therefore *transfer* we our *tabernacle* (our *devotions)* through some of those *steps* which *God* the *Lord* made to his *issue of death* that *day*. Take in the *whole day* from the *hour* that *Christ received* the *passover* upon *Thursday, unto* the *hour* in which he *died* the *next day*. Make *this* present *day* that *day* in thy *devotion*, and consider what *he did*, and remember what *you have done*. Before he *instituted* and *celebrated* the *Sacrament*, (which was *after* the *eating of the passover)* he proceeded to that act of *humility*, to *wash his disciples feet*, even *Peters, who* for a while *resisted* him; In thy *preparation* to the holy and blessed *Sacrament*, hast thou with a sincere *humility* sought a *reconciliation* with all the *world*, even with those that have been *averse* from it, and *refused* that *reconciliation* from thee? If so, and not else thou hast spent that *first part* of his *last day*, in a *conformity* with him. After the *Sacrament* he spent the time till night in *prayer*, in *preaching*, in *Psalms;* Hast thou considered that a *worthy receiving* of the *Sacrament* consists in a *continuation* of *holiness after*, as well as in a *preparation* before? If so, thou hast therein also *conformed* thy self to him, so *Christ* spent his time till night; *At night* he *went into the garden* to *pray*, and he prayed *prolixius* he spent *much time* in *prayer*. How much? Because it is literally expressed, that *he prayed there three several times*, and that *returning to his Disciples* after his *first prayer*, and *finding them asleep* said, *could ye not watch with me one hour*, it is collected that he *spent three hours* in *prayer*. I dare scarce ask thee *whither* thou *went* or *how* thou *disposed of thy self*, when it *grew dark* and after *last night:* If that time were spent in a *holy recommendation* of thy self to God, and a *submission of thy will* to *his*, It was spent in a *conformity* to him. In that *time* and in those *prayers* was *his agony* and *bloody sweat*. I will *hope* that thou didst *pray*, but not *every ordinary* and *customary prayer*, but *prayer actually* accompanied *with shedding of tears*, and *dispositively* in a readiness to *shed blood* for *his glory* in *necessary cases*, puts thee into a *conformity* with him; About midnight he was *taken* and *bound with a kiss?* from thence he was *carried back* to *Jerusalem*, first to *Annas*, then to *Caiphas*, and (as late as it was) then he was *examined* and *buffeted*, and *delivered over* to the custody of those *officers*, from whom he received all those *irrisions*, and *violences*, the *covering of his face*, the *spitting upon his face*, the *blasphemies of words*, and the *smartness of blows* which that *Gospel* mentions. In which compass fell that *Gallicinium*, that *crowing of the Cock* which *called up Peter* to his *repentance*. How thou passed all that time last night thou knowest. If thou didst any thing that needed *Peters tears*, and hast *not shed them*, let me be thy *Cock*, do it now, Now thy *Master* (in the unworthiest of his servants) *looks back upon thee,* do it now; *Betimes,* in the morning, so soon as it was day, the *Jews held a counsel* in the *high Priests hall,* and *agreed upon their evidence* against him, and then carried him to *Pilate,* who was to be his *Judge;* didst thou *accuse* thy self when thou *wakedst this morning,* and wast thou content even with *false accusations* (that is) rather to *suspect actions* to have been sin, which were not, than to *smother* and *justify* such as were *truly sins?* then thou spent that *hour* in *conformity* to him: *Pilate* found *no evidence against him,* and therefore to ease himself, and to pass a *compliment* upon *Herod, Tetrarch of Galilee,* who was at that time at *Jerusalem* (because *Christ* being a *Galilean* was of *Herods jurisdiction*) *Pilate sent him* to *Herod,* and rather as a *madman* than a *malefactor, Herod* remanded him *(with scorn)* to Pilate to proceed against him; And this was about *eight* of the *clock.* Hast thou been content to come to this *Inquisition,* this examination, this agitation, this cribration, this pursuit of thy *conscience,* to *sift* it, to follow it from the *sins* of thy *youth* to thy *present sins,* from the *sins* of thy *bed,* to the *sins* of thy *board,* and from the *substance* to the *circumstance* of thy *sins?* That's *time spent* like thy *Saviors. Pilate* would have *saved Christ,* by using the *privilege of the day* in his behalf, because that *day* one *prisoner was to be delivered,* but they *chose Barrabas.* He would have *saved him from death,* by *satisfying their fury,* with *inflicting* other *torments* upon him, *scourging* and *crowning with thorns,* and *loading* him with many *scornful* and *ignominous contumelies;* But they regarded him not, they pressed a *crucifying.* Hast thou gone about to *redeem thy sin,* by *fasting,* by *Alms,* by *disciplines* and *mortifications,* in way of *satisfaction* to the *Justice of God?* that will not serve, that's not the right way, *we press* an utter *Crucifying* of that *sin* that governs thee; and that *conforms* thee to *Christ.* Toward *noon Pilate* gave *judgment,* and they made such *haste* to execution, as that by *noon* he was *upon the Cross.* There now hangs that *sacred Body* upon the *Cross, rebaptized* in his own *tears* and *sweat,* and *embalmed* in his *own blood alive.* There are those *bowels of compassion,* which are so conspicuous, so manifested, as that you may *see them through his wounds.* There those *glorious eyes* grew faint in their light: so as the *Sun ashamed* to survive them, *departed with his light too.* And then that *Son of God,* who was *never from us,* and yet had now come a *new way unto* us in *assuming our nature,* delivers that *soul* (which was *never out* of his *Fathers hands*) by a *new way,* a *voluntary emission* of it into his Fathers hands; For though to this *God our Lord,* *belonged these issues of death,* so that considered in his own contract, he *must* necessarily *die,* yet at *no breach* or *battery,* which they had made upon his *sacred Body,* issued his soul, but *emisit,* he *gave up the Ghost,* and as *God breathed a soul into* the *first Adam,* so this *second Adam breathed his soul into God, into the hands of God.* There we leave you in that *blessed dependency,* to *hang* upon *him* that *hangs* upon the *Cross,* there *bathe* in his *tears,* there *suck* at his *wounds,* and *lie down in peace* in his *grave,* till he vouchsafe you a *resurrection,* and an *ascension* into that *Kingdom,* which he *hath purchased for you,* with the *inestimable price* of his *incorruptible blood.* Amen.

William Perkins

1558–1602

*A*broad and looser type of Puritanism than that proposed by the Presbyterian form for the organization of the Church of England under Elizabeth I broke out of the clerical theory of the equality of ministers, which Presbyterianism had advocated in the early seventeenth century. William Perkins, educated like many laymen at Cambridge, concentrated on the Church's essential teaching, the sorting of the sheep from the goats, and an integral place in the cosmic drama of God versus ill-doers as played out in England and on the Continent. Their passion was religious; their role, as they saw it, was frequently that of lawyers in the layman's tradition in which many of them were trained. A minister like Perkins, who had great influence on the thought of the Puritan settlements in Massachusetts, saw churches as places not for liturgical processions but as auditoriums for the pulpit. Cotton Mather's New England would become the laboratory for their intellectual and spiritual experiments.

Perkins was at the forefront of the problems raised in the mass hysteria of his day by a post-Reformation diabolism and a demoralization of the accused, which has become hideously familiar in the enlightened twentieth century. England, in Perkins's century, was by no means exceptionally vicious in its persecution of witches. The morbid fascination of the subject had a hungrier audience on the Continent and in Scotland; Perkins was concerned (in a society in which it was perilous to question belief in the existence of witches) with what seems to us a legal quibble. He insisted that goodness is not godly when springing from a contract with darkness; the servants of the fiend who commit crimes grounded in sheer malevolence are more harmless. Subtracting Perkins's sermon from the ferment of its bigoted and ravening belief in servants of the Devil, it is possible to find a reiteration of the old belief about the pavement of the road to hell. The New World, however, took Perkins's legalistic distinction even further, into a period of atrocity and greater persecution than took place in East Anglia, from which many of its preachers came.

The Good Witch Must Also Die

The *good Witch,* is he or she that by consent in a league with the devil, doth use his help, for the doing of good only. This cannot hurt, torment, curse, or kill, but only heal and cure the hurts inflicted upon men or cattle, by bad Witches. For as they can do no good, but only hurt: so this can do no hurt, but good only. And this is that order which the devil hath set in his kingdom, appointing to several persons their several offices and charges. And the good Witch is commonly termed the *unbinding Witch.*

Now howsoever both these be evil, yet of the two, the more horrible and detestable Monster is the good Witch, for look in what place soever there be any bad Witches that hurt only, there also the devil hath his good ones, who are better known than the bad, being commonly called *Wisemen,* or *Wise-women.* This will appear by experience in most places in these countries. For let a mans child, friend, or cattle be taken with some sore sickness, or strangely tormented with some rare and unknown disease, the first thing he doth, is to bethink himself and inquire after some Wiseman or Wise-woman, and thither he sends and goes for help. When he comes, he first tells him the state of the sick man: the Witch then being certified of the disease, prescribeth either Charms of words to be used over him, or other such counterfeit means, wherein there is no virtue; being nothing else but the devils Sacraments, to cause him to do the cure, if it come by Witchcraft. Well, the means are received, applied, and used, the sick party accordingly recovereth, and the conclusion of all is, the usual acclamation; Oh happy is the day, that ever I met with such a man or woman to help me!

Men of learning have observed, that all Witches through Europe, are of like carriage and behavior in their examinations, and convictions: they use the same answers, refuges, defenses, protestations. In a word, look what be the practices and courses of the Witches in England, in any of these particulars, the same be the practices of the Witches in Spain, France, Italy, Germany, &c. Wherefore the case is clear, they are not deluded by Satan, through the force of humor, as is avouched; for such persons, according as they are diversly taken, would show themselves diversly affected, and vary in their speeches, actions, and conceits, both public and private. Fourthly, our Witches are wont to communicate their skill to others by tradition, to teach and instruct their children and posterity, and to initiate them in the grounds and practices of their own trade, while they live, as may appear by the confessions recorded in the Courts of all countries. But if they were persons troubled with melancholy, their conceits would die with them. For conceits, and imaginary fancies, which rise of any humor, cannot be conveyed from party to party, no more than the humor it self. Lastly, if this sleight might serve to defend Witches under pretence of delusion through corrupted humors, then here were a cover for all manner of sins. For example: a felon is apprehended for robbery or murder, and is brought before the Judge: Upon examination he confesseth the fact, being convicted the law proceeds to condemnation. The same mans friends come in, and allege before the Judge in this manner; This man hath a crazy brain, and is troubled with melancholy, and though he hath confessed the fact, yet the truth is, it was not he, but the devil, who himself committed the murder, and made him think he did it, when he did it not, and hereupon he hath confessed. Would any man think, that this were a reasonable allegation, and a sufficient mean to move the Judge to acquit him? Assuredly if it were, upon the same ground might any sin be laid upon the devils back, and all good laws and judicial proceedings be made void.

Therefore howsoever the patrons of Witches be learned men, yet they are greatly deceived in fathering the practises of Sorcery upon a melancholic humor.

But for the further ratifying of their assertion, they proceed, and use this argument: They which confess of themselves things false, and impossible, must needs be parties deluded, but our Witches do this, when they be examined or consulted with, as that they can raise tempests, that they are carried through the air in a moment, from place to place, that they pass through keyholes, and clefts of doors, that they be sometimes turned into cats, hares, and other creatures; lastly, that they are brought into fair countries, to meet with Herodias, Diana, and the Devil, and such like; all which are mere fables, and things impossible.

Ans. We must make a difference of Witches in regard of time. There is a time, when they first begin to make a league with Satan, and a time also after the league is made and confirmed.

When they first begin to grow in confederacy with the devil, they are sober, and their understanding found, they make their match waking, and as they think wisely enough, knowing both what they promise the devil, and upon what conditions, and therefore all this while it is no delusion. But after they be once in the league, and have been entangled in compact with the devil (considerately as they think, for their own good and advantage) the case may be otherwise. For then reason and understanding may be depraved, memory weakened and all the powers of their soul blemished. Thus becoming his vassals they are deluded, and so intoxicated by him that they will run into thousands of fantastical imaginations, holding themselves to be transformed into the shapes of other creatures, to be transported into the air into other countries, yea, to do so many strange things which in truth they do not.

Touching the manner of Examination, there be two kinds of proceeding; either by a single Question, or by some Torture. A single question is, when the Magistrate himself only maketh inquiry, what was done or not done, by bare and naked interrogations. A torture is, when besides the inquiry in words, he useth also the rack, or some other violent means to urge confession. This course hath been taken in some countries, and may no doubt lawfully and with good conscience be used, how be it not in every case, but only upon strong and great presumptions going before, and when the party is obstinate. And thus much for Examination: now followeth Conviction.

Conviction, is an action of the Magistrate, after just examination, discovering the Witch. This action must proceed from just and sufficient proofs, and not from bare presumptions. For though presumptions give occasion to examine, yet they are no sufficient causes of conviction. Now in general the proofs used for conviction are of two sorts, some be less sufficient, some be more sufficient.

The less sufficient proofs are these. First, in former ages, the party suspected of Witchcraft, was brought before the Magistrate, who caused red-hot iron, and scalding water to be brought, and commanded the party to put his hand in the one, or to take up the other, or both; and if he took up the iron in his bare hand without burning, or endured the water without scalding, hereby he was cleared, and judged free, but if he did burn or scald, he was then convicted, and condemned for a Witch. But this manner of conviction, hath long ago been condemned for wicked and diabolical, as in truth it is, considering that thereby many times, an innocent man may be condemned and a rank witch escape unpunished.

But some witches there be that cannot be convicted of killing any: what shall become of them? *Ans.* As the killing witch must die by another Law, though he were no Witch: so the healing and harmless Witch must die by this Law, though he kill not, only for a covenant made with Satan. For this must always be remembered, as a conclusion, that by Witches we understand not those only which kill and torment: but all Diviners, Charmers, Jugglers, all Wizards, commonly called Wisemen and Wise-women; yea, whatsoever do any thing (knowing what they do) which cannot be effected by nature or art; and in the same number we reckon all good Witches, which do no hurt but good, which do not spoil and destroy, but save and deliver. All these come under this sentence of *Moses,* because they deny God, and are confederates with Satan. By the laws of England, the thief is executed for stealing, and we think it just and profitable: but it were a thousand times better for the land, if all Witches, but specially the blessing Witch might suffer death. For the thief by his stealing, and the hurtful Enchanter by charming, bring hindrance and hurt to the bodies and goods of men; but these are the right hand of the devil, by which he taketh and de-

stroyeth the souls of men. Men do commonly hate and spit at the damnify-
ing Sorcerer, as unworthy to live among them; whereas the other is so dear
unto them, that they hold themselves and their country blessed that have
him among them, they fly unto him in necessity, they depend upon him as
their god, and by this means, thousands are carried away to their final confusion. Death therefore is the just and deserved portion of the good Witch.

Thomas Grantham

fl. 1641

*E*ight years before the violent end of the reign of Charles I, the Stu-
art King executed at the end of the English Civil War, the country
curate and schoolmaster Thomas Grantham preached a compassionate, domestic, and quietly humane sermon on making the best of an imperfect
marriage. The political polemics of the years shortly before the war (or the
Great Rebellion) engaged the clergy of Caroline England as well as Parliament and army. Most of Grantham's fellow ministers, Anglican, Puritan, or
Presbyterian, took vehement and warring sides in the tense and bitter conflict between King and commons.

    Grantham's sermon seems unconventional for a period of bitter strife
and contentiousness in street and pulpit alike; he was an unconventional ed-
ucator for the age as well, abolishing corporal punishment in his school and
restricting the school day to five hours. His sermon on the reconciliation of
spouses to an imperfect union was considered scandalous and led to his ex-
pulsion from the curacy of Barnet, now a part of the borough of Greater
London. Reading between the lines three centuries later, it doesn't seem
unreasonable to guess that Grantham may have had in mind not only the disappointment of Jacob with his Leah but the disillusion and frustration citi-

zens have always felt with the body politic. Perhaps the unorthodox Thomas Grantham intended a parable about not only human marriage but the imperfect union of church and state.

❦

A Wife Mistaken, or a Wife and No Wife

A sermon on being reconciled to marital imperfection by Thomas Grantham, curate of High Barnet, 1641

And it came to pass that in the morning behold it was Leah. And he said unto Laban, What is this thou hast done unto me? did not I serve with thee for Rachel? wherefore then hast thou beguiled me?

—GENESIS 29:25

In the text you may observe a Conjunction and a division: a Conjunction, here are two together that should be asunder, *Jacob* and *Leah*. And in the morning behold it was *Leah*. A division, here are two asunder that should be together, *Jacob* and *Rachel:* and first of the Conjunction as fittest for this season, and opportunity; you have seen the quality of this conjunction, it was an ill Conjunction, a great deal of deceit in it, and where is there a Conjunction, a Marriage, but there is deceit in it, and least this deceit should cause a separation, the Church bindeth them together before God and man, for better for worse, for richer for poorer. And unless this course were taken, how soon would there be a partition, their qualities being almost as different as heaven and hell, as the good Angels and the bad. *Nabal* and *Abigail, Nabal* a fool and churl, and of so base a disposition, such a man of *Belial,* that his own servants said a man could not tell how to speak to him: and she a kind complemental woman, she fell at *Davids* feet, and offered to wash the feet of his servants. *David* and *Michal, Michal* a scoffing woman, deriding *David* for dancing before the *Ark,* and he a man after Gods own heart; *Socrates* with *Xantippe,* she is like a *Quotidian Ague,* or at the best she is like *Sauls* evil spirit that comes too often upon him. *Moses* and *Zipporah,* she a terrible fiery woman, Thou art a bloody husband to me, saith she, and *Moses* the meekest man above all the men of the earth. The learned distinguish a fourfold deceit in Marriage, the first is *error personae,* when *Leah* is given in stead of *Rachel,* one party for another, as to *Jacob,* and this mistake doth hinder and nullify Marriage: for in Marriage there is a mutual love and consent One to another, but this is not where *Leah* is given in stead of *Rachel,* and therefore no Marriage. But will some say, is it possible that *Jacob* (who was so subtle a man) should be so deceived, he was noted for a supplanter by his Brother *Esau;* Is he not rightly called *Jacob,* for he hath supplanted me these two times of my birthright and blessing. He was so grave, so arch a supplanter, that he could deceive his father although his voice betrayed him, and although his father told him it was the voice of *Jacob,* yet he pressed him to bless him in stead of his brother *Esau.* We say that man is an excellent *Hocus-Pocus,* excellent in legerdemain, and slight of hand that can deceive one that looks upon him. But he that can deceive the hearing, and the feeling, he is far more excellent: my sight may be deceived for I may take that which is Pictured to be lively and real, but my hearing, my feeling cannot be so easily deceived. *Thomas* would not believe his seeing, his hearing, but when he came to feeling to lay his hand in our Saviors side, then he cried out, My Lord and my God. And now I suppose you are ready to ask, how this Subtle man was deceived? The deceit was thus: In those days the Brides came veiled and Masked to their Marriage Beds, for modesty sake, and it was a sign of Modesty to be silent. And thus much for the first deceit, which is *error personae,* a mistake of the person, as this text represents to you. There is another deceit, which is *error qualitatis,* when a man takes as he thinks he hath, one thrifty, honest, fair, and she proves a painted whorish, liquorish slut. And this deceit is general, for many women show like the Egyptian Temples, very beautiful without and built, and adorned with precious stones, saith, *Lucian,* but if you seek what god they worship within, you shall find him to be a Cat, or a Goat, or an Ape, or some such ridiculous ill-favored creature: so, many women, although they be fair and beautiful without, are full of many vanities, fickle, unconstant, lascivious affections: many a man thinks he hath a saint, when he hath a Devil, a fair woman, when she is a painted plastered faced *Jezabel;* I will not speak of these painted tombs and sepulchers, beautiful without, but loathsome within, these Apples of Sodom, that seem fair to the sight but at the least touch they fall to dust: so the least approaching discovers the corruption of these creatures, so great is their corruption it corrupts the sweetest perfumes, and makes them loathsome as themselves: but I will not rake any longer in this unsavory dunghill. There are two other errors, or deceits in Marriage, as *error Conditionis,* and *error fortunæ:* but I let them pass, for fear I should run into the error of being tedious to this assembly. I come now to the division, or separation; there is discovery of an ill Conjunction, therefore I will cast my meditations a little upon this appearance, or discovery of this Conjunction. In the morning behold it was *Leah.* There is many a man sleeps with *Leah* and thinks it is *Rachel,* there is many a man so blinded in his love and affection that he is as much or more mistaken in the qualities of his wife than *Jacob* was in the person of *Leah:* many a man thinks he hath a wife that loves him, when she cares not for him, and he may think that she is sighing and sorrowing in his absence, when she is Reveling and Dancing. You may read *Prov.* 7:18. there's a woman speaks to a man in her husbands absence to take his fill of love with her: he (may be) thinks, she is weeping in his absence, when she is tumbling in her perfumed bed, as you may read there, verse 17. *I have perfumed my bed with Myrrh, Aloes and Cinnamon; I have decked it with coverings of tapestry, and fine linen of Egypt:* no question this woman embraces her husband when he comes home, and he discovers nothing: for the way of a whorish woman (as *Solomon* saith), *is like the flight of a Bird in the air, like the passage of a ship upon the sea, like a serpent creeping into a rock:* no sign of the birds flying, of the serpents creeping, of the ships passage.

Look upon *Joseph's* Mistress, she hath his coat to show for honesty, *Ecce signum, Behold the coat of this Hebrew:* did *Sampson* think those hands would have clipped his locks, that had so often embraced his body? Some rash men do maintain, that the reason why men think there are so many good women, is, because they are so blind and ignorant themselves; if they had but the eyes of the Wife, to see with *Solomons* eyes, may be they would say, There was not one good of a thousand, and he had told them one by one. And how does *Solomon* define a good woman? just as the Philosopher does, *Vacuum ex supposito quod detur;* if there be a *Vacuum,* it is *Locus non repletus corpore;* if there be, or shall ever be such a thing in the world as a good woman, then she is this and that, she is like a merchants Ship that bringeth her food from far:

and what of greater value! she is like to precious jewels, she is like to them, but there is none like to her, none of equal value with her. *Solomon* saith, *She is a crown to her husband, she is the glory of her husband,* saith Saint *Paul,* the very scarlet she clothes her servants in does show her honorable, God himself calls her a helper, and such a helper she is, that man could not have been capable of that blessing, *Increase and multiply,* without her, then it was *The Seed of the woman that broke the Serpents head:* she was *Deipora,* she brought forth a God, and here I will be bold to say out of the due honor to that Sex, that there have been women have deserved these praises of *Solomon:* What was that *Esther?* that Cherubin of the Church under whose wings it was safe: the Papists call the Virgin *Mary, Regina Cœli,* Queen of Heaven, and they pray to her to command our Savior, *Mater impera Filio,* Mother command thy Son; She hath more Churches dedicated to her than our Savior, than all the Trinity, although she paid her Fine in milk, but He in blood, (as a great Divine saith). How happy hath this Kingdom been under a Queen, there are many eyes now living that have seen it, and not a man but knows it; I need not instance in particulars the elect Lady and her sister, to whom Saint *John* wrote, *Priscilla* able to inform a learned man *Apollos* in the Scripture: these women were highly honored by that Apostle called from Heaven, *Greet Priscilla and Aquila, Rom.* 16:3. *Aquila and Priscilla salute you,* 1 *Cor.* 16:19. *Salute Priscilla and Aquila,* 2 *Tim.* 4:19. *Priscilla went with him into Syria, Acts* 18:18. and thus much for the discovery, how long may a man sleep before he knows with whom, or what she is he sleeps withall, before he knows whether it be *Leah* or *Rachel.* I am come now to the division or separation, and you see it is a high and great division, *Jacob* begins to word it, to fall to terms with *Laban* (who was his Master) What is this thou hast done unto me; did not I serve with thee for *Rachel?* wherefore then hast thou beguiled me? And indeed the inconveniences were very many that befell *Jacob* by this wicked act of *Laban:* first of all he made his daughter a whore, and a whore is odious to the children of God, she was either to be burned, or to be stoned. Then the wrong done to *Rachel,* being deceived of her expectation, was enough to make her weep her self blear eyed like *Leah,* then he brought an inconvenience upon *Jacob,* having more wives than one; some say it was a sin, some hold it a great Inconvenience to have one, therefore much more to have two.

The married man is entangled like a fish in a net; he comes merrily in, but he is mightily perplexed when he cannot get out; then this action of *Laban* was enough to set the sisters at variance, and what joy could *Jacob* have when his wives were divided, it was enough to divide his heart: then the desire of rule, and jealousies, and distrusts that one hath of the other; then the charges to maintain two, whereas *Jacob* if he had had but one, he would never have sought further. God made but one for *Adam*, and *Lamech* was the first that had two Wives, and he had no more than two, and he was of the posterity of *Cain*, and condemned by the fathers: and from *Adam* to *Abraham*, none of the posterity of *Seth* had more than one wife (that we read of); they two shall be one flesh, and how can that be if a man have many wives. God made only male and female, and he took but one rib, and made of one rib, One Woman, not many. I will not say, it was a sin to have many wives, for I find it in the Law, *Deut.* 21:15. *If a man have two wives, one that he loveth, and another that he hateth,* and there the Law speaks of both their sons as legitimate, *Deut.* 17:17. The Law does forbid the King to have many wives which may draw away his mind, and Saint *Augustine* (upon that place) saith, *permissum & Regi habere plures uxores non plurimas,* he may have more than one or two, but not many, and *Iehoiada* that was a most holy Priest, took two wives, for King *Ioash*, 2 *Chron.* 24:3. But me thinks I hear some say, *Laban* is unjustly condemned for dealing so strictly with *Jacob:* was it not a great kindness in *Laban* to take *Jacob*, *Jacob* that had cousined [i.e., duped] his Father, his Brother, and to trust him with his flock? And then it was a kindness that he gave him his daughter, and for ought I know the better of the two, the fairest is not always the best. Beautiful *Rachel* sold *Jacob* for Mandrakes, whereas blear eyed *Leah* bought him and went out to meet him, *Gen.* 30:16. Tender eyed Leah will be weeping at my misfortunes, when beautiful *Rachel* will be laughing with another: *Abraham* went in danger with beautiful *Sarah*, but *Jacob* liveth secure with tender eyed *Leah*. *Rachel* stole her fathers gods, and could see her Father and husband quarrel the while, when *Leah* was continually weeping. *Rachel* will be impatient if she have not what she desires (give me Children or else I die) and what is beauty with such disquietness, but like a fair house haunted with sprites, or a bed of violets with a serpent. But look upon *Leah,* she is more moderate, tender eyed, she will be weeping in stead of scolding. *Rachel* will be subject to be wandering like *Dina*. *Leah* is tender eyed, and the wind will hurt her. *Venium spectantur ut Ipse,* they delight to be looked upon. What are these many fancies in their dressings but so many signs to invite a man to Inn there if he please, whereas the Passenger else had gone on his way? What does the fowler whistle for but to catch the Bird, and such is the end of their enchantments. Thus you see the danger of beauty, there is more danger in it than in the most unruly Elements. The fire hath no power of a man if he do not touch it; nor the water; but if a man look but upon beauty, it will endanger him, and it is kept with a great deal of danger and care, as the Apples of the *Hesperides* with a watchful *Dragon*. But will some say, why do you maintain blear eyed *Leah* against beautiful *Rachel? Leahs* fault was great in lying with *Jacob.* To this I answer, fornication was held no sin among the Gentiles, and the Church of *Rome* holds, *fornicationem non vagam,* that if a man keep constantly to one woman it is no sin: and here let no man be harsh against *Leah,* for she is tender eyed, and can weep tears enough to wash away her sin, tears enough to wash our Saviors feet. Alas, be not harsh against her, she is blear eyed already and too much weeping will make her blind. What if *Leah* have a blemish in the eye of her body, yet her understanding, the eye of her soul may be clear, and beautiful; and if men consider rightly, the greatest deformity and blemish in a woman is, to be blear eyed in her understanding, to mistake a mans actions, not to see them clearly. If her husband be sociable, then he is given to drunkenness, if silent, then he hath no discourse in him, if merry, not that gravity that becomes him, if he put not himself upon hard adventures to raise his fortunes, she is disquieted, and if he do, and be foiled, then she condemns him; give me the eye of the understanding, let the other be as clear as crystal, if this be blemish there is no joy. For ought I know, this *Laban,* this Idolater, shall rise up against many Christians. How usual is it for many a man to make fair promises, to promise a man *Rachel;* he shall have this and that, and any thing his heart can desire if he will serve them; but when a man hath done all he can, they will put *Leah* upon him, some blear eyed unhandsome thing, upon which so soon as a man can but look, he shall find it to be *Leah.* It's plain enough to be seen (behold it was *Leah)* it is a hard thing for a man to get a *Rachel* of his Master, to get any thing that hath any delight or pleasure in it, great men will not part with their *Rachels.* And still I say, this *Laban* had more honesty and goodness than many a Christian, for although he had done *Jacob* a little wrong, yet he had so much mildness, and Gentleness, and Gentility, as he did suffer *Jacob* to speak to him and to tell him of it (why hast thou beguiled me thus?). Now there are rich men, if they have done a man a displeasure, will not be told of it. Nay if a poor man trust a rich man with money, if he be not disposed to give it, or is unwilling, will be angry if the poor man ask it, and do him all the mischief that may be, and what is this but like thieves that do not only rob a man, but bind a man too, and gag him that he shall not speak, or like Rogues that murder a man because they shall not betray them? God send me to deal with *Laban,* with an Idolater; I shall find a man that I dare speak to, I shall find a mate that will give me *Leah,* that will give me something and cousin me of all.

God complained of his vineyard, that when he had taken a great deal of pains with it, it brought forth wild grapes, *ecce Labruscus,* behold wild grapes plain enough to be seen. And here if I should show to the world with an *Ecce,* the wild grapes, the Basest actions of men, I make no question but men would pass the same judgment that *David* did upon the rich man that took the poor mans Lamb. And here let every man be exhorted not to deceive his servant or his kinsman or his friend. *Jacob* for deceiving his brother and his Father, was paid in his own Coin, and enjoyed not the blessing twenty years after: *Laban* deceived him in his wife, *Laban* for deceiving *Jacob,* was deceived by *Jacob,* with the rods he laid. *Rachel* stole *Labans* gods for deceiving her of her husband at first. *Jacob* deceived his Father with Goats skins, and he himself was deceived with the blood of a Goat. *David* cut off the lap of *Sauls* coat, and his clothes would not keep him warm in his old age. *Sampsons* eye lusted after a Philistine, and *Sampsons* eye was put out, *Jeroboams* hand reached to the Prophet, and that hand withered. Thus you see how God punisheth sin in the same act, in the same part, in the same kind. Time will not give me leave here to show you how many a man sleeps with *Leah,* with some ugly deformed sin, and being blinded in sin and darkness, thinks it is *Rachel,* (very beautiful) and loves it entirely, till the morning light of Gods grace arise, and then he sees the deformity of his sin, how blear eyed it is, how ill-favored, and now let every man consider how we are all servants to God, and we serve him for *Rachel,* for some pleasant thing we delight in, as the Apostles dreamt of a Kingdom, if it please God to give us *Leah,* in stead of *Rachel,* to give us that which pleaseth us not so well, let us be content with it and serve him on still, he will at the last give us *Rachel,* we shall be married to him in whom are all joys, such as eye hath not seen, nor ear heard, neither hath it entered into the heart of man to conceive. To which God of his mercy bring us: to God the Father, God the Son, and God the Holy Ghost be all honor, &c.

Jeremy Taylor

1613–1667

After Cromwell's triumphant campaigns in Ireland and Scotland, and his great victory over the Royalists at Worcester in 1651, his attention turned to the pulpit, where Puritan preachers, given a long leash on dissension, appeared to constitute a threat to the peace of the realm. The Protectorate, under Cromwell, has been described as a fallow period for the English pulpit; one of its most distinctive voices was that of Jeremy Taylor. The son of a barber, the protégé of Laud, and, in his first marriage, rumored to be the spouse of an illegitimate daughter of Charles I, Taylor was a loose cannon in the Cromwellian state Church.

Most ministers accepted Cromwell's measures, while a small minority, opposing the Commonwealth's savagely repressive policy in Ireland, formed Royalist resistance groups. The future Bishop Taylor made an active and moving plea for toleration in 1647 in "The Liberty of Prophesying" and crafted sermons during a period of battles, pillaging, burning, and betrayals. They make him not only one of the rare great Puritan divines to show a pacific temper but a brilliant original. His sermon on revenge was preached in the sequestered place made available by his patron, the Earl of Carbury, at Golden Grove in Wales, where the simplicity and exquisiteness of his style, expressed in sermons to a remote and rustic congregation, produced not only a subtle instrument of moral theology but the manual of prayers, *The Golden Grove,* for which both the place and his "gentle wizardry," as one historian calls it, are known. He chose, in his sermons, to speak on topics which are seemingly innocuous, but many of his generalities refer to the butchery of the English Civil War. Jeremy Taylor refers here to a text by the second-century Stoic philosopher Epictetus, whose belief that wrongdoers are more to be pitied than their victims later became part of the Christian canon of belief.

ℭ

Lust for Revenge

. . . What man can give a reasonable account of such a man, who to prosecute his revenge will do himself an injury, that he may do a lesse to him that troubles him. Such a man hath given me ill language; *oute tēn kephalion algei, oute ton ophthalmon, oute to iskhion, oute ton agron apollyei;* My head aches not for his language, nor hath he broken my thigh, nor carried away my land. But yet this man must be requited. Well, suppose that. But then let it be proportionable; you are not undone, let not him be so. Oh yes; for else my revenge triumphs not. Well, if you do, yet remember he will defend himself, or the Law will right him; at least do not do wrong to yourself by doing him wrong. This were but Prudence, and Self-interest. And yet we see, that the heart of some men hath betrayed them to such furiousness of Appetite, as to make them willing to die, that their enemy may be buried in the same Ruins. Jovius Pontanus tells of an Italian slave (I think) who being enraged against his Lord, watched his absence from home, and the employment and inadvertency of his fellow-servants: he locked the doors, and secured himself for a while, and Ravished his Lady; then took her three sons up to the battlements of the house, and at the return of his Lord, threw one down to him upon the pavement, and then a second, to rend the heart of their sad Father, seeing them weltering in their blood and brains. The Lord begged for his third, and now his only Son, promising pardon and liberty, if he would spare his life. The slave seemed to bend a little, and on condition his Lord would cut off his own Nose, he would spare his Son. The sad Father did so, being willing to suffer anything, rather than the loss of that Child; But as soon as he saw his Lord all bloody with his wound, he threw the third Son, and himself down together upon the pavement. The story is sad enough, and needs no lustre and advantages of sorrow to represent it:

But if a man sets himself down, and considers sadly, he cannot easily tell upon what sufficient inducement, or what principle the slave should so certainly, so horridly, so presently, and then so eternally ruin himself. What could he propound to himself as a recompense to his own so immediate Tragedy? There is not in the pleasure of the revenge, nor in the nature of the thing, any thing to tempt him; we must confess our ignorance, and say, that The Heart of man is desperately wicked; and that is the truth in general, but we cannot fathom it by particular comprehension.

For when the heart of man is bound up by the grace of God, and tied in golden bands, and watched by Angels, tended by those Nurse-keepers of the soul; it is not easy for a man to wander: And the evil of his heart is but like the ferity and wildness of Lions-whelps: But when once we have broken the hedge, and got into the strengths of youth, and the licentiousness of an ungoverned age, it is wonderful to observe, what a great inundation of mischief in a very short time will overflow all the banks of Reason and Religion. *Vice* first is *pleasing,* then it grows *easy,* then *delightful,* then *frequent,* then *habitual,* then *confirmed,* then the *man is impenitent,* then he is *obstinate,* then he *resolves never to Repent,* and then he is *Damned.* And by that time he is come halfway in this progress, he confutes the Philosophy of the old Moralists; For they, not knowing the vileness of man's Heart, not considering its desperate amazing Impiety, knew no other degree of wickedness but This, That men preferred Sense before Reason, and their understandings were abused in the choice of a temporal before an intellectual and eternal good: But they always concluded, that the Will of man must of necessity follow the last dictate of the understanding, declaring an object to be good in one sense or other. Happy men they were that were so Innocent; that knew no pure and perfect malice, and lived in an Age, in which it was not easy to confute them. But besides that, now the wells of a deeper iniquity are discovered, we see by too sad experience, that there are some sins proceeding from the heart of man, which have nothing but simple, and unmingled malice; Actions of mere spite; doing evil, because it is evil; sinning without sensual pleasures: sinning with sensual pain, with hazard of our lives: with actual torment, and sudden deaths, and certain and present damnation: sins against the Holy Ghost: open hostilities, and professed enmities against God and all virtue. I can go no further: because there is not in the world, or in the nature of things, a greater Evil. And that is the Nature and Folly of the

Devil: he tempts men to ruin, and hates God, and only hurts himself, and those he tempts: and does himself no pleasure, and some say, he increases his own accidental torment.

William Laud

1573–1645

This British prelate was born the son of a clothier and rose to the rank of Archbishop of Canterbury in 1633, supporting the doomed Charles I and absolutism in church and state. His Puritan adversaries were implacable in their opposition, and when Laud was impeached for treason by the Long Parliament, he was sentenced to death by beheading. He defended the Anglican Church as a national institution and warred with Rome over issues of papal infallibility and universality; his enemies' enemies were rarely his friends. William Laud took difficult and hopelessly unpopular positions during his career as Charles I's chief minister and was a steadfast opponent of enclosure (the consolidation of sheep farmers' land into compact holdings, which depopulated the English countryside).

Although Laud declined a cardinal's hat and despite his English patriotism, he was accused of popery; he also rejected the Puritan view that God intended the betterment of man's life on earth and a cooperation, to that end, with His purposes.

When William Laud's uncompromising but not easily politicized views became part of the bitter scenario of the oncoming English Civil War, he was hunted down by a drummer boy (who then became one of the last prisoners in England to endure the rack) as "William the Fox." His episcopacy was abolished a year after his death on the scaffold. When he preached at the Inauguration of Charles I in 1625, it is apparent he knew trouble was on its way and that his exceptional tolerance of the right of ordinary men to enjoy their social liberties was in peril. He lay in the Tower in his last days, tired and alone, convicted as an archidolator. His wit in his last speech glitters like a metaphysical poet's in the penumbra of death. His enemies, as a contemporary editor has remarked, would have danced with joy, had dancing not been sinful.

ᑫ

The Last Words of the Archbishop of Canterbury

A Sermon from the Scaffold on Tower Hill, 1645

Good people,

You'll pardon my old Memory, and upon so sad occasions as I am come to this place, to make use of my Papers, I dare not trust my self otherwise. This is a very uncomfortable place to Preach in, and yet I shall begin with a Text of Scripture, in the twelfth of the Hebrews,

Let us run with patience that race that is set before us, looking unto Jesus the author and finisher of our faith, who for the joy that was set before him, endured the Cross, despising the shame, and is set down at the right hand of the Throne of God.

I have been long in my race, and how I have looked unto Jesus the Author and finisher of my Faith, is best known to him: I am now come to the end of my race, and here I find the Cross, a death of shame, but the shame must be despised, or there is no coming to the right hand of God; Jesus despised the shame for me, and God forbid but I should despise the shame for him; I am going apace, as you see, toward the red Sea, and my feet are upon the very brinks of it, an Argument, I hope, that God is bringing me to the Land of Promise, for that was the way by which of old he led his people; But before they came to the Sea, he instituted a Passover for them, a Lamb it was, but it was to be eaten with very sour Herbs, as in the twelfth of *Exodus.*

I shall obey, and labor to digest the sour Herbs, as well as the Lamb, and I shall remember that it is the Lords Passover; I shall not think of the Herbs, nor be angry with the hands which gathered them, but look up only to him who instituted the one, and governeth the other: For men can have no more power over me, than that which is given them from above; I am not in love with this passage through the red Sea, for I have the weakness and infirmity of flesh and blood in me, and I have prayed as my Savior taught me, and exampled me, *Ut transiret calix ista,*

That this Cup of red Wine might pass away from me, but since it is not that my will may, his will be done; and I shall most willingly drink of this Cup as deep as he pleases, and enter into this Sea, aye and pass through it, in the way that he shall be pleased to lead me.

And yet (Good People) it would be remembered, That when the Servants of God, old *Israel,* were in this boisterous Sea, and *Aaron* with them, the Egyptians which persecuted them, and did in a manner drive them into that Sea, were drowned in the same waters, while they were in pursuit of them: I know my God whom I serve, is as able to deliver me from this Sea of Blood, as he was to deliver the three Children from the furnace, *Daniel* 3.

And I most humbly thank my Savior for it, my Resolution is now, as theirs was then; their Resolution was, They would not worship the Image which the King had set up; nor shall I the Imaginations which the People are setting up, nor will I forsake the Temple, and the Truth of God, to follow the Bleating of *Jeroboams* Calves in *Dan* and in *Bethel.*

And I pray God bless all this People, and open their eyes, that they may see the right way; for if it fall out that the blind lead the blind, doubtless they will both into the ditch: For my self, I am, (and I acknowledge it in all humility) a most grievous sinner many ways, by thought, word and deed, and therefore I cannot doubt but that God hath mercy in store for me a poor penitent, as well as for other sinners; I have, upon this sad occasion, ransacked every corner of my heart, and yet I thank God, I have not found any of my sins that are there, any sins now deserving death by any known Law of this Kingdom; and yet thereby I charge nothing upon my Judges (I humbly beseech you I may rightly be understood, I charge nothing in the least degree upon my Judges) for they are to proceed by proof, by valuable Witnesses, and in that way I or any Innocent in the world may justly be condemned: And I thank God, though the weight of the Sentence lie very heavy upon me, yet I am as quiet within, as (I thank Christ for it) I ever was in my life: And though I am not only the first Archbishop, but the first man that ever died in this way, yet some of my Predecessors have gone this way, though not by this means: for *Elfegus* was hurried away and lost his head by the *Danes;* and *Simon Sudbury* in the fury of *Wat Tyler* and his fellows: And long before these Saint John Baptist had his head danced off by a lewd woman; and Saint *Cyprian* Archbishop of Carthage submitted his head to a persecuting sword. Many examples great and good, and they teach me patience, for I hope my cause in Heaven will look of another dye than the color that is put upon it here upon earth; and some comfort it is to me, not only that I go the way of these great men in their several Generations, but also that my charge (if I may not be partial) looks somewhat like that against Saint *Paul* in the twenty-fifth of the *Acts,* for he was accused for the Law and the Temple, that is the Law and Religion; and like that of Saint *Stephen* in the sixth of the *Acts,* for breaking the Ordinances which *Moses* gave us, which Ordinances were Law and Religion: but you'll say, do I then compare my self with the integrity of Saint *Paul,* and Saint *Stephen?* no, God forbid, far be it from me; I only raise a comfort to my self, that these great Saints and servants of God were thus laid up in their several times; And it is very memorable that Saint *Paul,* who was one of them, and a great one, that helped on the accusation against Saint *Stephen,* fell afterward into the selfsame accusation himself, yet both of them great Saints and servants of God; Aye, but perhaps a great clamor there is, that I would have brought in Popery, I shall answer that more fully by and by; in the mean time, you know what the Pharisees said against Christ himself, in the eleventh of *John, If we let him alone, all men will believe on him, Et veniunt Romani, and the Romans will come and take away both our place and the Nation.* Here was a causeless cry against Christ that the Romans would come, and see how just the Judgment of God was, they crucified Christ for fear lest the Romans should come, and his death was that that brought in the Romans upon them, God punishing them with that which they most feared: and I pray God this clamor of *veniunt Romani,* (of which I have given to my knowledge no just cause) help not to bring him in; for the Pope never had such a Harvest in England since the Reformation, as he hath now upon the Sects and divisions that are among us; in the mean time, *by honor and dishonor, by good report and evil report, as a deceiver and yet true,* am I now passing out of this world.

Some particulars also I think not amiss to speak of: and first this I shall be bold to speak of the King, our gracious Sovereign, He hath been much traduced by some for laboring to bring in Popery, but upon my Conscience (of which I am now going to give God a present account) I know him to be as free from this Charge I think as any man living, and I hold him to be as sound a Protestant, according to the Religion by Law established, as any man in this Kingdom, and that He will venture His Life as far and as freely for it; and I think I do or should know both His affection to Religion, and His grounds upon which that affection is built, as fully as any man in England.

The second particular is concerning this great and populous City, which God, bless; here hath been of late a fashion taken up to gather hands, and then go to the Honorable and great Court of the Kingdom, the Parliament, and clamor for Justice, as if that great and wise Court, (before whom the causes come which are unknown to the many;) could not, or would not do Justice, but at their call and appointment; a way which may endanger many an innocent man, and pluck innocent blood upon their own heads, and perhaps upon this City also, which God forbid: and this hath been lately practiced against my self, God forgive the setters of this, with all my heart I beg it, but many well-meaning people are caught by it: In Saint *Stephens* case, when nothing else would serve, they stirred up the people against him, *Acts* 6, and *Herod* went just the selfsame way, for when he had killed Saint *James,* he would not venture upon Saint *Peter* too, till he saw how the people took it, and were pleased with it, in the twelfth of the *Act.* But take heed of having your hands full of blood, in the first of *Isaiah;* for there is a time best known to himself, when God among other sin makes inquisition for blood; and when Inquisition is on foot, the Psalmist tells us, *Psalm* 9, that God remembers, that is not all, *that God remembers and forgets not* (saith the Prophet) *the complaint of the poor;* and he tells you what poor they are in the ninth verse, the poor whose blood is shed by such kind of means: Take heed of this, *It is a fearful thing* (at any time) *to fall into the hands of the living God,* in the twelfth of the *Hebrews:* but it is fearful indeed, and then especially, when he is making his Inquisition for blood, and therefore with my prayers to avert the Prophecy from the City, let me desire that this City would remember the Prophecy that is expressed, *Jer.* 26:15.

The third particular, is this poor Church of England, that hath flourished and been a shelter to other neighboring Churches, when storms have driven upon them; but alas, now it is in a storm it self and God knows whether, or how it shall get out; and which is worse than a storm from without, it is become like an Oak cleft to shivers with wedges made out of its own body, and that in every cleft, profaneness and irreligion is creeping in apace; while as *Prosper* saith, Men that introduce profaneness are cloaked with a name of imaginary religion; for we have in a manner almost lost the substance, and dwell much, nay too much a great deal in Opinion; and that Church which all the Jesuits machinations in these parts of Christendom could not ruin is now fallen into a great deal of danger by her own.

The last particular (for I am not willing to be tedious, I shall hasten to go out of this miserable world) is my self, and I beseech you, as many as are within hearing, observe me. I was born and baptized in the bosom of the Church of *England,* as it stands yet established by Law, in that profession I have ever since lived, and in that profession of the Protestant Religion here established I come now to die; this is no time to dissemble with God, least of all in matter of Religion, and therefore I desire it may be remembered; I have always lived in the Protestant Religion established in *England;* and in that I come now to die: What Clamors and Slanders I have endured for laboring to keep an Uniformity in the external service of God according to the Doctrine and Discipline of this Church all men know and I have abundantly felt: Now at last I am accused of high Treason in Parliament, a crime which my soul ever abhorred; this Treason was charged upon me to consist of two parts; an endeavor to subvert the Law of the Realm, and a like endeavor to overthrow the true Protestant Religion established by those Laws. Besides my Answers which I gave to the several Charges, I protested my innocency in both Houses. It was said, Prisoners protestations at the Bar must not be taken *de ipso;* I can bring no witness of my heart, and the intentions thereof, therefore I must come to my Protestation, not at the Bar, but to my Protestation at this hour and instant of my death, in which (as I said before) I hope all men will be such charitable Christians as not to think I would die and dissemble my Religion, I do therefore here, with that caution that I delivered before, without all prejudice in the world to my Judges, that are to proceed *secundum allegata and probata,* and so to be understood, I die in the presence of Almighty God and all his holy and blessed Angels, and I take it now on my death, That I never endeavored the subversion of the Laws of the Realm, nor never any change of the Protestant Religion into Popish super-

stition: and I desire you all to remember this Protest of mine, for my innocency in these and from all manner of Treasons whatsoever.

I have been accused likewise as an enemy to Parliaments; no, God forbid, I understood them, and the benefits that comes by them, a great deal
too well to be so, but I did indeed dislike some mis-governments (as I conceived) of some few one or two Parliaments; and I did conceive humbly that
I might have reason for it, for *corruptio optimi est pessima:* There is no corruption in the world so bad as that which is of the best thing in it self for the
better the thing is in nature, the worse it is corrupted; and this being the
highest and greatest Court, over which no other can have any jurisdiction in
the Kingdom, if by any way a mis-government (which God forbid) should
any ways fall upon it the Subjects of this Kingdom are left without all manner of remedy, and therefore God preserve them, and bless them, and direct them, that there may be no mis-conceit, much less mis-government
among them. I will not enlarge my self any further, I have done, I forgive all
the world, all and every of those bitter enemies, or others whatsoever they
have been which have any ways prosecuted me in this kind and I humbly desire to be forgiven first of God, and then of every man, whether I have offended him or no, if he do but conceive that I have; Lord, do thou forgive
me, and I beg forgiveness of him, and so I heartily desire you to join with
me in prayer.

John Bunyan

1628–1688

*T*he Pilgrim's Progress, written during the imprisonment of a Dissenting
preacher in Bedford jail, was once so widely popular an allegorical
work that it was obligatory reading for middle-class Victorian children. Its

prolific author, John Bunyan, who took the commonplace metaphor of life as a journey and charged an ordinary English landscape with spiritual significance, had little schooling himself. The son of a tinker, Bunyan was educated by the popular literature of the English Puritans, by John Foxe's *Book of Martyrs,* and by the authorized version of the English Bible. His own spiritual autobiography describes his emergence from a period of dissoluteness and spiritual darkness, his conversion, and his vocation as a lay preacher in the Bedford Separatist Church.

The restoration of Charles II ended the relative freedom of worship allowed the separated churches and Puritan Seekers, Ranters, and Quakers of Cromwellian England; Bunyan was charged with holding a service deemed Nonconformist by the Church of England and was jailed for twelve years. After his release, he began to preach again, earning the nickname "Bishop Bunyan," only to be detained again during a renewal of persecution. That confinement was short, and for the rest of his life Bunyan was free to preach and write and publish the allegorical works which have survived as the narratives of a born storyteller and natural genius later compared by the Romantics to Robert Burns.

The search for salvation, the understanding of life as a quest, and the resources of symbol and parable are evident in Bunyan's last sermon, in which plain metaphors of darkness and dungeons, children and fathers, birth and rebirth are turned to his evangelical purpose. He avoided literary adornment and affectation, stating that God and the Devil did not play with him, thus, "wherefore I may not play in my relating of them, but lay down the thing as it was."

Mr. Bunyan's Last Sermon
July 1688

Which were born, not of blood, nor of the will of the flesh, nor
of the will of man, but of God.

—JOHN 1:13

The words have a dependence on what goes before, and therefore I must direct you to them for the right understanding of it. You have it thus: "He came to his own but his own received him not; but as many as believed on him, to them gave he power to become the sons of God, even to them which believe on his name; which were born not of blood, nor of the will of the flesh, but of God." In the words before, you have two things:

First. Some of his own rejecting him when he offered himself to them.

Secondly. Others of his own receiving him and making him welcome; those that reject him he also passes by; but those that receive him, he gives them power to become the sons of God. Now, lest any one should look upon it as a good luck or fortune, says he, "They were born not of blood, nor of the will of the flesh, nor of the will of man, but of God": They that did not receive him, they were only born of flesh and blood: but those that receive him, they have God to their Father, they receive the doctrine of Christ with a vehement desire.

First. I'll show you what he means by blood. They that believe are born to it, as an heir is to an inheritance; they are born of God; not of flesh, nor of the will of man, but of God; not of blood, that is, not by generation, not born to the kingdom of heaven by the flesh; not because I am the son of a godly man or woman—that is meant by blood. He has made of one blood all nations; but when he says here, *Not of blood* he rejects all carnal privileges they did boast of. They boasted they were Abraham's seed: No, no, says he, it is not of blood; think not to say you have Abraham as your father, you must be born of God, if you go to the kingdom of heaven.

Secondly. "Nor of the will of the flesh": What must we understand by that?

First. It is taken for those vehement inclinations that are in man to all manner of looseness; fulfilling the desires of the flesh—that must be understood here: Men are not made the children of God by fulfilling their lustful desires, it must be understood here in the best sense; there is not only in carnal men a will to be vile, but there is in them a will to be saved also, a will to go to heaven also: But this it will not do, it will not privilege a man in the things of the kingdom of God, natural desires after the things of another world, they are not an argument to prove a man shall go to heaven whenever he dies. I am not a free-willer, I do abhor it; yet there is not the wickedest man, but he desires some time or other to be saved; he will read some time or other, or it may be, pray; but this will not do: "It is not in him that will, nor in him that runs, but in God that sheweth mercy"; there is willing and running, and yet to no purpose. (Rom. 9:16.) "Israel, which followed after the law of righteousness, have not obtained it"; here I do not understand, as if the apostle had denied a virtuous course of life to be the way to heaven; but that a man without grace, though he have natural gifts, yet he shall not obtain privilege to go to heaven, and be the son of God. Though a man without grace may have a will to be saved, yet he cannot have that will God's way: Nature, it cannot know any thing but the things of nature; the things of God knows no man, but by the Spirit of God; unless the Spirit of God be in you, it will leave you on this side the gates of heaven: "Not of blood, nor of the will of the flesh, nor of the will of man, but of God." It may be some may have a will, a desire that Ishmael may be saved; know this, it will not save thy child. If it was our will, I would have you all go to heaven: How many are there in the world that pray for their children, and cry for them, and ready to die, and this will not do? God's will is the rule of all, it is only through Jesus Christ, "Which were born not of flesh, nor of the will of man, but of God." Now I come to the doctrine.

Men that believe in Jesus Christ, to the effectual receiving of Jesus Christ, they are born to it: He does not say they shall be born to it, but they are born to it; born of God unto God, and the things of God, before he receives God to eternal salvation: "Except a man be born again he cannot see the kingdom of God." Now unless he be born of God he cannot see it! Suppose the kingdom of God be what it will, he cannot see it before he be begotten of God; suppose it be the Gospel, he cannot see it before he be brought into a state of regeneration; believing is the consequence of the new birth: "Not of blood, nor of the will of man, but of God."

First. I will give you a clear description of it under one similitude or two: A child, before it be born into the world, is in the dark dungeon of its mother's womb; so a child of God, before he be born again, in the dark dungeon of sin, sees nothing of the kingdom of God, therefore it is called a new birth; the same soul has love one way in its carnal condition, another way when it is born again.

Secondly. As it is compared to a birth—resembling a child in its mother's womb—so it is compared to a man being raised out of the grave; and to be born again, is to be raised out of the grave of sin: "Awake thou that sleepest, and arise from the dead, and Christ shall give thee life." To be raised from the grave of sin, is to be begotten and born. Revelation 1:5, there is a famous instance of Christ: "He is the first begotten from the dead, the first born from the dead," unto which our regeneration alludeth; that is, if you be born again by seeing those things that are above, then there is a similitude betwixt Christ's resurrection and the new birth: which was born, which was restored out of this dark world, and translated out of the kingdom of this dark world into the kingdom of his dear Son, and made us live a new life; this is to be born again; and he that is delivered from the mother's womb, it is by the help of the mother; so he that is born of God, it is by the Spirit of God: I must give you a few consequences of a new birth.

First of all: A child, you know, is incident to cry as soon as it comes into the world; for, if there be no noise, they say it is dead; you that are born of God, and Christians, if you be not criers, there is no spiritual life in you; if you be born of God, you are crying ones; as soon as he has raised you out of the dark dungeon of sin, you cannot but cry to God, What shall I do to be saved? As soon as ever God had touched the jailor, he cries out, "Men and brethren, what must I do to be saved?" Oh! how many prayerless professors are there in London, that never pray? Coffeehouses will not let you pray; trades will not let you pray; looking glasses will not let you pray; but if you were born of God, you would.

Secondly. It is not only natural for a child to cry, but it must crave the breast, it cannot live without the breast, therefore Peter makes it the true trial of a newborn babe: the newborn babe desires the sincere milk of the word, that he may grow thereby; if you be born of God, make it manifest by desiring to be nourished of God: do you long for the milk of promises? A man lives one way when he is in the world—another way when he is brought unto Jesus Christ. (Isa. 66.) "They shall suck and be satisfied!" If you be born again, there is no satisfaction till you get the milk of God's word into your souls. "To suck and be satisfied with the breasts of consolation." (Isa. 66:11.) Oh, what is a promise to a carnal man! a brothel it may be is more sweet to him; but if you be born again, you cannot live without the milk of God's word. What is a woman's breast to a horse? but what is it to a child? There is its comfort night and day, there is its succor night and day; O how loath are they it should be taken from them. Minding heavenly things, says a carnal man, is but vanity; but to a child of God, there is his comfort.

Thirdly. A child that is newly born, if it have not other comforts to keep it warm than it had in its mother's womb, it dies—it must have some thing got for its succor; so Christ had swaddling clothes prepared for him—so those that are born again, they must have some promise of Christ to keep them alive; those that are in a carnal state, they warm themselves with other things; but those that are born again, they cannot live without some promise of Christ to keep them alive, as he did to the poor infant in Ezekiel 17: "I covered thee with embroidered gold," and when women are with child what fine things will they prepare for their child? O but what fine things has Christ prepared to wrap all in that are born again! O what wrappings of gold has Christ prepared for all that are born again! Women will dress their children that every one may see them how fine they are; so he, in Ezekiel 16:11: "I decked thee also with ornaments, and I also put bracelets upon thine hand, and a chain on thy neck, and I put a jewel on thy forehead, and earrings in thine ears, and a beautiful crown upon thine head"; and, says he in the 13th verse, "Thou didst prosper to a kingdom." This is to set out nothing in the world but the righteousness of Christ and the graces of the Spirit, without which a newborn babe cannot live, unless it have the golden righteousness of Christ.

Fourthly. A child when it is in his mother's lap, the mother takes great delight to have that which will be for its comfort; so it is with God's children; they shall be kept on his knee. (Isa. 66:11.) "They shall suck and be satisfied with the breasts of her consolation." (Verse 13th.) "As one whom his mother comforteth, so will I comfort you." There is a similitude in these things that nobody knows of but those that are born again.

Fifthly. There is usually some similitude betwixt the father and the child, it may be the child looks like its father; so those that are born again, they have a new similitude, they have the image of Jesus Christ. (Gal. 4.) Every one that is born of God, has something of the features of heaven upon him: Men love those children that are likest them most usually; so does God his children, therefore they are called the children of God; but others do not look like him, therefore they are called Sodomites. Christ describes children of the devil by their features; the children of the devil, his works they will do; all works of unrighteousness, they are the devil's works; if you are earthly, you have bore the image of the earthly, if heavenly you have bore the image of the heavenly.

Sixthly. When a man has a child, he trains him up to his own liking; such children have learned the custom of their father's house; so are those that are born of God, they have learned the custom of the true church of God; there they learn to cry, My Father and my God; they are brought up in God's house, they learn the method and form of God's house, for regulating their lives in this world.

Seventhly. Children—it is natural for them to depend upon their father for what they want: if they want a pair of shoes, they go and tell him; if they want bread, they go and tell him; so should the children of God do. Do you want spiritual bread? Go tell God of it. Do you want strength of grace? Ask it of God. Do you want strength against Satan's temptations? Go and tell God of it. When the devil tempts you, run home and tell your heavenly Father: go pour out your complaints to God; this is natural to children—if any wrong them, they go and tell their father; so do those that are born of God, when they meet with temptations, go and tell God of them.

The first use is this, to make a strict inquiry whether you be born of God or not. Examine by those things I laid down before, of a child of nature, and a child of grace; are you brought out of the dark dungeon of this world into Christ? Have you learned to cry, My Father! (Jer. 3:16:) "And I said, thou shalt call me thy Father." All God's children are criers; cannot you be quiet without you are filled with the milk of God's word; cannot you be satisfied without you have peace with God? Pray you consider it, and be serious with yourselves; if you have not these marks, you will fall short of the kingdom of God, you shall never have an interest there; there is no intruding; they will say, "Lord, Lord, open to us, and he will say, I know you not";

no child of God, no heavenly inheritance. We sometimes give something to those that are not our children, but not our lands. O do not flatter yourselves with a portion among the sons, unless you live like sons. When we see a king's son playing with a beggar, this is unbecoming; so if you be the king's children, live like the king's children; if you be risen with Christ, set your affections on things above and not on things below; when you come together, talk of what your Father promised you; you should all love your Father's will, and be content and pleased with the exercises you meet with in the world; if you are the children of God, live together lovingly; if the world quarrel with you, it is no matter: but it is sad if you quarrel together, if this be among you it is a sign of ill breeding; it is according to no rules you have in the word of God. Dost thou see a soul that has the image of God in him? Love him, love him; say, this man and I must go to heaven one day; serve one another, do good for one another; and, if any wrong you, pray to God to right you, and love the brotherhood.

Lastly. If you be the children of God, learn that lesson, gird up the loins of your mind as obedient children, not fashioning yourselves according to your former conversation, but be ye holy in all manner of conversation; consider that the holy God is your Father, and let this oblige you to live like the children of God, that you may look your Father in the face with comfort another day.

Isaac Barrow

1630–1677

*S*uch connoisseurs of rhetoric as Alexander Pope, Samuel Taylor Coleridge, and Daniel Webster called Isaac Barrow the English Bossuet; others considered him the greatest English orator before Burke. In his novel *Amelia,* Henry Fielding has his heroine say of Barrow's sermons, "If ever an angel might be thought to guide the pen of a writer, surely the pen of that great and good man had such an assistant." He certainly had the résumé for it.

Barrow began unpromisingly enough as a London linen draper's son whose tendencies toward untidiness and fighting once made his widower father exclaim that, if it pleased the Lord to take any one of his children, he hoped it would be Isaac. He soon settled down as a student at Cambridge and would have risen in prominence there except that his Royalist leanings blocked the way in the new era of Oliver Cromwell. So instead he sold his books and began a five-year sojourn abroad in Europe, with a side trip to Constantinople, where he read in their original Greek the works of his own favorite preacher, John Chrysostom.

After the Restoration, Barrow's brilliance was readily acknowledged, first by his being appointed Regius professor of Greek at Trinity College, Cambridge; then by his being made the first Lucasian professor of mathematics. (Isaac Newton was his even more brilliant student, to whom he eventually resigned his chair.) Finally, in 1672, Charles II made him Master of Trinity, declaring he had given the post to "the best scholar in Europe." Barrow's final project in his short life would be to lay the foundation for that college's magnificent library.

In 1671, Barrow was appointed college preacher. He typically wrote his sermons out. They were long, but he delivered them in stalwart fashion, once complaining after three and a half hours of speaking that he was a bit tired from *standing*. Perhaps because he took such care in their composition, Barrow's sermons represent some of the finest examples extant of seventeenth-century prose, a fact that surely deserves to be better known. More than that, the range and vigor of his thought are evident in every paragraph. Once Charles II, after hearing Barrow preach, called him unfair because, after he was finished, there was nothing on his subject left for anyone to say.

In the following sermon, in which he compares the divine will with its fickle human counterpart, Barrow's searching intellect locates for us with mathematical precision and vigorous language exactly where, as he inimitably puts it, "the business pincheth."

Of Submission to the Divine Will

Nevertheless let not my will, but thine be done.
—LUKE 22:42

The great controversy, managed with such earnestness and obstinacy between God and Man, is this, whose will shall take place, his or ours: Almighty God, by whose constant protection and great mercy we subsist, doth claim to himself the authority of regulating our practice, and disposing our fortunes; but we affect to be our own masters and carvers; not willingly admitting any law, not patiently brooking any condition, which doth not sort with our fancy and pleasure. To make good his right, God bendeth all his forces, and applieth all proper means both of sweetness and severity (persuading us by arguments, soliciting us by entreaties, alluring us by fair promises, scaring us by fierce menaces, indulging ample benefits to us, inflicting sore corrections on us, working in us and upon us by secret influences of grace, by visible dispensations of providence), yet so it is, that commonly nothing doth avail, our will opposing itself with invincible resolution and stiffness.

Here indeed the business pincheth; herein as the chief worth, so the main difficulty of religious practice consisteth, in bending that iron sinew; in bringing our proud hearts to stoop, and our sturdy humors to buckle, so as to surrender and resign our wills to the just, the wise, the gracious will of our God, prescribing our duty, and assigning our lot unto us. We may accuse our nature, but it is our pleasure; we may pretend weakness, but it is willfulness, which is the guilty cause of our misdemeanors; for by God's help (which doth always prevent our needs, and is never wanting to those who seriously desire it) we may be as good as we please, if we can please to be good; there is nothing within us that can resist, if our wills do yield themselves up to duty: to conquer our reason is not hard; for what reason of man can withstand the infinite cogency of those motives, which induce to obedience? What can be more easy, than by a thousand arguments, clear as day, to convince any man, that to cross God's will is the greatest absurdity in the world, and that there is no madness comparable thereto? Nor is it difficult, if we resolve upon it, to govern any other part or power of our nature; for what cannot we do, if we are willing? what inclination cannot we check, what appetite cannot we restrain, what passion cannot we quell or moderate; what faculty of our soul or member of our body is not obsequious to our will? Even half the resolution with which we pursue vanity and sin, would serve to engage us in the ways of wisdom and virtue.

Wherefore in overcoming our will the stress lieth; this is that impregnable fortress, which everlastingly doth hold out against all the batteries of reason and of grace; which no force of persuasion, no allurement of favor, no discouragement of terror can reduce: this puny, this impotent thing it is, which grappleth with Omnipotency, and often in a manner baffleth it. And no wonder; for that God doth not intend to overpower our will, or to make any violent impression on it, but only to "draw it" (as it is in the Prophet) "with the cords of a man," or by rational inducements to win its consent and compliance; our service is not so considerable to him, that he should extort it from us; nor doth he value our happiness at so low a rate as to obtrude it on us. His victory indeed were no true victory over us, if he should gain it by main force, or without the concurrence of our will; our works not being our works, if they do not issue from our will; and our will not being our will, if it be not free; to compel it were to destroy it, together with all the worth of our virtue and obedience: wherefore the Almighty doth suffer himself to be withstood, and beareth repulses from us; nor commonly doth he master our will otherwise than by its own spontaneous conversion and submission to him. If ever we be conquered, as we shall share in the benefit, and wear a crown; so we must join in the combat, and partake of the victory, by subduing ourselves: we must take the yoke upon us; for God is only served by volunteers; he summoneth us by his Word, he attracteth us by his Grace, but we must freely come unto him.

Our will indeed of all things is most our own; the only gift, the most proper sacrifice we have to offer; which therefore God doth chiefly desire, doth most highly prize, doth most kindly accept from us. Seeing then our duty chiefly moveth on this hinge, the free submission and resignation of our will to the will of God; it is this practice, which our Lord (who came to guide us in the way to happiness, not only as a teacher by his word and excellent doctrine, but as a leader, by his actions and perfect example) did especially set before us; as in the constant tenor of his life, so particularly in that great

exigency which occasioned these words, wherein, renouncing and deprecat-
ing his own will, he did express an entire submission to God's will, a hearty
complacence therein, and a serious desire that it might take place.

For the fuller understanding of which case, we may consider, that our
Lord, as partaker of our nature, and, "in all things" (bating sin) "like unto
us," had a natural human will, attended with senses, appetites, and affections, apt from objects incident to receive congruous impressions of pleasure and pain; so that whatever is innocently grateful and pleasant to us, that
he relished with delight, and thence did incline to embrace; whatever is distasteful and afflictive to us, that he resented with grief, and thence was
moved to eschew; to this probably he was liable in a degree beyond our ordinary rate; for that in him nature was most perfect, his complexion very
delicate, his temper exquisitely sound and fine; for so we find, that by how
much any man's constitution is more sound, by so much he hath a smarter
gust of what is agreeable or offensive to nature. If perhaps sometimes infirmity of body, or distemper of soul (a savage ferity, a stupid dullness, a fondness of conceit, or stiffness of humor, supported by wild opinions, or vain
hopes) may keep men from being thus affected by sensible objects; yet in
him pure nature did work vigorously, with a clear apprehension and lively
sense, according to the design of our Maker, when into our constitution he
did implant those passive faculties, disposing objects to affect them so and
so, for our need and advantage: if this be deemed weakness, it is a weakness
connected with our nature, which he therewith did take, and "with which"
(as the Apostle saith) "he was encompassed." Such a will our Lord had, and
it was requisite that he should have it; that he thence might be qualified to
discharge the principal instances of obedience, for procuring God's favor to
us, and for setting an exact pattern before us; for God imposing on him duties to perform, and dispensing accidents to endure, very cross to that natural will, in his compliance, and acquiescence thereto, his obedience was
thoroughly tried; his virtue did shine most brightly; therefore (as the Apostle saith) "he was in all points tempted"; thence, as to meritorious capacity,
and exemplary influence, "he was perfected through suffering."

Hence was the whole course of his life and conversation among men,
so designed, so modeled, as to be one continual exercise of thwarting that
human will, and closing with the Divine pleasure: it was predicted of him,
"Lo, I come to do thy will, O God"; and of himself he affirmed, "I came

down from heaven not to do my own will, but the will of him that sent me";
whereas therefore such a practice is little seen in achieving easy matters, or
in admitting pleasant occurrences; it was ordered for him, that he should
encounter the roughest difficulties, and be engaged in circumstances most
harsh to natural apprehension and appetite; so that if we trace the footsteps
of his life from the sordid manger to the bloody cross, we can hardly mark
anything to have befallen him apt to satisfy the will of nature. Nature liketh
respect, and loatheth contempt; therefore was he born of mean parentage,
and in a most homely condition; therefore did he live in no garb, did assume
no office, did exercise no power, did meddle in no affairs, which procure to
men consideration and regard; therefore an impostor, a blasphemer, a sorcerer, a loose companion, a seditious incendiary were the titles of honor,
and the eulogies of praise conferred on him; therefore was he exposed to
the lash of every slanderous, every scurrilous, every petulant and ungoverned tongue.

Nature doth affect the good opinion, and goodwill of men, especially
when due in grateful return for great courtesy and beneficence; nor doth
anything more grate thereon than abuse of kindness; therefore, could he
(the world's great friend and benefactor) say, "the world hateth me"; therefore were those, whom he, with so much charity and bounty had instructed,
had fed, had cured of diseases (both corporal and spiritual) so ready to
clamor, and commit outrage upon him; therefore could he thus expostulate,
"Many good works have I showed you from my Father; for which of those
works do ye stone me?" therefore did his kindred slight him, therefore did
his disciples abandon him, therefore did the grand traitor issue from his own
bosom; therefore did that whole nation, which he chiefly sought and labored to save, conspire to persecute him, with most rancorous spite and
cruel misusage.

Nature loveth plentiful accommodations, and abhorreth to be pinched
with any want; therefore was extreme penury appointed to him; he had no
revenue, no estate, no certain livelihood, not "so much as a house where to
lay his head," or a piece of money to discharge the tax for it; he owed his
ordinary support to alms, or voluntary beneficence; he was to seek his food
from a fig tree on the way; and sometimes was beholden for it to the courtesy of publicans; *di hēmas eptocheuse,* "he was" (saith St. Paul) "a beggar
for us."

Nature delighteth in ease, in quiet, in liberty; therefore did he spend his days in continual labor, in restless travel, in endless vagrancy, "going about and doing good"; ever hastening thither, whither the needs of men did call, or their benefit invite; therefore did he "take on him the form of a servant," and was among his own followers "as one that ministereth"; therefore he "pleased not himself," but suited his demeanor to the state and circumstances of things, complied with the manners and fashions, comported with the humors and infirmities of men.

Nature coveteth good success to its design and undertakings, hardly brooking to be disappointed and defeated in them: therefore was he put to water dry sticks; that is, to instruct a most dull and stupid, to reform a most perverse and stubborn generation; therefore his ardent desires, his solicitous cares, his painful endeavors for the good of men did obtain so little fruit; had indeed a contrary effect, rather aggravating their sins than removing them, rather hardening than turning their hearts, rather plunging them deeper into perdition, than rescuing them from it: therefore so much in vain did he, in numberless miraculous works, display his power and goodness, convincing few, converting fewer by them; therefore although he taught with most powerful authority, with most charming gracefulness, with most convincing evidence, yet, "Who" (could he say) "hath believed our report?" Though he most earnestly did invite and allure men to him, offering the richest boons that heaven itself could dispense, yet, "Ye will not" (was he forced to say) "come unto me, that ye may be saved"; although with assiduous fervency of affection he strove to reclaim them from courses tending to their ruin, yet how he prospered, sad experience declareth, and we may learn from that doleful complaint, "How often would I have gathered thy children together, as a hen doth gather her brood under her wings, and ye would not"; *ouk ēthelasate,* your will did not concur, your will did not submit.

In fine, natural will seeketh pleasure, and shunneth pain; but what pleasure did he taste; what inclination, what appetite, what sense did he gratify? How did he feast, or revel? How, but in tedious fastings, in frequent hungers, by passing whole nights in prayer, and retirement for devotion upon the cold mountains? What sports had he, what recreation did he take, but feeling incessant gripes of compassion, and wearisome roving in quest of the lost sheep? In what conversation could he divert himself, but among those, whose doltish incapacity, and froward humor, did wring from his patience those words, "How long shall I be with you, how long shall I suffer you?" What music did he hear? What but the rattlings of clamorous obloquy, and furious accusations against him? to be desperately maligned, to be insolently mocked, to be styled a King, and treated as a slave; to be spit on, to be buffeted, to be scourged, to be drenched with gall, to be crowned with thorns, to be nailed to a cross; these were the delights which our Lord enjoyed, these the sweet comforts of his life, and the notable prosperities of his fortune: such a portion was allotted to him, the which he did accept from God's hand with all patient submission, with perfect contentedness, with exceeding alacrity, never repining at it, never complaining of it, never flinching from it, or fainting under it; but proceeding on in the performance of all his duty, and prosecution of his great designs, with undaunted courage, with unwearied industry, with undisturbed tranquillity and satisfaction of mind.

Had indeed his condition and fortune been otherwise framed; had he come into the world qualified with a noble extraction; had he lived in a splendid equipage, had he enjoyed a plentiful estate and a fair reputation, had he been favored and caressed by men; had he found a current of prosperous success, had safety, ease and pleasure waited on him, where had been the pious resignation of his will, where the precious merit of his obedience, where the glorious luster of his example? how then had our frailty in him become victorious over all its enemies; how had he triumphed over the solicitations and allurements of the flesh; over the frowns and flatteries of the world; over the malice and fury of hell; how then could he have so demonstrated his immense charity toward us, or laid so mighty obligations upon us?

Such in general was the case, and such the deportment of our Lord; but there was somewhat peculiar, and beyond all this occurring to him, which drew forth the words of our text: God had tempered for him a potion of all the most bitter and loathsome ingredients that could be; a drop whereof no man ever hath, or could endure to sip; for he was not only to undergo whatever load human rage could impose, of ignominious disgrace, and grievous pain; but to feel dismal agonies of spirit, and those unknown sufferings, which God alone could inflict, God only could sustain; "Behold, and see," he might well say, "if there be any sorrow like unto my sorrow, which is done unto me; wherewith the Lord hath afflicted me in the day of his fierce anger?" He was to labor with pangs of charity, and through his heart to be pierced with deepest commiseration of our wretched case: he was to crouch under the burden of all the sins (the numberless most heinous sins and abominations) ever committed by mankind: he was to pass through the hottest furnace of divine vengeance, and by his blood to quench the wrath of Heaven flaming out against iniquity; he was to stand (as it were) before the mouth of Hell, belching fire and brimstone on his face: his grief was to supply the defects of our remorse, and his suffering in those few moments to countervail the eternal torments due to us: he was to bear the hiding of God's face, and an eclipse of that favorable aspect, in which all bliss doth reside; a case which he that so perfectly understood, could not but infinitely resent: these things with the clearest apprehension he saw coming on him; and no wonder that our nature started at so ghastly a sight; or that human instinct should dictate that petition, "Father, if thou wilt, let this cup pass from me"; words implying his most real participation of our infirmity; words denoting the height of those sad evils which encompassed him with his lively and lowly resentment of them; words informing us, how we should entertain God's chastisements, and whence we must seek relief of our pressures (that we should receive them, not with a scornful neglect or sullen insensibility, but with a meek contrition of soul; that we should entirely depend on God's pleasure for support under them, or a releasement from them), words which in conjunction with those following do show how instantly we should quash and overrule any insurrection of natural desire against the command or providence of God. We must not take that prayer to signify any purpose in our Lord to shift off his passion, or any wavering in resolution about it; for he could not anywise mean to undo that, which he knew done with God before the world's foundation; he would not unsettle that, which was by his own free undertaking, and irreversible decree; he that so often with satisfaction did foretell this event, who with so "earnest desire" longed for its approach; who with that sharpness of indignation did rebuke his friend offering to divert him from it; who did again repress St. Peter's animosity with that serious expostulation, "The cup which my Father hath given me, shall I not drink it?" who had advisedly laid such trains for its accomplishment, would he decline it? Could that heart all burning with zeal for God and charity to men admit the least thought or motion of averseness from drinking that cup, which was the sovereign medicine administered by divine wisdom for the recovery of God's creation? No; had he spake with such intent, legions of Angels had flown to his rescue; that word, which framed the worlds, which stilled the tempests, which ejected devils, would immediately have scattered his enemies, and dashed all their projects against him; wherefore those words did not proceed from intention, but as from instinct, and for instruction; importing, that what our human frailty was apt to suggest, that his divine virtue was more ready to smother; neither did he vent the former, but that he might express the latter.

He did express it in real effect; immediately with all readiness addressing himself to receive that unsavory potion; he reached out his hand for it, yielding fair opportunity and advantages to his persecutors; he lifted it up to his mouth, innocently provoking their envy and malice; he drank it off with a most steady calmness, and sweet composure of mind, with the silence, the simplicity, the meekness of a lamb, carried to the slaughter; no fretful thought rising up, no angry word breaking forth, but a clear patience, enlivened with a warm charity, shining in all his behavior, and through every circumstance of his passion.

Such in his life, such at his death was the practice of our Lord; in conformity whereto we also readily should undertake whatever God proposeth, we gladly should accept whatever God offereth, we vigorously should perform whatever God enjoineth, we patiently should undergo whatever God imposeth or inflicteth, how cross soever any duty, any dispensation, may prove to our carnal sense or humor.

To do thus, the contemplation of this example may strongly engage us: for if our Lord had not his will, can we in reason expect, can we in modesty desire to have ours? must we be cockered and pleased in everything, when he was treated so coarsely, and crossed in all things? can we grudge at any kind of service, or sufferance; can we think much (for our trial, our exercise, our correction) to bear a little want, a little disgrace, a little pain, when the Son of God was put to discharge the hardest tasks, to endure the sorest adversities?

But farther to enforce these duties, be pleased to cast a glance on two considerations. 1. What the will is, to which, 2. Who the willer is, to whom, we must submit.

1. What is the will of God? is it anything unjust, unworthy, or dishonorable, anything incommodious or hurtful, anything extremely difficult, or intolerably grievous that God requireth of us, to do or bear? No: he willeth nothing from us, or to us, which doth not best become us, and most behove us; which is not attended with safety, with ease, with the solidest profit, the fairest reputation, and the sweetest pleasure.

Two things he willeth, that we should be good, and that we should be happy; the first in order to the second, for that virtue is the certain way, and a necessary qualification to felicity.

"The will of God," saith St. Paul, "is our sanctification"; what is that? what, but that the decays of our frame, and the defacements of God's image within us should be repaired; that the faculties of our soul should be restored to their original integrity and vigor; that from most wretched slaveries we should be translated into a happy freedom, yea, into a glorious kingdom; that from despicable beggary and baseness we should be advanced to substantial wealth, and sublime dignity; that we should be cleansed from the foulest defilements, and decked with the goodliest ornaments; that we should be cured of most loathsome diseases, and settled in a firm health of soul; that we should be delivered from those brutish lusts, and those devilish passions, which create in us a hell of darkness, of confusion, of vexation; which dishonor our nature, deform our soul, ruffle our mind, and wrack our conscience; that we should be endowed with those worthy dispositions and affections, which do constitute in our hearts a heaven of light, of order, of joy and peace; dignify our nature, beautify our soul, clarify and cheer our mind; that we should eschew those practices, which never go without a retinue of woeful mischiefs and sorrows, embracing those which always yield abundant fruits of convenience and comfort; that, in short, we should become friends of God, fit to converse with Angels, and capable of paradise.

"God" (saith St. Paul again) "willeth all men to be saved"; "He willeth not" (saith St. Peter) "that any man should perish"; he saith it himself, yea, he sweareth it, "that he hath no pleasure in the death of the wicked, but that the wicked should turn from his way and live." And what is this will? what, but that we should obtain all the good whereof we are capable; that we should be filled with joy, and crowned with glory; that we should be fixed in an immovable state of happiness, in the perpetual enjoyment of God's favor, and in the light of his blissful presence: that we should be rid of all the evils to which we are liable; that we should be released from inextricable chains of guilt, from incurable stings of remorse, from being irrecoverably engaged to pass a disconsolate eternity in utter darkness, and extreme woe? Such is God's will; to such purposes every command, every dispensation of God (how grim, how rough soever it may seem) doth tend: and do we refuse to comply with that goodwill; do we set against it a will of our own, affecting things unworthy of us, things unprofitable to us, things prejudicial to our best interests; things utterly baneful to our souls? Do we reject the will that would save us, and adhere to a will that would ruin us; a foolish and a senseless will, which slighting the immense treasures of Heaven, the unfading glories of God's Kingdom, the ineffable joys of eternity, doth catch at specious nothings, doth pursue mischievous trifles; a shadow of base profit, a smoke of vain honor, a flash of sordid pleasure; which passeth away like "the mirth of fools," or "the crackling of thorns," leaving only soot, black and bitter behind it.

2. But at least ere we do thus, let us consider, whose will it is, that requireth our compliance.

It is the will of him, whose will did found the earth, and rear the Heaven; whose will sustaineth all things in their existence and operation; whose will is the great law of the world, which universal nature in all its motions doth observe; which reigneth in Heaven, the blessed spirits adoring it, which swayeth in Hell itself, the cursed fiends trembling at it. And shall we alone (we pitiful worms crawling on earth) presume to murmur, or dare to kick against it?

It is the will of our Maker, who together with all our other faculties did create and confer on us the very power of willing: and shall we turn the work of his hands, the gift of his bounty against him?

It is the will of our Preserver, who together with all that we are, or have, continually doth uphold our very will itself; so that without employing any positive force, merely by letting us fall out of his hand, he can send us and it back to nothing: and shall our will clash with that, on which it so wholly dependeth; without which it cannot subsist one moment, or move one step forward in action?

It is the will of our sovereign Lord, who upon various indisputable accounts hath a just right to govern us, and an absolute power to dispose of us: ought we not therefore to say with old Eli, "It is the Lord, let him do to me as it seemeth good to him"? Is it not extreme iniquity, is it not monstrous arrogance for us, in derogation to his will, to pretend giving law, or picking a station to ourselves? Do we not manifestly incur high treason against the King of Heaven by so invading his office, usurping his authority, snatching his scepter into our hands, and setting our wills in his throne?

It is the will of our Judge, from whose mouth our doom must proceed, awarding life or death, weal or woe unto us; and what sentence can we expect, what favor can we pretend to, if we presumptuously shall offend, oppose that will, which is the supreme rule of justice, and sole fountain of mercy?

It is the will of our Redeemer, who hath bought us with an inestimable price, and with infinite pains hath rescued us from miserable captivity under most barbarous enemies, that obeying his will we might command our own, and serving him we might enjoy perfect freedom. And shall we, declining his call and conduct out of that unhappy state, bereave him of his purchase, frustrate his undertakings, and forfeit to ourselves the benefit of so great redemption?

It is the will of our best friend; who loveth us much better than we do love ourselves; who is concerned for our welfare, as his own dearest interest, and greatly delighteth therein; who by innumerable experiments hath demonstrated an excess of kindness to us; who in all his dealings with us purely doth aim at our good, never charging any duty on us, or dispensing any event to us, so much with intent to exercise his power over us, as to express his goodness toward us; who never doth afflict or grieve us more against our will, than against his own desire; never indeed but when goodness itself calleth for it, and even mercy doth urge thereto; to whom we are much obliged, that he vouchsafeth to govern and guide us, our service being altogether unprofitable to him, his governance exceedingly beneficial to us. And doth not such a will deserve regard, may it not demand compliance from us? to neglect or infringe it, what is it; is it not palpable folly, is it not foul disingenuity, is it not detestable ingratitude?

So doth every relation of God recommend his will to us; and each of his attributes doth no less: for,

It is the will of him who is most holy, or whose will is essential rectitude: how then can we thwart it, without being stained with the guilt, and wounded with a sense of great irregularity and iniquity?

It is the will of him who is perfectly just; who therefore cannot but assert his own righteous will, and avenge the violation thereof: is it then advisable to drive him to that point by willful provocation; or to run upon the edge of necessary severity?

It is the will of him who is infinitely wise; who therefore doth infallibly know what is best for us, what doth most befit our capacities and circumstances; what in the final result will conduce to our greatest advantage and comfort: shall we then prefer the dreams of our vain mind before the oracles of his wisdom; shall we, forsaking the direction of his unerring will, follow the impulse of our giddy humor?

It is the will of him who is immensely good and benign; whose will therefore can be no other than goodwill to us; who can mean nothing thereby but to derive bounty and mercy on us. Can we then fail of doing well, if we put ourselves entirely into his hands; are we not our own greatest enemies, in withstanding his gracious intentions?

It is finally the will of him who is uncontrollably powerful; whose will therefore must prevail one way or other: either with our will, or against it, either so as to bow and satisfy us, or so as to break and plague us: for "My counsel" (saith he) "shall stand, and I will do all my pleasure." As to his dispensations, we may fret, we may wail, we may bark at them, but we cannot alter or avoid them: sooner may we by our moans check the tides, or by our cries stop the sun in his career, than divert the current of affairs, or change the state of things established by God's high decree; what he layeth on, no hand can remove; what he hath destined, no power can reverse; our anger therefore will be ineffectual, our impatience will have no other fruit than to aggravate our guilt, and augment our grief.

As to his commands, we may "lift up ourselves against them," we may fight stoutly, we may in a sort prove conquerors; but it will be a miserable victory, the trophies whereof shall be erected in Hell, and stand upon the ruins of our happiness; for while we insult over abused grace, we must fall under incensed justice. If God cannot fairly procure his will of us in way of due obedience, he will surely execute his will upon us in way of righteous vengeance; if we do not surrender our wills to the overtures of his goodness, we must submit our backs to the strokes of his anger. He must reign over us, if not as over loyal subjects to our comfort, yet as over stubborn rebels to our confusion; for this in that case will be our doom, and the last words God will design to spend upon us: "Those mine enemies, which would not that I should reign over them, bring them hither, and slay them before me."

Now the God of peace, that brought again from the dead our Lord Jesus, that great Shepherd of the sheep, through the blood of the everlasting Covenant, make you perfect in every good work to do his will, working in you that which is well pleasing in his sight, through Jesus Christ; to whom be glory for ever and ever. Amen.

Jacques Bénigne Bossuet

1627–1704

Bossuet, considered the greatest of French orators on the basis of his sermons alone, died in the same year in which Voltaire entered a Jesuit college, missing a collision with an intellectual adversary at least as formidable as the Protestants with whom he fought duel after duel. So dogmatic that he is remembered for remarking that he defined a heretic as "he who has an opinion," and so brilliant a rhetorician that French *lycée* students still model their essays on his prose, Bossuet was distinguished by a directness and dignity which reached their highest moments in his funeral orations. The eulogy in the religious tradition has its roots in the classical world as well as the scriptural; at its highest level, it evokes the glory of the world and its heroes, and the transience of both.

Intellectually precocious like many marked out in childhood for the Church, Jacques Bénigne Bossuet opened the Bible one day, came upon the prophecies of Isaiah, and found in the voice and prosodic style of the Old Testament writer one that suited the high commission of the preacher he became as bishop of Meaux. Louis XIV was enchanted by his oratory despite Bossuet's chastisement, in the vein of the same biblical prophet, of the dissolute King and court. His funeral sermon on the great Condé, the most celebrated French soldier of the seventeenth century, was preached at Notre Dame Cathedral. Widely considered a masterpiece of French literature, it stands beside the famous sermon on ambition in which Bossuet complains (quoting St. Augustine) that "we abandon rule, and sigh for power."

Funeral Oration for Louis Bourbon, Prince of Condé

The Lord is with thee, thou mighty man of valor.
Go in this thy might. Surely I will be with thee.

—JUDGES 6:12, 14, 16

At the moment that I open my lips to celebrate the immortal glory of Louis Bourbon, Prince of Condé, I find myself equally overwhelmed by the greatness of the subject, and, if permitted to avow it, by the uselessness of the task. What part of the habitable world has not heard of the victories of the Prince of Condé, and the wonders of his life? Everywhere they are rehearsed. The Frenchman, in extolling them, can give no information to the stranger. And although I may remind you of them today, yet, always anticipated by your thoughts, I shall have to suffer your secret reproach for falling so far below them. We feeble orators can add nothing to the glory of extraordinary souls. Well has the sage remarked that their actions alone praise them; all other praise languishes by the side of their great names. The simplicity of a faithful narrative alone can sustain the glory of the Prince of Condé. But expecting that history, which owes such a narrative to future ages, will make this appear, we must satisfy, as we can, the gratitude of the public, and the commands of the greatest of kings. What does the empire not owe to a prince who has honored the house of France, the whole French name, and, so to speak, mankind at large! Louis the Great himself has entered into these sentiments. After having mourned that great man, and given by his tears, in the presence of his whole court, the most glorious eulogy which he could receive, he gathers together in this illustrious temple whatever is most august in his kingdom, to render public acknowledgments to the memory of the Prince; and he desires that my feeble voice should animate all these mournful signs—all this funeral array. Let us then subdue our grief and make the effort.

God has revealed to us that He alone makes conquerors, that He alone causes them to subserve His designs. Who made Cyrus but God, who, in the prophecies of Isaiah, named him two hundred years before his birth? "Thou hast not known Me," said He to him, "but I have even called thee by thy name, and surnamed thee. I will go before thee and make the crooked places straight; I will break in pieces the gates of brass, and cut in sunder the bars of iron. I am the Lord, and there is none else, there is no God beside Me. I form the light and create darkness"; as if He had said, "I the Lord do everything, and from eternity know everything that I do." Who could have formed an Alexander but the same God who made him visible from afar to the prophet Daniel, and revealed by such vivid images his unconquerable ardor? "See," said He, "that conqueror, with what rapidity he advances from the west, as it were by bounds and without touching the earth." Resembling, in his bold movements and rapid march, certain vigorous and bounding animals, he advances, only by quick and impetuous attacks, and is arrested neither by mountains nor precipices. Already the King of Persia falls into his power. At sight of him, he is "moved with anger—rushes upon him, stamps him under his feet; none can defend him from his attacks, or deliver him out of his hand." Listening only to these words of Daniel, whom do you expect to see under that image—Alexander or the Prince of Condé? God had given him that indomitable valor for the salvation of France during the minority of a king of four years. But let that king, cherished of heaven, advance in life, everything will yield to his exploits. Equally superior to his friends and his enemies, he will hasten now to employ, now to surpass his most distinguished generals; and under the hand of God, who will ever befriend him, he will be acknowledged the firm bulwark of his kingdom. But God had chosen the Prince of Condé to defend him in his childhood.

I have seen him (and do not imagine that I exaggerate here) deeply moved with the perils of his friends; I have seen him, simple and natural, change color at the recital of their misfortunes, entering into their minutest as well as most important affairs, reconciling contending parties, and calming angry spirits with a patience and gentleness which could never have been expected from a temper so sensitive, and a rank so high. Far from us be heroes without humanity! As in the case of all extraordinary things, they might force our respect and seduce our admiration, but they could never win our love. When God formed the heart of man He planted goodness there, as the proper characteristic of the Divine nature, and the mark of that beneficent hand from which we sprang. Goodness, then, ought to be the principal element of our character, and the great means of attracting the affection of others. Greatness, which supervenes upon this, so far from diminishing goodness, ought only to enable it, like a public fountain, to diffuse itself more extensively. This is the price of hearts! For the great, whose goodness is not diffusive, as a just punishment of their haughty indifference, remain forever deprived of the greatest good of life, the fellowship of kindred souls. Never did one less fear that familiarity would diminish respect. Is this the man that stormed cities and gained battles? Have I forgotten the high rank he knew so well to defend? Let us acknowledge the hero, who, always equal to himself, without rising to appear great, or descending to be civil and kind, naturally appeared everything that he ought to be toward all men, like a majestic and beneficent river, which peacefully conveys from city to city, the abundance which it has spread through the countries which it waters; which flows for the benefit of all, and rises and swells only when some violent opposition is made to the gentle current which bears it on its tranquil course. Such was the gentleness and such the energy of the Prince of Condé. Have you an important secret? Confide it freely to that noble heart; your affair becomes his by that confidence. Nothing was more inviolable to that Prince than the rights of friendship. When a favor was asked of him, it was he that appeared obliged; and never was his joy so natural or lively, as when he conferred pleasure upon others.

Let us now look at the qualities of his intellect; and since, alas! that which is most fatal to human life, namely, the military art, admits of the greatest genius and talent, let us in the first place consider the great genius of the Prince with reference to that department. And in the first place, what general ever displayed such far-reaching foresight? One of his maxims was, that we ought to fear enemies at a distance, in order not to fear them near at hand—nay more, to rejoice in their approach. See, as he considers all the advantages which he can give or take, with what rapidity he comprehends times, places, persons, and not only their interests and talents, but even all their humors and caprices! See how he estimates the cavalry and infantry of his enemies, by the nature of the country, or the resources of the confederated princes! Nothing escapes his penetration. With what prodigious comprehension of the entire details and general plan of the war, he is ever awake to the occurrence of the slightest incident; drawing from a deserter, a prisoner, a passer-by, what he wishes him to say or to conceal, what he knows, and, so to speak, what he does not know, so certain is he in his conclusions. His patrols repeat to him the slightest things: he is ever on the watch, for he holds it as a maxim, that an able general may be vanquished, but ought never to suffer himself to be surprised. And it is due to him to say that this never occurred in his case. At whatever, or from whatever quarter his enemies come, they find him on his guard, always ready to fall upon them, and take advantage of their position; like an eagle, which, whether soaring in midair, or perched upon the summit of some lofty rock, sweeps the landscape with his piercing eyes, and falls so surely upon his prey, that it can neither escape his talons, nor his lightning glance. So keen his perception, so quick and impetuous his attack, so strong and irresistible the hands of the Prince of Condé. In his camp vain terrors, which fatigue and discourage more than real ones, are unknown. All strength remains entire for true perils; all is ready at the first signal, and as saith the prophet, "All arrows are sharpened, all bows bent." While waiting, he enjoys as sound repose as he would under his own roof.

But if ever he appeared great, and by his wondrous self-possession, superior to all exigencies, it was in those critical moments upon which victory turns, and in the deepest ardor of battle. In all other circumstances he deliberates—docile, he lends an ear to the counsels of all; but here everything is presented to him at once; the multiplicity of objects confounds him not; in an instant his part is taken; he commands, he acts together; everything is made to subserve his purpose. Shall I add, for why fear the reputation of so great a man should be diminished by the acknowledgment, that he was distinguished not only by his quick sallies which he knew so promptly and agreeably to repair, but that he sometimes appeared, on ordinary occasions, as if he had in him another nature, to which his great soul abandoned minor details, in which he himself deigned not to mingle. In the fire, the shock, the confusion of battle, all at once sprung up in him—I know not what firmness and clearness, what ardor and grace—so attractive to his friends, so terrible to his enemies—a combination of qualities and contrasts, at once singular and striking. In that terrible engagement, when before the gates of the city, and in the sight of the citizens, Heaven seemed to decide the fate of the Prince; when he had against him choice troops and a powerful general—when, more than once, he saw himself exposed to the caprices of fortune—when, in a word, he was attacked on every side, those who were fighting near him have told us that if they had an affair of importance to transact with him, they would have chosen for it that very moment when the fires of battle were raging around him; so much did his spirit appear elevated above them, and, as it were, inspired in such terrible encounters; like those lofty mountains, whose summits, rising above clouds and storms, find their serenity in their elevation, and lose not a single ray of the light by which they are enveloped.

Such, messieurs, are the spectacles which God gives to the world, and the men whom He sends into it, to illustrate, now in one nation, now in another, according to His eternal counsels, His power and His wisdom. For, do His Divine attributes discover themselves more clearly in the heavens which His fingers have formed, than in the rare talents which He has distributed, as it pleases Him, to extraordinary men? What star shines more brilliantly in the firmament, than the Prince de Condé has done in Europe? Not war alone gave him renown; but his resplendent genius which embraced everything, ancient as well as modern, history, philosophy, theology the most sublime, the arts and the sciences. None possessed a book which he had not read; no man of excellence existed, with whom he had not, in some speculation or in some work, conversed; all left him instructed by his penetrating questions or judicious reflections. His conversation, too, had a charm, because he knew how to speak to everyone according to his talents; not merely to warriors on their enterprises, to courtiers on their interests, to politicians on their negotiations, but even to curious travelers on their discoveries in nature, government or commerce; to the artisan on his inventions, and in fine to the learned of all sorts, on their productions. That gifts like these come from God, who can doubt?

That they are worthy of admiration, who does not see? But to confound the human spirit which prides itself upon these gifts, God hesitates not to confer them upon His enemies. St. Augustine considers among the heathen, so many sages, so many conquerors, so many grave legislators, so many excellent citizens—a Socrates, a Marcus Aurelius, a Scipio, a Caesar, an Alexander, all deprived of the knowledge of God, and excluded from His eternal kingdom. Is it not God then who has made them? Who else could do so but He who made everything in heaven, and in the earth? But why has He done so? what in this case are the particular designs of that infinite wisdom which makes nothing in vain? Hear the response of St. Augustine. "He has made them," says he, "that they might adorn the present world." He has made the rare qualities of those great men, as He made the sun. Who admires not that splendid luminary; who is not ravished with his mid-day radiance, and the gorgeous beauty of his rising or decline? But as God has made it to shine upon the evil and upon the good, such an object, beautiful as it is, can not render us happy; God has made it to embellish and illumine this great theater of the universe. So also when He has made, in His enemies as well as in His servants, those beautiful lights of the mind, those rays of His intelligence, those images of His goodness; it is not that these alone can secure our happiness. They are but a decoration of the universe, an ornament of the age. See moreover the melancholy destiny of those men who are chosen to be the ornaments of their age. What do such rare men desire but the praise and the glory which men can give? God, perhaps to confound them will refuse that glory to their vain desires! No: He confounds them rather by giving it to them, and even beyond their expectation. That Alexander who desired only to make a noise in the world, has made it even more than he dared to hope. Thus he must find himself in all our panegyrics, and, by a species of glorious fatality, so to speak, partake of all the praises conferred upon every prince. If the great actions of the Romans required a recompense, God knows how to bestow one correspondent to their merits as well as their desires. For a recompense He gives them the empire of the world, as a thing of no value. O kings! humble yourselves in your greatness: conquerors, boast not your victories! He gives them, for recompense, the glory of men; a recompense which never reaches them; a recompense which we endeavor to attach to—what? To their medals or their statues disinterred from the dust, the refuse of years and barbarian violence; to the ruins of their monuments and works, which contend with time, or rather to their idea, their shadow, or what they call their name! Such is the glorious prize of all their labors; such, in the very attainment of their wishes is the conviction of their error! Come, satisfy yourselves, ye great men of earth! Grasp, if you can, that phantom of glory, after the example of the great men whom ye admire. God, who punishes their pride in the regions of despair, envies them not, as St. Augustine says, that glory so much desired: "vain, they have received a recompense as vain as their desires."

But not thus shall it be with our illustrious Prince. The hour of God is come; hour anticipated, hour desired, hour of mercy and of grace. Without being alarmed by disease, or pressed by time, He executes what He designed. A judicious ecclesiastic, whom he had expressly called, performs for him the offices of religion; he listens, humble Christian, to his instructions; indeed, no one ever doubted his good faith. From that time he is seen seriously occupied with the care of vanquishing himself; rising superior to his insupportable pains, making, by his submission, a constant sacrifice. God, whom he invoked by faith, gave him a relish for the Scriptures; and in that Divine Book, he found the substantial nurture of piety. His counsels were more and more regulated by justice; he solaced the widow and orphan, the poor approached him with confidence. A serious as well as an affectionate father, in the pleasant intercourse which he enjoyed with his children, he never ceased to inspire them with sentiments of true virtue; and that young prince, his grandchild, will forever feel himself indebted to his training. His entire household profited by his example.

These, messieurs, these simple things—governing his family, edifying his domestics, doing justice and mercy, accomplishing the good which God enjoins, and suffering the evils which He sends—these are the common practices of the Christian life which Jesus Christ will applaud before His Father and the holy angels. But histories will be destroyed with empires; no more will they speak of the splendid deeds with which they are filled. While he passed his life in such occupations, and carried beyond that of his most famous actions the glory of a retreat so good and pious, the news of the illness of the Duchess de Bourbon reached Chantilly [the residence of the Prince of Condé] like a clap of thunder. Who was not afraid to see that rising light extinguished? It was apprehended that her condition was worse than it proved. What, then, were the feelings of the Prince of Condé, when he saw himself threatened with the loss of that new tie of his family to the person of the king? Was it on such an occasion that the hero must die? Must he who had passed through so many sieges and battles perish through his tenderness? Overwhelmed by anxieties produced by so frightful a calamity, his heart, which so long sustained itself alone, yields to the blow; his strength is exhausted. If he forgets all his feebleness at the sight of the king approaching the sick princess; if transported by his zeal, he runs, without assistance, to avert the perils which that great king does not fear, by pre-venting his approach, he falls exhausted before he has taken four steps—a new and affecting way of exposing his life for the king. Although the Duchess d'Enghien, a princess, whose virtue never feared to perform her duty to her family and friends, had obtained leave to remain with him, to solace him, she did not succeed in assuaging his anxieties: and after the young princess was beyond danger, the malady of the king caused new troubles to the Prince. The Prince of Condé grew weaker, but death con-cealed his approach. When he seemed to be somewhat restored, and the Duke d'Enghien, ever occupied between his duties as a son and his duties as a subject, had returned by his order to the king, in an instant all was changed, and his approaching death was announced to the Prince. Chris-tians, give attention, and here learn to die, or rather learn not to wait for the last hour, to begin to live well. What! expect to commence a new life when, seized by the freezing grasp of death, ye know not whether ye are among the living or the dead? Ah! prevent, by penitence, that hour of trou-ble and darkness! Thus, without being surprised at that final sentence com-municated to him, the Prince remains for a moment in silence, and then all at once exclaims, "Thou dost will it, O my God; Thy will be done! Give me grace to die well!" What more could you desire? In that brief prayer you see submission to the will of God, reliance on His providence, trust in His grace, and all devotion. From that time, such as he had been in all combats, serene, self-possessed, and occupied without anxiety, only with what was necessary to sustain them—such also he was in that last conflict. Death appeared to him no more frightful, pale and languishing, than amid the fires of battle and in the prospect of victory. While sobbings were heard all around him, he continued, as if another than himself were their object, to give his orders; and if he forbade them weeping, it was not because it was a distress to him, but simply a hindrance. At that time, he extended his cares to the least of his domestics. With a liberality worthy of his birth and of their services, he loaded them with gifts, and honored them still more with mementos of his regard.

The manner in which he began to acquit himself of his religious duties, deserves to be recounted throughout the world; not because it was particularly remarkable; but rather because it was, so to speak, not such;—for it seemed singular that a Prince so much under the eye of the world, should furnish so little to spectators. Do not then, expect those magniloquent words which serve to reveal, if not a concealed pride, at least an agitated soul, which combat or dissemble its secret trouble. The Prince of Condé knew not how to utter such pompous sentences; in death, as in life, truth ever formed his true grandeur. His confession was humble, full of penitence and trust. He required no long time to prepare it; the best preparation for such a confession is not to wait for it as a last resort. But give attention to what follows. At the sight of the holy Viaticum, which he so much desired, see how deeply he is affected. Then he remembers the irreverence with which, alas! he had sometimes dishonored that divine mystery. Calling to mind all the sins which he had committed, but too feeble to give utterance to his intense feelings, he borrowed the voice of his confessor to ask pardon of the world, of his domestics, and of his friends. They replied with their tears. Ah! reply ye now, profiting by that example! The other duties of religion were performed with the same devotion and self-possession. With what faith and frequency did he, kissing the cross, pray the Savior of the world that His blood, shed for him, might not prove in vain. This it is which justifies the sinner, which sustains the righteous, which reassures the Christian! Three times did he cause the prayers for those in anguish to be repeated, and ever with renewed consolation. In thanking his physicians, "See," said he, "my true physicians," pointing to the ecclesiastics to whose teachings he had listened, and in whose prayers he joined. The Psalms were always upon his lips, and formed the joy of his heart. If he complained, it was only that he suffered so little in reparation for his sins. Sensible to the last of the tenderness of his friends, he never permitted himself to be overcome by it; on the contrary, he was afraid of yielding too much to nature. What shall I say of his last interview with the Duke d'Enghien? What colors are vivid enough to represent to you the constancy of the father, the extreme grief of the son? Bathed in tears, his voice choked with sobs, he clasps his dying father, then falls back, then again rushes into his arms, as if by such means he would retain that dear object of his affection; his strength gives way, and he falls at his feet. The Prince, without being moved, waits for his recovery; then calling the Duchess, his daughter-in-law, whom he also sees speechless, and almost without life, with a tenderness in which nothing of weakness is visible, he gives them his last commands, all of which are instinct with piety. He closes with those prayers which God ever hears, like Jacob, invoking a blessing upon them, and upon each of their children in particular. Nor shall I forget thee, O Prince, his dear nephew, nor the glorious testimony which he constantly tendered to your merit, nor his tender zeal on your behalf, nor the letter which he wrote, when dying, to reinstate you in favor of the king—the dearest object of your wishes—nor the noble qualities which made you worthy to occupy, with so much interest, the last hours of so good a life. Nor shall I forget the goodness of the king, which anticipated the desires of the dying Prince; nor the generous cares of the Duke d'Enghien, who promoted that favor, nor the satisfaction which he felt in fulfilling the wishes of his dying father. While his heart is expanded, and his voice animated in praising the king, the Prince de Conti arrives, penetrated with gratitude and grief. His sympathies are renewed afresh; and the two Princes hear what they will never permit to escape from their heart. The Prince concludes, by assuring them that they could never be great men, nor great princes, nor honorable persons, except so far as they possessed real goodness, and were faithful to God and the king. These were the last words which he left engraven on their memory—this was the last token of his affection—the epitome of their duties.

All were in tears, and weeping aloud. The Prince alone was un-moved; trouble came not into that asylum where he had cast himself. O God, Thou wert his strength and his refuge, and as David says, the im-movable rock upon which he placed his confidence. Tranquil in the arms of his God, he waited for his salvation, and implored His support, until he fi-nally ceased to breathe. And here our lamentations ought to break forth at the loss of so great a man. But for the love of the truth, and the shame of those who despise it, listen once more to that noble testimony which he bore to it in dying. Informed by his confessor that if our heart is not entirely right with God, we must, in our addresses, ask God Himself to make it such as He pleases, and address Him in the affecting language of David, "O God, create in me a clean heart." Arrested by these words, the Prince pauses, as if occupied with some great thought; then calling the ecclesiastic who had suggested the idea, he says: "I have never doubted the mysteries of religion, as some have reported." Christians, you ought to believe him; for in the state he then was, he owed to the world nothing but truth. "But," added he, "I doubt them less than ever. May these truths," he continued, "reveal and develop themselves more and more clearly in my mind. Yes!" says he, "we shall see God as He is, face to face!" With a wonderful relish he repeated in Latin those lofty words—"As He is—face to face!" Nor could those around him grow weary of seeing him in so sweet a transport. What was then taking place in that soul? What new light dawned upon him? What sudden ray pierced the cloud, and instantly dissipated, not only the darkness of sense, but the very shadows, and if I dare to say it, the sacred obscurities of faith? What then became of those splendid titles by which our pride is flattered? On the very verge of glory, and in the dawning of a light so beautiful, how rapidly vanish the phantoms of the world! How dim appears the splendor of the most glorious victory! How profoundly we despise the glory of the world, and how deeply regret that our eyes were ever dazzled by its radiance. Come, ye people, come now—or rather ye Princes and Lords, ye judges of the earth, and ye who open to man the portals of heaven; and more than all others, ye Princes and Princesses, nobles descended from a long line of kings, lights of France, but today in gloom, and covered with your grief, as with a cloud, come and see how little remains of a birth so august, a grandeur so high, a glory so dazzling. Look around on all sides, and see all that magnificence and devotion can do to honor so great a hero; titles and inscriptions, vain signs of that which is no more—shadows which weep around a tomb, fragile images of a grief which time sweeps away with every thing else; columns which appear as if they would bear to heaven the magnificent evidence of our emptiness; nothing, indeed, is wanting in all these honors but he to whom they are rendered! Weep then over these feeble remains of human life; weep over that mournful immortality we give to heroes. But draw near especially ye who run, with such ardor, the career of glory, intrepid and warrior spirits! Who was more worthy to command you, and in whom did ye find command more honorable? Mourn then that great Captain, and weeping, say: "Here is the man that led us through all hazards, under whom were formed so many renowned captains, raised by his example, to the highest honors of war; his shadow might yet gain battles, and lo! in his silence, his very name animates us, and at the same time warns us, that to find, at death, some rest from our toils, and not arrive unprepared at our eternal dwelling, we must, with an earthly king, yet serve the King of Heaven." Serve then that immortal and ever merciful King, who will value a sigh or a cup of cold water, given in His name, more than all others will value the shedding of your blood. And begin to reckon the time of your useful services from the day on which you gave yourselves to so beneficent a Master. Will not ye too come, ye whom he honored by making you his friends? To whatever extent you enjoyed his confidence, come all of you, and surround his tomb. Mingle your prayers with your tears; and while admiring, in so great a prince, a friendship so excellent, an intercourse so sweet, preserve the remembrance of a hero whose goodness equalled his courage. Thus may he ever prove your cherished instructor; thus may you profit by his virtues; and may his death, which you deplore, serve you at once for consolation and example. For myself, if permitted, after all others, to render the last offices at this tomb, O prince, the worthy subject of our praises and regrets, thou wilt live forever in my memory. There will thy image be traced, but not with that bold aspect which promises victory. No, I would see in you nothing which death can efface. You will have in that image only immortal traits. I shall behold you such as you were in your last hours under the hand of God, when His glory began to dawn upon you. There shall I see you more triumphant than at Fribourg and at Rocroy; and ravished by so glorious a triumph, I shall give thanks in the beautiful words of the well-beloved disciple, "This is the victory that overcometh the world, even our faith." Enjoy, O prince, this victory, enjoy it forever, through the everlasting efficacy of that sacrifice. Accept these last efforts of a voice once familiar to you. With you these discourses shall end. Instead of deploring the death of others, great prince, I would henceforth learn from you to render my own holy; happy, if reminded by these white locks of the account which I must give of my ministry; I reserve for the flock, which I have to feed with the word of life, the remnants of a voice which falters, and an ardor which is fading away.

Saul Levi Morteira

fl. 1619–1660

*M*orteira's second of two eulogies on the death of one of the early leaders of the Portuguese community in Amsterdam gives us an example of the sermon as narrative, as a historical biography from the Sephardic Diaspora, and as a kind of classical eulogy. His subject, Dr. David Farar, was born in Lisbon, a medical student and scholar, and one of the founders of the synagogue in Amsterdam; he appears to have been an apt student of the literature of Christianity and a late discoverer of his Jewish identity. Farar also seems to have been controversial in his day, and the task of delivering his eulogy must have been a formidable challenge even for Saul Levi Morteira.

Contemporary translators of this eulogistic sermon from Hebrew into English have remarked on its use of a rabbinic belief that listeners who hear praise of a worthy man but fail to learn thereby of their own need for penitence "deserve to be buried alive," i.e., are beyond hope. The sermon's structure is tripartite, based on a well-known rabbinic lament which metaphorically, with images of burning cedars, the hauling in of a monster of the deep, and the slipping of a hook into the torrent, expresses the relationship of a great leader (*tsaddiq* or "righteous man") to the crowd. The sermon moves with a great intellectual agility, which does not preclude deep feeling and a sense of grief, from an earlier Sabbath sermon to explorations of the root meaning of a Hebrew word to Genesis and to a peroration based on Psalm 15.

Second Farar Eulogy:
"The Tsaddiq Is Lost"

An innocent man, dwelling in tents.

—GENESIS 25:27

Mo'ed Qatan, the chapter [beginning] "These may shave": When the soul of Rav Ashi departed, a certain eulogizer began to speak of him as follows: "If the cedars have caught fire, what hope is there for the moss on the wall? If Leviathan has been hauled in by a fishhook, what hope is there for the minnows? If the hook has fallen into the mighty river, what hope is there for the waterholes?" Bar Abbin said to him, "God forbid that I should talk of 'hook' or 'flame' in connection with the righteous. Rather, 'Weep for the losers, not for the lost, for he is at rest, while we are in distress.' "

The sages spoke hyperbolically about the obligation of eulogizing a decent man, saying "Whoever is slothful regarding the eulogy of a decent man deserves to be buried alive." Now they revealed the reason for their hyperbole in the formulation of their statement. They did not say "whoever does not eulogize a decent man," but "whoever is slothful regarding the eulogy, etc." This teaches us the great benefit that comes to us from the eulogy, for in it the qualities of the deceased are made public and recalled to memory. Furthermore, the listener will fear for his own judgment and strive to emulate the *tsaddiq* who has died. Thus, whether one strives to emulate those fine qualities, or whether one thinks "If this happens to the *tsaddiq,* how much worse will it be for the wicked," he will be impelled to return to God, who will have compassion upon him, and thereby become invigorated to perform God's commandments.

Now the statement "Whoever is slothful regarding the eulogy of a decent man" does not mean "whoever is slothful in *delivering* the eulogy"; it means whoever is slothful regarding the commandments at the eulogy of a decent man. When one hears the eulogy given for a decent man, when one hears about those fine qualities, and yet remains slothful, there is no more hope for him, for he has not arisen or budged from his sloth even in the face of such a great stimulus as the death of the *tsaddiq*. That is why "he deserves to be buried alive," for he must indeed be totally wicked, his heart made of stone, incapable of melting. Now the evil are called "dead" even when alive, and the dead are to be buried. Therefore such a person is like a wicked man; he deserves to be buried alive. That is why they said "whoever is slothful," rather than saying "whoever does not deliver a eulogy, etc."

Both of these beneficial lessons were derived by that eulogist with whose words we began from the eulogy for Rav Ashi. He recounted the praises of the deceased, and he taught the listeners a lesson: that they should apply the message *a fortiori* to themselves. He thereby brought benefit both to the listeners and to the deceased: to the listeners, because they will return from their evil way, and to the deceased, because this will be a source of great merit for him in facing his Maker, since even in his death he remains God's servant as he was during his life, bringing his people back to the right path.

The eulogist divided his words into three, providing three metaphors for the *tsaddiq,* calling him a cedar, Leviathan, and a mighty river. These are intended to express the perfection of the deceased in each of the three areas of human behavior: governing of oneself, of a state, and of a household. From these he derived an *a fortiori* lesson: if this is what happened to one who was perfect in all areas, what hope is there for those who are imperfect in all?

(He began by saying, "If the cedars have caught fire, what hope is there for the moss on the wall?") He began by saying, "If the cedars have caught fire." He compared him to a cedar, in which alone there are a number of fine qualities similar to the human soul, as I explained at length in my sermon for the lesson *Huqqat* on the verse *The priest shall take cedar wood* (Num. 19:6).

First, the cedar is the most distinguished of all trees, as in the message sent by the king of Israel to the king of Judea: "The moss on the wall sent to the cedar in Lebanon," meaning the most distinguished to the lowly. This is a unique quality of the human soul among everything created on the six days of creation. Of it alone the Bible says *Let us make [man]* (Gen. 1:26); into it life was exhaled by God, and consultation was required. All this clearly shows its eternality, as we have explained many times.

How fitting, then, in this respect is the metaphor of the cedar for this *tsaddiq* who has departed, for he was designated as outstanding in this congregation, the first among the founders of Judaism, established as a pillar of iron to this day. He did not hesitate in his labor and toil until it was established in its proper place. Therefore it is fitting to call him an outstanding cedar.

Now what can be said "if the cedars have caught fire"? Not that the flame can prevail over the righteous! We may deduce *a fortiori* from the golden altar and from Hananiah, Mishael and Azariah, over whom fire did not prevail—that is, over their bodies—that the flame does not prevail over a *tsaddiq*. No, we speak of fire to express the quickness of his passing. If the designated cedars, the pillars of the diaspora, have caught fire, what hope is there for the lowly moss generated upon the wall, when the wall is devastated and destroyed by their behavior? What will become of them in their punishment, what will become of them when their protecting wall has been removed?

The cedar also serves as an example of height, for example in the verse *whose stature was like the cedar's?* (Amos 2:9). Similar to this is the human soul in that its source is lofty, elevated above all other created beings, for it was exhaled by God. The sages said, "Whoever exhales exhales something of his own essence." In this respect too we may say and apply the word "cedar" to this *tsaddiq,* thinking of his stature during the year when he walked with God. This too God showed us as a sign of his love, for he was leader, officer, *parnas* and *memmuneh,* elevated above all others. When one rises to greatness, all his sins are pardoned. If the cedars have caught fire—one who could lead the congregation and unify it—what hope is there for the moss of the wall, those who in their lowliness cause divisiveness and remove from the congregation good leadership?

The cedar was also taken for the building of things pertaining to the divine, as we see in the verse, *The cedar of the interior of the house . . . was all cedar, no stone was exposed; . . . he overlaid its cedar altar* (1 Kings 6:18, 20). This is a particular quality of the human soul, which alone can serve to apprehend spiritual things, not the body from which they are in a different category. That is why the prophets used figurative language in apprehending spiritual things. In this too, our righteous departed may be compared to the cedar, for he served all things of a spiritual nature, and was first for everything pertaining to holiness: judging in peace, gathering charitable funds to redeem the captive and marry off the orphan, passing ordinances for a voluntary society, establishing an academy, annulling transgressions, involving himself in communal necessities, speaking before Gentile scholars. In short, he was like a cedar, serving in all matters pertaining to God. If the divine cedars have caught fire, what hope is there for the moss on the wall, those whose social life is represented by a wall: material things, food and drink, prostitutes, swearing, and all other sins?

The cedar is always associated with the name of God, as in the verses, *the cedars of God by its boughs* (Ps. 80:11), *[The trees of the Lord drink their fill,] the cedars of Lebanon, His own planting* (Ps. 104:16). This quality also is to be found in the human soul, which is called the spirit of God, *the soul of Shaddai* (Job 32:8), *the lamp of the Eternal* (Prov. 20:27), and many similar expressions. How fitting too is this quality for the *tsaddiq* who was called by God's name wherever he went. During the first years in this land, when people used to conceal their [Jewish] names, he would proclaim his in public, as events occurred every day. That is why many Gentiles from the ends of the earth came to seek him out. Even in Spain, in a place of danger, he did not conceal it; he identified himself as a Jew, a word in which the name of God is contained. If the cedars have caught fire, what hope is there for the moss on the wall which, because of excessive fear and insufficient trust, spurned it and denied it and voluntarily went to a place where they had to hope not to be recognized, lying to God by denying His name.

The cedar is a simile for the *tsaddiq*, as we see in the verse, *The righteous (tsaddiq) flourish like a date-palm, they thrive like a cedar in Lebanon* (Ps. 92:13). This is indeed a quality of the soul, which finds no true serenity or joy except in justice, honesty, and truth. It rejoices not in physical pleasures, but rather in the disciplines of wisdom and the apprehension of truth. So with this *tsaddiq:* we know that he flourished like a date-palm, straightforward, without deviousness, never diverting himself to left or right as he walked. And his truthfulness: speaking what was in his heart, not saying one thing and thinking another. How he rejoiced in truth and justice, how distant he was from falsehood! If the cedars have caught fire, what hope is there for the moss on the wall, which has no roots? Sometimes they will be there and sometimes not, and truth is absent from their lips.

The cedar is also a tree into which no worm can enter, which does not decay, a quality indeed present in the human soul, which does not decay and is not destroyed. So it is that this *tsaddiq* was like a cedar which did not decay. We see this in the verses, *we will panel it with cedar* (Cant. 8:9), *for the name of the righteous (tsaddiq) is invoked in blessing, but the fame of the wicked rots* (Prov. 10:7). His memory is for the world to come; it will not rot or be destroyed throughout the generations. This is a clear indication of his perfect rest, for all those with whom the spirit of their fellow human beings are pleased, the spirit of the Omnipresent is pleased with. His memory will always be blessed, *the tsaddiq will be remembered forevermore* (Ps. 112:6). If the cedars have caught fire, what hope is there for the moss on the wall—the ordinary people who have no memorial, who have never performed an act to be mentioned with blessing—after their death. Such acts are extremely beneficial, as we see in the verse, *the name of the righteous is invoked in blessing, but the fame of the wicked rots* (Prov. 10:7). What blessing and rotting can be meant here, except for reward and punishment? Thus in the first part of the metaphorical statement, using the cedar, we see explained some of the qualities of the *tsaddiq* pertaining to personal conduct.

Secondly, he said, "If Leviathan has been hauled in by a fish-hook, what hope is there for the minnows?" This statement too applies essentially to this *tsaddiq*. For "Leviathan" has four meanings. The first is the name of a great fish, as in the verses, *Leviathan that You formed to sport with* (Ps. 104:26), *Leviathan the elusive serpent* (Isa. 27:1), and so forth. Now it is said, if Leviathan—a healthy man, handsome, looking like royalty, like an angel of God (cf. Judg. 8:18; 13:6), *whose eyes were undimmed and his vigor unabated* (Deut. 34:7), who never had pain in his head and was healthy—was "hauled in by a fishhook"—by such a minor illness, "what hope is there for the minnows"—the elderly, the weak, frail in body and emaciated? How easily *the wind shall carry them off, the whirlwind shall scatter them* (Isa. 41:16), unless they *look to their ways* (Ps. 119:15).

A second meaning for "Leviathan" is derived from the word *yelalah*, "wailing." The Aramaic translation of the word in the verse *those prepared to rouse up Leviathan* (Job 3:8) is "wailing." Thus the meaning of "If Leviathan . . ." is, if one who causes wailing and grief for the entire people at his illness, as all of them prayed to God to cure him, and at his death the entire household of Israel wept—an unambiguous indication of his righteousness—"what hope is there for the minnows," at whose death people will rejoice because of their lowliness and wickedness? We see this in the verse, *When the wicked perish there are shouts of joy* (Prov. 11:10).

A third meaning for "Leviathan" is derived from the word *livvuy,* "accompaniment." Thus he said, "If Leviathan," who was *a graceful wreath (leviyyat ḥen) upon our head, a necklace upon our throat* (cf. Prov. 1:9), he who used to honor us by his accompaniment, who was at the head of the funeral procession, the voluntary society, the academy—if he "has been hauled in by a fishhook, what hope is there for the minnows," from whom people keep their distance because of their stench.

A fourth meaning is derived from "Levite." He said, "If such a great man, of distinguished ancestral lineage, linked with the chosen tribe of Levi on his mother's side, for that is why he was not redeemed although he was a firstborn—if Leviathan reaching such a level of perfection has been hauled in by a fishhook, what hope is there for the minnows" of ordinary families, having no merit from their ancestors?

He concluded by saying, "If the hook has fallen into the mighty river *(naḥal),* what hope is there for the waterholes?" This too can be interpreted in five ways, each one of them proclaiming the kinds of excellence in character and mind found together in this *tsaddiq.* First, *naḥal* has the meaning "river," for his excellence was like a river flowing continuously day and night, never ceasing to do the will of his heavenly Father. Who has not seen him on many days? When his ships arrived, the poor, the orphan and the widow would rejoice when they went forth from his house. People entered and left carrying many gifts, such that *his food was given* [away], *his drink was assured* (Isa. 33:16), always consistently, like a flowing river. "If the hook has fallen into the mighty river, what hope is there for the waterholes," which are not of benefit to all others?

The word can also be derived from *naḥalah,* inheritance, for he was a lion whose father was a lion, a good man whose father was good, a priest whose father was a priest. His goodness was a legacy from his ancestors. He was the son of the esteemed R. Abraham Farar the Elder, of blessed memory, a model of goodness, such that there was a constantly flowing inheritance *(naḥalah).* If even into this "the hook has fallen, what hope is there for the waterholes," that have no origins to speak of?

In addition, *naḥal* can be derived from *ḥoli,* "sickness," as we see in the biblical phrase *my wound is grievous (naḥlah makati)* (Jer. 10:19). He therefore says, "If in the mighty *naḥal*"—if one whose passing has caused a general sickness *(ḥoli),* a universal weeping, *for every head is ailing (le-ḥoli) and every heart is sick* (Isa. 1:5), for our heads and our hearts have been wounded—despite it all "the hook has fallen, what hope is there for the waterholes," at whose passing no one will pay any attention?

Furthermore, *naḥal* is etymologically linked with music, as in the biblical phrase *For the leader, on the neḥilot* (Ps. 5:1). Thus the eulogist spoke of continuous, harmonious music—for this *tsaddiq* was composed of all the qualities that combine as yet another fine quality to make beautiful music: wisdom, reverence, beauty, decency, love, justice, strength, eloquence, healing. All the sounds of this music were played continuously with a sweetness that brought joy to God and man. If with such a man "the hook has fallen, what hope is there for the waterholes," that lack any element of perfection?

Finally, *naḥal* can be derived from the Talmudic phrase for a swarm *(naḥil)* of bees. He therefore said, if this mighty *naḥal,* the entire congregation—for he was the one who unified it, in him alone the entire congregation was represented, he perfected it, he brought it together, he was the source of its joy—if here too "the hook has fallen, what hope is there for the waterholes," who fail to manifest even their own individual potential? In short, whoever can think of all these things and not fear for his soul, but remains slothful in the fear of God during the eulogy for a decent man, such a person deserves to be buried alive.

Young children have no thought or concern about the provisions they need for survival so long as their father, at whose table they eat, remains alive, for they rely upon him. But when he dies, they must necessarily begin to fear and make an effort to find provisions for themselves. So at the loss of a shelter like this, a protecting father for all, about whom we once said, *in his shade we live among the nations* (cf. Lam. 4:20), the people as a whole must begin to think that now he is missing, each person needs to face the burdens of individual work. This is the meaning of the statement, "Weep for the losers, not for the lost, for he is at rest—about to receive the reward for his actions—while we are in distress." Instead of being protected by his merit, we are now left in distress, each one to be helped by his own efforts. That is why we say, "They have departed for their resting places, leaving us to our sighs." For he is certainly at rest, at perfect rest. Even though "not every man is worthy of two tables," through the beauty and decency of his deeds he earned both. He had success in this world, and it will be good for him in the next.

This is as we began in our theme verse, *An innocent man (tam)* (Gen. 25:27), meaning a complete man *(tamim),* perfect in everything, *dwelling in tents* (Gen. 25:27), dwelling peacefully in two tents, this world and the world to come, for both of them are called "tents." This world, in the verse, *stretched them out like a tent to dwell in* (Isa. 40:22). The world to come, in the verse, *Lord, who may sojourn in Your tent, who may dwell on Your holy mountain? He who lives without blame, who does what is right, and in his heart acknowledges the truth, whose tongue is not given to evil, who has never done harm to his fellow, or borne reproach for his neighbor; for whom a contemptible man is abhorrent, but who honors those who fear the Lord; who stands by his oath even to his hurt; who has never lent money at interest, or accepted a bribe against the innocent* (Ps. 15:1–5): all qualities openly manifest and recognized in this *tsaddiq.* He will therefore receive their reward with the conclusion of the Psalm: *He who acts thus shall never be shaken* (Ps. 15:5). May God remember his merit on our behalf and put an end to our sorrows. But our duty is to accept this judgment, and to say "Blessed is the Judge of Truth."

PART VI

"Errand into the
Wilderness"

Colonial America

John Winthrop

1 5 8 8 – 1 6 4 9

*T*he Puritans who set sail from old England did not think of New England as being "new." It appeared to them to be much like the benighted island they left behind, a familiar world of sin and struggle, vacant except for a few Indians. John Winthrop was the first governor of Massachusetts Bay, an unrelenting preacher, fierce searcher of souls, and one of the great speakers in the pantheon of the founders of the New World. He began as an attorney in London, a gentleman resident at Groton Manor in England occupied with the passing of parliamentary bills. In 1629 he joined in the Cambridge Agreement, pledging along with his Puritan fellow signers to remove to New England, where he was twelve times chosen governor by annual election in the new colony.

The American historian Perry Miller has explained that John Winthrop, speaking from the deck of his storm-tossed flagship *Arbella* in 1630, saw the immigration of Puritans not as a retreat from Europe but as a flank attack of English scholars, soldiers, and statesmen, building the foundation of the "city on a hill" as a means to a greater end. In Winthrop's view, the citizens of New England entered into a new covenant between men and God like that between rulers and subjects, to which his conservative and aristocratic mind was already sealed.

In this sermon, delivered to a captive audience on shipboard, wondering if they could possibly survive the transatlantic crossing and the rigors of the coasts and forests of Plymouth Plantation, Winthrop's argument offers more than survival: he proposed the city on a hill as a new Jerusalem and a new Rome, with a sense of high purpose as to what another preacher, Samuel Danforth, later called "an errand into the wilderness."

Another historian, Samuel Eliot Morison, has remarked of Winthrop and the Pilgrim Fathers that their "range was narrow, but within it they were supreme."

A Model of Christian Charity

Written
on Board the Arbella,
on the Atlantic Ocean
by the Honorable John Winthrop Esquire

In His passage (with the great Company of Religious people,
of which Christian Tribes he was the Brave Leader and famous
Governor) from the Island of Great Britain to New England in
the North America
Anno 1630

. . . From the former Considerations ariseth these Conclusions.

1 First, This love among Christians is a real thing not Imaginary.

2ly. This love is as absolutely necessary to the being of the body of Christ, as the sinews and other ligaments of a natural body are to the being of that body.

3ly. This love is a divine spiritual nature free, active strong Courageous permanent under valuing all things beneath its proper object, and of all the graces this makes us nearer to resemble the virtues of our heavenly father.

4ly. It rests in the love and welfare of its beloved, for the full and certain knowledge of these truths concerning the nature use, [and] excellency of this grace, that which the holy ghost hath left recorded 1 Cor. 13. may give full satisfaction which is needful for every true member of this lovely body of the Lord Jesus, to work upon their hearts, by prayer meditation continual exercise at least of the special [power] of this grace till Christ be formed in them and they in him all in each other knit together by this bond of love.

It rests now to make some application of this discourse by the present design which gave the occasion of writing of it. Herein are 4 things to be propounded: first the persons, 2ly, the work, 3ly, the end, 4ly the means.

1. For the persons, we are a Company professing ourselves fellow members of Christ, In which respect only though we were absent from each other many miles, and had our employments as far distant, yet we ought to account our selves knit together by this bond of love, and live in the exercise of it, if we would have comfort of our being in Christ, this was notorious in the practice of the Christians in former times, as is testified of the Waldenses from the mouth of one of the adversaries Aeneas Sylvius, *mutuo [solent amare] penè antequam norint,* they use to love any of their own religion even before they were acquainted with them.

2ly. For the work we have in hand, it is by a mutual consent through a special overruling providence, and a more than an ordinary approbation of the Churches of Christ to seek out a place of Cohabitation and Consortship under a due form of Government both civil and ecclesiastical. In such cases as this the care of the public must oversway all private respects, by which not only conscience, but mere Civil policy doth bind us; for it is a true rule that particular estates cannot subsist in the ruin of the public.

3ly. The end is to improve our lives to do more service to the Lord the comfort and increase of the body of Christ whereof we are members that our selves and posterity may be the better preserved from the Common corruptions of this evil world to serve the Lord and work out our Salvation under the power and purity of his holy Ordinances.

4ly. For the means whereby this must be effected, they are 2fold, a Conformity with the work and end we aim at, these we see are extraordinary, therefore we must not content our selves with usual ordinary means whatsoever we did or ought to have done when we lived in England, the same must we do and more also where we go: That which the most in their Churches maintain as a truth in profession only, we must bring into familiar and constant practice, as in this duty of love we must love brotherly without dissimulation (Rom. 12:9–10), we must love one another with a pure heart fervently (1 Peter 1:22) we must bear one anothers burdens (Gal. 6:2), we must not look only on our own things, but also on the things

of our brethren, neither must we think that the lord will bear with such fail-
ings at our hands as he doth from those among whom we have lived, and
that for 3 Reasons.

1. In regard of the more near bond of marriage, between him and us,
wherein he hath taken us to be his after a most strict and peculiar manner
which will make him the more Jealous of our love and obedience so he tells
the people of Israel, you only have I known of all the families of the Earth
therefore will I punish you for your Transgressions. (Amos 3:2.)

2ly. Because the lord will be sanctified in them that come near him.
We know that there were many that corrupted the service of the Lord some
setting up Altars before his own, others offering both strange fire and
strange Sacrifices also; yet there came no fire from heaven, or other sudden
Judgment upon them as did upon Nadab and Abihu (Lev. 10:1–2) who yet
we may think did not sin presumptuously.

3ly. When God gives a special Commission he looks to have it strictly
observed in every Article, when he gave Saul a Commission to destroy
Amaleck he indented with him upon certain Articles and because he failed
in one of the least, and that upon a fair pretense, it lost him the kingdom,
which should have been his reward, if he had observed his Commission
(1 Sam. 15; 28:16–18): Thus stands the cause between God and us, we are
entered into Covenant with him for this work, we have taken out a Commission, the Lord hath given us leave to draw our own Articles we have professed to enterprise these Actions upon these and these ends, we have
hereupon besought him of favor and blessing: Now if the Lord shall please
to hear us, and bring us in peace to the place we desire, then hath he rati-
fied this Covenant and sealed our Commission, [and] will expect a strict
performance of the Articles contained in it, but if we shall neglect the observation of these Articles which are the ends we have propounded, and dis-
sembling with our God, shall fall to embrace this present world and
prosecute our carnal intentions, seeking great things for our selves and our
posterity, the Lord will surely break out in wrath against us be revenged of
such a perjured people and make us know the price of the breach of such a
Covenant.

Now the only way to avoid this shipwreck and to provide for our posterity is to follow the Counsel of Micah, to do Justly, to love mercy, to

walk humbly with our God (Micah 6:8), for this end, we must be knit together in this work as one man, we must entertain each other in brotherly
Affection, we must be willing to abridge our selves of our superfluities, for
the supply of others necessities, we must uphold a familiar Commerce
together in all meekness, gentleness, patience and liberality, we must delight in each other, make others Conditions our own, rejoice together,
mourn together, labor, and suffer together, always having before our eyes
our Commission and Community in the work, our Community as members of the same body, so shall we keep the unity of the spirit in the bond
of peace (Eph. 4:3), the Lord will be our God and delight to dwell among
us, as his own people and will command a blessing upon us in all our ways,
so that we shall see much more of his wisdom power goodness and truth
then formerly we have been acquainted with, we shall find that the God of
Israel is among us, when ten of us shall be able to resist a thousand of our
enemies, when he shall make us a praise and glory, that men shall say of
succeeding plantations: the Lord make it like that of New England: for we
must Consider that we shall be as a City upon a Hill, the eyes of all people
are upon us; so that if we shall deal falsely with our god in this work we
have undertaken and so cause him to withdraw his present help from us,
we shall be made a story and a byword through the world, we shall open
the mouths of enemies to speak evil of the ways of God and all professors
for Gods sake; we shall shame the faces of many of Gods worthy servants,
and cause their prayers to be turned into Curses upon us till we be consumed out of the good land whether we are going: And to shut up this discourse with that exhortation of Moses that faithful servant of the Lord in
his last farewell to Israel Deut. 30. Beloved there is now set before us life,
and good, death and evil in that we are Commanded this day to love the
Lord our God, and to love one another to walk in his ways and to keep his
Commandments and his Ordinance, and his laws, and the Articles of our
Covenant with him that we may live and be multiplied, and that the Lord
our God may bless us the land whether we go to possess it: But if our
hearts shall turn away so that we will not obey, but shall be seduced and
worship [serve *canceled*] other Gods our pleasures, and profits, and serve
them; it is propounded unto us this day, we shall surely perish out of the
good Land whether we pass over this vast Sea to possess it; Therefore let

us choose life, that we, and our Seed, may live; by obeying his voice, and cleaving to him, for he is our life, and our prosperity.

Cotton Mather

1663–1728

*O*f all American preachers associated in the public imagination with New England Puritanism, fiery preaching, and witch hunting, Cotton Mather is preeminent. Yet the rich complexity of his life and times belie such clichéd generalizations. The offspring of generations of preachers on both the Cotton and Mather sides, he grew up in the shadow of his father's, Increase Mather's, Boston pulpit. As a child, his precocity was demonstrated by the ability to take down in Latin a sermon as it was being preached in English. At the age of eleven and a half he entered Harvard College and began his religious vocation in earnest. There he developed a severe, humiliating stammer, from which he prayed for release. By sixteen he was informally preaching to his neighbors.

On the day of his ordination, in 1685, Mather preached a sermon, on John 21:17 ("He saith unto him the third time, Simon, son of Jonah, lovest thou me? Peter was grieved because he said unto him the third time, Lovest thou me? And he said unto him, Lord, thou knowest all things; thou knowest that I love thee. Jesus saith unto him, Feed my sheep"). It lasted for one and three quarter hours, a not uncommon length at the time. He and his father (whom he outlived by only five years) both preached in the Old North Church. It had three tiers of galleries, and on any given Sunday could and did hold nearly half the adult population of Boston.

The variety of Mather's preaching was wide, including "execution sermons," to which the condemned would be brought in chains and holding a Bible. Some of the hapless even requested a Mather sermon. Published sermons were the best-sellers of the day, and Mather's first was "The Call of the Gospel" (1686), which "sold exceedingly."

Throughout a long life of fervor and controversy, Mather produced thousands of sermons and at his death was easily, given the tally of his other writings, the most prolific author the New World had yet produced. He was confined to his bed the last weeks of his life and even so used the occasion to exemplify to his visiting admirers the art of dying. His burial took place in Copp's Hill, the Old North Church cemetery, observed by a "Vast Concourse, [an] Exceeding long Procession and numberless Spectators. Every heart Sad."

Mather's interest reached well beyond the subjects of fire and brimstone and included a lively pursuit of medicine and science. In the excerpt here, he preaches to us across the centuries his delight at God's wonderful fashioning of the universe.

𝒸ℛ

Thanksgiving

Praises bespoke for the God of Heaven, in a Thanksgiving Sermon delivered on December 19, 1689, containing just Reflections upon the Excellent Things done by the Great God, more generally in Creation and Redemption, and in the Government of the World, but more particularly in the Remarkable Revolutions of Providence which are everywhere the matter of present Observation . . .

And O that we might all *stir up our selves* this Day to *Sing* and *Spread* the *praises* due to the Eternal God for the *excellent things* which He has done. . . .

First, the Excellent Things done by God, in the Works of *Creation,* call for our Praises. It was once the outcry of the Psalmist, in a Rapture, *Praise the Lord from the Heavens, praise the Lord from the Earth, praise the Lord all ye His Armies.* Truly, 'Tis our Business to *praise* Him, *for* the Heavens, and *for* the Earth, and *for* all those Armies which He has replenished the World withal. We have a good pattern for us, in Psalm 104:14, 33. Says the Psalmist, *O*

Lord, how manifold are thy Works! In wisdom hast thou made them all. Well, and what is now incumbent upon us, that have the view thereof? It follows, *I will sing praise unto my God, while I have any Being.* Methinks the Children of Men too much imitate the Spider, when they Look after nothing but building a little House for themselves, and concern themselves with nothing but the petty Affairs thereof. We should remember that we are Citizens of the World, and as far as we can, we should visit every Corner of it, with our Praises to Him, *of whom and for whom is all.* I make no question, but that we do in a blessed manner Antedate Heaven, by doing so. The *Praises* of God are Exhibited in every part of the World, and we forfeit the privilege of *Reason,* if we do not put as many of them as we can, into our Acknowledgments. There are above six Thousand *Plants* growing on that little Spot of the World, which we tread upon; and yet a Learned Man, has more than once, found *One* Vegetable enough to make a Subject for a *Treatise* on it. What might then be said upon the Hundred and fifty *Quadrupeds,* the Hundred and fifty *Volatils,* the five and twenty *Reptiles,* besides the vast multitudes of *Aquatils,* added unto the rich variety of *Gems* and *Minerals,* in our World? Our own *Bodies* are, to use the Phrase of the Psalmist, *So Fearfully and Wonderfully made,* that one of the Ancient Heathen at the sight thereof, could not forbear breaking forth into a *Hymn* unto the *praise* of the great Creator; 'Tis impossible that anything should be better shaped! Indeed, All the Things that we have every Day before our eyes, have a most charming prospect in them, and the very Deformities which the Flood has brought upon this *Terraqueous* Globe, are made *Beauties,* by the Disposals of *the Lord that sat upon the Flood.* There is not a Fly, but what may confuse an *Atheist.* And the Little things which our Naked Eyes cannot penetrate into, have in them a *Greatness* not to be seen without Astonishment. By the Assistance of Microscopes have I seen *Animals* of which many Hundreds would not Equal a Grain of Sand. How Exquisite, How stupendous must the Structure of them be! The *Whales* that are sometimes found more than an *Hundred Foot* in length, methinks those *moving Islands,* are not such *Wonders* as these minute Fishes are.

But alas, All this *Globe* is but as a Pins point, if compared with the mighty *Universe.* Never did any man yet make a tolerable Guess at its Dimensions: but were we among the *Stars,* we should utterly lose the sight of our *Earth,* although it be above twenty-six thousand *Italian* Miles in the compass of it. Look upon the *Wandering Stars,* and you shall see so many

Worlds, that swallow up all our Conjectures at the circumstances of them, and of their *Satellites.* Look upon the *Fixed Stars,* and what shall we say about the *Bigness* of them? Doubtless they many scores of times exceed the Bulk of this poor Lump of Clay, about a few Foot whereof the Inhabitants are so Quarrelsome. Or what shall we say about the *Number* of them? For though they are but a few above a Thousand, that we ever see, without a *Telescope,* yet that will tell us, that the *Six,* which we commonly call, *The Seven Stars,* have above *Sixty* among them, and the rest are like the *Sand* of the Sea, innumerable. But above all, the *Sun,* that principal Engine, which the whole *Visible Creation* hath such a manifest Dependence on; *This* declares *the Glory of God,* at such a Rate, that the Philosopher once thought himself born on purpose, to Behold the *Splendors of it. This* at last hath glared out my Eyes, that at this time, I can look no further upon the *Marvels of the Creation.* But, my Brethren, Let us take our Time to Travel over the *World* (I hope, we shall one Day have *Bodies* more able to do it, than our *Spirits* at present are!) and then let us give many Thousands of Praises to Him, Whose Omnipotent and Omniscient Hand hath Created all. *O Sing unto the Lord, because He hath done Excellent Things,* in making and managing the vast *Fabrick* of the World.

Jonathan Edwards

1703–1758

In the 1740s Jonathan Edwards preached to a new congregation in Enfield, Connecticut; the occasion inspired, two hundred years later, two poems by New England American poet Robert Lowell: "After the Surprising Conversions" and "Mr. Edwards and the Spider." When Edwards spoke, his sermons frequently stressed the word "fire" and the ordinary sinner's precarious strut over the abyss. The notion of hellfire was well emblazoned on the minds of his susceptible audience, one already pitched to the heights of a religious panic and seemingly sympathetic to Edwards's Calvin-istic theology. Edwards, a precocious scholar and brilliant student of the English idealist John Locke, believed in a covenant between God and man in which salvation was the outcome for which sinners must strive, and in which the fires of hell awaited the unrepentant.

In the dangerous paradise of the New World in which Edwards preached, his audience was ready to believe itself well along the slope to damnation, and his vision of depravity and sulphur is in the tradition of the jeremiad—an instance of what the historian Perry Miller has called the "tyranny of form over thought." But revivalism and the fear of the flame are ongoing themes in American society and rhetoric, and Edwards's dream of Judgment Day and our suspension between life and unending apocalyptic terror continue to haunt much of America's political, religious, and moral life.

ᥴᕽ

Sinners in the Hands of an Angry God

Their foot shall slide in due time.

—DEUTERONOMY 32:35

In this verse is threatened the vengeance of God on the wicked unbe-lieving Israelites, who were God's visible people, and who lived under the means of grace; but who, notwithstanding all God's wonderful works to-ward them, remained (as ver. 28) void of counsel, having no understanding in them. Under all the cultivations of heaven, they brought forth bitter and poisonous fruit; as in the two verses next preceding the text—The expres-sion I have chosen for my text, *Their foot shall slide in due time,* seems to imply the following things, relating to the punishment and destruction to which these wicked Israelites were exposed.

1. That they were always exposed to *destruction;* as one that stands or walks in slippery places is always exposed to fall. This is implied in the man-ner of their destruction coming upon them, being represented by their foot sliding. The same is expressed, Psalm 73:18. "Surely thou didst set them in slippery places; thou castedst them down into destruction."

2. It implies, that they were always exposed to sudden unexpected destruction. As he that walks in slippery places is every moment liable to fall, he cannot foresee one moment whether he shall stand or fall the next; and when he does fall, he falls at once without warning: Which is also expressed in Psalm 73:18, 19. "Surely thou didst set them in slippery places; thou castedst them down into destruction: How are they brought into desolation as in a moment!"

3. Another thing implied is, that they are liable to fall *of themselves*, without being thrown down by the hand of another; as he that stands or walks on slippery ground needs nothing but his own weight to throw him down.

4. That the reason why they are not fallen already, and do not fall now, is only that God's appointed time is not come. For it is said, that when that due time, or appointed time comes, *their foot shall slide*. Then they shall be left to fall, as they are inclined by their own weight. God will not hold them up in these slippery places any longer, but will let them go; and then, at that very instant, they shall fall into destruction; as he that stands on such slippery declining ground, on the edge of a pit, he cannot stand alone, when he is let go he immediately falls and is lost.

The observation from the words that I would now insist upon is this.—"There is nothing that keeps wicked men at any one moment out of hell, but the mere pleasure of God"—By the *mere* pleasure of God, I mean his *sovereign* pleasure, his arbitrary will, restrained by no obligation, hindered by no manner of difficulty, any more than if nothing else but God's mere will had in the least degree, or in any respect whatsoever, any hand in the preservation of wicked men one moment.—The truth of this observation may appear by the following considerations.

1. There is no want of *power* in God to cast wicked men into hell at any moment. Men's hands cannot be strong when God rises up. The strongest have no power to resist him, nor can any deliver out of his hands.—He is not only able to cast wicked men into hell, but he can most easily do it. Sometimes an earthly prince meets with a great deal of difficulty to subdue a rebel, who has found means to fortify himself, and has made himself strong by the numbers of his followers. But it is not so with God. There is no fortress that is any defense from the power of God. Though hand join in hand, and vast multitudes of God's enemies combine and associate them-

selves, they are easily broken in pieces. They are as great heaps of light chaff before the whirlwind; or large quantities of dry stubble before devouring flames. We find it easy to tread on and crush a worm that we see crawling on the earth; so it is easy for us to cut or singe a slender thread that any thing hangs by: thus easy is it for God, when he pleases, to cast his enemies down to hell. What are we, that we should think to stand before him, at whose rebuke the earth trembles, and before whom the rocks are thrown down?

2. They *deserve* to be cast into hell; so that divine justice never stands in the way, it makes no objection against God's using his power at any moment to destroy them. Yea, on the contrary, justice calls aloud for an infinite punishment of their sins. Divine justice says of the tree that brings forth such grapes of Sodom, "Cut it down, why cumbereth it the ground?" Luke 13:7. The sword of divine justice is every moment brandished over their heads, and it is nothing but the hand of arbitrary mercy, and God's mere will, that holds it back.

3. They are already under a sentence of *condemnation* to hell. They do not only justly deserve to be cast down thither, but the sentence of the law of God, that external and immutable rule of righteousness that God has fixed between him and mankind, is gone out against them, and stands against them; so that they are bound over already to hell. John 3:18. "He that believeth not is condemned already." So that every unconverted man properly belongs to hell; that is his place; from thence he is, John 8:23. "Ye are from beneath": And thither he is bound; it is the place that justice, and God's word, and the sentence of his unchangeable law assign to him.

4. They are now the objects of that very same *anger* and wrath of God, that is expressed in the torments of hell. And the reason why they do not go down to hell at each moment, is not because God, in whose power they are, is not then very angry with them; as he is with many miserable creatures now tormented in hell, who there feel and bear the fierceness of his wrath. Yea, God is a great deal more angry with great numbers that are now on earth: yea, doubtless, with many that are now in this congregation, who it may be are at ease, than he is with many of those who are now in the flames of hell.

So that it is not because God is unmindful of their wickedness, and does not resent it, that he does not let loose his hand and cut them off. God is not altogether such an one as themselves, though they may imagine him to be so. The wrath of God burns against them, their damnation does not slumber; the pit is prepared, the fire is made ready, the furnace is now hot, ready to receive them; the flames do now rage and glow. The glittering sword is whet, and held over them, and the pit hath opened its mouth under them.

5. The *devil* stands ready to fall upon them, and seize them as his own, at what moment God shall permit him. They belong to him; he has their souls in his possession, and under his dominion. The scripture represents them as his goods, Luke 11:12. The devils watch them; they are ever by them at their right hand; they stand waiting for them, like greedy hungry lions that see their prey, and expect to have it, but are for the present kept back. If God should withdraw his hand, by which they are restrained, they would in one moment fly upon their poor souls. The old serpent is gaping for them; hell opens its mouth wide to receive them; and if God should permit it, they would be hastily swallowed up and lost.

6. There are in the souls of wicked men those hellish *principles* reigning, that would presently kindle and flame out into hellfire, if it were not for God's restraints. There is laid in the very nature of carnal men, a foundation for the torments of hell. There are those corrupt principles, in reigning power in them, and in full possession of them, that are seeds of hellfire. These principles are active and powerful, exceeding violent in their nature, and if it were not for the restraining hand of God upon them, they would soon break out, they would flame out after the same manner as the same corruptions, the same enmity does in the hearts of damned souls, and would beget the same torments as they do in them. The souls of the wicked are in scripture compared to the troubled sea, Isa. 57:20. For the present, God restrains their wickedness by his mighty power, as he does the raging waves of the troubled sea, saying, "Hitherto shalt thou come, but no further"; but if God should withdraw that restraining power, it would soon carry all before it. Sin is the ruin and misery of the soul; it is destructive in its nature; and if God should leave it without restraint, there would need nothing else to make the soul perfectly miserable. The corruption of the heart of man is immoderate and boundless in its fury; and while wicked men live here, it is like fire pent up by God's restraints, whereas if it were let loose, it would set on fire the course of nature; and as the heart is now

a sink of sin, so if sin was not restrained, it would immediately turn the soul into a fiery oven, or a furnace of fire and brimstone.

7. It is no security to wicked men for one moment, that there are no visible means of death at hand. It is no security to a natural man, that he is now in health, and that he does not see which way he should now immediately go out of the world by any accident, and that there is no visible danger in any respect in his circumstances. The manifold and continual experience of the world in all ages, shows this is no evidence, that a man is not on the very brink of eternity, and that the next step will not be into another world. The unseen, unthought-of ways and means of persons going suddenly out of the world are innumerable and inconceivable. Unconverted men walk over the pit of hell on a rotten covering, and there are innumerable places in this covering so weak that they will not bear their weight, and these places are not seen. The arrows of death fly unseen at noonday; the sharpest sight cannot discern them. God has so many different unsearchable ways of taking wicked men out of the world and sending them to hell, that there is nothing to make it appear, that God had need to be at the expense of a miracle, or go out of the ordinary course of his providence, to destroy any wicked man, at any moment. All the means that there are of sinners going out of the world, are so in God's hands, and so universally and absolutely subject to his power and determination, that it does not depend at all the less on the mere will of God, whether sinners shall at any moment go to hell, than if means were never made use of, or at all concerned in the case.

8. Natural men's prudence and care to preserve their own lives, or the care of others to preserve them, do not secure them a moment. To this, divine providence and universal experience do also bear testimony. There is this clear evidence that men's own wisdom is no security to them from death; that if it were otherwise we should see some difference between the wise and politic men of the world, and others, with regard to their liableness to early and unexpected death: but how is it in fact? Eccles. 2:16. "How dieth the wise man? even as the fool."

9. All wicked men's pains and *contrivance* which they use to escape hell, while they continue to reject Christ, and so remain wicked men, do not secure them from hell one moment. Almost every natural man that

hears of hell, flatters himself that he shall escape it; he depends upon himself for his own security; he flatters himself in what he has done, in what he is now doing, or what he intends to do. Every one lays out matters in his own mind how he shall avoid damnation, and flatters himself that he contrives well for himself, and that his schemes will not fail. They hear indeed that there are but few saved, and that the greater part of men that have died heretofore are gone to hell; but each one imagines that he lays out matters better for his own escape than others have done. He does not intend to come to that place of torment; he says within himself, that he intends to take effectual care, and to order matters so for himself as not to fail.

But the foolish children of men miserably delude themselves in their own schemes, and in confidence in their own strength and wisdom; they trust to nothing but a shadow. The greater part of those who heretofore have lived under the same means of grace, and are now dead, are undoubtedly gone to hell; and it was not because they were not as wise as those who are now alive: it is not because they did not lay out matters as well for themselves to secure their own escape. If we could speak with them, and inquire of them, one by one, whether they expected, when alive, and when they used to hear about hell, ever to be the subjects of that misery: we doubtless, should hear one and another reply, "No, I never intended to come here: I had laid out matters otherwise in my mind; I thought I should contrive well for myself: I thought my scheme good. I intended to take effectual care; but it came upon me unexpected; I did not look for it at that time, and in that manner; it came as a thief: Death outwitted me: God's wrath was too quick for me. Oh, my cursed foolishness! I was flattering myself, and pleasing myself with vain dreams of what I would do hereafter; and when I was saying, Peace and safety, then suddenly destruction came upon me."

10. God has laid himself under *no obligation,* by any promise to keep any natural man out of hell one moment. God certainly has made no promises either of eternal life, or of any deliverance or preservation from eternal death, but what are contained in the covenant of grace, the promises that are given in Christ, in whom all the promises are yea and amen. But surely they have no interest in the promises of the covenant of grace who are not the children of the covenant, who do not believe in any of the promises, and have no interest in the Mediator of the covenant.

So that, whatever some have imagined and pretended about promises made to natural men's earnest seeking and knocking, it is plain and manifest, that whatever pains a natural man takes in religion, whatever prayers he makes, till he believes in Christ, God is under no manner of obligation to keep him a moment from eternal destruction.

So that, thus it is that natural men are held in the hand of God, over the pit of hell; they have deserved the fiery pit, and are already sentenced to it; and God is dreadfully provoked, his anger is as great toward them as to those that are actually suffering the executions of the fierceness of his wrath in hell, and they have done nothing in the least to appease or abate that anger, neither is God in the least bound by any promise to hold them up one moment; the devil is waiting for them, hell is gaping for them, the flames gather and flash about them, and would fain lay hold on them, and swallow them up; the fire bent up in their own hearts is struggling to break out: and they have no interest in any Mediator, there are no means within reach that can be any security to them. In short, they have no refuge, nothing to take hold of; all that preserves them every moment is the mere arbitrary will, and uncovenanted, unobliged forbearance of an incensed God.

Application

The use of this awful subject may be for awakening unconverted persons in this congregation. This that you have heard is the case of every one of you that are out of Christ.—That world of misery, that lake of burning brimstone, is extended abroad under you. There is the dreadful pit of the glowing flames of the wrath of God; there is hell's wide gaping mouth open; and you have nothing to stand upon, nor any thing to take hold of; there is nothing between you and hell but the air; it is only the power and mere pleasure of God that holds you up. . . .

The God that holds you over the pit of hell, much as one holds a spider, or some loathsome insect over the fire, abhors you, and is dreadfully provoked: his wrath toward you burns like fire; he looks upon you as worthy of nothing else, but to be cast into the fire; he is of purer eyes than to bear to have you in his sight; you are ten thousand times more abominable in his eyes, than the most hateful venomous serpent is in ours. You have offended him infinitely more than ever a stubborn rebel did his prince; and yet it is nothing but his hand that holds you from falling into the fire every moment. It is to be ascribed to nothing else, that you did not go to hell the last night; that you were suffered to awake again in this world, after you closed your eyes to sleep. And there is no other reason to be given, why you have not dropped into hell since you arose in the morning, but that God's hand has held you up. There is no other reason to be given why you have not gone to hell, since you have sat here in the house of God, provoking his pure eyes by your sinful wicked manner of attending his solemn worship. Yea, there is nothing else that is to be given as a reason why you do not this very moment drop down into hell.

O sinner! Consider the fearful danger you are in: it is a great furnace of wrath, a wide and bottomless pit, full of the fire of wrath, that you are held over in the hand of that God, whose wrath is provoked and incensed as much against you, as against many of the damned in hell. You hang by a slender thread, with the flames of divine wrath flashing about it, and ready every moment to singe it, and burn it asunder; and you have no interest in any Mediator, and nothing to lay hold of to save yourself, nothing to keep off the flames of wrath, nothing of your own, nothing that you ever have done, nothing that you can do, to induce God to spare you one moment. . . .

Are there not many here who have lived long in the world, and are not to this day born again? and so are aliens from the commonwealth of Israel, and have done nothing ever since they have lived, but treasure up wrath against the day of wrath? Oh, sirs, your case, in an especial manner, is extremely dangerous. Your guilt and hardness of heart is extremely great. Do you not see how generally persons of your years are passed over and left, in the present remarkable and wonderful dispensation of God's mercy? . . .

And let every one that is yet of Christ, and hanging over the pit of hell, whether they be old men and women, or middle-aged, or young people, or little children, now hearken to the loud calls of God's word and providence. This acceptable year of the Lord, a day of such great favors to some, will doubtless be a day of as remarkable vengeance to others. Men's hearts harden, and their guilt increases apace at such a day as this, if they neglect their souls; and never was there so great danger of such persons being given up to hardness of heart and blindness of mind. God seems now to be hastily gathering in his elect in all parts of the land; and probably the greater part of adult persons that ever shall be saved, will be brought in now in a little time, and that it will be as it was on the great outpouring of the Spirit upon the Jews in the apostles' days; the election will obtain, and the rest will be blinded. If this should be the case with you, you will eternally curse this day, and will curse the day that ever you were born, to see such a season of the pouring out of God's Spirit, and will wish that you had died and gone to hell before you had seen it. Now undoubtedly it is, as it was in the days of John the Baptist, the axe is in an extraordinary manner laid at the root of the trees, that every tree which brings not forth good fruit, may be hewn down and cast into the fire.

Therefore, let every one that is out of Christ, now awake and fly from the wrath to come. The wrath of Almighty God is now undoubtedly hanging over a great part of this congregation: Let every one fly out of Sodom: "Haste and escape for your lives, look not behind you, escape to the mountain, lest you be consumed."

PART VII

"Preach Ye upon the Housetops"

Eighteenth-Century England and Europe

John Tillotson

1630–1694

Though he began as a Puritan (he would marry a niece of Oliver Cromwell's), lived through the English Civil War, the Restoration, and the Revolution of 1689, Tillotson eventually died as Archbishop of Canterbury, a most successful rise to power and testimony to his general tolerance and likability. He is placed first in the section of this book devoted to the eighteenth century because he is in every way the inaugurator of, and transition figure to, the preaching style and spirit of that later age. His popular, collected sermons commonly appeared on the private reading shelves of educated readers for generations. Their publication made his widow rich, though he had died penniless.

The end of the seventeenth century saw the final, unsuccessful effort, by Catholic James II, to hold on to some notion of a divine monarchy. Summoned by Parliament, William of Orange, a Dutch Protestant, ascended the throne in 1688 and benignly opened the era of British constitutional monarchy, in place to this day. The religious message of a brilliant preacher like Tillotson perfectly fitted the new era: "The immense popularity of Archbishop Tillotson's sermons told in favour of a type of faith which stressed practice, minimized theology, and leaned heavily on reason."[1]

He favored a plain style, akin to his politics and his Low Church religion—in contrast to that of his illustrious predecessors John Donne and Lancelot Andrewes. Baroque sentence construction and exceeding length were replaced, in the words of his entry in the *Dictionary of National Biography*, "by clearness and what passed in that age for brevity." His eulogist,

---

[1] Gerald R. Cragg, *The Church and the Age of Reason, 1648–1789,* Vol. 4 of *The Penguin History of the Church* (London: 1960; Penguin ed. 1990), p. 77.

Bishop Gilbert Burnet, described this new way of proclaiming the Word: "He said what was just necessary to give clear ideas of things, and no more: He laid aside all long and affected Periods . . . the whole Thread was of a piece, plain, and distinct. No affectation of Learning, no squeezing of Texts, no superficial Strains, no false thought nor bold flights, all was solid and yet lively, and grave as well as fine."

Tillotson studied the Church Fathers, particularly Basil the Great and John Chrysostom. He gave the appearance of effortless, spontaneous preaching. However, as he told a colleague, his actual approach was to write out every word and memorize them all by heart—until the strain forced a more reasonable method. His literary contemporaries and admirers included Andrew Marvell, John Locke, Samuel Pepys, and Poet Laureate John Dryden, who generously credited whatever talent he had for English prose to reading Tillotson's sermons.

The example included here concerns a subject (malicious sniping) close to the heart of that age of sectarian polemic and anonymous religious pamphleteering. Nor does it lose application to our own bad habits of gossip, slander, and innuendo.

↶

Against Evil-Speaking

Speak evil of no man.

—TITUS 3:2

General persuasives to repentance and a good life, and invectives against sin and wickedness at large, are certainly of good use to recommend religion and virtue, and to expose the deformity and danger of a vicious course. But it must be acknowledged, on the other hand, that these general discourses do not so immediately tend to reform the lives of men, because they fall among the crowd, but do not touch the conscience of particular persons in so sensible and awakening a manner as when we treat of particular duties and sins, and endeavor to put men upon the practice of the one and to reclaim them from the other, by proper arguments taken from the Word of God and from the nature of particular virtues and vices. . . . And to this end I have pitched upon one of the common and reigning vices of the age, calumny and evil-speaking, by which men contract so much guilt to themselves and create so much trouble to others, and from which, it is to be feared, few or none are wholly free.

I. This vice consists in saying things of others which tend to their disparagement and reproach, to the taking away or lessening of their reputation and good name. And this, whether the things said be true or not. If they be false and we know it, then it is downright calumny; and if we do not know it, but take it upon the report of others, it is however a slander, and so much the more injurious because really groundless and undeserved. If the thing be true, and we know it to be so, yet it is a defamation, and tends to the prejudice of our neighbor's reputation. And it is a fault to say the evil of others which is true, unless there be some good reason for it. Besides, it is contrary to that charity and goodness which Christianity recognizes, to divulge the faults of others, though they be really guilty of them, without necessity or some very good reason for it.

Again, it is evil-speaking and the vice condemned in the text, whether we be the first authors of the report or relate it from others, because the man that is evil spoken of is equally defamed either way.

Again, whether we speak evil of a man to his face or behind his back. The former may indeed seem to be the more generous, but yet is a great fault, and that which we call *reviling;* the latter is more mean and base, and that which we properly call *slander* or *backbiting.*

And lastly, whether it be done directly and in express terms, or more obscurely and by way of oblique insinuation, whether by way of downright reproach or with some crafty preface of commendation; for, so it have the effect to defame, the manner of address does not much alter the case; the one may be the more dexterous but is not one jot less faulty. For many times the deepest wounds are given by these smoother and more artificial ways of slander, as by asking questions—"Have you not heard so and so of such a man? I say no more. I only ask the question"—or by general intimations that "they are loath to say what they have heard of such a one, are very sorry for it, and do not at all believe it" (if you will believe them)—and this many times without telling the thing, but leaving you in the dark to suspect the worst.

II. We will now consider the extent of this prohibition, *to speak evil of no man,* and the due bounds and limitations of it. For it is not to be understood absolutely to forbid us to say anything concerning others that is bad. This in some cases may be necessary and our duty, and in several cases very fit and reasonable. . . .

It is not only lawful but very commendable and many times our duty to do this in order to the probable amendment of the person of whom evil is spoken. In such a case we may tell a man of his faults privately, or, when it may not be fit for us to use that boldness and freedom, we may reveal his faults to one that is more fit and proper to reprove him and will probably make no other use of this discovery but in order to his amendment. And this is so far from being a breach of charity that it is one of the best testimonies of it. For perhaps the party may not be guilty of what hath been reported of him, and then it is a kindness to give him the opportunity of vindicating himself. Or, if he be guilty, perhaps being privately and prudently told of it he may repent. . . . But then we must take care that this be done out of kindness, and that nothing of our own passion be mingled with it, and that, under pretense of reproving and reforming men, we do not reproach and revile them, and tell them of their faults in such a manner as if we did it to show our authority rather than our charity. It requires a great deal of address and gentle application so to manage the business of reproof as not to irritate and exasperate the person whom we reprove, instead of curing him.

This likewise is not only lawful but our duty, when we are legally called to bear witness concerning the faults and crime of another. A good man would not be an accuser, unless the public good or the prevention of some great evil should require it. And then the plain reason of the thing will sufficiently justify a voluntary accusation; otherwise it hath always among well-mannered people been esteemed very odious for a man to be officious in this kind and a forward informer concerning the misdemeanors of others. But when a man is called to give testimony in this kind, in obedience to the laws, and out of reverence to the oaths taken, in such cases he is so far free from deserving blame for so doing, that it would be an unpardonable fault in him to conceal the truth or any part of it.

It is lawful to publish the faults of others in our own necessary defense and vindication. When a man cannot conceal another's faults without betraying his own innocence, no charity requires a man to suffer himself to be defamed, to save the reputation of another man. . . .

This also is lawful for caution and warning to a third person, that is in danger to be infected by the company or the example of another, or may be greatly prejudiced by reposing too much confidence in him, having no knowledge or suspicion of his bad qualities. But even in this case we ought to take great care that the ill character we give of any man may be spread no further than is necessary to the good end we designed in it.

Besides these more obvious and remarkable cases, this prohibition doth not, I think, hinder but that in ordinary conversation men may mention that ill of others which is already made as public as it well can be, or that one friend may not in freedom speak to another of the miscarriage of a third person, where he is secure no ill use will be made of it, and that it will go no further to his prejudice, provided always that we take no delight in hearing or speaking ill of others. And the less we do it, though without any malice or design of harm, still the better, because this shows that we do not feed upon ill reports and take pleasure in them.

These are all the usual cases in which it may be necessary for us to speak evil of other men. And these are so evidently reasonable that the prohibition in the text cannot with reason be extended to them. And if no man would allow himself to say anything to the prejudice of another man's good name but in these and the like cases, the tongues of men would be very innocent and the world would be very quiet.

III. I proceed in the third place to consider the evil of this practice, both in the causes and the consequences of it. . . .

One of the deepest and most common causes of evil-speaking is ill nature and cruelty of disposition. Men do commonly incline to the censorious and uncharitable side. . . . To speak evil of others is almost become the general entertainment of all companies, and the great and serious business of most meetings and visits, after the necessary ceremonies and compliments are over, is to sit down and backbite all the world. 'Tis the sauce of conversation, and all discourse is counted but flat and dull which hath not something of piquancy and sharpness in it against somebody.

But especially if it concerns one of another party, and that differs from us in matters of religion; in this case all parties seem to be agreed that they do God good service in blasting the reputation of their adversaries. And though they all pretend to be Christians and the disciples of him who taught nothing but kindness and meekness and charity, yet it is strange to see with what a savage and murderous disposition they will fly at one another's reputation and tear it in pieces. . . . To speak impartially, the zealots of all parties have got a scurvy trick of lying for the truth. . . .

Another cause of the commonness of this vice is that many are so bad themselves in one kind or other. For to think and speak ill of others is not only a bad thing but a sign of a bad man. When men are bad themselves, they are glad of any opportunity to censure others, and are always apt to suspect that evil of other men which they know by* themselves. They cannot have a good opinion of themselves, and therefore are very unwilling to have so of anybody else. And for this reason they endeavor to bring men to a level, hoping it will be some justification of them if they can but render others as bad as themselves.

Another source of this vice is malice and revenge. When men are in heat and passion, they do not consider what is true but what is spiteful and mischievous, and speak evil of others in revenge of some injury which they have received from them; and when they are blinded by their passions, they lay about them madly and at a venture, not much caring whether the evil they speak be true or not. Nay, many are so devilish as to invent and raise false reports on purpose to blast men's reputations. . . .

Another cause of evil-speaking is envy. Men look with an evil eye upon the good that is in others. This makes them greedy to entertain and industriously to publish anything that may serve to that purpose, thereby to raise themselves upon the ruins of other men's reputations. And therefore, as soon as they have got an ill report of any good man by the end, to work they presently go, to send it abroad by the first post. For the string is always ready upon their bow to let fly this arrow with an incredible swiftness through city and country, for fear the innocent man's justification should overtake it.

Another cause of evil-speaking is impertinence and curiosity, an itch of talking and meddling in the affairs of other men which do nowise concern them. Some persons love to mingle themselves in all business, and are loath to seem ignorant of so important a piece of news as the faults and follies of men, or any bad thing that is talked of in good company. And therefore they do with great care pick up ill stories as good

---

*I.e., about or against. The same usage occurs in the King James Version of 1 Corinthians 4:4: "For I know nothing by myself."

matter of discourse in the next company that is worthy of them. And this, perhaps, not out of any great malice but for want of something better to talk of. . . .

I proceed to consider the ordinary but very pernicious consequences and effects of it, both to others and to ourselves. First to others, the parties I mean that are slandered. To them it is certainly a great injury, and commonly a high provocation, but always matter of no small grief and trouble. . . . Secondly, the consequences of this vice are as bad or worse to ourselves. Whoever is wont to speak evil of others gives a bad character of himself even to those whom he desires to please, who, if they be wise enough, will conclude that he speaks of them to others as he does of others to them. . . .

IV. I proceed in the fourth place to add some arguments and considerations to take men off from this vice. . . .

Consider how cheap a kindness it is to speak well—at least, not to speak ill of any. A good word is an easy obligation, but not to speak ill requires only our silence, which costs us nothing. Some instances of charity are chargeable, as to relieve the wants and necessities of others; the expense deters many from this kind of charity. But, were a man never so covetous, he might afford another man his good word; at least he might refrain from speaking ill of him, especially if it be considered how dear many have paid for a slanderous and reproachful word. . . .

Consider that no quality doth ordinarily recommend one more to the favor and goodwill of men than to be free from this vice. Every one desires such a man's friendship and is apt to repose a great trust and confidence in him. . . .

When ye are going to speak reproachfully of others, consider whether ye do not lie open to just reproach in the same or some other kind. There are very few so innocent and free either from infirmities or greater faults as not to be obnoxious to reproach upon one account or other; even the wisest and most virtuous and most perfect among men have some little vanity or affectation which lays them open to the raillery of a mimical* and malicious wit. Therefore we should often turn our thoughts upon ourselves and

---

*I.e., characteristic of a "mimic," who excites laughter by a ludicrous mimicry of someone or something.

look into that part of the wallet which men commonly fling over their shoulders and keep behind them, that they may not see their own faults. And when we have searched that well, let us remember our Savior's rule, *He that is without sin, let him first cast the stone.* . . .

V. I shall in the last place give some rules and directions for the prevention and cure of this great evil among men.

Never say any evil of any man but what you certainly know. Whenever you positively accuse and indict any man of any crime, though it be in private and among friends, speak as if you were upon your oath, because God sees and hears you. . . . Never speak evil of any man upon common fame, which for the most part is false but almost always uncertain whether it be true or not. Not but that it is a fault in most cases to report the evil of men which is true, and which we certainly know to be so; but if I cannot prevail to make men wholly to abstain from this fault, I would be glad to compound with some persons to gain this point of them, however, because it will retrench nine parts in ten of evil-speaking in the world.

Before you speak evil of any man, consider whether he hath not obliged you by some real kindness; and then it is a bad return to speak ill of him who has done us good. Consider also whether you may not come hereafter to be acquainted with him, related to him, or obliged by him whom you have thus injured. And how will you then be ashamed when you reflect upon it, and perhaps have reason also to believe that he to whom you have done this injury is not ignorant of it. . . .

Let us accustom ourselves to pity the faults of men and to be truly sorry for them; and then we shall take no pleasure in publishing them. He is not a good Christian who is not heartily sorry for the faults even of his greatest enemies. And if he will be so, he will discover [lay bare] them no further than is necessary to some good end.

Whenever we hear any man evil-spoken of, if we know any good of him, let us say that. It is always the more human and the more honorable part to stand up in defense and vindication of others than to accuse and bespatter them. Possibly the good you have heard of them may not be true; but it is much more probable that the evil which you have heard of them is not true neither. . . .

That you may not speak ill of any, do not delight to hear ill of them. Give no countenance to busybodies and those who love to talk of other

men's faults. Or, if you cannot decently reprove them because of their quality, then divert the discourse some other way. Or, if you cannot do that, by
seeming not to mind it you may sufficiently signify that you do not like it.

Let every man mind himself and his own duty and concernment. Do
but endeavor in good earnest to mend thyself, and it will be work enough
for one man, and leave thee but little time to talk of others. . . .

Lastly, let us set a watch before the door of our lips, and not speak but
upon consideration—I do not mean to speak finely, but fitly. Especially
when thou speakest of others, consider of whom and what thou art going
to speak. Use great caution and circumspection in this matter; look well
about thee, on every side of the thing and on every person in the company,
before thy words slip from thee, which, when they are once out of thy lips,
are for ever out of thy power. . . . If we have a mind wise enough and good
enough, we may easily find a field large enough for innocent conversation,
such as will harm nobody and yet be acceptable enough to the better and
wiser part of mankind. . . .

All that now remains is to reflect upon what hath been said, and to
urge you and myself to do accordingly. For all is nothing, if we do not practice what we so plainly see to be our duty. Many are so taken up with the
deep points and mysteries of religion that they never think of the common
duties and offices of human life. But faith and a good life are so far from
clashing with one another that the Christian religion hath made them inseparable. True faith is necessary to a good life, and a good life is the genuine product of a right belief; and therefore the one ought never to be
pressed to the prejudice of the other.

I foresee what will be said, because I have heard it so often said in the
like case, that there is not a word of Jesus Christ in all this. No more is there
in the text. And yet I hope that Jesus Christ is truly preached whenever his
will and laws and the duties enjoined by the Christian religion are inculcated upon us.

Jonathan Swift

1667–1745

S wift was an Anglican clergyman for fifty of his seventy-eight years
and dean of St. Patrick's Cathedral in Dublin for thirty of those fifty.
It is accordingly a surprise to learn that his entire surviving sermon output
consists of eleven examples. He once gave a bundle of his sermons to his
friend Dr. Sheridan, noted an early biographer, the Earl of Orrery: "They
were held in such low esteem in his own thoughts, that some years before
he died, he gave away the whole collection to Dr. Sheridan, with the utmost
indifference: 'Here,' says he, 'are a bundle of my old sermons; you may have
them if you please: they may be of use to you, they have never been of any
to me.' "

Despite his self-deprecation, Swift's sermons are not only edifying but
offer a clear window into his early-eighteenth-century world. He preached
at a time when maintaining the primacy of the national church against the
combined assaults of evangelical religion—and worse, indifference to religion altogether—was of vital political importance to him and most others
of Tory persuasion. The pulpit style of the seventeenth century—ornate,
abstract, larded with untranslated snippets of Greek and Latin—had given
way to a simpler ideal, to preach "plain honest stuff," as he put it. He wanted
his hearers to experience the gospel message directly, without the dangerous distractions of emotion or needless preoccupation with the manner or
person of the preacher himself. Then he knew minds and hearts would respond with right thinking and action.

Even with such concerns, it is hardly surprising that Swift, the greatest satirist and wit of his age, and the creator in 1726 of *Gulliver's Travels*,
would choose "Upon Sleeping in Church" for a subject, taking a passage

from the Acts of the Apostles in which Paul keeps his audience up so late with his preaching that a poor fellow named Eutychus (something like "Lucky" in Greek) falls asleep and tumbles almost to his death from his high perch. Swift uses the occasion to tell his congregation that, while ridicule of and indifference to true religion may be bad, complete insensibility to it is far worse!

ᘓ

Upon Sleeping in Church

And there sat in a Window a certain young Man named Eutychus, being fallen into a deep sleep; and while Paul was long preaching, he sunk down with Sleep, and fell down from the third Loft, and was taken up dead.

—ACTS 20:9

I have chosen these Words with Design, if possible, to disturb some Part in this Audience of half an Hour's Sleep, for the Convenience and Exercise whereof this Place, at this Season of the Day, is very much celebrated.

There is indeed one mortal Disadvantage to which all preaching is subject; that those who, by the Wickedness of their Lives, stand in greatest Need, have usually the smallest Share; for, either they are absent upon the Account of Idleness, or Spleen, or Hatred to Religion, or in order to doze away the Intemperance of the Week; or, if they do come, they are sure to employ their Minds rather any other Way, than regarding or attending to the Business of the Place.

The Accident which happened to this young Man in the Text, hath not been sufficient to discourage his Successors: But, because the Preachers now in the World, however they may exceed St. *Paul* in the Art of setting Men to Sleep, do extremely fall short of him in the Working of Miracles; therefore Men are become so cautious as to choose more safe and convenient Stations and Postures for taking their Repose, without Hazard of their Persons; and upon the whole Matter, choose rather to trust their Destruction to a Miracle, than their Safety. However, this being not the only Way by which the lukewarm Christians and Scorners of the Age discover their Neglect and Contempt of Preaching, I shall enter expressly into Consideration of this Matter, and order my Discourse in the following Method.

> *First,* I shall produce several Instances to shew the great Neglect of Preaching now among us.
>
> *Secondly,* I shall reckon up some of the usual Quarrels Men have against Preaching.
>
> *Thirdly,* I shall set forth the great Evil of this Neglect and Contempt of Preaching, and discover the real Causes from whence it proceedeth.
>
> *Lastly,* I shall offer some Remedies against this great and spreading Evil.

First, I shall produce certain Instances to shew the great Neglect of Preaching now among us.

These may be reduced under two Heads. First, Men's Absence from the Service of the Church; and, Secondly, their Misbehavior when they are here.

The first Instance of Men's Neglect, is in their frequent Absence from the Church.

There is no Excuse so trivial, that will not pass upon some Men's Consciences to excuse their Attendance at the public Worship of God. Some are so unfortunate as to be always indisposed on the Lord's Day, and think nothing so unwholesome as the Air of a Church. Others have their Affairs so oddly contrived, as to be always unluckily prevented by Business. With some it is a great Mark of Wit, and deep Understanding, to stay at Home on *Sundays.* Others again discover strange Fits of Laziness, that seize them, particularly on that Day, and confine them to their Beds. Others are absent out of mere Contempt of Religion. And, lastly, there are not a few who look upon it as a Day of Rest, and therefore claim the Privilege of their Castle, to keep the Sabbath by eating, drinking, and sleeping, after the Toil and Labor of the Week. Now, in all this the worst Circumstance is, that these Persons are such whose Companies are most required, and who stand most in *Need of a Physician.*

Secondly, Men's great Neglect and Contempt of Preaching, appear by their Misbehavior, when at Church.

If the Audience were to be ranked under several Heads, according to their Behavior, when the Word of God is delivered, how small a Number would appear of those who receive it as they ought? How much of the Seed then sown would be found to fall by the Way Side, upon stony Ground, or among Thorns? And how little good Ground would there be to take it? A Preacher cannot look around from the Pulpit, without observing, that some are in a perpetual Whisper, and, by their Air and Gesture, give Occasion to suspect, that they are in those very Minutes defaming their Neighbor. Others have their Eyes and Imagination constantly engaged in such a Circle of Objects, perhaps to gratify the most unwarrantable Desires, that they never once attend to the Business of the Place; the Sound of the Preacher's Words doth not so much as once interrupt them. Some have their Minds wandering among idle, worldly, or vicious Thoughts. Some lie at Catch to ridicule whatever they hear, and with much Wit and Humor provide a Stock of Laughter, by furnishing themselves from the Pulpit. But, of all Misbehavior, none is comparable to that of those who come here to sleep; Opium is not so stupefying to many Persons as an Afternoon Sermon. Perpetual Custom hath so brought it about, that the Words of whatever Preacher, become only a Sort of uniform Sound at a Distance, than which nothing is more effectual to lull the Senses. For, that it is the very Sound of the Sermon which bindeth up their Faculties, is manifest from hence, because they all awake so very regularly as soon as it ceaseth, and with much Devotion receive the Blessing, dozed and besotted with Indecencies I am ashamed to repeat.

I proceed, *Secondly,* to reckon up some of the usual Quarrels Men have against Preaching, and to shew the Unreasonableness of them.

Such unwarrantable Demeanor as I have described, among Christians in the House of God, in a solemn Assembly, while their Faith and Duty are explained and delivered, have put those who are guilty, upon inventing some Excuses to extenuate their Fault: This they do by turning the Blame either upon the particular Preacher, or upon Preaching in general. First, they object against the particular Preacher; his Manner, his Delivery, his Voice are disagreeable; his Style and Expression are flat and low, sometimes improper and absurd; the Matter is heavy trivial and insipid; sometimes despicable, and perfectly ridiculous, or else, on the other Side, he runs up into unintelligible Speculation, empty Notions, and abstracted Flights, all clad in Words above usual Understandings.

Secondly, They object against Preaching in general; it is a perfect Road of Talk; they know already whatever can be said; they have heard the same an hundred Times over. They quarrel that Preachers do not relieve an old beaten Subject with Wit and Invention; and that now the Art is lost of moving Men's Passions, so common among the Orators of *Greece* and *Rome*. These, and the like Objections, are frequently in the Mouths of Men who despise the Foolishness of Preaching. But let us examine the Reasonableness of them.

The Doctrine delivered by all Preachers is the same: *So we preach, and so ye believe:* But the Manner of delivering is suited to the Skill and Abilities of each, which differ in Preachers just as in the rest of Mankind. However, in personal Dislikes of a particular Preacher, are these Men sure they are always in the right? Do they consider how mixed a Thing is every Audience, whose Taste and Judgment differ, perhaps every Day, not only from each other, but themselves? And how to calculate a Discourse, that shall exactly suit them all, is beyond the Force and Reach of human Reason, Knowledge or Invention. Wit and Eloquence are shining Qualities, that God hath imparted, in great Degrees, to very few, nor any more to be expected, in the Generality of any Rank among Men, than Riches and Honor. But further: If Preaching in general be all old and beaten, and that they are already so well acquainted with it, more Shame and Guilt to them who so little edify by it. But, these Men, whose Ears are so delicate as not to endure a plain Discourse of Religion, who expect a constant Supply of Wit and Eloquence on a Subject handled so many thousand Times; what will they say when we turn the Objection upon themselves, who with all the lewd and profane Liberty of Discourse they take, upon so many thousand Subjects, are so dull as to furnish nothing but tedious Repetitions, and little paltry, nauseous Commonplaces, so vulgar, so worn, or so obvious, as upon any other Occasion, but that of advancing Vice, would be hooted off the Stage. Nor, lastly, are Preachers justly blamed for neglecting human Oratory to move the Passions, which is not the Business of a Christian Orator, whose Office it is only to work upon Faith and Reason. All other Eloquence hath been a perfect Cheat, to stir up Men's Passions against Truth and Justice, for the Service of a Faction, to put false Colors upon Things, and by an Amusement of agreeable Words, make the worse Reason appear to be the better. This is certainly not to be allowed in Christian Eloquence, and therefore, St. *Paul* took quite the other Course; he *came not with Excellency of Words, or enticing Speeches of Men's Wisdom, but in plain Evidence of the Spirit, and Power:* And, perhaps, it was for that Reason the young Man *Eutychus,* used to the *Grecian* Eloquence, grew tired, and fell so fast asleep.

I go on *Thirdly,* to set forth the great Evil of this Neglect and Scorn of Preaching, and to discover the real Causes from whence it proceedeth.

I think it is obvious to believe, that this Neglect of Preaching hath very much occasioned the great Decay of Religion among us. To this may be imputed no small Part of that Contempt some Men bestow on the Clergy; for whoever talketh without being regarded, is sure to be despised. To this we owe in a great Measure, the spreading of Atheism and Infidelity among us; for, Religion, like all other Things, is soonest put out of Countenance by being ridiculed. The Scorn of Preaching might perhaps, have been at first introduced by Men of nice Ears and refined Taste; but it is now become a spreading Evil, through all Degrees, and both Sexes; for, since Sleeping, Talking and Laughing are Qualities sufficient to furnish out a Critick, the meanest and most Ignorant have set up a Title, and succeeded in it, as well as their Betters. Thus are the last Efforts of reforming Mankind rendered wholly useless: *How shall they hear,* saith the Apostle, *without a Preacher?* But, if they have a Preacher, and make it a Point of Wit or Breeding not to hear him, what Remedy is left? To this Neglect of Preaching, we may also entirely impute that gross Ignorance among us in the very Principles of Religion, which is amazing to find in Persons who very much value their own Knowledge and Understanding in other Things; yet it is a visible, inexcusable Ignorance, even in the meanest among us, considering the many Advantages they have of learning their Duty. And, it hath been the great Encouragement to all Manner of Vice: For, in vain we preach down Sin to a People, *whose Hearts are waxed gross, whose Ears are dull of Hearing,* and *whose Eyes are closed.* Therefore Christ himself, in his Discourses, frequently rouseth up the Attention of the Multitude, and of his Disciples themselves, with this Expression, *He that hath Ears to hear, let him hear.* But, among all Neglects of Preaching, none is so fatal as that of sleeping in the House of God; a Scorner may listen to Truth and Reason, and in Time grow serious; an Unbeliever may feel the Pangs of a guilty Conscience; one whose Thoughts or Eyes wander among other Objects, may, by a lucky Word, be called back to Attention: But the Sleeper shuts up all Avenues to his Soul: He is *like the deaf*

Adder, that hearkeneth not to the Voice of the Charmer, charm he never so wisely. And we may preach with as good Success to the Grave that is under his Feet.

But the great Evil of this Neglect will further yet appear, from considering the real Causes whence it proceedeth; whereof the first, I take to be, an evil Conscience. Many Men come to Church to save or gain a Reputation; or because they will not be singular, but comply with an established Custom; yet all the while, they are loaded with the Guilt of old rooted Sins. These Men can expect to hear of nothing but Terrors and Threatenings, their Sins laid open in true Colors, and eternal Misery the Reward of them; therefore no Wonder they stop their Ears, and divert their Thoughts, and seek any Amusement, rather than stir the Hell within them.

Another Cause of this Neglect, is a Heart set upon worldly Things. Men whose Minds are much enslaved to earthly Affairs all the Week, cannot disengage or break the Chain of their Thoughts so suddenly, as to apply to a Discourse that is wholly foreign to what they have most at Heart. Tell a Usurer of Charity, and Mercy, and Restitution, you talk to the Deaf; his Heart and Soul, with all his Senses, are got among his Bags, or he is gravely asleep, and dreaming of a Mortgage. Tell a Man of Business, that the Cares of the World *choak the good Seed;* that we must not encumber ourselves with much serving; that the Salvation of his Soul is the one Thing necessary: You see, indeed, the Shape of a Man before you, but his Faculties are all gone off among Clients and Papers, thinking how to defend a bad Cause, or find Flaws in a good one; or, he weareth out the Time in drowsy Nods.

A Third Cause of the great Neglect and Scorn of Preaching, ariseth from the Practice of Men who set up to decry and disparage Religion; these, being zealous to promote Infidelity and Vice, learn a Rote of Buffoonery that serveth all Occasions, and refutes the strongest Arguments for Piety and good Manners. These have a Set of Ridicule calculated for all Sermons and all Preachers, and can be extreme witty as often as they please upon the same Fund.

Let me now in the last Place, offer some Remedies against this great Evil.

It will be one Remedy against the Contempt of Preaching, rightly to consider the End for which it was designed. There are many who place Abundance of Merit in going to Church, although it be with no other Prospect but that of being well entertained, wherein if they happen to fail, they return wholly disappointed. Hence it is become an impertinent Vein among People of all Sorts, to hunt after what they call a good Sermon, as if it were a Matter of Pastime and Diversion. Our Business, alas, is quite another Thing, either to learn, or at least be reminded of our Duty, to apply the Doctrines delivered, compare the Rules we hear with our Lives and Actions, and find wherein we have transgressed. These are the Dispositions Men should bring into the House of God, and then they will be little concerned about the Preacher's Wit or Eloquence, nor be curious to enquire out his Faults of Infirmities, but consider how to correct their own.

Another Remedy against the Contempt of Preaching is, that Men would consider, whether it be not reasonable to give more Allowances for the different Abilities of Preachers than they usually do? Refinements of Style, and Flights of Wit, as they are not properly the Business of any Preacher, so they cannot possibly be the Talents of all. In most other Discourses, Men are satisfied with sober Sense and plain Reason; and, as Understandings usually go, even that is not over frequent. Then why should they be so overnice in expectation of eloquence, where it is neither necessary nor convenient, is hard to imagine.

Lastly, The Scorners of Preaching would do well to consider, that this Talent of Ridicule, they value so much, is a Perfection very easily acquired, and applied to all Things whatsoever; neither is it any Thing at all the worse, because it is capable of being perverted to Burlesque: Perhaps it may be the more perfect upon that Score; since we know, the most celebrated Pieces have been thus treated with greatest Success. It is in any Man's Power to suppose a Fool's Cap on the wisest Head, and then laugh at his own Supposition. I think there are not many Things cheaper than supposing and laughing; and if the uniting these two Talents can bring a Thing into Contempt, it is hard to know where it may end.

To conclude, these Considerations may, perhaps, have some Effects while Men are awake; but what Argument shall we use to the Sleeper? What Methods shall we take to hold open his Eyes? Will he be moved by Considerations of common Civility? We know it is reckoned a Point of very bad Manners to sleep in private Company, when, perhaps, the tedious Impertinence of many Talkers would render it at least as excusable as at the dullest Sermon. Do they think it a small Thing to watch four Hours at a Play, where all Virtue and Religion are openly reviled; and can they not watch one half

Hour to hear them defended? Is this to deal like a Judge, (I mean like a good Judge) to listen on one Side of the Cause, and sleep on the other? I shall add but one Word more: That this indecent Sloth is very much owing to that Luxury and Excess Men usually practice upon this Day, by which half the Service thereof is turned into Sin; Men dividing the Time between God and their Bellies, when after a gluttonous Meal, their Senses dozed and stupefied, they retire to God's House to sleep out the Afternoon. Surely, Brethren, these Things ought not so to be.

He that hath Ears to hear, let him hear. And God give us all Grace to hear and receive his holy Word to the Salvation of our own Souls.

Laurence Sterne

1713–1768

The vicar of a small town in eighteenth-century Yorkshire was also the author of what most critics consider to be the first "stream of consciousness" novel. *The Life and Opinions of Tristram Shandy, Gentleman* owes something, in its eccentricities of punctuation, pauses, long-winded digressions, and willful chaos, to Laurence Sterne's life as vicar at Sutton-in-the-Forest. Before *Tristram Shandy* made Sterne so famous that even a letter addressed to "Tristram Shandy, in Europe" would reach its author, the Irish preacher's antic, witty, and laconic sermons had been published in his *Sermons of Mr. Yorick*. (In *Tristram Shandy,* "Yorick" is a parson whose japery comes from his direct descent from the dead jester in *Hamlet.*) His congregation didn't find the country parson Sterne's preaching as compelling as readers and critics have found his novels: when Sterne ascended the pulpit, half the congregation of his church (or later, his cathedral) walked out.

Sterne's private life was tumultuous to the point of scandal; his attentions to ladies were notorious. A first wife became insane, and chronic illness and depression attended his fame. The originality of his mind, the influence on Sterne of the philosopher John Locke's theory of the irrational association of ideas, and the way in which his fractured syntax expressed complexity, in both the pulpit and his fiction, made him the target of denunciation and scorn by Samuel Johnson, Horace Walpole, and the more fashionable writer of *Clarissa Harlowe,* Samuel Richardson. In his sermon on the Prodigal Son, there is room for comparison with Sterne's unfinished *Sentimental Journey,* a playful fiction which moralizes, like this text, on human fallibility, one of Sterne's favorite themes. The journey of the Prodigal Son becomes a metaphor for the trajectory of a mismanaged life, refashioned by Sterne as a Shandyesque commentary on human reality and the drollery of its predicament.

The Prodigal Son

I know not whether the remark is to our honor or otherwise, that lessons of wisdom have never such power over us, as when they are wrought into the heart, through the groundwork of a story which engages the passions: Is it that we are like iron, and must first be heated before we can be wrought upon? or, Is the heart so in love with deceit, that where a true report will not reach it, we must cheat it with a fable, in order to come at truth?

Whether this parable of the prodigal (for so it is usually called) is really such, or built upon some story known at that time in Jerusalem, is not much to the purpose; it is given us to enlarge upon, and turn to the best moral account we can.

"A certain man, says our Savior, had two sons, and the younger of them said to his father, Give me the portion of goods which falls to me: and he divided unto them his substance. And not many days after, the younger son gathered all together and took his journey into a far country, and there wasted his substance with riotous living."

The account is short: the interesting and pathetic passages with which such a transaction would be necessarily connected, are left to be supplied by the heart: the story is silent—but nature is not: much kind advice, and many a tender expostulation would fall from the father's lips, no doubt, upon this occasion.

He would dissuade his son from the folly of so rash an enterprise, by showing him the dangers of the journey, the inexperience of his age, the hazards of his life, his fortune, his virtue would run, without a guide, without a friend: he would tell him of the many snares and temptations which he had to avoid, or encounter at every step, the pleasures which would solicit him in every luxurious court, the little knowledge he could gain—except that of evil; he would speak of the seductions of women, their charms, their poisons: what helpless indulgences he might give way to, when far from restraint, and the check of the giving his father pain.

The dissuasive would but inflame his desire.

He gathers all together.—

—I see the picture of his departure—the camels and asses laden with his substance, detached on one side of the piece, and already on their way: the prodigal son standing on the foreground with a forced sedateness, struggling against the fluttering movement of joy, upon his deliverance from restraint: the elder brother holding his hand, as if unwilling to let it go:—the father,—sad moment! with a firm look, covering a prophetic sentiment, "that all would not go well with his child,"—approaching to embrace him, and bid him adieu. Poor inconsiderate youth! From whose arms art thou flying? From what a shelter art thou going forth into the storm? Art thou weary of a father's affection, of a father's care? or, Hopest thou to find a warmer interest, a truer counselor, or a kinder friend in a land of strangers, where youth is made a prey, and so many thousands are confederated to deceive them, and live by their spoils.

We will seek no further than this idea, for the extravagancies by which the prodigal son added one unhappy example to the number: his fortune wasted, the followers of it fled in course, the wants of nature remain,—the hand of God gone forth against him—*"For when he had spent all, a mighty famine arose in that country."* Heaven! have pity upon the youth, for he is in hunger and distress, strayed out of the reach of a parent, who counts every hour of his absence with anguish, cut off from all his tender offices, by his folly, and from relief and charity from others, by the calamity of the times.

Nothing so powerfully calls home the mind as distress: the tense fiber then relaxes, the soul retires to itself, sits pensive and susceptible of right impressions: if we have a friend, 'tis then we think of him; if a benefactor, at that moment all his kindnesses press upon our mind. Gracious and bountiful God! Is it not for this, that they who in their prosperity forget thee, do yet remember and return to thee in the hour of this sorrow? When our heart is in heaviness, upon whom can we think but thee, who knowest our necessities afar off, puttest all our tears in thy bottle, seest every careful thought, hearest every sigh and melancholy groan we utter.

Strange!—that we should only begin to think of God with comfort, when with joy and comfort we can think of nothing else.

Man surely is a compound of riddles and contradictions: by the law of his nature he avoids pain, and yet *unless he suffers in the flesh, he will not cease from sin,* though it is sure to bring pain and misery upon his head forever.

While all went pleasurably on with the prodigal, no pang of remorse for the sufferings in which he had left him, or resolution of returning, to make up the account of his folly: his first hour of distress, seemed to be his first hour of wisdom:—*When he came to himself, he said, How many hired servants of my father have bread enough and to spare, whilst I perish!*

Of all the terrors of nature, that of one day or another dying by hunger, is the greatest, and it is wisely wove into our frame to awaken man to industry, and call forth his talents; and though we seem to go on carelessly, sporting with it as we do with other terrors—yet, he that sees this enemy fairly, and in his most frightful shape, will need no long remonstrance, to make him turn out of the way to avoid him.

It was the case of the prodigal—he arose to go unto his father. Alas! How shall he tell his story? Ye who have trod this round, tell me in what words he shall give in to his father, the sad *Items* of his extravagancy and folly;

The feasts and banquets which he gave to whole cities in the east, the costs of Asiatic rarities, and of Asiatic cooks to dress them, the expenses of singing men and singing women, the flute, the harp, the sackbut, and of all kinds of music the dress of the Persian courts, how magnificent! their slaves, how numerous! their chariots, their horses, their palaces, their furniture, what immense sums they had devoured! what expectations from strangers of condition! what exactions!

How shall the youth make his father comprehend, that he was cheated at Damascus by one of the best men in the world; that he had lent a part of his substance to a friend at Nineveh, who had fled off with it to the Ganges; that a whore of Babylon swallowed his best pearl, and anointed the whole city with his balm of Gilead: that he had been sold by a man of honor for twenty shekels of silver, to a worker in graven images; that the images he had purchased had profited him nothing; that they could not be transported across the wilderness, and had been burned with fire at Shusan; that the apes *(vide 2 Chron.* 9:21) and peacocks, which he had sent for from Tharsis, lay dead upon his hands; and that the mummies had not been dead long enough which had been brought him out of Egypt: that all had gone wrong since the day he forsook his father's house.

Leave the story—it will be told more concisely. *When he was yet afar off, his father saw him*—compassion told it in three words—*he fell upon his neck and kissed him.*

Great is the power of eloquence: but never is it so great as when it pleads along with nature, and the culprit is a child strayed from his duty, and returned to it again with tears: Casuists may settle the point as they will: But what could a parent see more in the account, than the natural one, of an ingenuous heart too open for the world, smitten with strong sensations of pleasures, and suffered to sally forth unarmed in the midst of enemies stronger than himself?

Generosity sorrows as much for the overmatched, as pity herself does.

The idea of a son so ruined, would double the father's caresses: every effusion of his tenderness would add bitterness to his son's remorse. "Gracious heaven! what a father have I rendered miserable!"

And he said, I have sinned against heaven, and in thy sight, and am no more worthy to be called thy son.

But the father said, Bring forth the best robe.

O ye affections! How fondly do you play at cross-purposes with each other?—'Tis the natural dialogue of true transport: joy is not methodical, and where an offender, beloved, overcharges itself in the offense, words are too cold; and a conciliated heart replies by tokens of esteem.

And he said unto his servants, Bring forth the best robe and put it on him; and put a ring on his hand, and shoes on his feet, and bring hither the fatted calf, and let us eat and drink and be merry.

When the affections so kindly break loose, Joy is another name for Religion.

We look up as we taste it: the cold Stoic without, when he hears the dancing and the music, may ask sullenly, (with the elder brother) What it means? and refuse to enter: but the humane and compassionate all fly impetuously to the banquet, given *for a son who was dead and is alive again—who was lost and is found.* Gentle spirits, light up the pavilion with a sacred fire; and parental love, and filial piety lead in the mask with riot and wild festivity! Was it not for this that God gave man music to strike upon the kindly passions; that nature taught the feet to dance to its movements, and as chief governess of the feast poured forth wine into the goblet, to crown it with gladness?

The intention of this parable is so clear from the occasion of it, that it will not be necessary to perplex it with any tedious explanation: it was designed by way of indirect remonstrance to the Scribes and Pharisees, who animadverted upon our Savior's conduct, for entering so freely into conferences with sinners, in order to reclaim them. To that end, he proposes the parable of the shepherd, who left his ninety and nine sheep that were safe in the fold, to go and seek for one sheep that was gone astray, telling them in other places, that they who were whole wanted not a physician, but they that were sick: and here, to carry on the same lesson, and to prove how acceptable such a recovery was to God, he relates this account of the prodigal son and his welcome reception.

I know not whether it would be a subject of much edification to convince you here, that our Savior, by the prodigal son, particularly pointed at those who were *sinners of the Gentiles,* and were recovered by divine Grace to repentance; and by the elder brother, he intended as manifestly the more froward of the Jews, who envied their conversion; and thought it a kind of wrong to their primogeniture, in being made fellow heirs with them of the promises of God.

These uses have been so ably set forth, in so many good sermons upon the prodigal son, that I shall turn aside from them at present, and content myself with some reflections upon that fatal passion which led him, and so many thousands after the example, *to gather all he had together, and take his journey into a far country.*

The love of variety, or curiosity of seeing new things, which is the same, or at least a sister passion to it, seems wove into the frame of every son and daughter of Adam; we usually speak of it as one of nature's levities, though planted within us for the solid purposes of carrying forward the mind to fresh inquiry and knowledge: strip us of it, the mind (I fear) would doze forever over the present page: and we should all of us rest at ease with such objects as presented themselves in the parish or province where we first drew our breath.

It is to this spur which is ever on our sides, that we owe the impatience of this desire for traveling: the passion is no way bad but as others are, in its mismanagement or excess; order it rightly, the advantages are worth the pursuit; the chief of which are—to learn the languages, the laws and customs, and understand the government and interest of other nations, to acquire an urbanity and confidence of behavior, and fit the mind more easily for conversation and discourse; to take us out of the company of our aunts and grandmothers, and from the track of nursery mistakes; and by showing us new objects, or old ones in new lights; to reform our judgment—by tasting perpetually the varieties of nature; to know what *is good*—by observing the address and arts of men, to conceive what is *sincere*—and by seeing the difference of so many various humors and manners—to look into ourselves and form our own.

This is some part of the cargo we might return with; but the impulse of seeing new sights, augmented with that of getting clear from all lessons both of wisdom and reproof at home—carries our youth too early out, to turn this venture to much account; on the contrary, if the scene painted of the prodigal in his travels, looks more like a copy than an original, will it not be well if such an adventurer, with so unpromising a setting out—without *carte*, without compass—be not cast away forever,—and may he not be said to escape well—if he returns to his country, only as naked, as he first left it?

But you will send an able pilot with your son—a scholar.

If wisdom can speak in no other language but Greek or Latin—you do well—or if mathematics will make a man a gentleman—or natural philosophy but teach him to make a bow—he may be of some service in introducing your son into good societies, and supporting him in them when he has done—but the upshot will be generally this, that in the most pressing occasions of address, if he is a mere man of reading, the unhappy youth will have the tutor to carry—and not the tutor to carry him.

But you will avoid this extreme; he shall be escorted by one who

knows the world, not merely from books—but from his own experience—
a man who has been employed on such services, and thrice made the *tour of
Europe, with success.*

That is, without breaking his own, or his pupil's neck; for if he is such
as my eyes have seen! some broken *Swiss valet de chambre,* some general undertaker, who will perform the journey in so many months "IF GOD PERMIT,"
much knowledge will not accrue; some profit at least, he will learn the
amount to a halfpenny, of every stage from Calais to Rome; he will be carried to the best inns, instructed where there is the best wine, and sup a livre
cheaper, than if the youth had been left to make the tour and the bargain
himself. Look at our governor! I beseech you: see, he is an inch taller as he
relates the advantages.

And here endeth his pride, his knowledge and his use.

But when your son gets abroad, he will be taken out of his hand, by
his society with men of rank and letters, with whom he will pass the greatest part of his time.

Let me observe in the first place, that company which is really good,
is very rare—and very shy: but you have surmounted this difficulty; and
procured him the best letters of recommendation to the most eminent and
respectable in every capital.

And I answer, that he will obtain all by them, which courtesy strictly
stands obliged to pay on such occasions, but no more.

There is nothing in which we are so much deceived, as in the advantages proposed from our connections and discourse with the literati, etc. in
foreign parts; especially if the experiment is made before we are matured
by years or study.

Conversation is a traffic; and if you enter into it, without some stock
of knowledge, to balance the account perpetually betwixt you, the trade
drops at once: and this is the reason, however it may be boasted to the contrary, why travelers have so little (especially good) conversation with na-
tives, owing to their suspicion, or perhaps conviction, that there is nothing
to be extracted from the conversation of young itinerants, worth the trouble of their bad language or the interruption of their visits.

The pain on these occasions is usually reciprocal; the consequence of
which is, that the disappointed youth seeks an easier society; and as bad

company is always ready, and ever lying in wait, the career is soon finished; and the poor prodigal returns the same object of pity, with the prodigal in the gospel.

Samuel Johnson

1709–75

One of his biographers, John Hawkins, said that Johnson "was never greedy of money, but without money could not be stimulated to write." Among the numerous odd jobs he undertook was the anonymous writing of sermons, for which he was usually paid two guineas apiece. Some twenty-eight have been posthumously identified, including one signed and written on the occasion of the funeral of his beloved wife, Tetty. Most of them were composed for a lifelong London clergyman friend he met when they were children at school in Litchfield, John Taylor. Boswell described the latter as "a hearty English 'Squire, with the parson superinduced," so it must have seemed a bit odd to hear him preach Johnson on the institution of marriage when his own was breached.

Samuel Johnson was a devout Anglican who, like many of his countrymen, found good preaching was an important part of his life. He once asserted, "Why, Sir, you are to consider, that sermons make a considerable branch of English literature; so that a library must be very imperfect if it has not a numerous collection of sermons." Themes in his sermons often mirror those of his literary works but certainly both proceeded from his fervent efforts to attain a spiritual life. Given the widespread and perfectly accepted contemporary practice of borrowing, adapting, reading, and otherwise using the sermons of others without acknowledgment—a practice, by the way, that can be found justified as far back as (and indeed *by*) St. Augustine—he would have had no compunction about his role as a ghostwriter.

The text of the sermon that follows is taken from Ecclesiastes, the title of whose Hebrew author, Qoheleth, is often fittingly translated as "the Preacher." Its theme, vanity, would lead any reader familiar with Johnson to reread his majestic poetic jeremiad, *The Vanity of Human Wishes* (1749), in which the poet seems at one point almost to make self-reference:

> Deign on the passing world to turn thine eyes,
> And pause awhile from letters, to be wise;
> There mark what ills the scholar's life assail,
> Toil, envy, want, the patron, and the jail.

All Is Vanity

I have seen all the works that are done under the sun; and behold, all is vanity and vexation of spirit.

—ECCLESIASTES 1:14

That all human actions terminate in vanity, and all human hopes will end in vexation, is a position, from which nature withholds our credulity, and which our fondness for the present life, and worldly enjoyments, disposes us to doubt; however forcibly it may be urged upon us, by reason or experience.

Every man will readily enough confess, that his own condition discontents him; and that he has not yet been able, with all his labor, to make happiness, or, with all his inquiries, to find it. But he still thinks, it is some where to be found, or by some means to be procured. His envy sometimes persuades him to imagine, that others possess it; and his ambition points the way, by which he supposes, that he shall reach, at last, the station to which it is annexed. Every one wants something to happiness, and when he has gained what he first wanted, he wants something else; he wears out life in efforts and pursuits, and perhaps dies, regretting that he must leave the world, when he is about to enjoy it.

So great is our interest, or so great we think it, to believe ourselves able to procure our own happiness, that experience never convinces us of our impotence; and indeed our miscarriages might be reasonably enough imputed by us, to our own unskillfulness, or ignorance; if we were able to derive intelligence, from no experience but our own. But surely we may be content to credit the general voice of mankind, complaining incessantly of general infelicity; and when we see the restlessness of the young, and the peevishness of the old; when we find the daring and the active combating misery, and the calm and humble lamenting it; when the vigorous are exhausting themselves, in struggles with their own condition, and the old and the wise retiring from the contest, in weariness and despondency; we may be content at last to conclude, that if happiness had been to be found, some would have found it, and that it is vain to search longer for what all have missed.

But though our obstinacy should hold out, against common experience and common authority, it might at least give way to the declaration of Solomon, who has left this testimony to succeeding ages; that all human pursuits and labors, are vanity. From the like conclusion made by other men, we may escape; by considering, that *their* experience was small, and *their* power narrow; that they pronounced with confidence upon that, which they could not know; and that many pleasures might be above their reach, and many more beyond their observation; *they* may be considered, as uttering the dictates of discontent, rather than persuasion; and as speaking not so much of the general state of things, as of their own share, and their own situation.

But the character of Solomon leaves no room for subterfuge; he did not judge of what he did not know. He had in his possession, whatever power and riches, and, what is still more, whatever wisdom and knowledge could confer. As he understood the vegetable creation, from the cedar of Libanus, to the hysop on the wall; so there is no doubt, but he had taken a survey of all the gradations of human life, from the throne of the prince, to the shepherd's cottage. He had in his hand, all the instruments of happiness, and in his mind, the skill to apply them. Every power of delight which others possessed, he had authority to summon, or wealth to purchase; all that royal prosperity could supply, was accumulated upon him; at home he had peace, and in foreign countries he had honor; what every nation could supply, was poured down before him. If power be grateful, he was a king; if there be pleasure in knowledge, he was the wisest of mankind; if wealth can purchase happiness, he had so much gold, that silver was little regarded. Over all these advantages, presided a mind, in the highest degree disposed to magnificence and voluptuousness; so eager in pursuit of gratification, that alas! after every other price had been bid for happiness, religion and virtue were brought to the sale. But after the anxiety of his inquiries, the weariness of his labors, and the loss of his innocence, he obtained only this conclusion: "I have seen all the works that are done under the sun, and behold, all is vanity and vexation of spirit."

That this result of Solomon's experience thus solemnly bequeathed by him to all generations, may not be transmitted to us without its proper use; let us diligently consider,

First, in what sense we are to understand, that all is vanity.

Secondly, how far the conviction, that all is vanity, ought to influence the conduct of life.

Thirdly, what consequences the serious and religious mind may deduce from the position, that all is vanity.

When we examine first, in what sense we are to understand, that all is vanity; we must remember, that the Preacher is not speaking of religious practices, or of any actions immediately commanded by God, or directly referred to him; but of such employments as we pursue by choice, and such works as we perform, in hopes of a recompense in the present life; such as flatter the imagination with pleasing scenes, and probable increase of temporal felicity; of this he determines that all is vanity, and every hour confirms his determination.

The event of all human endeavors is uncertain. He that plants, may gather no fruit; he that sows, may reap no harvest. Even the most simple operations are liable to miscarriage, from causes which we cannot foresee; and if we could foresee them, cannot prevent. What can be more vain, than the confidence of man, when the annual provision made for the support of life is not only exposed to the uncertainty of the weather, and the variation of the sky, but lies at the mercy of the reptiles of the earth, or the insects of the air? The rain and the wind, he cannot command; the caterpillar he cannot destroy, and the locust he cannot drive away.

But these effects, which require only the concurrence of natural causes, though they depend little upon human power, are yet made by Providence regular and certain, in comparison with those extensive and complicated undertakings, which must be brought to pass by the agency of man, and which require the union of many understandings, and the cooperation of many hands. The history of mankind is little else than a narrative of designs which have failed, and hopes that have been disappointed. In all matters of emulation and contest, the success of one implies the defeat of another, and at least half the transaction terminates in misery. And in designs not directly contrary to the interest of another, and therefore not opposed either by artifice or violence, it frequently happens, that by negligence or mistake, or unseasonable officiousness, a very hopeful project is brought to nothing.

To find examples of disappointment and uncertainty, we need not raise our thoughts to the interests of nations, nor follow the warrior to the field, or the statesman to the council. The little transactions of private families are entangled with perplexities; and the hourly occurrences of common life are filling the world with discontent and complaint. Every man hopes for kindness from his friends, diligence from his servants, and obedience from his children; yet friends are often unfaithful, servants negligent, and children rebellious. Human wisdom has, indeed, exhausted its power, in giving rules for the conduct of life; but those rules are themselves but vanities. They are difficult to be observed, and though observed, are uncertain in the effect.

The labors of man are not only uncertain, but imperfect. If we perform what we designed, we yet do not obtain what we expected. What appeared great when we desired it, seems little when it is attained; the wish is still unsatisfied, and something always remains behind, without which, the gratification is incomplete. He that rises to greatness, finds himself in danger; he that obtains riches, perceives that he cannot gain esteem. He that is caressed, sees interest lurking under kindness; and he that hears his own praises, suspects that he is flattered. Discontent and doubt are always pursuing us. Our endeavors end without performance, and performance ends without satisfaction.

But since this uncertainty and imperfection is the lot which our Creator has appointed for us, we are to inquire,

Secondly, how far the conviction, that all is vanity, ought to influence the conduct of life.

Human actions may be distinguished into various classes. Some are actions of duty, which can never be vain, because God will reward them. Yet these actions, considered as terminating in this world, will often produce vexation. It is our duty to admonish the vicious, to instruct the ignorant, and relieve the poor; and our admonitions will, sometimes, produce anger, instead of amendment; our instructions will be sometimes bestowed upon the perverse, the stupid, and the inattentive; and our charity will be sometimes misapplied, by those that receive it, and, instead of feeding the hungry, will pamper the intemperate; but these disappointments do not make good actions vain, though they show us, how much all success depends upon causes, on which we have no influence.

There are likewise actions of necessity; these are often vain and vexatious; but such is the order of the world, that they cannot be omitted. He that will eat bread, must plow and sow; though it is not certain, that he who plows and sows shall eat bread. It is appointed, that life should be sustained by labor; and we must not sink down in sullen idleness, when our industry is permitted to miscarry. We shall often have occasion to remember the sentence, denounced by the Preacher, upon all that is done under the sun; but we must still prosecute our business, confess our imbecility, and turn our eyes upon him, whose mercy is over all his works, and who, though he humbles our pride, will succor our necessities.

Works of absolute necessity, are few and simple; a very great part of human diligence is laid out, in accommodations of ease, or refinements of pleasure; and the further we pass beyond the boundaries of necessity, the more we lose ourselves in the regions of vanity, and the more we expose ourselves to vexation of spirit. As we extend our pleasures, we multiply our wants. The pain of hunger is easily appeased, but to surmount the disgust of appetite vitiated by indulgence, all the arts of luxury are required, and all are often vain. When to the enjoyments of sense, are superadded the delights of fancy, we form a scheme of happiness that never can be complete, for we can always imagine more than we possess. All social pleasures put us more or less in the power of others, who sometimes cannot, and sometimes will not, please us. Conversations of argument often end in bitterness of controversy, and conversations of mirth, in petulance and folly. Friendship is violated by interest, or broken by passion, and benevolence finds its kindness bestowed on the worthless and ungrateful.

But most certain is the disappointment of him, who places his happiness in comparative good, and considers, not what he himself wants, but what others have. The delight of eminence must, by its own nature, be rare, because he that is eminent, must have many below him, and therefore if we suppose such desires general, as very general they are, *the happiness of a few must arise from the misery of many.* He that places his delight in the extent of his renown, is, in some degree, at the mercy of every tongue; not only malevolence, but indifference, may disturb him; and he may be pained, not only by those who speak ill but by those likewise that say nothing.

As every engine of artificial motion, as it consists of more parts, is in more danger of deficience and disorder; so every effect, as it requires the agency of greater numbers, is more likely to fail. Yet what pleasure is granted to man, beyond the gross gratifications of sense, common to him with other animals, that does not demand the help of others, and the help of greater numbers, as the pleasure is sublimated and enlarged? And since such is the constitution of things, that whatever can give pleasure, can likewise cause uneasiness, there is little hope that uneasiness will be long escaped. Of them, whose offices are necessary to felicity, some will be perverse, and some will be unskillful; some will negligently withhold their contributions, and some will enviously withdraw them. The various and opposite directions of the human mind, which divide men into so many different occupations, keep all the inhabitants of the earth perpetually busy; but when it is considered, that the business of every man is to counteract the purpose of some other man, it will appear, that universal activity cannot contribute much to universal happiness. Of those that contend, one must necessarily be overcome, and he that prevails, never has his labor rewarded to his wish, but finds, that he has been contending for that which cannot satisfy, and engaged in a contest where even victory is vanity.

What then is the influence which the conviction of this unwelcome truth ought to have upon our conduct? It ought to teach us humility, patience, and diffidence. When we consider how little we know of the distant consequences of our own actions, how little the greatest personal qualities can protect us from misfortune, how much all our importance depends upon the favor of others, how uncertainly that favor is bestowed, and how easily it is lost, we shall find, that we have very little reason to be proud. That which is most apt to elate the thoughts, height of place, and greatness of power, is the gift of others. No man can, by any natural or intrinsic faculties, maintain himself in a state of superiority; he is exalted to his place, whatever it be, by the concurrence of those, who are for a time content to be counted his inferiors, he has no authority in himself; he is only able to control some, by the help of others. If dependence be a state of humiliation, every man has reason to be humble, for every man is dependent.

But however unpleasing these considerations may be, however unequal our condition is to all our wishes or conceptions, we are not to admit impatience into our bosoms, or increase the evils of life, by vain throbs of discontent. To live in a world where all is vanity, has been decreed by our Creator to be the lot of man, a lot which we cannot alter by murmuring, but may soften by submission.

The consideration of the vanity of all human purposes and projects, deeply impressed upon the mind, necessarily produces that diffidence in all worldly good, which is necessary to the regulation of our passions, and the security of our innocence. In a smooth course of prosperity, an unobstructed progression from wish to wish, while the success of one design facilitates another, and the opening prospect of life shows pleasures at a distance, to conclude that the passage will be always clear, and that the delights which solicit from far, will, when they are attained, fill the soul with enjoyments, must necessarily produce violent desires, and eager pursuits, contempt of those that are behind, and malignity to those that are before. But the full persuasion that all earthly good is uncertain in the attainment, and unstable in the possession, and the frequent recollection of the slender supports on which we rest, and the dangers which are always hanging over us, will dictate inoffensive modesty, and mild benevolence. *He* does not rashly treat another with contempt, who doubts the duration of his own superiority: *he* will not refuse assistance to the distressed, who supposes that he may quickly need it himself. He that considers how imperfectly human wisdom can judge of that, which has not been tried, will seldom think any possibilities of advantage worthy of vehement desire. As his hopes are moderate, his endeavors will be calm. He will not fix his fond hopes upon things which he knows to be vanity, but will enjoy this world, as one who knows that he does not possess it: and that this is the disposition, which becomes our condition, will appear, when we consider,

Thirdly, what consequences the serious and religious mind may draw from the position, that all is vanity.

When the present state of man is considered, when an estimate is made of his hopes, his pleasures, and his possessions; when his hopes appear to be deceitful, his labors ineffectual, his pleasures unsatisfactory, and his possessions fugitive, it is natural to wish for an abiding city, for a state more constant and permanent, of which the objects may be more proportioned to our wishes, and the enjoyments to our capacities; and from this wish it is reasonable to infer, that such a state is designed for us by that infinite wisdom, which, as it does nothing in vain, has not created minds with comprehensions never to be filled. When revelation is consulted, it appears that such a state is really promised, and that, by the contempt of worldly pleasures, it is to be obtained. We then find, that instead of lamenting the imperfection of earthly things, we have reason to pour out thanks to him who orders all for our good, that he has made the world, such as often deceives, and often afflicts us; that the charms of interest are not such, as our frailty is unable to resist, but that we have such interruptions of our pursuits, and such languor in our enjoyments, such pains of body and anxieties of mind, as repress desire, and weaken temptation: and happy will it be, if we follow the gracious directions of Providence, and determine, that no degree of earthly felicity shall be purchased with a crime: if we resolve no longer to bear the chains of sin, to employ all our endeavors upon transitory and imperfect pleasures, or to divide our thoughts between the world and heaven; but to bid farewell to sublunary vanities, to endure no longer an unprofitable vexation of spirit, but with pure heart and steady faith to "fear God, and to keep his commandments, and remember that this is the whole of man." (Eccles. 12:13.)

John Wesley

1703–91

John Wesley's biographers have sometimes focused on his identity as the fifteenth son of an intense and politically Tory mother whose personal religion was bent on "breaking the will of the child." As an undergraduate at Oxford, the salvation seeker Wesley formed a Holy Club with his brother Charles and George Whitefield, who was to become another great popular preacher of the day. Austerity, an appetite for frost, prisons, and pest houses, gave their "Methodist" sect great notoriety, but Wesley himself left Oxford in 1735 for a missionary trip to Georgia in the American colonies. A fierce determination, on his return, inspired him to bring to others his own experience of salvation. In Wesley's words, he had a mystical encounter in which his heart was ". . . strangely warmed. I felt that I did trust in Christ, Christ alone for salvation; and an assurance was given me that he had taken *my* sins, even *mine,* and saved me from the law of sin and death."

Wesley's evangelical vision sent him into a different spiritual wilderness from that of the Americas. For the next fifty-three years he traveled on horseback into countless villages and towns and preached out of doors after his exclusion from the Church of England. The preaching circuit of the energetic and fervent Wesley took him over many thousands of miles of rural eighteenth-century England and resulted in the building of hundreds of Methodist chapels devoted to communal confession of sin and mutual exhortation and prayer. An inevitable breach with the Anglican Church came in 1784, when Methodism, in keeping with Wesley's political conservatism and belief in the transformation of the will of the individual, crystallized as a separatist movement and social force for good works. Its ideals were thrift, abstinence, and relentless hard work—a road to salvation, as one historian has called it, which made it not a religion *of* the poor but *for* the poor.

Restless energy—poured not only into his vast collection of sermons but into translating Thomas à Kempis and into the kind of daily exhortation which made Samuel Johnson describe him as a good conversationalist, but "never at leisure"—gave Wesley's language a flamelike quality. His last words were "I'll praise, I'll praise." His impact on society was enormous, too, while his conception of "the great assize" or high court in this famous sermon unites the notion of private and public scrutiny which made Methodism so transcendent and quixotic a force in an England at the threshold of the Industrial Revolution.

☙

The Great Assize

We shall all stand before the judgment-seat of Christ.
—ROMANS 14:10

How many circumstances concur to raise the awfulness of the present solemnity! The general concourse of people of every age, sex, rank, and condition of life, willingly or unwillingly gathered together, not only from the neighboring, but from distant parts; criminals, speedily to be brought forth, and having no way to escape; officers, waiting in their various posts, to execute the orders which shall be given; and the representative of our gracious sovereign, whom we so highly reverence and honor. The occasion, likewise, of this assembly, adds not a little to the solemnity of it: to hear and determine causes of every kind, some of which are of the most important nature; on which depends no less than life or death; death that uncovers the face of eternity! It was, doubtless, in order to increase the serious sense of these things, and not in the minds of the vulgar only, that the wisdom of our forefathers did not disdain to appoint even several minute circumstances of this solemnity. For these also, by means of the eye or ear, may more deeply affect the heart: and when viewed in this light, trumpets, staves, apparel, are no longer trifling or significant, but subservient, in their kind and degree, to the most valuable ends of society.

But, awful as this solemnity is, one far more awful is at hand. For yet a little while, and "we shall all stand before the judgment seat of Christ." "For, as I live, saith the Lord, every knee shall bow to Me, and every tongue shall confess to God." And in that day "every one of us shall give account of himself to God."

Had all men a deep sense of this, how effectually would it secure the interests of society! For what more forcible motive can be conceived to the practice of genuine morality, to a steady pursuit of solid virtue, and a uniform walking in justice, mercy and truth? What could strengthen our hands in all that is good, and deter us from all that is evil, like a strong conviction of this, "The judge standeth at the door"; and we are shortly to stand before him?

It may not, therefore, be improper, or unsuitable to the design of the present assembly, to consider,

I. The chief circumstances which will precede our standing before the judgment seat of Christ.

II. The judgment itself; and

III. A few of the circumstances which will follow it.

1. Let us, in the first place, consider the chief circumstances which will precede our standing before the judgment seat of Christ.

And, first, "God will show signs in the earth beneath," particularly He will "arise to shake terribly the earth." "The earth shall reel to and fro like a drunkard, and shall be removed like a cottage." "There shall be earthquakes" (not in divers only, but) "in all places"; not in one only, nor in a few, but in every part of the habitable world, even "such as were not since men were upon the earth, so mighty earthquakes and so great." In one of these "every island shall flee away, and the mountains will not be found."

Meantime all the waters of the terraqueous globe will feel the violence of those concussions; "the sea and waves roaring," with such an agitation as had never been known before, since the hour that "the fountains of the great deep were broken up," to destroy the earth, which then "stood out of the water and in the water." The air will be all storm and tempest, full of dark vapors and pillars of smoke, resounding with thunder from pole to pole, and torn with ten thousand lightnings. But the commotion will not stop in the region of air; "the powers of heaven also shall be shaken. There shall be signs in the sun, and in the moon, and in the stars"; those fixed as well as those that move around them. "The sun shall be turned into darkness, and the moon into blood, before the great and terrible day of the Lord come." "The stars shall withdraw their shining," yea, and "fall from heaven," being thrown out of their orbits. And then shall be heard the universal shout, from all the companies of heaven, followed by the "voice of the archangel," proclaiming the approach of the Son of God and man, "and the trumpet of God" sounding an alarm to all that sleep in the dust of the earth. In consequence of this, all the graves shall open, and the bodies of men arise. The sea, also, shall give up the dead which are therein, and everyone shall rise with "his own body"; his own in substance, although so changed in its properties as we cannot now conceive. "For this corruptible will (then) put on incorruption, and this mortal put on immortality." Yea, "death and hades," the invisible world, shall "deliver up the dead that are in them," so that all who ever lived and died, since God created man, shall be raised incorruptible and immortal.

2. At the same time, "the Son of man shall send forth His angels" over all the earth; "and they shall gather His elect from the four winds, from one end of heaven to the other." And the Lord Himself shall come with clouds, in His own glory, and the glory of His Father, with ten thousand of His saints, even myriads of angels, and shall sit upon the throne of His glory. "And before Him shall be gathered all nations, and He shall separate them one from another, and shall set the sheep (the good) on His right hand, and the goats (the wicked) upon the left." Concerning this general assembly it is that the beloved disciple speaks thus: "I saw the dead (all that had been dead), small and great, stand before God. And the books were opened (a figurative expression, plainly referring to the manner of proceeding among men), and the dead were judged out of those things which were written in the books, according to their works."

II. These are the chief circumstances which are recorded in the oracles of God as preceding the general judgment. We are, secondly, to consider the judgment itself, so far as it hath pleased God to reveal it.

1. The Person by whom God will judge the world is His only-begotten Son, whose "goings forth are from everlasting"; "who is God over all, blessed forever." Unto Him, being "the out-beaming of His Father's glory, the express image of His Person," the Father "hath committed all judgment, because He is the Son of man"; because, though He was "in the

form of God, and thought it not robbery to be equal with God, yet He emptied Himself, taking upon Him the form of a servant, being made in the
likeness of man"; yea, because, "being found in fashion as a man, He humbled Himself (yet further), becoming obedient unto death, even the death
of the cross. Wherefore God hath highly exalted Him," even in His human
nature, and "ordained Him," as man, to try the children of men, "to be the
Judge both of the quick and dead"; both of those who shall be found alive at
His coming and of those who were before gathered to their fathers.

2. The time, termed by the prophet "the great and the terrible day," is
usually in Scripture styled "the day of the Lord." The space from the creation
of man upon the earth to the end of all things, is "the day of the sons of
men"; the time that is now passing is properly "our day"; when this is ended,
"the day of the Lord" will begin. But who can say how long it will continue?
"With the Lord one day is as a thousand years, and a thousand years as one
day." And from this very expression some of the ancient Fathers drew that
inference that what is commonly called the day of judgment would be a
thousand years; and it seems they did not go beyond the truth; very probably they did not come up to it. For, if we consider the number of persons
who are to be judged, and of actions which are to be inquired into, it does
not appear that a thousand years will suffice for the transactions of that day;
so that it may not, improbably, comprise several thousand years. But God
shall reveal this also in its season.

3. With regard to the place where mankind will be judged, we have no
explicit account in Scripture. An eminent writer (but not alone: many have
been of the same opinion) supposes it will be on earth, where the works
were done, according to which they shall be judged; and that God will, in
order thereto, employ the angels of His strength

To smooth and lengthen out the boundless space,
And spread an area for all human race.

But perhaps it is more agreeable to our Lord's own account of His
coming in the clouds to suppose it will be on earth, if not "twice a plane-
tary height." And this supposition is not a little favored by what St. Paul
writes to the Thessalonians: "The dead in Christ shall rise first. Then we who
remain alive shall be caught up together with them, in the clouds, to meet

the Lord in the air." So that it seems most probable the great white throne will be high exalted above the earth.

4. The persons to be judged who can count, any more than the drops of rain, or the sands of the sea? "I behold," saith St. John, "a great multitude, which no man can number, clothed with white robes, and palms in their hands." How immense, then, must be the total multitude of all nations, and kindreds, and people, and tongues; of all that have sprung from the loins of Adam, since the world began till time shall be no more! If we admit the common supposition, which seems no ways absurd, that the earth bears at any one time no less than four hundred millions of living souls, men, women, and children, what a congregation must all these generations make who have succeeded each other for seven thousand years!

> Great Xerxes' world in arms, proud Cannae's host,
> They all are here; and here they all are lost,
> Their numbers swell to be discerned in vain,
> Lost as a drop in the unbounded main.

Every man, every woman, every infant of days that ever breathed the vital air, will then hear the voice of the Son of God, and start into life, and appear before Him. And this seems to be the natural import of that expression, "the dead, small and great"; all universally, all without exception, all of every age, sex, or degree, all that ever lived and died, or underwent such a change as will be equivalent with death. For long before that day the phantom of greatness disappears and sinks into nothing. Even in the moment of death that vanishes away. Who is rich or great in the grave?

5. And every man shall there "give an account of his own works"; yea, a full and true account of all that he ever did while in the body, whether it was good or evil.

Nor will all the actions alone of every child of man be then brought to open view, but all their words; seeing "every idle word which men shall speak, they shall give account thereof in the day of judgment"; so that "by thy words" as well as works, "thou shalt be justified; and by thy words thou shalt be condemned." Will not God then bring to light every circumstance also that accompanied every word or action, and if not altered the nature, yet lessened or increased the goodness or badness of them? And how easy is this to Him who is "about our bed, and about our path, and spieth out all our ways"? We know "the darkness is no darkness to Him, but the night shineth as the day."

6. Yea, He will bring to light, not the hidden works of darkness only, but the very thoughts and intents of the hearts. And what marvel? For He "searcheth the reins and understandeth all our thoughts." "All things are naked and open to the eye of Him with whom we have to do." "Hell and destruction are before Him, without a covering. How much more the hearts of the children of men?"

7. And in that day shall be discovered every inward working of every human soul; every appetite, passion, inclination, affection, with the various combinations of them, with every temper and disposition that constitute the whole complex character of each individual. So shall it be clearly and infallibly seen who was righteous and who was unrighteous; and in what degree every action, or person, or character, was either good or evil.

8. "Then the King will say to them upon His right hand, Come ye, blessed of My Father. For I was hungry, and ye gave Me meat; thirsty, and ye gave Me drink; I was a stranger, and ye took me in; naked, and ye clothed Me." In like manner, all the good they did upon earth will be recited before men and angels; whatsoever they had done either in word or deed, in the name or for the sake of the Lord Jesus. All their good desires, intentions, thoughts, all their holy dispositions, will also be then remembered; and it will appear that though they were unknown or forgotten among men, yet God noted them in His book. All their sufferings, likewise, for the name of Jesus, and for the testimony of a good conscience, will be displayed, unto their praise from the righteous Judge, their honor before saints and angels, and the increase of that "far more exceeding and eternal weight of glory."

9. But will their evil deeds too (since, if we take in his whole life, there is not a man on earth that liveth and sinneth not), will these be remembered in that day, and mentioned in the great congregation? Many believe they will, and ask "Would not this imply that their sufferings were not at an end, even when life ended—seeing they would still have sorrow and shame, and confusion of face to endure?" They ask further, "How can this be reconciled with God's declaration by the prophet, 'If the wicked will turn from all his sins that he hath committed, and keep all My statutes, and do that which is lawful and right, all his trangressions that he hath committed, they shall not

be once mentioned unto him,' how is it consistent with the promise which God has made to all who accept of the Gospel covenant, 'I will forgive their iniquities, and remember their sins no more,' or as the Apostle expresses it, 'I will be merciful to their unrighteousness, and their sins and iniquities will I remember no more'?"

10. It may be answered, it is apparently and absolutely necessary for the full display of the glory of God, for the clear and perfect manifestation of His wisdom, justice, power and mercy, toward the heirs of salvation, that all the circumstances of this life should be placed in open view, together with all their tempers, and the desires, thoughts, and intents of their hearts, otherwise how would it appear out of what a depth of sin and misery the grace of God had delivered them. And indeed if the whole lives of all the children of men were not manifestly discovered, the whole amazing con-texture of Divine Providence could not be manifested, nor should we yet be able, in a thousand instances "to justify the ways of God to man," unless our Lord's words were fulfilled in their utmost sense, without any restric-tion or limitation, "There is nothing covered that shall not be revealed, or hid that shall not be known," abundance of God's dispensations under the sun would still appear without their reasons. And then only when God hath brought to light all the hidden things of darkness, whosoever were the ac-tors therein, will it be seen that wise and good were all His ways, that He saw through the thick cloud, and governed all things by the wise counsels of His own will, that nothing was left to chance, or the caprice of men, but God disposed all strongly and sweetly, and wrought all into one connected chain of justice, mercy and truth.

11. And in the discovery of the Divine perfections, the righteous will rejoice with joy unspeakable, far from feeling any painful sorrow or shame; for any of those past transgressions which were long since blotted out as a cloud, and washed away by the blood of the Lamb. It will be abundantly suf-ficient for them that all the transgressions which they had committed shall not be once mentioned unto them to their disadvantage; that their sins, and transgressions, and iniquities shall be remembered no more to their con-demnation. This is the plain meaning of the promise, and this all the chil-dren of God shall find true, to their everlasting comfort.

12. After the righteous are judged, the King will turn to them upon His left hand, and they shall also be judged, every man according to his

works. But not only their outward works will be brought into the account, but all the evil words which they have ever spoken, yea, all the evil desires, affections, tempers which have or have had a place in their souls, and all the evil thoughts or designs which were ever cherished in their hearts. The joyful sentence of acquittal will then be pronounced upon those upon the right hand, the dreadful sentence of condemnation upon those on the left, both of which must remain fixed and unmovable as the throne of God.

III. 1. We may, in the third place, consider a few of the circumstances which will follow the general judgment. And the first is the execution of the sentence pronounced on the evil and the good. "These shall go away into eternal punishment, and the righteous into life eternal." It should be observed it is the very same word which is used, both in the former and in the latter clause: it follows that either the punishment lasts forever, or the reward too will come to an end. No, never, unless God could come to an end, or His mercy and truth could fail. "Then shall the righteous shine forth as the sun, in the kingdom of their Father," "and shall drink of those rivers of pleasure which are at God's right hand for evermore." But here all description falls short, all human language fails! Only one who is caught up into the third heaven can have a just conception of it. But even such a one cannot express what he hath seen, these things it is not possible for man to utter.

The wicked, meantime, shall be turned into hell, even all the people that forget God. They will be "punished with everlasting destruction from the presence of the Lord, and from the glory of His power." They will be "cast into the lake of fire, burning with brimstone," originally "prepared for the devil and his angels," where they will gnaw their tongues for anguish and pain, they will curse God and look upward. There the dogs of hell, pride, malice, revenge, rage, horror, despair, continually devour them. There "they have no rest, day or night, but the smoke of their torment ascendeth for ever and ever." For "their worm dieth not, and the fire is not quenched."

2. Then the heavens will be shriveled up as a parchment scroll, and pass away with a great noise; they will "flee from the face of Him that sitteth on the throne, and there will be found no place for them." The very manner of their passing away is disclosed to us by the apostle Peter: "In the day of God, the heavens being on fire, shall be dissolved." The whole beautiful fabric will be overthrown by that raging element, the connection of all its parts destroyed, and every atom torn asunder from the others. By the same, "the

earth also, and the works that are therein shall be burned up." The enormous works of nature, the everlasting hills, mountains that have defied the rage of time, and stood unmoved so many thousand years, will sink down in fiery ruin. How much less will the works of art, though of the most durable kind, the utmost effort of human industry, tombs, pillars, triumphal arches, castles, pyramids, be able to withstand the flaming conqueror! All, all will die, perish, vanish away, like a dream when one awaketh!

3. It has indeed been imagined by some great and good men that as it requires that same Almighty Power to annihilate things as to create; to speak into nothing or out of nothing; so no part of no atom in the universe will be totally or finally destroyed. Rather, they suppose that, as the last operation of fire, which we have yet been able to observe, is to reduce into glass what, by a smaller force, it had reduced to ashes; so, in the day God hath ordained, the whole earth, if not the material heavens also, will undergo this change, after which the fire can have no further power over them. And they believe this is intimated by that expression in the Revelation made to St. John, "Before the throne there was a sea of glass like unto crystal." We can not now either affirm or deny this; but we shall know hereafter.

4. If it be inquired by the scoffers, the minute philosophers, how can these things be? Whence should come such an immense quantity of fire as would consume the heavens and the whole terraqueous globe? We would beg leave first to remind them that this difficulty is not peculiar to the Christian system. The same opinion almost universally obtained among the unbigoted heathens. But, secondly, it is easy to answer, even from our slight and superficial acquaintance with natural things, that there are abundant magazines of fire ready prepared, and treasured up against the day of the Lord. How soon may a comet, commissioned by Him, travel down from the most distant parts of the universe! And were it to fix upon the earth, in its return from the sun, when it is some thousand times hotter than a red-hot cannonball; who does not see what must be the immediate consequence? But, not to ascend so high as the ethereal heavens, might not the same lightnings which "give shine to the world," if commanded by the Lord of nature, give ruin and utter destruction? Or to go no further than the globe itself; who knows what huge reservoirs of liquid fire are from age to age contained in the bowels of the earth? Etna, Hecla, Vesuvius, and all the other volcanoes that belch out flames and coals of fire, what are they but so many proofs and

mouths of those fiery furnaces; and at the same time so many evidences that
God hath in readiness wherewith to fulfill His word? Yea, were we to observe no more than the surface of the earth, and the things that surround us
on every side, it is most certain (as a thousand experiments prove, beyond
all possibility of denial) that we, ourselves, our whole bodies, are full of fire,
as well as everything around us. Is it not easy to make this ethereal fire visible even to the naked eye, and to produce thereby the very same effects on
combustible matter which are produced by culinary fire? Needs there then
any more than for God to unloose that secret chain, whereby this irresistible
agent is now bound down, and lies quiescent in every particle of matter?
And how soon would it tear the universal frame in pieces, and involve all in
one common ruin!

5. There is one circumstance more which will follow the judgment
that deserves our serious consideration: "We look," says the apostle, "according to His promise, for new heavens and a new earth, wherein dwelleth
righteousness." The promise stands in the prophecy of Isaiah: "Behold: I create new heavens and a new earth; and the former shall not be remembered,"
so great shall the glory of the latter be! These St. John did behold in the visions of God. "I saw," saith he, "a new heaven and a new earth, for the first
heaven and the first earth were passed away. And I heard a great voice from
(the third) heaven, saying: Behold the tabernacle of God is with men; and
He will dwell with them, and they shall be His people; and God Himself
shall be with them, and be their God!" Of necessity therefore they will all
be happy. "God shall wipe away all tears from their eyes, and there shall be
no more death, neither sorrow, nor crying; neither shall there be any more
pain." "There shall be no more curse, but they shall see His face," shall have
the nearest access to, and thence the highest resemblance of Him. This is the
strongest expression in the language of Scripture to denote the most perfect happiness. "And His name shall be on their foreheads"; they shall be
openly acknowledged as God's own property, and His glorious nature shall
most visibly shine forth in them. "And there shall be no night there; and they
need no candle, neither the light of the sun, for the Lord God giveth them
light, and they shall reign for ever and ever."

Suffer me to add a few words to all of you who are at this present before the Lord. Should not you bear it in your minds all the day long, that a
more awful day is coming? A large assembly this! But what is it to that which

every eye will then behold, this general assembly of all the children of men that ever lived on the face of the whole earth! A few will stand at the judgment seat this day, to be judged touching what shall be laid to their charge; and they are now reserved in prison, perhaps in chains, till they are brought forth to be tried and sentenced. But we shall all, I that speak, and you that hear, "stand at the judgment-seat of Christ." And we are now reserved on this earth, which is not our home, in this prison of flesh and blood, perhaps many of us in chains of darkness too, till we are ordered to be brought forth. Here a man is questioned concerning one or two acts which he is supposed to have committed: there we are to give an account of all our works, from the cradle to the grave; of all our words, of all our desires and tempers, all the thoughts and intents of our hearts; of all the uses we have made of our various talents, whether of mind, body, or fortune, till God said, "Give an account of their stewardship, for thou mayest be no longer steward." In this count, it is possible some who are guilty may escape for want of evidence; but there is no want of evidence in that court. All men with whom you had the most secret intercourse, who were privy to all your designs and actions, are ready before your face. So are all the spirits of darkness, who inspired evil designs, and assisted in the execution of them. So are all the angels of God, those eyes of the Lord, that run to and fro over all the earth, who watched over your soul, and labored for your good, so far as you would permit. So is your own conscience a thousand witnesses in one, now no more capable of being either blinded or silenced, but constrained to know and to speak the naked truth, touching all your thoughts, and words, and actions. And is conscience as a thousand witnesses?—yea, but God is as a thousand witnesses. Oh, who can stand before the face of the great God, even our Savior Jesus Christ?

See! see! He cometh! He maketh the clouds His chariot! He rideth upon the wings of the wind! A devouring fire goeth before Him, and after Him a flame burneth! See! He sitteth upon His throne, clothed with light as with a garment, arrayed with majesty and honor! Behold His eyes are as a flame of fire, His voice as the sound of many waters! How will ye escape? Will ye call to the mountains to fall on you, the rocks to cover you? Alas, the mountains themselves, the rocks, the earth, the heavens, are just ready to flee away! Can ye prevent the sentence? Wherewith? With all the substance of thy house, with thousands of gold and silver? Blind wretch! Thou camest naked from thy mother's womb, and more naked into eternity. Hear the Lord, the Judge! "Come, ye blessed of my Father! inherit the kingdom prepared for you from the foundation of the world." Joyful sound! How widely different from that voice which echoes through the expanse of heaven, "Depart, ye cursed, into everlasting fire, prepared for the devil and his angels!" And who is he that can prevent or retard the full execution of either sentence? Vain hope! Lo, hell is moved from beneath to receive those who are ripe for destruction! And the everlasting doors lift up their heads, that the heirs of Glory may come in!

"What manner of persons, then, ought we to be, in all conversation and godliness?" We know it cannot be long before the Lord will descend with the voice of the archangel, and the trumpet of God; when everyone of us shall appear before Him, and give an account of his own works. "Wherefore, behold; seeing ye look for these things," seeing ye know He will come, and will not tarry, "be diligent, that ye may be found of Him in peace, without spot and blemish." Why should ye not? Why should one of you be found on the left hand at His appearing? He willeth not that any should perish, but that all should come to repentance; by repentance, to faith in a bleeding Lord; by faith, to spotless love; to the full image of God renewed in the heart, and producing all holiness of conversation. Can you doubt of this, when you remember the Judge of all is likewise the Savior of all? Hath He not bought you with His own blood, that ye might not perish, but have everlasting life? Oh make proof of His mercy, rather than His justice; of His love, rather than the thunder of His power! He is not far from everyone of us; and He is now come, not to condemn, but to save the world. He standeth in the midst! Sinner, doth He not now, even now, knock at the door of thy heart? Oh that thou mayest know, at least in this thy day, the things that belong unto thy peace! Oh that ye may now give yourselves to Him who gave Himself for you, in humble faith, in holy, active, patient love! So shall ye rejoice with exceeding joy in His day, when He cometh in the clouds of heaven!

Charles Wesley

1707–1788

*I*n the company of his brother John and George Whitefield, Charles Wesley founded a "methodist" society of young men at Christ Church, Oxford. Their circle of pious young scholars was dedicated to fasting and prayer. The origin of the term "Methodism" may come from a letter by the young Charles Wesley in which he remarks on having persuaded several young "scholars to accompany me and to observe the method of study prescribed by the statutes of the university." Other sources have suggested a different origin for what began as a derisive nickname for their methodical religious association: Charles Wesley, divine and hymn writer, responded once to pressure from his surviving and energetic siblings by asking, "What, would you have me to be a saint all at once?"

Charles Wesley kept a journal, which records his ministry to Indians and colonists in Georgia, his stormy voyages during the mission to America, and his own itinerant ministry on horseback from Newcastle-on-Tyne to the workers in the tin mines of Cornwall. In 1748 he reported that "the presbyterians say I am a presbyterian; the churchgoers that I am a minister of theirs; and the catholics are sure I am a good catholic in my heart."

Most of Charles Wesley's sermons were unpublished in his lifetime. He is remembered chiefly as the composer of a very large number of hymns, the father of two children of interesting accomplishment, one a composer in the school of Handel, the other a woman of letters. His own quiet brand of spiritual genius was probably best realized in his music, along with a gift for verse in both Latin and English. The topics of his hymns, which are no doubt his greatest legacy, are wide-ranging. Five hundred of them are in constant use, although much attention is devoted to his lyrical underscoring of the "real presence" in his sacramental hymns. Something of the quality of this gifted younger son, and perhaps his own obscure biography in relation to an autocratic older brother (in the best biblical tradition of warring siblings), is retained in the volume of *Sermons* issued by his widow after his death.

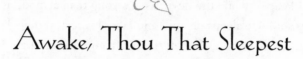

Awake, Thou That Sleepest

Preached on Sunday, April 4, 1742,
before the University of Oxford

Awake, thou that sleepest, and arise from the dead, and Christ shall give thee light.

—EPHESIANS 5:14

In discoursing on these words, I shall, with the help of God—

I. Describe the sleepers, to whom they are spoken:

II. Enforce the exhortation, "Awake, thou that sleepest, and arise from the dead": and,

III. Explain the promise made to such as do awake and arise: "Christ shall give thee light."

I. 1. And first, as to the sleepers here spoken to. By sleep is signified the natural state of man; that deep sleep of the soul, into which the sin of Adam hath cast all who spring from his loins; that supineness, indolence, and stupidity, that insensibility of his real condition, wherein every man comes into the world, and continues till the voice of God awakes him.

2. Now, "they that sleep, sleep in the night." The state of nature is a state of utter darkness; a state wherein "darkness covers the earth, and gross darkness the people." The poor unawakened sinner, how much knowledge soever he may have as to other things, has no knowledge of himself: in this respect "he knoweth nothing yet as he ought to know." He knows not that he is a fallen spirit, whose only business in the present world is, to recover from his fall, to regain that image of God wherein he was created. He sees

no necessity for the *one thing needful,* even that inward universal change, that "birth from above," figured out by baptism, which is the beginning of that total renovation, that sanctification of spirit, soul, and body, "without which no man shall see the Lord."

3. Full of all diseases as he is, he fancies himself in perfect health. Fast bound in misery and iron, he dreams that he is [happy and] at liberty. He says, "Peace! Peace!" while the devil, as "a strong man armed," is in full possession of his soul. He sleeps on still, and takes his rest, though hell is moved from beneath to meet him; though the pit from whence there is no return hath opened its mouth to swallow him up. A fire is kindled around him, yet he knoweth it not; yea, it burns him, yet he lays it not to heart.

4. By one who sleeps, we are, therefore, to understand (and would to God we might all understand it!) a sinner satisfied in his sins; contented to remain in his fallen state, to live and die without the image of God; one who is ignorant both of his disease, and of the only remedy for it; one who never was warned, or never regarded the warning voice of God, "to flee from the wrath to come"; one that never yet saw he was in danger of hellfire, or cried out in the earnestness of his soul, "What must I do to be saved?"

5. If this sleeper be not outwardly vicious, his sleep is usually the deepest of all: whether he be of the Laodicean spirit, "neither cold nor hot," but a quiet, rational, inoffensive, good-natured professor of the religion of his fathers; or whether he be zealous and orthodox, and, "after the most straitest sect of our religion," live "a Pharisee"; that is, according to the scriptural account, one that justifies himself; one that labors to establish his own righteousness, as the ground of his acceptance with God.

6. This is he, who, "having a form of godliness, denies the power thereof"; yea, and probably reviles it, wheresoever it is found, as mere extravagance and delusion. Meanwhile, the wretched self-deceiver thanks God, that he is "not as other men are; adulterers, unjust, extortioners"; no, he doeth no wrong to any man. He "fasts twice in a week," uses all the means of grace, is constant at church and sacrament; yea, and "gives tithes of all that he has"; does all the good that he can: "touching the righteousness of the law," he is "blameless": he wants nothing of godliness, but the power; nothing of religion, but the spirit; nothing of Christianity, but the truth and the life.

7. But know ye not, that, however highly esteemed among men such

a Christian as this may be, he is an abomination in the sight of God, and an heir of every woe which the Son of God, yesterday, today, and for ever, denounces against "scribes and Pharisees, hypocrites"? He hath "made clean the outside of the cup and the platter," but within is full of all filthiness. "An evil disease cleaveth still unto him, so that his inward parts are very wickedness." Our Lord fitly compares him to a "painted sepulchre," which "appears beautiful without"; but, nevertheless, is "full of dead men's bones, and of all uncleanness." The bones indeed are no longer dry; the sinews and flesh are come upon them, and the skin covers them above: but there is no breath in them, no Spirit of the living God. And, "if any man have not the Spirit of Christ, he is none of His." "Ye are Christ's, if so be that the Spirit of God dwell in you": but, if not, God knoweth that ye abide in death, even until now.

8. This is another character of the sleeper here spoken to. He abides in death, though he knows it not. He is dead unto God, "dead in trespasses and sins." For, "to be carnally minded is death." Even as it is written, "By one man sin entered into the world, and death by sin; and so death passed upon all men"; not only temporal death, but likewise spiritual and eternal. "In that day that thou eatest," said God to Adam, "thou shalt surely die": not bodily (unless as he then became mortal), but spiritually: thou shalt lose the life of thy soul, thou shalt die to God; shalt be separated from Him, thy essential life and happiness.

9. Thus first was dissolved the vital union of our soul with God; insomuch that "in the midst of" natural "life, we are" now in spiritual "death." And herein we remain till the Second Adam becomes a quickening Spirit to us; till He raises the dead, the dead in sin, in pleasure, riches, or honors. But, before any dead soul can live, he "hears" (hearkens to) "the voice of the Son of God": he is made sensible of his lost estate, and receives the sentence of death in himself. He knows himself to be "dead while he liveth"; dead to God, and all the things of God; having no more power to perform the actions of a living Christian, than a dead body to perform the functions of a living man.

10. And most certain it is, that one dead in sin has not "senses exercised to discern spiritual good and evil." "Having eyes, he sees not; he hath ears, and hears not." He doth not "taste and see that the Lord is gracious." He "hath not seen God at any time," nor "heard His voice," nor "handled the

word of life." In vain is the name of Jesus "like ointment poured forth, and all His garments smell of myrrh, aloes, and cassia." The soul that sleepeth in death hath no perception of any objects of this kind. His heart is "past feeling," and understandeth none of these things.

11. And hence, having no spiritual senses, no inlets of spiritual knowledge, the natural man receiveth not the things of the Spirit of God; nay, he is so far from receiving them, that whatsoever is spiritually discerned is mere foolishness unto him. He is not content with being utterly ignorant of spiritual things, but he denies the very existence of them. And spiritual sensation itself is to him the foolishness of folly. "How," saith he, "can these things be? How can any man *know* that he is alive to God?" Even as you know that your body is now alive. Faith is the life of the soul; and if ye have this life abiding in you, ye want no marks to evidence it *to yourself,* but *elenchos Pneúmatos,* that divine consciousness, that *witness of* God, which is more and greater than ten thousand human witnesses.

12. If He doth not now bear witness with thy spirit, that thou art a child of God, O that He might convince thee, thou poor unawakened sinner, by His demonstration and power, that thou art a child of the devil! O that, as I prophesy, there might now be "a noise and a shaking"; and may "the bones come together, bone to his bone!" Then "come from the four winds, O Breath! and breathe on these slain, that they may live!" And do not ye harden your hearts, and resist the Holy Ghost, who even now is come to convince you of sin, "because you believe not on the name of the only begotten Son of God."

II. 1. Wherefore, "awake, thou that sleepest, and arise from the dead." God calleth thee now by my mouth; and bids thee know thyself, thou fallen spirit, thy true state and only concern below. "What meanest thou, O sleeper? Arise! Call upon thy God, if so be thy God will think upon thee, that thou perish not." A mighty tempest is stirred up round about thee, and thou art sinking into the depths of perdition, the gulf of God's judgments. If thou wouldest escape them, cast thyself into them. "Judge thyself, and thou shalt not be judged of the Lord."

2. Awake, awake! Stand up this moment, lest thou "drink at the Lord's hand the cup of His fury." Stir up thyself to lay hold on the Lord, the Lord thy Righteousness, mighty to save! "Shake thyself from the dust." At least, let the earthquake of God's threatenings shake thee. Awake, and cry out

with the trembling jailer, "What must I do to be saved?" And never rest till thou believest on the Lord Jesus, with a faith which is His gift, by the operation of His Spirit.

3. If I speak to any one of you, more than to another, it is to thee, who thinkest thyself unconcerned in this exhortation. "I have a message from God unto thee." In His name, I warn thee "to flee from the wrath to come." Thou unholy soul, see thy picture in condemned Peter, lying in the dark dungeon, between the soldiers, bound with two chains, the keepers before the door keeping the prison. The night is far spent, the morning is at hand, when thou art to be brought forth to execution. And in these dreadful circumstances thou art fast asleep; thou art fast asleep in the devil's arms, on the brink of the pit, in the jaws of everlasting destruction!

4. O may the Angel of the Lord come upon thee, and the light shine into thy prison! And mayest thou feel the stroke of an Almighty Hand, raising thee, with, "Arise up quickly, gird thyself, and bind on thy sandals, cast thy garment about thee, and follow Me."

5. Awake, thou everlasting spirit, out of thy dream of worldly happiness! Did not God create thee for Himself? Then thou canst not rest till thou restest in Him. Return, thou wanderer! Fly back to thy ark. This is not thy home. Think not of building tabernacles here. Thou art but a stranger, a sojourner upon earth; a creature of a day, but just launching out into an unchangeable state. Make haste. Eternity is at hand. Eternity depends on this moment. An eternity of happiness, or an eternity of misery!

6. In what state is thy soul? Was God, while I am yet speaking, to require it of thee, art thou ready to meet death and judgment? Canst thou stand in His sight, who is of "purer eyes than to behold iniquity"? Art thou "meet to be partaker of the inheritance of the saints in light"? Hast thou "fought a good fight, and kept the faith"? Hast thou secured the one thing needful? Hast thou recovered the image of God, even righteousness and true holiness? Hast thou put off the old man, and put on the new? Art thou clothed upon with Christ?

7. Hast thou oil in thy lamp? grace in thy heart? Dost thou "love the Lord thy God with all thy heart, and with all thy mind, and with all thy soul, and with all thy strength"? Is that mind in thee, which was also in Christ Jesus? Art thou a Christian indeed; that is, a new creature? Are old things passed away, and all things become new?

8. Art thou a "partaker of the divine nature"? Knowest thou not that "Christ is in thee, except thou be reprobate"? Knowest thou that God "dwelleth in thee, and thou in God, by His Spirit, which He hath given thee"? Knowest thou not that "thy body is a temple of the Holy Ghost, which thou hast of God"? Hast thou the witness in thyself? the earnest of thine inheritance? (Art thou sealed by that Spirit of Promise, unto the day of redemption?) Hast thou "received the Holy Ghost"? Or dost thou start at the question, not knowing "whether there be any Holy Ghost"?

9. If it offends thee, be thou assured, that thou neither art a Christian, nor desirest to be one. Nay, thy very prayer is turned into sin; and thou hast solemnly mocked God this very day, by praying for the inspiration of His Holy Spirit, when thou didst not believe there was any such thing to be received.

10. Yet, on the authority of God's Word, and our own Church, I must repeat the question, "Hast thou received the Holy Ghost?" If thou hast not, thou art not yet a Christian. For a Christian is a man that is "anointed with the Holy Ghost and with power." Thou art not yet made a partaker of pure religion and undefiled. Dost thou know what religion is?—that it is a participation of the divine nature; the life of God in the soul of man; Christ formed in the heart; "Christ in thee, the hope of glory"; happiness and holiness; heaven begun upon earth; "a kingdom of God within thee; not meat and drink," no outward thing; "but righteousness, and peace, and joy in the Holy Ghost"; an everlasting kingdom brought into thy soul; a "peace of God, that passeth all understanding"; a "joy unspeakable, and full of glory"?

11. Knowest thou, that "in Jesus Christ, neither circumcision availeth anything, nor uncircumcision; but faith that worketh by love"; but a new creation? Seest thou the necessity of that inward change, that spiritual birth, that life from the dead, that holiness? And art thou thoroughly convinced, that without it no man shall see the Lord? Art thou laboring after it?—"giving all diligence to make thy calling and election sure," "working out thy salvation with fear and trembling," "agonizing to enter in at the strait gate"? Art thou in earnest about thy soul? And canst thou tell the Searcher of hearts, "Thou, O God, art the thing that I long for! Lord, Thou knowest all things; Thou knowest that I *would* love Thee!"

12. Thou hopest to be saved; but what reason hast thou to give of the hope that is in thee? Is it because thou hast done no harm? or, because thou

hast done much good? or, because thou art not like other men; but wise, or learned, or honest, and morally good; esteemed of men, and of a fair reputation? Alas! all this will never bring thee to God. It is in His account lighter than vanity. Dost thou know Jesus Christ, whom He hath sent? Hath He taught thee, that "by grace we are saved through faith; and that not of ourselves: it is the gift of God: not of works, lest any man should boast"? Hast thou received the faithful saying, as the whole foundation of thy hope, "that Jesus Christ came into the world to save sinners"? Hast thou learned what that meaneth, "I came not to call the righteous, but sinners to repentance? I am not sent, but unto the lost sheep"? Art thou (he that heareth, let him understand!) lost, dead, *damned already?* Dost thou know thy deserts? Dost thou feel thy wants? Art thou "poor in spirit"? mourning for God, and refusing to be comforted? Is the prodigal "come to himself," and well content to be therefore thought "beside himself" by those who are still feeding upon the husks which he hath left? Art thou willing to live godly in Christ Jesus? And dost thou therefore suffer persecution? Do men say all manner of evil against thee falsely, for the Son of Man's sake?

13. O that in all these questions ye may hear the voice that wakes the dead; and feel that hammer of the Word, which breaketh the rocks in pieces! "If ye will hear His voice to-day, while it is called to-day, harden not your hearts." Now, "awake, thou that sleepest" in spiritual death, that thou sleep not in death eternal! Feel thy lost estate, and "arise from the dead." Leave thine old companions in sin and death. Follow thou Jesus, and let the dead bury their dead. "Save thyself from this untoward generation." "Come out from among them, and be thou separate, and touch not the unclean thing, and the Lord shall receive thee." "Christ shall give thee light."

III. 1. This promise, I come, lastly, to explain. And how encouraging a consideration is this, that whosoever thou art, who obeyest His call, thou canst not seek His face in vain! If thou even now "awakest, and arisest from the dead," He hath bound Himself to "give thee light." "The Lord shall give thee grace and glory"; the light of His grace here, and the light of His glory when thou receivest the crown that fadeth not away. "Thy light shall break forth as the morning, and thy darkness be as the noon-day." "God, who commanded the light to shine out of darkness, shall shine in thy heart; to give the knowledge of the glory of God in the face of Jesus Christ." "On them that fear the Lord shall the Sun of Righteousness arise with healing in His wings." And in that day it shall be said unto thee, "Arise, shine; for thy light is come, and the glory of the Lord is risen upon thee." For Christ shall reveal Himself in thee: and He is the true Light.

2. God is light, and will give Himself to every awakened sinner that waiteth for Him; and thou shalt then be a temple of the living God, and Christ shall "dwell in thy heart by faith": and, "being rooted and grounded in love, thou shalt be able to comprehend with all saints, what is the breadth, and length, and depth, and height of that love of Christ which passeth knowledge" (that thou mayest be filled with all the fullness of God).

3. Ye see your calling, brethren. We are called to be "an habitation of God through His Spirit"; and, through His Spirit dwelling in us, to be saints here, and partakers of the inheritance of the saints in light. So exceeding great are the promises which are given unto us, actually given unto us who believe! For by faith "we receive, not the spirit of the world, but the Spirit which is of God"—the sum of all the promises—"that we may know the things that are freely given to us of God."

4. The Spirit of Christ is that great gift of God which, at sundry times, and in divers manners, He hath promised to man, and hath fully bestowed since the time that Christ was glorified. Those promises, before made to the fathers, He hath thus fulfilled: "I will put My Spirit within you, and cause you to walk in My statutes." (Ezek. 36:27.) "I will pour water upon him that is thirsty, and floods upon the dry ground: I will pour My Spirit upon thy seed, and My blessing upon thine offspring." (Isa. 44:3.)

5. Ye may all be living witnesses of these things: of remission of sins, and the gift of the Holy Ghost. "If thou canst believe, all things are possible to him that believeth." "Who among you is there that feareth the Lord, and" yet walketh "in darkness, and hath no light"? I ask thee, in the name of Jesus, Believest thou that His arm is not shortened at all? that He is still mighty to save? that He is the same yesterday, today, and for ever? that He hath now power on earth to forgive sins? "Son, be of good cheer: thy sins are forgiven." God, for Christ's sake, hath forgiven thee. Receive this, "not as the word of man; but as it is indeed, the word of God"; and thou art justified freely through faith. Thou shalt be sanctified also through faith which is in Jesus, and shalt set to thy seal, even thine, that "God hath given unto us eternal life, and this life is in His Son."

6. Men and brethren, let me freely speak unto you; and suffer ye the

word of exhortation, even from one the least esteemed in the Church. Your conscience beareth you witness in the Holy Ghost, that these things are so, if so be ye have tasted that the Lord is gracious. "This is eternal life, to know the only true God, and Jesus Christ, whom He hath sent." This experimental knowledge, and this alone, is true Christianity. He is a Christian who hath received the Spirit of Christ. He is not a Christian who hath not received Him. Neither is it possible to have received Him, and not know it. "For, at that day" (when He cometh, saith our Lord), "ye shall know that I am in My Father, and you in Me, and I in you." This is that "Spirit of Truth, whom the world cannot receive, because it seeth Him not, neither knoweth Him: but ye know Him; for He dwelleth with you, and shall be in you." (John 14:17.)

7. The world cannot receive Him, but utterly rejecteth the Promise of the Father, contradicting and blaspheming. But every spirit which confesseth not this is not of God. Yea, "this is that spirit of Antichrist, whereof ye have heard that it should come into the world; and even now it is in the world." He is Antichrist whosoever denies the inspiration of the Holy Ghost, or that the indwelling Spirit of God is the common privilege of all believers, the blessing of the gospel, the unspeakable gift, the universal promise, the criterion of a real Christian.

8. It nothing helps them to say, "We do not deny the *assistance* of God's Spirit; but only this *inspiration,* this *receiving the Holy Ghost,* and being *sensible* of it. It is only this *feeling* of the Spirit, this being *moved* by the Spirit, or *filled* with it, which we deny to have any place in sound religion." But, in *only denying this,* you deny the whole Scriptures; the whole truth, and promise, and testimony of God.

9. Our own excellent Church knows nothing of this devilish distinction; but speaks plainly of "feeling the Spirit of Christ"; of being "moved by the Holy Ghost" and knowing and "feeling there is no other name than that of Jesus," whereby we can receive life and salvation. She teaches us all to pray for the "inspiration of the Holy Spirit"; yea, that we may be "filled with the Holy Ghost." Nay, and every Presbyter of hers professes to receive the Holy Ghost by the imposition of hands. Therefore, to deny any of these, is, in effect, to renounce the Church of England, as well as the whole Christian revelation.

10. But "the wisdom of God" was always "foolishness with men." No

marvel, then, that the great mystery of the gospel should be now also "hid from the wise and prudent," as well as in the days of old; that it should be almost universally denied, ridiculed, and exploded, as mere frenzy; and that all who dare avow it still are branded with the names of madmen and enthusiasts! This is "that falling away" which was to come; that general apostasy of all orders and degrees of men, which we even now find to have overspread the earth. "Run to and fro in the streets of Jerusalem, and see if ye can find a man," a man that loveth the Lord his God with all his heart, and serveth Him with all his strength. How does our own land mourn (that we look no farther) under the overflowings of ungodliness! What villanies of every kind are committed day by day; yea, too often with impunity, by those who sin with a high hand, and glory in their shame! Who can reckon up the oaths, curses, profaneness, blasphemies; the lying, slandering, evil-speaking; the Sabbath-breaking, gluttony, drunkenness, revenge; the whoredoms, adulteries, and various uncleanness; the frauds, injustice, oppression, extortion, which overspread our land as a flood?

11. And even among those who have kept themselves pure from these grosser abominations, how much anger and pride, how much sloth and idleness, how much softness and effeminacy, how much luxury and self-indulgence, how much covetousness and ambition, how much thirst of praise, how much love of the world, how much fear of man, is to be found! Meanwhile, how little of true religion! For, where is he that loveth either God or his neighbor, as He hath given us commandment? On the one hand, are those who have not so much as the form of godliness; on the other, those who have the form only: there stands the *open,* there the *painted,* sepulchre. So that in very deed, whosoever were earnestly to behold any public gathering together of the people (I fear those in our churches are not to be excepted), might easily perceive, "that the one part were Sadducees, and the other Pharisees": the one having almost as little concern about religion, as if there were "no resurrection, neither angel nor spirit"; and the other making it a mere lifeless form, a dull round of external performances, without either true faith, or the love of God, or joy in the Holy Ghost!

12. Would to God I could except *us* of this place! "Brethren, my heart's desire, and prayer to God, for you is, that ye may be saved" from this overflowing of ungodliness; and that here may its proud waves be stayed! But is it so indeed? God knoweth, yea, and our own consciences, it is not. Ye have

not kept yourselves pure. Corrupt are we also and abominable; and few are there that understand any more; few that worship God in spirit and in truth. We, too, are "a generation that set not our hearts aright, and whose spirit cleaveth not steadfastly unto God." He hath appointed us indeed to be "the salt of the earth: but if the salt hath lost its savor, it is thenceforth good for nothing; but to be cast out, and to be trodden underfoot of men."

13. And "shall I not visit for these things, saith the Lord? Shall not My soul be avenged on such a nation as this?" Yea, we know not how soon He may say to the sword, "Sword go through this land!" He hath given us long space to repent. He lets us alone this year also: but He warns and awakens us by thunder. His judgments are abroad in the earth; and we have all reason to expect the heaviest of all, even that He "should come unto us quickly, and remove our candlestick out of its place, except we repent and do the first works"; unless we return to the principles of the Reformation, the truth and simplicity of the gospel. Perhaps we are now resisting the last effort of divine grace to save us. Perhaps we have well nigh "filled up the measure of our iniquities," by rejecting the counsel of God against ourselves, and casting out His messengers.

14. O God, "in the midst of wrath, remember mercy"! Be glorified in our reformation, not in our destruction! Let us "hear the rod, and Him that appointed it"! Now that Thy "judgements are abroad in the earth, let the inhabitants of the world learn righteousness"!

15. My brethren, it is high time for us to awake out of sleep before the "great trumpet of the Lord be blown," and our land become a field of blood. O may we speedily see the things that make for our peace, before they are hid from our eyes! "Turn Thou us, O good Lord, and let Thine anger cease from us. O Lord, look down from heaven, behold and visit this vine"; and cause us to know "the time of our visitation." "Help us, O God of our salvation, for the glory of Thy name! O deliver us, and be merciful to our sins, for Thy name's sake! And so we will not go back from Thee. O let us live, and we shall call upon Thy name. Turn us again, O Lord God of Hosts! Show the light of Thy countenance, and we shall be whole."

"Now unto Him that is able to do exceeding abundantly above all that we can ask or think, according to the power that worketh in us, unto Him be glory in the Church by Christ Jesus throughout all ages, world without end. Amen!"

Rabbi Nachman
of Bratislava

1772–1811

*I*n the Jewish tradition, for many centuries, the prohibition of writing on the Sabbath made any transcript of the sermons of even the Hasidic master Rabbi Nachman a matter of memory, opportunity, and chance. Nachman's homiletic discourses were sometimes dictated, then written from memory at the end of the Sabbath, and, although delivered in Yiddish, recorded by a disciple in Hebrew. The absence of a conventional institutional structure and hierarchy did not mandate the recording of a sermon, but Nachman's charismatic preaching has survived to inform scholars, philosophers, and even literary fiction.

Nachman himself was the great-grandson of the Baal Shem Tov (Master of the Wondrous Name; 1700–1760) and legendary founder of the Hasidim, whose own name implies intense piety, religious fervor, and an ecstatic relation to the natural world. By Nachman's time, the Hasidim comprised half the Jewish population of Eastern Europe and contributed to a brilliant revival of folk literature and fable. Rabbi Nachman preached in parables, whether walking through a Galician forest with his pupils or sitting at the Sabbath table.

He populated his tales with symbols as accessible and as simple as the parables of Christ, although his meanings, which preoccupied the twentieth-century German philosopher Martin Buber, take the audience into a labyrinth. In the tale "The Lost Princess," the King was meant to be understood as God; the daughter, the Schechina, or Glory of God; and the earth, the place where Evil resides. The prince (the Israel of the Messiah) waits twice in the deserts of Egypt and Babylon and then again must wander, in an image of the present exile, over the earth until she is found in a Holy Land represented by the Golden Mountain.

The estrangement on earth of the soul from God and the mystical possibility of the soul finding God's Living Glory (the Schechina) as sparks in all living things are implicit in Nachman's story, as moving and evocative as the Christian fairy tales of Oscar Wilde or the parables of Franz Kafka, who admired and imitated their allegorical mystery and sense of a magical relationship with the Divine.

The Lost Princess

And How She Was Found in the Palace of Pearls

There was a King who had six sons and but one daughter; he loved his daughter more than any of his other children, and passed many hours in her company; but one day while they were together the princess displeased the King, and he cried out, "May the devil take you!"

There seemed nothing amiss that night when the princess went to bed. But in the morning she could not be found.

Then the King tore his hair for grief and guilt. "It is because of what I cried out," he said, "that she is gone."

Then the Second to the Throne, seeing the King in despair, arose and cried, "Give me a servant, and a steed, and gold, and I will go out and seek the princess."

For a long time he rode through wasteland and desert in search of the missing maiden. Once as he passed in a desert he saw a road at the edge of the sand, and he thought, "I have ridden so long in the desert without meeting anyone. Perhaps the road will lead me to the city."

The road led him to a great castle guarded by hosts of warriors. The prince was afraid they would not allow him to enter the castle, but nevertheless he dismounted from his steed, and went up to them; and they allowed him to pass through the gate. Then he came in upon a magnificent courtyard, and saw a marble palace before him. He went into the palace, and walked through halls that were studded with alabaster pillars. Guards stood in all the passageways, but no one questioned him, and he went from room to room until he came to the chamber of the throne, and there a king was seated. Tables laden with delicate foods were along the walls of the room; the prince ate of the delicacies; then he lay down in a corner of the chamber where he might not easily be seen, and he watched to see what would happen.

Musicians played upon their instruments, and sang before the king; soon the king held out his hand and commanded that the queen be brought. Then the music became more joyous, and people danced in the court, and made merry, and drank, for the queen would soon appear.

When the queen came into the chamber she was given a smaller seat next to the throne; the wanderer looked upon her and saw that she was indeed the princess he sought. And as she looked out over the room she saw the man withdrawn into an obscure corner, and she recognized him. She got down from her throne and went to him and said, "Do you not know me?"

"You are the princess!" he said. "But how have you come to this place?"

"The King let fall an angry word," she said. "He cried, 'May the evil one take you!' and this is the palace of evil."

"The King is grief-stricken because of what he has done, and I have sought for you these many years," the wanderer told her. "How may I take you away?"

"You cannot take me from this place," she said, "except that you first go and select a place for yourself, and there you must remain for an entire year, thinking only of my deliverance, longing and hoping to rescue me, and on the last day of the year you must not eat a particle of food, but must fast, and on the last night of the year you must not sleep; then you may come to me."

He did as she told him to do. He went into the desert and remained there an entire year, and at the end of the year he did not sleep, and did not eat, but returned toward the palace of the evil one. On the way, he passed a beautiful tree heavily laden with ripe fruit, and a terrible desire came over him to taste of the apples, so he went and ate. At once he fell into a deep sleep, and he slept for a very long time. When he awoke he saw his servant standing beside him, and he cried out, "Where am I?"

"You have slept many years," the servant said; "I have waited by you, while I lived on the fruit."

Then the wanderer went to the palace and came to the princess; and she cried, "See what you have done! Because of a single day, you have lost eternity! For if you had come on that day, you might have rescued me. I know that it is difficult to refrain from eating, and it is especially difficult on the last day, for the evil spirit was strong in you on that last day. But you must go again and choose a place and remain there another year, praying, and longing, and hoping to deliver me; on the last day of that year you may eat, but you must drink no wine, for wine will cause you to sleep, and the most important thing of all is not to sleep."

He went back to the wilderness, and did as she had told him to do, but on the last day, as he was returning toward the palace, he saw a flowing spring. He said to his servant, "Look, the fountain of water is red, and it has an odor as of wine!" Then he knelt and tasted of the spring, and at once fell to the ground and slept. He slept for many years.

And in that time a great army of warriors passed on the road, among them were mounted riders, and carriages, and at last there came a great carriage drawn by fourteen steeds. The princess was in that carriage; but when she saw the wanderer's servant on the road, she ordered the carriage to be halted, and she went down and saw the wanderer sleeping, and she sat by him and wept. "Poor man," she said; "so many years you have sought me, and wandered so far, and endured so much pain, and yet because of a single day you have lost me, and see how you must suffer, and how I suffer because of that day!" Then she took her veil from her face; she wrote upon the veil with her tears, and left it beside him; and she got into her carriage and rode away.

After he had slept seventy years, the man awoke and asked his servant, "Where am I?" The servant told him what had happened, of the army that had passed, and how the princess had wept over him. Just then the wanderer saw the veil lying beside him, and he cried, "Where does this come from?"

"The princess left it for you," the servant said. "She wrote upon it with her tears."

He who was Second to the Throne held the veil up to the sun, and saw the marks of her weeping, and read of her grief at finding him so, and read that she was gone from the first palace of the evil one, but that he must now seek her in a palace of pearls that stood on a golden mountain. "Only there, you may find me," the princess had written.

Then the wanderer left his servant and went alone in search of the princess.

For many years he wandered among mankind, asking and seeking for the palace of pearls upon the mountain of gold, until he knew that it was to be found upon no chart, and in no land inhabited by men, and in no desert, for he had been everywhere. But still he searched in the wilderness, and in the wilderness he came upon a giant who carried a tree that was greater than any tree that grew in the world of men. The giant looked upon the wanderer and said, "Who are you?"

He answered, "I am a man."

"I have been so long in the wilderness," said the giant, "that it is many years since I have seen a man." And he looked at the man.

The man said, "I seek a palace built of pearls upon a golden mountain."

The giant laughed, and said, "There is no such place on earth!"

But the man cried, "There is! There must be!" and he would not give up his seeking.

Then the giant said, "Since you are so obstinate, I'll prove to you that there is no such place on earth. I am the lord over all the animal kingdom, and every beast that runs over the earth, from the greatest to the tiniest, answers to my call. Surely if there were such a place as you seek, one of my creatures would have seen it." So he bent and blew on the ground, making a sound that was narrow as the call of wind in the grass, and wide as the rustling of leaves; his call spread like spreading water, and at once the beasts of the earth came running, leaping toward him: the timid gazelle and the wild tiger and every creature from the beetle to the great elephant, all came, and he asked of them: "Have you seen a palace of pearls built on a golden mountain?"

The creatures all answered him, "No."

Then the giant said to the man, "You see, my friend, there is no such place at all. Spare yourself, and return home."

But the man cried, "There is, there must be such a place! And I must find it!"

The giant pitied him, and told him, "I have a brother who is lord over all the creatures of the air; perhaps one of them has seen this place, for birds fly high."

Then the man went further into the wilderness, until he found another giant who carried a great tree in his hand. "Your brother has sent me to you," he said. And he told the giant of his quest. The giant whistled into the air, and his cry was like the sound of all the winds that murmur and shriek high over the earth; at once every winged creature, insect and eagle, answered his call. But none had seen a palace of pearls upon a golden mountain.

"You see," said the giant, "there is no such place at all. You had better return home, and rest yourself."

But the man cried, "There is, there must be such a place, and I will not rest until I find it!"

At last the second giant said, "I have a brother who is lord over all the winds. Go to him, perhaps he can help you."

After many years the wanderer came to the third giant, who carried a still greater tree in his hand; and the wanderer told the giant what he sought.

Then the giant opened wide his mouth, and the call he hurled over the world was like the tumult of colliding heavens. In that instant, all the winds over the earth came rushing to him, and he asked them, "Have you seen a palace of pearls upon a mountain of gold?" But none of them had seen such a thing.

"Someone is jesting with you, and has sent you on a fool's quest," the giant said to the man. "Better go home, and rest yourself."

But the man cried, "There is, there must be such a place!" Just then another wind came hastening to the giant, and lay breathless and weary at his feet.

"You have come late!" the giant cried angrily, and he lifted the great tree to lash the wind. "Why did you come tardily to my call?"

"Master," the wind said, "I came as soon as I could, but I could not come sooner, for I had to carry a princess to a mountain of gold on which there stands a palace built of pearls."

The man heard, and was overjoyed. "Can you take me there?" he begged. The wind answered, "I can."

Then the master of the winds said to the man, "You will have need of gold, where you are going, for in that city all things are of high worth." And he took a wonderful purse, and gave it to the wanderer. "Whenever you put your hand into this bag," the giant said, "you will find it filled with gold, no matter how much gold you draw out of it."

Then the wind took up the wanderer and set him down upon the golden mountain.

The wanderer saw the palace of pearls that stood within a wonderful city, and the city was surrounded by many walls guarded by warriors. But he put his hand into his marvelous purse, and gave them gold, and they let him pass, and when he came into the city he found that it was a pleasant and beautiful place. Then he lived there for a long while, and there the princess lived, but in the end, with wisdom and righteousness, he took her home to the King.

Ezekiel Landau

1713–1793

When the Hapsburg Emperor Joseph II issued his Edict of Toleration in 1781, Ezekiel Landau praised its end of discriminatory legislation against the Jews in a sermon which made the emperor the antithesis of Pharaoh. Landau, the Chief Rabbi of Prague and the supreme authority for Bohemian Jewry, had delivered a eulogy for the Empress Maria Theresa two years earlier before a gathering of the leaders of the Jewish community and a number of powerful Christian representatives of both the government and the army.

The eulogy as genre in Jewish preaching, its traditional structure, and its place within the service are undefined in the Talmud; yet it is known that eulogies were delivered over the dead although not included until the middle of the fifteenth century in collections of model sermons. This sermon, composed in Hebrew but reworked in German, is replete with ironies. Landau apologizes profusely for the eight-day delay between the death of the empress and his response in the synagogue, and Maria Theresa's personal antipathy toward the Jews was no secret. She shaped the imperial policy which drove the Jews from Prague in 1744, condoned a punitive rate of taxation on Jewish subjects, and called the Jewish people "a plague . . . to be kept away and avoided."

Landau's sermon, delivered in the deep and resonant voice for which he was famous, may be a political and even moral masterpiece, praising the empress for her courage and her charitable works, and subtly extolling her for her son, Joseph II, the architect of tolerance and reform who was about to ascend the throne. Its interest is not merely historical, for it suggests the mix of the temporal and spiritual which aimed at survival without extinguishing the beacon a pulpit provides for the faithful in dangerous times.

Eulogy for Empress Maria Theresa

And you, O mortal, sigh; with tottering limbs and bitter grief, sigh before their eyes. When they ask you, "Why do you sigh?" answer, "Because of the tidings that come." Every heart sinks and all hands hang limp; every spirit grows faint and all knees turn to water. It has indeed come to pass, declares the Lord God.

—EZEKIEL 21:11–13

Today is the eighth day since the evil tidings came that the crown has fallen from our head. (Lam. 5:16.) It was my obligation to see that we should immediately have arranged a great memorial service, following the biblical text, *In every square there shall be lamenting, in every street cries of "Ah, woe!" The farm hand shall be called to mourn, and those skilled in wailing to lament.* (Amos 5:16.) We should have fulfilled the verse, *I was bowed with gloom, like one mourning for his mother.* (Ps. 35:14.) For the mother of the realm has fallen, our sovereign, pious, humble and righteous, the Queen and Empress

Maria Theresa, may her soul rest in the Garden of Eden. She was indeed the mother of the realm; from her loins royalty has gone forth (cf. Gen. 35:11).

However, I delayed until now, not out of laziness, God forbid, but because of several reasons. First, because of the intense grief that overwhelmed me when I heard the news, I had no strength to speak, and I knew not what to say. In me was fulfilled the verse that applies to the friends of Job: *They sat with him on the ground seven days and seven nights. None spoke a word to him for they saw how very great was the suffering.* (Job 2:13.) So with me: so great was the pain of my grief that I could not collect my thoughts to speak coherently for seven days, until today. That is one reason.

The second reason is that nothing confounds a physician who comes to attend a sick man more than discovering two opposite conditions, such that whatever diminishes one intensifies the other. He is hard-pressed to know what to do without making things worse. That is our situation today. Now Kohelet spoke of twenty-eight different times, saying, *A season is set for everything, a time for every experience under heaven: a time to give birth and a time to die . . . a time to weep and a time to laugh, a time of mourning and a time of dancing.* (Eccles. 3:1–2, 4.) He specified twenty-eight times, fourteen good and fourteen bad. In all he used the infinitive: to be born, to die, to plant, to uproot. But with mourning and dancing he did not use the infinitive, saying *a time of mourning and a time of dancing.*

I interpret this to suggest . . . that it is as if the time itself is mourning, and the same with its opposite, dancing. This means, if not everyone realizes how much is lost in the death of a certain person, someone must stand up in public and inform the others about the significance of the loss and the mourning that is appropriate. However, at the loss of a great individual, highly esteemed and unique, whose great and glorious splendor is obvious to everyone, all will feel the loss spontaneously. It is as if the sun were to set at noontime: darkness would cover the earth, and all would recognize the absence of the sun's light.

This is our situation today. It is a *time of mourning:* no one needs to stand and preach and inspire, for the sun of our monarch the Empress Maria Theresa shined brilliantly; the power of her fine personality, the fairness of her heart, the abundance of her graciousness were known throughout the world. Now her sun has set, her radiance has been extinguished. Will not all grow faint, and each one of us say, *Oh that my head were water, my eyes a fount of tears; then would I weep day and night* (Jer. 8:23), for the mother of the nation has died, the queen who was as a mother to all the nations. That is why it is a *time of mourning.*

Yet, by contrast, it is also a *time of dancing,* for in us has been fulfilled the verse, *The sun rises, and the sun sets* (Eccles. 1:5), which the sages interpreted to mean: when the sun of one righteous person sets, the sun of another rises; when David's sun set, Solomon's began to shine. So it is now: when the sun of our mighty and gracious sovereign the empress set, there shines that of her son, the great and mighty, wise and pious, more precious than gold and gems, the Emperor Joseph, may His splendid Majesty be exalted. In him is fulfilled the verse, *His throne as the sun before Me.* (Ps. 89:37.) Just as the radiant sun is seen throughout the world, all welcoming its light, so the fame of our emperor is known throughout the world, his praises sung in every kingdom, near and far. Happy are we, how goodly is our lot that we have been deemed worthy of such a fine and noble king. May our eyes behold the king in his beauty (Isa. 33:17), the king who sustains the land through his justice (Prov. 29:4), the king who reigns in righteousness (Isa. 32:1).

Now *in the light of the king's face there is life* (Prov. 16:15) for the subjects of his realms. This is "dancing" out of abundant joy. Thus at present, two opposing and mutually incompatible times have come together: a time of mourning for the great sorrow, of anguished grief and weeping over the death of Her Majesty the Empress, and a time of joyous and delightful celebration over the accession to her throne of our gracious sovereign the Emperor. For this reason I did not know how to direct my mood; I was uncertain how to act. That is why Solomon did not say, "A time to mourn and a time to dance," for a person cannot perform two contradictory actions simultaneously, but the time can combine them both. What impelled me now to summon this memorial assembly I shall divulge a bit later.

The third consideration that led me to silence until now is that I thought it unbefitting the glory of our gracious Majesty the Empress to eulogize her. One does not give a eulogy for the living, only for the dead. And I say that we should not attribute death to our gracious Majesty. Let me explain by citing a passage from the Talmud (B. Taʿan. 5b):

> Rabbi Johanan said, Our ancestor Jacob did not die. R. Nahman replied, Was it for nothing that the wailers wailed and the embalmers

embalmed and the buriers buried? He answered, I am interpreting a biblical verse: *Have no fear, My servant Jacob declares the Lord, Be not dismayed, O Israel! I will deliver you from far away, your descendants from their land of captivity* (Jer. 30:10). This verse establishes an analogy between Jacob and his descendants: just as his descendants are living, so he is living.

All the commentators have worn themselves out trying to explain this passage: why this message is derived from the verse, and how it answers the question, Was it for nothing that the wailers wailed, and they embalmed and buried him?

It seems to me that the meaning is to be found in another Talmudic passage (B. B. Bat. 115a):

Rabbi Phinehas ben Hama interpreted the verse, *Hadad heard in Egypt that David had been laid to rest with his fathers and that Joab the army commander was dead* (1 Kings 11:21). Why does it say that David was laid to rest, and that Joab was dead? David, who left a son like him, is said to have been laid to rest, whereas Joab, who did not leave a son like him is said to be dead.

Thus one who leaves a son like him is not said to be dead. I would give a philosophical explanation for this. We know that a living human being is composed of matter and form, namely, the body, which is matter, and the soul, which is its form. Death applies primarily to matter, while the soul returns to God who gave it (cf. Eccles. 12:7). Even during the period of human life, life is applied primarily to the form. We must therefore try to understand how death can pertain to the soul, if even after death it returns to its origin, the root of all life.

The answer is that the soul comes into this world in order to cleave to this matter so that it may become worthy of acquiring a level of perfection. The more a person attains this perfection, the higher is the level to which the soul ascends. This is how we should understand the rabbinic statement that the righteous human being is superior to the angel. Truly, Gentile scholars have repudiated this statement as altogether bizarre, and indeed, basic principles of philosophy make it seem surprising. The explanation is that the angel is pure form without any material component, and it therefore has no capacity for any kind of sin, for every sin and transgression originates in matter following its own tendency. The angel, pure form, has no evil inclination; it always remains at the same level, never ascending or descending from the moment of its creation.

By contrast, the righteous person who serves God and overcomes the material component ascends from one level to the next, and in this respect is superior to the angel. The righteous person is described as moving, the angel as standing, for the righteous person moves from level to level. That is his true life, and that is why he was created. All this applies throughout a lifetime. However, at death, when the form (which is the soul) is separated from the matter (which is the body) and the body is buried in a grave while the spirit returns to God, then the soul has no evil inclination, and it can no longer ascend to any level higher than that which it attained at the time of its separation from matter. That is why we speak of death with regard to the form, for it has died from the status of being able to ascend higher.

Now a father can bestow merit upon his son; the righteousness of the blameless one can smooth the way of his child. Father and mother are always looking out for their children from the day they have a mind of their own, guiding them in the right path and teaching them to be ethical. Thus every good deed of the child follows the principles learned from the parents. Whatever good the child does throughout life is counted toward the merit of the parents, as if they themselves had done it. In this sense, even after their death, they can still ascend to a higher status.

In this regard, I offer an interpretation of the following verses:

He further showed me Joshua, the high priest, standing before the angel of the Lord. . . . Now Joshua was clothed in filthy garments when he stood before the angel. The latter spoke up and said to his attendants, " Take the filthy garments off him!" And he said to him, "See I have removed your guilt from you, and you shall be clothed in [priestly] robes." Then he gave the order, "Let a pure diadem be placed on his head." . . . And the angel of the Lord charged Joshua as follows: "Thus said the Lord of Hosts, If you walk in My paths and keep

My charge, you in turn will rule My House and guard My courts, and I will permit you to move about among these attendants." (Zech. 3:1–7.)

The Aramaic translation of Jonathan renders the phrase "filthy garments" as referring to the sons of the priest who were married to women disqualified from the priesthood. The phrase "You shall be clothed in [priestly] robes" means that they should put aside their improper wives and take proper ones. Thus God announced to the Prophet in a prophetic vision that Joshua should rebuke his sons and make them repent, taking proper wives in place of the improper ones. He certainly hinted that through Joshua's act of rebuking his sons, they would so act. That is why he said "You [Joshua] shall be clothed in [priestly] robes." If his sons would repent of their own accord, he would have no [priestly] robes, which allude to merit, as Jonathan's Aramaic translation of the verse shows.

This interpretation fits the end of the passage, *I will permit you to move about among these attendants.* The righteous person is called a "mover," for he is always moving from one level to the next, as I already indicated. The angel is called an attendant, one who stands in place. At the death of the righteous one, as his spirit ascends to the place of the angels, then his soul too remains stationary among the attendants. But if he has children whom he guided to be themselves righteous, then even after this he may "move about" to a higher level. So long as Joshua failed to inspire his sons to repent, even though he was fully righteous, a priest of the most high God, moving ever upward throughout his life, his upward movement ceased with his death, and he was stationary. But once he acted to bring about the repentance of his sons, the promise was *I will permit you to move about among these attendants,* namely the angels: even after death I will allow you to move.

Therefore, the homiletical interpretation of R. Phinehas in Baba Batra is appropriate: "David, who left a son like him, is not said to be dead," except in relation to his material component, his body, which was buried in the earth. But as for his formal component, the soul, he is not said to be dead, for he commanded his son Solomon before his death to walk in God's ways. The Bible says, *When David's life was drawing to a close, he instructed his son Solomon as follows: I am going the way of all the earth; be strong and show your-*

self a man. Keep the charge of the Lord your God, walking in His ways and follow-ing His laws, His commandments, His rules, and His admonitions. . . . (1 Kings 2:1–3.) Therefore all of Solomon's additional achievements redounded to the credit of his father, and even after his death he ascended higher. That is why he was not said to be dead.

Now let us return to the statement of R. Johanan in tractate Ta'anit that our ancestor Jacob did not die. R. Nahman replied, Was it for nothing that they wailed and embalmed and buried? He answered, I am interpreting a biblical verse . . . which establishes an analogy between Jacob and his de-scendants: just as his descendants are living, so he is living. Now Jacob left a son like him. Even though all twelve sons were equal in goodness, never-theless there was one most blessed, whom he himself toiled to teach all he had learned from his own masters, to transmit to him all his wisdom: his most beloved son, *the fruitful vine* (Gen. 49:22), Joseph. This is how the sages interpreted the verses, *These are the generations of Jacob: Joseph* (Gen. 37:2) and *He was the child of his old age* (Gen. 37:3).

Thus so long as Joseph was alive—and by "alive" I mean ascending from one level to the next, all because of the influence of Jacob who guided him properly—Jacob continued to ascend, even after his death, and was called "alive." Therefore R. Johanan replied, "I am interpreting a biblical verse." The meaning is, indeed the wailers and the embalmers and the buri-ers performed their tasks, but so long as his offspring is alive, he thereby re-mains alive.

Let us now look at our gracious sovereign the Empress Maria Theresa, may she be remembered for good. She was worthy of leaving a son like this: our sovereign, who excels in all virtues and achievements, the Emperor Joseph, may His Majesty be exalted. It was his mother who guided him from his youth in every fine virtue. She therefore should not be called dead, for even though she has departed from us, her subjects, her splendor and majesty have not departed. They are her son, this esteemed emperor. He is her splendor, he is her majesty, about him it is fitting to say, *in the light of the king's face there is life* (Prov. 16:15), for in the light of his face is the life of his gracious mother after her death.

All of this I thought about, and I was inwardly torn, whether to de-liver a eulogy or to remain silent. What made me decide to deliver a public eulogy was the verse with which I began. Let us examine it in detail. It says,

And you, O mortal, sigh; with tottering limbs and bitter grief, sigh before their eyes.
When they ask you, "Why do you sigh?" answer, "Because of the tidings that come."
Every heart sinks and all hands hang limp; every spirit grows faint and all knees turn
to water. It has indeed come to pass, declares the Lord God. (Ezek. 21:11–13.)

This passage certainly requires explication. The statement, *When they*
ask you, "Why do you sigh?" implies that if someone else had been sighing no
one would have asked; it is a particular individual who is asked "Why do you
sigh?" This is highlighted by a redundancy in the wording: *When they ask you,*
"Why do you sigh?" when it would have been enough to say, "When they ask,
'Why do you sigh?' " Since it says, *When they ask you,* it indicates that the
question is directed specifically to you. This requires an explanation.

Furthermore, if the tidings had been about an unknown disaster, then
the Prophet would have had to sigh in order to bring it to the attention of
the asker and to communicate the seriousness of the calamity. But the disaster was to be perceptible, even obvious to all, as it says, *Because of the tid-*
ings that come. Every heart sinks and all hands hang limp. Thus everyone would
recognize it by themselves. Why then did the Prophet need to sigh in their
presence? If it was simply to mourn about the disaster, he could have
mourned privately, by himself.

Furthermore, what is the function of the question, *Why do you sigh?*
After all, the disaster is obvious to all, for we are told, *every heart sinks. . . ."*
Note that the Masoretes were sensitive, indicating by the position of the
cantillation mark that the word *ba'ah* is in the present tense, not the past,
indicating it was not something that already occurred. This resolves a problem in the verse. I once gave a sermon interpreting the phrase *Why do you*
sigh? in its own context. However, on this occasion, we shall interpret it as
applying to us.

I am the man about whom it is said. My name is Ezekiel. *And you, O*
mortal, sigh! You must certainly remember that sixteen years have passed
since a certain *Shabbat ha-Gadol*—it was the year 5524 [1764]—when God
bestowed strength to our king, the Emperor Joseph, may His Majesty be exalted, and elevated him while his father, the gracious Emperor Francis, was
still alive, may he be remembered for good. Our sovereign the Emperor
Joseph was then given the royal crown in Frankfurt am Main and made
Römischerkönig. This was on the first day of Nisan in 5524 [April 3, 1764].
Soon after that, on *Shabbat ha-Gadol,* I delivered a public sermon, proclaim-

ing the praises of this tower of strength, our sovereign the Emperor, who was then king, for his praises were known from his youth.

I gave praise and thanks to God for having established such an excellent, good king. And I said that heaven had given a sign that he was a fine and decent king, for the rabbis said in tractate Rosh Hashanah that good, ethical kings count their reign from the month of Nisan. An example is Cyrus, about whom the Prophet said, *Thus said the Lord to Cyrus, His anointed one, whose right hand He grasped.* (Isa. 45:1.) Now if the Prophet called him God's anointed, he was certainly an ethical king. And they counted his reign from the month of Nisan, as is demonstrated in tractate Rosh Hashanah. Since it was an act of heaven that this Emperor was anointed and the royal crown set upon his head in the month of Nisan, it is certainly a sign from heaven that all who see him will recognize that he is recognized from heaven as a fine and decent king, and that God would grasp his right hand and exalt him. I then proclaimed publicly some of his praises, for they are too numerous to complete.

But now I feel pain deep inside me over the death of our sovereign, the Empress. *I sigh with tottering limbs and bitter grief* (Ezek. 21:11) before the entire congregation. *When they ask you, "Why do you sigh?,"* that is, why do you in particular sigh? They ask me, as it were, "If it is because of the death of the queen, why you yourself proclaimed publicly the praise of our sovereign the Emperor who has arisen now in place of his mother. It is therefore as if the queen is still here."

The answer is, *Because of the tidings that come. Every heart sinks.* (Ezek. 21:12.) The human being is a microcosm, the organs are like people within a society. The heart is compared to the royal sovereign, for it rules over all the other organs. We find this in the Kuzari, Part IV, section 25, where it says, "The heart is not mentioned, because it is sovereign." Now we have heard the tidings that our sovereign the Emperor, may His Majesty be exalted, has himself been overcome with grief over the death of his mother the Empress. Now he certainly knows his own outstanding valor and strength; he knows his consummate wisdom; he knows that he is the equal of his ancestors and his mother in every good trait. Nevertheless, the love for his mother and her immense glory were overpowering for him, to the point that he is engaged in profound mourning and lament.

What then should we do? Should we not mourn for this glorious mother, who was the mother of her realms, who reigned for so many years? Since the heart sinks, alluding to the king, the mighty Emperor, who has been overcome and has sunk into grief at the death of the queen, all the organs that depend upon the heart, all the subjects of the realms, should also engage in profound mourning and lament. For *all hands hang limp, every spirit grows faint, all knees turn to water.* Therefore, when I heard of the extensive mourning in Vienna, involving everyone, led by the Emperor himself, I was inspired to stand before the congregation and offer a eulogy. However, I was seized with fear and trembling at the thought that I, an insignificant creature, would utter words in praise of our gracious sovereign, the Empress, until the government graciously granted me permission to do so.

Now my dear friends, our sages debated whether the eulogy is an honor for the living or an honor for the dead. In the category of "honor for the dead" is included two things: celebration of the glory of the person being eulogized, and also celebration of the glory of that person's ancestors according to their respective merits.

How shall I begin? Time does not suffice to express even a minute portion of praise that is due. Well known is the splendor of this great dynasty, the House of Austria, from the day when its radiant majesty began to shine. How many Emperors reigned, one after the other, each one exalted, each one a gracious monarch who dealt beneficently with all. We Jews as well have always found refuge in their realms. May God reward the goodness and graciousness of each one in the world of truth. Thus for the honor of the dead we should indulge in deep lamenting and grief.

Also in the category of "honor for the dead" is the glory of her highness, the Empress, may she be remembered for good in her own right because of her outstanding personal qualities. Alas for the splendor that has been lost to this generation! How shall we begin to tell her praises? Her conduct as a reigning monarch? It is indeed amazing that one woman could rule over so many great states with such goodness and integrity, appointing worthy and qualified judges, promulgating edicts throughout her realms, all with wondrous wisdom. It is almost beyond belief that all this could have been done by this woman for forty-one years! In this regard, she was indeed *a woman of valor* (Prov. 31:10), the crowning glory of all the realms.

There was also her eloquence, the logical manner of her speech with nobles and officials of the various realms, always with intelligence, insight, and knowledge. *Her mouth was full of wisdom, her tongue with kindness.* (Prov. 31:26.) She did not speak in fury, rage, or anger. All was in good taste and refinement. *Her mouth produced wisdom, her lips knew what is pleasing* (cf. Prov. 10:31–32). Maria Theresa, Maria Theresa! I apply to you the verse, *You are more beautiful than all men, your speech is endowed with grace, rightly has God given you an eternal blessing.* (Ps. 45:3.) Eternal, because even after your death, your good name is like fine oil (cf. Cant. 1:3), your name will not be forgotten, your good reputation will endure for all time.

And her heroic counsel in military matters. How strong she showed herself to be! Her resolute heroism is indeed well known. At the very beginning of her reign, several kings and rulers gathered against her with forces like the sands of the sea. But she *was not dismayed by their shouts, not cowed by their numbers.* (Isa. 31:4.) This fearlessness enabled her to drive them away from her lands with heroic power. Truly it is amazing that a woman should array herself in the adornments of a man, wearing the spirit of heroism! She should be praised for having confidence in the righteousness of her cause. Cowardice is a great flaw, especially for sovereigns. We find that the Torah warns against cowardice and fear in battle: *You are about to join battle with your enemy. Let not your courage falter, do not fear or panic.* (Deut. 20:3.) This is how the Queen then clothed herself in fortitude. Her star strode forth, her scepter rose and smashed the brow of all her enemies (cf. Num. 24:17).

As for her kindness and compassion over all her subjects, this is so well known it needs no demonstration. Never have we heard that she became full of vengeful spite to punish sinners with cruelty. To the contrary, she was quite ready to forgive and deal graciously with the guilty.

Her concern for all the states of her empire, especially in times of suffering? We saw with our own eyes during the year of dearth and famine [1771] the extent of her devotion. Indeed, she found no pleasure in eating or drinking herself until, with vigorous and decisive action, she brought food to these realms from afar. She did not rest throughout the period of famine, nor did she desist from sending wheat and foodstuffs time after time. Remember her, O God, and reward her in the world of reward, in fulfillment of the verse, *You offer your compassion to the hungry, and satisfy the fam-*

ished creature, therefore shall your light shine in the darkness and your gloom shall be like noonday. (Isa. 58:10.) Let also the name of our sovereign, Emperor Joseph II, be remembered for good in this context. He acted energetically at the time of dearth, opening the warehouses like the biblical Joseph. May God prolong his days and make his years pleasant for having saved many lives. Also for us, the Jews, there was an edict from the Queen to provide food in accordance with their needs.

Her commitment to the welfare of the realms? Look at how she spread learning throughout the land; look how many schools she established. Surely this deserves the praise, *Many women have done well, but you surpass them all.* (Prov. 31:29.)

As for the Queen's conduct of her own palace and court, the nobles and the attendants: with all her servants it is known that she never made their burden too harsh. She spoke to them with calm respect and never humiliated a single one, male or female.

In addition to the splendor of royalty, bestowed upon her from heaven, she had the adulation of all the inhabitants of her realms, near and far. They served her with devotion, not out of fear but out of love. In times of war we saw that all her subjects actually risked their lives for her. Those in the army, from the highest nobles to the lowly privates, stood their ground and fought her battle with all their might. Nobles and officials responsible for purveying supplies, whether for war or for other imperial needs, together with the rest of those associated with the affairs of state, both non-Jews and Jews—all of us eagerly awaited the opportunity of serving our Queen with all our strength, not because of any expectation of reward, but because of genuine love. This is how we all acted during the siege of the year 1757. I myself labored then with all my might; indeed, I placed my life in grave danger, as was well known then, all because of love. This is nothing but the gift of God, who graciously implanted the love of the Queen in the hearts of all her subjects.

Her personal qualities? She was modest and withdrawn, abstaining from all physical desires and lusts. For many years, she did not participate in games or listen to music, either vocal or instrumental; she did not attend the comedy or the operas. Has such a thing ever been heard or seen: that a queen as powerful as she was, raised from birth in royal luxury, should totally spurn all temporal pleasures? She was humble in a position of greatness. In her humility she would listen to the great and the small alike and receive their petition.

Her beneficent acts? She supported many charitable causes while denying herself, as is known from the regular allotment of food she provided for so many. Look at all the orphanages, called *Waisenhäuser,* look at all the poor houses, called *Armenhäuser,* look at the money she contributed to this! May God remember her for good.

Every aspect of her departure from this world was blessed. She died with a good name, with a mind clear to the final hour, speaking sensibly before her death, giving instructions that testify to her consummate perfection. For a woman with all these qualities, we may weep day and night for many days, indulging in deep mourning and lament, yet we will not fulfill even a small part of our obligation. Never has there been such a degree of royal splendor as we see in her death: the daughter of an emperor, the wife of an emperor, the mother of an emperor. Yet she took no pride in any of these. Not only her subjects but also this entire generation throughout the whole world cannot imagine what we have lost in the death of our noble Queen, our sovereign, Empress Maria Theresa, may her memory be for good.

Alas! I cry out bitterly, not knowing how to find solace, citing the words of the lamenter, *What can I take as witness or liken to you . . . what can I match with you to console you?* (Lam. 2:13.) The commentators explain that when sorrow befalls a person, those who try to console often say, "A similar tragedy befell so and so, and he accepted consolation; so you should do the same." But if a tragedy befell someone that had never occurred to anyone else, the comforters would have no basis for consolation. So I say, if we were able to find a woman of comparable stature, even several generations ago, whose memory was preserved in the history books of bygone ages—a woman comparable in greatness, lineage, achievements, personal qualities, humility and abstinence—and had she died before reaching the age of seventy, and her contemporaries been consoled, then we too might have listened to words of consolation. But if we search and are unable to find her peer, I know not how we can be comforted.

Up to this point we have spoken in our eulogy about honor to the deceased. As for honor to the living: see how her immense praiseworthiness is obvious from her offspring. All of her children are blessed, monarchs have issued from her loins (cf. Gen. 35:11). There is a maxim that states, "If one cannot see the tree, let him look at its fruits." One who has never seen a particular field but sees only its produce and praises the fruits and vegetables knows that the tree must be flourishing and the field blessed by God. Happy is the one who bore and raised such children, monarchs of various peoples, spread through states far and near, primed for sovereignty or for high positions in the governments of great nations. Supreme over them all is *the fruitful vine, Joseph* (Gen. 49:22), our noble monarch, consummate in every character trait, the Emperor, may his majestic splendor be exalted. Now all these, her offspring, suffer the sorrow and distress of mourning for the Queen. We must share in their sorrow, to feel pain for the pearl without price that has been lost to us. Alas for those who are lost but not forgotten.

And so, every consideration requires us to deepen our mourning. There is no comforter at hand except for the Lord of Hosts, who brings healing even before the affliction. God exalted the Emperor during his mother's lifetime, and we have recognized his enormous merit, seen that he is a great and noble king. This is the source of our consolation: that there has come forth a shoot from the stump of Queen Maria Theresa, a twig has sprouted from her stock (cf. Isa. 11:1). From her has blossomed a radiant flower, producing glorious fruit. He will be for us and for all the states of his empire a source of consolation, for nothing of all the fine qualities found in his gracious mother, of blessed memory, are lacking in him. God has bestowed upon him *the spirit of wisdom and insight, the spirit of counsel and valor.* (Isa. 11:2.) He shall *judge the poor with equity and decide with justice for the lowly of the land.* (Isa. 11:4.) He will be a source of refuge for every one of his realms, the great eagle under whose wings all will find shelter and live securely. For he is a valiant king, a man who wages war with both strength and wisdom so as to prevail against his enemies, exulting in the shouts of victory. He will succeed in every enterprise to which he turns.

And now, my brothers and friends, Jews and indeed everyone who hears these words, whether Jews or non-Jews: is this not the fruit of all the good that has come to us, to repay our sovereign, the gracious Queen Maria Theresa, for all the good things she did throughout her life by serving wholeheartedly her son, our noble sovereign the Emperor, with all our heart and with all our soul (cf. Deut. 6:5), with abundant love as we served his mother the queen, the Empress? It is incumbent upon us to pray to the King of Kings, whose throne is in the heavens above and who bestows sovereignty to kings, that He will give strength to our king the Emperor, and exalt his reign on high.

May God make his throne greater than that of any other emperor. May He set his hand upon the sea, his right hand upon the rivers (cf. Ps. 89:26). O God, let the king rejoice in Your strength and exult in Your victory (cf. Ps. 21:2). Give him what his heart desires, do not deny him the request of his lips (cf. Ps. 21:3). Proffer him blessing of good things, set upon his head a crown of fine gold (cf. Ps. 21:4). Increase his glory, endow him with splendor and majesty; make him blessed forever, gladden him with joy (cf. Ps. 21:6–7). Let him accept with good cheer comfort for the loss of his mother, and let him sit upon his throne in happiness. May power leap before him (Job 41:14), may the king rejoice in God. Add days to the days of our king (cf. Ps. 61:7), the noble Emperor, long years to his life, O God, that he may judge Your people righteously. Make us worthy of his compassion that he may favor us, watch over us in mercy, and act toward us with kindness. And we shall bless our gracious sovereign, the Emperor, as all of us say together (and the entire congregation responded and said), "Long live our sovereign, Emperor Joseph the Second! Amen."

PART VIII

"The Bringing of Truth
Through Personality"

The Nineteenth Century

Isaac Meir Rothenberg
of Ger

1789–1866

*T*he transmission of this famous preaching from the early first century B.C. through the nineteenth is emblematic of many long links
in the chain of survival of texts on the sacred. The theologian and scholar
Martin Buber (1878–1965) preserved it in his collections of tales from the
Hasidic masters; a Hasidic master from Poland who died a decade before
Buber was born had transmitted it to his own assembly of the faithful on the
eve of Yom Kippur. Isaac Meir, a relatively obscure descendant of a long
dynasty of rabbis in the Jewish Pale, is typical of the late Hasidic masters
whose work Buber translated into German from the Yiddish texts, work
marked by its learning, playfulness, and passion for the Torah. When he
spoke to those sitting around his table at the last meal before the Yom Kippur fast, he took Hillel's famous ethical proclamation and underscored its
enigmatic words with the "learned wit" and gravity which have made him
the model of a Jewish sage and source of many of the most popular Talmudic tales in Jewish literature and folklore.

Hillel's birth and death dates are uncertain; the memory of the sage's
words is more reliable. We know that he was born in Babylonia (c. 60 B.C.)
into a family of Davidic ancestry and studied in Jerusalem. During the period of the second Temple he became a great interpreter of Torah, summing
up its wisdom in a negative "Golden Rule." "What is hateful to you, do not
to others. That is the whole of Torah; the rest is commentary on it. Now go
and learn." His homilies were elliptical and doubtless demanding even for
his fervent and learned audience: his exegetical discipline and its "Seven
Rules" of hermeneutics came to be known as the "House of Hillel." Much of

his life has become encrusted with legend, a heady mix of intellectual rigor, aphorism, anecdote, and riddle.

In the oral tradition, Hillel's famous utterance became proverbial as "If I am not for myself, who will be for me? But if I am for myself alone, what am I?" The company sitting around the table for a repast on the eve of Yom Kippur, attending to every word of the master, would have noted and been amused by the intellectual sport which, in this homily, reversed the original order of Hillel's words, turning its third question into the second for reasons which surely they considered and debated inwardly during the long High Holy Day which followed.

On the Eve of the Day of Atonement

Before the Day of Atonement, the rabbi of Ger said to the hasidim gathered around his table:

Hillel, our teacher, says, "If I am not for myself, who will be for me?" If I do not perform my service, who will perform it for me? Everyone must perform his own service. And further along, he says: "And if not now, when? When will this Now be?" The Now that is now, this instant in which we are speaking, did not exist at any time since the world was created, and it will never exist again. Formerly there was another Now, and later will be another Now, and every Now has its own service; as we read in the Book of Splendor: "The garments of morning are not the garments of evening."

Strive for the Torah with all your strength and you will be linked to the Torah—but the sixty myriad letters in the Torah correspond to the sixty myriad souls in Israel, of whom the Torah is speaking: in this way you will become related to the whole. And if you proffer yourself to the whole, you receive from the whole; you receive even more than you put into it. And so to your own. Now you can add something of your neighbor's Now, of the good he accomplishes in that Now. Furthermore Hillel, our teacher, says: "And if I am only for myself, what am I?" If—God forbid—I should be separated from the community, when could I catch up on my Now? No other Now can make up for this Now, for every moment is concentrated in its particular light.

He who has done ill and talks about it and thinks about it all the time does not cast the base thing he did out of his thoughts, and whatever one thinks, therein one is; one's soul is wholly and utterly in what one thinks and so much a man dwells in baseness. He will certainly not be able to turn, for his spirit will grow coarse and his heart stubborn, and in addition to this he may be overcome by gloom. What would you? Rake the muck this way, rack the muck that way—it will always be muck. Have I sinned, or have I not sinned—what does Heaven get out of it? In the time I am brooding over it, I could be stringing pearls for the delight of Heaven. That is why it is written: "Depart from evil and do good"—turn wholly away from evil, do not dwell upon it, and do good. You have done wrong? Then counteract it by doing right.

And so on this day before the Day of Atonement let us feel a withdrawal from sin and a strengthening of the spirit, feel it in our innermost heart and not through forced ecstasy, receive it in our hearts for all future time, and be merry. Let us recite the list of our sins as quickly as possible, and not dwell upon it, but rather dwell upon the words of the prayer: "And thou, O Lord, shalt reign, thou alone. . . ."

St. Jean Baptiste Marie Vianney

1786–1869

*T*he Curé of Ars, like St. Bernadette of Lourdes, was born to a family of French peasants and spent his childhood tending sheep. Jean Baptiste Marie Vianney's history—after his career as a deserter from Napoleon's army, a failed seminarian in Lyons whose ordination came late because of both the closing of French churches by the government and his own inability to learn Latin—has many parallels with the life of the young girl who discovered the miraculous spring of Lourdes, had visions of the Virgin Mary, and was admitted at last to a convent, with some reluctance on the part of Church authorities. A reader of Zola's novel about Lourdes, and Franz Werfel's enormously successful historical novel on the same subject, *The Song of Bernadette,* can easily imagine both the Curé of Ars and Bernadette Soubirous coexisting as characters in the same book, and in the same chapter of religious and cultural history in nineteenth-century France.

The bitter anticlerical climate of Napoleonic France and the secularist conflicts of the Second Empire may have provoked a reactionary emphasis on miracle working, mass pilgrimages, public penances, and psychic powers. Vianney, sent as the curé of a backwater called Ars, not far from Lyons, became the focus of something resembling a cult of personality. His sermons against drunkenness, fornication, and violation of the Sabbath contributed to his enormous celebrity. By 1855, twenty thousand pilgrims a year made their way to Ars, and the curé spent sixteen to eighteen hours a day in the confessional, absorbed in the direction of souls for which his humility, gentleness, patience, and common sense earned him, more than his fame, an elevation from Venerable to Blessed in less than a quarter of a century after his death. The miracles attributed to him include his remarkable powers of obtaining money for the charitable institutions he founded, his apparently prescient knowledge of past and future in the confessional box, and the mortifications and self-imposed daily penances of his own exemplary private life. His sermon on temptation is suggestive of the high quality of consolation he must have offered as a confessor of sins. When the Curé of Ars was canonized in 1925, Pope Pius XI declared him the patron saint of parish priests.

ↂ

Beware If You Have No Temptations

Whom does the devil pursue most? Perhaps you are thinking that it must be those who are tempted most; these would undoubtedly be the habitual drunkards, the scandalmongers, the immodest and shameless people who wallow in moral filth, and the miser, who hoards in all sorts of ways.

No, my dear brethren, no, it is not these people. On the contrary, the Devil despises them, or else he holds onto them, lest they not have a long enough time in which to do evil, because the longer they live, the more their bad example will drag souls into hell. Indeed, if the Devil had pursued this lewd and shameless old fellow too closely, he might have shortened the latter's life by fifteen or twenty years, and he would not then have destroyed the virginity of that young girl by plunging her into the unspeakable mire of his indecencies; he would not, again, have seduced that wife, nor would he have taught his evil lessons to that young man, who will perhaps continue to practice them until his death. If the Devil had prompted this thief to rob on every occasion, he would long since have ended on the scaffold and so he would not have induced his neighbor to follow his example. If the Devil had urged this drunkard to fill himself unceasingly with wine, he would long ago have perished in his debaucheries, instead of which, by living longer, he has made many others like himself. If the Devil had taken away the life of this musician, or that dancehall owner, of this cabaret keeper, in some raid or scuffle, or on any other occasion, how many souls would there be who, without these people, would not be damned and who now will be? St. Augustine teaches us that the Devil does not bother these people very much; on the contrary, he despises them and spits upon them.

So, you will ask me, who then are the people most tempted? They are these, my friends; note them carefully. The people most tempted are those who are ready, with the grace of God, to sacrifice everything for the salvation of their poor souls, who renounce all those things which most people eagerly seek. It is not one devil only who tempts them, but millions seek to entrap them. We are told that St. Francis of Assisi and all his religious were gathered on an open plain, where they had built little huts of rushes. Seeing the extraordinary penances which were being practiced, St. Francis ordered that all instruments of penance should be brought out, whereupon his religious produced them in bundles. At this moment there was one young man to whom God gave the grace to see his Guardian Angel. On the one side he saw all of these good religious, who could not satisfy their hunger for penance, and, on the other, his Guardian Angel allowed him to see a gathering of eighteen thousand devils, who were holding counsel to see in what way they could subvert these religious by temptation. One of the devils said: "You do not understand this at all. These religious are so humble; ah, what wonderful virtue, so detached from themselves, so attached to God! They have a superior who leads them so well that it is impossible to succeed in winning them over. Let us wait until their superior is dead, and then we shall try to introduce among them young people without vocations who will bring about a certain slackening of spirit, and in this way we shall gain them."

A little further on, as he entered the town, he saw a devil, sitting by himself beside the gate into the town, whose task was to tempt all of those who were inside. This saint asked his Guardian Angel why it was that in order to tempt this group of religious there had been so many thousands of devils while for a whole town there was but one—and that one sitting down. His good angel told him that the people of the town had not the same need of temptations, that they had enough bad in themselves, while the religious were doing good despite all the traps which the Devil could lay for them.

The first temptation, my dear brethren, which the Devil tries on anyone who has begun to serve God better is in the matter of human respect. He will no longer dare to be seen around; he will hide himself from those with whom heretofore he had been mixing and pleasure seeking. If he should be told that he has changed a lot, he will be ashamed of it! What people are going to say about him is continually in his mind, to the extent that he no longer has enough courage to do good before other people. If the Devil cannot get him back through human respect, he will induce an extraordinary fear to possess him that his confessions are not good, that his confessor does not understand him, that whatever he does will be all in vain, that he will be damned just the same, that he will achieve the same result in the end by letting everything slide as by continuing to fight, because the occasions of sin will prove too many for him.

Why is it, my dear brethren, that when someone gives no thought at all to saving his soul, when he is living in sin, he is not tempted in the slightest, but that as soon as he wants to change his life, in other words, as soon as the desire to give his life to God comes to him, all Hell falls upon him? Listen to what St. Augustine has to say: "Look at the way," he tells us, "in which the Devil behaves towards the sinner. He acts like a jailer who has a great many prisoners locked up in his prison but who, because he has the key in his pocket, is quite happy to leave them, secure in the knowledge that they cannot get out. This is his way of dealing with the sinner who does not consider the possibility of leaving his sin behind. He does not go to the trouble of tempting him. He looks upon this as time wasted because not only is the sinner not thinking of leaving him, but the Devil does not desire to multiply his chains. It would be pointless, therefore, to tempt him. He allows him to live in peace, if, indeed, it is possible to live in peace when one is in sin. He hides his state from the sinner as much as is possible until death, when he then tries to paint a picture of his life so terrifying as to plunge him into despair. But with anyone who has made up his mind to change his life, to give himself up to God, that is another thing altogether."

While St. Augustine lived in sin and evil, he was not aware of anything by which he was tempted. He believed himself to be at peace, as he tells us himself. But from the moment that he desired to turn his back upon the Devil, he had to struggle with him, even to the point of losing his breath in the fight. And that lasted for five years. He wept the most bitter of tears and employed the most austere of penances: "I argued with him," he says, "in my chains. One day I thought myself victorious, the next I was prostrate on the earth again. This cruel and stubborn war went on for five years. However, God gave me the grace to be victorious over my enemy."

You may see, too, the struggle which St. Jerome endured when he desired to give himself to God and when he had the thought of visiting the Holy Land. When he was in Rome, he conceived a new desire to work for his salvation. Leaving Rome, he buried himself in a fearsome desert to give himself over to everything with which his love of God could inspire him. Then the Devil, who foresaw how greatly his conversion would affect others, seemed to burst with fury and despair. There was not a single temptation that he spared him. I do not believe that there is any saint who was as strongly tempted as he. This is how he wrote to one of his friends:

> My dear friend, I wish to confide in you about my affliction and the state to which the Devil seeks to reduce me. How many times in this vast solitude, which the heat of the sun makes insupportable, how many times the pleasures of Rome have come to assail me! The sorrow and the bitterness with which my soul is filled cause me, night and day, to shed floods of tears. I proceed to hide myself in the most isolated places to struggle with my temptations and there to weep for my

sins. My body is all disfigured and covered with a rough hair shirt. I have no other bed than the naked ground and my only food is coarse roots and water, even in my illnesses. In spite of these rigors, my body still experiences thoughts of the squalid pleasures with which Rome is poisoned; my spirit finds itself in the midst of those pleasant companionships in which I so greatly offended God. In this desert to which I have condemned myself to avoid Hell, among these somber rocks, where I have no other companions than the scorpions and the wild beasts, my spirit still burns my body, already dead before myself, with an impure fire; the Devil still dares to offer it pleasures to taste. I behold myself so humiliated by these temptations, the very thought of which makes me die with horror, and not knowing what further austerities I should exert upon my body to attach it to God, that I throw myself on the ground at the foot of my crucifix, bathing it with my tears, and when I can weep no more I pick up stones and beat my breast with them until the blood comes out of my mouth, begging for mercy until the Lord takes pity on me. Is there anyone who can understand the misery of my state, desiring so ardently to please God and to love Him alone? Yet I see myself constantly prone to offend Him. What sorrow this is for me! Help me, my dear friend, by the aid of your prayers, so that I may be stronger in repelling the Devil, who has sworn my eternal damnation.

These, my dear brethren, are the struggles to which God permits his great saints to be exposed. Alas, how we are to be pitied if we are not fiercely harried by the Devil! According to all appearances, we are the friends of the Devil: he lets us live in a false peace, he lulls us to sleep under the pretense that we have said some good prayers, given some alms, that we have done less harm than others. According to our standard, my dear brethren, if you were to ask, for instance, this pillar of the cabaret if the Devil tempted him, he would answer quite simply that nothing was bothering him at all. Ask this young girl, this daughter of vanity, what her struggles are like, and she will tell you laughingly that she has none at all, that she does not even know what it is to be tempted. There you see, my dear brethren, the most terrifying temptation of all, which is not to be tempted. There you see the state of those whom the Devil is preserving for Hell. If I dared, I would tell you that he takes good care not to tempt or torment such people about their past lives, lest their eyes be opened to their sins.

The greatest of all evils is not to be tempted because there are then grounds for believing that the Devil looks upon us as his property and that he is only awaiting our deaths to drag us into Hell. Nothing could be easier to understand. Just consider the Christian who is trying, even in a small way, to save his soul. Everything around him inclines him to evil; he can hardly lift his eyes without being tempted, in spite of all his prayers and penances. And yet a hardened sinner, who for the past twenty years has been wallowing in sin, will tell you that he is not tempted! So much the worse, my friend, so much the worse! That is precisely what should make you tremble—that you do not know what temptations are. For to say that you are not tempted is like saying the Devil no longer exists or that he has lost all his rage against Christian souls. "If you have no temptations," St. Gregory tells us, "it is because the devils are your friends, your leaders, and your shepherds. And by allowing you to pass your poor life tranquilly, to the end of your days, they will drag you down into the depths." St. Augustine tells us that the greatest temptation is not to have temptations because this means that one is a person who has been rejected, abandoned by God, and left entirely in the grip of one's own passions.

Theodore Parker

1810–1860

In Theodore Parker's New England, the Unitarian Church's affirmation of the brotherhood of mankind received its greatest test with the rise of the abolitionist movement and the political debates of the decade before the Civil War. Parker, clergyman, author, and theologian, served in the 28th Congregational Society of Boston from 1845 until his death in Flor-

ence, Italy, and was a celebrity on the lecture circuit of the day. A passionate orator who dissented from the view of conservative churchmen that the
affairs of church and state must remain separate, Parker's prophetic wrath
was uncompromising in its refusal to tolerate the institution of slavery, and
he was a great attraction in a mid-nineteenth-century world where femi-
nists and spiritualists competed to claim public attention. The national debate on slavery and states' rights was another form of public entertainment,
filling Boston's Music Hall.

Parker supported the antislavery raids of John Brown in the 1850s, arguing that zealotry and force alone would shatter the complicity and acceptance of holding human beings in bondage. Here, the Unitarian minister
whose controversial influence spread far beyond his parish engaged the attention of Charles Sumner and Abraham Lincoln. His allusion in this text to
the "forlorn children of Adam" is a subtle and clever stab at those clergymen
and apologists for slavery who commonly invoked in its defense a biblical
reference not only to "the children of Ham" but to the curse of Cain. The
rationalist Unitarian Dr. Parker wants his audience, as true Christians, to
grasp a point both genealogical and moral.

A Sermon of Slavery

Know ye not that to whom ye yield yourselves servants to obey,
his servants ye are to whom ye obey; whether of sin unto death, or
of obedience unto righteousness?

—ROMANS 6:16

In our version of the New Testament the word *servant* often stands for
a word in the original, which means *slave*. Such is the case in this passage just
read, and the sense of the whole verse is this: "If a man yields unconditional
service to sin, he is the *slave* of sin, and gets death for his reward." Here,
however, by a curious figure of speech, not uncommon in this apostle, he
uses the word *slave* in a good sense—*slave* of obedience unto righteousness.
I now ask your attention to a short sermon of slavery.

A popular definition has sometimes been given of common bodily slavery, that it is the holding of property in man. In a kindred language it is called body-property. In this case, a man's body becomes the possession, property, chattel, tool, or thing of another person, and not of the man who lives in it. This foreign person, of course, makes use of it to serve his own ends, without regard to the true welfare, or even the wishes, of the man who lives in that body, and to whom it rightfully belongs. Here the relation is necessarily that of force on one side and suffering on the other, though the force is often modified and the suffering sometimes disguised or kept out of sight.

Now man was made to be free, to govern himself, to be his own master, to have no cause stand between him and God, which shall curtail his birthright of freedom. He is never in his proper element until he attains this condition of freedom; of self-government. Of course, while we are children, not having reached the age of discretion, we must be under the authority of our parents and guardians, teachers, and friends. This is a natural relation. There is no slavery in it; no degradation. The parents, exercising rightful authority over their children, do not represent human caprice, but divine wisdom and love. They assume the direction of the child's actions, not to do themselves a service, but to benefit him. The father restrains his child, that the child may have more freedom, not less. Here the relation is not of force and suffering, but of love on both sides; of ability, which loves to help, and necessity, which loves to be directed. The child that is nurtured by its parent gains more than the parent does. So it is the duty of the wise, the good, the holy, to teach, direct, restrain the foolish, the wicked, the ungodly. If a man is wiser, better, and holier than I am, it is my duty, my privilege, my exaltation to obey him. For him to direct me in wisdom and love, not for his sake but for my own, is for me to be free. He may gain nothing by this, but I gain much.

As slavery was defined to be holding property in man, so freedom may be defined as a state in which the man does of his own consent, the best things he is capable of doing at that stage of his growth. Now there are two sorts of obstacles which prevent, or may prevent, man from attaining to this enviable condition of freedom. These are:—

I. Obstacles external to ourselves, which restrict our freedom; and
II. Obstacles internal to ourselves, which restrict our freedom.

A few words may be said on the condition to which men are brought by each of these classes of objects.

I. Of the slavery which arises from a cause external to ourselves. By the blessing of Providence, seconding the efforts, prayers, tears of some good men, there is no bodily, personal slavery sanctioned by the law amongst us in New England. But at the South we all know that some millions of our fellow-citizens are held in bondage; that men, women, and children are brought and sold in the shambles of the national capital; are owned as cattle; reared as cattle; beaten as cattle. We all know that our fathers fought through the War of Independence with these maxims in their mouths and blazoned on their banners: that all men are born free and equal, and that the God of eternal justice will at last avenge the cause of the oppressed, however strong the oppressor may be; yet it is just as well known that the sons of those very fathers now trade in human flesh, separating parent and child, and husband and wife, for the sake of a little gain; that the sons of those fathers eat bread not in the sweat of their own brow, but in that of the slave's face; that they are sustained, educated, rendered rich, and haughty, and luxurious by the labor they extort from men whom they have stolen, or purchased from the stealer, or inherited from the purchaser. It is known to you all, that there are some millions of these forlorn children of Adam, men whom the Declaration of Independence declares "born free and equal" with their master before God and the Law; men whom the Bible names "of the same blood" with the prophets and apostles; men "for whom Christ died," and who are "statues of God in ebony"—that they are held in this condition and made to feel the full burden of a corrupt society, and doomed from their birth to degradation and infamy, their very name a mock-word; their life a retreat, not a progress—for the general and natural effect of slavery is to lessen the qualities of a man in the slave as he increases in stature or in years—their children, their wives, their own bones and sinews at the mercy of a master! That these things are so, is known to all of us; well known from our childhood.

Every man who has ever thought at all on any subject, and has at the same time a particle of manhood in him, knows that this state of slavery would be to him worse than a thousand deaths; that set death in one scale, and hopeless slavery for himself and children in the other, he would not hesitate in his choice, but would say, "Give me death, though the life be ground out of me with the most exquisite tortures of lingering agony that malice can invent or tyranny inflict." To the African thus made the victim of American cupidity and crime, the state of slavery, it will be said, may not appear so degrading as to you and me, for he has never before been civilized, and though the untaught instinct of man bid him love freedom, yet Christianity has not revealed to him the truth, that all men are brothers before God, born with equal rights. But this fact is no excuse or extenuation of our crime. Who would justify a knave in plundering a little girl out of a fortune that she inherited, on the ground that she was a little girl "of tender years," and had never enjoyed or even beheld her birthright? The fact, that the injured party was ignorant and weak, would only enhance and aggravate the offense, adding new baseness and the suspicion of cowardice to guilt. If the African be so low, that his condition of slavery is tolerable in his eyes, and he can dance in his chains—happy in the absence of the whip—it is all the more a sin, in the cultivated and the strong, in the Christian(!) to tyrannize over the feeble and defenseless. Men at the South with the Bible in one hand—with the Declaration of Independence in the other hand—with the words of Jesus, "Love your neighbor as yourself," pealing upon them from all quarters, attempt to justify slavery; not to excuse, to cloak, or conceal the thing, but to vindicate and defend it. This attempt, when made by reflecting men in their cool moments, discovers a greater degree of blackness of heart than the kidnapping of men itself. It is premeditated wickedness grown conscious of itself. The plain truth of the matter is this: Men who wish for wealth and luxury, but hate the toil and sweat, which are their natural price, brought the African to America; they make his chains; they live by his tears; they dance to the piping of his groans; they fatten on his sweat and are pampered by his blood. If these men spoke as plainly as they must needs think, they would say openly, "our sin captured these men on the African sands; our sin fettered them in slavery; and, please God, our sin shall keep them in slavery till the world ends." This has been thought long enough, it is high time it was said also that we may know what we are about and where we stand.

Men at the North sometimes attempt to gloss the matter over, and hush it up by saying the least possible on the subject. They tell us that some masters are "excellent Christians." No doubt it is so, estimating these masters by the common run of Christians—you find such on the deck of pirate ships; in the dens of robbers. But suppose some slaveholders are as good Christians as Fenelon or St. Peter; still a sin is a sin, though a Christian commit it. Our fathers did not think "taxation without representation" any the less an evil because imposed by "his most Christian Majesty," a King of Christians.

Then, too, it is said, "the slaves are very happy, and it is a great pity to disturb them," that "the whole mass are better fed and clothed, and are troubled with fewer cares, than working men at the North." Suppose this true also, what then? Do you estimate your welfare in pounds of beef; in yards of cloth; in exemption from the cares of a man! If so all appeal to you is vain, your own soul has become servile. The Savior of the world was worse fed and clothed, no doubt, than many a Georgian slave, and had not where to lay his head, wearied with many cares; but has your Christianity taught you that was an evil, and the slave's hutch at night, and pottage by day, and exemption from a man's cares by night and day, are a good, a good to be weighed against freedom! Then are you unworthy the soil you stand on; you contaminate the air of New England, which free men died to transmit to their children free!

Still further it is said, "the sufferings of slaves are often exaggerated." This may be true. No doubt there have been exaggerations of particular cases. Every slave-owner is not a demon, not a base man. No doubt there are what are called good Christians, men that would be ornaments to a Christian church, among slaveholders. But though there have been exaggerations in details, yet the awful sum of misery, unspeakable wretchedness, which hangs over two millions of slaves is such that eye hath not seen it; nor ear heard it; nor heart conceived of it. It were so if all their masters were Christians in character, in action, still retaining slaves. How much deeper and wilder must swell that wide weltering sea of human agony, when the masters are what we know so many are, hard-hearted and rapacious, insolent and brutal!

This attempt to gloss the matter over and veil the fact, comes from two classes of men.

1. Some make the attempt from a real design to promote peace. They see no way to abate this mischief; they see "the folly and extravagance" of such as propose "dangerous measures," and therefore they would have us say nothing about it. The writhing patient is very sick; the leech more venture-

some than skillful; and the friends, fearful to try the remedy, unwilling to summon wiser advice, declare the sick man is well as ever if you will only let him alone! These men mourn that anyone should hold another in bondage; they think our fathers were illustrious heroes, for fighting dreadful wars with the parent country rather than pay a little tax against their will, but that this evil of slavery can never be healed; therefore, in the benevolence of their heart, they refuse to believe all the stories of suffering that reach their ears. The imagination of a kind man recoils at the thought of so much wretchedness; still more, if convinced that it cannot be abated. Now these men are governed by the best of motives, but it does not follow that their opinions are so just as their motives are good.

2. But there are others, who are willing to countenance the sin and continue it, well knowing that it is a sin. They would not have it abated. They tell you of the stupidity of the African; that he is made for nothing but a slave; is allied to the baboon and the ape, and is as much in his place when fettered, ignorant and savage, in a rice field, to toil under a taskmaster's whip, as a New Englander, free and educated, is in his place, when felling forests, planning railroads, or "conducting" a steam-engine. Hard treatment and poor fare, say they, are the black man's due. Besides, they add, there is a natural antipathy between the black race and the white, which only the love of money, or the love of power, on the part of the white is capable of overcoming; that the blacks are an inferior race, and therefore the white Saxons are justified in making them slaves. They think the strong have a right to the services of the weak, forgetting that the rule of reason, the rule of Christianity, is just the other way; "We that are strong ought to bear the infirmities of the weak." They would have us follow the old rule, "that they should get who have the power, and they should keep who can." Of this class nothing further need be said save this: that they are very numerous, and quote the New Testament in support of slavery, thus contriving to pass for Christians, and have made such a stir in the land that it is scarce safe to open one's mouth and strip the veil from off this sin. . . .

The opinion of good and religious men here amongst us seems to be, that slavery is a great sin and ought to be abolished as soon as possible; that the talent and piety of the nation cannot be better employed than in devising the speediest and most effectual way of exterminating the evil. Such of them as see a way to abolish the wrong cry aloud and publish the tidings;

others who see no way to state that fact also, not failing to express their dread of all violent measures. Such is the conviction of good and religious men at the North. But there is another opinion a little different, which is held by a different class of men at the North; they think that slavery is a great sin, and ought to be kept up so long as men can make money by it. But if the suppression of slavery could be effected—not as our fathers won their freedom, by blood and war—so gently as not to ruffle a sleeping baby's eyelid, yet if it diminished the crop of rice, or cotton, or tobacco, or corn, a single quintal a year, it would be a great mistake to free, cultivate, Christianize, and bless these millions of men! No one, I take it, will doubt this is a quite common opinion here in New England. The cause of this opinion will presently be touched upon. To show what baseness was implied in holding such opinions, would be simply a waste of time.

We all know there is at the North a small body of men, called by various names, and treated with various marks of disrespect, who are zealously striving to procure the liberation of slaves, in a peaceable and quiet way. They are willing to make any sacrifice for this end. They start from the maxim, that slavery is sin, and that sin is to be abandoned at once, and forever, come what will come of it. These men, it is said, are sometimes extravagant in their speech; they do not treat the "patriarchal institution" with becoming reverence; they call slave-holders hard names, and appeal to all who have a heart in their bosoms, and to some who find none there, to join them and end the patriarchal institution by wise and Christian measures. What wonder is it that these men sometimes grow warm in their arguments! What wonder that their heart burns when they think of so many women exposed to contamination and nameless abuse; of so many children reared like beasts, and sold as oxen; of so many men owning no property in their hands, or their feet, their hearts, or their lives! The wonder is all the other side, that they do not go to further extremities, sinful as it might be, and like St. John in his youth, pray for fire to come down from heaven and burn up the sinners, or like Paul, when he had not the excuse of youthful blood, ask God to curse them. Yet they do none of these things, never think of an appeal to the strong arm, but the Christian heart. . . . There is no doubt that these men are sometimes extravagant! There need be no wonder at that fact. The best of men have their infirmities, but if this extravagance be one of them, what shall we call the deadness of so many more amongst us? An infirmity? What shall we say of the sin itself? An infirmity also? Honest souls engaged in a good work, fired with a great idea, sometimes forget the settled decorum of speech, commonly observed in forum and pulpit, and call sin SIN. If the New Testament tell truth, Paul did so, and it was thought he would "turn the world upside down," while he was only striving to set it right. John the Baptist and Jesus of Nazareth did the same thing, and though one left his head in a charger, and the other his body on a cross, yet the world thinks at this day they did God's great work with their sincerity of speech.

The men who move in this matter encounter opposition from two classes of men; from the moderate, who do not see the wisdom of their measures, and who fear that the slave if set free will be worse off than before, or who think that the welfare of the masters is not sufficiently cared for. These moderate men think "we had better not meddle with the matter at present," but by and by, at a convenient season, they will venture to look into it. . . .

Then too they encounter opposition from the selfish, who see, or think they see, that the white masters will lose some thousands of millions of dollars, if slavery be abolished! Who has forgotten the men that opposed the introduction of Christianity at Ephesus, the craftsmen that made silver shrines for Diana!

I know some men say, "we have nothing to do with it. Slavery is the affair of the slave-owners and the slaves, not yours and mine. Let them abate it when they will." A most unchristian saying is this. Slavery! we have something to do with it. The sugar and rice we eat, the cotton we wear, are the work of the slave. His wrongs are imported to us in these things. We eat his flesh and drink his blood. I need not speak of our political connection with slavery. You all know what that is, and its effect on us here. But socially, individually, we are brought into contact with it every day. If there is a crime in the land known to us, and we do not protest against it to the extent of our ability, we are partners of that crime. It is not many years since it was said, temperate men had nothing to do with the sin of drunkenness; though they paid for it out of their purse! When they looked they found they had much to do with it, and sought to end it. . . .

Such then is slavery at the South; such the action of men at the North to attack or to defend it. But look a moment at the cause of this sin, and of its defense. It comes from the desire to get gain, comfort, or luxury; to have power over matter, without working or paying the honest price of that gain, comfort, luxury, and power; it is the spirit which would knowingly and of set purpose injure another for the sake of gaining some benefit to yourself. Such a spirit would hold slaves everywhere, if it were possible. Now when the question is put to any fair man, Is not this spirit active at the North as well as the South? there is but one answer. The man who would use his fellow-man as a tool merely, and injure him by that use; who would force another in any way to bend to his caprice; who would take advantage of his ignorance, his credulity, his superstition, or his poverty, to enrich and comfort himself; in a word, who would use his neighbor to his neighbor's hurt, that man has the spirit of slave-holding, and were circumstances but different, he would chain his brethren with iron bonds. If you, for your own sake, would unjustly put any man in a position which degrades him in your eyes, in his own eyes, in the eyes of his fellow-men, you have the spirit of the slave-holder. There is much of this spirit with us still. . . . Doubtless we have still social institutions which eyes more Christian than ours shall one day look upon as evils, only less than that of slavery itself. But it is gradually that we gain light; he that converts it to life as fast as it comes, does well.

II. Let a word be said on the other kind of slavery; that which comes from a cause internal to ourselves. This is common at the North, and South, and East, and West. In this case the man is prevented from doing what is best for him, not by some other man who has bound him, but by some passion or prejudice, superstition or sin. Here the mischief is in his own heart. If you look around you, you find many that bear the mark of the beast; branded on the forehead and the right hand; branded as slaves. "He that committeth sin is the slave of sin." The avaricious man is a slave. He cannot think a thought but as his master bids. He cannot see a truth if a dollar intervene. He cannot relieve the poor, nor sympathize with the distressed, nor yield to the humane impulse of his natural heart. If he sees in the newspaper a sentence on the wastefulness or the idleness of the poor, he remembers it forever; but a word in the Bible to encourage charity—he never finds that.

The passionate man is a slave; he lies at the mercy of the accidents of a day. If his affairs go well he is calm and peaceful; but if some little mistake arise he is filled with confusion, and the demon that rules him draws the chain. This master has many a slave under his yoke. He is more cruel than any planter in Cuba or Trinidad. He not only separates friend from friend, parent from child, and husband from wife, but what is worse yet, prevents their loving one another while they are together. This makes man a tyrant, not a husband; woman a fiend, not an angel, as God made her to be. This renders marriage a necessary evil, and housekeeping a perpetual curse, for it takes the little trifles which happen everywhere, except between angels, and makes them very great matters; it converts mistakes into faults, accidents into vices, errors into crimes; and so rends asunder the peace of families, and in a single twelvemonth disturbs more marriages than all the slave-holders of Carolina in a century.

So the peevish man is a slave. His ill humor watches him like a demon. Ofttimes it casteth him into the fire, and often into the water. In the morning he complains that his caprice is not complied with; in the evening that it is. He is never peaceful except when angry; never quiet but in a storm. He is free to do nothing good; so he acts badly, thinks badly, feels badly— three attributes of a devil. A yoke of iron and fetters of brass were grievous to bear, no doubt; the whip of a task-master makes wounds in the flesh; but God save us from the tyranny of the peevish, both what they inflict and what they suffer.

The intemperate man also is a slave; one most totally subjugated. His vice exposes him to the contempt and insult of base men, as well as to the pity of the good. Not only this, but his master strips him of his understanding; takes away his common sense, conscience, his reason, religion—qualities that make a man differ from a beast; on his garments, his face, his wife and child, is written in great staring letters, so that he may read that runs— This man also has sold his birthright and become a slave. . . .

Bodily slavery is one of the greatest wrongs that man can inflict on man; an evil not to be measured by the external and visible woe which it entails on the victim, but by the deep internal ruin which it is its direct tendency to produce. If I had the tongue of the Archangel I could not give utterance to the awfulness of this evil. There is no danger that this be exaggerated, no more than that the sun in a picture be painted too bright. . . .

I know men say that you and I ought not to move in this matter; that we have nothing to do with it. They urge in argument that the Constitution of the United States is the supreme law of the land, and that sanctions slavery. But it is the supreme law made by the voters, like the statutes denouncing capital punishment. What voters have made can voters unmake. There is no supreme law but that made by God; if our laws contradict that, the sooner they end or the sooner they are broken, why, the better. It seems to be thought a very great thing to run counter to a law of man, written on parchment; a very little thing to run counter to the law of Almighty God, Judge of the quick and the dead. Has He sanctioned slavery? "Oh yes," say some, and cite Old Testament and New Testament in proof thereof. It has been said, "The devil can quote Scripture for his purpose." We need not settle that question now, but it is certain that men can quote it to support despotism when that is the order of the day, or freedom when that is the "law of the land"; certain that men defend drunkenness and war, or sobriety and peace, out of its pages. A man finds what he looks for. . . .

Bodily slavery, though established by the powers that be, is completely in the hands of the voters, for they are the powers that be, is no more sanctioned by the supreme law of the land than stealing or murder. No enactment of man can make that right which was wrong before. It can never be abstractly right in any circumstances to do what is abstractly wrong.

But that other slavery, which comes from yourself, that is wholly within your power. And which, think you, is the worse, to be unwillingly the slave of a man and chained and whipped, or to be the voluntary slave of avarice, passion, peevishness, intemperance! It is better that your body be forcibly constrained, bought and sold, than that your soul, yourself, be held in thraldom. The spirit of a slave may be pure as an angel's; sometimes as lofty and as blessed too. The comforts of religion, when the heart once welcomes them, are as beautiful in a slave's cabin as in a king's court. When death shakes off the slave's body, the chain falls with it, and the man, disenthralled at last, goes where the wicked cease from troubling, where the weary are at rest, where the slave is free from his master; yes, where faithful use of the smallest talent and humblest opportunity has its reward, and unmerited suffering finds its ample recompense. But the voluntary slavery under sin—it has no bright side. None in life; in death no more. You may flee from a taskmaster, not from yourself.

Bodily slavery is so bad that the sun might be pardoned if it turned back, refusing to shine on such a sin; on a land contaminated with its stain.

But soul-slavery, what shall we say of that? Our fathers bought political freedom at a great price; they sailed the sea in storms; they dwelt here aliens on a hostile soil, the world's outcasts; in cold and hunger, in toil and want they dwelt here; they fought desperate wars in freedom's name! Yet they bought it cheap. You and I were base men, if we would not give much more than they paid, sooner than lose the inheritance.

But freedom for the soul to act right, think right, feel right, you cannot inherit; that you must win for yourself. Yet it is offered you at no great price. You may take it who will. It is the birthright of you and me and each of us; if we keep its conditions it is ours. Yet it is only to be had by the religious man—the man true to the nature God gave him. Without His Spirit in your heart you have no freedom. Resist His law, revealed in nature, in the later scripture of the Bible, in your own soul; resist it by sin, you are a slave, you must be a slave. Obey that law, you are Christ's freeman; nature and God are on your side. How strange it would be that one man should be found on all the hills of New England, of soul so base, of spirit so dastardly, that of his own consent took on him the yoke of slavery; went into the service of sin; toiled with that leprous host, in hopeless unrecompensed misery, without God, without heaven, without hope. Strange, indeed, that in this little village there should be men who care not for the soul's freedom, but consent to live, no, to die daily, in the service of sin.

Charles Grandison Finney

1792–1875

The Great Revival in nineteenth-century American religious history included the controversial figure of Charles Finney, trained in the law, eventually the president of Oberlin College, and after a late conversion, so persuasive and expressive in his language and in his direct appeal to the consciences of his audiences that his enemies found him blasphemous and theatrical. His reputation was enormous in his time, mingled with the cross-currents of the day in which his lawyerly logic fed a revivalist anxiety over the accountability of men and women, and a historic break with the Calvin-ist notion of free will.

Finney read Scripture like the lawyer that he was, while deeply moved by its tides of language. The upright New Englander found in the Bible a level of religious worship which compelled him to write in his memoirs, "I shall die if these waves continue to pass over me." When he preached, mem-bers of his congregation wept, fainted, and fell into ecstatic trances. Part of his mission as pastor of the Second Free Presbyterian Church in New York in 1832 involved taking a decided stand against slavery, although he de-clined, as he said, "to make it a hobby."

The sermon on stewardship is typical of Finney's rational, litigious search for truth, for individual accountability, and for his exalted ideal of the state of spiritual stability he called "sanctification." There is no spirit of com-promise in Charles Grandison Finney's spiritual court of law; his body of belief, now known as "Oberlin theology," is still part of American discourse on freedom, perfectibility, and human frailty.

Stewardship

Give an account of thy stewardship.

—LUKE 16:2

A steward is one who is employed to transact the business of another, as his agent or representative in the business in which he is employed.

His duty is to promote, in the best possible manner, the interest of his employer. He is liable, at any time, to be called to an account for the man-ner in which he has transacted his business, and to be removed from his of-fice at the pleasure of his employer.

One important design of the parable of which the text is a part is to teach that all men are God's stewards. The Bible declares that the silver and gold are his, and that he is, in the highest possible sense, the proprietor of the universe. Men are mere stewards, employed by him for the transaction of his business, and required to do all they do for his glory. Even their eating and drinking are to be done for his glory, i.e., that they be strengthened for the best performance of his business.

That men *are* God's stewards, is evident from the fact that God treats them as such, and removes them at his pleasure, and disposes of the property in their hands, which he could not do, did he not consider them merely his agents, and not the owners of the property.

1. If men are God's stewards, they are bound to account to him for their *time.* God has created them and keeps them alive and their time is his. Hearer, should you employ a steward and pay him for his time, would you not expect him to employ that time in your service? Would you not consider it fraud and dishonesty, for him, while in your pay, to spend his time in idleness, or in promoting his private interests? Suppose he were often idle, that would be bad enough; but suppose that he *wholly* neglected your business, and that, when called to an account, and censured for not doing his duty, he should say, "Why, what have I done?" would you not suppose that for him to have done *nothing,* and let your business suffer, was great wickedness, for which he deserved to be punished?

Now, you are God's steward, and if you are an impenitent sinner, you have wholly neglected God's business, and have remained idle in his vineyard, or have been only attending to your own private interest; and now are you ready to ask what you have done? Are you not a knave, thus to neglect the business of your great employer, and go about your own private business, to the neglect of all that justice and duty and God require of you?

But suppose *your* steward should employ his time in *opposing* your interest, using your capital and time in driving at speculations directly opposed to the business for which he was employed? Would you not consider this great dishonesty? Would you not think it very ridiculous for him to account himself an honest man? Would you not suppose yourself *obliged* to call him to an account? And would you not account anyone a villain who should approve such conduct? Would you not think yourself *bound* to publish him abroad, that the world might know his character, and that you might clear yourself from the charge of upholding such a person?

How, then, shall God dispose of you, if you employ your time in *opposing* his interest, and use his capital in your hands, to drive at speculation directly opposed to the business for which he has employed you? Are you not ashamed, then, to account yourself an honest man; and will not God consider himself under an *obligation* to call you to an account? Should he not do this, would not the omission be an evidence, on his part, of an approval of your abominable wickedness? Must he not feel himself constrained to make you a public example, that the universe may know how much he abhors your crimes?

2. Stewards are bound to give an account of their *talents.* By talents, I mean here the powers of their minds. Suppose you should educate a man to be your steward, should support him during the time that he was engaged in study, and be at all the expense of his education, and that then he should either neglect to employ his mind in your service, or should use the powers of his cultivated intellect for the promotion of his own interests; would you not consider this as fraud and villainy? Now, God created your minds, and has been at the expense of your education, and has trained you up for his service; and do you either let your mind remain in idleness, or pervert the powers of your cultivated intellect, to the promotion of your own private interest, and then ask what you have done to deserve the wrath of God?

But suppose your steward should use his education in *opposition* to your interest, and use all the powers of his mind to destroy the very interest for which he was educated, and which he is employed to sustain; would you not look upon his conduct as marked with horrid guilt? And do *you,* sinner, employ the powers of your mind, and whatever education God may have given you, in *opposing* his interest; perverting his truth; scattering "firebrands, arrows and death" all around you, and think to escape his curse? Shall not the Almighty be avenged upon such a wretch?

3. A steward is bound to give an account for the *influence he exerts* upon mankind around him.

Suppose you should employ a steward, should educate him until he possessed great talents, should put a large capital in his hands, should exalt him high in society, and place him in circumstances to exert an immense influence in the commercial community, and that then he should refuse or neglect to exert this influence in promoting your interest; would you not consider this default a perpetual fraud practiced upon you?

But suppose he should exert all this influence against you, and array himself with all his weight of character and talent and influence, and even employ the capital with which he was intrusted, in *opposing* your interest—what language, in your estimation, could then express your sense of his guilt?

Hearer, whatever influence God has given you, if you are an impenitent sinner, you are not only neglecting to use it for God, to build up his kingdom, but you are employing it in *opposition* to his interest and glory; and for this, do you not deserve the damnation of hell? Perhaps you are rich, or learned, or have, on other accounts, great influence in society, and are refusing to use it to save the souls of men, but are bringing all your weight of character and talents and influence and example, to drag all who are within the sphere of your influence, down to the gates of hell.

4. You must give an account for the manner in which you use *the property in your possession.* Suppose your steward should refuse to employ the capital with which you intrusted him, for the promotion of your interest, or suppose he were to account it his own, and to use it for his own private interest, or apply it to the gratification of his lusts, or the aggrandizement of his family; in bestowing large portions upon his daughters, or in ministering to the lusts and pride of his sons; while at the same time your business was suffering for the want of this very capital; or suppose that this steward held the purse-strings of your wealth, and that you had multitudes of other servants, whose necessities were to be supplied out of the means in his hands, and that their welfare, and even their lives, depended on these supplies; and yet this steward should minister to his own lusts, and those of his family, and suffer those, your other servants, to perish—what would you think of such wickedness? You entrusted him with your money, and enjoined him to take care of your other servants, and, through his neglect, they were all dead men.

Now, you have God's money in your hands, and are surrounded by God's children, whom he commands you to love as you do yourself. God might, with perfect justice, have given his property them instead of you. The world is full of poverty, desolation, and death; hundreds and millions are perishing, body and soul; God calls on you to exert yourself as his steward, for their salvation; to use all the property in your possession, so as to promote the greatest possible amount of happiness among your fellow-creatures. The Macedonian cry comes from the four winds of heaven, "Come over and help us"; and yet you refuse to help; you hoard up the wealth in your possession, live in luxury, and let your fellow-men go down to hell. What language can describe your guilt?

But suppose your servant, when you called him to account, should say, "Have I not acquired this property by my own industry?" would you not answer, "You have employed my capital to do it, and my time, for which I have paid you; and the money you have gained is mine." So when God calls upon you to use the property in your possession for him, do you say it is yours, that you have obtained it by your own industry? Pray, whose time have you used, and whose talents and means? Did not God create you? Has he not sustained you? Has he not prospered you, and given you all his success? Yes; your time is his; your all is his: you have no right to say that wealth you have is yours; it is his, and you are bound it use it for his glory. You are a traitor to your trust if you do not so employ it.

If your clerk take only a little of your money, his character is gone, and he is branded as a villain. But sinners take not only a dollar or so, but all they can get, and use it for themselves. Don't you see that God would do wrong not to call you to account, and punish you for filling both your pockets with his money, and calling it your own? Professor of religion, if you are doing so don't call yourself a Christian.

5. You must give an account of your *soul*. You have no right to go to hell. God has a right to your soul; your going to hell would injure the whole universe. It would injure hell, because it would increase its torments. It would injure heaven, because it would wrong it out of your services. Who shall take the harp in your place, in singing praises to God? Who shall contribute your share to the happiness of heaven?

Suppose you had a steward to whom you had given life, and educated him at a very great expense, and then he should willfully throw that life away; has he a right thus to dispose of a life of so much value to you? Is it not as just to rob you of the same amount of property in anything else? God has made your soul, sustained and educated you, till you are now able to render him important services, and to glorify him forever; and have you a right to go to hell, and throw away your soul, and thus rob God of your services? Have you a right to render hell more miserable, and heaven less happy, and thus injure God and all the universe?

Do you still say, What if I do lose my soul, it is nobody's business but my own? That is false; it is everybody's business. Just as well might a man bring a contagious disease into a city, and spread dismay and death all around, and say it was nobody's business but his own.

6. You must give an account for the *souls of others*. God commands you to be a co-worker with him in converting the world. He needs your services, for he saves souls only through the agency of men. If souls are lost, or the gospel is not spread over the world, sinners charge all the blame upon Christians, as if they only were bound to be active in the cause of Christ, to exercise benevolence, to pray for a lost world, to pull sinners out of the fire. I wonder who has absolved *you* from these duties? Instead of doing your duty, you lie as a stumbling-block in the way of other sinners. Thus, instead of helping to save a world, all your actions help to send souls to hell.

7. You are bound to give an account of the *sentiments you entertain and propagate*. God's kingdom is to be built up by truth and not by error. Your sentiments will have an important bearing upon the influence you exert over those around you.

Suppose the business in which your steward was employed required that he should entertain right notions concerning the manner of doing it, and the principle involved in it, of your will and of his duty. And suppose you had given him, in writing, a set of rules for the government of his conduct, in relation to all the affairs with which he was intrusted; then if he should neglect to examine those rules, or should pervert their plain meaning, and should thus pervert his own conduct, and be instrumental in deceiving others, leading them in the way of disobedience, would you not look upon this as criminal and deserving the severest reprobation?

God has given you rules for the government of your conduct. In the Bible you have a plain revelation of his will in relation to all your actions. And now, do you either neglect or pervert it, and thus go astray yourself, and lead others with you in the way of disobedience and death, and then call yourself an honest man? For shame!

8. You must give an account of your *opportunities of doing good*.

If you employ a steward to transact your business, you expect him to take advantage of the state of the market and of things in general, to improve every opportunity to promote your interest. Suppose at the busy seasons of the year, he should spend his time in idleness, or in his own private affairs, and not have an eye at all to the most favorable opportunities of promoting your interest, would you not soon say to him, "Give an account of thy stewardship, for thou mayest be no longer steward"? Now, sinner, you have always neglected opportunities of serving God, of warning your fellow-sinners, of promoting revivals of religion, and advancing the interests of truth. You have been diligent merely to promote your own private interests, and have entirely neglected the interests of your great employer; and are you not a wretch, and do you not deserve to be put out of the stewardship, as a dishonest man, and to be sent to the state prison of the universe? How can you escape the damnation of hell?

Remarks. From this subject you can see why the business of this world is a snare that drowns men's souls in destruction and perdition.

Sinners transact business to promote their own private interests, and not as God's stewards; and thus act dishonestly, defraud God, grieve the Spirit, and promote their own sensuality, pride and death. If men considered themselves as God's clerks, they would not lie, and overreach, and work on the Sabbath, to make money for *Him;* they would be sure that such conduct would not please him. God never created this world to be a snare to men—it is abused; he designed it to be a delightful abode for them—but how perverted!

Should all men's business be done as for God, they would not find it such a temptation to fraud and dishonesty, as to ensnare and ruin their souls; it would have no tendency to wean the soul from him, or to banish him from their thoughts. When holy Adam dressed God's garden and kept it, had that a tendency to banish God from his mind? If your gardener should all day be very busy in your presence, dressing your plants, consulting your views, and doing your pleasure continually, asking how shall this be done, and how shall that be done, would this have a tendency to banish you from his thoughts? So, if you were busy all the day, seeking God's glory, and transacting all your business for him, acting as his steward, sensible that his eyes were upon you, and were this your constant inquiry, how will this please him? and how will that please him? your being busy in such employment would have no tendency to distract your mind, and turn your thoughts from God.

Or, suppose a mother, whose son was in a distant land, was busy all day in putting up clothes, and books, and necessaries for him, continually questioning, how will this please him? and how will that please him? would that employment have a tendency to divert her mind from her absent son?

Now if you consider yourself as God's steward, doing his business; if you are in all things consulting his interests and his glory, and consider all your possessions as his, your time and your talents; the more busily you are engaged in his service, the more will God be present to all your thoughts.

Again. You see why idleness is a snare to the soul. A man that is idle, is dishonest, forgets his responsibility, refuses to serve God, and gives himself up to the temptations of the devil. Nay the idle man tempts the devil to tempt him.

Again. You see the error of the maxim, that men cannot attend to business and religion at the same time. A man's business ought to be a part of his religion. He cannot be religious in idleness. He must have some business, to be religious at all, and if it is performed from a right motive, his lawful and necessary business is as much a necessary part of religion as prayer, or going to church, or reading his Bible. Anyone who pleads this maxim is a knave by his own confession, for no man can believe that an honest employment, and pursued for God's glory, is inconsistent with religion. The objection supposes in the face of it that he considers his business either as unlawful in itself, or that he pursues it in a dishonest manner. If this be true, he cannot be religious, while thus pursuing his business; if his employment be wicked, he must relinquish it; or if honest and pursued in an unlawful manner, he must pursue it lawfully; or in either case he will lose his soul. But if his business is lawful, let him pursue it honestly, and from right motives, and he will find no difficulty in attending to his business, and being religious at the same time. A life of business is best for Christians, as it exercises their graces and makes them strong.

That most men do not account themselves as God's stewards is evident from the fact that they consider the losses they sustain in business as their own losses. Suppose that some of your debtors should fail, and your clerks should speak of it as their loss, and say they had met with great losses, would you not look upon it as ridiculous in the extreme? And is it not quite as ridiculous for you, if any of your Lord's debtors fail, to make yourself very uneasy and unhappy about it? Is it your loss, or his? If you have done your duty, and taken suitable care of his property, and a loss is sustained, it is not your loss, but his. You should look at your sins and your duty, and not be frightened lest God should become bankrupt. If you acted as God's steward or as his clerk, you would not think of speaking of the loss as your own loss. But if you have considered the property in your possession as your own, no wonder that God has taken it out of your hands.

Again. You see that in the popular acceptation of the term, it is ridiculous to call institutions for the extension of the Redeemer's kingdom in the world, *charitable institutions.* In one sense, indeed, they may be called such. Should you give your steward orders to appropriate a certain amount of funds for the benefit of the poor in a certain parish—this would be charity in *you,* but not in *him,* it would be ridiculous in *him* to pretend that the charity was *his.* So, institutions for the promotion of religion are the charities of God, and not of man. The funds are God's, and it is his requirement that they be expended according to his directions, to relieve the misery, or advance the happiness of our fellow-men. God, then, is the giver, and not *men,* and to consider the charities as the gift of *men* is to maintain that the funds belong to *men* and not to God. To call them charitable institutions, in the sense in which they are usually spoken of, is to say that men confer a favor upon God; that they give him *their* money and consider *him* as an object of charity.

Suppose that a company of merchants in the city should employ a number of agents to transact their business in India, with an immense capital, and suppose these agents should claim the funds as their property, and whenever a draft was made upon them, should consider it *begging,* and asking *charity* at their hands, and should call the servant by whom the order was sent a *beggar;* and farther, suppose they should get together, and form a *charitable society* to pay these drafts, of which they should become "life members" by paying each a few dollars of their employers' money into a common fund, and then hold themselves exonerated from all farther calls; so that, when an agent was sent with drafts, they might direct the treasurer of their society to let him have a little, as a matter of almsgiving. Would not this be vastly ridiculous? What then do you think of yourself, when you talk of supporting these *charitable institutions,* as if God, the owner of the universe, was to be considered as soliciting charity and his servants as the agents of an infinite *beggar?* How wonderful it is that God does not take such presumptuous men and put them in hell in a moment, and then with the money in their hands execute his plans for converting the world.

Nor is it less ridiculous for them to suppose that by paying over the funds in their hands for this purpose, *they* confer a charity upon *men:* for it should all along be borne in mind, that the money is not *theirs*. They are God's stewards and only pay it over to his order—in doing this, therefore, *they* neither confer a charity upon the servants who are sent with the orders nor upon those for whose benefit the money is to be expended.

Again. When the servants of the Lord come with a draft upon you, to pay over some of the money in your possession into his treasury, to defray the expenses of his government and kingdom, why do you call it your own, and say you can't spare it? What do you mean by calling the agents beggars and saying you are sick of seeing so many beggars—disgusted with those agents of *charitable* institutions? Suppose your steward under such circumstances should call your agents beggars and say he was sick of so many beggars; would you not call him to an account, and let him see that the property in his possession was yours and not his?

Again. You see the great wickedness of men's hoarding up property as long as they live, and at death leaving a part of it to the church. What a will! To leave God half of his own property. Suppose a clerk should do so, and make a will, leaving his employer part of his own property! Yet this is called *piety*. Do you think that Christ will always be a beggar? And yet the church is greatly puffed up with their great charitable donations and legacies to Jesus Christ.

Again. You see the wickedness of laying up money for your children, and why money so laid up is a *curse* to them. Suppose your steward should lay up your money for his children, would you not consider him a knave? How then dare you take God's money and lay it up for your children, while the world is sinking down to hell? But will you say, Is it not my duty to provide for my "own household"? Yes, it is your duty *suitably* to provide for them, but what is a suitable provision? Give them the best education you can for the service of God. Make all *necessary* provision for the supply of their *real* wants, "till they become of sufficient age to provide for themselves"— and then if *you see them disposed to do good in serving God and their generation,* give them all the advantages for *doing this* in your power. But to make them rich—to gratify their pride—to enable them to live in luxury or ease—or to provide that they may become rich—to give your daughters what is called a genteel education—to allow them to spend their time in dress, idleness, gossiping, and effeminacy, you have no right—it is defrauding God, ruining your own soul, and greatly endangering theirs.

Again. Impenitent sinners will be finally and eternally disgraced. Do you not account it a disgrace to a man, to be detected in fraud and every species of knavery in transacting the business of his employer? Is not such a man deservedly thrown out of business; is he not a disgrace to himself and his family; can anybody trust him? How then will you appear before an injured God and an injured universe—a God whose laws and rights you have despised—a universe with whose interests you have been at war? How will you, in the solemn judgment, be disgraced, your name execrated, and you become the hissing and contempt of hell, for the numberless frauds and villainies you have practiced upon God and upon his creatures! But perhaps you are a professor of religion: Will your profession cover up your selfishness and vile hypocrisy, while you have defrauded God, spent his money upon your lusts, and accounted those as beggars who came with drafts upon you to pay over into his treasury? How will you hold up your head in the face of heaven? How dare you now pray; how dare you sit at the communion table; how dare you profess the religion of Jesus Christ, if you have set up a private interest, and do not consider all that you have as his, and use it all for his glory?

Again. We have here a true test of Christian character. True Christians *consider themselves* as God's stewards: they act for him, live for him, transact business for him, eat and drink for his glory, live and die to please him. But sinners and hypocrites live for themselves; account their time, their talents, their influence, as their own; and dispose of them all for their own private interest and thus drown themselves in destruction and perdition.

At the judgment, we are informed that Christ will say to those who are accepted, "Well done, good and faithful servants." Hearer! could he truly say this of you, "Well done, good and faithful servant; thou hast been faithful over a few things," i.e., over the things committed to your charge. He will pronounce no false judgment, put no false estimate upon things; and if he cannot say this truly, "Well done, good and faithful servant," you will not be accepted, but will be thrust down to hell. Now, what is your character, and what has been your conduct? God will soon call you to give an account of your stewardship. Have you been faithful to God, faithful to your own soul, and the souls of others? Are you ready to have your accounts examined, your conduct scrutinized, and your life weighed in the balance of the sanctuary? Are you interested in the blood of Jesus Christ? If not, repent, *repent now,* of all your wickedness, and lay hold upon the hope that is set before you; for, hark! a voice cries in your ears, "Give an account of thy stewardship, for thou mayest be no longer a steward."

Ralph Waldo Emerson

1803–1882

*H*erman Melville once observed of Emerson that in him he could readily see, "notwithstanding his merit, a gaping flaw. It was, the insinuation, that had he lived in those days when the world was made, he might have offered some valuable suggestions." Drollery aside, the days Emerson did live in abundantly received his valuable suggestions; and, in fact, they showed a remarkable consistency from beginning to end. We may tend to think him, as he certainly did become, a denizen of the lecture hall rather than the Church. Indeed in his famous Harvard Divinity School Address (1838) he talked of "the famine of the churches . . . the sleep of indolence . . . the din of routine." Nonetheless, each chamber in the nautilus of his life can be seen emerging from his beginnings in the Unitarianism of his youth.

Though he preached his final sermon in 1837 (still leaving behind enough, all told, to fill four thick modern volumes), no one would have denied Emerson's early destiny for the pulpit. He had sprung from an unbroken line of Puritan preachers extending back to the early seventeenth century. His father, William, had preached at the First Church of Boston; after a trial period as a "supply," or fill-in, preacher, he himself would stand in the pulpit of the Second Church, where such illustrious predecessors as the Mathers, father and son, Increase and Cotton, had stood before him.

Emerson's religious formation occurred at a time and a place when the old New England Calvinism, with its notion of man's radical inability to change God's eternal plan for him, had begun to give way to the more liberal thought that this life was, rather, a testing place for the next, that man's soul and his character were granted some purchase for development; otherwise, belief in free will had to be abandoned.

From the beginning, Emerson saw Christianity as pointing to something larger than itself. Its forms and rituals, even in their symbolic and abstracted Unitarian versions, troubled him. He once gave a famous sermon, "The Lord's Supper," demurring at his ability and sincerity to conduct the communion service, after which he was released from his pastorate. Such misgivings, however, did not deny his strong belief in the moral message of Jesus and in God's presence in each man and woman's heart and soul.

The sermon chosen here is the very first one he wrote out for delivery (in 1826) and is based on a powerful and suggestive verse taken from the oldest preserved Christian writing, St. Paul's Epistle to the Thessalonians: "Pray without ceasing." For Emerson, every secret wish or desire has to be seen as a prayer, regardless of its worthy or unworthy object, and God in turn will always answer every prayer, either in this world or the next. Under such terms, the consequences of our acts take on their moral freight.

⪜

"Pray Without Ceasing"

It is the duty of men to judge men only by their actions. Our faculties furnish us with no means of arriving at the motive, the character, the secret self. We call the tree good from its fruits, and the man, from his works. Since we have no power, we have no right, to assign for the actions of our neighbor any other than those motives which ought in similar circumstances to guide our own. But because *we* are not able to discern the processes of thought, to see the soul—it were very ridiculous to doubt or deny that any beings can. It is not incredible, that, the thoughts of the mind are the subjects of perception to some beings, as properly, as the sounds of the voice, or the motions of the hand are to us. Indeed, every man's feeling may be appealed to on this question, whether the idea, that other beings can read his thoughts, has not appeared so natural and probable, that he has checked sometimes a train of thoughts that seemed too daring or indecent, for any unknown beholders to be trusted with.

It ought to be distinctly felt by us that we stand in the midst of two worlds, the world of matter and the world of spirit. Our bodies belong to one; our thoughts to the other. It has been one of the best uses of the Christian religion to teach, that the world of spirits is more certain and stable than the material universe. Every thoughtful man has felt, that there was a more awful reality to thought and feeling, than to the infinite panorama of nature around him. The world he has found indeed consistent and uniform enough throughout the mixed sensations of thirty or forty years, but it seems to him at times, when the intellect is invigorated, to ebb from him, like a sea, and to leave nothing permanent but thought. Nevertheless it is a truth not easily nor early acquired, and the prejudice that assigns greater fixture and certainty to the material world is a source of great practical error. I need hardly remind you of the great points of this error. I need not ask you if the objects that every day are the cause of the greatest number of steps taken, of the greatest industry of the hands and the feet, the heart and the head, are the perishable things of sense, or the imperishable things of the soul; whether all this stir from day to day, from hour to hour of all this mighty multitude, is to ascertain some question dear to the understanding concerning the nature of God, the true Constitution and destination of the human soul, the proper balance of the faculties and the proper office of each; or (what of immortal thought comes nearer to practical value) whether all men are eagerly intent to study the best systems of education for themselves and their children? Is it not rather the great wonder of all who think enough to wonder that almost all that sits near the heart, all that colors the countenance, and engrosses conversation at the family board are these humble things of mortal date, and in the history of the universe absolutely insignificant? Is it not outside shows, the pleasures of appetite, or at best of pride; is it not bread and wine and dress, and our houses, and our furniture, that give the law to the great mass of actions and words? This is the great error which the strong feeling of the reality of things unseen must correct. It is time greater force should be given to the statement of this doctrine; it is time men should be instructed that their inward is more valuable than their outward estate; that thoughts and passions, even those to which no language is ever given, are not fugitive undefined shadows, born in a moment, and in a moment blotted from the soul, but are so many parts of the imperishable universe of morals; they should be taught that they do not think *alone;* that when they retreat from the public eye, and hide themselves to conceal in solitude guilty recollections or guilty wishes, the great congregation of moral natures, the spirits of just men made perfect; angels and archangels; the Son of God, and the Father everlasting, open their eyes upon them and speculate on these clandestine meditations.

I. The necessary inference from these reflections, is the fact which gives them all their importance, and is the doctrine I am chiefly anxious to inculcate. It is not only when we audibly and in form, address our petitions to the Deity, that we pray. We pray without ceasing. Every secret wish is a prayer. Every house is a church, the corner of every street is a closet of devotion. There is no rhetoric, let none deceive himself; there is no rhetoric in this. There *is* delusion of the most miserable kind, in that fiction on which the understanding pleads to itself its own excuse, when it knows not God and is thoughtless of him. I mean that outward respect, that is paid to the name and worship of God, whilst the thoughts and the actions are enlisted in the service of sin. "I will not swear by God's name," says the wary delinquent; "I will not ask him to lend his aid to my fraud, to my lewdness, to my revenge; nor will I even give discountenance to the laws I do not myself observe. I will not unmask my villainy to the world, that I should stand in the way of others, more scrupulous, nay, better than I."

And it is by this paltry counterfeit of ignorance that you would disguise from yourselves the truth? And will you really endeavor to persuade yourself, that, God is such a one as you yourself, and will be amused by professions, and may, by fraudulent language, be kept out of the truth? Is it possible, that men of discretion in common affairs, can think so grossly? Do you not know that the knowledge of God is perfect and immense; that it breaks down the fences of presumption, and the arts of hypocrisy; that night, and artifice, and time, and the grave, are naked before it; that the deep gives up its dead, that the gulfs of Chaos are disemboweled before him; that the minds of men are not so much independent existences, as they are ideas present to the mind of God; that he is not so much the observer of your actions, as he is the potent principle by which they are bound together; not so much the reader of your thoughts, as the active Creator by whom they are aided into being; and casting away the deceptive subterfuges of language, and speaking with strict philosophical truth, that every faculty is but a mode of his action; that your reason is God, your virtue is God, and nothing but your liberty, can you call securely and absolutely your own?

Since, then, we are thus, by the inevitable law of our being, surrendered unreservedly to the unsleeping observation of the Divinity, we cannot shut our eyes to the conclusion, that, *every desire of the human mind, is a prayer uttered to God and registered in heaven.*

II. The next fact of sovereign importance in this connection is, that *our prayers are granted.* Upon the account I have given of prayer, this ulterior fact is a faithful consequence. What then! If I pray that fire shall fall from heaven to consume mine enemies, will the lightning come down? If I pray that the wealth of India may be piled in my coffers, shall I straightway become rich? If I covet my neighbor's beauty, or wit, or honorable celebrity—will these desirable advantages be at once transferred from being the sources of his happiness, to become the sources of mine? It is plain there is a sense in which this is not true. But it is equally undeniable that in the sense in which I have explained the nature of prayer, and which seems the only proper sense, the position is universally true. For those are not prayers, which begin with the ordinary appellatives of the Deity and end with his son's name, and a ceremonial word—those are not prayers, if they utter no one wish of our hearts, no one real and earnest affection, but are formal repetitions of sentiments taken at second hand, in words the supple memory has learned of fashion; O my friends, these are not prayers, but mockeries of prayers. But the true prayers are the daily, the hourly, momentary desires, that come without impediment, without fear, into the soul, and bear testimony at each instant to its shifting character. And these prayers are granted.

For is it not clear that what we strongly and earnestly desire we shall make every effort to obtain; and has not God so furnished us with powers of body and of mind that we can acquire whatsoever we seriously and unceasingly strive after?

For it is the very root and rudiment of the relation of man to this world, that we are in a condition of wants which have their appropriate gratifications *within our reach;* and that we have faculties which can bring us to our ends; that we are full of capacities that are near neighbors to their objects, and our free agency consists in this, that we are able to reach those sources of gratification, on which our election falls. And if this be so, will not he who thinks lightly of all other things in comparison with riches; who thinks little of the poor man's virtue, or the slave's misery as they cross his path in life, because his observant eye is fixed on the rich man's manners and is searching in the lines of his countenance, with a sort of covetousness, the tokens of a pleased contemplation of the goods he has in store, and the consideration that, on this account, is conceded to him in society; will not such a one, if his thoughts daily point towards this single hope, if no exertion is grateful to him which has not this for its aim; if the bread is bitter to him that removes his riches one day farther from his hand, and the friends barren of comfort to him that are not aiding to this dishonorable ambition; will not such a one arrive at the goal, such as it is, of his expectation and find, sooner or later, a way to the heaven where he has garnered up his heart? Assuredly he will.

And will not the votary of other lusts, the lover of animal delight, who is profuse of the joys of sense, who loveth meats and drinks, soft raiment and the wine when it moveth itself aright, and giveth its color in the cup; or the more offensive libertine who has no relish left for any sweet in moral life, but only waits opportunity to surrender himself over to the last damning debauchery; will not these petitioners who have knocked so loudly at heaven's doors, receive what they have so importunately desired? Assuredly they will. There is a commission to nature, there is a charge to the elements made out in the name of the Author of events, whereby they shall help the purposes of man, a pre-existent harmony between thoughts and things whereby prayers shall become effects, and these warm imaginations settle down into events.

And if there be, in this scene of things, any spirit of a different complexion, who has felt, in the recesses of his soul, "how awful goodness is, and virtue in her own shape how lovely," who has admired the excellence of others, and set himself by precepts of the wise, and by imitation, which, a wise man said, is "a globe of precepts," to assimilate himself to the model in the Universe, beneath God, level with his venerated idea of virtue; who looks with scorn at the cheap admiration of crowds, and loves the applause of good men, but values more his own; and has so far outstripped humanity, that he can appreciate the love of the Supreme; if he aspire to do signal service to mankind, by the rich gift of a good example, and by unceasing and sober efforts to instruct and benefit men; will this man wholly fail, and waste his requests on the wind? Assuredly he will not. His prayers, in a certain sense, are like the will of the Supreme Being:

> His word leaps forth to its effect at once,
> He calls for things that are not, and they come.

His prayers are granted; all prayers are granted. Unceasing endeavors always attend true prayers, and, by the law of the Universe, unceasing endeavors do not fail of their end.

Let me not be misunderstood as thinking lightly of the positive duty of stated seasons of prayer. That solemn service of man to his maker is a duty of too high authority and too manifest importance to excuse any indifference to its claims. It is because that privilege is abused, because men in making prayers forget the purpose of prayer, forget that praying is to make them leave off sinning, that I urge it in its larger extent when it enters into daily life.

I have attempted to establish two simple positions, that, we are always praying, and that it is the order of Providence in the world, that our prayers should be granted. If exceptions can be quoted to me out of the book of common life, to the universality of either of these doctrines, I shall admit them in their full force, nor shall I now detain you by any inquiry into the abstract metaphysical nature of that happiness human beings are permitted to derive from what are called possessions, and how far it belongs to the imagination. I shall content myself, at present, with having stated the general doctrine and with adverting to its value as a practical principle.

And certainly, my friends, it is not a small thing that we have learned. If we have distinctly apprehended the fact which I have attempted to set in its true light, it cannot fail to elevate very much our conception of our relations and our duties. Weep no more for human frailty, weep no more, for what there may be of sorrow in the past or of despondency in the present hour. Spend no more unavailing regrets for the goods of which God in his Providence has deprived you. Cast away this sickly despair that eats into the soul debarred from high events and noble gratification. Beware of easy assent to false opinion, to low employment, to small vices, out of a reptile reverence to men of consideration in society. Beware (if it teach nothing else let it teach this), beware of indolence, the suicide of the soul, that lets the immortal faculties, each in their orbit of light, wax dim and feeble, and star by star expire. These considerations let our doctrine enforce. Weep not for man's frailty—for if the might of Omnipotence has made the elements obedient to the fervency of his daily prayers, he is no puny sufferer tottering, ill at ease, in the Universe, but a being of giant energies, architect of his fortunes, master of his eternity. Weep not for the past; for this is duration over which the secret virtue of prayer is powerless, over which the Omnipotence of God is powerless; send no voice of unprofitable wailing back into the depths of time; for prayer can reverse in the future the events of the past. Weep not for your wasted possessions, for the immeasurable future is before you and the wealth of the Universe invites your industry. Nor despair that your present daily lot is lowly, nor succumb to the shallow understanding or ill example of men whose worldly lot is higher. Be not deceived; for what is the Past? It is nothing worth. Its value, except as means of wisdom, is, in the nature of things actually nothing. And what is the imposing present? what are the great men and great things that surround you? All that they can do for you is dust, and less than dust to what you can do for yourself. They are like you stretching forward to an infinite hope, the citizens in trust of a future world. They think little of the present; though they seem satisfied, they are not satisfied but repine and endeavor after greater good. They, like you, are born to live when the sun has gone down in darkness and the moon is turned to blood.

My friends, in the remarks that have just been made I have already in part anticipated the third great branch of our subject, which is that *our prayers are written in Heaven.*

III. The great moral doctrines we have attempted to teach would be of limited worth if there were no farther consideration in this series of thought. You are pleased with the acquisition of property; you pray without ceasing to become rich. You lay no tax of conscience on the means. You desire to become rich by dint of virtue or of vice; of force or of fraud. And in virtue of the order of things that prevails in the world, as I have stated, you come to your ends. Is this all? Is the design of Providence complete? Is there no conclusion to this train of events, thus far conducted?

The wicked has flourished up to his hope. He has ground the faces of the poor. He has the tears of the widow and the curse of the fatherless but they lie light on his habitation; for he has built his house where these can-

not come, in the midst of his broad lands, on a pleasant countryside, sheltered by deep ornamental woods, and the voices of the harp and the viol tin-
kle in his saloons; the gay and the grave, the rich and the fair swarm to him
in crowds and though they salute him and smile often upon him they do not
utter one syllable of reproach nor repeat one imprecation of the poor. But
far away, too far to be any impediment to his employment, the wretches he
has cruelly stripped of their last decent comforts, and the well-saved means
with which sinking poverty yet strives to bear up, and make a respectable
appearance in society—are now, in small unaccommodated tenements, eating a morsel of bread, and uttering in unvisited, unremembered solitude,
the name of the oppressor. And have we seen all, my friends, and is poor
struggling worth to be rewarded only with worth, and be poor and vile beside, and is Vice to go triumphing on to the grave? Aye; to the grave. Hitherto, shalt thou go, and no farther, and here shall thy proud waves be staid.
My friends, there is another world. After death there is life. After death in
another state, revives your capacity of pleasure and of pain, the evil memory of evil actions, revives yourself, the man within the breast, the gratified
petitioner in the exact condition to which his fulfilled desires have, by the
inevitable force of things, contracted or expanded his character. There is another world; a world of remuneration; a world to which you and I are going
and which it deeply behooves us to survey and scrutinize as faithfully as we
can, as it lies before us, "though shadows, clouds, and darkness rest upon it."
It is plain that *as* we die in this world, we shall be born into that. It is plain,
that, it is, if it be anything, a world of spirits; that body, and the pleasures
and pains appertaining to body can have no exercise, no mansion there; that
it can be the appropriate home only of high thought and noble virtue. Hence
it must happen, that, if a soul can have access to that ethereal society, fleshed
over with bodily appetites, in which no love has grown up of thought and
moral beauty, and no sympathy and worship of virtue, but in their place
gnawing lusts have coiled themselves with a serpent's trail into the place of
every noble affection that God set up in the recesses of the soul when he
balanced the parts and modulated the harmony of the whole. And these
pampered appetites that grew in the soil of this world, find no aliment for
them in heaven, no gaudy vanities of dress, no riotous excitement of songs
and dances, no filthy gluttony of meats and drinks, no unclean enjoyments,
finding none of all this, it must happen, that these appetites will turn upon

their master, in the shape of direst tormentors; and if the economy of the universe provide no natural issue, whereby these mortal impurities can be purged with fire out of the texture of the soul, they must continue from hour to hour, from age to age, to arm the principles of his nature against the happiness of man.

Of this mysterious eternity, about to open upon us, of the nature of its employments and our relation to it, we know little. But of one thing be certain, that if the analogies of time can teach aught of eternity, if the moral laws taking place in this world, have relation to those of the next, and even the forecasting sagacity of the Pagan philosopher [Plato] taught him that the Laws below were sisters of the Laws above—then the riches of the future are dealt out on a system of compensations. That great class of human beings who in every age turned aside from temptation to pursue the bent of moral nature shall now have *their* interests consulted. They have cast their bread on the waters (for the choice lay often between virtue and their bread), trusting that after many days a solemn retribution of good should be rendered to them in the face of the world. Insult and sorrow, rags and beggary they have borne; they have kept the faith though they dwelled in the dust, and now, the pledge of God that supported them in the trial must be redeemed, and shall be, to the wonder of themselves, through the furthest periods of their undying existence.

Their joy and triumph is that revelation of the gospel which is most emphatically enforced by images borrowed from whatever was most grand and splendid in the imaginations of men; but crowns and thrones of judgment, and purple robes are but poor shadows of that moral magnificence, with which in the company of souls disembodied, Virtue asserts its majesty, and becomes the home and fountain of unlimited happiness.

Nothing remains but the obligation there is on each of us to make what use we can of this momentous doctrine. Is it to another condition than yours, to some removed mode of life, to the vices of some other class of society that this preaching, with strict propriety, belongs? No, my friends, if you are of the great household of God; if you are distinguishers of good and evil; if you believe in your own eternity; if you are tempted by what you feel to be evil attractions; if you are mortal, it belongs to you. If you have ever felt a desire for what Conscience, God's vicegerent, enthroned within you, condemned; if impelled by that desire, and willfully deaf to that condemnation, you swerved towards the gratification, and obtained the object, and stifled the monitor—then it is you, and not another; then you have uttered these unseemly prayers; the prayer is granted and is written in heaven; and at that moment, though men are not privy to all the passages of your life, and will salute you respectfully, and though it may be your own violated memory has ceased to treasure heedfully the number of your offenses—yet every individual transgression has stamped its impress on your character, and moral beings in all the wide tracts of God's dominion and God over all fasten their undeceived eyes on this spectacle of moral ruin. To you therefore it belongs, to everyone who now hears me, to look anxiously to his ways; to look less at his outward demeanor, his general plausible action, but *to cleanse his thoughts*. The heart is pure or impure, and out of it, are the issues of life and of DEATH.

Henry Ward Beecher

1813–1887

When a group of Congregationalists opened Plymouth Church of the Pilgrims in the leafy "borough of churches," in Brooklyn Heights in 1847, they chose a great speaker with a national platform of the day to conduct their services. Henry Ward Beecher was the brother of Harriet Beecher Stowe, author of *Uncle Tom's Cabin,* a spellbinding expositor of the political and social issues of the day, fiercely opposed to slavery, and an advocate of women's suffrage and free trade. The interior of the church, where Beecher conducted a famous mock slave auction in 1856 to stun and move his congregation to frenzied sympathy for the abolitionist cause, still houses a theatrical interior within its brick meetinghouse facade. A silver plaque designates the place where Abraham Lincoln once sat; church archives and newspapers record the thrill of Beecher's Sunday sermons.

Special ferries, known as "Beecher's boats," took the citizens of New York, before the building of the Brooklyn Bridge, across the East River to hear him appeal to his audience to consider Jesus Christ in "His personal relations to individual men."

Beecher's very first sermon at Plymouth Church outlined his agenda for the pulpit: he believed that a minister should deal with topics of trade, morals, and politics. (During a period of violence in the Kansas Territory over slavery and freedom, Beecher raised so much money and weaponry for "Bloody Kansas" that Plymouth Church was known as "Church of the Holy Rifles," and the rifles themselves as "Beecher's Bibles.") The intensity of his emotional appeal on the topical themes he preached on while pacing around his elevated pulpit was shadowed by the public scandal of his personal life. The yellow press of the 1880s, covering Beecher's trial for adultery with a parishioner's wife, made sensational news of his steady denial of guilt. The elders of the Congregational Church stood by the minister, maintaining him in his pulpit until his death.

A stenographer recorded Beecher's peripatetic sermons, many delivered on a trip to England where he promoted the Union cause during the Civil War. Most of his preachings, so highly praised during his lifetime that he was frequently compared to St. Paul on the Areopagus in Athens, denounce evil and evildoing; in his sermon on Ezekiel's vision we have a contemporary sense of Beecher's own inwardness and self-reproach, of a view of God and man which transcended the mere rhetoric for which he is most celebrated.

❦

Spared!

I was left.

—EZEKIEL 9:8

The vision of Ezekiel, which is recorded in the previous chapter, brought to light the abominations of the house of Judah. The vision which follows in this chapter shows the terrible retribution that the Lord God brought upon the guilty nation, beginning at Jerusalem.

He beheld the slaughtermen come forth with their weapons, he marked them being the destroying work at the gate of the Temple, he saw them proceed through the main streets, and not omit a single lane; they slew utterly all those who were not marked with the mark of the writer's inkhorn on their brow. He stood alone—that Prophet of the Lord—himself spared in the midst of universal carnage; and as the carcasses fell at his feet, and the bodies stained with gore lay all around him, he said, "I was left." He stood alive amongst the dead, because he was found faithful among the faithless; he survived in the midst of universal destruction, because he had served his God in the midst of universal depravity.

We shall now take the sentence apart altogether from Ezekiel's vision, and appropriate it to ourselves, and I think when we read it over and repeat it, "I was left," it very naturally invites us to take a *retrospect* of the past, very readily also it suggests a *prospect* of the future, and, I think, it permits also a terrible *contrast* in reserve for the impenitent.

1. First of all, then, my brethren, we have here a pathetic reflection, which seems to invite us to take a solemn retrospect—"I was left." You remember, many of you, times of sickness, when cholera was in your streets. You may forget that season of pestilence, but I never can; when the duties of my pastorate called me continually to walk among your terror-stricken households, and to see the dying and the dead. Impressed upon my young heart must ever remain some of those sad scenes I witnessed when I first came to this metropolis, and was rather employed at that time to bury the dead than to bless the living. Some of you have passed through not only one season of cholera but many, and you have been present, too, perhaps, in climates where fever has prostrated its hundreds, and where the plague and other dire diseases have emptied out their quivers, and every arrow has found its mark in the heart of some one of your companions. Yet you have been left. You walked among the graves, but you did not stumble into them. Fierce and fatal maladies lurked in your path, but they were not allowed to devour you. The bullets of death whistled by your ears, and yet you stood alive, for his bullet had no billet for your heart. You can look back, some of you, through fifty, sixty, seventy years. Your bald and gray heads tell the story that you are no more raw recruits in the warfare of life. You have become veterans, if not invalids, in the army. You are ready to retire, to put off your armor, and give place to others. Look back, brethren, I say, you have

come into the sere and yellow leaf; remember the many seasons in which you have seen death hailing multitudes about you; and think—"I was left." And we, too, who are younger, in whose veins our blood still leaps in vigor, can remember times of peril, when thousands fell about us, yet we can say in God's house with great emphasis, "I was left"—preserved, great God, when many others perished; sustained, standing on the rock of life when the waves of death dashed about me, the spray fell heavy upon me, and my body was saturated with disease and pain, yet am I still alive—permitted still to mingle with the busy tribes of men.

Now, then, what does such a retrospect as this suggest? Ought we not each one of us to ask the question, What was I spared for? Why was I left? Many of you were at that time, and some of you even now are dead in trespasses and sins. You were not spared because of your faithfulness, for you brought forth nothing but the grapes of Gomorrah. Certainly God did not stay his sword because of anything good in you. A multitude of clamorous evils in your disposition if not in your conduct might well have demanded your summary execution. You were spared. Let me ask you why? Was it that mercy might yet visit you—that grace might yet renew your soul? Have you found it so? Has sovereign grace overcome you, broken down your prejudices, thawed your icy heart, broken your stony will in pieces? Say, sinner, in looking back upon the times when you have been left, were you spared in order that you might be saved with a great salvation? And if you cannot say "Yes" to that question, let me ask you whether it may not be so yet? Soul, why has God spared you so long, while you are yet his enemy, a stranger to him, and far off from him by wicked works? Or, on the contrary, has he spared you—I tremble at the bare mention of the possibility—has he prolonged your days, to develop your propensities, that you may grow riper for damnation—that you may fill up your measure of crying iniquity, and then go down to the pit a sinner seared and dry, like wood that is ready for the fire? Can it be so? Shall these spared moments be spoiled by misdemeanors, or shall they be given up to repentance, and to prayer? Will you now, ere the last of your suns shall set in everlasting darkness, will you now look unto him? If so, you will have reason to bless God through all eternity that you were left, because you were left that you might yet seek and might yet find him who is the Savior of sinners.

Do I speak to many of you who are Christians—and you, too, have been left? When better saints than you were snatched away from earthly ties and creature kindred—when brighter stars than you were enclouded in night, were you permitted still to shine with your poor flickering ray? Why was it, great God? Why am I now left? Let me ask myself that question. In sparing me so long, my Lord, has thou not something more for me to do? Is there not some purpose as yet unconceived in my soul which thou wilt yet suggest to me, and to carry out which thou wilt yet give me grace and strength, and spare me again a little while? Am I yet immortal, or shielded at least from every arrow of death, because my work is incomplete? Is the tale of my years prolonged because the full tale of the bricks hath not been made up? Then show me what thou wouldst have me do? Since thus I have been left, help me to feel myself a specially consecrated man, left for a purpose, reserved for some end, else I had been worms' meat years ago, and my body had crumbled back to its mother earth. Christian, I say, always be asking yourself this question; but especially be asking it when you are preserved in times of more than ordinary sickness and mortality. If I am left, why am I left? Why am I not taken home to heaven? Why do I not enter into my rest? Great God and Master, show me what thou wouldst have me do, and give me grace and strength to do it.

Let us change the retrospect for a moment, and look upon the sparing mercy of God in another light. "I was left." Some of you now present, whose history I well know, can say, "I was left"; and say it with peculiar emphasis. You were born of ungodly parents; the earliest words you can recollect were base and blasphemous, too bad to repeat. You can remember how the first breath your infant lungs received was tainted air—the air of vice, of sin, and iniquity. You grew up, you and your brothers and your sisters, side by side; you filled the home with sin, you went on together in your youthful crimes, and encouraged each other in evil habits. Thus you grew up to manhood, and then you were banded together in ties of obliquity as well as in ties of consanguinity. You added to your number; you took in fresh associates. As your family circle increased, so did the flagrancy of your conduct. You all conspired to break the Sabbath; you devised the same scheme, and perpetrated the same improprieties. Perhaps you can recollect the time when Sunday invitations used always to be sent, a sneer at godliness was couched in the invitations. You recollect how one and another of your old comrades died; you followed them to their graves and your merriment was checked a little while, but it soon broke out again. Then a sister died, steeped to the mouth in infidelity; after that a brother was taken; he had no hope in his death; all was darkness and despair before him. And so, sinner, thou has outlived all thy comrades. If thou are inclined to go to hell, thou must go there along a beaten track: a path which, as thou lookest back upon the way thou has trodden, is stained with blood; for thou canst remember how all that have been before thee have gone to the long home in dismal gloom, without a glimpse or ray of joy. And now thou are left, sinner; and, blessed by God, it may be you can say, "Yes, and I am not only left, but I am here in the house of prayer; and if I know my own heart, there is nothing I should hate so much as to live my old life over again. Here I am, and I never believed I should ever be here. I look back with mournfulness indeed upon those who have departed; but though mourning them, I express my gratitude to God that I am not in torments—not in hell—but still here; yea, not only here, but having a hope that I shall one day see the face of Christ, and stand amidst blazing worlds robed in his righteousness and preserved by his love." You have been left, then, and what ought you to say? Ought you to boast? Oh no; be doubly humble. Should you take the honor to yourself? No; put the crown upon the head of free, rich, undeserved grace. And what should you do above all other men? Why, you should be doubly pledged to serve Christ. As you have served the devil through thick and thin, until you came to serve him alone, and your company had all departed, so by divine grace may you be pledged to Christ—to follow him, though all the world should despise him, and to hold on to the end, until, if every professor should be an apostate, it might yet be said of you at the last, "He was left; he stood alone in sin while his comrades died; and then he stood alone in Christ when his companions deserted him." Thus of you it should ever be said, "He was left."

This suggests also one more form of the same retrospect. What a special providence has watched over some of us, and guarded our feeble frames! There are some of you, in particular, who have been left to such an age that as you look back upon your youthful days you revoke far more of kinsfolk in the tomb than remain in the world, more under the earth than above it. In your dreams you are the associates of the dead. Still you are left. Preserved amidst a thousand dangers of infancy, then kept in youth, steered safely over the shoals and quicksands of an immature age, and over the rocks and reefs of manhood, you have been brought past the ordinary period of mortal life, and yet you are still here. Seventy years exposed to perpetual death, and yet preserved till you have come almost, perhaps, to your fourscore years. You have been left, my dear brother, and why are you left? Why is it that brothers and sisters are all gone? Why is it that your old school-companions have gradually thinned? You cannot recollect one, now alive, who was your companion in youth. How is that now, you, who have lived in a certain quarter so long, see new names there on all the shop doors, new faces in the streets, and everything new to what you once saw in your young days? Why are you spared? Are you an unconverted man? are you an unconverted woman? To what end are you spared? Is it that you may at the eleventh hour be saved?—God grant it may be so—or art thou spared till thou shalt have sinned thyself into the lowest depths of hell that thou mayest go there the most aggravated sinner because of oft-repeated warnings as often neglected—art thou spared for this, or is it that thou mayest be saved? But art thou a Christian? Then is it not hard for thee to answer the question, Why art thou spared? I do not believe there is an old woman on earth, living in the most obscure cot in England, and sitting this very night in the dark garret, with her candle gone out, without means to buy another—I do not believe that old woman would be kept out of heaven five minutes unless God had something for her to do on earth; and I do not think that yon gray-headed man now would be preserved here unless there was somewhat for him to do. Tell it out, tell it out, thou aged man; tell the story of that preserving grace which has kept thee up till now. Tell to thy children and to thy children's children what a God he is whom thou hast trusted. Stand up as a hoary patriarch and tell how he delivered thee in six troubles, and in seven suffered no evil to touch thee, and bear to coming generations thy faithful witness that his word is true, and that his promise cannot fail. Lean on thy staff, and say ere thou diest in the midst of thy family, "Not one good thing hath failed of all that the Lord God hath promised." Let thy ripe days bring forth a mellow testimony to his love; and as thou hast more and more advanced in years, so be thou more and more advanced in knowledge and in confirmed assurance of the immutability of his counsel, the truthfulness of his oath, the preciousness of his blood, and the sureness of the salvation of all those who put their trust in him. Then shall we know that thou art spared for a high and noble purpose indeed. Thou shalt say it with tears of gratitude, and we will listen with smiles of joy—"I was left."

2. I must rather suggest these retrospects than follow them up, though, did time permit, we might well enlarge abundantly, and therefore I must hurry on to invite you to a *prospect*. "And I was left." You and I shall soon pass out of this world into another. This life is, as it were, but the ferry boat; we are being carried across, and we shall soon come to the true shore, the real *terra firma,* for here there is nothing that is substantial. When we shall come into the next world we have to expect by and by a resurrection—a resurrection both of the just and of the unjust; and in that solemn day we are to expect that all that dwell upon the face of the earth shall be gathered together in one place. And he shall come, who came once to suffer, "he shall come to judge the world in righteousness, and the people in equity." He who came as an infant shall come as the Infinite. He who lay wrapped in swaddling bands shall come girt about the paps with a golden girdle, with a rainbow wreath, and robes of storm. There shall we all stand a vast innumerable company; earth shall be crowned from her valley's deepest base to the mountain's summit, and the sea's waves shall become the solid standing-place of men and women who have slept beneath its torrents. Then shall every eye be fixed on him, and every ear shall be open to him, and every heart shall watch with solemn awe and dread suspense for the transactions of that greatest of all days, that day of days, that sealing up of the ages, that completing of the dispensation. In solemn pomp the Savior comes, and his angels with him. You hear his voice as he cries, "Gather together the tares in bundles to burn them." Behold the reapers, how they come with wings of fire! see how they grasp their sharp sickles which have long been grinding upon the mill-stone of God's long-suffering, but have become sharpened at the last. Do you see them as they approach? And there they are mowing down a nation with their sickles. The vile idolaters have just now fallen, and yonder a family of blasphemers has been crushed beneath the feet of the reapers. See there a bundle of drunkards being carried away upon the reapers' shoulders to the great blazing fire. See again in another place the whoremonger, the adulterer, the unchaste, and such like, tied up in vast bundles—bundles the withes of which shall never be rent—and see them cast into the fire, and see how they blaze in the unutterable torments of that pit: and shall I be left? Great God, shall I stand there wrapped in his righteousness alone, the righteousness of him who sits my Judge erect upon the judgment seat? Shall I, when the

wicked shall cry, "Rocks hide us, mountains on us fall," shall this eye look up, shall this face dare to turn itself to the face of him that sits upon the throne? Shall I stand calm and unmoved amidst universal terror and dismay? Shall I be numbered with the godly company, who, clothed with the white linen which is the righteousness of the saints, shall await the shock, shall see the wicked hurled to destruction, and feel and know themselves secure? Shall it be so, or shall I be bound up in a bundle to burn, and swept away forever by the breath of God's nostrils, like the chaff driven before the wind? It must be one or the other; which shall it be? Can I answer that question? Can I tell? I can tell it—tell it now—for I have in this very chapter that which teaches me how to judge myself. They who are preserved have the mark in their foreheads, and they have a character as well as a mark, and their character is, that they sigh and cry for all the abominations of the wicked. Then, if I hate sin, and if I sigh because others love it—if I cry because I myself through infirmity fall into it—if the sin of myself and the sin of others is a constant source of grief and vexation of spirit to me, then have I that mark and evidence of those who shall neither sigh nor cry in the world to come, for sorrow and sighing shall flee away. Have I the blood mark on my brow today? Say, my soul, hast thou put thy trust in Jesus Christ alone, and as the fruit of the faith, has thy faith learned how to love; not only him that saveth thee; but others too, who as yet are unsaved? And do I sigh and cry within while I bear the blood mark without? Come, brother, sister, answer this for thyself, I charge thee; I charge thee do so, by the tottering earth, and by the ruined pillars of heaven, that shall surely shake. I pray thee by the cherubim and seraphim that shall be before the throne of the great Judge; by the blazing lightnings, that shall then kindle the thick darkness, and make the sun amazed and turn the moon into blood; by him whose tongue is like a flame—like a sword of fire; by him who shall judge thee, and try thee, and read thy heart and declare thy ways, and divide unto thee thine eternal portion. I conjure thee, by the certainties of death, by the sureness of judgment, by the glories of heaven, by the solemnities of hell—I beseech, implore, command, entreat thee— ask thyself now, "Shall I be left?" Do I believe in Christ? Have I been born again? Have I a new heart and a right spirit? Or, am I still what I always was—God's enemy, Christ's despiser, cursed by the law, cast out from the gospel, without God and without hope, a stranger to the commonwealth of Israel? Oh, I cannot speak to thee as earnestly as I would to God I could. I want to thrust this question into your very loins, and stir up your heart's deepest thoughts with it. Sinner, what will become of thee when God shall winnow the chaff from the wheat, what will be thy portion? Thou that standest in the aisle yonder, what will by thy portion, thou who are crowded there what will be thy portion, when he shall come, and nothing shall escape his eye? Say, shalt thou hear him? Say, and shall thy heart-strings crack whilst he utters the thundering sound, "Depart, ye cursed"; or shall it by thy happy lot—thy soul transported all the while with bliss unutterable—to hear him say, "Come ye blessed of my Father, inherit the kingdom prepared for you from the foundations of the world." Our text invites a prospect. I pray you take it, and look across the narrow stream of death, and say, "Shall I be left?"

> When thou, my righteous Judge, shalt come,
> To fetch thy ransom'd people home,
>   Shall I among them stand?
> Shall such a worthless worm as I,
> Who sometimes am afraid to die,
>   Be found at thy right hand?

3. But now we come to a terrible *contrast,* which I think is permitted in the text—"I was left." Then there will be some who will not be left in the sense we have been speaking of, and yet who will be left after another and more dreadful manner. They will be left by mercy, forsaken by hope, given up by friends, and become a prey to the implacable fury, to the sudden, infinite, and unmitigated severity and justice of an angry God. But they will not be left or exempted from judgment, for the sword shall find them out, the vials of Jehovah shall reach even to their hearts. And the flame, the pile whereof is wood, and much smoke shall suddenly devour them, and that without remedy. Sinner, thou shalt be left. I say, thou shalt be left of all those fond joys that thou huggest now—left of that pride which now steels thy heart: thou wilt be low enough then. Thou wilt be left of that iron constitution which now seems to repel the dart of death. Thou shalt be left of those companions of thine that entice thee on to sin and harden thee in iniquity. Thou shalt be left then of that pleasing fancy of

thine, and of that merry wit which can make sport of Bible truths and mock at divine solemnities. Thou shalt be left then of all thy buoyant hopes, and of all thy imaginary delights. Thou shalt be left of that sweet angel, Hope, who never forsaketh any but those who are condemned to hell. Thou shalt be left of God's Spirit, who sometimes now pleads with thee. Thou shalt be left of Jesus Christ, whose gospel hath been so often preached in thine ear. Thou shalt be left of God the Father; he shall shut his eyes of pity against thee, his bowels of compassion shall no more yearn over thee; nor shall his heart regard thy cries. Thou shalt be left; but oh! again I tell thee, thou shalt not be left as one who hath escaped, for when the earth shall open to swallow up the wicked, it shall open at thy feet and swallow thee up. When the fiery thunderbolt shall pursue the spirit that falls into the pit that is bottomless, it shall pursue thee and reach thee and find thee. When God rendeth the wicked in pieces, and there shall be none to deliver, he shall rend thee in pieces, he shall be unto thee as a consuming fire, thy conscience shall be full of gall, thy heart shall be drunken with bitterness, thy teeth shall be broken even with gravel stones, thy hopes riven with his hot thunderbolts, and all thy joys withered and blasted by his breath. Oh! careless sinner, mad sinner, thou who art dashing thyself now downward to destruction, why wilt thou play the fool at this rate? There are cheaper ways of making sport for thyself than this. Dash thy head against the wall; go scrabble there, and, like David, let thy spittle fall upon thy beard, but let not thy sin fall upon thy conscience, and let not thy despite of Christ be like a millstone hanged about thy neck, with which thou shalt be cast into the sea forever. Be wise, I pray thee. Oh, Lord, make the sinner wise; hush his madness for awhile; let him be sober and hear the voice of reason; let him be still and hear the voice of conscience; let him be obedient and hear the voice of Scripture. "Thus saith the Lord, because I will do this, consider thy ways." "Prepare to meet thy God." "Oh, Israel, set thine house in order, for thou shalt die and not live." "Believe on the Lord Jesus Christ and thou shalt be saved." I do feel I have a message for someone tonight. Though there may be some who think the sermon not appropriate to a congregation where there is so large proportion of converted men and women, yet what a large portion of ungodly ones there are here too! I know that you come here, many of you, to hear some funny tale, or to catch at some strange, extravagant speech of one whom you repute to be an eccentric man. Ah, well, he is eccentric, and hopes to be so till he dies; but it is simply eccentric in being in earnest, and wanting to win souls. Oh, poor sinners, there is no odd tale I would not tell if I thought it would be blessed to you. There is no grotesque language which I would not use, however it might be thrown back at me again, if I thought it might but be serviceable to you. I set not my account to be thought a fine speaker; they that use fine language may dwell in the king's palaces. I speak to you as one who knows he is accountable to no man, but only to God; as one who shall have to render his account at the last great day. And I pray you now go not away to talk of this and that which you have remarked in my language. Think of this one thing, "Shall I be left? Shall I be saved? Shall I be caught up and dwell with Christ in heaven? or shall I be cast down to hell forever and ever?" Turn over these things. Think seriously of them. Hear that voice which says, "Him that cometh to me I will in no wise cast out." Give heed to the voice which expostulates—"Come now, let us reason together, saith the Lord: though your sins be as scarlet, they shall be as white as snow; though they be red like crimson, they shall be as wool." How else shall you find shelter when the tempest of divine wrath rages? How else shall you stand in the lot of the righteous at the end of the days?

Gerard Manley Hopkins

1844–1889

In the Victorian poet-priest Gerard Manley Hopkins we encounter a figure of remarkable contradictions: physical frailty and iron will; aesthete and humble servant of God; gorgeous, innovative, and, during his lifetime largely unpublished, poet and obscure cleric.

He was born, the eldest of eight, to middle-class Anglican parents.

When he went up to Oxford he was all at once exposed to an extraordinary multiplicity of influences, including Matthew Arnold, Walter Pater, Benjamin Jowett, and, most importantly, John Henry Newman, famous convert from the Oxford Movement to Roman Catholicism. Eventually Hopkins, too, was received into the Catholic Church and indeed entered the Society of Jesus as a novice soon after. His subsequent dual career as priest, teaching classics, first, at the English public school Stonyhurst and then, for the rest of his short life, at University College, Dublin, gave him both much happiness and cause for melancholy.

Hopkins's long friendship with fellow poet Robert Bridges provided the posthumous occasion in 1918 for the latter to prepare an edition of the former's poems that burst upon the literary world with reverberations that continue to this day.

The same poet whose original concepts of "sprung rhythm" and "inscape" and whose poems such as "The Windhover" and "The Grandeur of God" have had such influence was also described by a contemporary as "not cut out physically to be an orator; he was small of stature and his voice tended to be shrill." He gave the sermon that follows early in his priestly life when briefly but happily assigned to Bedford Leigh, a "smoke-sodden little town" near the city of Manchester in northern England. In it, he focuses on three unique aspects of Jesus—his physical person, his mind, and his character. Moving through a beautiful series of insights into our understanding of the gospel descriptions, he ends with a rising litany of acclamations of praise for Christ.

Hopkins will always be better known for his poetry, but of his sermons, the consensus is that this is his best.

And Joseph and His Mother Marveled

For Sunday evening Nov. 23, 1879, at Bedford Leigh

Et erat ejus et mirantes super his quae dicebantur de illo.
("And Joseph and his mother marveled at those things which
were spoken of him.")

—LUKE 2:33 (TEXT TAKEN AT RANDOM)

St. Joseph though he often carried our Lord Jesus Christ in his arms
and the Blessed Virgin though she gave him birth and suckled him at her
breast, though they seldom either of them had the holy child out of their
sight and knew more of him far than all others, yet when they heard what
Holy Simeon a stranger had to say of him the Scripture says they wondered.
Not indeed that they were surprised and had thought to hear something different but that they gave their minds up to admiration and dwelt with rev-
erent wonder on all God's doings about the child their sacred charge.
Brethren, see what a thing it is to hear about our Lord Jesus Christ, to think
of him and dwell upon him; it did good to these two holiest people, the
Blessed Virgin and St. Joseph, even with him in the house of God thought
fit to give them lights by the mouth of strangers. It cannot but do good to
us, who have more need of holiness, who easily forget Christ, who have not
got him before our eyes to look at. And though we do have him before our
eyes, masked in the Sacred Host, at mass and Benediction and within our
lips receive him at communion, yet to hear of him and dwell on the thought
of him will do us good.

Our Lord Jesus Christ, my brethren, is our hero, a hero all the world
wants. You know how books of tales are written, that put one man before
the reader and shew him off handsome for the most part and brave and call
him My Hero or Our Hero. Often mothers make a hero of a son; girls of a
sweetheart and good wives of a husband. Soldiers make a hero of a great
general, a party of its leader, a nation of any great man that brings it glory,
whether king, warrior, statesman, thinker, poet, or whatever it shall be. But

Christ, he is the hero. He too is the hero of a book or books, of the divine
Gospels. He is a warrior and a conqueror; of whom it is written he went
forth conquering and to conquer. He is a king, Jesus of Nazareth king of the
Jews, though when he came to his own kingdom his own did not receive
him, and now, his people having cast him off, we Gentiles are his inheritance. He is a statesman, that drew up the New Testament in his blood and
founded the Roman Catholic Church that cannot fail. He is a thinker, that
taught us divine mysteries. He is an orator and poet, as in his eloquent
words and parables appears. He is all the world's hero, the desire of nations.
But besides he is the hero of single souls; his mother's hero, not out of
motherly foolish fondness but because he was, as the angel told her, great
and the son of the Most High and all that he did and said was done and said
about him she laid up in her heart. He is the true-love and the bridegroom
of men's souls: the virgins follow him whithersoever he goes; the martyrs
follow him through a sea of blood, through great tribulation; all his servants
take up their cross and follow him. And those even that do not follow him,
yet they look wistfully after him, own him a hero, and wish they dared answer to his call. Children as soon as they can understand ought to be told
about him, that they may make him the hero of their young hearts. But there
are Catholic parents that shamefully neglect their duty: the grown children
of Catholics are found that scarcely know or do not know his name. Will
such parents say they left instruction to the priest or the schoolmaster?
Why, if they sent them very early to the school they might make that excuse, but when they do not what will they say then? It is at the father's or
mother's mouth first the little one should learn. But the parents may be gossiping or drinking and the children have not heard of their lord and savior.
Those of you, my brethren, who are young and yet unmarried resolve that
when you marry, if God should bless you with children, this shall not be but
that you will have more pity, will have pity upon your own.

There met in Jesus Christ all things that can make man lovely and love-
able. In his body he was most beautiful. This is known first by the tradition
in the Church that it was so and by holy writers agreeing to suit those words
to him / Thou art beautiful in mold above the sons of men: we have even accounts of him written in early times. They tell us that he was moderately
tall, well built and tender in frame, his features straight and beautiful, his
hair inclining to auburn, parted in the midst, curling and clustering about

the ears and neck as the leaves of a filbert, so they speak, upon the nut. He wore also a forked beard and this as well as the locks upon his head were never touched by razor or shears; neither, his health being perfect, could a hair ever fall to the ground. The account I have been quoting (it is from memory, for I cannot now lay my hand upon it) we do not indeed for certain know to be correct, but it has been current in the Church and many generations have drawn our Lord accordingly either in their own minds or in his images. Another proof of his beauty may be drawn from the words *proficiebat sapientia et aetate et gratia apud Deum et homines* (Luke 2:52)/he went forward in wisdom and bodily frame and favor with God and men; that is/he pleased both God and men daily more and more by his growth of mind and body. But he could not have pleased by growth of body unless the body was strong, healthy, and beautiful that grew. But the best proof of all is this, that his body was the special work of the Holy Ghost. He was not born in nature's course, no man was his father; had he been born as others are he must have inherited some defect of figure or of constitution, from which no man born as fallen men are born is wholly free unless God interfere to keep him so. But his body was framed directly from heaven by the power of the Holy Ghost, of whom it would be unworthy to leave any the least botch or failing in his work. So the first Adam was molded by God himself and Eve built up by God too out of Adam's rib and they could not but be pieces, both, of faultless workmanship: the same then and much more must Christ have been. His constitution too was tempered perfectly, he had neither disease nor the seeds of any: weariness he felt when he was wearied, hunger when he fasted, thirst when he had long gone without drink, but to the touch of sickness he was a stranger. I leave it to you, brethren, then to picture him, in whom the fullness of the godhead dwelt bodily, in his bearing how majestic, how strong and yet how lovely and lissome in his limbs, in his look how earnest, grave but kind. In his Passion all this strength was spent, this lissomeness crippled, this beauty wrecked, this majesty beaten down. But now it is more than all restored, and for myself I make no secret I look forward with eager desire to seeing the matchless beauty of Christ's body in the heavenly light.

I come to his mind. He was the greatest genius that ever lived. You know what genius is, brethren—beauty and perfection in the mind. For perfection in the bodily frame distinguishes a man among other men his fellows: so may the mind be distinguished for its beauty above other minds and that is genius. Then when this genius is duly taught and trained, that is wisdom; for without training genius is imperfect and again wisdom is imperfect without genius. But Christ, we read, advanced in wisdom and in favor with God and men: now this wisdom, in which he excelled all men, had to be founded on an unrivaled genius. Christ then was the greatest genius that ever lived. You must not say, Christ needed no such thing as genius; his wisdom came from heaven, for he was God. To say so is to speak like the heretic Apollinaris, who said that Christ had indeed a human body but no soul, he needed no mind and soul, for his godhead, the Word of God, that stood for mind and soul in him. No, but Christ was perfect man and must have mind as well as body and that mind was, no question, of the rarest excellence and beauty; it was genius. As Christ lived and breathed and moved in a true and not a phantom human body and in that labored, suffered, was crucified, died, and was buried; as he merited by acts of his human will; so he reasoned and planned and invented by acts of his own human genius, genius made perfect by wisdom of its own, not the divine wisdom only.

A witness to his genius we have in those men who being sent to arrest him came back empty handed, spellbound by his eloquence, saying / Never man spoke like this man.

A better proof we have in his own words, his sermon on the mount, his parables, and all his sayings recorded in the Gospel. My brethren, we are so accustomed to them that they do not strike us as they do a stranger that hears them first, else we too should say / Never man etc. No stories or parables are like Christ's, so bright, so pithy, so touching; no proverbs or sayings are such jewelry: they stand off from other men's thoughts like stars, like lilies in the sun; nowhere in literature is there anything to match the Sermon on the Mount: if there is let men bring it forward. Time does not allow me to call your minds to proofs or instances. Besides Christ's sayings in the Gospels a dozen or so more have been kept by tradition and are to be found in the works of the Fathers and early writers and one even in the Scripture itself: It is more blessed etc. When these sayings are gathered together, though one cannot feel sure of every one, yet reading all in one view they make me say / These must be Christ's, never man etc. One is: Never rejoice but when you look upon your brother in love. Another is: My mystery is for me and for the children of my house.

And if you wish for another still greater proof of his genius and wisdom look at this Catholic Church that he founded, its ranks and constitution, its rites and sacraments.

Now in the third place, far higher than beauty of the body, higher than
genius and wisdom the beauty of the mind, comes the beauty of his character, his character as man. For the most part his very enemies, those that do
not believe in him, allow that a character so noble was never seen in human
mold. Plato the heathen, the greatest of the Greek philosophers, foretold of
him: he drew by his wisdom a picture of the just man in his justice crucified
and it was fulfilled in Christ. Poor was his station, laborious his life, bitter
his ending: through poverty, through labor, through crucifixion his majesty
of nature more shines. No heart as his was ever so tender, but tenderness
was not all: this heart so tender was as brave, it could be stern. He found
the thought of his Passion past bearing, yet he went through with it. He was
feared when he chose: he took a whip and singlehanded cleared the temple.
The thought of his gentleness towards children, towards the afflicted, towards sinners, is often dwelt on; that of his courage less. But for my part I
like to feel that I should have feared him. We hear also of his love, as for John
and Lazarus; and even love at first sight, as of the young man that had kept
all the commandments from his childhood. But he warned or rebuked his
best friends when need was, as Peter, Martha, and even his mother. For, as
St. John says, he was full both of grace and of truth.

But, brethren, from all that might be said of his character I single out
one point and beg you to notice that. He loved to praise, he loved to reward. He knew what was in man, he best knew men's faults and yet he was
the warmest in their praise. When he worked a miracle he would grace it
with / Thy faith hath saved thee, that it might almost seem the receiver's
work, not his. He said of Nathanael that he was an Israelite without guile;
he that searches hearts said this, and yet what praise that was to give! He
called the two sons of Zebedee Sons of Thunder, kind and stately and honorable name! We read of nothing thunderlike that they did except, what was
sinful, to wish fire down from heaven on some sinners, but they deserved
the name or he would not have given it, and he has given it them for all
time. Of John the Baptist he said that his greater was not born of women.
He said to Peter / Thou art Rock / and rewarded a moment's acknowledgment of him with the lasting headship of his Church. He defended Magdalen

and took means that the story of her generosity should be told forever. And though he bids *us* say we are unprofitable servants, yet he himself will say to each of us / Good and faithful servant, well done.

And this man whose picture I have tried to draw for you, brethren, is your God. He was your maker in time past; hereafter he will be your judge. Make him your hero now. Take some time to think of him; praise him in your hearts. You can over your work or on your road praise him, saying over and over again / Glory be to Christ's body; Glory to the body of the Word made flesh; Glory to the body suckled at the Blessed Virgin's breasts; Glory to Christ's body in its beauty; Glory to Christ's body in its weariness; Glory to Christ's body in its Passion, death and burial; Glory to Christ's body risen; Glory to Christ's body in the Blessed Sacrament; Glory to Christ's soul; Glory to his genius and wisdom; Glory to his unsearchable thoughts; Glory to his saving words; Glory to his sacred heart; Glory to its courage and manliness; Glory to its meekness and mercy; Glory to its every heartbeat, to its joys and sorrows, wishes, fears; Glory in all things to Jesus Christ God and man. If you try this when you can you will find your heart kindle and while you praise him he will praise you—a blessing etc.

John Henry Newman

1801–1890

The Oxford Movement in England of the 1830s was an intellectual and religious earthquake, restoring to the Anglican Church much of the richness of liturgy, ornament, and practice of the sacraments its leaders lost in the ferment of the Reformation. John Henry Newman's conversion to the Roman Catholic Church in the middle of the next decade was equally dramatic; by 1876 the convert was made a cardinal. Earlier, as a vicar in the Anglican Church of St. Mary the Virgin at Oxford, Newman's sermons

drew great attention; the shock of his conversion was paralleled by the opposition and controversy raised by Newman's famous *Apologia pro Vita Sua,*
written in answer to Charles Kingsley, who had denounced Newman as a
theologian who did not consider truth "a necessary virtue." As a spiritual autobiography, it impressed even writers like George Eliot, who sought truth-
telling in the form of moral fiction, but acknowledged the book had
"breathed much life" into her.

In addition to six volumes of sermons Newman published novels (now
forgotten), poetry (the hymn "Lead, Kindly Light" is far from forgotten),
lectures, essays, and the lives of saints.

His powers of argument are indisputable, and his attempt to reconcile
the Church of Rome with the Church of England is as vividly controversial
today as it was in the contentious deaneries of Victorian England. His mind
was one of great penetration and power, allied to a poetic sensibility capable of overly subtle refinements which sometimes obscured the genuine
candor of his convictions.

Newman in the pulpit was astonishing, and remains influential in both
the Anglican and the Roman Catholic churches. He read his sermons in a
voice which is described as having a "gentle and haunting sweetness." But
throughout his career he remained provocative, whether reminding his audience of new ways in which they could encounter the real deposit of truth
over superstition in the Christian faith, or serving the ecumenical purpose
which built a hundred-year bridge between Canterbury and Rome.

The Powers of Nature
(The Feast of St. Michael and All Angels)

Who maketh His Angels spirits, His ministers a flaming fire.

—PSALM 104:4

On today's Festival it well becomes us to direct our minds to the
thought of those Blessed Servants of God, who have never tasted of sin; who
are among us, though unseen, ever serving God joyfully on earth as well as

in heaven; who minister, through their Maker's condescending will, to the redeemed in Christ, the heirs of salvation.

There have been ages of the world, in which men have thought too much of Angels, and paid them excessive honor; honored them so perversely as to forget the supreme worship due to Almighty God. This is the sin of a dark age. But the sin of what is called an educated age, such as our own, is just the reverse: to account slightly of them, or not at all; to ascribe all we see around us, not to their agency, but to certain assumed laws of nature. This, I say, is likely to be our sin, in proportion as we are initiated into the learning of this world; and this is the danger of many (so-called) philosophical pursuits, now in fashion, and recommended zealously to the notice of large portions of the community, hitherto strangers to them, chemistry, geology, and the like; the danger, that is, of resting in things seen, and forgetting unseen things, and our ignorance about them.

I will attempt to say what I mean more at length. The text informs us that Almighty God makes His Angels spirits or winds, and His Ministers a flame of fire. Let us consider what is implied in this.

1. What a number of beautiful and wonderful objects does nature present on every side of us! and how little we know concerning them! In some indeed we see symptoms of intelligence, and we get to form some idea of what they are. For instance, about brute animals we know little, but still we see they have sense, and we understand that their bodily form which meets the eye is but the index, the outside token of something we do not see. Much more in the case of men: We see them move, speak, and act, and we know that all we see takes place in consequence of their will, because they have a spirit within them, though we do not see it. But why do rivers flow? Why does rain fall? Why does the sun warm us? And the wind, why does it blow? Here our natural reason is at fault; we know, I say, that it is the *spirit* in man and in beast that makes man and beast move, but reason tells us of no spirit abiding in what is commonly called the natural world, to make it perform its ordinary duties. Of course, it is *God's* will which *sustains* it all; so does God's will enable *us* to move also, yet this does not hinder, but, in one sense we may be truly said to move ourselves: but how do the wind and water, earth and fire, move? Now here Scripture interposes, and seems to tell us, that all this wonderful harmony is the work of Angels. Those events which we ascribe to chance as the weather, or to nature as the seasons, are

duties done to that God who maketh His Angels to be winds, and His Ministers a flame of fire. For example, it was an Angel which gave to the pool
at Bethesda its medicinal quality; and there is no reason why we should
doubt that other health-springs in this or other countries are made such by
a like unseen ministry. The fires on Mount Sinai, the thunders and lightnings, were the work of Angels; and in the Apocalypse we read of the Angels restraining the four winds. Works of vengeance are likewise attributed
to them. The fiery lava of the volcanoes, which (as it appears) was the cause
of Sodom and Gomorrah's ruin, was caused by the two Angels who rescued
Lot. The hosts of Sennacherib were destroyed by an Angel, by means (it is
supposed) of a suffocating wind. The pestilence in Israel when David numbered the people, was the work of an Angel. The earthquake at the resurrection was the work of an Angel. And in the Apocalypse the earth is smitten
in various ways by Angels of vengeance (John 5:4; Exod. 19:16–18; Gal.
3:19; Acts 7:53; Rev. 7:1; Gen. 19:13; 2 Kings 19:35; 2 Sam. 24:15–17;
Matt. 28:2; Rev. 8, 9, 16).

Thus, as far as the Scripture communications go, we learn that the
course of nature, which is so wonderful, so beautiful, and so fearful, is effected by the ministry of those unseen beings. Nature is not inanimate; its
daily toil is intelligent; its works are *duties*. Accordingly, the Psalmist says,
"The heavens declare the glory of God, and the firmament showeth His
handy-work." "O Lord, Thy word endureth forever in heaven. Thy truth also
remaineth from one generation to another; Thou hast laid the foundation of
the earth, and it abideth. They continue this day according to Thine ordinance for *all things serve thee*." (Ps. 19:1; 119:89–91.)

I do not pretend to say, that we are told in Scripture what matter is;
but I affirm, that as our souls move our bodies, be our bodies what they
may, so there are Spiritual Intelligences which move those wonderful and
vast portions of the natural world which seem to be inanimate; and as the
gestures, speech, and expressive countenances of our friends around us enable us to hold intercourse with them, so in the motions of universal nature,
in the interchange of day and night, summer and winter, wind and storm,
fulfilling His word, we are reminded of the blessed and dutiful Angels. Well
then, on this day's Festival, may we sing the hymn of those Three Holy Children whom Nebuchadnezzar cast into the fiery furnace. The Angels were
bid to change the nature of the flame, and make it harmless to them; and

they in turn called on all the creatures of God, on the Angels especially, to glorify Him. Though many hundreds of years have passed since that time, and the world now vainly thinks it knows more than it did, and that it has found the real causes of the things it sees, still may we say, with grateful and simple hearts, "O all ye works of the Lord, O ye Angels of the Lord, O ye sun and moon, stars of heaven, showers and dew, winds of God, light and darkness, mountains and hills, green things upon the earth, bless ye the Lord, praise Him, and magnify Him forever." Thus, whenever we look abroad, we are reminded of those most gracious and holy Beings, the servants of the Holiest, who deign to minister to the heirs of salvation. Every breath of air and ray of light and heat, every beautiful prospect, is, as it were, the skirts of their garments, the waving of the robes of those whose faces see God in heaven. And I put it to anyone, whether it is not as philosophical, and as full of intellectual enjoyment, to refer the movements of the natural world to them, as to attempt to explain them by certain theories of science; useful as these theories certainly are for particular purposes, and capable (in subordination to that higher view) of a religious application.

2. And thus I am led to another use of the doctrine under consideration. While it raises the mind, and gives it a matter of thought, it is also profitable as a humbling doctrine, as indeed I have already shown. Vain man would be wise, and he curiously examines the works of nature, as if they were lifeless and senseless; as if he alone had intelligence, and they were base inert matter, however curiously contrived at the first. So he goes on, tracing the order of things, seeking for Causes in that order, giving names to the wonders he meets with, and thinking he understands what he has given a name to. At length he forms a theory, and recommends it in writing, and calls himself a philosopher. Now all these theories of science, which I speak of, are useful, as classifying, and so assisting us to *recollect,* the works and ways of God and of His ministering Angels. And again, they are ever most useful, in enabling us to *apply* the course of His Providence, and the ordinances of His will, to the benefit of man. Thus we are enabled to enjoy God's gifts; and let us thank Him for the knowledge which enables us to do so, and honor those who are His instruments in communicating it. But if such a one proceeds to imagine that, because he knows something of this world's wonderful order, he therefore knows *how* things really go on, if he treats the miracles of nature (so to call them) as mere mechanical processes,

continuing their course by themselves—as works of man's contriving (a clock, for instance) are set in motion, and go on, as it were, of themselves—if in consequences he is, what may be called, irreverent in his conduct towards nature, thinking (if I may so speak) that it does not hear him, and see how he is bearing himself towards it; and if, moreover, he conceives that the Order of Nature, which he partially discerns, will stand in the place of the God who made it, and that all things continue and move on, not by His will and power, and the agency of the thousands and ten thousands of His unseen Servants, but by fixed laws, self-caused and self-sustained, what a poor weak worm and miserable sinner he becomes! Yet such, I fear, is the condition of many men nowadays who talk loudly, and appear to themselves and others to be oracles of science, and, as far as the detail of facts goes, do know much more about the operations of Nature than any of us.

Now let us consider what the real state of the case is. Supposing the inquirer I have been describing, when examining a flower, or a herb, or a pebble, or a ray of light, which he treats as something so beneath him in the scale of existence, suddenly discovered that he was in the presence of some powerful being who was hidden behind the visible things he was inspecting, who, though concealing his wise hand, was giving them their beauty, grace, and perfection, as being God's instrument for the purpose, nay whose robe and ornaments those wondrous objects were, which he was so eager to analyze, what would be his thoughts? Should we but accidentally show a rudeness of manner towards our fellow-man, tread on the hem of his garment, or brush roughly against him, are we not vexed, not as if we had hurt him, but from the fear we may have been disrespectful? David had watched the awful pestilence three days, doubtless not with curious eyes, but with indescribable terror and remorse; but when at length he "lifted up his eyes and saw the *Angel* of the Lord" (who caused the pestilence) "stand between the earth and the heaven, having a drawn sword in his hand stretched out over Jerusalem, *then* David and the elders, who were clothed in sackcloth, *fell* upon their faces." (1 Chron. 21:16.) The mysterious, irresistible pestilence became still more fearful when the cause was known; and what is true of the terrible, is true on the other hand of the pleasant and attractive operations of nature. When then we walk abroad, and "meditate in the field at eventide," how much has every herb and flower in it to surprise and overwhelm us! For even did we know as much about them as the wisest of men,

yet there are those around us, though unseen, to whom our greatest knowledge is as ignorance; and, when we converse on subjects of nature scientif-
ically, repeating the names of plants and earths, and describing their
properties, we should do so religiously, as in the hearing of the great Servants of God, with the sort of diffidence which we always feel when speaking before the learned and wise of our own mortal race, as poor beginners
in intellectual knowledge, as well as in moral attainments.

Now I can conceive persons saying all this is fanciful; but if it appears
so, it is only because we are not accustomed to such thoughts. Surely we are
not told in Scripture about the Angels for nothing, but for practical purposes; nor can I conceive a use of our knowledge more practical than to
make it connect the sight of the world with the thought of another. Nor one
more consolatory; for surely it is a great comfort to reflect that, wherever
we go, we have those about us, who are ministering to all the heirs of salvation, though we see them not. Nor one more easily to be understood and
felt by all men; for we know that at one time the doctrine of Angels was received even too readily. And if any one would argue hence against it as dangerous, let him recollect the great principle of our Church, that the abuse
of a thing does not supersede the use of it; and let him explain, if he can, St.
Paul's exhorting Timothy not only as "before God and Christ," but before
"the elect Angels" also. Hence, in the Communion Service, our Church
teaches us to join our praises with that of "Angels and Archangels, and all
the Company of heaven"; and the early Christians even hoped that they
waited on the Church's seasons of worship and glorified God with her. Nor
are these thoughts without their direct influence on our faith in God and His
Son; for the more we can enlarge our view of the next world, the better.
When we survey Almighty God surrounded by His Holy Angels, His thousand thousands of ministering Spirits, and ten thousand times ten thousand
standing before Him, the idea of His awful Majesty rises before us more
powerfully and impressively. We begin to see how little we are, how altogether mean and worthless in ourselves, and how high He is, and fearful.
The very lowest of His Angels is indefinitely above us in this our present
state; how high then must be the Lord of Angels! The very Seraphim hide
their faces before His glory, while they praise Him; how shamefaced then
should sinners be, when they come into His presence!

Lastly, it is a motive to our exertions in doing the will of God, to think

that, if we attain to heaven, we shall become the fellows of the blessed Angels. Indeed, what do we know of the courts of heaven, but as peopled by
them? and therefore doubtless they are revealed to us, that we may have
something to fix our thoughts on, when we look heavenwards. Heaven indeed is the palace of Almighty God, and of Him doubtless we must think in
the first place; and again of His Son our Savior, who died for us, and who is
manifested in the Gospels, in order that we may have something definite to
look forward to: for the same cause, surely, the Angels also are revealed to us,
that heaven may be as little as possible an unknown place in our imaginations.

Let us then entertain such thoughts as these of the Angels of God; and
while we try to think of them worthily, let us beware lest we make the contemplation of them a mere feeling, and a sort of luxury of the imagination.
This world is to be a world of practice and labor; God reveals to us glimpses
of the Third Heaven for our comfort; but if we indulge in these as the end
of our present being, not trying day by day to purify ourselves for the future enjoyment of the fullness of them, they become but a snare of our
enemy. The Services of religion, day by day, obedience to God in our calling
and in ordinary matters, endeavors to imitate our Savior Christ in word and
deed, constant prayer to Him, and dependence on Him, these are the due
preparation for receiving and profiting by His revelations; whereas many a
man can write and talk beautifully about them, who is not at all better or
nearer heaven for all his excellent words.

Holiness Necessary for Future Blessedness

Holiness, without which no man shall see the Lord.

—HEBREWS 12:14

In this text it has seemed good to the Holy Spirit to convey a chief truth
of religion in a few words. It is this circumstance which makes it especially
impressive; for the truth itself is declared in one form or other in every part
of Scripture. It is told us again and again, that to make sinful creatures holy
was the great end which our Lord had in view in taking upon Him our na-

ture, and thus none but the holy will be accepted for His sake at the last day. The whole history of redemption, the covenant of mercy in all its parts and provisions, attests the necessity of holiness in order to salvation; as indeed even our natural conscience bears witness also. But in the text what is elsewhere implied in history, and enjoined by precept, is stated doctrinally, as a momentous and necessary fact, the result of some awful irreversible law in the nature of things, and the inscrutable determination of the Divine Will.

Now someone may ask, "Why is it that holiness is a necessary qualification for our being received into heaven? why is it that the Bible enjoins upon us so strictly to love, fear, and obey God, to be just, honest, meek, pure in heart, forgiving, heavenly-minded, self-denying, humble, and resigned? Man is confessedly weak and corrupt; *why* then is he enjoined to be so religious, so unearthly? *why* is he required (in the strong language of Scripture) to become 'a new creature'? Since he is by nature what he is, would it not be an act of greater mercy in God to save him altogether without this holiness, which it is so difficult, yet (as it appears) so necessary for him to possess?"

Now we have no right to ask this question. Surely it is quite enough for a sinner to know, that a way has been opened through God's grace for his salvation, without being informed why that way, and not another way, was chosen by Divine Wisdom. Eternal life is "the *gift* of God." Undoubtedly He may prescribe the terms on which He will give it; and if He has determined holiness to be the way of life, it is enough; it is not for us to inquire why He has so determined.

Yet the question may be asked reverently, and with a view to enlarge our insight into our own condition and prospects; and in that case the attempt to answer it will be profitable, if it be made soberly. I proceed therefore, to state one of the reasons, assigned in Scripture, why present holiness is necessary, as the text declares to us, for future happiness.

To be holy is, in our Church's words, to have "the true circumcision of the Spirit", that is, to be separate from sin, to hate the works of the world, the flesh, and the devil; to take pleasure in keeping God's commandments; to do things as He would have us do them; to live habitually as in the sight of the world to come, as if we had broken the ties of this life, and were dead already. Why cannot we be saved without possessing such a frame and temper of mind?

I answer as follows: That, even supposing a man of unholy life were suffered to enter heaven, *he would not be happy there:* so that it would be no mercy to permit him to enter.

We are apt to deceive ourselves, and to consider heaven a place like this earth; I mean, a place where everyone may choose and take his *own* pleasure. We see that in this world, active men have their own enjoyments, and domestic men have theirs; men of literature, of science, of political talent, have their respective pursuits and pleasures. Hence we are led to act as if it will be the same in another world. The only difference we put between this world and the next, is that *here* (as we know well), men are *not always sure,* but *there,* we suppose they *will be always sure,* of obtaining what they seek after. And accordingly we conclude, that *any man,* whatever his habits, tastes, or manner of life, if *once admitted* into heaven, would be happy there. Not that we altogether deny, that some preparation is necessary for the next world; but we do not estimate its real extent and importance. We think we can reconcile ourselves to God when we will; as if nothing were required in the case of men in general, but some temporary attention, more than ordinary, to our religious duties—some strictness, during our last sickness, in the services of the Church, as men of business arrange their letters and papers on taking a journey or balancing an account. But an opinion like this, though commonly acted on, is refuted as soon as put into words. For heaven, it is plain from Scripture, is not a place where many different and discordant pursuits can be carried on at once, as is the case in this world. Here every man can do his *own* pleasure, but there he must do *God's* pleasure. It would be presumption to attempt to determine the employments of that eternal life which good men are to pass in God's presence, or to deny that the state which eye hath not seen, nor ear heard, nor mind conceived, may comprise an infinite variety of pursuits and occupations. Still so far we are distinctly told, that the future life will be spent in God's *presence,* in a sense which does not apply to our present life; so that it may be best described as an endless and uninterrupted worship of the Eternal Father, Son, and Spirit. "They serve Him day and night in His temple, and He that sitteth on the throne shall dwell among them. . . . The Lamb which is in the midst of the throne shall feed them, and shall lead them unto living fountains of waters." Again. "The city had no need of the sun, neither of the moon to shine in it, for the glory of God did lighten it, and the Lamb is the light thereof. And the nations of them which are saved shall walk in the light of it, and the kings of the earth do bring their glory and honour into it." (Rev. 7:15, 17; 21:23, 24.) These passages from St. John are sufficient to remind us of many others.

Heaven then is not like this world; I will say what it is much more like—*a church*. For in a place of public worship no language of this world is heard; there are no schemes brought forward for temporal objects, great or small; no information how to strengthen our worldly interests, extend our influence, or establish our credit. These things indeed may be right in their way, so that we do not set our hearts upon them; still (I repeat), it is certain that we hear nothing of them in a church. Here we hear solely and entirely of *God*. We praise Him, worship Him, sing to Him, thank Him, confess to Him, give ourselves up to Him, and ask His blessing. And *therefore,* a church is like heaven; viz. because both in the one and the other, there is one single sovereign subject—religion—brought before us.

Supposing, then, instead of it being said that no irreligious man could serve and attend on God in heaven (or see Him, as the text expresses it), we were told that no irreligious man could worship, or spiritually see Him in church; should we not at once perceive the meaning of the doctrine? viz. that, were a man to come hither, who had suffered his mind to grow up in its own way, as nature or chance determined, without any deliberate habitual effort after truth and purity, he would find no real pleasure here, but would soon get weary of the place; because, in this house of God, he would hear only of that one subject which he cared little or nothing about, and nothing at all of those things which excited his hopes and fears, his sympathies and energies. If then a man without religion (supposing it possible) were admitted into heaven, doubtless he would sustain a great disappointment. Before, indeed, he fancied that he could be happy there; but when he arrived there, he would find no discourse but that which he had shunned on earth, no pursuits but those he had disliked or despised, nothing which bound him to aught *else* in the universe, and made him feel at home, nothing which he could enter into and rest upon. He would perceive himself to be an isolated being, cut away by Supreme Power from those objects which were still entwined around his heart. Nay, he would be in the presence of that Supreme Power, whom he never on earth could bring himself steadily to think upon, and whom now he regarded only as the destroyer of all that was precious and dear to him. Ah! he could not *bear* the face of the Living God; the Holy God would be no object of joy to him. "Let us alone! What have we to do with thee?" is the sole thought and desire of unclean souls, even while they acknowledge His majesty. None but the holy can look upon the Holy One; without holiness no man can endure to see the Lord.

When, then, we think to take part in the joys of heaven without holiness, we are as inconsiderate as if we supposed we could take an interest in the worship of Christians here below without possessing it in our measure. A careless, a sensual, an unbelieving mind, a mind destitute of the love and fear of God, with narrow views and earthly aims, a low standard of duty, and a benighted conscience, a mind contented with itself, and unresigned to God's will, would feel as little pleasure, at the last day, at the words, "Enter into the joy of thy Lord," as it does now at the words, "Let us pray." Nay, much less, because, while we are in a church, we may turn our thoughts to other subjects, and contrive to forget that God is looking on us; but that will not be possible in heaven.

We see, then, that holiness, or inward separation from the world, is necessary to our admission into heaven, because heaven is *not* heaven, is not a place of happiness *except* to the holy. There are bodily indispositions which affect the taste, so that the sweetest flavors become ungrateful to the palate; and indispositions which impair the sight, tingeing the fair face of nature with some sickly hue. In like manner, there is a moral malady which disorders the inward sight and taste; and no man laboring under it is in a condition to enjoy what Scripture calls "the fullness of joy in God's presence, and pleasures at His right hand for evermore."

Nay, I will venture to say more than this—it is fearful, but it is right to say it—that if we wished to imagine a punishment for an unholy, reprobate soul, we perhaps could not fancy a greater than to *summon it to heaven*. Heaven would be hell to an irreligious man. We know how unhappy we are apt to feel at present, when alone in the midst of strangers, or of men of different tastes and habits from ourselves. How miserable, for example, would it be to have to live in a foreign land, among a people whose faces we never saw before, and whose language we could not learn. And this is but a faint illustration of the loneliness of a man of earthly dispositions and tastes, thrust into the society of saints and angels. How forlorn would he wander through the courts of heaven! He would find no one like himself; he would see in every direction the marks of God's holiness, and these would make him shudder. He would feel himself always in His presence. He could no longer turn his thoughts another way, as he does now, when conscience reproaches him. He would know that the Eternal Eye was ever upon him; and that Eye of holiness, which is joy and life to holy creatures, would seem to him an Eye of wrath and punishment. God cannot change His nature. Holy He must ever be. But while He is holy, no unholy soul can be happy in heaven. Fire does not inflame iron, but it inflames straw. It would cease to be fire if it did not. And so heaven itself would be fire to those, who would fain escape across the great gulf from the torments of hell. The finger of Lazarus would but increase their thirst. The very "heaven that is over their head" will be "brass" to them.

And now I have partly explained why it is that holiness is prescribed to us as the condition on our part for our admission into heaven. It seems to be necessary from the very nature of things. We do not see how it could be otherwise. Now then I will mention two important truths which seem to follow from what has been said.

1. If a certain character of mind, a certain state of the heart and affections, be necessary for entering heaven, our *actions* will avail for our salvation, chiefly as they tend to produce or evidence this frame of mind. Good works (as they are called) are required, not as if they had anything of merit in them, not as if they could of themselves turn away God's anger for our sins, or purchase heaven for us, but because they are the means, under God's grace, of strengthening and showing forth that holy principle which God implants in the heart, and without which (as the text tells us) we cannot see Him. The more numerous are our acts of charity, self-denial, and forbearance, of course the more will our minds be schooled into a charitable, self-denying, and forbearing temper.

The more frequent are our prayers, the more humble, patient, and religious are our daily deeds, this communion with God, these holy works, will be the means of making our hearts holy, and of preparing us for the future presence of God. Outward acts, done on principle, create inward habits. I repeat, the separate acts of obedience to the will of God, good works as they are called, are of service to us, as gradually severing us from this world of sense, and impressing our hearts with a heavenly character.

It is plain, then, what works are *not* of service to our salvation: all those which either have no effect upon the heart to change it, or which have a bad effect. What then must be said of those who think it an easy thing to please God, and to recommend themselves to Him; who do a few scanty services, call these the walk of faith, and are satisfied with them? Such men, it is too evident, instead of being themselves profited by their acts, such as they are, of benevolence, honesty, or justice, may be (I might even say) injured by them. For these very acts, even though good in themselves, are made to foster in these persons a bad spirit, a corrupt state of heart; viz. self-love, self-conceit, self-reliance, instead of tending to turn them from this world to the Father of spirits. In like manner, the mere outward acts of coming to church, and saying prayers, which are, of course, duties imperative upon all of us, are really serviceable to those only who do them in a heavenward spirit. Because such men only use these good deeds to the improvement of the heart; whereas even the most exact outward devotion avails not a man, if it does not improve it.

2. But observe what follows from this. If holiness be not merely the doing a certain number of good actions, but is an inward character which follows, under God's grace, from doing them, how far distant from that holiness are the multitude of men! They are not yet even obedient in outward deeds, which is the first step towards possessing it. They have even to learn to practice good works, as the means of changing their hearts, which is the end. It follows at once, even though Scripture did not plainly tell us so, that no one is able to prepare himself for heaven, that is, make himself holy, in a short time—at least we do not see how it is possible; and this, viewed merely as a deduction of the reason, is a serious thought. Yet, alas! as there are persons who think to be saved by a few scanty performances, so there are others who suppose they may be saved all at once by a sudden and easily acquired faith. Most men who are living in neglect of God, silence their consciences, when troublesome, with the promise of repenting some future day. How often are they thus led on till death surprises them! But we will suppose they *do* begin to repent when that future day comes. Nay, we will even suppose that Almighty God were to forgive them, and to admit them into His holy heaven. Well, but is nothing more requisite? are they in a fit state to *do Him service in heaven?* is not this the very point I have been so insisting on, that they are *not* in a fit state? has it not been shown that, even if admitted there without a change of heart, they would find no pleasure in

heaven? and is a change of heart wrought in a day? Which of our tastes or likings can we change at our will in a moment? Not the most superficial. Can we then at a word change the whole frame and character of our minds? Is not holiness the result of many patient, repeated efforts after obedience, gradually working on us, and first modifying and then changing our hearts? We dare not, of course, set bounds to God's mercy and power in cases of repentance late in life, even where He has revealed to us the general rule of His moral governance; yet, surely, it is our duty ever to keep steadily before us, and act upon, those general truths which His Holy Word has declared. His Holy Word in various ways warns us, that, as no one will find happiness in heaven, who is not holy, so no one can learn to be so, in a short time, and when he will. It implies it in the text, which names a qualification, which we know in matter of fact does ordinarily take time to gain. It propounds it clearly, though in figure, in the parable of the wedding garment, in which inward sanctification is made a condition distinct from our acceptance of the proffer of mercy, and not negligently to be passed over in our thoughts as if a necessary consequence of it; and in that of the ten virgins, which shows us that we must meet the bridegroom with the oil of holiness, and that it takes time to procure it. And it solemnly assures us in St. Paul's Epistles, that it is possible so to presume on Divine grace, as to let slip the accepted time, and be sealed even before the end of life to a reprobate mind. (Heb. 6:4–6; 26–29. Vide also 2 Pet. 2:20, 22.)

I wish to speak to you, my brethren, not as if aliens from God's mercies, but as partakers of His gracious covenant in Christ; and for this reason in especial peril, since those only can incur the sin of making void His covenant, who have the privilege of it. Yet neither on the other hand do I speak to you as willful and obstinate sinners, exposed to the imminent risk of forfeiting, or the chance of having forfeited, your hope of heaven. But I fear there are those, who, if they dealt faithfully with their consciences, would be obliged to own that they had not made the service of God their first and great concern; that their obedience, so to call it, has been a matter of course, in which the heart has had no part; that they have acted uprightly in worldly matters chiefly for the sake of their worldly interest. I fear there are those, who, whatever be their sense of religion, still have such misgivings about themselves, as lead them to make resolve to obey God more exactly some future day, such misgivings as convict them of sin, though not

enough to bring home to them its heinousness or its peril. Such men are trifling with the appointed season of mercy. To obtain the gift of holiness is the
work of a *life*. No man will ever be perfect here, so sinful is our nature.
Thus, in putting off the day of repentance, these men are reserving for a few
chance years, when strength and vigor are gone, that WORK for which a
whole life would not be enough. That work is great and arduous beyond expression. There is much of sin remaining even in the best of men, and "if the
righteous scarcely be saved, where shall the ungodly and the sinner appear?"
(1 Pet. 4:13.) Their doom may be fixed any moment; and though this
thought should not make a man despair today, yet it should ever make him
tremble for tomorrow.

Perhaps, however, others may say: "We know something of the power
of religion—we love it in a measure—we have many right thoughts—we
come to church to pray; this is a proof that we are prepared for heaven: we
are safe, and what has been said does not apply to us." But be not you, my
brethren, in the number of these. One principal test of our being true servants of God is our wishing to serve Him better; and be quite sure that a
man who is contented with his own proficiency in Christian holiness, is at
best in a dark state, or rather in great peril. If we are really imbued with the
grace of holiness, we shall abhor sin as something base, irrational, and pol-
luting. Many men, it is true, are contented with partial and indistinct views
of religion, and mixed motives. Be you content with nothing short of perfection; exert yourselves day by day to grow in knowledge and grace; that,
if so be, you may at length attain to the presence of Almighty God.

Lastly, while we thus labor to mold our hearts after the pattern of the
holiness of our Heavenly Father, it is our comfort to know, what I have already implied, that we are not left to ourselves, but that the Holy Ghost is
graciously present with us, and enables us to triumph over, and to change
our own minds. It is a comfort and encouragement, while it is an anxious
and awful thing, to know that God works in and through us. (Phil. 2:12,
18.) We are the instruments, but we are only the instruments, of our own
salvation. Let no one say that I discourage him, and propose to him a task
beyond his strength. All of us have the gifts of grace pledged to us from our
youth up. We know this well; but we do not use our privilege. We form
mean ideas of the difficulty, and in consequence never enter into the greatness of the gifts given us to meet it. Then afterwards, if perchance we gain

a deeper insight into the work we have to do, we think God a hard master, who commands much from a sinful race. Narrow, indeed, is the way of life, but infinite is His love and power who is with the Church, in Christ's place, to guide us along it.

John J. Jasper

1812–1901

Ministerial students at the University of Richmond were called "Jaspers" not long ago. The idiom honored the memory of John Jasper, who was born into slavery in Virginia and worked after his emancipation, at the end of the Civil War, cleaning mortar from old bricks to rebuild the city amid rubble, before founding the Sixth Mount Zion Church. Interstate 95 makes a slight detour around the brick building where Jasper's rhetoric, his eidetic memory of most of the Bible, and his resonant preaching with tongue and hands made him the great minister of his flock during the tumult of Reconstruction. (During the Civil War, Jasper pastored churches in the South and conducted services for wounded Confederates in Richmond's military hospitals.) A white minister who heard his extraordinary performance in the pulpit remarked that he "was the preacher; likewise the church and the choir and the deacons and the congregation."

Contemporary theologians would probably call John Jasper a fundamentalist; his understanding of the Bible was severely literal, adjudicating any seeming dispute between the Word of God and scientific disclosures in favor of the Divine. His most famous sermon was a response, delivered over ninety minutes, in reply to a question from a parishioner about whether or not the sun moved. At the end of the service Jasper polled the congregation to learn if they were convinced that the sun moved: the vote was unanimous that it did. He preached this sermon more than two hundred and fifty times in the South as well as the North; once the Virginia General Assembly stopped its session to have Jasper preach "De Sun Do Move."

This great oral presentation from an African-American folk church falls into the category defined in the tradition as "call and response." Its incantation and synchronization of a phrase and a verbal response from the congregation, in a ritual which is as highly controlled and sustained as a bardic performance, in its patterning and native poetry, have survived through the recording of many hands. Langston Hughes selected Jasper's oratory for his famous anthology of the 1930s, *The Book of Negro Folklore,* coedited with Arna Bontemps; William Faulkner's prose is in debt to its passionate and cadenced language, although the decision to preserve Jasper's speech in dialect, given his self-taught literacy, remains a puzzle.

De Sun Do Move

The Lord is a man of war; the Lord God is His name.

—EXODUS 15:3

'Low me to say dat when I was a young man and a slave, I knowed nothin worth talkin bout concernin books. Dey was sealed mysteries to me, but I tell you I longed to break de seal. I thirsted for de bread of learnin. When I seen books I ached to git in to 'em for I knowed dat dey had de stuff for me and I wanted to taste dere contents, but most of de time dey was barred against me.

By de mercy of de Lord a thing happened. I got a roomfeller—he was a slave, too and he had learned to read. In de dead of de night he give me lessons outen de New York Spellin Book. It was hard pullin, I tell you; harder on him, for he know'd just a little and it made him sweat to try to beat somethin into my hard head. It was worse with me. Up de hill every step, but when I got de light of de lesson into my noodle I fairly shouted, but I know'd I was not a scholar. De consequence was I crept long mighty tedious, gittin a crumb here and dere until I could read de Bible by skippin de long words, tolerable well. Dat was de start of my education—dat is what little I got. I make mention of dat young man. De years have fled away since den but I ain't forgot my teacher and never shall. I thank my Lord for him and I carries his memory in my heart.

Bout seven months after my gittin to readin, God converted my soul and I reckon bout de first and main thing dat I begged de Lord to give me was de power to understand His Word. I ain't braggin and I hates self-praise, but I bound to speak de thankful word. I believes in my heart dat my prayer to understand de Scriptur was heard. Since dat time I ain't cared bout nothin 'cept to study and preach de Word of God.

Not, my brothren, dat I's de fool to think I knows it all. Oh, my Father, no! Far from it. I don't hardly understand myself nor half of de things round me and dere is millions of things in de Bible too deep for Jasper and some of 'em too deep for everybody. I don't carry de keys to de Lord's closet and He ain't tell me to peep in and if I did I'm so stupid I wouldn't know it when I see it. No, friends, I knows my place at de feet of my Master and dere I stays.

But I can read de Bible and get de things what lay on de top of de soil. Outen de Bible I know nothin extry bout de sun. I seen its course as he rides up dere so gran and mighty in de sky, but dere is heaps bout dat flamin orb dat is too much for me. I know dat de sun shines powerfully and pours down its light in floods and yet dat is nothin compared with de light dat flashes in my mind from de pages of God's book. But you knows all dat. I knows dat de sun burns—oh, how it did burn in dem July days! I tell you he cooked de skin on my back many a day when I was hoein in de corn field. But you knows all dat—and yet dat is nothing to de divine fire dat burns in de souls of God's chillun. Can't you feel it, brothren?

But bout de course of de sun, I have got dat. I have done ranged through de whole blessed Book and scoured down de last thing de Bible has to say bout de movement of de sun. I got all dat pat and safe. And lemme say dat if I don't give it to you straight, if I gits one word crooked or wrong, you just holler out, "Hold on dere, Jasper, you ain't got dat straight" and I'll beg pardon. If I don't tell de truth, march up on dese steps here and tell me I's a liar and I'll take it. I fears I do lie sometimes— I'm so sinful, I find it hard to do right; but my God don't lie and He ain't put no lie in de Book of eternal truth and if I give you what de Bible say, den I bound to tell de truth.

I got to take you all dis afternoon on an excursion to a great battle-field. Most folks like to see fights—some is mighty fond of gittin into fights and some is mighty quick to run down de back alley when dere is a battle goin on for de right. Dis time I'll 'scort you to a scene where you shall witness a curious battle. It took place soon after Israel got in de Promise Land. You 'member de people of Gideon make friends with God's people when dey first entered Canaan and dey was monstrous smart to do it. But, just de same, it got 'em in to an awful fuss. De cities round bout dere flared up at dat and dey all joined dere forces and say dey gwine to mop de Bigyun people off de ground and dey bunched all dere armies together and went up for to do it. When dey come up so bold and brace de Gideonites was scared outen dere senses and dey sent word to Joshua dat dey was in trouble and he must run up dere and git 'em out. Joshua had de heart of a lion and he was up dere directly. Dey had an awful fight, sharp and bitter but you might know dat General Joshua was not dere to get whipped. He prayed and he fought and de hours got away too fast for him and so he asked de Lord to issue a special order dat de sun hold up awhile and dat de moon furnish plenty of moonshine down on de lowest part of de fightin grounds. As a fact, Joshua was so drunk with de battle, so thirsty for de blood of de enemies of de Lord and so wild with de victory dat he tell de sun to stand still till he could finish his job.

What did de sun do? Did he glare down in fiery wrath and say, "What you talking bout my stoppin for, Joshua? I ain't never started yet. Been here all de time and it would smash up everything if I was to start." No, he ain't say dat. But what de Bible say? Dat's what I ask to know. It say dat it was at de voice of Joshua dat it stopped. I don't say it stopped; tain't for Jasper to say dat, but de Bible, *de Book of God,* say so. But I say dis; nothin can stop until it has first started. So I knows what I'm talkin bout. De sun was travelin long dere through de sky when de order come. He hitched his red ponies and made quite a call on de land of Gideon. He perch up dere in de skies just as friendly as a neighbor what comes to borrow somethin and he stand up dere and he look like he enjoyed de way Joshua waxes dem wicked armies. And de moon, she wait down in de low grounds dere and pours out her light and look just as calm and happy as if she was waitin for her escort. Dey never budged, neither of 'em long as de Lord's army needed a light to carry on de battle.

I don't read when it was dat Joshua hitch up and drove on, but I suppose it was when de Lord told him to go. Anybody knows dat de sun didn't stay dere all de time. It stopped for business and went on when it got through. Dis is bout all dat I has to do with dis particular case. I done showed you dat dis part of de Lord's word teaches you dat de sun stopped which show dat he was movin before dat and dat he went on afterwards. I told you dat I would prove dis and I's done it and I defies anybody to say dat my point ain't made.

I told you in de first part of dis discourse dat de Lord God is a man of war. I expect by now you begin to see it is so. Don't you admit it? When de Lord come to see Joshua in de day of his fears and warfare and actually make de sun stop stone still in de heavens so de fight can rage on till all de foes is slain, you're obliged to understand dat de God of peace is also de man of war. He can use both peace and war to heap de riches and to scatter de host of de aliens. A man talked to me last week bout de laws of nature and he say dey can't possibly be upset and I had to laugh right in his face. As if de laws of anything was greater dan my God who is de lawgiver for everything. My Lord is great! He rules in de heavens, in de earth and down under de ground. He is great and greatly to be praised. Let all de people bow down and worship before Him! Dere you are! Ain't dat de movement of de sun? Bless my soul! Hezekiah's case beat Joshua. Joshua stop de sun, but here de Lord make de sun walk back ten degrees; and yet dey say dat de sun stand stone still and never move a peg. It look to me he move round mighty brisk and is ready to go any way dat de Lord orders him to go. I wonder if any of dem philosophers is round here dis afternoon? I'd like to take a square look at one of dem and ask him to explain dis matter. He can't do it, my brothren. He knows a heap bout books, maps, figgers and long distances but I defy him to take up Hezekiah's case and explain it off. He can't do it, my brothren. De Word of de Lord is my defense and bulwark and I fears not what men say nor do—my God give me my victory.

Low me, my friends, to put myself square bout dis movement of de sun. It ain't no business of mine whether de sun move or stan still, or whether it stop or go back or rise or set. All dat is out of my hand entirely and I got nothin to say. I got no the-o-ry on de subject. All I ask is dat we will take what de Lord say bout it and let His will be done bout everything. What dat will is I can't know except He whisper into my sould or write it in a book. Here's de Book. Dis is enough for me and with it to pilot me, I can't get far astray.

But I ain't done with you yet. And de song says, dere's more to follow. I invite you to hear de first verse in de seventh chapter of de Book of Revelations. What do John under de power of de Spirit say? He says he saw four angels standin on de four corners of de earth, holdin de four winds of de earth and so forth. Low me to ask if de earth is round where do it keep its corners? A flat square thing has corners, but tell me where is de corner of an apple or a marble or a cannon ball or a silver dollar. If dere is anyone of dem philosophers what's been takin so many cracks at my old head bout here, he is cordially invited to step forward and square up dis vexin business. I hear tell dat you can't square a circle but it looks like dese great scholars done learn how to circle a square. If dey can do it, let 'em step to de front and do de trick. But, my brothren, in my poor judgment, dey can't do it; tain't in 'em to do it. Dey is on de wrong side of de Bible—dat's on de outside of de Bible, and dere's where de trouble comes in with 'em. Dey done got out of de breastworks of de truth and as long as dey stay dere de light of de Lord will not shine on dere path. I ain't care so much bout de sun, though it's mighty convenient to have it but my trust is in de Word of de Lord. Long as my feet is flat on de solid rock, no man can move me. I's gettin my orders from de God of my salvation.

The other day a man with a high collar and side whiskers come to my house. He was one nice Northern gentleman what think a heap of us colored people in de South. Dey are lovely folks and I honors 'em very much. He seem from de start kinder strict and cross with me and after a while he broke out furious and fretted and he says: "Allow me Mister Jasper to give you some plain advice. Dis nonsense bout de sun movin where you are gettin is disgracin your race all over de country and as a friend of your people I come to say it's got to stop." . . . Ha! Ha! Ha! . . . Mars Sam Hargrovenever hardly smash me dat way. It was equal to one of dem old overseers way back yonder. I tell him dat if he'll show me I's wrong, I give it all up. . . . My! My! . . . Ha! Ha! . . . He sail in on me and such a storm bout science, new discoveries and de Lord only knows what all, I hever hear before and den he tel me my race is urgin me and poor old Jasper must shut up his fool mouth.

When he got through—it look like he never would—I tell him John

Jasper ain't set up to be no scholar and don't know de philosophies and ain't trying to hurt his people but is workin day and night to lift 'em up but his foot is on de rock of eternal truth. Dere he stand and dere he is going to stand till Gabriel sounds de judgment note. So I say to de gentleman what scolded me up so dat I hear him make his remarks but I ain't hear where he get his Scripture from and that between him and de Word of de Lord, I take my stand by de Word of God every time. Jasper ain't mad; he ain't fighting nobody; he ain't been appointed janitor to run de sun; he nothin but de servant of God and a lover of de Everlasting Word. What I care bout de sun? De day comes on when de sun will be called from his race track and his light squinched out forever; de moon shall turn to blood and this earth be consumed with fire. Let 'em go; dat won't scare me nor trouble God's elected people, for de word of de Lord shall endure forever and on dat Solid Rock we stand and shall not be moved!

Is I got you satisfied yet? Has I proven my point? Oh, ye whose hearts is full of unbelief! Is you still holding out? I reckon de reason you say de sun don't move is cause you are so hard to move yourself. You is a real trial to me, but, never mind, I ain't given you up yet and never will. Truth is mighty; it can break de heart of stone and I must fire another arrow of truth out of de quiver of de Lord. If you has a copy of God's Word bout your person, please turn to dat minor prophet, Malachi, what write de last book in de whole Bible and look at chapter one, verse eleven. What do it say? I better read it for I got a notion you critics don't carry any Bible in your pockets every day in de week. Here is what it says: "For from de rising of de sun even unto de goin down of de same, My name shall be great among de Gentiles . . . My name shall be great among de heathen, says de Lord of hosts!" How do dat suit you? It looks like dat ought to fix it! Dis time it is de Lord of Hosts hisself dat is doin de talkin and He is talkin on a wonderful and glorious subject. He is telling of de spreadin of His Gospel of de comin of His last victory over de Gentiles and de world-wide glories dat at de last He is to get. Oh, my brothren, what a time dat will be! My soul takes wing as I anticipate with joy dat millennium day! De glories as dey shine before my eyes blinds me and I forget de sun and moon and stars. I just remembers dat long bout dose last days dat de sun and moon will go out of business for dey won't be needed no more. Den will King Jesus come back to see His people and He will be de sufficient light of de world. Joshua's battles will be over. Hezekiah won't need no sun dial and de sun and moon will fade out before de glorious splendors of de New Jerusalem.

But what de matter with Jasper? I most forgot my business and most gone to shoutin over de far away glories of de second comin of my Lord. I beg pardon and will try to get back to my subject. I have to do as de sun in Hezekiah's case—fall back a few degrees. In dat part of de Word dat I'm given you from Malachi—dat de Lord hisself spoke—he declares dat His glory is gwine to spread. Spread? Where? From de rising of de sun to de goin down of de same. What? Don't say dat, does it? Dat's exactly what it says. Ain't dat clear enough for you? De Lord pity dese doubtin Thomases. Here is enough to settle it all and cure de worse cases. Wake up here, wise folks, and get your medicine. Where is dem high collared philosophers now? What dey skulkin round in de brush for? Why don't you get out in de broad afternoon light and fight for your collars? Ah, I understand it; you got no answer. De Bible is against you and in your consciences you are convicted.

But I hears you back dere. What you whisperin bout? I know! You say you sent me some papers and I never answer dem . . . Ha, ha, ha! . . . I got 'em. De difficulty bout dem papers you sent me is dat dey did not answer me. Dey never mention de Bible one time. You think so much of yourself and so little of de Lord God and thinks what you say is so smart dat you can't even speak of de Word of de Lord. When you ask me to stop believing in de Lord's Word and to pin my faith to your words, I ain't goin to do it. I take my stand by de Bible and rest my case on what it says. I take what de Lord says bout my sins, bout my Savior, bout life, bout death, bout de world to come and I take what de Lord say bout de sun and moon and I cares little what de haters of my God chooses to say. Think dat I will forsake de Bible? It is my only Book, my hope, de arsenal of my soul's supplies and I wants nothin else.

But I got another word for you yet. I done work over dem papers dat you sent me without date and without name. You deals in figures and thinks you are bigger dan de archangels. Lemme see what you done say. You set yourself up to tell me how far it is from here to de sun. You think you got it down to a nice point. You say it is 3,339,002 miles from de earth to de sun. Dat's what you say. Another one say dat de distance is 12,000,000; another got it to 27,000,000. I hears dat de great Isaac Newton worked it up to 28,000,000 and later on de philosophers gone another rippin rise to

50,000,000. De last one gets it bigger dan all de others, up to 90,000,000. Don't any of 'em agree and so dey runs a guess game and de last guess is always de biggest. Now, when dese guessers can have a convention in Richmond and all agree upon de same thing, I'd be glad to hear from you again and I does hope dat by dat time you won't be ashamed of your name.

Heaps of railroads has been built since I saw de first one when I was fifteen years old but I ain't hear tell of a railroad built yet to de sun. I don't see why if dey can measure de distance to de sun, dey might not get up a railroad or a telegraph and enable us to find something else bout it dan merely how far off de sun is. Dey tell me dat a cannon ball could make de trip to de sun in twelve years. Why don't dey send it? It might be rigged up with quarters for a few philosophers on de inside and fixed up for a comfortable ride. Dey would need twelve years' rations and a heap of changes of raiment—mighty thick clothes when dey start and mighty thin ones when dey git dere.

Oh, my brothren, dese things make you laugh and I don't blame you for laughing except it's always sad to laugh at de follies of fools. If we could laugh 'em out of countenance we might well laugh day and night. What cuts into my soul is dat all dese men seem to me dat dey is hitting at de Bible. Dat's what stirs my soul and fills me with righteous wrath. Little cares I what dey says bout de sun, provided dey let de Word of de Lord alone. But never mind. Let de heathen rage and de people imagine a vain thing. Our King shall break 'em in pieces and dash 'em down. But blessed be de name of our God, de Word of de Lord endureth forever! Stars may fall, moons may turn to blood and de sun set to rise no more, but Thy kingdom, oh, Lord, is from everlastin to everlastin!

But I has a word dis afternoon for my own brothren. Dey is de people for whose souls I got to watch—for dem I got to stand and report at de last—dey is my sheep and I's dere shepherd and my soul is knit to dem forever. Ain't for me to be troublin you with dese questions bout dem heavenly bodies. Our eyes goes far beyond de smaller stars. Our home is clean out of sight of dem twinklin orbs. De chariot dat will come to take us to our Father's mansion will sweep out by dem flickerin lights and never halt till it brings us in clear view of de throne of de Lamb. Don't hitch your hopes to no sun nor stars. Your home is got Jesus for its light and your hopes must travel up dat way. I preach dis sermon just for to settle the minds of my few brothren and I repeats it cause kind friends wish to hear it, and I hopes it will do honor to de Lord's Word. But nothin short of de Pearly Gates can satisfy me and I charge my people, fix your feet on de Solid Rock, your hearts on Calvary, and your eyes on de throne of de Lamb. Dese strifes and griefs will soon get over; we shall see de King in His glory and be at ease. Go on, go on, ye ransomed of de Lord! Shout His praises as you go! And I shall meet you in de city of de New Jerusalem where ye shan't need de light of de sun—for de Lamb of de Lord is de light of de saints!

Phillips Brooks

1835–1893

On the day of his Boston funeral, the coffin of this "Prince of Preachers," Bishop Phillips Brooks, containing the mortal remains of his nearly six-and-a-half-foot, three-hundred-pound frame, was carried from Trinity Church, which he had built a generation earlier, on the shoulders of eight Harvard oarsmen, who had practiced the day before in the college gym with a coffin full of iron. Ten thousand people attended locally, but the whole nation mourned the passing of the man who was doubtless its best-known religious figure, and who most conceded was its best preacher.

It was not always so clear that Brooks would attain such signal success in the Episcopal priesthood and pulpit. His first career as an usher, or teacher in training, at his alma mater, the Boston Latin School, had ended in disaster and dismissal. In later years, reflecting on this failed beginning, he delivered one of his most famous sermons, "The Symmetry of Life," which would eventually be adapted by Martin Luther King, Jr., as the basis of a favorite sermon of his own, "The Dimensions of a Complete Life" (see page 638).

Brooks left behind ten volumes of posthumously published sermons as well as what has for most of us now become a nearly anonymous legacy, the Christmas carol "O Little Town of Bethlehem," written in 1865 on a visit to Palestine. His preaching was widely praised during and after his life and tended to focus on moral messages and the importance of individual character formation. He was not a theologian or a dogmatist and in fact showed a remarkable absence of denominational prejudice. One commentator has noted that his "sermons deal with the suburban territory of Christian truth; but in that field they are among the best." In a series of talks at Yale in 1877, later published as *Lectures on Preaching* and still consulted by students of homiletics as one of the best summaries of its kind, he memorably defined what preaching is: "the communication of truth through a man to a man. . . . Preaching is the bringing of truth through personality."

He composed his sermons to a set routine, picking a topic on Monday and discussing it with colleagues, beginning to write loosely on Tuesday and with more care and compression on Wednesday. On Thursday he began the final version, writing it out in the most perfect copperplate hand and ensuring that its length—even with his well-known rapid delivery—did not exceed twenty-seven to twenty-nine minutes. Finishing on Saturday morning, he gathered the sheets specially cut for his use and sewed them together himself for easy and silent turning in the pulpit.

The Brooks sermon included here is on a text from Exodus and has an uncannily modern feel to it. The theme is a familiar one in this preacher's work: the failure to take personal responsibility for what we do—and the means Jesus freely offers us to do so.

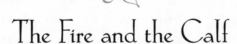

The Fire and the Calf

So they gave it me: then I cast it into the fire, and there came out this calf.

—EXODUS 32:24

In the story from which these words are taken we see Moses go up into the mountain to hold communion with God. While he is gone the Israelites begin to murmur and complain. They want other gods, gods of their own. Aaron, the brother of Moses, was their priest. He yielded to the people, and when they brought him their golden earrings he made out of them a golden calf for them to worship. When Moses came down from the mountain he found the people deep in their idolatry. He was indignant. First he destroyed the idol, "He burnt it in the fire, and ground it to powder, and strewed it upon the water, and made the children of Israel drink of it." Then he turned to Aaron: "What did this people unto thee that thou hast brought so great a sin upon them?" And Aaron meanly answered: "Let not the anger of my Lord wax hot: thou knowest the people, that they are set on mischief. For they said unto me, Make us gods which shall go before us. . . . And I said unto them, Whosoever hath any gold, let them break it off. So they gave it me: then I cast it into the fire, and there came out this calf." That was his mean reply. The real story of what happened had been written earlier in the chapter. When the people brought Aaron their golden earrings "he received them at their hand, and fashioned it with a graving tool, after he had made it a molten calf; and they said, These be thy gods, O Israel, which brought thee up out of the land of Egypt." That was what really happened, and this is the description which Aaron gave of it to Moses: "So they gave it me: then I cast it into the fire, and there came out this calf."

Aaron was frightened at what he had done. He was afraid of the act itself, and of what Moses would say. Like all timid men, he trembled before the storm which he had raised. And so he tried to persuade Moses, and perhaps in some degree even to persuade himself, that it was not he that had done this thing. He lays the blame upon the furnace. "The fire did it," he declares. He will not blankly face his sin, and yet he will not tell a lie in words. He tells what is literally true. He had cast the earrings into the fire, and this calf had come out. But he leaves out the one important point, his own personal agency in it all; the fact that he had molded the earrings into the calf's shape, and that he had taken it out and set it on its pedestal for the people to adore. He tells it so that it shall all look automatic. It is a curious, ingenious, but transparent lie.

Let us look at Aaron's speech a little while this morning and see what it represents, for it does represent something. There never was a speech more true to our human nature. We are all ready to lay the blame upon the furnaces. "The fire did it," we are all of us ready to say. Here is a man all gross and sensual, a man still young, who has lost the freshness and the glory and the purity of youth. He is profane; he is cruel; he is licentious; all his brightness has grown lurid; all his wit is ribaldry. You know the man. As far as a man can be, he is a brute. Suppose you question him about his life. You expect him to be ashamed, repentant. There is not a sign of anything like that! He says, "I am the victim of circumstances. What a corrupt, licentious, profane age is this in which we live! When I was in college I got into a bad set. When I went into business I was surrounded by bad influences. When I grew rich, men flattered me. When I grew poor, men bullied me. The world has made me what I am, this fiery, passionate, wicked world. I had in my hands the gold of my boyhood which God gave me. Then I cast it into the fire, and there came out this calf." So the poor wronged miserable creature looks into your face with his bleared eyes and asks your pity. Another man is not a profligate, but a miser, or a mere business machine. "What can you ask of me?" he says. "This is a mercantile community. The business man who does not attend to his business goes to the wall. I am what this intense commercial life has made me. I put my life in there, and it came out this." And he gazes fondly at his golden calf and his knees bend under him with the old habit of worshipping it, and he loves it still, even when he abuses and disowns it. And so with the woman of society. "The fire made me this," she says of her frivolity and pride. And so of the politician and his selfishness and partisanship. "I put my principles into the furnace and this came out." And so of the bigot and his bigotry, the one-sided conservative with his stubborn resistance to all progress, the one-sided radical with his ruthless iconoclasm. So of all partial and fanatical men. "The furnace made us," they are ready to declare. "These things compel us to be this. In better times we might have been better, broader men; but, now behold, God put us into the fire, and we came out this." It is what one is perpetually hearing about disbelief. "The times have made me skeptical. How is it possible for a man to live in days like these and yet believe in God and Jesus and the Resurrection? You ask me how I, who was brought up in the faith and in the Church, became a disbeliever." "Oh, you remember that I lived five years here," or "three years there." "You know I have been very much thrown with this set or with that. You know the temper of our town. I cast myself into the fire, and I came out this." One is all ready to understand, my friends, how the true soul, struggling for truth, seems often to be worsted in the struggle.

One is ready to have tolerance, respect, and hope for any man who, reaching after God, is awed by God's immensity and his own littleness, and falls
back crushed and doubtful. His is a doubt which is born in the secret chambers of his own personal conscientiousness. It is independent of his circumstances and surroundings. The soul which has truly come to a personal
doubt finds it hard to conceive of any ages of the most implicit faith in which
it could have lived in which that doubt would not have been in it. It faces its
doubt in a solitude where there is none but it and God. All that one understands, and the more he understands it the more unintelligible does it seem
to him, that any earnest soul can really lay its doubt upon the age, the set,
or the society it lives in. No; our age, our society is what, with this figure
taken out of the old story of Exodus, we have been calling it. It is the furnace. Its fire can set and fix and fasten what the man puts into it. But, properly speaking, it can create no character. It can make no truly faithful soul a
doubter. It never did. It never can.

Remember that the subtlety and attractiveness of this excuse, this
plausible attributing of power to inanimate things and exterior conditions
to create what only man can make, extends not only to the results which we
see coming forth in ourselves; it covers also the fortunes of those for whom
we are responsible. The father says of his profligate son whom he has never
done one wise or vigorous thing to make a noble and pure-minded man: "I
cannot tell how it has come. It has not been my fault. I put him into the
world and this came out." The father whose faith has been mean and selfish
says the same of his boy who is a skeptic. Everywhere there is this cowardly
casting off of responsibilities upon the dead circumstances around us. It is a
very hard treatment of the poor, dumb, helpless world which cannot answer
to defend itself. It takes us as we give ourselves to it. It is our minister fulfilling our commissions for us upon our own souls. If we say to it, "Make us
noble," it does make us noble. If we say to it, "Make us mean," it does make
us mean. And then we take the nobility and say, "Behold, how noble I have
made myself." And we take the meanness and say, "See how mean the world
has made me."

You see, I am sure, how perpetual a thing the temper of Aaron is, how
his excuse is heard everywhere and always. I need not multiply illustrations.
But now, if all the world is full of it, the next question is, What does it mean?
Is it mere pure deception, or is there also delusion, self-deception in it? Take

Aaron's case. Was he simply telling a lie to Moses and trying to hide the truth from his brother whom he dreaded, when he said, "I cast the earrings into the fire, and this calf came out"? Or was he in some dim degree, in some half-conscious way, deceiving himself? Was he allowing himself to attribute some power to the furnace in the making of the calf? Perhaps as we read the verse above in which it is so distinctly said that Aaron fashioned the idol with a graving tool, any such supposition seems incredible. But yet I cannot but think that some degree, however dim, of such self-deception was in Aaron's heart. The fire was mysterious. He was a priest. Who could say that some strange creative power had not been at work in the heart of the furnace which had done for him what he seemed to do for himself. There was a human heart under that ancient ephod, and it is hard to think that Aaron did not succeed in bringing himself to be somewhat imposed upon by his own words, and hiding his responsibility in the heart of the hot furnace. But however it may have been with Aaron, there can be no doubt in almost all cases this is so. Very rarely indeed does a man excuse himself to other men and yet remain absolutely unexcused in his own eyes. When Pilate stands washing the responsibility of Christ's murder from his hands before the people, was he not feeling himself as if his hands grew cleaner while he washed? When Shakespeare paints Macbeth with the guilty ambition which was to be his ruin first rising in his heart, you remember how he makes him hide his new-born purpose to be king even from himself, and pretend, that he is willing to accept the kingdom only if it shall come to him out of the working of things, for which he is not responsible, without an effort of his own.

> If chance will have me king, why, chance may crown me,
> Without my stir.

That was the first stage of the growing crime which finally was murder. Often it takes this form. Often the very way to help ourselves most to a result which we have set before ourselves is just to put ourselves into a current which is sweeping on that way, and then lie still and let the current do the rest; and in all such cases it is so easy to ignore or to forget the first step, which was that we chose that current for our resting place, and so to say that it is only the drift of the current which is to blame for the dreary shore on which at last our lives are cast up by the stream. Suppose you are today a scornful man, a man case-hardened in conceit and full of disbelief in anything generous or supernatural, destitute of all enthusiasm, contemptuous, supercilious. You say the time you live in has made you so. You point to one large tendency in the community which always sets that way. You parade the specimens of enthusiastic people whom you have known who have been fanatical and silly. You tell me what your favorite journal has been saying in your ears every week for years. You bid me catch the tone of the brightest people whom you live among, and then you turn to me and say, "How could one live in such an atmosphere and not grow cynical? Behold, my times have made me who I am." What does that mean? Are you merely trying to hide from me, or are you also hiding from yourself, the certain fact that you have chosen that special current to launch your boat upon, that you have given your whole attention to certain kinds of facts and shut your eyes to certain others, that you have constantly valued the brightness which went to the depreciation of humanity and despised the urgency with which a healthier spirit has argued for the good in man and for his everlasting hope? Is it not evident that you yourself have been able to half forget all this, and so when the stream on which you launched your boat at last drives it upon the beach to which it has been flowing all the time, there is a certain lurking genuineness in the innocent surprise with which you look around upon the desolate shore on which you land, and say to yourself, "How unhappy I am that I should have fallen upon these evil days, in which it is impossible that a man should genuinely respect or love his fellowmen"?

For there are currents flowing always in all bad directions. There is a perpetual river flowing towards sensuality and vice. There is a river flowing perpetually towards skepticism and infidelity. And when you once have given yourself up to either of these rivers, then there is quite enough in the continual pressure, in that great movement like a fate beneath your keel, to make you lose the sense and remembrance that it is by your own will that you are there, and only think of the resistless flow of the river which is always in your eyes and ears. This is the mysterious, bewildering mixture of the consciousness of guilt and the consciousness of misery in all our sin. We live in a perpetual confusion of self-pity and self-blame. We go up to the scaffolds where we are to suffer, half like culprits crawling to the gallows and half like martyrs proudly striding to their stakes. When we think of what sort of reception is to meet us in the other world as the sum and judgment of the life we have been living here, we find ourselves ready, according to the moment's mood, either for the bitterest denunciation, as of souls who have lived in deliberate sin; or for tender petting and refreshment, as of souls who have been buffeted and knocked about by all the storms of time, and for whom now there ought to be soft beds in eternity. The confusion of men's minds about the judgments of the eternal world is only the echo of their confusion about the responsibilities of the life which they are living now.

Suppose there is a man here this morning who committed a fraud in business yesterday. He did it in a hurry. He did not stop to think about it then. But now, in this quiet church with everything calm and peaceful round him, with the words of prayer which have taken God for granted sinking into his ears, he has been thinking it over. How does it look to him? Is he not certainly sitting in the mixture of self-pity and self-reproach of which I spoke? He did the sin, and he is sorry as a sinner. The sin did itself, and he is sorry as a victim. Nay, perhaps in the next pew to him, or perhaps in the same pew, or perhaps in the same body, there is sitting a man who means to do a fraud tomorrow. In him too is there not the same confusion? One moment he looks it right in the face, and says, "Tomorrow night I shall despise myself." The next moment he is quietly thinking that the sin will do itself and give him all its advantage, and he need not interfere. "If chance will make me cheat, why chance may crown me, without my stir." Both thoughts are in his mind, and if he has listened to our service, it is likely enough that he has found something in it—even in the words of the Bible—for each thought to feed upon.

I own this freely, and yet do I believe, and I call you to bear me witness, that such self-deception almost never is absolutely complete. We feel its incompleteness the moment anyone else attempts to excuse us with the same excuse with which we have excused ourselves. Suppose that some one of the Israelites who stood by had spoken up in Aaron's behalf and said to Moses: "Oh, he did not do it. It was not his act. He only cast the gold into the fire, and there came out this calf." Must not Aaron as he listened have felt the wretchedness of such a telling of the story, and been ashamed, and even cried out and claimed his responsibility and his sin? Very often it is good for us to imagine someone saying aloud in our behalf what we are silently saying to ourselves in self-apology. We see its thinness when another hand holds it up against the sun, and we stand off and look at it. If I might turn again to Shakespeare and his wonderful treasury of human character, there is a scene in Hamlet which exactly illustrates what I mean. The king has determined that Hamlet must die, and is just sending him off upon the voyage from which he means that he is never to return. And the king has fully explained the act of his own conscience, and accepted the crime as a necessity. And then he meets the courtiers, Rosencrantz and Guildenstern, who are to have the execution of the base commission. And they, like courtiers, try to repeat to the king the arguments with which he has convinced himself. One says—

> Most holy and religious fear it is
> To keep those many many bodies safe
> That live and feed upon your majesty.

And the other takes up the strain and says—

> The single and peculiar life is bound,
> With all the strength and armor of the mind,
> To keep itself from 'noyance; but much more
> That spirit upon whose weal depend and rest
> The lives of many.

They are the king's own arguments. With them he has persuaded his own soul to tolerate the murder. But when they come to him from these other lips, he will none of them. He cuts them short. He cannot hear from others what he has said over and over to himself.

> Arm you, I pray you, to this speedy voyage.

So he cries out and interrupts them. Let the deed be done, but let not these echoes of his self-excuse parade before him the way in which he is trifling with his own soul.

So it is always. I think of the mysterious judgment day, and sometimes it appears to me as if our souls would need no more than merely that voices outside ourselves should utter in our ears the very selfsame pleas and apologies with which we, here upon the earth, have extenuated our own wickedness. They of themselves, heard in the open air of eternity, would let us see how weak they were, and so we should be judged. Is not that partly the reason why we hate the scene of some old sin? The room in which we did it seems to ring forever with the sophistries by which we persuaded ourselves that it was right, and will not let us live in comfortable delusion. Our life there is an anticipated judgment day.

I doubt not that this tendency to self-deception and apology with reference to the sins which they commit differs exceedingly with different men. Men differ, perhaps, nowhere else more than in their disposition to face the acts of their lives and to recognize their own personal part and responsibility for the things they do. Look, for instance, at this Aaron and his brother Moses. The two men are characterized by their own sins. The sin of Aaron was a denial or concealment of his own personal agency: "I cast it into the fire, and there came out this calf." The sin of Moses, you remember, was just the opposite. As he stood with his thirsty people in front of the rock of Horeb, he intruded his personal agency where it had no right. "Hear now, ye rebels; must we fetch water out of this rock?" To be sure, in the case of Moses it was a good act of mercy to which he put his claim, while in Aaron's case it was a wicked act whose responsibility he desired to avoid. And men are always ready to claim the good deeds in which they have the slightest share, even when they try to disown the sins which are entirely their own. But still the actions seem to mark the men. Moses is the franker, manlier, braver man. In Aaron the priest there is something of that oversubtle, artificial, complicated character, that power of being morally confused even in the midst of pious feeling, that lack of simplicity, and of the disposition to look at things frankly in the eye; in a word, that vague and defective sense of personality and its responsibilities which has often in the history of religion made the very name of priestcraft a reproach. Moses is the prophet. His distinct mission is the utterance of truth. He is always simple; never more simple than when he is most profound; never more sure of the fundamental principles of right and wrong, of honesty and truth, than when he is deepest in the mystery of God; never more conscious of himself and his responsibilities than when he is most conscious of God and His power.

And this brings me to my last point, which I must not longer delay to reach. If the world is thus full of the Aaron spirit, of the disposition to throw the blame of wrong-doing upon other things and other people, to represent to others, and to our own souls, that our sins do themselves, what is the spiritual source of such a tendency, and where are we to look to find its cure? I have just intimated what seems to me to be its source. It is a vague and defective sense of personality. Anything which makes less clear to a man the fact that he, standing here on his few inches of the earth, is a distinct separate being, in whom is lodged a unit of life, with his own soul, his own character, his own chances, his own responsibilities, distinct and separate from any other man's in all the world; anything that makes all that less clear demoralizes a man, and opens the door to endless self-excuses. And you know, surely, how many tendencies there are today which are doing just that for men. Every man's personality, in his clear sense of himself, seems to be standing where almost all the live forces of the time are making their attacks upon it. It is like a tree in the open field from which every bird carries away some fruit. The enlargement of our knowledge of the world, the growing tendency of men to work in large companies, the increased despotism of social life, the interesting studies of hereditation, the externality of a large part of our action, the rush and competition for the prizes which represent the most material sort of success, the spread of knowledge by which at once all men are seen to know much, and, at the same time, no man is seen to know everything; all these causes enfeeble the sense of personality. The very prominence of the truth of a universal humanity, in which our philanthropy justly glories, obscures the clearness of the individual human life. Once it was hard to conceive of man, because the personalities of men were so distinct. Once people found it hard, as the old saying was, to see the forest for the trees. Now it is the opposite. To hundreds of people it is almost impossible to see the trees for the forest. Man is so clear that men become obscure. As the Laureate of the century sings of the time which he so well knows: "The individual withers and the race is more and more." These are the special causes, working in our time, of that which has its general causes in our human nature working everywhere and always.

And if this is the trouble, where then, is the help? If this is the disease, where is the cure? I cannot look for it anywhere short of that great assertion of the human personality which is made when a man personally enters into the power of Jesus Christ. Think of it! Here is some Aaron of our modern life trying to cover up some sin which he has done. The fact of the sin is clear enough. It stands out wholly undisputed. It is not by denying that the thing was done but by beclouding the fact that he did it with his own hands, with his own will; thus it is that the man would cover up his sin. He has been nothing but an agent, nothing but a victim; so he assures his fellowmen, so he assures himself. And now suppose that while he is doing that, the great change comes to that man by which he is made a disciple and servant of Jesus Christ. It becomes known to him as a certain fact that God loves him individually, and is educating him with a separate personal education which is all his own. The clear individuality of Jesus stands distinctly out and says to him, "Follow me!" Jesus stops in front of where he is working just as evidently as He stopped in front of the booth where Matthew was sitting collecting taxes, and says, "Follow me." He is called separately, and separately he does give himself to Christ. Remember all that is essential to a Christian faith. You cannot blur it all into indistinctness and generality. In the true light of the redeeming Incarnation, every man in the multitude stands out as every blade of grass on the hillside stands distinct from every other when the sun has risen. In this sense, as in many another, this is the true light which lighteneth every man that cometh into the world.

The Bible calls it a new birth, and in that name too there are many meanings. And among other meanings in it must there not be this—the separateness and personality of every soul in Christ? Birth is the moment of distinctness. The meanest child in the poorest hovel of the city, who by and by is to be lost in the great whirlpool of human life, here at the outset where his being comes, a new fact, into the crowded world, is felt in his distinctness, has his own personal tending, excites his own personal emotion. When he is born and when he dies, but perhaps most of all when he is born, the commonest, the most commonplace and undistinguished of mankind asserts the fact of privilege of his separateness. And so when the possession of the soul by Christ is called the "New Birth," one of the meanings of that name is this, that then there is a reassertion of personality, and the soul which had lost itself in the slavery of the multitude finds itself again in the obedience of Christ.

And now what will be the attitude of this man, with his newly-awakened selfhood, towards that sin which he has been telling himself that his hands did, but that he did not do? May he not almost say that he will need that sin for his self-identification? Who is he? A being whom Christ has for-given, and then in virtue of that forgiveness made His servant. All his new life dates from and begins with his sin. He cannot afford to find his con-sciousness of himself only in the noble parts of his life, which it makes him proud and happy to remember. There is not enough of that to make for him a complete and continuous personality. It will have great gaps if he disowns the wicked demonstrations of his selfhood and says, "It was not I," wherever he has done wrong. No! Out of his sin, out of the bad, base, cowardly acts which are truly his, out of the weak and wretched passages of his life which it makes him ashamed to remember, but which he forces himself to recol-lect and own, out of these he gathers the consciousness of a self all astray with self-will, which he then brings to Christ and offers in submission and obedience to His perfect will.

You try to tell some soul rejoicing in the Lord's salvation that the sins over whose forgiveness by its Lord it is gratefully rejoicing, were not truly its; and see what strange thing comes. The soul seems to draw back from your assurance as if, if it were true, it would be robbed of all its surest con-fidence and brightest hope. You meant to comfort the poor penitent, and he looks into your face as if you were striking him a blow. And you can see what such a strange sight means. It is not that the poor creature loves those sins or is glad that he did them, or dreams for an instant of ever doing them again. It is only that through those sins, which are all the real experience he has had, he has found himself, and finding himself has found his Savior and the new life.

So the only hope for any of us is in a perfectly honest manliness to claim our sins. "I did it! I did it," let me say of all my wickedness. Let me refuse to listen for one moment to any voice which would make my sins less mine. It is the only honest and the only hopeful way, the only way to know and be ourselves. When we have done that, then we are ready for the Gospel, ready for all that Christ wants to show us that we may become, and for all the powerful grace by which He wants to make us be it perfectly.

Dwight Lyman Moody

1837–1899

*H*is uncertain dreamy youth, and its rebellious false starts, could have made this descendant of the Puritans and son of a brick-mason in Northfield, Massachusetts, a model for a character in a naturalist tragic novel by Theodore Dreiser. But his evangelical career, after his job in a shoestore in Boston and a conversion in the Mount Vernon Congregational Church, made him one of the great American preachers of the nineteenth century. (His work as traveling salesman for a firm dealing in shoes is really no more unpromising than St. Paul's turns as a Temple policeman or tent-maker in first-century Palestine.) The personality of the salesman remained part of his persuasive force: for Moody, securing a decision for Christ was like "closing a sale." Undereducated and sometimes ungrammatical, a nervous stammerer, and one of the founders of the YMCA in America, he was a brilliant teacher in the Sunday school programs in Chicago, where he lived and worked after 1856. They eventually blossomed into the Moody Bible Institute, begun in 1889.

Moody emphasized, in a preaching style notable for its directness, forcefulness, and ready intimacy, the gospel of God's fatherly love. His personal integrity made him volunteer as a chaplain on the battlefields of the Civil War, and a prison visitor whose wide activism in problems of social welfare was matched by the executive ability of a born businessman. He was, however, no Elmer Gantry, building a financial empire on the salvation of souls, but a layman who inspired ministers, combining a largeness of spirit with common sense. The colloquial language of his sermons was as genuine as his refusal to profit personally from the proceeds of his work. Its slogan was "The evangelization of the world in this generation," its summons articulated in this well-known sermon, one which, like the body of his speeches and writings, has never gone out of print.

Come

Incline your ear, and come unto me: hear, and your soul shall live; and I will make an everlasting covenant with you, even the sure mercies of David.

—ISAIAH 55:3

We have for our subject this afternoon the precious little word "Come." I want to call your attention first to the "Come" in the 55th chapter of the prophecies of Isaiah. "Incline your ear, and come unto me: hear, and your soul shall live; and I will make an everlasting covenant with you, even the sure mercies of David."

"Incline your ear, and come unto me; hear, and your soul shall live." Now, I find if we get people to listen—to pause and hear the voice of God, it isn't long before they are willing to follow that voice; but it is so hard to get people to stop and listen for a moment. The din of the world makes such a noise that the people don't hear the voice—that still small voice. He says, "Incline your ear, and come unto me." Now, if we could only get all the friends in this audience to incline their ears this afternoon—not only your natural ears but the ears of your soul, you could be saved today. But Satan does not want you to do this; he does all he can to keep your ears from hearing. He makes you think about yourself, about your sons, your homes; but, my friends, let us forget all those things today—let us forget all our surroundings, and close our eyes to the world, and just try and listen to the word of God, and come and hear what He has to say. "Incline your ear, and come unto me: hear, and your soul shall live." Now, let us turn to the tenth chapter of Romans, where we see, "Faith cometh by hearing, and hearing by the word of God." Now, it is not my words I want you to hear this afternoon, but I want you to hear the words of this loving King who calls you to Himself. What does He say? In another place he says: "Behold, I stand at the door, and knock; if any man hear my voice, and open the door, I will come in to him, and sup with him, and he with me," or "if any woman," or any one; that's what it means, my friends—"hear my voice, and open the door, I will come in to her, and will sup with her and she with me." I heard of a little child some time ago who was burned. The mother had gone out and left her three children at home. The eldest left the room, and the remaining two began to play with the fire, and set the place a blaze. When the youngest of the two saw what she had done she went into a little cupboard and fastened herself in. The remaining child went to the door and knocked and knocked, crying to her to open the door and let her take her out of the burning building, but she was too frightened to do it. It seems to me as if this was the way with hundreds and thousands in this city. He stands and knocks, but they've got their hearts barred and bolted, because they don't know that He has come only to bless them. May God help you to hear, and if you listen to Him and bring your burdens to Him, He will bless you. He is able to open the ears of everyone here if you let Him in. I was up here at the hotel the other night, and I had the door locked and bolted, and someone came and rapped. I shouted "Come in!" The man tried to come in, but he couldn't; I had to get up and unlock the door before he could enter. That's the way with many people today. They've got the door bolted and barred; but if you only open it to Him, He will come in.

"If any man hear my voice, and open the door, I will come in and sup with him and he with me." Now, my friends, can you hear it? Can you hear God's voice speaking through His own Word? "Incline your ear, and come unto me." Just listen. You know sometimes, when you hear a man speaking whose voice you don't hear very well, and you want to hear every word the man says, you put your hand up to your ear to catch the sound clearer. Now listen. God says, "Incline your ear, and come unto me: hear, and your soul shall live; and I will make an everlasting covenant with you." Now, is it not true? Can't you hear that loving voice speaking to you, and won't you obey that voice and let Him save you? But I can imagine some of you saying, "I can't hear anything." Take your ears to Him and He will make you hear.

Now let me take you to another course. While John and his disciples were standing, Jesus came along, and John said: "Behold the Lamb of God!" and Jesus said: "What seek ye?" "Where dwellest thou?" he asked; to which He replied: "Come and see"; and they just obeyed Him and never left Him. My friends, if I could introduce you to Christ—could just get you to catch one glimpse of Him; if you could but see the King in all His beauty; if you could but see Him in all His loveliness, you would never forsake Him, for we "shall grow up before him as a tender plant, and as a root out of a dry ground: he hath no form nor comeliness; and when we shall see him, there is no beauty that we should desire him." Follow Him as your Savior. In order to appreciate Him you have to be brought to Him, but if sin has come between you and Him, I cannot tell you anything about Him. It is just like telling a blind man about the beauties of nature, the loveliness of the flowers, or of the world. That is the way, if sin stands between you and Him, and when Christians try to tell you about the beauties of Christianity they fail, but if you come and have an interview with Him you will see that you cannot help but love Him; you will see that you cannot but forsake all and follow Him. I remember once hearing of a child who was born blind. He grew up to be almost a man, when a skillful physician thought he could give the man his sight. He was put under the doctor's treatment, and for a long time he worked, till at last he succeeded. But he wouldn't let the man see the light of the sun all at once, lest it would strike him blind. It had to be done gradually. So he put a lot of bandages upon his eyes and removed one after another until the last one was reached, and when it was taken off the young man began to see. When he saw the beauties of the world he upbraided his friends for not telling him about the beauties of nature. "Why, we tried to tell you about the beauties of the world, but we could not," they said. And so it is with us. All that we can do is to tell you to come and see—come and see the loveliness of Christ.

I can imagine some of you saying, "I am blind, I cannot see any beauty in Him." Bring your blindness to Him as you bring your deafness and He will give you sight, as He did with the blind Bartimaeus—as He did with all the blind men on earth. There was never a blind man who came to Him requesting his sight whose request was not granted, and there is not a blind soul in this assembly but will be healed if you come to Him. He says that's what He came for, to give sight to the blind. If you cannot see any beauty in Him pray to God to give you sight.

The next "Come" is in the prophecies of Isaiah. "Come now, and let us reason together, saith the Lord: though your sins be as scarlet, they shall be as white as snow; though they be red like crimson, they shall be as wool." I find a great many people say their reason stands between them and God.

Now, let me say here, the religion of Jesus is a matter of revelation, not of investigation. No one ever found out Christ by reason. It is a matter of revelation. Now see what He says, "Come now"—that means this afternoon—"though your sins be as scarlet, they shall be as white as snow." Now He puts a pardon in the sinner's face. "Your sins may be as scarlet, they shall be as white as snow." Take the scarlet in that lady's shawl. It is a fast color. You cannot wash it out and make it white; if you tried you would only destroy the shawl. But He will make your sins white as snow, though they be as scarlet, if you come to Him. Just come to Him as you are, and instead of reasoning, ask Him to take them away. Then He will reason it out with you. The natural man does not understand spiritual things, but when a man is born of the Spirit, then it is that the spiritual things are brought out to him. A great many people want to investigate—want to reason out the Bible from back to back, but He wants us first to take a pardon. That's God's method of reasoning. He puts a pardon in the face of the sinner. "Come now." Do you think there is not reason in this? Suppose the whole plan of salvation was reasoned out to you, why death might step in before the end of the reasoning was reached. So God puts a pardon first. If you will be influenced today you will just bring your reason to Him, and ask Him to give you wisdom to see divine things, and He will do it. "If any of you lack wisdom, let him ask of God, that giveth to all men liberally, and upbraideth not; and it shall be given liberally." The idea, that this reason that God hath given should keep him from Christ.

A number of years ago as I was coming out of a daily prayer meeting in one of our Western cities, a lady came up to me and said, "I want to have you see my husband and ask him to come to Christ." She said, "I want to have you go and see him." She told me his name, and it was of a man I had heard of before. "Why," said I, "I can't go and see your husband. He is a booked infidel. I can't argue with him. He is a good deal older than I am, and it would be out of place. Then I am not much for infidel argument." "Well, Mr. Moody," she says, "that ain't what he wants. He's got enough of that. Just ask him to come to the Savior." She urged me so hard and so strong, that I consented to go. I went to the office where the Judge was doing business, and told him what I had come for. He laughed at me. "You are very foolish," he said, and began to argue with me. I said, "I don't think it will be profitable for me to hold an argument with you. I have just one favor I want to ask of you, and that is, that when you are converted you will let me know." "Yes," said he, "I will do that. When I am converted, I will let you know," with a good deal of sarcasm.

I went off, and requests for prayer were sent here and to Fulton Street, New York, and I thought the prayer there and of that wife would be answered if mine were not. A year and a half after I was in that city, a servant came to the door and said: "There is a man in the front parlor who wishes to see you." I found the Judge there. He said: "I promised I would let you know when I was converted. I've been converted." "Well," said I, "I'm glad to hear it! Tell me all about it." I had heard it from other lips, but I wanted to hear it from his own. He said his wife had gone out to a meeting one night and he was home alone, and while he was sitting there by the fire he thought, "Supposing my wife is right, and my children are right: suppose there is a heaven and hell, and I shall be separated from them." His first thought was: "I don't believe a word of it." The second thought came, "You believe in the God that created you, and that the God that created you is able to teach you. You believe that God can give you life." "Yes, the God that created me can give me life. I was too proud to get down on my knees by the fire, and I said, 'O God, teach me.' And as I prayed, I don't understand it, but it began to get very dark, and my heart got very heavy. I was afraid to tell my wife when she came to bed and I pretended to be asleep. She kneeled down beside that bed and I knew she was praying for me. I kept crying, 'O God, save me; O God, take away this burden,' but it grew darker, and the load grew heavier and heavier. All the way to my office I kept crying, 'O God, take away this load of guilt.' I gave my clerks a holiday, and just closed my office and locked the door. I fell down on my face: I cried in agony to the Lord, 'O Lord, for Christ's sake, take away this guilt.' I don't know how it was, but it began to grow very light. I said, I wonder if this isn't what they call conversion. I think I will go and ask the minister if I am not converted. I met my wife at the door and said, 'My dear, I've been converted.' She looked in amazement. 'Oh it's a fact, I've been converted!' We went into that drawing-room and knelt down by the sofa and prayed to God to bless us." The old Judge said to me, the tears trickling down his cheeks, "Mr. Moody, I've enjoyed life more in the last three months than in all the years of my life put together." If there is an infidel here—if there is a skeptical one here, ask God to give wisdom to come now. Let us reason together, and if you become acquainted with God the day will not go before you receive light from Him.

The next "Come" I want to call your attention to is a very sweet one. He says, "Come and reason," "Come and see," and now we have "Come and rest." What this world wants is rest. Every man, every woman is in pursuit of it, and how many of us have found it? How many are bearing burdens about our hearts always—how many have come into this hall today with a great burden on their hearts? What does He say: "Come unto me, all ye that labour and are heavy laden, and I will give you rest." Now a great many people have an idea that they get rid of their burdens themselves, but they must come to Him if they want to be relieved. That's what Christ came for. Come to Him. "He hath borne our griefs and carried our sorrows." There could not be a sweeter "Come" than this. How many mothers are bearing burdens for their children—how many because of their sons, or perhaps you have husbands who have proved unfaithful, or maybe you are widows who have been without support. The future may look dark to you: but hear the loving voice of the Savior, "Come unto me, all ye that labor and are heavy laden, and I will give you rest." There is not a soul here—I don't care what the burden may be—in this vast audience, but can lay their burden on the Lord Jesus Christ, and He will bear it for you. We can be released; we have found a resting place, and that is in the loving bosom of the Lord Jesus Christ. There is a hymn written by Dr. Andrew Bonar which can express this much better than I can. Let me read it:

> I heard the voice of Jesus say:
>   "Come unto me and rest;
> Lay down, thou weary one, lay down
>   Thy head upon my breast."

> I came to Jesus as I was,
>   Weary and worn and sad;
> I found in Him a resting-place,
>   And He has made me glad.

> I heard the voice of Jesus say:
>   "Behold I freely give

The living water—thirsty one,
    Stoop down and drink and live!"

I came to Jesus and I drank
    Of that life-giving stream;
My thirst was quenched, my soul revived
    And now I live in Him.

I heard the voice of Jesus say:
    "I am this dark world's light;
Look unto Me, thy morn shall rise,
    And all thy day be bright."

I looked at Jesus and I found
    In Him my Star, my Sun.
And in that light of Life I'll walk
    Till traveling days are done.

Oh, my friends, if you want to rest today, come to Him. He stands with His arms outstretched, and says: "Come to me and rest." Does the world satisfy you? Are not the griefs of this world crushing many a heart here? Hear the voice of Jesus: "Come and rest." The world cannot take it from you; the world's crosses and trials will not tear it from you; He will give you peace and comfort and rest if you but come.

The next "Come" is "come and drink and eat." You don't have to pay anything. You know it is hard for a man to get a tax on water unless when it has to be brought into the city. But this water is always without price, and salvation is like a river, flowing at the feet of everyone; and all you have to do is to stoop down and drink of this living water and never die. The world cannot give you comfort—cannot give you water to satisfy your thirst, and every man and woman in this world is thirsty. That's the way our places of amusement are filled. People are constantly thirsting for something. But how are they filled with those amusements? They are as thirsty as ever. But if they drink the waters that He offers they will have a fountain in them springing up into everlasting life. I remember coming down a river with some wounded soldiers. The water was very muddy, and as we had no filters they had to drink the dirty water, which did not satisfy their thirst. I re-member a soldier saying, "O that I had a draught of water from my father's well." If you drink of the living water your soul will never thirst again. Not only does He say, "Come and drink of that living water," but He says, "Come and eat." In the fifty-fifth chapter of Isaiah you are invited to come and eat. You know all that the children of Israel had to do in the wilderness was just to pick up the manna and eat. They didn't have to make it. And people had just to stoop down and pick up the manna and eat, and drink from the flinty rock when the water flowed. And today the provision is brought to the door of your hearts. You haven't to go down to the earth for it, or to go up to the skies for it. It is here, and all you've got to do is eat.

You know almost the last words of Christ after His resurrection, when, having a little fish, He said to His disciples, "Come and dine." Oh, what a sweet invitation—the invitation of the Master to His disciples, "Come and dine." I invite you now to come and dine with Him; He will quench that thirst; He will satisfy your hunger, and all you've got to do is take Him at His word.

Is there a poor thirsty one here today? I bid you come and drink of the fountain of living water; I bid you come and eat of the heavenly bread; yes, the bread made in heaven, the bread that angels feed on—Christ Himself is the bread of life.

Now, many people make a great mistake about accepting Christ. They think they've got something to do; think they've got to do some work, or that they've got to pray and wrestle before taking Him; they think it is a question of performances whether they are saved or not. Now, it is a question of simply taking what God offers you. I remember when I was out on the Pacific coast, a man took me through his house, out on his lands, and showed me his orchards, and then said: "Mr. Moody, you are a guest of mine, and I want you to feel perfectly at home, do what you like." Well, after this man said this, you don't suppose if I wanted an orange I was going under the tree to pray that it would fall into my pocket? I just went up boldly and plucked what I wanted. And so the bread of heaven is offered to us, and all we've got to do is to go boldly up and take it. This is what God wants you to do. Everything is prepared for you.

There is a class, too, who say: "But I'm afraid I'll not hold out." How many people are stumbling over this! Now, if you come boldly up to the throne you'll get all the support you need—"Let us therefore come boldly unto the throne of grace, that we may obtain mercy, and find grace to help in time of need." There is a passage for you; that ought to be sufficient. And there is not a woman here today but can be kept, from this very day and this very hour, from evil—"For I the Lord thy God will keep you, without spot or wrinkle, and without blemish." Some of the vilest men who have ever trodden this earth have been saved with the grace of God. Some have been kept sixty or seventy years merely by the grace of God, and never wavered. "Come boldly to the throne of grace" and you will get power. That is sufficient. Won't you take Him at His word? It seems to me that it is madness not to take the gift offered us by God.

Let me call attention to another "Come." My friends, the Bible is full of them, and you can't say if you don't come there have been no invitations. He says: "Come to the marriage." Now, you young ladies like marriages pretty well. Let a marriage come off in a church, and hundreds will be there; and probably next night, at the prayer meeting, there will scarcely be a dozen of you present. Now here is a marriage, and there is not a lady here whom God does not want to be present at the marriage feast. There is an invitation. And here is another "Come": "Come and inherit the kingdom prepared for you from the foundation of the world." God has got an inheritance for every one of you. The time will soon come, if you accept Christ and become as His bride, when you shall hear the voice of Him saying to you: "Come and inherit the kingdom prepared for you from the foundation of the world." What a mistake it will be, my friends, if you will not hear that invitation given to you! There is an inheritance incorruptible in the heavens, a building not made with hands, and He wants everyone to enter into this inheritance, and so it is your privilege to be present at the marriage feast and receive the inheritance if you will.

You know the first "Come" in the Bible is in regard to salvation. It was given to Noah; God said, "Come thou, and all thy house into the ark," not a part of them, but "all thy house." That is the first "Come" in the Bible, and all through that blessed book it is repeated; and now we come to the last one. It seems as if the Bible was created by this word "come." "The Spirit and the bride say, Come. And let him that is athirst come. And whosoever will, let him taste the water of life freely." There is our invitation, as broad as the world itself. And if God says you are to come in there, no power in heaven, or earth, or hell can stop you! He bids you come. Now bear in mind it is your sins God wants, and not your faith. You have nothing about you that He wants except your sins. People are continually trying to come to Him by their faith, by their feelings, by their tears, by their good deeds, by their works; but you have to come to Him just as you are. There is not a woman present but can roll off every sin and leave them in this tabernacle.

Now the question comes, What right have you to come? Why, because the King invites you. Suppose Queen Victoria had sent me an invitation to be present at Windsor at a feast given in honor of the marriage of one of her sons to a princess of Russia. I take the cars to New York, then the boat to Liverpool, then I would run down to London, where I would get the train to Windsor Castle. There is a sentry walking up and down in front of the gate. If I hadn't my invitation he would refuse me admittance; but there is not a soldier in the British army can keep me out, because I've got the Queen's invitation. But suppose the man looks at me and says: "You can't go into the presence of the Queen with those clothes; you are not fit to stand before the Queen." That is none of his business; that's hers. So the invitation comes from Him, and He wants you to come and He will clothe you in garments fit for His presence. You will be stripped of every rag of self-righteousness, and a robe of spotlessness will be put upon you.

A great many people say, "I want to become clean before I come to Christ." Now, my friends, that is the devil's work. He tries to get people to believe that they can't come without getting rid of their sins, but as I've said, all through the Scriptures He bids you come as you are. We cannot take away our sins; come to Him and He will blot them out. A few years ago in London, there used to be a good many little children stolen to act as chimney sweeps. A child was stolen from a wealthy family, and a great reward was offered, but he couldn't be found. This child had been kidnapped. One day he was sent up a chimney and came down on the other side, and into a beautiful room. The little fellow was bewildered. A lady was sitting there, and recognized him as her son, and although the little fellow was covered with smut, she ran to him, and drew him to her bosom, and that is the way Christ will receive you. You needn't try to get rid of one particle of sin. He wants to save you as you are. "Whosoever will, let him come and drink of the waters of life freely." Will you come today? The Spirit and the bride invite you this afternoon. Now I want to ask you what are you going to do with these ten loving invitations today—"Come and hear," "Come and see," "Come and reason," "Come and rest," "Come and eat and drink," "Come and dine," "Come and find grace," "Come unto the marriage," "Come and inherit the kingdom prepared for you from the foundation of the world," "Whosoever will, let him come." Ask God to help you to come today. If I were in your place I would settle this question before I left this building; I would just press up to the kingdom of God and take Him at His word. Now would you just all lift up your hearts in prayer. Let every Christian pray for every soul here today out of Christ. Let us now just unite in this one petition that every soul in this building may come to Christ today.

Sabine Baring-Gould

1834–1924

Whether or not clerical life can actually confer longevity, in the case of Baring-Gould it certainly permitted literary fecundity. His published works between 1857 and 1920 number 159, most of them intended for a popular readership and, while predictably covering religious topics, also included such titles as *Book of Were-Wolves* and *Devonshire Characters and Strange Events*.

After Cambridge and his ordination in 1864 he was assigned as a curate at Horbury in the West Riding of Yorkshire, where wool mills and child labor abounded. There he began a mission school, and on one Whitsun wrote a processional hymn for his students called "Onward, Christian Soldiers." Among his charges was a poor girl aptly named Grace, whom Baring-Gould would later marry and who bore him fourteen children.

He brought out numerous books of sermons with titles like *Village*

Preaching for a Year, recommended by the *Church Times* "to the Clergy, who will gather from them many a hint how to make use of anecdote, illustration, scraps of personal experience, &c., in their pulpit teaching." He published a small book called *Sermons to Children* (1882) in which he made ample use of all of the foregoing, declaring in the Preface, "If I do not greatly err, in preaching to children, the best possible models are Æsop's Fables. The truth the teacher desires to impress on the minds of his little hearers should not occupy nakedly the major portion of his address, but be appended to the story as a Moral." While their chapter titles generally declare a tone of high Victorian earnestness—"Tidiness," "Willfulness," "Idle Talk," "The Baits of Satan," etc.—they belie the considerable charm, insight, and effectiveness with which they are composed. Baring-Gould's speaking voice is almost audible on the page, suggesting how delightful it must have been to hear him preach.

Perseverance

Be not weary in well-doing.

—2 THESSALONIANS 3:13

There was, at the beginning of the 7th century, a famous bishop of Seville, a great writer whose works have descended to us; his name was Isidore. When he was a boy at school, he was wearied and disgusted with the drudgery of learning. He could not master the principles of grammar, and the propositions of Euclid. He despaired of ever getting on at his lessons, and he ran away from school, probably with the intention of becoming a soldier. The sun grew hot, and he became exhausted; so he sat down to rest beside a little spring that gushed over a rock. As he reposed in the shade, he noticed that the continual dropping of the water had worn away a large stone beneath the jet. Then he thought if the light rain of the spring could scoop out the hard heart of the stone, then assuredly constant learning would at last overcome his natural inaptitude to acquire knowledge. He turned back, and re-appeared at school; seated himself once more at his desk, and went on at the weary round of duties. The result was that he became a great doctor of the Church, and that now, twelve hundred years after his death, his books are still studied.

Long after the days of St. Isidore, an apprentice ran away from his master in London. He got as far as Highgate, and there, as he sat on a milestone, he heard Bow bells chiming, and thought they called him back, bade him turn, and promised that he should become Lord Mayor of London. You all know the story of Richard Whittington.

You are often dispirited and down-hearted about your schoolwork. It seems so hard and so uninteresting, such tedious, unprofitable drudgery. You feel disposed to give it up; the difficulties are more than you can master.

In the British Museum are a great many carved alabaster slabs from Nineveh, and stamped bricks from Babylon. They are written over with lines of characters, made of little arrowheads turned in all conceivable directions; it looks as if arrowheads had been showered over these bricks and stones, and that, except for their being in lines, their arrangement was haphazard. But it is not so. They are writing. When the slabs and bricks were collected and brought to England, nobody knew what the characters meant, and no one knew in what language the writing was. What could be more impossible a task than to find out the meaning of these strange arrowhead lines? However, patient students set to work, compared, and classified, and at last they found out what collection of arrowheads appeared to be verbs, and what to be substantives. Then they tried them with various languages, and at last got the key. Now these writings can be read and interpreted. Is not this wonderful? It is the fruit of patient perseverance. It might have been thought absolutely impossible to read inscriptions in an unknown and dead language, written in unknown characters, but patience and resolution not to be discouraged can work wonders, can do things that appear impossible.

There are in your head reason and memory; and both these faculties have to be cultivated. This is why you have to work at mathematics, and to learn so much by heart. Your reason is educated by means of mathematics, so that you may grow up to think, and think problems out. And you learn by heart a great deal, you learn what may perhaps be of no use to you; but still your memory is being trained. This is a most valuable faculty, and it is one that is very inadequately cultivated among us. Among savage people the powers of the memory are very great indeed, for they are obliged to remember things, whereas we have notebooks, and can dot things down in them, and save ourselves the trouble of storing them in our heads.

In India the sacred books of the Hindus are taught to the Brahmans, and they have to learn them with the greatest nicety, to know every word and stop. It is marvelous how much and how accurately they can remember the minutest particulars.

No doubt you feel it very hard to work at your mathematics, and to learn much by heart. But be not discouraged; these are most necessary things for you to do for the education of your minds. Those who have not been taught to think clearly when young, are rather troublesome in maturity, they are so confused in their notions, they do not "go to the bottom of things" as the saying is. And such as have not had their memories trained to be exact, labor, in afterlife, under great disadvantages. They remember about events, but do not grasp the particulars, which are exactly what are most needed. They remember that something happened, for instance, but not the day on which it happened.

But I will speak no more to you about perseverance in your school-work, but of perseverance in other matters.

First, let me exhort you never to undertake anything, till you have well weighed it, and seen that you can finish it. Then, when you have taken it in hand, as a matter of principle, go through with it to the end. Some people are always beginning things and leaving them incomplete. They want the gift of perseverance. Or, they begin a thing well, tire of it, and finish it off roughly and carelessly. I will tell you what their undertakings are like. They are like the image that was seen by Nebuchadnezzar. The head of the image was of fine gold. So is the beginning of the undertaking of a person without much moral resolution and determination to persevere. There is the grandest start made. Everything is to be excellent, splendid and superfine. The breast and the arms were of silver. Interest begins to slacken; still the work is good, but not as good as before; it is as inferior as silver is to gold. The belly and the thighs were of brass. Here is a still greater falling off. The legs of iron. Worse

still. The feet, part of iron, and finishing off with clay. Here indeed is a picture of imperfection, of good intention, and bad execution, of grandest beginning, and wretched termination. The head gold—the toes clay.

Now take care before you undertake anything, that it shall not resemble Nebuchadnezzar's image. Make a resolution to carry out to the end
whatever you begin, in quality equal to the beginning. "Whatsoever your
hand findeth to do, do it with all your might."

It is better to do a little well, than a great deal badly. It is better to
begin a little matter and finish it, than to start a great one and leave it incomplete.

If this be good advice in ordinary matters, it is still better advice in
your spiritual concerns. In your religious life as in your worldly life, never
attempt more than you feel sure you can go on with. It is much better to
begin with the clay, and mount up through iron and brass to silver, and finish off with gold, than to begin with gold and come down to clay.

If you undertake any good work, finish it. But do not undertake one
till you have turned over in your mind your capabilities of carrying it out.
Nothing is more common than for children to resolve to do this or that
good thing, and to leave it undone, forget about it, or tire of it. Far better,
I say, never to have made the resolution, than not to carry it through. I
would not have you aim very high. Find out what you can hit, and try to
strike the bull's-eye, but do not make shots at the moon.

Many a man has failed in his Christian course, because he has been too
ambitious at first. When running for a race you are warned to run quietly
at first, and to quicken speed at the end, and go to the goal with a rush. If
you put out your full strength at starting, you soon get out of breath, lag,
and probably come in last. The head is gold and the feet clay. I have known
a good many precociously pious children, and they have grown languid in
their religious profession when youth came on, and have ended in complete
indifference and an ungodly life. The head gold, the feet clay. A river always
has a small head, and widens as it goes on. A tree begins as a small plant, and
increases its bulk and height as it grows. The day begins with a little streak
of white, that widens and brightens till the sun arises. So it is in the Christian life. The beginnings are small, the results are great. A river does not
stop flowing, nor a tree arrest its growth, nor the day halt in its dawning; so

the true Christian life is one of gradual progress. And it is one of progress, because the Christian soul is endowed with the grace of perseverance. Without perseverance it gives up increasing, it ceases from the struggle that attends its growth, and comes to naught.

The grace of perseverance is then a very precious one. It is the continuance of life in your soul. Without it the good begun in you at Baptism will never be perfected; the seed sown in your heart will bear no fruit, the work begun will never be completed. I have seen little chickens that have died in their shells, without hatching out. They did not peck vigorously enough, or resolutely enough, at the thin white wall that shut them from the sun and air. They gave it up as hopeless, the breaking through of the shell, in which they could see no rift, and so they died. There is many a good intention, children, that dies like an unhatched chick. All that is wanted to perfect it, is perseverance, a determination to go on in spite of obstacles, to work on in spite of restraint. Persevere in good, and obstacles will give way, and obstruction crack and fall before you, and good resolves will end in living works.

Perseverance is a grace, that is, it is a gift of God. As such you must pray for it, pray that you may persevere unto the end, for it is only to such that the crown of life is promised: pray that He who has begun the good work in you may finish it. It is only he that endures to the end that shall be saved; only he who fights the good fight of faith, and having done all he can, stands on his ground, not driven from it, who will be rewarded as a victor.

When Jesus Christ died on the Cross, He bowed His head, and said, "It is finished!" What was finished? Why, the purpose for which He had come into the world, the Redemption of mankind. He went through with it at the cost of bitter agony, shame, and death; at the cost of the scourge, the crown of thorns, the nails, the spear. "The work which My Father hath given Me shall I not do it?" Take that text as your maxim through life. You have a work set you by your heavenly Father, the work of spreading His glory and making your immortal souls to grow. Pray God to give you His best gift of perseverance, that you may, all through life, continue doing the work of God, both without and within, till death comes: and then your perseverance in well-doing will be rewarded with Eternal Life.

My Lord in glory reigning,
  Upon the glassy sea,
By angel-hosts surrounded
  Is thinking still on me.
My heart for joy is dancing,
  My lamp is burning clear,
The Bridegroom bids me enter,
  If I but persevere.

My Lord a land is ruling,
  The Land of Pure Delight,
Whence hate and night are banished,
  And all is love and light.
What though my lot be lowly!
  What though my way be drear!
'Tis mine, 'tis mine, that Kingdom,
  If I but persevere.

My Lord a home is building,
  A mansion passing fair,
Of orient pearl and burnished gold,
  Of jewels, costly, rare.
A home where nothing wanteth,
  Away with doubt and fear!
'Tis mine, 'tis mine, that mansion,
  If I but persevere.

My Lord a crown is binding,
  Of flowers in heaven that blow,
Of ruby red, and turquoise,
  Of flames, and flakes of snow.
In sorest fight, hard driven,
  This thought my heart will cheer,
'Tis mine, 'tis mine, that garland,
  If I but persevere.

My Lord a song is teaching
　The angel-choirs on high,
They strike their harps and cymbals,
　And sound the psaltery;
A song to greet the wanderer,
　To heaven's gate drawing near,
'Tis mine, 'tis mine, that welcome,
　If I but persevere.

William Jennings Bryan

1 8 6 0 – 1 9 2 5

The court trial in Dayton, Tennessee, in July 1925, in which the agnostic Clarence Darrow defended a high school biology teacher, John Scopes, who was found guilty of violating a state law that forbade the teaching of the theory of evolution, was prosecuted by William Jennings Bryan, the Boy Orator of the Platte, the Great Commoner and unsuccessful agrarian candidate for the presidency against William McKinley. He had won the nomination with a galvanizing speech, as an advocate of the free coinage of silver, which concluded with the words, "You shall not press down upon the brow of labor this crown of thorns, you shall not crucify mankind upon a cross of gold." His gift for rhetoric, as displayed in the Scopes trial (and dramatized in the 1950s play *Inherit the Wind* by Jerome Lawrence and Robert E. Lee), made him a poignant figure in American history as well as the theater; his simple fundamentalism was mocked during Darrow's cross-examination. The stress of the trial, and the journalistic whiplashing he endured throughout it at the pens of reporters like H. L. Mencken, probably contributed to his death five days later.

　　Bryan was an immensely influential lecturer, touring America to

champion a number of public causes, risking ridicule for his complex be-
liefs. He was committed to a literal interpretation of the Bible, finding in
evolutionary theory a cheapening of the meaning of human existence on
earth and a flat contradiction of the words of Genesis. His public humiliation during the Scopes trial provides little testimony to the simplicity,
rather than the naiveté, of his faith in Christian dogma or to his sense of
humor. In a long state of conflict about the issue of prohibition of alcohol,
Bryan remarked of a diplomatic luncheon at the end of the First World War,
where the beverages of choice were water or grape juice, that "the glasses
for plain and mineral water looked a little lonesome."

Historians and theologians alike have questioned Bryan's wisdom; the
question of his integrity remains beyond doubt. The oration that follows was
solicited by the editors of the *New York Times* and was printed there on February 26, 1922.

God and Evolution

I appreciate your invitation to present the objections to Darwinism, or
evolution applied to man, and beg to submit to your readers the following:

The only part of evolution in which any considerable interest is felt is
evolution applied to man. A hypothesis in regard to the rocks and plant life
does not affect the philosophy upon which one's life is built. Evolution applied to fish, birds and beasts would not materially affect man's view of his
own responsibilities except as the acceptance of an unsupported hypothesis
as to these would be used to support a similar hypothesis as to man. The
evolution that is harmful—distinctly so—is the evolution that destroys
man's family tree as taught by the Bible and makes him a descendant of the
lower forms of life. This, as I shall try to show, is a very vital matter.

I deal with Darwinism because it is a definite hypothesis. In his "Descent of Man" and "Origin of Species" Darwin has presumed to outline a
family tree that begins, according to his estimate, about two hundred million years ago with marine animals. He attempts to trace man's line of descent from this obscure beginning up through fish, reptile, bird, and animal
to man. He has us descend from European, rather than American, apes and

locates our first ancestors in Africa. Then he says, "But why speculate?"—a very significant phrase because it applies to everything that he says. His entire discussion is speculation.

Darwin's "Laws"

Darwin set forth two (so-called) laws by which he attempts to explain the changes which he thought had taken place in the development of life from the earlier forms to man. One of these is called "natural selection" or "survival of the fittest," his argument being that a form of life which had any characteristic that was beneficial had a better chance of survival than a form of life that lacked that characteristic. The second law that he assumed to declare was called "sexual selection," by which he attempted to account for every change that was not accounted for by natural selection. Sexual selection has been laughed out of the classroom. Even in his day Darwin said (see note to "Descent of Man" 1874 edition, page 625) that it aroused more criticism than anything else he had said, when he used sexual selection to explain how man became a hairless animal. Natural selection is being increasingly discarded by scientists. John Burroughs, just before his death, registered a protest against it. But many evolutionists adhere to Darwin's *conclusions* while discarding his *explanations*. In other words, they accept the line of descent which he suggested *without any explanation whatever* to support it.

Other scientists accept the family tree which he outlined, but would have man branch off to a point below, or above, the development of apes and monkeys instead of coming through them. So far as I have been able to find, Darwin's line of descent has more supporters than any other outlined by evolutionists. If there is any other clearly defined family tree supported by a larger number of evolutionists, I shall be glad to have information about it that I may investigate it.

The first objection to Darwinism is that it is only a guess and was never anything more. It is called a "hypothesis," but the word "hypothesis," though euphonious, dignified, and high-sounding, is merely a scientific synonym for the old-fashioned word "guess." If Darwin had advanced his views as a *guess* they would not have survived for a year, but they have floated for a half a century, buoyed up by the inflated word "hypothesis." When it is understood that "hypothesis" means "guess," people will inspect it more carefully before accepting it.

No Support in the Bible

The second objection to Darwin's guess is that it has not one syllable in the Bible to support it. This ought to make Christians cautious about accepting it without thorough investigation. The Bible not only describes man's creation, but gives a reason for it; man is a part of God's plan and is placed on earth for a purpose. Both the Old and New Testament deal with man and with man only. They tell of God's creation of him, of God's dealings with him and of God's plans for him. Is it not strange that a Christian will accept Darwinism as a substitute for the Bible when the Bible not only does not support Darwin's hypothesis but directly and expressly contradicts it?

Third—Neither Darwin nor his supporters have been able to find a fact in the universe to support their hypothesis. With millions of species, the investigators have not been able to find *one single instance* in which one species has changed into another, although, according to the hypothesis, *all* species have developed from one or a few germs of life, the development being through the action of "resident forces" and without outside aid. Whenever a form of life, found in the rocks, is found among living organisms, there is no material change from the earliest form in which it is found. With millions of examples, nothing imperfect is found—nothing in the process of change. This statement may surprise those who have accepted evolution without investigation, as most of those who call themselves evolutionists have done. One preacher who wrote to me expressing great regret that I should dissent from Darwin said that he had not investigated the matter for himself, but that nearly all scientists seemed to accept Darwinism.

The latest word that we have on this subject comes from Professor Bateson, a high English authority, who journeyed all the way from London to Toronto, Canada, to address the American Association for the Advancement of Science the 28th day of last December. His speech has been published in full in the January issue of *Science*.

Professor Bateson is an evolutionist, but he tells with real pathos how every effort to discover the origin of species has failed. He takes up different lines of investigation, commenced hopefully but ending in disappointment. He concludes by saying, "Let us then proclaim in precise and unmistakable language that our faith in evolution is unshaken," and then he adds, "our doubts are not as to the reality or truth of evolution, but as to the origin of species, a technical, almost domestic problem. Any day that mystery may be solved." Here is optimism at its maximum. They fall back on faith. They have not yet found the origin of species, and yet how can evolution explain life unless it can account for change in species? Is it not more rational to believe in creation of man by separate act of God than to believe in evolution without a particle of evidence?

Fourth—Darwinism is not only without foundation, but it compels its believers to resort to explanations that are more absurd than anything found in the "Arabian Nights." Darwin explains that man's mind became superior to woman's because, among our brute ancestors, the males fought for their females and thus strengthened their minds. If he had lived until now, he would not have felt it necessary to make so ridiculous an explanation, because woman's mind is not now believed to be inferior to man's.

As to Hairless Men

Darwin also explained that the hair disappeared from the body, permitting man to become a hairless animal, because among our brute ancestors, the females preferred the males with the least hair and thus in the course of ages, bred the hair off. It is hardly necessary to point out that these explanations conflict: the males and females could not both select at the same time.

Evolutionists, not being willing to accept the theory of creation, have to explain everything, and their courage in this respect is as great as their efforts are laughable. The eye, for instance, according to evolutionists, was brought out by "the light beating upon the skin"; the ears came out in response to "air waves"; the leg is the development of a wart that chanced to appear on the belly of an animal; and so the tommyrot runs on *ad infinitum* and sensible people are asked to swallow it.

Recently a college professor told an audience in Philadelphia that a baby wiggles its big toe without wiggling its other toes because its ancestors climbed trees; also that we dream of falling because our forefathers fell out of trees fifty thousand years ago, adding that we are not hurt in our dreams of falling because we descended from those that were *not killed.* (If we descended from animals at all, we certainly did not descend from those that were killed in falling.) A professor in Illinois has fixed as the great day in history the day when a water puppy crawled upon the land and decided to stay there, thus becoming man's first progenitor. A dispatch from Paris recently announced that an eminent scientist had reported having communicated with the soul of a dog and learned that the dog was happy.

I simply mention these explanations to show what some people can believe who cannot believe the Bible. Evolution seems to close the heart of some to the plainest spiritual truths while it opens the mind to the wildest of guesses advanced in the name of science.

Guessing Is Not Science

Guesses are not science, Science is classified knowledge, and a scientist ought to be the last person to insist upon a guess being accepted until proof removes it from a field of hypothesis into the field of demonstrated truth. Christianity has nothing to fear from any *truth;* no *fact* disturbs the Christian religion or the Christian. It is the unsupported *guess* that is substituted for science to which opposition is made, and I think the objection is a valid one.

But, it may be asked, why should one object to Darwinism *even though it is not true?* This is a proper question and deserves a candid answer. There are many guesses which are perfectly groundless and at the same time entirely harmless; and it is not worthwhile to worry about a guess or to disturb the guesser so long as his guess does not harm others.

The objection to Darwinism is that it is *harmful,* as well as groundless. It entirely changes one's view of life and undermines faith in the Bible. Evolution has no place for the miracle or the supernatural. It flatters the egoist to be told that there is nothing that his mind cannot understand. Evolution proposed to bring all the processes of nature within the comprehension of man by making it the explanation of everything that is known. Creation implies a Creator and the finite mind cannot comprehend the infinite. We can understand some things, but we run across mystery at every point. Evolution attempts to solve the mystery of life by suggesting a process of development commencing "in the dawn of time" and continuing uninterrupted up until now. Evolution does not explain creation: it simply diverts attention from it by hiding it behind eons of time. If a man accepts Darwinism, or evolution applied to man, and is consistent, he rejects the miracle and the supernatural as impossible. He commences with the first chapter of Genesis and blots out the Bible story of man's creation, not because the evidence is insufficient, but because the miracle is inconsistent with evolution. If he is consistent, he will go through the Old Testament step by step and cut out all the miracles and the supernatural. He will then take up the New Testament and cut out all the supernatural—the virgin birth of Christ, His miracles, and His resurrection, leaving the Bible a storybook without binding authority upon the conscience of man. Of course, not all evolutionists are consistent; some fail to apply their hypothesis to the end just as some Christians fail to apply their Christianity to life.

Evolution and God

Most of the evolutionists are materialists; some admitting that they are atheists, others calling themselves agnostics. Some call themselves "theistic evolutionists," but the theistic evolutionist puts God so far away that He ceases to be a present influence in the life. Canon Barnes of Westminster, some two years ago, interpreted evolution as to put God back of the time when the electrons came out of "stuff" and combined (about 1740 of them) to form an atom. Since then, according to Canon Barnes, things have been developing to God's plan without God's aid.

It requires measureless credulity to enable one to believe that all that we see about us came by chance, by a series of happy-go-lucky accidents. If only an infinite God could have formed hydrogen and oxygen and united them in just the right proportions to produce water—the daily need of every living thing—scattered among the flowers all the colors of the rainbow and every variety of perfume, adjusted the mockingbird's throat to its musical scale, and fashioned a soul for man, why should we want to imprison God in an impenetrable past? This is a living world. Why not a living God upon the throne? Why not allow Him to work now?

Theistic evolutionists insist that they magnify God when they credit

Him with devising evolution as a plan of development. They sometimes characterize the Bible God as a "carpenter god" who is described as repairing His work from time to time at man's request. The question is not whether God could have made the world according to the plan of evolution—of course, an all-powerful God could make the world as He pleased. The real question is, Did God use evolution as His plan? If it could be shown that man, instead of being made in the image of God, is a development of beasts we would have to accept it, regardless of its effect, for truth is truth and must prevail. But, when there is no proof we have a right to consider the effect of the acceptance of an unsupported hypothesis.

Darwin's Agnosticism

Darwinism made an agnostic out of Darwin. When he was a young man he believed in God; before he died he declared that the beginning of all things is a mystery insoluble by us. When he was a young man he believed in the Bible; just before his death he declared that he did not believe that there had ever been any revelation; that banished the Bible as the inspired Word of God, and with it, the Christ of whom the Bible tells. When Darwin was young he believed in a future life; before he died he declared that each must decide the question for himself from vague, uncertain probabilities. He could not throw any light upon the great questions of life and immortality. He said that he "must be content to remain an agnostic."

And then he brought the most terrific indictment that I have read against his own hypothesis. He asks (just before his death): "Can the mind of man, which has, as I fully believe, been developed from a mind as low as that possessed by the lowest animal, be trusted when it draws such grand conclusions?" He brought man down to the brute level and then judged man's mind by brute standards.

This is Darwinism. This is Darwin's own testimony against himself. If Darwinism could make an agnostic of Darwin, what is its effect likely to be upon students to whom Darwinism is taught at the very age when they are throwing off parental authority and becoming independent? Darwin's guess gives the student an excuse for rejecting the authority of God, an excuse that appeals to him more strongly at this age than at any other age in life. Many of them come back after a while as Romanes came back. After feeding upon husks for twenty-five years, he began to feel his way back, like a prodigal son, to his father's house, but many never return.

Professor Leuba, who teaches psychology at Bryn Mawr, Pennsylvania, wrote a book about six years ago entitled "Belief in God and Immortality," . . . in which he declared that belief in God and immortality is dying out among the educated classes. As proof of this he gave the results which he obtained by submitting questions to prominent scientists in the United States. He says that he found that more than half of them, according to their own answers, do not believe in a personal God or a personal immortality. To reinforce his position, he sent questions to students of nine representative colleges and found that unbelief increases from 15 per cent in the freshman year to 30 per cent in the junior class, and to 40 to 45 per cent (among the men) at graduation. This he attributes to the influence of the scholarly men under whose instruction they pass in college.

Religion Waning Among Children

Anyone desiring to verify these statistics can do so by inquiry at our leading state institutions and even among some of our religious denominational colleges. Fathers and mothers complain of their children losing interest in religion and speaking lightly of the Bible. This begins when they come under the influence of a teacher who accepts Darwin's guess, ridicules the Bible story of creation and instructs the child upon the basis of the brute theory. In Columbia a teacher began his course in geology by telling the children to lay aside all that they had learned in Sunday School. A teacher of philosophy in the University of Michigan tells students that Christianity is a state of mind and that there are only two books of literary value in the Bible. Another professor in that university tells students that no thinking man can believe in God or in the Bible. A teacher in the University of Wisconsin tells his students that the Bible is a collection of myths. Another state university professor diverts a dozen young from the ministry and the president of a prominent state university tells his students in a lecture on religion to throw away religion if it does not harmonize with the teaching of biology, psychology, etc.

The effect of Darwinism is seen in the pulpits; men of prominent denominations deny the virgin birth of Christ and some even His resurrection. Two Presbyterians, preaching in New York state, recently told me that agnosticism was the natural attitude of old people. Evolution naturally leads to agnosticism. Those who teach Darwinism are undermining the faith of Christians; they are raising questions about the Bible as an authoritative source of truth; they are teaching materialistic views that rob the life of the young of spiritual values.

Christians do not object to freedom of speech; they believe that Biblical truth can hold its own in a fair field. They concede the right of ministers to pass from belief to agnosticism or atheism, but they contend that they should be honest enough to separate themselves from the ministry and not attempt to debase the religion which they profess.

And so in the matter of education. Christians do not dispute the right of any teacher to be agnostic or atheistic, but Christians do deny the right of agnostics and atheists to use the public school as a forum for the teaching of their doctrines.

The Bible has in many places been excluded from the schools on the ground that religion should not be taught by those paid by public taxation. If this doctrine is sound, what right have the enemies of religion to teach irreligion in the public schools? If the Bible cannot be taught, why should Christian taxpayers permit the teaching of guesses that make the Bible a lie? A teacher might just as well write over the door of his room, "Leave Christianity behind you, all ye who enter here," as to ask his students to accept a hypothesis directly and irreconcilably antagonistic to the Bible.

Our opponents are not fair. When we find fault with the teaching of Darwin's unsupported hypothesis, they talk about Copernicus and Galileo and ask whether we shall exclude science and return to the dark ages. Their evasion is a confession of weakness. We do not ask for the exclusion of any scientific truth, but we do protest an atheist teacher being allowed to blow his guesses in the face of the student. The Christians who want to teach religion in their schools furnish the money for denominational institutions. If atheists want to teach atheism, why do they not build their own schools and employ their own teachers? If a man really believes that he has brute blood in him, he can teach that to his children at home or he can send them to atheistic schools, where his children will not be in danger of losing their brute philosophy, but why should he be allowed to deal with other people's children as if they were little monkeys?

We stamp upon our coins "In God We Trust"; we administer to witnesses an oath in which God's name appears, our President takes his oath of
office upon the Bible. Is it fanatical to suggest that public taxes should not
be employed for the purpose of undermining the nation's God? When we
defend the Mosaic account of man's creation and contend that man has no
brute blood in him, but was made in God's image by separate act and placed
on earth to carry out a divine decree, we are defending the God of the Jews
as well as the God of the Gentiles, the God of the Catholics as well as the
God of the Protestants. We believe that faith in a Supreme Being is essential
to civilization as well as to religion and that abandonment of God means
ruin to the world and chaos to society.

Let these believers in "the tree man" come down out of the trees and
meet the issue. Let them defend the teachings of agnosticism or theism if
they dare. If they deny that the natural tendency of Darwinism is to lead
many to a denial of God, let them frankly point out the portions of the Bible
which they regard as consistent with Darwinism, or evolution applied to
man. They weaken faith in God, discourage prayer, raise doubt as to a future
life, reduce Christ to the stature of a man, and make the Bible a "scrap of
paper." As religion is the only basis of morals, it is time for Christians to protect religion from its most insidious enemy.

PART IX

"Woe Is Unto Me If I Preach Not the Gospel"

The Twentieth Century

Billy Sunday

1862–1935

I walked down State Street in Chicago one Sunday afternoon about forty years ago with some baseball players whose names were world renowned. We entered a saloon and drank, and then walked to the corner of State and Van Buren streets, which was then a vacant lot and where afterward Siegel & Cooper's big department store was erected.

I never pass that spot to this day that I do not stop, take off my hat, bow my head, and thank God for saving me and keeping me. I was passing that corner one day at the noon hour as hundreds of people were pouring out of the stores and office buildings for lunch. I stepped to the edge of the sidewalk, removed my hat and bowed my head. A policeman came up and asked, "Pardner, are you sick? I saw you step to the edge of the sidewalk and remove your hat. If you are, I'll call the wagon."

"No, my name is Billy Sunday. I was converted on this spot nearly forty years ago and I never pass here that I do not stop and pray and thank God for saving me. I was praying—that's why I removed my hat."

The policeman removed his cap, and stretching out his hand he said, "Put her there, Bill. I know who you are; you stay and pray as long as you want to and I'll keep the gang away from you."

By the time William Ashley Sunday took his stroll down State Street he could count nearly a quarter of a million additional conversions to his credit—and to the credit of his flamboyant, aw-shucks style of preaching. Estimates of his lifetime audiences—for the most part in the pre-radio age—come to a hundred million strong, a figure that eighteenth-century Titan of preaching George Whitefield could only have dreamed of reaching.

What he had originally seen on State Street was a "Gospel Wagon," a curbside music and preaching invitation to attend a mission nearby, which he did and which led to his conversion. Sunday the preacher, however, was a career superadded to that of Sunday the center fielder for the Chicago White Stockings, for whom he played from 1883 to 1891. Though his lifetime batting average was only .254, he was capable of circumnavigating the bases in fourteen seconds flat and so had other means of compensating for poor hitting.

As a preacher, Sunday took his place in a tradition of conversion-oriented, emotion-centered Baptist gospel reform. His most obvious immediate predecessor was Dwight L. Moody (1837–99), another, earlier Chicago-based preacher with a mass ministry. The second half of the nineteenth century was an age of constant European immigration to the United States, especially to the Northeast and Upper Midwest. Among the real problems that arose among these new citizens was the evil of drink—a probable trade-off for low wages and the absence of sufficient female companionship. Accordingly, the Anti-Saloon League, the temperance movement, and other meliorist efforts tried to cut off the problem at the source. Eventually a Pyrrhic victory—the Volstead Act banning alcohol consumption—was achieved during the First World War, and a decade and a half of Prohibition ensued until 1933. Billy Sunday became a tireless protagonist of the war on booze.

While temperance may have been his most intense proximate goal, it is clear that heaven remained his ultimate goal. The Sunday sermon that follows, later reprinted in the *Omaha Daily News,* has heaven for its subject and between its lines permits the attentive reader for a moment to visualize Billy sliding into home one final time.

Heaven

First, what do I want most of all? A man in Chicago said to me one day, "If I could have all I wanted of any one thing I would take money." He would be a fool, and so would you if you would make a similar choice. There are lots of things money can't do. Money can't buy life. Money can't buy health. I want to show you the absolute and utter futility of pinning your hope to a lot of fool things that will damn your soul to hell. There is only one hope to escape:

"As Moses lifted up the serpent in the wilderness, even so must the Son of Man be lifted up, that whosoever believeth in Him should not perish but have everlasting life. For God so loved the world that He gave His only begotten Son, that whosoever believeth in Him should not perish, but have everlasting life."

You can't hire a substitute in religion. You can't do some deed of kindness or act of philanthropy and substitute that for the necessity of repentance and faith in Jesus Christ. Lots of people will acknowledge their sin in the world, struggle on without Jesus Christ, and do their best to lead honorable, upright lives. Your morality will make you a better man or woman, but it will never save your soul. Morality doesn't save anybody. Your culture doesn't save you. I don't care who you are or how good you are, if you reject Jesus Christ you are doomed.

God hasn't one plan of salvation for the millionaire and another for the hobo. He has the same plan for everybody. God isn't going to ask you whether you like it or not. He isn't going to ask your opinion of His plan. There it is and we'll have to take it as God gives it. Simply ridding your life of the weeds of sin and not planting Jesus Christ is of no more value to you than a piece of ground is to a farmer without seed in it. And yet that is exactly what multitudes of people are doing.

Dismiss the idea that God owes you salvation. He gives you the opportunity, and if you don't improve it you will go to hell. Get out of your head the idea that God owes you salvation. Some people think God is like a great big Bookkeeper in heaven, and that He has a lot of angels as assistants. Every time you do a good thing He writes it down on one page, and every time you do a bad deed He writes it down on the opposite page. When you die He draws a line and adds them up. If you have done more good things than bad, you go to heaven; more bad things than good, you go to hell.

You moral man, you may be just as well off as the Christian until death knocks you down. Then you are lost, because you trust in your morality. The Christian is saved because he trusts in Jesus Christ. Some people want to wash their sins, and they whitewash them, but God wants them white. There's a lot of difference between being whitewashed and being washed white. Not only does God promise you salvation on the ground that you repent and accept Jesus Christ. He offers you eternal life as a gift.

I stand here and tell you that God offers you salvation through repentance and faith in Jesus Christ, and that you must accept it or be lost. You will stand up and argue the question, as though your argument could change God's plan. You can never do that. Not only has God promised you salvation on the ground of your acceptance of Jesus Christ as your Savior. He has promised to give you a home in which to spend eternity. Listen! "In my Father's house are many mansions. If it were not so I would have told you. I go to prepare a place for you."

Some people say heaven is a state or condition. I don't believe it. It might possibly be better to be in a heavenly state than in a heavenly place. It might be better to be in hell in a heavenly state than to be in heaven in a hellish state. That may be true. But heaven is as much a place as the home to which you are going when I dismiss this meeting. "I go to prepare a place for you."

Heaven will be free from everything that curses and damns this old world here. Wouldn't this be a grand old world if it weren't for a lot of things in it? The only thing that makes Omaha a decent place to live in is the religion of Jesus Christ. There isn't a man that would live in it if you took religion out.

There will be no sickness in heaven, no pain, no sin, no poverty, no want, no death, no grinding toil. There are many poor men and women that never have any rest. They have to get up early and work all day. But in heaven there remaineth a rest for the people of God. Weary women that start out early to your daily toil, you will not have to get out and toil all day. No toil in heaven, no sickness there!

Heaven, that is a place. He has gone to prepare it for those who do His will and keep His commandments and turn away from their sin. Isn't it great? Everything will be perfect in heaven. Down here we know only in part but there we shall know even as we are known. It is a city that hath foundations.

Among the last declarations of Jesus is "In my Father's house are many mansions." What a comfort to the bereaved and afflicted! Not only has God provided salvation through faith in Jesus Christ as a gift of God's out-stretched hand. He has also provided a home in which you can spend eternity.

Surely, friends of Omaha, from the beginning of the history of man, from the time Enoch walked with God and was not, until on the Isle of Patmos John saw let down by God out of heaven the new Jerusalem, surely we have ample proof that heaven is a place. Although we cannot see it with the natural eye, it is a place, the dwelling place of God and of the angels and of the redeemed through faith in the Son of God. He says, "I go to prepare a place for you." Oh, what a time we'll have in heaven!

In heaven they never mar the hillsides with spades, for they dig no graves. In heaven they never get sick. In heaven no one carries handker-chiefs, for nobody cries. In heaven they never phone for the undertaker, for nobody dies. In heaven you will never see a funeral procession going down the street, or crepe hanging from the door knob.

None of the things that enter your home here will enter there. "Former things have passed away." All things have become new. In heaven the flowers never fade, the winter winds and blasts never blow. The rivers never congeal, for it never gets cold.

Don't let God hang a "For Rent" sign in the mansion that He has prepared for you. Just send up word tonight, "Jesus, I've changed my mind. Put down my name for that. I'm coming, I'm coming home!"

"In my Father's house are many mansions. If it were not so I would have told you. I go to prepare a place for you."

Send Him word tonight to reserve one of those mansions for you!

Dietrich Bonhoeffer

1906–1945

*B*onhoeffer, eminent Protestant theologian whose principal concern was the role of Christianity in a secular world, was also a remarkable individual whose life in Hitlerian Germany engaged the even more difficult question of the attitude of the Christian toward a tyrannical state. Active in protests against the Nazi regime from its earliest days and especially against its anti-Semitism, Bonhoeffer was a leading spokesman for the Confessing Church, an organization of Protestant churches which became a center of resistance to totalitarian rule. In 1939 he considered taking refuge in New York City, but returned after two weeks, writing to Reinhold Niebuhr, "I will have no right to participate in the reconstruction of Germany after the war if I do not share the trials of this time with my people." His involvement in the resistance after his return became a conspirator's role when he was implicated in the July 19, 1944, plot to overthrow Hitler.

In this almost prescient sermon, preached on March 13, 1937, on the enigma of Judas's betrayal of Jesus Christ at the Last Supper, Bonhoeffer's theological concerns, which emphasized the "table fellowship" of the Lord's Supper and the final fellowship of the kingdom of God, converge with his own fate. Christianity has always grappled with the figure of the false disciple Judas as the terrible and necessary instrument of human redemption, since without his treachery the Crucifixion would not have taken place. Similarly, had Bonhoeffer himself not been likewise betrayed by a Gestapo informer, his own heroic testimony to the power of the Holy Spirit in the face of evil would not have received the seal of martyrdom. He was hanged in Flössenberg Prison a few days before the end of the war in Europe.

The Judas Sermon

...and the Son of man is betrayed into the hands of sinners.
Rise, let us be going: behold, he is at hand that doth betray me.
And while he yet spake, lo, Judas, one of the twelve, came, and
with him a great multitude with swords and staves, from the chief
priests and elders of the people.
Now he that betrayed him gave them a sign, saying, Whomsoever
I shall kiss, that same, is he: hold him fast.
And forthwith he came to Jesus, and said, Hail, master; and
kissed him.
And Jesus said unto him, Friend, wherefore art thou come? Then
came they, and laid hands on Jesus, and took him.

—MATTHEW 26:45b–50

Jesus had kept one thing from his disciples right up to the Last Supper. He had left them in no doubt about the path of suffering he was to tread. Three times he had told them that the Son of Man had to be delivered into the hands of sinners. But he had not yet revealed the deepest mystery to them. Only in their last hours together in the Passover meal could he say to them, The Son of Man is delivered into the hands of sinners—by treachery. "One of you will betray me."

By themselves, the enemy can have no power over him. It takes a friend for that: a close friend to give him up, a disciple to betray him. The most fearful thing of all happens not from the outside, but from within. Jesus' path to Golgotha begins with the disciples' betrayal. Some sleep, that incomprehensible sleep in Gethsemane, one betrays him, and in the end "all the disciples forsook him and fled."

The night of Gethsemane comes to an end. *"Behold the hour is at hand"*—the hour which Jesus had prophesied earlier, the hour of which the disciples had long known and at whose advent they trembled, the hour for which Jesus was so ready and for which the disciples were so utterly unprepared, the hour which nothing in the world could postpone any longer. "Behold the hour is at hand, *and the Son of Man is delivered into the hands of sinners.*"

"Delivered," says Jesus. That means that it is not the world that gets him in its grasp. Jesus himself is now handed over, surrendered, given up by his own. He is refused protection. No one will bother with him any more—leave him to the others. That is, Jesus is thrown aside, the protecting hands of his friends are lowered. Let the hands of the sinners do what they will with him now. Let them assault him, those whose impious hands should never have touched him. Let them make sport of him, mock him, smite him. We cannot change that now. This is what delivering up Jesus means, no longer to take his part, to surrender him to mockery and the power of the public, to let the world take its feelings out on him, not to stand by him any more. Jesus is handed over to the world by his own. That is his death.

Jesus knows what is before him. Firmly and decisively he summons his disciples, *"Rise, let us be going."* Often his threatening foes had to fall back before him, he went out freely through their midst, their hands fell. Then his hour had not yet come. Now it is here. Now he goes out to meet them of his own free will. And so that there shall be no doubt, so that it is absolutely clear that the hour has come in which he is to be delivered up, he says, *"See, my betrayer is at hand."* Not a glance at the great crowd that is approaching, nor at the swords and clubs of the enemy. By themselves they would have had no power! Jesus fixes his gaze solely on the one who has brought to pass this hour of darkness. His disciples too are to know where the enemy stands. For a moment everything, the history of salvation, the history of the world, lies in the hands of one man—the traitor. "See, my betrayer is at hand"—and in the darkness the disciples recognize him with horror—Judas, the disciple, the brother, the friend. With horror, for when Jesus that self-same evening had said to them, "One of you will betray me," none had dared to accuse another. None had been able to imagine another capable of such an action. And so each had to ask the other, "Lord, is it I?" "Lord, is it I?" Each in his own heart was more capable than his brother of such an action.

"While he was still speaking, Judas came, one of the twelve, and with him a great crowd with swords and clubs." Now we see only the two persons concerned. The disciples and the mob fall back—both do their work badly. Only two do their work as it had to be done.

Jesus and Judas. Who is Judas? That is the question. It is one of the oldest and most troublesome questions in Christianity. First of all let us keep to what the Evangelist himself tells us about Judas: he is *Judas, one of the twelve*. Can we feel something of the horror with which the Evangelist wrote this tiny clause? Judas, one of the twelve—what more was there to say here? And does this not really say everything? The whole of the dark mystery of Judas, and at the same time the deepest shock at his deed? Judas, one of the twelve. That means that it was impossible for this to happen; it was absolutely impossible—and yet it happened. No, there is nothing more to explain or to understand here. It is completely and utterly inexplicable, incomprehensible, it is an unfathomable riddle—and yet it was done. Judas, one of the twelve. That does not just mean that he was one who was with Jesus day and night, who had followed Jesus, who had sacrificed something, who had given up all to be with Jesus, a brother, a friend, a confidant of Peter, of John, of the Lord himself. It means something far more incomprehensible: Jesus himself called and chose Judas! That is the real mystery. For Jesus knew who would betray him from the beginning. In St. John's Gospel Jesus says, "Did I not choose you, the twelve, and one of you is a devil?" Judas, one of the twelve, and now the reader must look not only at Judas, but rather in great bewilderment at the Lord who chose him. And those whom he chose, he loved. He shared his whole life with them, he shared with them the mystery of his person, and in the same way he sent them out to preach the Gospel. He gave them authority to drive out demons and to heal—and Judas was in their midst. In fact, by his office of keeping charge of the disciples' purse, Judas seemed to have been marked out above the others.

True, John once says that Judas was a thief. But is that not meant to be just a dark hint that Judas was a thief in the case of Jesus, that he stole and surrendered to the world Jesus, who did not belong to him? And are not the thirty pieces of silver, too, simply a sign of how common and small the gift of the world is for him who knows the gift of Jesus? And yet Jesus knew from the beginning who would betray him! John has one more completely mysterious sign of Jesus' closeness with Judas to tell. On the night of the Last Supper, Jesus offers Judas a sop dipped in the dish, and with this sign of the closest community Satan enters into Judas. Thereupon Jesus says to Judas, half as a request, half as a command, "What you are going to do, do quickly." No one else understood what was happening. Everything remained between Jesus and Judas.

"Friend, why are you here?" Do you hear how Jesus still loves Judas, how he still calls him his friend at this hour? Even now Jesus will not let Judas go. He lets himself be kissed by him. He does not push him away. No, Judas must kiss him. His communion with Jesus must reach its consummation. "Why are you here?" Jesus knows well why Judas is here, and yet, "Why are you here?" And "Judas, would you betray the Son of Man with a kiss?" A last expression of a disciple's faithfulness, coupled with betrayal. A last sign of passionate love, joined with far more passionate hate. A last enjoyment of a subservient gesture, in consciousness of the superiority of the victory over Jesus which it brings. An action divided to its uttermost depths, this kiss of Judas. Not to be able to be abandoned by Christ, and yet to give him up. Judas, would you betray the Son of Man with a kiss? Who is Judas? Should we not also think here of the name that he bore? "Judas," does he not stand here for the people, divided to its uttermost depths, from which Jesus came, for the chosen people, that had received the promise of the Messiah and yet had rejected him? For the people of Judah, that loved the Messiah and yet could not love him in this way? "Judas"—his name in German means "thanks." Was this kiss not the thanks offered by the divided people and yet at the same time the eternal renunciation? Who is Judas? Who is the traitor? Faced with this question, are we to be able to do anything but say with the disciples, "Lord, is it I?" "Is it I?"

"Then they came and laid hands on Jesus and seized him"

> 'Tis I, whose sin now binds thee,
>   With anguish deep surrounds thee,
>   And nails thee to the tree;
>   The torture thou art feeling,
>   Thy patient love revealing,
> 'Tis I should bear it, I alone.

Let us now see the final end. At the same hour as Jesus accomplishes his redemptive suffering on the cross on Golgotha, Judas went and hanged himself, damned himself in fruitless repentance. What terrible community! Christendom has always seen in Judas the dark mystery of divine rejection and eternal damnation. It has recognized and borne witness with fear to the earnestness and judgment of God on the traitor. For precisely this reason, however, it has never looked on him with pride and arrogance, but has in trembling and in recognition of its own tremendous sin sung, "O poor Judas, what is this that thou hast done?" and would take refuge with him who hung upon the cross for all our sins and brought about our redemption, praying,

> In thy most bitter passion,
> My heart to share doth cry,
> With thee for my salvation
> Upon the cross to die.
> Ah, keep my heart thus moved
> To stand thy cross beneath,
> To mourn thee well-beloved
> Yet thank thee for thy death.

Ronald Knox

1 8 8 8 – 1 9 5 7

The novelist Evelyn Waugh wrote only two biographies, one on the Jesuit martyr Sir Edmund Campion, the other on Ronald Knox. Born into an evangelical Church of England family of missionaries, Knox was a dazzlingly precocious scholar, took a First at Oxford, and was briefly a leader in the Anglo-Catholic movement before, as his era would have called it, he "went over to Rome," in 1917. After his conversion, like John Henry Newman's several generations earlier, he entered a life which shared some of the difficult renunciations and the fine accomplishments of his great Victorian model. The autobiographical *A Spiritual Aeneid* (1918) describes his decision to become a Roman Catholic, while Knox's new translation of the Bible, based on the Vulgate, kept alive the promise of the brilliant academic career begun at Oxford.

Knox successfully published detective stories and later acquired a reputation as a broadcaster and journalist. The first years of his transition from the Anglican to the Roman Catholic faith involved isolation and schoolmastering before he returned to Oxford as chaplain to Catholic undergraduates. His homilies at Sunday mass were celebrated for what a contemporary scholar calls his "formation in a culture where literature and religion shared a common grammar." Always in high demand as a preacher, a formidable apologist in the Roman Catholic tradition (his famed correspondence with Sir Arnold Lunn charmed a generation), and a historian of religion who once compared John Wesley to King Lear, Knox kept his spiritual life hidden, confiding once that in the great bulk of his prayers "I have not felt . . . as I was talking to God in His presence, but rather apostrophizing Him in his absence."

During the Second World War, Knox lived in the countryside with aristocratic friends whom he was preparing for reception into the Catholic Church, while serving as chaplain to a group of evacuees from a girls' convent school. There he preached some of his most elegant and beguiling sermons, including a slow but never halting exposition of the Nicene Creed.

The Creed in Slow Motion

I Believe in the Holy Ghost (1)

I've always been rather fond of the story, which I should think is almost certainly untrue, of a small boy in the East End of London who came to confession, and reduced his confession to the shortest possible limits by saying, "Bless me, Father, for I have sinned; thrown mud at the buses and don't believe in the Holy Ghost." I don't know what your experience may have been, but personally I have never been assailed by any temptation to throw mud at buses, and therefore I can't say what excuses the penitent may have had for this inconsiderate treatment of public property. But I think he was obviously a fool not to believe in the Holy Ghost. If you are going to believe in the Christian religion at all, and indeed in a sense if you are going to believe in any religion at all, I don't see how you can help believing in the Holy Ghost.

Suppose you come across one of those people, who are getting rather common in England nowadays, who don't quite like to describe themselves as Christians, but say they believe in God; yes, of course they believe in God. Suppose you try to pin them down, and find out what they really mean by it; suppose you ask, for example, "Do you believe that God is a Person, in the same sense as you and me?"—you will find that they reply, "Oh, dear no; not a person; that would be anthromophorphism." And you say, "Well, let's cut that part out; what do you really think God is like? How would you describe him?" And what's their answer? Why, that God is a Spirit, a sort of Force or Influence which manifests itself in various ways in and through this visible world of ours, but particularly manifests itself in the religious aspirations of human beings. To which you may very sensibly reply, "Oh, I see, you believe in the Holy Ghost, but not in the Father or the Son."

Well, we believe in the Holy Ghost as well as the Father and the Son; and this afternoon we want to get some rough idea, at any rate, of what we mean by that. I think we are all rather apt, at the back of our minds, to forget that the Holy Spirit existed from all eternity, and to think of him as having come into existence on the Day of Pentecost. Well, of course that can't be true, because the Blessed Trinity has existed from all eternity, and it wouldn't be a Trinity without the Holy Spirit. So we've got to go right back, and think of God existing altogether outside time, independently of any worlds, or any angels for that matter. From all eternity there has been a multiplicity of life within the unity of the Godhead. God the Father, from all eternity, has spoken a Word; or if you prefer to put it in a rather more luminous way, from all eternity he has thought a thought of himself. When you or I think, the thought has no existence outside our own minds; but when the eternal Mind thinks of itself, it produces a Thought as eternal as itself, and that Thought is, like the eternal Mind, a Person. And so you get two persons within the Blessed Trinity, the eternal Mind and its eternal Thought. And now, you can't imagine two Divine Persons as existing side by side, can you, without their having some relation to each other, some attitude towards each other; and what that attitude will be it is not difficult to guess; they will love one another. And this Love, which springs at once from the eternal Mind and its eternal Thought, binding them to one another, is the Holy Spirit. That is why we say that the Holy Spirit proceeds from the Father and the Son. He is the conscious response of Love which springs up between them; he goes out from each of them to the other. That is not intended to be an explanation of the doctrine of the Blessed Trinity, because you cannot explain a mystery. But I think that is as near as our minds will get to understanding what the doctrine of the Trinity is about.

"Well," you say, "thank you very much; I expect one ought to know about all that, but it seems rather abstruse theology; now let's get on to Pentecost." You're quite wrong again; we haven't nearly got on to Pentecost yet. You didn't really think, did you, that the Holy Spirit had nothing at all to do with the visible creation until A.D. 30? If you did think that, you were very badly out in your dates. Let's go back to the second verse of the Bible, which tells us about a time millions and millions of years ago. It says, "the earth was void and empty, and darkness was upon the face of the deep. And the Spirit of God moved over the waters." The Hebrew for that is even jollier; it says that the earth was all *tohu* and *bohu,* which is a very good way of describing emptiness and confusion. Try to imagine the earth, or the universe if you prefer it, without any light at all, just undulations of matter, a great formless sea; no birds, no animals, no plants. And even then, "the Spirit of God moved over the waters." As soon as there was any creation at all, even when it was all *tohu* and *bohu,* it gave out a kind of dumb response to its Creator; it was like a mist rising in a river valley at evening; and what was it? It was the Spirit of God.

When God created the universe, it was a sort of extension, you may say, of that eternal Thought of his, which we call his Word. That is why we always think of the Second Person of the Blessed Trinity as specially concerned in the work of creation. And as, within the Godhead itself, the answer to that act of Thought was an eternal Act of Love, the Holy Spirit; so, when God created things outside himself, there was an immediate response of love from his creatures; and that response was inspired in them by the Holy Spirit. And all through the Old Testament you get the idea of God's Spirit as pervading nature; "the Spirit of the Lord fills the whole world, and that which containeth all things hath knowledge of the Voice."

What I'm saying just now isn't strict Catholic doctrine, all defined and printed in handbooks. But I think it's quite impossible to understand the Old Testament until you see that the Jews thought of the brute creation and even inanimate creation, mountains and valleys and sun and stars and beasts and birds and fishes—they always make a great point of the fishes—as conspiring to praise God all the time. And the medieval attitude was to accept that point of view about the response of creation to God, and to say, "Of course, that's the Holy Spirit; that's the response to God in nature. The Love which binds the Father and the Son overflows into created things, and makes them, too, aspire lovingly to God."

But whether you value that idea about God in nature or not, it's quite certain that once *man* has come into being, the Holy Spirit has an office to perform here on earth. No, not on the Day of Pentecost; do stop being in such a hurry to get on to the Day of Pentecost. If you think the Holy Spirit never interfered in human affairs between the time of Adam and the time of St. Peter, you are a heretic. Because although this Creed we are having sermons about doesn't mention it, the longer creed which is said at Mass, the Nicene Creed, goes out of its way at this point to say, "who spoke by the prophets." What does that mean? Well, in the first place what it says; it means that the Holy Spirit gave certain messages of warning to the Jews, by means of Isaias, Jeremy, Ezechiel, Daniel, Osee, Joel, Amos, Abdias, Jonas, Micheas, Naham, Habacuc, Sophonias, Aggaeus, Zachary and Malachy. They were moved to say various things, many of which it is difficult to understand, and some of which they probably didn't understand themselves. They were carried away by the impetus of the Holy Spirit, and the great point is that many of the things which they said, or rather which he said through them, were prophecies about the coming of Jesus Christ. I don't suppose that Isaias quite knew what he was talking about when he said, "Behold, a Virgin shall conceive and bear a Son." He just felt impelled, somehow, to say that, because that was what the Holy Spirit wanted him to say.

But, remember, this clause in the Nicene Creed means something more; it means that the *whole* of the Old Testament is inspired. And a lot of the books in the Old Testament are not prophecy exactly; they are pieces of history, and sometimes, like other pieces of history, it must be admitted, I think, that they are not very exciting to read, especially when you came across long lists of names. Well, all that is inspired. What do we mean when we say that it is inspired? Do we mean that the men who originally wrote those books, the books of Kings for example, simply sat down with a pen and took it all down as the Holy Spirit dictated it to them, just as you might take down a piece of dictation from one of the mistresses here? Must we picture them as saying, "Amasias, was five and twenty years old when he began to reign (yes, I've got that), and he reigned nine and twenty years in Jerusalem (yes, I've got that), and his mother's name was Joadan (how do you spell Joadan, please?)"—and so on and so on? There have been people before now who have thought of the inspiration of Holy Scripture as if it were a mere process of dictation, of that kind.

But of course that is not the way in which the Old Testament was written, and you can prove it. Because if you look at the second book of Machabees (a thing which very few people do) you will find that the author describes to us how he wrote his book. He says that he has abridged in one book all the history that was written in five books by somebody called Jason of Cyrene. Now, there is no reason whatever to think that Jason of Cyrene was inspired. But the man—we don't know his name, or anything about him—who got to work and boiled down those five books into one book, the second book of Machabees, *was* inspired. And inspiration didn't make it an easy job, like dictation is; you know how when one is doing dictation one can be thinking about all sorts of jolly things at the same time and do it more or less automatically. But no, this man says, "As to ourselves indeed in undertaking this work of abridging, we have taken in hand no easy task; yea, rather a business full of watching and sweat." It was like writing an essay, when you have to get the stuff out of books but put it down in your own words. And when he had finished, although it was an inspired book, this man wasn't in the least certain that it would be a best seller. He says at the end, "I will here make an end of my narration, which if I have done well, and as becometh the history, it is what I desired; but if not so perfectly, it must be pardoned me." Just what you feel inclined to say when you've finished writing an essay. He sat down and wrote quite an ordinary book, in quite an ordinary way; and yet it was inspired.

What do we mean when we say that it was inspired, or that any book of the Old Testament was inspired? Not that it was *dictated* by the Holy Spirit, but that the Holy Spirit helped the writers, watched over the process and saw they did it right; put ideas, perhaps, into their heads, which made them say, "That's rather a good idea; I never thought of that before"—but it all seemed to come out of their heads, and indeed it *did* come out of their heads; because the Holy Spirit works in our heads. That doesn't necessarily mean that every word in the Old Testament, taken quite literally, is infallibly accurate. You find it stated in the Psalms, for instance, that God has made the round world so sure that it cannot be moved. And when Galileo, or rather, first Copernicus and then Galileo, produced the idea which we all believe in nowadays, that the earth travels round and round on its own axis; that the sun doesn't really "set," all that happens is that we have lost sight of it because we've turned round the corner—when that idea was produced, a lot of people, chiefly Protestants, said, "That's heresy! The Bible tells us that the earth can't be moved, and here are these people wanting us to believe that it's speeding round and round like mad!" But of course that was idiotic of them. The Psalms weren't written to teach us lessons in geography; they were poetry, and the person who wrote that verse was just talking in the ordinary language of his time. So you can't be certain that every word of the Old Testament is *literally* true. But you can be certain that the theology of the Old Testament, once you have understood it properly and made allowances for the Hebrew way of saying things, *must* be true; because when it was written the Holy Spirit was at work to see that the thing got done right.

And remember, the Holy Spirit wasn't at work only amongst the Jews. All through those centuries before our Lord came, whenever a human heart aspired to God, it was the same old story; it was the Third Person of the Blessed Trinity carrying out in this visible, created world the same work which he carries out in the uncreated, invisible world of eternity. He was making, in us, that response of love towards the eternal Father which it is his nature to make. In spite of the Fall, there's a kind of instinct which makes man look up to God, try to get back to God, and that instinct is the silent working of the Holy Spirit, in the very heart even of unredeemed mankind.

There, now, we haven't got on to the Day of Pentecost after all; that's what comes of interrupting. But all this that I've been saying to you isn't really waste of time, because it's very difficult to get a right idea about the work of the Holy Spirit in the order of grace, until you've got some idea of what the Holy Spirit does in the order of nature. His essential office is to be the response of love in our hearts to the goodness of God.

I Believe in the Holy Ghost (2)

This Sunday, we really must get on to the Day of Pentecost. Try and imagine the picture of it; Jerusalem, quite a small town, with very narrow streets at that, crowded with thousands of Jewish pilgrims from all over the known world. They had come there to celebrate the Feast of Weeks, which was the Jewish harvest festival; because in that part of the world you get the wheat harvest in by Whit Sunday, and that must give you a nice long slack interval before the potatoes want picking. All these visitors from the parts of Libya about Cyrene—the General Montgomery country—and Elam, which would be right down somewhere in Iraq, and Pontus, not far from the southern end of where the Russians were fighting the Germans; nearly all Jews, but born and bred in a foreign country, so that they were familiar with the odd dialects the country people used in all these outlying parts of the world; Greek would be their natural language, but they'd have to know the local dialect so as to be able to talk to the people who came in to do business with them. I don't know if you've ever been to Lourdes, but I should think it must have been very much like Lourdes at the height of the pilgrimage season.

And what were they doing there, all these people? Were they really very much interested in thanking God for the harvest having been got in one rather unimportant district of the province of Syria? No, but it was the tradition to rally round when the great feasts came on in Jerusalem; their fathers had always done it, and they weren't going to give it up; they were devout men, and it was the thing to do. But it must have seemed rather pointless, rather out of the world-picture, now that Judea had become such a very unimportant place, and was ruled by foreign conquerors. So they drifted about the streets, a great tide of humanity, without any vital religious inspiration to rally them. It was rather like that tide of undifferentiated matter we were talking about last Sunday, the *tohu* and *bohu* which were the first result of God's creation. Was it possible that the Spirit of God would move on these sluggish waters, too?

And of course, quite suddenly, it did. Quite suddenly, here and there in the crowd, you saw the extraordinary sight of a working man from Galilee making his way to the temple, shouting out God's praises in an uncontrollable way that made you wonder whether he was drunk, though you had only just cleared away breakfast. And when you got nearer, you

found that it was St. Peter shouting out phrases in the language of Cappadocia, or St. Thomas talking fluent Parthian, and St. Matthew giving you
bits of his Gospel in the Berber dialect of Northern Africa. And the infec-
tion of their example spread; people took up their cries, hardly knowing
what they were doing, in a babel of strange tongues; from that *tohu* and *bohu*
of nationalities the response of the Holy Spirit went up once more in aspirations of love towards the God who had made all nations to dwell on the
face of the earth.

What did it mean? Well, it meant in general that, this day, the Catholic
Church was born. But we shall have to talk about the Catholic Church, I
suppose, about the end of September, so I won't enlarge on that subject just
now. The Holy Spirit does dwell in the Catholic Church as a whole, inspires
its official teachings infallibly, makes its doctors and theologians hit the right
nail on the head more often than not, and prevents popes and bishops, anyhow, from making the wrong move in practical politics all the time. But I
want to think more particularly this afternoon of the inspiration of the
Holy Spirit as it affects the life of the individual Christian, as it affects you
and me.

The first people to receive the Holy Spirit were, as we have seen, the
Apostles. And they needed his inspiration for a special reason; they were
going out all over the world to preach Jesus Christ, and they were going to
make themselves unpopular, because they would come up against a lot of
vested interests in doing so. They would be brought to trial before rulers
and magistrates, who would inquire rather unintelligently, as rulers and
magistrates do, "Here, what's all this?" And what were they going to say?
Our Lord himself warned them about that, if you remember; he told them,
"Don't bother about what you are going to say. When the time comes, it
won't be you that speak, it will be the spirit of your Heavenly Father that
speaks in you." That was the immediate office of the Holy Spirit, when he
came to earth on the Day of Pentecost to begin a new dispensation; he was
to enable the Apostles to put up an inspired defense when they were
brought to trial in courts of law. And that is why our Lord promised them
that he would send them a Paraclete. In the Protestant translation of the
Bible that word is translated, "the Comforter"; but that, I'm afraid, was a
howler made by the Protestant translators of the Bible; they mixed up the
active with the passive, the sort of thing I am sure any of you would scorn

to do. No, the Paraclete, a long and ugly word which you have come across before now in hymns, means primarily the lawyer who defends you in a court of justice; he has to explain that you did really mean to pay for the six yards of silk you took off the counter, and if you were found leaving the shop with the silk hidden in your umbrella, that was just absentmindedness. The Advocate, that is the primary meaning of Paraclete; though I don't think it makes a very pretty translation, because it suggests a rather prosy old gentleman, and a Scot at that.

But it goes deeper, of course. The Friend in Need—that is really what is meant by the word Paraclete. And you will find in St. Paul's writings that he didn't merely think of the Holy Spirit as suggesting to us useful things to say in a court of law; he makes suggestions to us about our prayers. "The Spirit," he says, "helps our weakness; we don't know how to pray as we ought to, but the Spirit himself makes petitions on our behalf, with groanings which cannot be uttered." So, you see, we don't have to think of the assistance of the Holy Spirit as something which we need when it is necessary for us to talk in public; like the Scots minister who began an extempore speech by saying, "When I'm called upon suddenly like this, I just say what the Holy Spirit puts into my mind; but if you give me an hour or two for preparation, I can do much better." The assistance of the Holy Spirit is something which we want every time we say our prayers; indeed, I suppose if you look at the thing properly the right way to put it is that every time we say our prayers it is the Holy Spirit who is praying *in* us.

What makes it difficult for us to realize that, is that we don't distinguish as carefully as we ought to between the extraordinary and the ordinary operations of the Holy Spirit. Except when the Holy Spirit makes his presence felt by outward manifestations, we forget that he's there. You see, when you were confirmed you received exactly the same gift which our Lady and the Apostles received on the Day of Pentecost. But you didn't thereupon get up and start praising God in Tamil or Choctaw; why was that? Because the Holy Spirit doesn't, as a rule, signalize his coming by these strange outward manifestations; he only does it occasionally, where it is specially important to call attention to what is happening. It's the same, after all, when you read the lives of the Saints. You read about Saints who went off into an ecstasy for five or six hours at a time, when they were saying their prayers, quite unconscious of what was going on around them. When that sort of thing happens, you can see at once that the Holy Spirit is taking a hand in it. But when *you* are kneeling there just going on saying, "Holy Mary, Mother of God, pray for us sinners now and at the hour of our death," you don't think of the Holy Spirit as having anything to do with *that;* it's just *you* trying to say your prayers, and not making much of it even so.

What we ought to try and realize much more than we do is that these very second-rate prayers of ours are really prayed in us, so far as they are prayers at all, by the Holy Spirit. No doubt our minds are in a rather confused state, full of distractions; there's a good deal of *tohu* and *bohu* about it. But the same echo of Divine Love which awoke in that formless creation, when the Spirit of God moved upon the face of the waters, awakes in you when you pray; the wind of Pentecost is blowing through the world still, and you are like a reed rustling in the wind; the motion, the activity, is his really, not yours; or rather, your activity conspires with his. And I think we sometimes make a mistake about that when our prayers aren't going too well. We try to make a tremendous effort at concentration, try to pump up more energy from somewhere inside ourselves, and reduce ourselves to a better state of prayer by sheer will-power. Whereas I think really the right attitude for us is to fall back more on the Holy Spirit, and leave things more to him. To say, "Go on praying in me, Holy Spirit; I can't do anything, I know I can't do anything, by these frantic efforts of my own. Every time I really try to settle down to it I find myself thinking about the holidays, or about that girl I've quarreled with, and nothing seems to come. But I *know* it's all right really, because it is *you* who do the praying; I am only a dumb instrument for you to make noises with. Since I find my own efforts make so little difference, let me keep still and leave room for you to go on praying, praying in me."

And it's the same with the inspirations of the Holy Spirit, with the guidance which he gives us. We all ought to pray to the Holy Spirit for guidance much more than we do. The reason, partly, why we don't do it more is that we expect too much of him and therefore we are disappointed. When we ask the Holy Spirit to show us what we ought to do on this occasion or that, we expect that a sudden, miraculous illumination will come into our minds; that we shall be told, as if by a voice speaking in our ears, what we ought to do. We have read about that kind of thing in the lives of the Saints, about St. Joan of Arc being told by her voices that she must go and tell the King of France to get himself crowned, and St. Catherine of Siena being suddenly inspired to tell the Pope to go back to Rome, and so on. Well, here again it's quite true that the Holy Spirit can, and sometimes does, give very holy people unexpected, miraculous guidance of this kind; it just comes to them—you can't imagine it as being the result of any human calculations of their own.

Sometimes, indeed, it hardly seems to make sense. There was St. Alexius, whose feast we kept yesterday. He left his home as a young man on a pilgrimage, and only came back years later, when they didn't recognize him. But they were good people, St. Alexius's parents, and they took pity on this rather half-witted, very holy young man who had dropped in on them, and let him stay in the house. So he lived in his father's house for seventeen years, without letting on who he was, and it was only found out by a written message which he left behind him when he died. The collect for yesterday asks God that as we celebrate St. Alexius's feast, so we may follow his example; but of course if we all did it would create a great deal of confusion and make our parents very unhappy. No, that was a special vocation which the Holy Spirit had for St. Alexius; and he put the idea into St. Alexius's head by a special, miraculous inspiration. But you and I mustn't expect that kind of thing.

We mustn't expect that kind of thing; but we must pray to the Holy Spirit for his guidance, all the same. Suppose you're leaving school, and can't make up your mind whether to apply for the Army or the Navy or the Air Force. It's perfectly reasonable to keep a novena to the Holy Spirit and ask for his guidance about it; but you mustn't expect to have a vision of your patron saint dressed in a sky-blue uniform, or something of that kind, so as to make you quite certain what it is God wants you to do. No, you keep your novena, and at the same time you take advice from your relations and friends, and you try to balance up in your own mind the arguments for and against this or that course. And when you have made up your mind in this way, you know that, if you kept your novena faithfully, the Holy Spirit *has* helped you to make up your mind, although there is nothing to show for it. Probably, sooner or later, you will come across a queer kind of Protestants who talk a great deal about "guidance," and think you ought never to do any-thing, not even cross the street or buy a new hat, unless you get a sudden, unaccountable indication that it is God's will for you to do so. They won't believe that if you've made up your mind to do a thing as the result of human calculations, the Holy Spirit can have had anything to do with it. And that, you see, is want of faith on their part. They imagine that the Holy Spirit can never interfere in the course of human affairs without making a splash about it and producing a kind of miraculous certainty in people's minds about what they ought to do. They can't believe that he has ordinary, as well as extraordinary, operations.

The primary office of the Holy Spirit is not to create a nine days' won-der by appearing suddenly in rushing winds, and tongues of fire. He is the eternal Love that proceeds from the Father and the Divine Word, produc-ing in human creatures and on behalf of human creatures, without their knowing it, a response of love to the Divine Love which created them.

C. S. Lewis

1898–1963

*W*ithin an hour or so of each other on the afternoon of Novem-ber 22, 1963, John F. Kennedy and Clive Staples Lewis died. A bit later in the day, in Los Angeles, so did Aldous Huxley. Of the three, a convincing case could be made that Lewis was the least remarkable. He spent the first quarter of his life in Belfast, where he was born to an Anglo-Irish family, that, like the families of so many interesting British writers, had plenty of clergy in its genealogy. He was a successful don teaching English literature at Oxford University during the second and third quarters of his life, and in the final quarter he did the same at Cambridge. He lived, inseparable, with his alcoholic older brother, Warnie, in the same house virtually all of his adult life, and it was there he died, an event nearly overlooked in the wake of the presidential assassination.

Despite the retrospective appearance of outward stability, and even dullness, in Lewis's life, his writings and those whose lives he directly affected provide far better testimony of the vivid and tumultuous personality within. The sermon (Lewis was often called upon to address religious assemblies of all sorts) that follows is about the meaning of the Christian's "membership" in Christ. Lewis's own life might usefully be seen as a chronicle of his quest for a satisfying membership in human society. First there was the shattering loss of his mother to cancer when he was nine, followed by an irreparable estrangement from his father. Then he set up his own household with his brother and Janie Moore, a woman seventeen years his senior. Next we note the establishment of the famous Inklings literary group, which included J. R. R. Tolkien. Finally, following Janie's death in 1951, he began his unusual relationship with, and then secret marriage to, Joy Gresham, an American Jewish convert to Christianity seventeen years his *junior,* who, like his mother, died of cancer not long after their union, and who also left behind two sons.

Although Lewis's literary criticism, his Narnia books for children, and his adult fiction would suffice to assure his place among the best writers of our century, it is the abundant and enduring stream of his spiritual and religious writing that will always attract us to him. Beginning with *The Pilgrim's Regress* (1933), his best-seller *The Screwtape Letters* (1942), and *Mere Christianity* (1952), a compilation of his wartime talks on the radio, he poured forth a Niagara of essays, talks, letters, and insights that fruitfully and practically instruct us about what it means to lead a life of the spirit. Special mention should be made of his autobiographical memoir, *Surprised by Joy* (1955), and his classic meditation on the meaning of his wife's death, *A Grief Observed* (1961).

Once, at a dinner party at which the subject arose of whom the guests would first like to meet in the afterlife, Lewis had no hesitation in naming Adam. At last in the company of his first ancestor, C. S. Lewis presumably looked forward to the privilege of an intimate, uninterrupted three-way conversation with the Deity.

Membership

No Christian and, indeed, no historian could accept the epigram which defines religion as "what a man does with his solitude." It was one of the Wesleys, I think, who said that the New Testament knows nothing of solitary religion. We are forbidden to neglect the assembling of ourselves together. Christianity is already institutional in the earliest of its documents. The Church is the Bride of Christ. We are members of one another.

In our own age the idea that religion belongs to our private life—that it is, in fact, an occupation for the individual's hour of leisure—is at once paradoxical, dangerous, and natural. It is paradoxical because this exaltation of the individual in the religious field springs up in an age when collectivism is ruthlessly defeating the individual in every other field. I see this even in a university. When I first went to Oxford the typical undergraduate society consisted of a dozen men, who knew one another intimately, hearing a paper by one of their own number in a small sitting-room and hammering out their problem till one or two in the morning. Before the war the typical undergraduate society had come to be a mixed audience of one or two hundred students assembled in a public hall to hear a lecture from some visiting celebrity. Even on those rare occasions when a modern undergraduate is not attending some such society he is seldom engaged in those solitary walks, or walks with a single companion, which built the minds of the previous generations. He lives in a crowd; caucus has replaced friendship. And this tendency not only exists both within and without the university, but is often approved. There is a crowd of busybodies, self-appointed masters of ceremonies, whose life is devoted to destroying solitude wherever solitude still exists. They call it "taking the young people out of themselves," or "waking them up," or "overcoming their apathy." If an Augustine, a Vaughan, a Traherne, or a Wordsworth should be born in the modern world, the leaders of a youth organization would soon cure him. If a really good home, such as the home of Alcinous and Arete in the *Odyssey* or the Rostovs in *War and Peace* or any of Charlotte M. Yonge's families, existed today, it would be denounced as *bourgeois* and every engine of destruction would be leveled against it. And even where the planners fail and someone is left physically by himself, the wireless has seen to it that he will be—in a sense not intended by Scipio—never less alone than when alone. We live, in fact, in a world starved for solitude, silence, and privacy, and therefore starved for meditation and true friendship.

That religion should be relegated to solitude in such an age is, then, paradoxical. But it is also dangerous for two reasons. In the first place, when the modern world says to us aloud, "You may be religious when you are alone," it adds under its breath, "and I will see to it that you never are alone." To make Christianity a private affair while banishing all privacy is to relegate it to the rainbow's end or the Greek calends. That is one of the enemy's stratagems. In the second place, there is the danger that real Christians who know that Christianity is not a solitary affair may react against that error by simply transporting into our spiritual life that same collectivism which has already conquered our secular life. That is the enemy's other stratagem. Like a good chess player, he is always trying to maneuver you into a position where you can save your castle only by losing your bishop. In order to avoid the trap we must insist that though the private conception of Christianity is an error, it is a profoundly natural one and is clumsily attempting to guard a great truth. Behind it is the obvious feeling that our modern collectivism is an outrage upon human nature and that from this, as from all other evils, God will be our shield and buckler.

This feeling is just. As personal and private life is lower than participation in the Body of Christ, so the collective life is lower than the personal and private life and has no value save in its service. The secular community, since it exists for our natural good and not for our supernatural, has no higher end than to facilitate and safeguard the family, and friendship, and solitude. To be happy at home, said Johnson, is the end of all human endeavor. As long as we are thinking only of natural values we must say that the sun looks down on nothing half so good as a household laughing together over a meal, or two friends talking over a pint of beer, or a man alone reading a book that interests him; and that all economies, politics, laws, armies, and institutions, save insofar as they prolong and multiply such scenes, are a mere ploughing the sand and sowing the ocean, a meaningless vanity and vexation of spirit. Collective activities are, of course, necessary, but this is the end to which they are necessary. Great sacrifices of this private happiness by those who have it may be necessary in order that it may be more widely distributed. All may have to be a little hungry in order that none may starve. But do not let us mistake necessary evils for good. The mistake is easily made. Fruit has to be tinned if it is to be transported and has to lose thereby some of its good qualities. But one meets people who have learned actually to prefer the tinned fruit to the fresh. A sick society must think much about politics, as a sick man must think much about his digestion; to ignore the subject may be fatal cowardice for the one as for the other. But if either comes to regard it as the natural food of the mind—if either forgets that we think of such things only in order to be able to think of something else—then what was undertaken for the sake of health has become itself a new and deadly disease.

There is, in fact, a fatal tendency in all human activities for the means to encroach upon the very ends which they were intended to serve. Thus money comes to hinder the exchange of commodities, and rules of art to hamper genius, and examinations to prevent young men from becoming learned. It does not, unfortunately, always follow that the encroaching means can be dispensed with. I think it probable that the collectivism of our life is necessary and will increase, and I think that our only safeguard against its deathly properties is in a Christian life, for we were promised that we could handle serpents and drink deadly things and yet live. That is the truth behind the erroneous definition of religion with which we started. Where it went wrong was in opposing to the collective mass mere solitude. The Christian is called not to individualism but to membership in the mystical body. A consideration of the differences between the secular collective and the mystical body is therefore the first step to understanding how Christianity without being individualistic can yet counteract collectivism.

At the outset we are hampered by a difficulty of language. The very word *membership* is of Christian origin, but it has been taken over by the world and emptied of all meaning. In any book on logic you may see the expression "members of a class." It must be most emphatically stated that the items or particulars included in a homogeneous class are almost the reverse of what St. Paul meant by *members* ([Greek]) [i.e., the usual translation from New Testament Greek] he meant what we should call *organs,* things essentially different from, and complementary to, one other, things differing not only in structure and function but also in dignity. Thus, in a club, the committee as a whole and the servants as a whole may both properly be regarded as "members"; what we should call the members of the club are merely units. A row of identically dressed and identically trained soldiers set side by side, or a number of citizens listed as voters in a constituency are not members of anything in the Pauline sense. I am afraid that when we describe a man as "a member of a church" we usually mean nothing Pauline; we mean only that he is a unit—that he is one more specimen of some kind of things as X and Y and Z. How true membership in a body differs from inclusion in a collective may be seen in the structure of a family. The grandfather, the parents, the grown-up son, the child, the dog, and the cat are true members (in the organic sense), precisely because they are not members or units of a homogeneous class. They are not interchangeable. Each person is almost a species in himself. The mother is not simply a different person from the daughter; she is a different kind of person. The grown-up brother is not simply one unit in the class children; he is a separate estate of the realm. The father and grandfather are almost as different as the cat and the dog. If you subtract any one member, you have not simply reduced the family in number; you have inflicted an injury on its structure. Its unity is a unity of unlikes, almost of incommensurables.

A dim perception of the richness inherent in this kind of unity is one reason why we enjoy a book like *The Wind in the Willows;* a trio such as Rat, Mole, and Badger symbolizes the extreme differentiation of persons in harmonious union, which we know intuitively to be our true refuge both from solitude and from the collective. The affection between such oddly matched couples as Dick Swiveller and the Marchioness, or Mr. Pickwick and Sam Weller pleases in the same way. That is why the modern notion that children should call their parents by their Christian names is so perverse. For this is an effort to ignore the difference in kind which makes for real organic unity. They are trying to inoculate the child with the preposterous view that one's mother is simply a fellow citizen like anyone else, to make it ignorant of what all men know and insensible to what all men feel. They are trying to drag the featureless repetitions of the collective into the fuller and more concrete world of the family.

A convict has a number instead of a name. That is the collective idea carried to its extreme. But a man in his own house may also lose his name, because he is called simply "Father." That is membership in a body. The loss of the name in both cases reminds us that there are two opposite ways of departing from isolation.

The society into which the Christian is called at baptism is not a collective but a Body. It is in fact that Body of which the family is an image on the natural level. If anyone came to it with the misconception that membership of the Church were membership in a debased modern sense—a massing together of persons as if they were pennies or counters—he would be corrected at the threshold by the discovery that the head of this Body is so unlike the inferior member that they share no predicate with Him save by analogy. We are summoned from the outset to combine as creatures with our Creator, as mortals with immortal, as redeemed sinners with sinless Redeemer. His presence, the interaction between Him and us, must always be the overwhelmingly dominant factor in the life we are to lead within the Body, and any conception of Christian fellowship which does not mean primarily fellowship with Him is out of court. After that it seems almost trivial to trace further down the diversity of operations to the unity of the Spirit. But it is very plainly there. There are priests divided from the laity, catechumens divided from those who are in full fellowship. There is authority of husbands over wives and parents over children. There is, in forms too subtle for official embodiment, a continual interchange of complementary ministrations. We are all constantly teaching and learning, forgiving and being forgiven, representing Christ to man when we intercede, and man to Christ when others intercede for us. The sacrifice of selfish privacy which is daily demanded of us is daily repaid a hundredfold in the true growth of personality which the life of the Body encourages. Those who are members of one another become as diverse as the hand and the ear. That is why the worldlings are so monotonously alike compared with the almost fantastic variety of the saints. Obedience is the road to freedom, humility the road to pleasure, unity the road to personality.

And now I must say something that may appear to you a paradox. You have often heard that though in the world we hold different stations, yet we are all equal in the sight of God. There are, of course, senses in which this is true. God is no acceptor of persons; His love for us is not measured by our social rank or our intellectual talents. But I believe there is a sense in which this maxim is the reverse of the truth. I am going to venture to say that artificial equality is necessary in the life of the State, but that in the Church we strip off this disguise, we recover our real inequalities, and are thereby refreshed and quickened.

I believe in political equality. But there are two opposite reasons for being a democrat. You may think all men so good that they deserve a share in the government of the commonwealth, and so wise that the commonwealth needs their advice. That is, in my opinion, the false, romantic doctrine of democracy. On the other hand, you may believe fallen men to be so wicked that not one of them can be trusted with any irresponsible power over his fellows.

That I believe to be the true ground of democracy. I do not believe that God created an egalitarian world. I believe the authority of parent over child, husband over wife, learned over simple to have been as much a part of the original plan as the authority of man over beast. I believe that if we had not fallen, Filmer would be right, and patriarchal monarchy would be the sole lawful government. But since we have learned sin, we have found, as Lord Acton says, that "all power corrupts, and absolute power corrupts absolutely." The only remedy has been to take away the powers and substitute a legal fiction of equality. The authority of father and husband has been rightly abolished on the legal plane, not because this authority is in itself bad (on the contrary, it is, I hold, divine in origin), but because fathers and husbands are bad. Theocracy has been rightly abolished not because it is bad that learned priests should govern ignorant laymen, but because priests are wicked men like the rest of us. Even the authority of man over beast has had to be interfered with because it is constantly abused.

Equality is for me in the same position as clothes. It is a result of the Fall and the remedy for it. Any attempt to retrace the steps by which we have arrived at egalitarianism and to reintroduce the old authorities on the political level is for me as foolish as it would be to take off our clothes. The Nazi and the nudist make the same mistake. But it is the naked body, still there beneath the clothes of each one of us, which really lives. It is the hierarchical world, still alive and (very properly) hidden behind a façade of equal citizenship, which is our real concern.

Do not misunderstand me. I am not in the least belittling the value of this egalitarian fiction which is our only defense against one another's cruelty. I should view with the strongest disapproval any proposal to abolish manhood suffrage, or the Married Women's Property Act. But the function of equality is purely protective. It is medicine, not food. By treating human persons (in judicious defiance of the observed facts) as if they were all the same kind of thing, we avoid innumerable evils. But it is not on this that we were made to live. It is idle to say that men are of equal value. If value is taken in a worldly sense—if we mean that all men are equally useful or beautiful or good or entertaining—then it is nonsense. If it means that all are of equal value as immortal souls, then I think it conceals a dangerous error. The infinite value of each human soul is not a Christian doctrine. God did not die for man because of some value He perceived in him. The value of each human soul considered simply in itself, out of relation to God, is zero. As St. Paul writes, to have died for valuable men would have been not divine but merely heroic; but God died for sinners. He loved us not because we were lovable, but because He is Love. It may be that He loves all equally—He certainly loved all to the death—and I am not certain what the expression means. If there is equality, it is in His love, not in us.

Equality is a quantitative term and therefore love often knows nothing of it. Authority exercised with humility and obedience accepted with delight are the very lines along which our spirits live. Even in the life of the affections, much more in the Body of Christ, we step outside that world which says "I am as good as you." It is like turning from a march to a dance. It is like taking off our clothes. We become, as Chesterton said, taller when we bow; we become lowlier when we instruct. It delights me that there should be moments in the services of my own Church when the priest stands and I kneel. As democracy becomes more complete in the outer world and opportunities for reverence are successively removed, the refreshment, the cleansing, and invigorating returns to inequality, which the Church offers us, become more and more necessary.

In this way then, the Christian life defends the single personality from the collective, not by isolating him but by giving him the status of an organ in the mystical Body. As the Book of Revelation says, he is made "a pillar in the temple of God"; and it adds, "he shall go no more out." That introduces a new side of our subject. That structural position in the Church which the humblest Christian occupies is eternal and even cosmic. The Church will outlive the universe; in it the individual person will outlive the universe. Everything that is joined to the immortal head will share His immortality.

We hear little of this from the Christian pulpit today. What has come of our silence may be judged from the fact that recently addressing the Forces on this subject, I found that one of my audience regarded this doctrine as "theosophical." If we do not believe it, let us be honest and relegate the Christian faith to museums. If we do, let us give up the pretense that it makes no difference. For this is the real answer to every excessive claim made by the collective. It is mortal; we shall live forever. There will come a time when every culture, every institution, every nation, the human race, all biological life is extinct and every one of us is still alive. Immortality is promised to us, not to these generalities. It was not for societies or states that Christ died, but for men. In that sense Christianity must seem to secular collectivists to involve an almost frantic assertion of individuality. But then it is not the individual as such who will share Christ's victory over death. We shall share the victory by being in the Victor. A rejection, or in Scripture's strong language, a crucifixion of the natural self is the passport to everlasting life. Nothing that has not died will be resurrected. That is just how Christianity cuts across the antithesis between individualism and collectivism. There lies the maddening ambiguity of our faith as it must appear to outsiders. It sets its face relentlessly against our natural individualism; on the other hand, it gives back to those who abandon individualism an eternal possession of their own personal being, even of their bodies. As mere biological entities, each with its separate will to live and to expand, we are apparently of no account; we are cross-fodder. But as organs of the Body of Christ, as stones and pillars in the temple, we are assured of our eternal self-identity and shall live to remember the galaxies as an old tale.

This may be put in another way. Personality is eternal and inviolable. But then, personality is not a datum from which we start. The individualism in which we all begin is only a parody or shadow of it. True personality lies ahead—how far ahead, for most of us, I dare not say. And the key to it does not lie in ourselves. It will not be attained by development from within outwards. It will come to us when we occupy those places in the structure of the eternal cosmos for which we were designed or invented. As a color first reveals its true quality when placed by an excellent artist in its pre-elected spot between certain others, as a spice reveals its true flavor when inserted just where and when a good cook wishes among the other ingredients, as the dog becomes really doggy only when he has taken his place in the household of man, so we shall then first be true persons when we have suffered ourselves to be fitted into our places. We are marble waiting to be shaped, metal waiting to be run into a mold. No doubt there are already, even in the unregenerate self, faint hints of what mold each is designed for, or what sort of pillar he will be. But it is, I think, a gross exaggeration to picture the saving of a soul as being, normally, at all like the development from seed to flower. The very words *repentance, regeneration, the New Man,* suggest something very different. Some tendencies in each natural man may have to be simply rejected. Our Lord speaks of eyes being plucked out and hands lopped off—a frankly Procrustean method of adaptation.

The reason we recoil from this is that we have in our day started by getting the whole picture upside down. Starting with the doctrine that every individuality is "of infinite value," we then picture God as a kind of employment committee whose business it is to find suitable careers for souls, square holes for square pegs. In fact, however, the value of the individual does not lie in him. He is capable of receiving value. He receives it by union with Christ. There is no question of finding for him a place in the living temple which will do justice to his inherent value and give scope to his natural idiosyncrasy. The place was there first. The man was created for it. He will not be himself till he is there. We shall be true and everlasting and really divine persons only in Heaven, just as we are, even now, colored bodies only in the light.

To say this is to repeat what everyone here admits already—that we are saved by grace, that in our flesh dwells no good thing, that we are, through and through, creatures not creators, derived beings, living not of ourselves but from Christ. If I seem to have complicated a simple matter, you will, I hope, forgive me. I have been anxious to bring out two points. I have wanted to try to expel that quite un-Christian worship of the human individual simply as such which is so rampant in modern thought side by side with our collectivism, for one error begets the opposite error and, far from neutralizing, they aggravate each other. I mean the pestilent notion (one sees it in literary criticism) that each of us starts with a treasure called "personality" locked up inside him, and that to expand and express this, to guard it from interference, to be "original," is the main end of life. This is Pelagian, or worse, and it defeats even itself. No man who values originality will ever be original. But try to tell the truth as you see it, try to do any bit of work as well as it can be done for the work's sake, and what men call originality will come unsought. Even on that level, the submission of the individual to the function is already beginning to bring true personality to birth. And secondly, I have wanted to show that Christianity is not, in the long run, concerned either with individuals or communities. Neither the individual nor the community as popular thought understands them can inherit eternal life, neither the natural self, nor the collective mass, but a new creature.

Paul Tillich

1886–1965

At the invitation of Reinhold Niebuhr, Paul Tillich came in 1933 from Germany, where his opposition to Nazism had put him at risk, to New York City. He taught at Union Theological Seminary from 1933 onward, introducing his own theological program and its goal of a radical rebuilding and transformation of society. His famous dictum, shaped by the horrors of World War I, in which he had served as a field chaplain, was "Religion is the substance of culture; culture is the form of religion."

Tillich valued, during his education in philosophy and classical culture, the goal of a personal synthesis, integrating his Christian faith with the ideals of classical humanism, leaving him "on the boundary" between opposing outlooks. Throughout his development as a theologian, he continued to occupy a paradoxical place, convinced that the believer is justified despite his unbelief: *"simul justus et dubitans."* The intellectual result of his struggle made him a Christian existentialist in mid-twentieth century. Tillich was heroically resigned to the notion that human beings can never know God's purpose, although they must be committed to its existence. They must make the "leap of faith," in which their estrangement from the divine, symbolized by the story in Genesis of the Fall, could achieve reunion through faith.

His classic books include *The Courage to Be* and the three-volume work *Systematic Theology.* His own inner conflicts, and his involvement with psychoanalytic theory, made him the great mentor of American theologians. Tillich established a critical notion of "theonomy," as opposed to "theocracy." He believed in dialectical struggle with extremes, whether they involved professional orthodoxy or, in his private life, issues of marital fidelity. His sermons bear the mark of Tillich's own complicated personality and are addressed to those alienated from their own religious traditions, earning him not only fame in America but the title "Apostle of the Skeptics."

Loneliness and Solitude

And when he had sent the multitudes away, he went up into a mountain apart to pray: and when the evening was come, he was there alone.

—MATTHEW 14:23

I.

"He was there, alone." So are we. Man is alone because he is man! In some way every creature is alone. In majestic isolation every star travels through the darkness of endless space. Each tree grows according to its own law, fulfilling its unique possibilities. Animals live, fight and die for themselves alone, confined to the limitations of their bodies. Certainly, they also appear as male and female, in families and in flocks. Some of them are gregarious. But all of them are alone! Being alive means being in a body—a body separated from all other bodies. And being separated means being alone.

This is true of every creature, and it is more true of man than of any other creature. He is not only alone; he also *knows* that he is alone. Aware of what he is, he asks the question of his aloneness. He asks why he is alone, and how he can triumph over his being alone. For this aloneness he cannot endure. Neither can he escape it. It is his destiny to be alone and to be aware of it. Not even God can take this destiny away from him.

In the story of paradise we read—"Then the Lord God said, It is not good that man should be alone." And He created the woman from the body of Adam. Here an old myth is used to show that originally there was no bodily separation between man and woman; in the beginning they were one. Now they long to be one again. But although they recognize each other as flesh of their own flesh, each remains alone. They look at each other, and despite their longing for each other as flesh of their own flesh, each remains alone. They look at each other, and despite their longing for each other, they see their strangeness. In the story, God Himself makes them aware of this fact when He speaks to each of them separately, when He makes each one responsible for his own guilt, when He listens to their excuses and mutual accusations, when He pronounces a separate curse over each, and leaves them to experience shame in the face of their nakedness. They are each alone. The creation of the woman has not overcome the situation which God describes as not good for man. He remains alone. And the creation of the woman, although it provides a helper for Adam, has only presented to the one human being who is alone another human being who is equally alone, and from their flesh all other men, each of whom will also stand alone.

We ask, however—is this really so? Did not God accomplish something better? Isn't our aloneness largely removed in the encounter of the sexes? Certainly it is during hours of communion and in moments of love. The ecstasy of love can absorb one's own self in its union with the other self, and separation seems to be overcome. But after these moments, the isolation of self from self is felt even more deeply than before, sometimes even to the point of mutual repulsion. We have given too much of ourselves, and now we long to take back what was given. Our desire to protect our aloneness is expressed in the feeling of shame. We feel ashamed when our intimate self, mental or bodily, is opened. We try to cover our nakedness, as did Adam and Eve when they became conscious of themselves. Thus, man and woman remain alone even in the most intimate union. They cannot penetrate each other's innermost center. And if this were not so, they could not be helpers to each other; they could not have human community.

This is why God Himself cannot liberate man from his aloneness: it is man's greatness that he is centered within himself. Separated from his world, he is thus able to look *at* it. Only because he can look at it can he know and love and transform it. God, in creating him the ruler of the earth, had to separate him and thrust him into aloneness. Man is also therefore able to be spoken to by God and by man. He can ask questions and give answers and make decisions. He has the freedom for good or evil. Only he who has an impenetrable center in himself is free. Only he who is alone can claim to be a man. This is the greatness and this is the burden of man.

II.

Our language has wisely sensed these two sides of man's being alone. It has created the word "loneliness" to express the pain of being alone. And it has created the word "solitude" to express the glory of being alone. Although, in daily life, we do not always distinguish these words, we should do so consistently and thus deepen our understanding of our human predicament.

In the twenty-fifth Psalm we read—"Turn thou to me and be gracious; for I am lonely and afflicted." The psalmist feels the pain of loneliness. We do not know the character of his particular loneliness, but we know the many faces that loneliness can have. We have all experienced some of them.

Most widespread is our loneliness after those who helped us to forget that we are alone have left us, either through separation or death. I refer not only to those nearest to us, but also to those human beings who give us the feeling of communion, groups with which we have worked, with which we have had social contact, with which we have had spiritual communication. For many people such loneliness becomes a permanent state and a continuous source of profound melancholy. The sighing of innumerable lonely people, all around us and over the world, fills the ears that are opened by love.

But let us also consider those among us who are surrounded by friends and neighbors, by co-workers and countrymen, who live in family groups and enjoy the communion of the sexes—everything that those others do *not* have. And let us ask—are they without the pain of loneliness? Is their aloneness covered up by the crowd in which they move? If we can number ourselves among these people, we might answer the question as follows: I never felt so lonely as in that particular hour when I was surrounded by people but suddenly realized my ultimate isolation. I became silent and retired from the group in order to be alone with my loneliness. I wanted my external predicament to match my internal one. Let us not minimize such an experience by asserting that some people are simply not strong enough to obtain a significant place in the group, and that their withdrawal is nothing but an expression of weakness, that may call for counseling or psychiatric help. Certainly, such people do exist in large numbers, and they need help. But I speak now of the strong ones, who have achieved their place in the crowd, and who nevertheless experience the terror of ultimate loneliness. They are aware, in a sudden break through the world around them, of man's real predicament. Let us also not minimize this experience by pointing out the fact that some people feel misunderstood despite their urgent desire to make themselves understandable, and therefore feel lonely in the crowd. No one can deny that there are such people, and further, that they even demonstrate a certain truth—for who is really understood, even by himself? The mystery of a person cannot be encompassed by a neat description of his character. Those, however, who always feel misunderstood confuse the mystery of each personality with imaginary treasures which they themselves believe they possess and which demand recognition from others. When such recognition is not forthcoming, they feel lonely and withdraw. They also need help. But again, there are those whose real treasures are great enough to find expression, to be understood and received, and yet who have this terrifying experience of ultimate loneliness. In such moments they break through the surface of their average life into the depth of man's predicament.

Many feel lonely because in spite of their effort to love and be loved, their love is rejected. This loneliness is often self-created. These people may be claiming as a right what can only come to them as a gift. They withdraw into a self-chosen loneliness, taking revenge through bitterness and hostility towards those they feel have rejected them, actually enjoying the pain of their loneliness. There are many such persons, and they contribute heavily to the growth of neurotic loneliness in our time. They above all need help, for they easily become the prey of a demonic force that secludes them completely within themselves.

But there is also the genuine experience of rejected love. No special claim is made, but hope yearns towards another, and is disappointed. A community of love comes to an end or fails to exist at all. Such loneliness cuts our ties with the world. We are indeed ultimately alone, and not even love from other directions or the power of our own love can lift this burden from us. He who can endure the loneliness of disappointed love without bitterness experiences the depth of man's predicament radically and creatively.

There are, finally, two forms of loneliness that cannot either be covered or escaped: the loneliness of guilt and the loneliness of death. Nobody can remove from us what we have committed against our true being. We feel both our hidden guilt and our open guilt as *ours,* and ours alone. We cannot really make anybody else responsible for what we have done. We cannot run away from our guilt, and we cannot honestly cover it up. We are alone with it. And it is a loneliness that permeates all other forms of loneliness, transforming them into experiences of judgment.

Then, there is that ultimate loneliness of having to die. In the anticipation of our death we remain alone. No communication with others can remove it, as no other's presence in the actual hour of our dying can conceal the fact that it is *our* death, and our death alone. In the hour of death we are cut off from the whole universe and everything in it. We are deprived of all the things and beings that made us forget our being alone. Who can endure this loneliness?

III.

Loneliness can be conquered only by those who can bear solitude. We have a natural desire for solitude because we are men. We want to feel what we are—namely, alone—not in pain and horror, but with joy and courage. There are many ways in which solitude can be sought and experienced. And each way can be called "religious," if it is true, as one philosopher said, that "religion is what a man does with his solitariness."

One of these ways is the desire towards the silence of nature. We can speak without voice to the trees and the clouds and the waves of the sea. Without words they respond through the rustling of leaves and the moving of clouds and the murmuring of the sea. This solitude we can have, but only for a brief time. For we realize that the voices of nature cannot ultimately answer the questions in our mind. Our solitude in nature can easily become loneliness, and so we return to the world of man.

Solitude can also be found in the reading of poetry, in listening to music, in looking at pictures, and in sincere thoughtfulness. We are alone, perhaps in the midst of multitudes, but we are not lonely. Solitude protects us without isolating us. But life calls us back to its empty talk and the unavoidable demands of daily routine. It calls us back to its loneliness and the cover that it, in turn, spreads over our loneliness.

Without a doubt, this last describes not only man's general predicament, but also, and emphatically, our time. Today, more intensely than in the preceding periods, man is so lonely that he cannot bear solitude. And he tries desperately to become a part of the crowd. Everything in our world supports him. It is a symptom of our disease that teachers and parents and the managers of public communication do everything possible to deprive us of the external conditions for solitude, the simplest aids to privacy. Even our houses, instead of protecting the solitude of each member of the family or group, are constructed to exclude privacy almost completely. The same holds true of the forms of communal life, the school, college, office and factory. An unceasing pressure attempts to destroy even our desire for solitude.

But sometimes God thrusts us out of the crowd into a solitude we did not desire, but which nonetheless takes hold of us. The prophet Jeremiah says—"I sit alone, because thy hand was upon me." God sometimes lays hands upon us. He wants us to ask the question of truth that may isolate us from most men, and that can be asked only in solitude. He wants us to ask the question of justice that may bring us suffering and death, and that can grow in us only in solitude. He wants us to break through the ordinary ways of man that may bring disrepute and hatred upon us, a breakthrough that can happen only in solitude. He wants us to penetrate to the boundaries of our being, where the mystery of life appears, and it can only appear in moments of solitude.

There may be some among you who long to become creative in some realm of life. But you cannot become or remain creative without solitude. One hour of conscious solitude will enrich your creativity far more than hours of trying to learn the creative process.

What happens in our solitude? Listen to Mark's words about Jesus' solitude in the desert—"And he was in the wilderness forty days, tempted by Satan; and he was with the wild beasts, and the angels ministered to him."

He is alone, facing the whole earth and sky, the wild beasts around him and within him, he himself the battlefield for divine and demonic forces. So, first, this is what happens in our solitude: we meet ourselves, not as ourselves, but as the battlefield for creation and destruction, for God and the demons. Solitude is not easy. Who can bear it? It was not easy even for Jesus. We read—"He went up into the hills to pray. When evening came, he was there alone." When evening comes, loneliness becomes more lonely. We feel this when a day, or a period, or all the days of our life come to an end. Jesus went up to pray. Is this the way to transform loneliness into solitude and to bear solitude? It is not a simple question to answer. Most prayers do not have this much power. Most prayers make God a partner in a conversation; we use Him to escape the only true way to solitude. Such prayers flow easily from the mouths of both ministers and laymen. But they are not born out of a solitary encounter of God with man. They are certainly not the kind of prayer for which Jesus went up into the hills. Better that we remain silent and allow our soul, that is always longing for solitude, to sigh without words to God. This we can do, even in a crowded day and a crowded room, even under the most difficult external conditions. This can give us moments of solitude that no one can take from us.

In these moments of solitude something is done to us. The center of our being, the innermost self that is the ground of our aloneness, is elevated to the divine center and taken into it. Therein can we rest without losing ourselves.

Now perhaps we can answer a question you may have already asked—how can communion grow out of solitude? We have seen that we can never reach the innermost center of another being. We are always alone, each for himself. But we can reach it in a movement that rises first to God and then returns from Him to the other self. In this way man's aloneness is not removed, but taken into the community with that in which the centers of all beings rest, and so into community with all of them. Even love is reborn in solitude. For only in solitude are those who are alone able to reach those from whom they are separated. Only the presence of the eternal can break through the walls that isolate the temporal from the temporal. One hour of solitude may bring us closer to those we love than many hours of communication. We can take them with us to the hills of eternity.

And perhaps when we ask—what is the innermost nature of solitude?

we should answer—the presence of the eternal upon the crowded roads of the temporal. It is the experience of being alone but not lonely, in view of the eternal presence that shines through the face of the Christ, and that includes everybody and everything from which we are separated. In the poverty of solitude all riches are present. Let us dare to have solitude—to face the eternal, to find others, to see ourselves.

Karl Barth

1886–1968

The Swiss theologian Karl Barth was ordained in the Swiss Evangelical Reformed Church after an education at four universities, where he immersed himself in philosophy and the thinking of the leaders of nineteenth-century liberal Protestantism.

Shaken by the inadequacy of his teachers to deal with the social questions of post–World War I Europe and with the war itself, Barth's radical interpretation of Paul's Epistle to the Romans shook in turn the theological establishment with his stress on the "wholly otherness of God." His reading of the Scriptures during a period as a country minister led Barth to a drastic revision of the relationship between God and man: Barth's Christocentric theology identified rational, historical Protestantism as a delusive cover for man's refusal to accept an unknowable God as He is and as He is revealed in Jesus Christ.

Barth's clarification of theological issues merged with the political in his resistance to National Socialism and in his rallying of other anti-Nazi churchmen at the Synod of Barmen. The meeting resulted in the Barmen Declaration, which became the basis of the Confessing Church, as opposed to the established Church, which was not adversarial to Hitler's regime. The first article of this text, as drafted by Barth, is the cornerstone of his theology: "Jesus Christ, as He is attested for us in Holy Scripture, is the one Word of God which we have to hear and which we have to trust and obey in life and in death." There is an implicit indictment here of Martin Luther's view of the relation of spiritual and temporal power, reflected in Barth's refusal to take an unconditional oath of allegiance to Hitler. Suspended from the University of Bonn, Barth accepted a chair of theology at Basel, in Switzerland, close to the German border.

After the end of the Third Reich, Barth's polemic continued, both in the pages of his massive *Church Dogmatics* and in the pulpit, where he preached, almost exclusively, in the Basel jail as "a prisoner among prisoners." This sermon on grace and deliverance comes from that long and remarkable pastoral commitment.

ᴄᴤ

Saved by Grace

By grace have you been saved.

—EPHESIANS 2:5

O Lord, our God! Through thy Son, our Lord Jesus Christ, thou hast made us thy children. We have heard thy voice and have gathered here to give thee praise, to listen to thy word, to call upon thee and to entrust to thy care our burdens and our needs. Be thou in our midst and be our teacher—that all anxiety and despair, all vanity and defiance within us, all our unbelief and superstition may diminish and thy greatness and goodness may show forth;

—that our hearts may be open to one another, that we may understand each other, and help one another;

—that this hour may be an hour of light wherein we may catch sight of the open sky and thus of the dawn on this dark earth.

The old has passed away, behold, the new has come. This is true, and it is true for us, as certainly as thou art in Jesus Christ the Savior of us all. But only thou canst truly tell us and show us that this is so. Speak and show then the truth to us and to all those who pray with us this Sunday morning. They pray for us. And we are praying for them. Grant their requests and ours! Amen.

My dear brothers and sisters, I now read a passage from the Letter of the Apostle Paul to the Ephesians: *By grace have you been saved*. This, I think, is brief enough for it to be remembered by all, for to impress itself upon you and, if it be God's will, to be understood.

We are gathered here this Sunday morning to hear this word: *By grace you have been saved!* Whatever else we do, praying and singing, is but an answer to this word spoken to us by God himself. The prophets and apostles wrote a strange book, called the Bible, for the very purpose of testifying to this fact before mankind. The Bible alone contains this sentence. We do not read it in Kant or in Schopenhauer, or in any book of natural or secular history, and certainly not in any novel, but in the Bible alone. In order to hear this word we need what is called the Church—the company of Christians, of human beings called and willing to listen together to the Bible and through it to the word of God. This is the word of God: *By grace you have been saved!*

Someone once said to me: "I need not go to church. I need not read the Bible. I know already what the Church teaches and what the Bible says: 'Do what is right and fear no one!' " Let me say at this point: If this were the message at stake, I would most certainly not have come here. My time is too precious and so is yours. To say that, neither prophets nor apostles, neither Bible, Jesus Christ nor God are needed. Anybody is at liberty to say this to himself. By the same token this saying is void of any new, of any very special and exciting message. It does not help anyone. I have never seen a smile on the face of a person reassuring himself with this kind of talk. As a rule, those who use it are a sad-looking lot, revealing all too easily that this word does not help them, does not comfort them, does not bring them joy.

Let us hear therefore what the Bible says and what we as Christians are called to hear together: *By grace you have been saved!* No man can say this to himself. Neither can he say it to someone else. This can only be said by God to each one of us. It takes Jesus Christ to make this saying true. It takes the apostles to communicate it. And our gathering here as Christians is needed to spread it among us. This is why it is truly news, and very special news, the most exciting news of all, the most helpful thing also, indeed the only helpful thing.

"By grace *you* have been saved!" How strange to have this message addressed to us! Who are we, anyway? Let me tell you quite frankly: we are all together great sinners. Please understand me: I include myself. I stand ready to confess being the greatest sinner among you all; yet you may then not exclude yourself from the group! Sinners are people who in the judgment of God, and perhaps of their own consciences, missed and lost their way, who are not just a little, but totally guilty, hopelessly indebted and lost not only in time, but in eternity. We are such sinners. And we are prisoners. Believe me, there is a captivity much worse than the captivity in this house. There are walls much thicker and doors much heavier than those closed upon you. All of us, the people without and you within, are prisoners of our own obstinacy, of our many greeds, of our various anxieties, of our mistrust and in the last analysis of our unbelief. We are all sufferers. Most of all we suffer from ourselves. We each make life difficult for ourselves and in so doing for our fellowmen. We suffer from life's lack of meaning. We suffer in the shadow of death and of eternal judgment toward which we are moving. We spend our life in the midst of a whole world of sin and captivity and suffering.

But now listen. Into the depth of our predicament the word is spoken from on high: *By grace you have been saved!* To be saved does not just mean to be a little encouraged, a little comforted, a little relieved. It means to be pulled out like a log from a burning fire. You have been saved! We are not told: you may be saved sometimes, or a little bit. No, you *have been* saved, totally and for all times. You? Yes, we! Not just any other people, more pious and better than we are, no, we, each one of us.

This is because Jesus Christ is our brother and, through his life and death, has become our Savior who has wrought our salvation. He is the word of God for us. And this word is: *By grace you have been saved!*

You probably all know the legend of the rider who crossed the frozen Lake of Constance by night without knowing it. When he reached the opposite shore and was told whence he came, he broke down, horrified. This is the human situation when the sky opens and the earth is bright, when we may hear: *By grace you have been saved!* In such a moment we are like that terrified rider. When we hear this word we involuntarily look back, do we not, asking ourselves: Where have I been? Over an abyss, in mortal danger! What did I do? The most foolish thing I ever attempted! What happened? I was doomed and miraculously escaped and now I am safe! You ask: "Do we really live in such danger?" Yes, we live on the brink of death. But we have been saved. Look at our Savior and at our salvation! Look at Jesus Christ on the cross, accused, sentenced and punished instead of us! Do you know for whose sake he is hanging there? For *our* sake—because of our sin—sharing *our* captivity—burdened with *our* suffering! He nails *our* life to the cross. This is how God had to deal with *us*. From this darkness he has saved *us*. He who is not shattered after hearing this news may not yet have grasped the word of God: *By grace you have been saved!*

But more important than the fear of sudden death is the knowledge of life imparted to us: "By grace you have been *saved!*" Therefore, we have reached the shore, the Lake of Constance is behind us, we may breathe freely, even though we still are in the grip of panic, and rightly so. This panic is but an aftermath. By virtue of the good news the sky truly opens and the earth is bright. What a glorious relief to be told that there I was, in the darkness, over that abyss, on the brink of death, but there I am no longer. Through this folly I lived, but I cannot and I will not do it again, never again. This happened, but it must not and it will not happen again. My sin, my captivity, my suffering are yesterday's reality, not today's. They are things of my past, not of the present nor of the future. I have been *saved!* Is this really so, is this the truth? Look once again to Jesus Christ in his death upon the cross. Look and try to understand that what he did and suffered he did and suffered for you, for me, for us all. He carried our sin, our captivity and our suffering, and did not carry it in vain. *He carried it away.* He acted as the captain of us all. He broke through the ranks of our enemies. He has already won the battle, our battle. All we have to do is to follow him, to be victorious with him. Through him, in him we are saved. Our sin has no longer any power over us. Our prison door is open. Our suffering has come to an end. This is a great word indeed. The word of God *is* indeed a great word. And we would deny him, we would deny the Lord Jesus Christ, were we to deny the greatness of this word: He sets us free. When he, the Son of God, sets us free, we are *truly* free.

Because we are saved by no other than Jesus Christ, we are saved *by grace*. This means that we did not deserve to be saved. What we deserved would be different. We cannot secure salvation for ourselves. Did you read in the newspapers the other day that man will soon be able to produce an artificial moon? But we cannot produce our salvation. No one can be proud of being saved. Each one can only fold his hands in great lowliness of heart and be thankful like a child. Consequently we shall never possess salvation as our property. We may only receive it as a gift over and over again, with hands outstretched. *"By grace* you have been saved!" This means constantly to look away from ourselves to God and to the man on the cross where this truth is revealed. This truth is ever anew to be believed and be grasped by faith. To believe means to look to Jesus Christ and to God and to trust that there is the truth for us, for our lives, for the life of all men.

Is it not a pity that we rebel against this very truth in the depth of our hearts? Indeed, we dislike hearing that we are saved by grace, and by grace alone. We do not appreciate that God does not owe us anything, that we are bound to live from his goodness alone, that we are left with nothing but the great humility, the thankfulness of a child presented with many gifts. For we do not like at all to look away from ourselves. We would much prefer to withdraw into our own inner circle, not unlike the snail into its shell, and to be with ourselves. To put it bluntly: we do not like to believe. And yet grace and therefore faith as I just described it is the beginning of the true life of freedom, of a carefree heart, of joy deep within, of love of God and neighbor, of great and assured hope! And yet grace and faith would make things so very simple in our lives!

Dear brothers and sisters, where do we stand now? One thing is certain: the bright day *has dawned,* the sun of God *does shine* into our dark lives, even though we may close our eyes to its radiance. His voice *does call* us from heaven, even though we may obstruct our ears. The bread of life *is offered* to us, even though we are inclined to clench our fists instead of opening our hands to take the bread and eat it. The door of our prison *is open,* even though, strangely enough, we prefer to remain within. God has put the house in order, even though we like to mess it up all over again. *By grace you have been saved!*—this is true, even though we may not believe it, may not accept it as valid for ourselves and unfortunately in so doing may forgo its benefits. *Why* should we want to forgo the benefits? *Why* should we not want to believe? *Why* do we not go out through the open door? *Why* do we not open our clenched fists? *Why* do we obstruct our ears? *Why* are we blindfolded? Honestly, *why?*

One remark in reply must suffice. All this is so because perhaps we failed to pray fervently enough for a change within ourselves, on our part. That God is God, not only almighty, but merciful and good, that he wills and does what is best for us, that Jesus Christ died for us to set us free, that by grace, in him, we have been saved—all this need *not* be a concern of our prayers. All these things are true apart from our own deeds and prayers. But to believe, to accept, to let it be true for us, to begin to live with this truth, to believe it not only with our minds and with our lips, but also with our hearts and with all our life, so that our fellowmen may sense it, and finally to let our total existence be immersed in the great divine truth, *by grace you have been saved,* this is to be the concern of our prayers. No human being has ever prayed for this in vain. If anyone asks for this, the answer is already being given and faith begins. And because no one has ever asked for this in vain, no one may omit praying like a little child for the assurance that God's truth, this terrible, this glorious truth, is shining even today, a small, yet increasingly bright light. *By grace you have been saved.* Ask that you may believe this and it will be given you; seek this, and you will find it; knock on this door, and it will be opened to you.

This, my dear friends, is what I have been privileged and empowered to tell you of the good news as the word of God today. Amen.

O Lord, our God! Thou seest and hearest us. Thou knowest each one of us far better than we know ourselves. Thou lovest us without our deserving it. Thou hast helped us and dost help us still, although we are ever again inclined to spoil thy work by wanting to help ourselves. Thou art the Judge, but thou art also the Savior of the poor and perplexed human race. For this we give thee thanks. For this we praise thee. We rejoice in the prospect of seeing with our own eyes on thy great day what we already now may believe if thou makest us free to do so.

Make us free to believe! Give us the true, honest and active faith in thee and in thy truth! Give it to many! Give it to all men! Give it to the peoples and their governments, to the rich and to the poor, to the healthy and to the sick, to the prisoners and to those who think they are free, to the old and to the young, to the joyful and to the sorrowful, to the heavy-laden and to the light-minded! There is no one who does not stand in need of faith, no one to whom the promise of faith is denied. Tell all our people, ourselves included, that thou art their merciful God and Father and ours! This we ask thee in the name of Jesus Christ who commanded us to pray: "Our Father . . ."

Martin Luther King, Jr.

1929–1968

When a skeptical James Baldwin went to hear King preach at his home church, Dexter Avenue Baptist, in Montgomery, Alabama, in 1958, he found a humble man who somehow intuited the needs of his audience, whether black or white, and who succeeded by "the forthrightness with which he speaks of those things which hurt and baffle them." Ten years earlier, far from confident he even had a vocation, an eighteen-year-old King stood up in his father's famous pulpit at Ebenezer Baptist in Atlanta and gave his maiden sermon.

The journey of Martin Luther King, Jr., from comfortable preacher's son to courageous civil rights martyr is one of this century's indelible tales. If it began obscurely in the segregated Southern precincts of the Black Church, it ended tragically in the corridors of national power and international recognition. In *The Souls of Black Folk* (1903) W. E. B. DuBois, whose long life ended the day before King's march on Washington in 1963, wrote presciently about "the Preacher" as "the most unique personality developed by the Negro on American soil. A leader, a politician, an orator, a 'boss,' an intriguer, an idealist—all these he is, and ever, too, the center of a group of men, now twenty, now a thousand in number."

King the preacher was certainly formed by the old emotional call-and-response tradition of the Black Church, but he was also formed by the example of Gandhi's nonviolence and by Reinhold Niebuhr's radical critique of liberal Protestantism. The latter's belief regarding race in America—"there is no problem of political life to which religious imagination can make a larger contribution"—was instrumental in forging King's mission to redeem the soul of his country.

Curiously, many of King's most stirring sermons—it is often hard, except, by their occasion, to distinguish them from his political exhortations—have still not been transcribed from their original tapes, many of which were made by Southern police-surveillance personnel. Who is not familiar at least with the usual sound snippet from "I Have a Dream" on the television news every January 15? Some may also have heard "A Knock at Midnight" or "The Drum Major Instinct." For our selection we have chosen the one he declared his own favorite: "The Dimensions of a Complete Life," which in centuries-old tradition he had adapted during his seminary days from another famous preacher's sermon, "The Symmetry of Life," by Phillips Brooks (*q.v.,* page 544).

ℭ℈

The Dimensions of a Complete Life

Many, many centuries ago, out on a lonely, obscure island called Patmos, a man by the name of John caught a vision of the new Jerusalem descending out of heaven from God. One of the greatest glories of this new city of God that John saw was its completeness. It was not partial and one-sided, but it was complete in all three of its dimensions. And so, in describing the city in the twenty-first chapter of the book of Revelation, John says this: "The length and the breadth and the height of it are equal." In other words, this new city of God, this city of ideal humanity, is not an unbalanced entity but it is complete on all sides.

Now John is saying something quite significant here. For so many of us the book of Revelation is a very difficult book, puzzling to decode. We look upon it as something of a great enigma wrapped in mystery. And certainly if we accept the book of Revelation as a record of actual historical occurrences it is a difficult book, shrouded with impenetrable mysteries. But if we will look beneath the peculiar jargon of its author and the prevailing apocalyptic symbolism, we will find in this book many eternal truths which continue to challenge us. One such truth is that of this text. What John is really saying is this: that life as it should be and life at its best is the life that is complete on all sides.

There are three dimensions of any complete life to which we can fitly give the words of this text: length, breadth, and height. The length of life as we shall think of it here is not its duration or its longevity, but it is the push of a life forward to achieve its personal ends and ambitions. It is the inward concern for one's own welfare. The breadth of life is the outward concern for the welfare of others. The height of life is the upward reach for God.

These are the three dimensions of life, and without the three being correlated, working harmoniously together, life is incomplete. Life is something of a great triangle. At one angle stands the individual person, at the other angle stand other persons, and at the top stands the Supreme, Infinite Person, God. These three must meet in every individual life if that life is to be complete.

Now let us notice first the length of life. I have said that this is the dimension of life in which the individual is concerned with developing his inner powers. It is that dimension of life in which the individual pursues personal ends and ambitions. This is perhaps the selfish dimension of life, and there is such a thing as moral and rational self-interest. If one is not concerned about himself he cannot be totally concerned about other selves.

Some years ago a learned rabbi, the late Joshua Liebman, wrote a book entitled *Peace of Mind*. He has a chapter in the book entitled "Love Thyself Properly." In this chapter he says in substance that it is impossible to love other selves adequately unless you love your own self properly. Many people have been plunged into the abyss of emotional fatalism because they did not love themselves properly. So every individual has a responsibility to be concerned about himself enough to discover what he is made for. After he discovers his calling he should set out to do it with all of the strength and power in his being. He should do it as if God Almighty called him at this particular moment in history to do it. He should seek to do his job so well that the living, the dead, or the unborn could not do it better. No matter how small one thinks his life's work is in terms of the norms of the world and the so-called big jobs, he must realize that it has cosmic significance if he is serving humanity and doing the will of God.

To carry this to one extreme, if it falls your lot to be a street sweeper, sweep streets as Raphael painted pictures, sweep streets as Michelangelo carved marble, sweep streets as Beethoven composed music, sweep streets as Shakespeare wrote poetry. Sweep streets so well that all the hosts of heaven and earth will have to pause and say, "Here lived a great street sweeper who swept his job well." In the words of Douglas Mallock:

If you can't be a highway, just be a trail;
If you can't be the sun, be a star
For it isn't by size that you win or you fail—
Be the best of whatever you are.

When you do this, you have mastered the first dimension of life—the length of life.

But don't stop here; it is dangerous to stop here. There are some people who never get beyond this first dimension. They are brilliant people; often they do an excellent job in developing their inner powers; but they live as if nobody else lived in the world but themselves. There is nothing more tragic than to find an individual bogged down in the length of life, devoid of the breadth.

The breadth of life is that dimension of life in which we are concerned about others. An individual has not started living until he can rise above the narrow confines of his individualistic concerns to the broader concerns of all humanity.

You remember one day a man came to Jesus and he raised some significant questions. Finally he got around to the question "Who is my neighbor?" This could easily have been a very abstract question left in midair. But Jesus immediately pulled that question out of midair and placed it on a dangerous curve between Jerusalem and Jericho. He talked about a certain man who fell among thieves. Three men passed; two of them on the other side. And finally another man came and helped the injured man on the ground. He is known to us as the good Samaritan. Jesus says in substance that this is a great man. He was great because he could project the "I" into the "thou."

So often we say that the priest and the Levite were in a big hurry to get to some ecclesiastical meeting and so they did not have time. They were concerned about that. I would rather think of it another way. I can well imagine that they were quite afraid. You see, the Jericho road is a dangerous road, and the same thing that happened to the man who was robbed and beaten could have happened to them. So I imagine the first question that the priest and the Levite asked was this: "If I stop to help this man, what will happen to me?" Then the good Samaritan came by, and by the very nature of his concern reversed the question: "If I do not stop to help this man, what will happen to him?" And so this man was great because he had the mental equipment for a dangerous altruism. He was great because he could surround the length of his life with the breadth of life. He was great not only because he had ascended to certain heights of economic security, but because he could condescend to the depths of human need.

All this had a great deal of bearing in our situation in the world today. So often racial groups are concerned about the length of life, their economic privileged position, their social status. So often nations of the world are concerned about the length of life, perpetuating their nationalistic concerns, and their economic ends. May it not be that the problem in the world today is that individuals as well as nations have been overly concerned with the length of life, devoid of the breadth? But there is still something to remind us that we are interdependent, that we are all involved in a single process, that we are all somehow caught in an inescapable network of mutuality. Therefore whatever affects one directly affects all indirectly.

As long as there is poverty in the world I can never be rich, even if I have a billion dollars. As long as diseases are rampant and millions of people in this world cannot expect to live more than twenty-eight or thirty years, I can never be totally healthy even if I just got a good checkup at Mayo Clinic. I can never be what I ought to be until you are what you ought to be. This is the way our world is made. No individual or nation can stand out boasting of being independent. We are interdependent. So John Donne placed it in graphic terms when he affirmed, "No man is an island entire of itself. Every man is a piece of the continent, a part of the main." Then he goes on to say, "Any man's death diminishes me because I am involved in mankind, and therefore never send to know for whom the bell tolls; it tolls for thee." When we discover this, we master the second dimension of life.

Finally, there is a third dimension. Some people never get beyond the first two dimensions of life. They master the first two. They develop their inner powers, they love humanity; but they stop right here. They end up with the feeling that man is the end of all things and that humanity is God. Philosophically or theologically, many of them would call themselves humanists. They seek to live without a sky. They find themselves bogged down on the horizontal plane without being integrated on the vertical plane. But if we are to live the complete life we must reach up and discover God. H. G. Wells was right: "The man who is not religious begins at nowhere and ends at nothing." Religion is like a mighty wind that breaks down doors and makes that possible and even easy which seems difficult and impossible.

In our modern world it is easy for us to forget this. We so often find ourselves unconsciously neglecting this third dimension of life. Not that we go up and say, "Good-by, God, we are going to leave you now." But we become so involved in the things of this world that we are unconsciously carried away by the rushing ride of materialism which leaves us treading in the confused waters of secularism. We find ourselves living in what Professor Sorokin of Harvard called a sensate civilization, believing that only those things which we can see and touch and to which we can apply our five senses have existence.

Something should remind us once more that the great things in this universe are things that we never see. You walk out at night and look up at the beautiful stars as they bedeck the heavens like swinging lanterns of eternity, and you think you can see all. Oh, no. You can never see the law of gravitation that holds them there. You walk around this vast campus and you probably have a great esthetic experience as I have had walking about and looking at the beautiful buildings, and you think you see all. Oh, no. You can never see the mind of the architect who drew the blueprint. You can never see the love and the faith and the hope of the individuals who made it so. You look at me and you think you see Martin Luther King. You don't see Martin Luther King; you see my body, but, you must understand, my body can't think, my body can't reason. You don't see the me that makes me me. You can never see my personality.

In a real sense everything that we see is a shadow cast by that which we do not see. Plato was right: "The visible is a shadow cast by the invisible." And so God is still around. All of our new knowledge, all of our new developments, cannot diminish his being one iota. These new advances have banished God neither from the microcosmic compass of the atom nor from the vast, unfathomable ranges of interstellar space. The more we learn about this universe, the more mysterious and awesome it becomes. God is still here.

So I say to you, seek God and discover him and make him a power in your life. Without him all of our efforts turn to ashes and our sunrises into darkest nights. Without him, life is a meaningless drama with the decisive scenes missing. But with him we are able to rise from the fatigue of despair to the buoyancy of hope. With him we are able to rise from the midnight of desperation to the daybreak of joy. Saint Augustine was right—we were made for God and we will be restless until we find rest in him.

Love yourself, if that means rational, healthy, and moral self-interest. You are commanded to do that. That is the length of life. Love your neighbor as you love yourself. You are commanded to do that. That is the breadth of life. But never forget that there is a first and even greater commandment, "Love the Lord thy God with all thy heart, and all thy soul and all thy mind." This is the height of life. And when you do this you live the complete life.

Thank God for John who, centuries ago, caught a vision of the new Jerusalem. God grant that those of us who still walk the road of life will catch this vision and decide to move forward to that city of complete life in which the length and the breadth and the height are equal.

O God, our gracious heavenly Father, we thank thee for all of the insights of the ages, and we thank thee for the privilege of having fellowship with thee. Help us to discover ourselves, to discover our neighbors, and to discover thee, and to make all part of our life. Grant that we will go now with grim and bold determination to live the complete life. In the name and spirit of Jesus, we pray. Amen.

Harry Emerson Fosdick

1878–1969

*A*nother graduate of the progressive Union Theological Seminary in New York City in the late nineteenth century, Harry Emerson Fosdick came of age in an undogmatic and bookish Baptist household. His homiletic talents established him as a religious liberal, who swiftly became the object of investigative committees during his tenure as a preaching minister at the First Presbyterian Church in New York City. The controversy over his view of the Apostles' Creed, and his refusal to assent to the orthodox Westminster Confession, dictated his inevitable resignation in the middle of the 1920s, a period of schism, acrimonious debate, and turbulence in the mainline American Protestant churches.

The dispute arising from the Scopes trial of 1925 and the division between advocates of the theory of evolution and "creationists" continue to divide Protestant denominations; in Fosdick's day it set in motion both the fundamentalist movement and the loosely affiliated league of churchmen who constituted themselves as liberals. Fosdick, who became a protégé of John D. Rockefeller, was given the shelter of an interdenominational sanctuary at Riverside Church in New York City, where his arguments for tolerance of those churchgoers skeptical of historical doctrine attracted thousands of parishioners.

Fosdick's religious liberalism and its sympathy with doubt over belief in the Virgin Birth, the Second Coming, and the resurrection of the body were popular but by no means facile. His loathing of militarism made him a pacifist during World War II; on November 3, 1935, this ecclesiastical modernist preached a famous sermon on modernism which indicted his contemporaries, and above all himself, of a cerebral, naive, and optimistic humanism which was complicit with evil, as he saw it, in the enlightened twentieth century. There is little evidence of complacency in Fosdick's view of religion and religious striving for the truth. His voice has an authenticity and moral rigor which still linger, while thirty years after his death debates over education, ethics, and doctrine continue to divide churchgoers and secularists alike.

The Church Must Go Beyond Modernism

If we are successfully to maintain the thesis that the church must go beyond modernism, we must start by seeing that the church had to go as far as modernism. Fifty years ago, a boy seven years of age was crying himself to sleep at night in terror lest, dying, he should go to hell, and his solicitous mother, out of all patience with the fearful teaching which had brought such apparitions to the mind, was trying in vain to comfort him. That boy is preaching to you today and you may be sure that to him the achievements of Christian modernism in the last half century seem not only important but indispensable.

Fifty years ago the intellectual portion of Western civilization had turned one of the most significant mental corners in history and was looking out on a new view of the world. The church, however, was utterly unfitted for the appreciation of that view. Protestant Christianity had been officially formulated in prescientific days. The Augsburg Confession was a notable statement but the men who drew it up, including Luther himself, did not even believe that the earth goes round the sun. The Westminster Confession, for the rigorous acceptance of which the Presbyterian rearguard still contends, was a memorable document but it was written forty years before Newton published his work on the law of gravitation. Moreover, not only were the mental patterns of Protestant Christianity officially formulated in prescientific days but, as is always true of religion, those patterns were sacred to their believers and the changes forced by the new science seemed impious and sacrilegious.

Youths like myself, therefore, a half century ago faced an appalling lag between our generation's intellect on the one side and its religion on the other, with religion asking us to believe incredible things. Behind his playfulness the author of *Through the Looking Glass* had this serious matter in mind when he represented the White Queen as saying to Alice, "I'm just one hundred and one, five months and a day." Said Alice, "I can't believe *that!*" Said the Queen pityingly, "Can't you? Try again: draw a long breath, and shut your eyes." So the church seemed to be speaking to us.

Modernism, therefore, came as a desperately needed way of thinking. It insisted that the deep and vital experience of the Christian soul with itself, with its fellows, with its God, could be carried over into this new world and understood in the light of the new knowledge. We refused to live bifurcated lives, our intellect in the late nineteenth century and our religion in the early sixteenth. God, we said, is a living God who has never uttered his final word on any subject; why, therefore, should prescientific frameworks of thought be so sacred that forever through them man seek the Eternal and the Eternal seek man? So we said, and thanks to modernism, it became true of many an anxious and troubled soul in our time that, as Sam Walter Foss expressed it,

> He saw the boundless scheme dilate,
> In star and blossom, sky and clod;
> And as the universe grew great,
> He dreamed for it a greater God.

The church thus had to go as far as modernism but now the church must go beyond it. For even this brief rehearsal of its history reveals modernism's essential nature; it is primarily an adaptation, an adjustment, an accommodation of Christian faith to contemporary scientific thinking. It started by taking the intellectual culture of a particular period as its criterion and then adjusted Christian teaching to that standard. Herein lies modernism's tendency toward shallowness and transiency; arising out of a temporary intellectual crisis, it took a special type of scientific thinking as standard and became an adaptation to, a harmonization with, the intellectual culture of a particular generation. That, however, is no adequate religion to represent the Eternal and claim the allegiance of the soul. Let it be a modernist who says that to you! Unless the church can go deeper and reach higher than that it will fail indeed.

In the first place, modernism has been excessively preoccupied with intellectualism. Its chosen problem has been somehow to adjust Christian faith to the modern intellect so that a man could be a Christian without throwing his reason away. Modernism's message to the church has been after this fashion: When, long ago, the new music came, far from clinging to old sackbuts and psalteries, you welcomed the full orchestra and such composers as Palestrina, Bach, Beethoven, to the glory of God; when the new art came you did not refuse it but welcomed Cimabue, Giotto, Raphael, and Michelangelo, to the enrichment of your faith; when the new architecture came, far from clinging to primitive catacombs or the old Romanesque, you greeted the Gothic with its expanded spaces and aspiring altitudes; so now, when the new science comes, take that in too, and, however painful the adaptations, adjust your faith to it and assimilate its truths into your Christian thinking.

Surely, that has been a necessary appeal but it centers attention on one problem only—intellectual adjustment to modern science. It approaches the vast field of man's experience and need head first, whereas the deepest experiences of man's soul, whether in religion or out of it, cannot be approached head first. List as you will the soul's deepest experiences and needs—friendship, the love that makes a home, the enjoyment of music, delight in nature, devotion to moral causes, the practice of the presence of God—it is obvious that, whereas, if we are wise, we use our heads on them, nevertheless we do not approach them mainly head first, but heart first, conscience first, imagination first. A man is vastly greater than his logic, and the sweep and ambit of his spiritual experience and need are incalculably wider than his rational processes. So modernism, as such, covers only a segment of the spiritual field and does not nearly compass the range of religion's meaning.

Indeed, the critical need of overpassing modernism is evident in the fact that our personal spiritual problems do not lie there any more. When I was a student in the seminary, the classrooms where the atmosphere grew tense with excitement concerned the higher criticism of the Bible and the harmonization of science and religion. That, however, is no longer the case.

The classrooms in the seminary where the atmosphere grows tense today concern Christian ethics and the towering question whether Christ has a moral challenge that can shake this contemporary culture to its foundations and save us from our deadly personal and social sins. So the world has moved far to a place where mere Christian harmonizers, absorbed with the intellectual attempt to adapt faith to science and accommodate Christ to prevalent culture, seem trivial and out of date. Our modern world, as a whole, cries out not so much for souls intellectually adjusted to it as for souls morally maladjusted to it, not most of all for accommodators and adjusters but for intellectual and ethical challengers.

When Paul wrote his first letter to the Corinthians, he said that he had become a Jew to the Jews that he might win the Jews, and he intimated that he had become a Greek to the Greeks that he might win the Greeks. "I am become," he said, "all things to all men, that I may by all means save some." This is a modernistic passage of adjustment and accommodation. But that is not all Paul said. Had it been all, Paul would have sunk from sight in an indistinguishable blend with the Greco-Roman culture of his day and we should never have heard of him. When he wrote the second time to the Corinthians he said something else:

> Come ye out from among them, and be ye separate,
> saith the Lord,
> And touch no unclean thing.

Church of Christ, take that to yourself now! Stop this endeavor to harmonize yourself with modern culture and customs as though they were a standard and criterion. Rather, come out from among them. Only an independent standing-ground from which to challenge modern culture can save either it or you.

In the second place, not only has modernism been thus predominantly intellectualistic and therefore partial, but, strange to say, at the same time it has been dangerously sentimental. The reason for this is easy to explain. One of the predominant elements in the intellectual culture of the late nineteenth and twentieth centuries, to which modernism adjusted itself, was illusory belief in inevitable progress. So many hopeful and promising things were afoot that two whole generations were fairly bewitched into thinking that every day in every way man was growing better and better. Scientific discovery, exploration and invention, the rising tide of economic welfare, the spread of democracy, the increase of humanitarianism, the doctrine of evolution itself, twisted to mean that automatically today has to be better than yesterday and tomorrow better than today—how many elements seduced us in those romantic days into thinking that all was right with the world!

In the intellectual culture to which modernistic Christianity adapted itself, such lush optimism was a powerful factor, and the consequences are everywhere present in the natural predispositions of our thought today. In the little village of Selborne, England, the visitor is shown some trees planted by a former minister near his dwelling, so that he might be spared the view of the village slaughter-house. Those trees are suggestive and symbolic of the sentimental illusions we plant to hide from our eyes the ugly facts of life. Especially we modernistic Christians, dealing, as we were, with thoughts of a kindly God by evolution lifting everything and everybody up, were deeply tempted to live in a fool's paradise behind our lovely trees.

For example, modernistic Christianity largely eliminated from its faith the God of moral judgment. To be sure, in the old theology, the God of moral judgment had been terribly presented so that little children did cry themselves to sleep at night for fear of him and of his hell. Modernism, however, not content with eliminating the excrescences of a harsh theology, became softer yet and created the general impression that there is nothing here to fear at all. One of the most characteristic religious movements of the nineteenth century heralded this summary of faith:

> The Fatherhood of God.
> The Brotherhood of Man.
> The Leadership of Jesus.
> Salvation by Character.
> The Progress of Mankind—
>   onward and upward forever.

Well, if that is the whole creed, this is a lovely world with nothing here to dread at all.

But there *are* things here to dread. Ask the physicians. They will tell us that in a law-abiding world are stern conditions whose fulfillment or non-fulfillment involve bodily destiny. Ask the novelists and dramatists, and at their best they are not lying to us as they reveal the inexorable fatality with which character and conduct work out their implied consequence. Ask the economists. They will tell us there are things to dread which lead to an inevitable economic hell. Ask even the historians and they will talk at times like old preachers about the God of moral judgment, as James Anthony Froude did when he said, "One lesson, and only one, history may be said to repeat with distinctness: that the world is built somehow on moral foundations; that, in the long run, it is well with the good; in the long run, it is ill with the wicked."

Indeed, cannot we use our own eyes to see that there are things here to fear? For this is no longer the late nineteenth and early twentieth centuries. This is the epoch after the first world war shook the earth to its foundations, and the God of judgment has spoken. My soul, what a world, which the gentle modernism of my younger ministry, with its kindly sentiments and limitless optimism, does not fit at all! We must go beyond that. Because I know that I am speaking here to many minds powerfully affected by modernism, I say to you as to myself: Come out of these intellectual cubicles and sentimental retreats which we built by adapting Christian faith to an optimistic era. Underline this: *Sin is real.* Personal and social sin is as terribly real as our forefathers said it was, no matter how we change their way of saying so. And it leads men and nations to damnation as they said it did, no matter how we change their way of picturing it. For these are times, real times, of the kind out of which man's great exploits have commonly been won, in which, if a man is to have a real faith he must gain it from the very teeth of dismay; if he is to have real hope, it must shine, like a Rembrandt portrait, from the dark background of fearful apprehension; if he is to have real character, he must achieve it against the terrific down-drag of an antagonistic world; and if he is to have a real church, it must stand out from the world and challenge it, not be harmonized with it.

In the third place, modernism has even watered down and thinned out the central message and distinctive truth of religion, the reality of God. One does not mean by that, of course, that modernists are atheists. One does mean, however, that the intellectual culture of the late nineteenth and early twentieth centuries, to which modernism adjusted itself, was predominantly man-centered. Man was blowing on his hands and doing such things at a rate as never had been done or dreamed on earth before. Man was pioneering new truth and building a new social order. You young people who were not here then can hardly imagine with what cheerful and confident trust we confided to man the saving of the world. So the temptation was to relegate God to an advisory capacity, as a kind of chairman of the board of sponsors of our highly successful human enterprise. A poet like Swinburne could even put the prevailing mood into candid words:

> Thou art smitten, thou God, thou art smitten; thy death is upon
>   thee, O Lord.
> And the love-song of earth as thou diest resounds through the wind
>   of her wings—
> Glory to Man in the highest! for Man is the master of things.

Look out on the world today and try, if you can, to repeat those words of Swinburne and still keep your face straight! At any rate, if ever I needed something deeper to go on than Swinburne's sentimental humanism, with man as the master of things, it is now—a philosophy, namely, a profound philosophy about what is ultimately and eternally real in this universe. We modernists were so disgusted with the absurdities of the old supernaturalistic theology that we were commonly tempted to visit our distaste on theology as a whole and throw it away. But theology means thinking about the central problem of existence—what is ultimately and eternally real in this universe. And in the lurid light of days like these it becomes clearer, as an increasing number of atheists are honestly saying, that if the eternally real is merely material, if the cosmos is a physical fortuity and the earth an accident, if there is no profounder reason for mankind's being here than just that at one stage in the planet's cooling the heat happened to be right, and if we ourselves are "the disease of the agglutinated dust," then to stand on this temporary and accidental earth in the face of this vast cosmos and try lyrically to sing,

> Glory to Man in the highest! for Man is the master of things,

is an absurd piece of sentimental tomfoolery. And because I have been and am a modernist it is proper that I should confess that often the modernistic

movement, adjusting itself to a man-centered culture, has encouraged this
mood, watered down the thought of the Divine, and, may we be forgiven
for this, left souls standing, like the ancient Athenians, before an altar to an
Unknown God!

On that point the church must go beyond modernism. We have been
all things to all men long enough. We have adapted and adjusted and accom-
modated and conceded long enough. We have at times gotten so low down
that we talked as though the highest compliment that could be paid
Almighty God was that a few scientists believed in him. Yet all the time, by
right, we had an independent standing-ground and a message of our own in
which alone is there hope for humankind. The eternally real is the spiritual.
The highest in us comes from the deepest in the universe. Goodness and
truth and beauty are not accidents but revelations of creative reality. God is!
On that point come out from among them and be ye separate! As the poet
imagined Paul saying:

Whoso has felt the Spirit of the Highest
cannot confound nor doubt Him nor deny:
yea with one voice, o world, tho' thou deniest,
Stand thou on that side, for on this am I.

Finally, modernism has too commonly lost its ethical standing-ground
and its power of moral attack. It is a dangerous thing for a great religion to
begin adjusting itself to the culture of a special generation. Harmonizing
slips easily into compromising. To adjust Christian faith to the new astronomy, the new geology, the new biology, is absolutely indispensable. But suppose that this modernizing process, well started, goes on and Christianity
adapts itself to contemporary nationalism, contemporary imperialism, contemporary capitalism, contemporary racialism—harmonizing itself, that is,
with the prevailing social status quo and the common moral judgments of
our time—what then has become of religion, so sunk and submerged in
undifferentiated identity with this world?

This lamentable end of a modernizing process, starting with indispensable adaptations and slipping into concession and compromise, is a
familiar phenomenon in religious history. For the word "modernism" may

not be exclusively identified with the adjustment of Christian faith and practice to the culture of a single era. Modernization is a recurrent habit in every living religion. Early Protestantism, itself, emerging along with a new nationalism and a new capitalism, was in its day modernism, involving itself and us in entanglements and compliances with political and economic ideas in whose presence we still are tempted to be servile. Every era with powerful originative factors in it evokes from religion indispensable adaptations, followed by further concessive acquiescences, which in time must be superseded and outgrown. Early Christianity went out from an old Jewish setting into a new Greek culture and never would have survived if it had not assimilated into its faith the profound insights of Greek philosophy. So in the classic creeds, like that of Nicaea, we have a blending of the old faith with the new philosophy, and in that process John and Paul themselves had already played a part. But, alas, early Christianity in its adjustment of its faith to Greek culture did not stop with adaptation to the insights of philosophy. At last it adapted itself to Constantine, to the licentious court, to war, to the lucrative enjoyment of imperial favors, to the use of bloody persecutions to coerce belief. One after another, it threw away the holiest things that had been entrusted to it by its Lord until, often hardly distinguishable from the culture it lived in, it nearly modernized itself into moral futility. Lift up that history, as it were a mirror, in which to see the peril of our American churches.

It is not in Germany alone that the church stands in danger of being enslaved by society. There the enslavement is outward, deliberate, explicit, organized. Here it is secret, quiet, pervasive, insidious. A powerful culture—social, economic, nationalistic, militaristic—impinging from every side upon the church, cries with persuasive voices, backed by all the sanctions and motives most urgent to the self-interest of man, Adjust yourself, adapt yourself, accommodate yourself!

When Great Britain was as mad about the Boer War as Italy is mad today about the Ethiopian War and all the forces of propaganda had whipped up the frenzy of the people to a fever heat, John Morley one night in Manchester faced an indignant, antagonistic crowd, and pleaded with his countrymen against the war. This in part is what he said: "You may carry fire and sword into the midst of peace and industry; it will be wrong. A war of the strongest government in the world with untold wealth and inexhaustible reserves against this little republic will bring you no glory: it will be wrong. You may make thousands of women widows and thousands of children fatherless: it will be wrong. It may add a new province to your empire: it will still be wrong." John Morley did not call himself a Christian. He called himself an agnostic. But he was far nearer standing where Christ intended his church to stand than the church has often been.

We modernists had better talk to ourselves like this. So had the fundamentalists—but that is not our affair. We have already largely won the battle we started out to win; we have adjusted the Christian faith to the best intelligence of our day and have won the strongest minds and the best abilities of the churches to our side. Fundamentalism is still with us but mostly in the backwaters. The future of the churches, if we will have it so, is in the hands of modernism. Therefore let all modernists lift a new battle cry: we must go beyond modernism! And in that new enterprise the watch-word will be not, Accommodate yourself to the prevailing culture! but, Stand out from it and challenge it! For this unescapable fact, which again and again in Christian history has called modernism to its senses, we face: we cannot harmonize Christ himself with modern culture. What Christ does to modern culture is to challenge it.

Reinhold Niebuhr

1892–1971

orn into the cultivated milieu of a German-American Protestant household in Missouri, where daily Bible readings, often in Greek and Hebrew, were coupled with a deep German Evangelical Church sense of moral and religious responsibility, it seemed inevitable that Reinhold Niebuhr would enter the ministry. After pastoral service in the Bethel Evangelical Church in Detroit, which fueled his activism in issues of management and labor, Niebuhr taught on the faculty of Union Theological Seminary in New York City. Remembering his tenure in Detroit, Niebuhr remarked of struggles involving issues of housing, job security, retirement benefits, and worker fatigue on the assembly lines, "I cut my eyeteeth fighting Ford."

He brought that experience into a serious reconsideration of the liberal and highly moralistic creed he inherited as Christian faith and returned, during his years at Union Theological Seminary, to the Bible as a source of reconsideration about its vision of the fallen nature of humanity. Niebuhr then began his long battle with both conservatives and liberals alike, over what he saw as moral smugness, naiveté, and facile optimism on both sides. His religious imagination, his sense of process and paradox allowed him a flirtation with Marxism in the late 1920s before he became highly critical of liberal and Marxist illusions. Niebuhr lived a difficult straddle through his long and distinguished career as theologian and preacher, too secular for many of his colleagues in religion, and too religious for many in his secular audience who approved of a technology and worldly power which, to his mind, contributed to the modern world's sense of meaninglessness and confusion.

Apart from his many famous sermons, including "The Wheat and the Tares" (the "tare" is a noxious weed sometimes called "darnel," which grows amid the wheat crop), Niebuhr's great fame is vividly reflected in his "Serenity Prayer," later adapted by Alcoholics Anonymous. Niebuhr wrote, on a summer Sunday in 1934, for his parishioners in Heath, Massachusetts, "O God, give us serenity to accept what cannot be changed, courage to change what should be changed, and wisdom to distinguish the one from the other." There is a hint of that now famous prayer in the distinction made here between two poles of human history and personal biography, in the parable of the wheat and the tares.

The Wheat and the Tares

Lord, thou hast been our dwelling place in all generations.
Before the mountains were brought forth,
   or ever thou hadst formed the earth and the world,
   even from everlasting to everlasting, thou art God.

Thou turnest man to destruction;
   and sayest, Return, ye children of men.
For a thousand years in thy sight
   are but as yesterday when it is past,
   and as a watch in the night.

Thou carriest them away as with a flood; they are as a sleep:
   in the morning they are like grass which groweth up.
In the morning it flourisheth, and groweth up;
   in the evening it is cut down, and withereth.

For we are consumed by thine anger,
   and by thy wrath are we troubled.
Thou hast set our iniquities before thee,
   our secret sins in the light of thy countenance.

For all our days are passed away in thy wrath:
    we spend our years as a tale that is told.
The days of our years are threescore years and ten;
    and if by reason of strength they be fourscore years,
yet is their strength labour and sorrow
    for it is soon cut off, and we fly away.

—PSALM 90:1–10

Another parable put he forth unto them, saying, The kingdom of
heaven is likened unto a man which sowed good seed in his field:
But while men slept, his enemy came and sowed tares among the
wheat, and went his way. But when the blade was sprung up, and
brought forth fruit, then appeared the tares also. So the servants of
the householder came and said unto him, Sir, didst not thou sow
good seed in thy field? from whence then hath it tares? He said
unto them, An enemy hath done this. The servants said unto him,
Wilt thou then that we go and gather them up? But he said,
Nay; lest while ye gather up the tares, ye root up also the wheat
with them. Let both grow together until the harvest: and in the
time of harvest I will say to the reapers, Gather ye together first
the tares, and bind them in bundles to burn them: but gather the
wheat into my barn.

—MATTHEW 13:24–30

I want to begin my sermon with the well-known ninetieth Psalm, and
end it with the parable of the wheat and the tares, which is the New Testament lesson of the morning. The ninetieth Psalm begins with the words,
"Lord, Thou hast been our dwelling place in all generations. Before the
mountains were brought forth, or ever thou hadst formed the earth and the
world, even from everlasting to everlasting, Thou art God." Then it goes on
to describe the human situation in typically biblical terms. "Thou carriest
them [that is, us] away as with a flood; . . . In the morning they are like
grass which groweth up. In the morning it flourisheth; . . . in the evening
it is cut down and withereth." The brevity of human life! "Thou carriest

them away as with a flood." We are like corks that bob up and down in the river of time. The brevity of human life may fill us with melancholy because it seems to reduce life to such insignificance. We bring our years to an end like a tale that is told, says the Psalmist.

The second point in the analysis of the human situation is implicit rather than explicit. Man is indeed like a cork that is drawn down the river of time, carried away as with a flood. But he could not be altogether that, because he knows about it; he speculates about it as the Psalmist does, and about the significance of it. Man stands outside of the river of time, so that he can anticipate his death either with hope or with melancholy. Also he can create. He is not only a creature, but he is a creator because he is not quite in the river of time; although he might forget how much of a creature he is when he begins to create. Therefore we come to the third point.

This drama of human history is indeed partly our construct, but it stands under a sovereignty much greater than ours. "A thousand years are in thy sight but as yesterday when it is past, and as a watch in the night." The drama of our individual life and the whole drama of human history stands under a mysterious and eternal sovereignty. It is a mysterious sovereignty which the prophets are always warning that we must not spell out too much. "My thoughts are not your thoughts, my ways are not your ways." But it is not complete mystery because—and this is the distinction between the biblical view and the philosophical view—in spite of the mystery, there are also glints of meaning in it. This God is the mysterious creator of the world, but he is also a just and merciful God.

The New Testament adds to this story by suggesting there is a clue to the mystery. This is the light that shineth in darkness, the drama of the life of our Lord Jesus Christ. Here we have a sense that the mystery of God's creativity and the mystery of his severe judgment and the mystery of his mercy are related, and the clue to the mystery lies in the combination of his justice and his mercy. How are they related; this is our question, and how are these all brought together and revealed? The light that shineth in darkness enables us to live our life, not merely in the sense of its brevity, but with a sense of a purpose for it, and also with the sense of a purpose, and judgment and ultimate fulfillment beyond any judgments or fulfillments that we can envisage.

There are various alternatives—modern and ancient—to what the biblical faith tells us about our human story. One of the great alternatives Aldous Huxley has defined as the "perennial philosophy," which many modern intellectuals, when they become religious, think is a plausible alternative to biblical faith.

According to this alternative view of life, attention is fastened on the second part of the human situation; man is in the river of time but is transcendent over it. This transcendence of his is indeterminate. He can rise higher and higher, and he can look at the whole thing and ask whether it has any meaning. Let him, therefore, rise higher and higher until he, in a sense, meets God. This is the strategy of detachment, according to which we all have our private airplanes, spiritually speaking, and these spiritual airplanes have indeterminate altitude records. There is no limit to how high you can go. You start, and raise yourself up from the human scene to the point where at first it seems creative, because you see, and are apologetic for, all your vanities and pretensions. You rise a little higher, and then you become apologetic for anything that you have done responsibly and creatively. And then you also begin to look at your fellowmen, and you see mothers caring for their children, scholars engaged in their enterprises, businessmen in the marketplace, politicians fighting for their causes, and you say, "What is the good of all this? This is all in the river of time. This is all so brief, and also it may corrupt."

Playing God to the universe, in other words, can be very exhilarating but very irresponsible. It is a strategy of weakness rather than of strength; if you happen to be very weak, you can look at the world from the highest altitude you can think of. If you get high enough in an airplane, you know that the farm of the good farmer and of the bad farmer look equally like garden plots. All distinctions disappear. All moral responsibilities disappear. Indeterminate extension of our freedom over time is certainly no answer to the problem of life.

Probably not many Christians are tempted to this alternative, yet it is a perennial temptation through the ages; if you would have a religious census of the world you would find that more people than the Christians or the Jews have some vision of this alternative to biblical religion.

Which brings us now again to the strategy of life as we have it in the faith of the Bible. We look at the brevity of our life. We admit that we are creatures. We know that we are unique creatures, that God has made us in his image, that we have a freedom to do something that nature does not know, that we can project goals beyond the limitations, ambitions, desires, and lusts of nature. We are the creatures who, gloriously, tragically, and pathetically, make history. As we make it, we have to make distinctions between good and evil. We know that selfishness is dangerous. We must be unselfish. The more we rise above our immediate situation and see the situation of the other person, the more creative we are. Therefore, our life story is concerned with making rigorous distinctions between right and wrong, between good and evil. Part of the Christian faith corresponds to this interpretation. Certainly a part of the Old Testament is not quite sure whether man is in relationship to God, or whether the primary job for the righteous is to war against the unrighteous. We have to admit that it makes a very big difference when we defend freedom against tyranny, and truth against the lies of the world. How else could we build history except by these rigorous distinctions between good and evil, right and wrong?

But now we come to the New Testament lesson, the puzzling lesson of the parable of the wheat and the tares. The man sowed a field of wheat and the enemy sowed tares among the wheat. And the servants, following the impulse of each one of us, asked if they should root out the tares so that the wheat could grow. This is a parable taken from agriculture to illustrate a point of morals, and it violates every principle of agriculture or of morals. After all, every farmer and every gardener makes ceaseless war against the tares. How else could the flowers and the wheat grow? And we have to make ceaseless war against evil within ourselves and in our fellowmen, or how could there be any kind of decency in the world? Against all moral impulse, we have this eschatological parable.

"Nay," said the householder. "Lest while ye gather up the tares, you root up also the wheat." The suggestion is that a great deal of evil may come from the selfishness of men, but perhaps more evil may come from the premature judgments of men about themselves and each other. "Let both grow together until the harvest." These wonderful words of Scripture suggest that while we have to judge, there is a judgment beyond our judgment, and there are fulfillments beyond our fulfillments.

Consider how much more evil and good, creativity and selfishness, are mixed up in actual life than our moralists, whether they be Christian or secular, realize. How little we achieve charity because we do not recognize this fact.

Let us consider the matter of creativity and the desire for approval. What could be more evil than the avaricious desire for the approval of our fellowmen? But how closely related it is to the impulse of creativity. The diary of Virginia Woolf notes that when she put out a new novel, she had an almost morbid interest in the reviews. She was an established artist. Was her anxiety justified? Could not she just take for granted that people would praise her or would accept her work? Yet she had a morbid concern, as anyone who has written a book understands. You may think that you are creative, but you suspect you may have slipped. You have to be approved in order to establish your creativity; the wheat and the tares are very mixed up. "Let both grow together until the harvest." When we think of ourselves, we ought to remember that there is an ultimate judgment against excessive self-concern. But when we deal with our fellowman, we must do so in charity.

How curiously are love and self-love mixed up in life, much more complexly than any scheme of morals recognizes. The simple words of the parable are more profound than the wisdom of all our moralists. There is a self-love which is the engine of creativity. It may not be justified ultimately for that reason, but when we look at history, we have to say that it is an engine of creativity.

There is a debate whether Cervantes wrote the great classic, *Don Quixote,* in order to pay his debts, or in order to get even with his critics. But now it does not make any difference what the motive was. *Don Quixote* is no less a great work of art.

In the field of politics we see very clearly the curious mixture of egotism and desire for public welfare. Winston Churchill, for example, was a very ambitious young man. His ambition gave him the chance to accomplish much. What he achieved was not only great statesmanship but had a quality of magnanimity that reminds us of the wisdom of the wheat and the tares. Churchill knew the mixture of good and evil in the dramas of history. We doubt whether he ever read or really heeded the parable of the wheat and the tares, yet in his magnanimity there was some of its wisdom. He showed the combination of creativity and self-love which we find particularly in politics, but is it not everywhere? There is a puzzling aspect to judgments about self-love or ambition. At what particular point do we think egotism so excessive that it becomes obviously corrupting? It is always rather corrupting, but when does it become *obviously* corrupting? We know certain people to be monstrous egoists, but can we put our finger on the spot where this mixture of love and self-love, which we all have, turns into monstrous egotism? We do have to make our judgments, but we cannot be exact in our moral measurement.

There are forms of self-love which are quite dangerous, but are enclosed in a great sea of vitality which robs them of some of their power. Let us compare America with Spain. In Spain, the somewhat medieval social and political order is according to the tradition of natural law and of the Catholic church. To us, it is stale and static. In this country, and in spite of all our weaknesses, our pride and pretensions, certainly there is life. Our national life is based upon the vitality of various interests balanced by various other interests. This is the heart of the free enterprise doctrine. These self-interests are not nearly as harmless as our conservative friends imagine them to be. Here we do have to violate the parable, and provisionally make judgments and say, "This form of self-interest must be checked." Or, "This form of self-interest must be balanced by other interest." Otherwise we will not have justice if the powerful man simply goes after his interest at the expense of the weak.

We make such provisional judgments, but all these provisional judgments stand ultimately under the truth of the parable of the wheat and the tares. "Let both grow together until the harvest." If we had more modesty about this, perhaps there would not have been such a debate between pure individualism and pure collectivism. On the one hand, this policy may be necessary. On the other hand, it may be dangerous. We had better try to find out how necessary and how dangerous it is, but not absolutely, or we will make the kind of judgment that will pull up the wheat with the tares.

What is Communism but a vast example of pulling up the tares, and not knowing the wheat that is among these tares of so-called self-interest or capitalistic injustice. Is it not surprising that we should have two great evils in our time, Nazism and Communism? Nazism represented such an obvious expression of collective egotism that we do not have to wait for the ultimate judgment. We all know that Nazism was evil! But Communism is a form of evil that comes from human beings forgetting that they are creatures, imagining themselves omniscient and righteous—absolutely righteous—and trying to rebuild the whole world in terms of their ideals, not knowing that their own sins are involved in it. The Communist knows nothing about the parable of the wheat and the tares, or about the ultimate judgment that stands over human existence, and above all nothing about the ambiguity of all human motives.

There is also that kind of selfishness which we might regard as an inadvertent and rather harmless corruption of the love impulse. Is it really inadvertent? Is it actually harmless? We do not know exactly. The sinfulness of parents in their love for their children gives us an example.

The love of parents for their children is one of the symbols of the kingdom of God. But we parents are not quite perfect. There are two crises which children face: one is in their youth when they find out that their parents are not as powerful as they thought; and the second is in their adolescence when they find out that the parents are not as good as they thought they were. No doubt every parent is better than an adolescent rebel imagines in the period of rebellion. The parent who claims to be absolutely loving and then insinuates into that love the old lust for power, which every human being has, obviously is vexatious. But it also must be recognized that there is some good in this evil.

Thus human history is a mixture of wheat and tares. We must make provisional distinctions, but we must know that there are no final distinctions. "Let both grow together until the harvest." Man is a creature and a creator. He would not be a creator if he could not overlook the human scene and be able to establish goals beyond those of nature and to discriminate between good and evil. He must do these things. But he must also remember that no matter how high this creativity may rise, he is himself involved in the flow of time, and he becomes evil at the precise point where he pretends not to be, when he pretends that his wisdom is not finite but infinite, and his virtue is not ambiguous but unambiguous.

From the standpoint of the biblical faith we do not have to despair because life is so brief, but we must not pretend to more because we are so great. Because we are both small and great, we have discerned a mystery and a meaning beyond our smallness and our greatness, and a justice and a love which completes our incompletions, which corrects our judgments, and which brings the whole story to a fulfillment beyond our power to fulfill any story.

We thank you, our God, for your judgments which are sterner than the judgments of man, Help us to remember them when mortal men speak well of us. We thank you for your mercy which is kinder than the goodness of men. Help us to discern this when we are overcome by the confusion of life, and despair about our own sin. Grant us, O Lord, always to worship you in all our doings in the greatness of your creativity and the wonder of your judgment and your mercy.

Harry Austryn Wolfson

1887–1974

Lithuanian born and the graduate of a yeshiva, Wolfson's earliest immersion was in the rigorous methodology of Talmudic textual interpretation; this approach to learning shaped the scholarly studies he continued as a young Jewish immigrant at Harvard University. Much of his vast learning in Semitic languages and literature and in philosophical works he later wrote on Spinoza and Philo was preoccupied with the conflict between faith and reason. His work was shaped by the conviction that any interpretation, including that of sacred texts, must try to clarify an individual philosopher's thinking by comprehending the philosopher's intellectual and social milieu. His investigations were vital to an interfaith community of thought in which a philosopher might make a powerful contribution toward the theological concerns of the great monotheistic religions.

Wolfson's long and reclusive career was spent at Harvard, where he taught, wrote, edited texts from Arabic, Hebrew, and Latin, and completed a major work on the philosophy of the Church Fathers. The sermon he preached by invitation at Harvard's Appleton Chapel in 1955 is an unusual testimony to the rigor and playfulness of the mind of a philosopher of religion whose impatience with facile certainties should never be confused with a simple dismissal of genuine religious faith. At the core of his "sermonette" may lie an echo of G. K. Chesterton's utterance that those who cease to believe in God are capable of believing anything.

The Professed Atheist and the Verbal Theist

The fool hath said in his heart,
There is no God.

—PSALM 14:1

The fool, who in the Scripture lesson this morning is quoted as saying to himself, There is no God, was not a fool in the ordinary sense of the term. He was not a fool in the sense of lacking in intelligence or lacking in knowledge. He was a fool in the sense of being perverse and contrary. He denied what others affirmed. But he was also a downright honest and plain-spoken fellow. People, he knew, believed in God; and by God, he knew, they meant a Being over and above and beyond the world, the creator and governor of the world, a God who revealed himself to men and told them what to do and what not to do and promised them reward for obedience and threatened them with punishment for disobedience. This, he knew, is what people believed in and this is what he did not believe in. And so, honestly and bluntly he said to himself and said to others, There is no God. He was quite willing to be known as an atheist. He did not start to quibble about the meaning of God. He did not offer a substitute God.

But, unlike him whom Scripture called fool, those who called themselves lovers of wisdom, philosophers, made quibbling about the meaning of God one of their chief occupations. Ever since Xenophanes rejected the gods of popular religion and put something else in their place to which he gave the name God, it became the practice of the Greek lovers of wisdom not to deny God but to change the meaning of God. Plato carried around a label, with the name God inscribed on it, even though he did not know where exactly in his philosophy to paste that label. Aristotle's God sat motionless on the top of the world, without, however, being able to detach himself from it. The God of the Stoics was imprisoned within the entrails of the world, from which he could not extricate himself. Even the Epicureans had their gods, ageless human beings, squatting on empty spaces between the worlds and, without a worry in their heads and without a care in their hearts, beholding with sublime indifference the happenings in the infinite worlds around them.

We are told that at the beginning of the Christian era Scripture-bred religious thinkers, on becoming acquainted with the array of deities of the Greek lovers of wisdom, were at a loss to know how to take them. They studied them, they examined them, they scrutinized them, and finally arrived at the conclusion that, while some of them were the paltry result of the blind groping of human reason for a truth which can be known only by faith and revelation, most of them were only polite but empty phrases for the honest atheism of the fool in the Scripture.

Nowadays, lovers of wisdom are still busily engaged in the gentle art of devising deities. Some of them offer as God a thing called man's idealized consciousness, others offer as God a thing called man's aspiration for ideal values or a thing called the unity of the ideal ends which inspire man to action, still others offer a thing called the cosmic consciousness or a thing called the universal nisus or a thing called the élan vital or a thing called the principle of concretion or a thing called the ground of being. I wonder, however, how many of the things offered as God by lovers of wisdom of today are not again only polite but empty phrases for the downright denial of God by him who is called fool in the Scripture lesson this morning!

Rudolf Bultmann

1884–1976

*R*udolf Bultmann, the New Testament scholar, theologian, and Existentialist philosopher, was a colleague of Martin Heidegger at the University of Marburg in the 1920s. Where Heidegger notoriously chose in 1933 to support the Nazi regime with a loyalty oath, Bultmann declined to modify his teaching in any fashion, and supported the Confessing Church and its passive resistance to Nazi ideology. His choice, as a Christian and son of a Lutheran minister, was that of a distinct number of German citizens whose life under the Third Reich from 1933 to 1945 has been described as an "interior emigration." After World War II, Bultmann was a major international figure, opening a global dialogue on his theory of Christian faith in the *kerygma* (proclamation of the Church), in which the risen Christ is transcendent through the Christian Church, with the Resurrection itself understood as a symbolic patterning of extinction and renewal.

Bultmann's scholarship pioneered this analysis of the Synoptic Gospels, moving away from a historical conception of Jesus Christ toward a program to "demythologize" the New Testament and interpret its teachings in a way that emphasized the human terms of its message. His farewell sermon to his colleagues and students at the University of Marburg considered the passing away of heaven and earth, but in an earlier sermon preached not long after the fall of the Third Reich (on July 17, 1945) Bultmann turned to the perplexing theme of the ability of humankind to live in two worlds—both heaven and earth—simultaneously, a task whose difficulties in Hitler's Germany may have been attested to by minister and congregation alike.

ᴄᴇ

This World and the Beyond
July 25, 1950

Heaven and earth will pass away, but my words will not pass away. But of that day or that hour no one knows, not even the angels in heaven, nor the Son, but only the Father. Take heed, watch; for you do not know when the time will come.

—MARK 13:31–33

This is the final service of the term. It is an hour of farewell, in which we bid goodbye to the term and all that it has brought us in the way of tasks completed. I hope also that it has enriched us with new joy, new impressions and new insights, with knowledge that has been inspiring and also perhaps a little frightening; in any event I hope that we have been both stirred and encouraged. For many also it is an hour of farewell to the place in which we have worked together, to the town of Marburg and its surrounding country. And the more our life is consciously or unconsciously molded and colored by the character of the environment in which we move, so much the more does our departure from it strike for us a solemn and significant note. Above all it is a time in which we bid farewell to each other, we who have been linked together as learners and teachers; and while for some it means only a temporary departure which will be followed by another term of work together, for many too it is a final farewell or at any rate a farewell for some considerable time, broken at most by occasional meetings later on.

This farewell service should unite us once again as we consider together and ask ourselves what such an hour as the present ought to mean in the light of God's word. Perhaps it may surprise us that in the Bible we do not easily find any message bearing directly on those moments in our life which to us are so important, as for example many an event in the circle of family or bourgeois life, or the alternation of the seasons, or even such an occasion as the end of a term. The word of God wishes to strike us on a deeper level of life than that of the natural feelings and thoughts which stir our minds in a moment of farewell; feelings of joyous thankfulness and sorrowful goodbye, of hopes for the future or even anxieties about the future—thoughts and feelings which certainly have their rightful place in our lives but which receive their true meaning only as we bring them into vital connection with that deeper level of life in which God's word strikes home to us and finds us.

God's word tell us in the first place that such an hour of farewell as the present implies nothing of particular significance in God's sight. Its meaning lies rather in the fact that it brings home to our minds the truth that our whole life is a constant process of bidding goodbye. It warns us to consider that we live immersed in the flux of time, and it teaches us to ask where eternity lies.

"Heaven and earth will pass away, but my words will not pass away." "Heaven and earth will pass away"—which means that at some time or other they will come to an end, for they are essentially transitory and at bottom they are passing away all the time. "But of that day or that hour no one knows, not even the angels in heaven, nor the Son, but only the Father"; that is, the day and the hour when this term will be reached. Do we then need to know it? Whether this end be near or far, the terrible thing is really not that our surrounding world will pass away, but that we ourselves who are framed and enclosed by it are frail perishable mortals; that our lives will reach their term, when heaven and earth will in any case pass away for us, even though they continue to subsist for a time as far as coming generations are concerned. Nor do we know the day and hour of our own end. *"Ultima latet"*—the last hour is hidden from our knowledge—this inscription on an old clock applies not only to the world in general but to us individuals in particular.

"Lord, so teach us to number our days that we may get a heart of wisdom." (Ps. 90:12.) Thus the Psalmist sings, and in that other psalm, whose solemn words ring forth so impressively in the German Requiem of Brahms, we read: "Lord, let me know my end, and what is the measure of my days; let me know how fleeting my life is! Behold, thou hast made my days a few handbreadths, and my lifetime is as nothing in thy sight. Surely every man stands as a mere breath! Surely man goes about as a shadow! Surely for nought are they in turmoil; man heaps up, and knows not who will gather!" (Ps. 39:4–6.)

But the fact that our days will come to their natural term is not the only solemn and fearful thought. There is also the further fact that the whole texture of our life is stamped by the mark of transitoriness. There is another inscription on a timepiece found by the Duke of York in a monastery at Amalfi and which he noted in his diary: *"dies nostri quasi umbra super terram, et nulla est mora"*—i.e. "Our days are like the shadow which moves over the face of the earth, and suffer no delay."

> Linger, and you'll regret it: time has sped
> How soon! day stands not still, nor comes again.
> How soon the earth's resplendent colors fade!
> The poplar sheds her silver leaf, how soon!

—so writes the ancient poet, Tibullus, and likewise the modern:

"This is a fact which none fully ponders, and far too awesome for weak complaining: the hours glide on, all fades in veils of mist" (Hoffmannsthal). Everywhere and at all times, men have known and been poignantly aware of this underlying truth of human life. Heathen as well as Jews and Christians have felt it, and the voices of the Old Testament, together with those of the heathen poets in the ancient east and classical antiquity and of the poets of modern times, form one vast choir singing in unison to this theme.

Now what follows from this? Firstly, the fact that it was not first the Christians, but before them the Jews and heathen too who sadly realized that the swift flight of time warns us of its preciousness, of the preciousness of the immediate present, the moment in which we stand. This realization, however, may be diversely interpreted:

"And I commend enjoyment, for man has no good thing under the sun but to eat, and drink, and enjoy himself, for this will go with him in his toil through the days of life which God gives him under the sun." (Eccles. 8:15.) "Go, eat your bread with enjoyment, and drink your wine with a merry heart. . . . Let your garments be always white; let not oil be lacking on your head. Enjoy life with the wife whom you love, all the days of your vain life. . . ." (9:7–9.) Thus speaks the so-called preacher, Solomon, and the very same note is struck in the *Carpe Diem* of Horace and our own "Gather ye rosebuds while ye may!"

All this, however, remains on the surface. Let us listen rather to the words of Pascal which he writes in the second section of his *Pensées* where he treats of the "Wretchedness of man without God," and in which he constantly speaks of the manifold distractions *(divertissements)* which absorb men's minds, of that spirit of frivolity which loses time because it loses the present moment:

> Never do we live whole-heartedly in the present. We anticipate the future, as though it were too slow in coming, as though we wished to hasten its advent; or else we recall the past, as though to arrest it in its swift flight. We are so foolish that we allow our thoughts to stray in periods of time which are not really ours, and we do not think of the sole point of time which veritably belongs to us. We are so stupid that we dwell on a past which no longer subsists, and thoughtlessly miss the time which is present with us. The truth is that the present is normally offensive to us. We refuse to face it because it vexes us; and if it is pleasant we idly deplore its passing. We try to keep it by merging it with the future, and we fondly think we can arrange matters which do not lie within our control, with a view to a point of time which we have no certainty of ever reaching. Let each one examine his thoughts. He will discover that they are all concerned either with the past or the future. We hardly ever think of the present; and when we do think of it, it is only to shed its light on the future. The present is never an end for us. Thus we never live, but only hope to live; and since we are always preparing ourselves to be happy, it is inevitable that we never in fact are happy.

What is it however that lends weight and meaning to our present, which, in spite of its swift passage, nevertheless lifts it out of the flux of time to fuse it with eternity? Might we answer: the fact that the present is to be used for the fulfillment of a task? But if this task is nothing more than the realization of a plan, the accomplishment of some piece of work, then the present is seen only from the standpoint of a future which will come and go; it is not yet seen in the light of eternity.

Or should we say that the present is determined by an unconditional obligation, that of the beautiful, the true and the good? That the present is the moment when we are faced by the call of duty, of responsibility? And is it not really the case that if we understand our present as confronting us with duty to be done and responsibility to be fulfilled, then we are freed from the melancholy of a retrospective glance into the past, as also from the anxious anticipation of the future? Is not the call to responsible action a call which comes to us from eternal horizons, a call which rescues our here-and-now from the inexorable flight of time, and sheds upon it the radiance of the eternal? Which gives abiding reality to what in itself is nothing?

I believe that we may and must say so much. And this call of eternity which delivers us from time into the here-and-now of responsibility, is understood by the Christian faith to be also the call of God. Nevertheless this is not the final and true answer which faith gives to the question: how is eternal reality imparted to our present?

For if we content ourselves with this answer, are we not eluding the mystery and the full scope of the problem of transience? Is our life entirely a matter of responsible action and the fulfillment of duty? Is it not also to an equal degree a matter of passive reception and suffering? Is it not also a life of encounter with others, who enrich and inspire us, who give us joy and dower us with love, or who test and train us through contradiction, and by compelling us to prove the genuineness of our thinking and willing? Is not our life also a life of pregnant destiny—harsh and cruel at times, at times also joyous and inspiring?

All this which gives content and substance to our life, passes away. And does not the curse of transience render it all vain and meaningless? Is life an exciting drama but a drama which dies away into nothingness? Or has it all an eternal import, or can it have such? Do not these questions press sorely on our minds when death snatches from us those to whom we were linked in the bonds of love? Do they not vex also today when we have seen the disappearance of so much that we thought great and beautiful and valuable, today, when we are caught up in a crisis which makes almost everything seem questionable, and which threatens with imminent destruction what hitherto seemed to give our life content and meaning? And can we truly comfort by such reference to duty and the call of responsibility those countless thousands whose lives have apparently become meaningless through loss of home and shelter, through servitude and misery, through want and hunger? Indeed, is it not the fact that for many people this very transitoriness of things has become their solace? That life for them has become dreamlike: "The most frightening dream is accompanied by a secret feeling that it all means nothing, howsoever we sweat with fear" (Hebbel).

And finally, what are we to say in the face of the realization that we fail to fulfill this summons of eternity? Are we not aware that we have often failed to obey it? Has not our time so often been misspent and wasted through our own fault? How seldom has been, how seldom is, our present time a genuinely fulfilled time, determined and enriched by obedience to the eternal will! Certainly the summons to responsibility and the call of duty are meant to give our present an eternal meaning; but does it not tax our inner resources to fulfill that meaning? And are we not presuming too much of ourselves in supposing that by our strength alone we can impart to our life an eternal quality? But is not the summons of God's eternal will not merely a demand but the promise of grace?

"Heaven and earth will pass away, but my words will not pass away." These words imply something further than the call to responsible existence; they imply also the call of grace which bestows upon our present that quality of eternal life in which we must live. How does this come about?

In the first place, because these words, sounding from eternity, remind us of that truth which of course we can become aware of in other ways: "Heaven and earth will pass away!" These words also emphasize our transience and ultimate nothingness; but the characteristic thing about them, what distinguishes them from the words of human insight and wisdom, is just this: that while in themselves they warn us of our transience and perishability, they are also words of promise. It is as if in the "no" which negates our existence is concealed God's secret "yes." These words declare to us: if our aspiration to eternity is genuine, then it is not to be satisfied by the possibility that the fleeting, to which we would fain cling, may receive permanence, but conversely by our surrendering it. They do not however suggest that in a mood of resignation we should surrender the aspiration itself. They declare rather that the confession of our transitoriness and perishability and the surrender of the fleeting things of time are precisely the ways of grasping the eternal; or better, of allowing it to become to us as a gift. They teach us to know God as the One who "gives life to the dead and calls into existence the things that do not exist" (Rom. 4:17); they bid us pronounce the death sentence on ourselves by refusing to place our trust in ourselves, by trusting rather in God who raises the dead (2 Cor. 1:9). As creatures we are called to recognize God as the Creator. But to come to have faith in God as the Creator we must, in the words of Luther, be dead to all things, to good and ill, to life and death, to heaven and hell, and from the depth of our hearts recognize that in our own power we can avail nothing. It is the very nature and way of God first to destroy and annihilate what is in us before He bestows on us His gift.

This is the truth which Jesus expresses not only in the words: "For whoever would save his life will lose it; and whoever loses his life for my sake, he will save it" (Luke 9:24)—but furthermore in His cross. And Paul confesses in the same sense: "Far be it from me to glory except in the cross of our Lord Jesus Christ, by which the world has been crucified to me, and I to the world" (Gal. 6:14); and elsewhere he aspires to become "like him in his death, that if possible I may attain the resurrection from the dead" (Phil. 3:10). The eternal reality which is to mold and color our present is not a reality immanent within it, which by our own resources we might elicit and express; it is a gift coming to us from the beyond, it is the resurrection of the dead. And as the passing away of heaven and earth is not something which is to be realized only in the future, so the resurrection of the dead is not simply an event which awaits future realization. "Truly, truly, I say to you, he who hears my word and believes him who sent me, has eternal life; he does not come into judgment, but has passed from death to life." (John 5:24.) For him who in faith has received in time the gift of eternity, the word of the poet becomes true: "Time is not, eternity alone is; eternity alone abides in time. The real which ever comes to birth in time, the true present ever enshrined in time" (Rückert).

Ludwig Tieck once said: "Time and eternity is a problem which constantly brings the religious and theologians into conflict with each other, and yet time is but articulated eternity. Otherwise it has no meaning." In fact, the religious and the theologians of whom Tieck is thinking are wrong and they see only one side of the matter. For that emancipation from the flux of time which eternity confers upon us does not signify a complete release from time, nor imply that we should flee from time with its duties and gifts. Neither in fact could we do so. Rather, the gift of eternal grace gives to our present in time that genuine truth and reality which man today, in the midst of our spiritual confusion, often so wistfully seeks. We are certainly not absolved from the burden of responsibility which the divine demand lays upon us, but now we can bear it, free from tension and anxiety, from self-deception and self-accusation. The more we are released from our self-preoccupation and concern, the more we are free and inspired in the accomplishment of our tasks, the more open we are to the encounters of life; for the richer is our life of love, when through self-surrender we are freed and sustained by the grace of eternity. And those words of Jesus, which declare that whosoever believes His message has passed from death to life, find their echo in the confession: "We know that we have passed out of death into life, because we love the brethren." (1 John 3:14.)

And what of the blows of fate, the sorrows of the present time and the future, which lie darkly and threateningly before us? Let us heed a word of Paul: "For all things are yours . . . and you are Christ's and Christ is God's." (1 Cor. 3:21, 23.) "All things are yours"—this does not mean that we can freely control all things, but that in all life's ways and in all the darkness of the future our weakness is precisely our strength to overcome all things. In Christ God meets us as our God, and to know and experience Him as our God and Father gives us the power to endure in whatever distress and pain come upon us. In his suffering Paul hears the word of the Master: "My grace is sufficient for you, for my power is made perfect in weakness" (literally: comes to fulfillment in weakness). And he answers: "For the sake of Christ, then, I am content with weaknesses, insults, hardships, persecutions, and calamities; for when I am weak, then I am strong." (2 Cor. 12:9ff.)

And the future towards which we are moving becomes then for us God's future. To move towards this future does not mean to desire to mold it by our human planning and carefulness. Equally little does it mean to expect from it the fulfillment of all our desires. But it does mean that we travel towards this unknown, this darkness, with our heart and mind open for what God wills to make of us. The extraordinary thing about the promise of the resurrection from the dead is just the faith which "believes in hope against hope," which is permitted to experience God as Him "who gives life to the dead." (Rom. 4:18, 17.)

And the wonderful thing is that for him who hopes not in his own future but in God's future, the present is blessed with peace and abiding reality. It is from God's future that the present receives its eternal meaning.

And what of the past? Has it forever vanished, is it lost beyond recall? I read recently a most moving characterization of the type of humanity which threatens to emerge today: "The volatile, inwardly motorized type of man is on the way. What was once part of his life, recedes into the distance, cuts itself adrift from him, and is dissolved in phantasmagoria. He has no inner texture which holds his being together with a deed, however dark it be. Deeds lie behind him forever lost in mist. . . . He divorces himself from his deeds and atrocities like one who has hidden mines in the earth and hurries away . . . what does it matter to him, what explodes behind him?" Thus will it be when men have lost the sense of the genuine and fulfilled present. But for him whose present is illuminated by the light of God's future springing from grace, both past and present begin to shine in a new light and become woven together in a genuine historical life. For such a one the past appears as guided by the hand of God.

And what of the time which not only has vanished but which we have misspent and lost? Those moments of which we are ashamed? Do they not make us realize that the gift of eternity is the gift of divine forgiving grace? Must not such recollections above all make us realize most plainly our powerlessness before God—that powerlessness in which alone we receive the gift of grace? And must not the pain of such recollections become for us an occasion of thanksgiving? Even in the hours of evil and degradation God's hand has held us and abased us, and we recognize His prevenient grace which wills to turn them into a blessing for us.

How much also which we did not formerly understand now becomes illuminated in its true significance! Each of us may question himself. I will only recall an episode from Proust's novel *A la recherche du temps perdu (Remembrance of Things Past)*. In a retrospective survey of his childhood, there emerges to the surface of the artist's mind a certain characteristic scene, namely the memory of his anguish which he suppressed before his father and to which he gave free expression when his mother came to kiss him good night. That time has long since been swallowed up in the mists of oblivion, and the child's sobs have long died away. "But in truth that anguish has never faded, and today I hear it afresh only because life around me has now grown silent—like those convent bells which in the daytime are so heavily drowned by the noises of the city that one might suppose they had ceased to sound, but which in the stillness of evening are once again heard."

In the stillness of evening! Let us not lose those moments of stillness and "sweet silent thought" in the confusions and bustle of the garish day.

"Eternity is silence. Change is feverish clamor. Silently sweeps God's will over the distant spaces of earth" (Wilhelm Raabe).

This thought brings us to the final words of our text. "Take heed, watch; for you do not know when the time will come." I think that there is no need for me to speak longer about it.

> Darkness reigns and all is silent;
>   O thou majesty on high
> Low my spirit bows before Thee
>   Where to enter is to die.
> Thee the Holy in the Holiest
>   Through the solemn night I seek.
> Silent let my soul await Thee:
>   Lord, I listen; do Thou speak.

—GERHARD TERSTEEGEN

Fulton J. Sheen

1895–1979

A kind of trajectory might be plotted to measure audience size for preachers across the centuries. Beginning with the Sermon on the Mount, continuing with the crowds who came to hear John Chrysostom, Savonarola, or John Donne; then the tremendous outdoor assemblies for the Wesley brothers; in the last century, the huge numbers attracted by Charles Spurgeon or Dwight L. Moody; finally, the attendance in our century at revivals held by evangelist Aimee Semple McPherson. You must total them all and then add on in order to approach the sum of those who watched and heard Bishop Fulton J. Sheen preach weekly on network television from 1951 to 1957. In one month, for example, a hundred million viewers tuned in, the number Billy Sunday is said to have reached over a forty-year career.

Media preaching, of course, did not begin with Sheen. His disreputable predecessor (actually, one of a number of disreputable Depression-era radio evangelists) was Father Charles E. Coughlin of the Shrine of the Little Flower in Royal Oak, Michigan. Coughlin's Sunday afternoon programs mixing Christian preaching with attacks on socialism and atheistic Jews were described by *Fortune* magazine in 1934 as "just about the biggest thing that ever happened to radio" and drew three to four million listeners.

By the 1940s, on the radio program "The Catholic Hour," a new voice was heard nationally. It belonged to Monsignor Fulton J. Sheen, born in Illinois, trained in neo-Thomism at the University of Louvain, a professor at Catholic University in Washington, D.C. His eloquence and ability to reach out to people of all faiths got him appointed national director of the Society for the Propagation of the Faith, which in turned prompted the producers at the DuMont television network to put him on the air. (He had in fact already conducted the first televised religious service in 1940 on Long Island, New York, a mass at which the candles all melted immediately when the bright, hot stage lights went on. Some one hundred viewers saw it on their primitive sets.)

One Tuesday in 1951, viewers used to watching a variety show starring the reigning King of Television, comedian Milton Berle, were greeted with something different:

> In mid-season, large numbers of adults began to turn from the *Texaco Star Theater* to a new, unexpected source of competition: God. DuMont, which prided itself—out of financial necessity—on producing "sensibly priced" entertainment, threw up against Berle a concept considered too ridiculously simple for the other networks to take seriously: a sermon. For thirty minutes each week on *Life Is Worth Living,* Roman Catholic Bishop Fulton J. Sheen delivered a strong but sensitive religious presentation. He was not plugging a particular doctrine, but rather was discussing everyday problems and the help a faith in God could bring. He even had a sense of humor,

often joking about his competition with Berle. One quip had it that both worked for the same boss, Sky Chief [a gasoline brand of Berle's sponsor].[1]

Dressed in his bishop's clericals, his piercing, deeply set eyes drilling through the camera lens, Sheen spoke movingly and with exceptional eloquence about a variety of subjects religious (Mary, the Mother of Jesus) and nonreligious (abortion, communism), appealing easily across denominational lines. That year his program won the coveted Emmy award, and he thanked his writers: Matthew, Mark, Luke, and John. His influence grew, and among those whom he could claim as his converts were Clare Boothe Luce, Fritz Kreisler, and Henry Ford II. In later years, after his television career was over, Sheen continued a course of itinerant preaching, especially at New York's St. Patrick's Cathedral on Good Fridays, until his death in 1979. He lies buried there, just down the street from the world headquarters of NBC, CBS, and ABC. In the sermon that follows he gives a good account of the Beatitudes.

The Beatitudes

The modern world talks of the Beatitudes as if they were just a kind of lecture and a very dull lecture at that, forgetful that the Beatitudes contain more dogma, more mortification, more hardships, more unmodernities than anything else in the Gospel. The Sermon on the Mount is just the prelude to the drama of Calvary.

Contrast the Beatitudes with what we might call the beatitudes of the world; the one is the antithesis of the other. The world says: "Blessed are the rich"; Christ says: "Blessed are the poor in spirit." The world says: "Blessed are the mighty"; Our Lord says: "Blessed are the meek." The world says: "Laugh and the world laughs with you"; Christ says: "Blessed are they that mourn." The world says: "Be for yourself and your country right or wrong";

---

[1]Harry Castleman and Walter J. Podrazik, *Watching TV: Four Decades of American Television* (New York: McGraw-Hill, 1982), p. 68.

Christ says: "Blessed are they that hunger and thirst after justice." The world says: "Sow your wild oats, you are only young once; blessed is the sex appeal"; Christ says: "Blessed are the clean of heart." The world says: "In time of peace prepare for war"; Christ says: "Blessed are the peacemakers." The world says: "Blessed are those who never suffer persecution"; Christ says: "Blessed are they that suffer persecution." The world says: "Blessed is popularity"; Christ says: "Blessed are ye when they shall revile you and persecute you and speak all that is evil against you for My sake."

In so many words the Sermon on the Mount placed an irreconcilable opposition between the world and Christ. He upset every maxim of the world as He upset the tables of the moneychangers in the temple, and said openly that He prayed not for the world: "If the world hate you, know ye that it hath hated Me before you. If you had been of the world, the world would love its own: but because you are not of the world, but I have chosen you out of the world, therefore the world hateth you."

Every standard the world ever held He upset with a ruthless abandon. He was the iconoclast of the world, smashing to fragments its false idols. He talked in the language of the paradox, for only the paradox could express the opposition between Himself and the world. The lofty, He said, shall be preferred; the scorned shall be reverenced; the needy shall possess all things; the reviled shall bless; the persecuted shall suffer patiently; the blasphemed shall entreat; the weak shall be strong, the strong shall be weak; the fool shall be wise, and the wise shall be foolish. He wrote the law of Christianity by the example of His own life, and that law is: The death of all things in their first stage is the necessary condition of infinite progress. Nothing is quickened unless it die.

Blessed Are the Meek

Our Lord both *preached* and *practiced* meekness.

He preached it in those memorable words that continue the Beatitudes: "You have heard that it hath been said: An eye for an eye and a tooth for a tooth. But I say to you not to resist evil; but if one strike thee on thy right cheek, turn to him also the other: and if a man will contend with thee in judgment, and take away thy coat, let go thy cloak also unto him. And whosoever shall force thee one mile, go with him another two. . . . You have heard that it hath been said: Thou shalt love thy neighbor and hate thy enemy. But I say to you: Love your enemies: do good to them that hate you: and pray for them that persecute and calumniate you that you may be the children of your Father who is in heaven, who maketh His sun to rise upon the good and bad, and raineth upon the just and the unjust. For if you love them that love you, what reward shall you have? do not even the tax collectors do this? And if you salute your brethren only, what do you more than others? do not also the pagans this? Be you therefore perfect, as also your heavenly Father is perfect."

But He not only preached meekness, He also *practiced* it. When His own people picked up stones to throw at Him, He threw none back in return; when His fellow townsmen brought Him to the brow of the hill to cast Him over the precipice, He walked through the midst of them unharmed; when the soldier struck Him with a mailed fist, He answered meekly: "If I have spoken evil, give testimony of the evil: but if well, why strikest thou me?"

When they swore to kill Him, He did not use His power to strike dead even a single enemy; and now on the Cross, meekness reaches its peak, when to those who pierce the hands that feed the world, and to those who pierce the feet that shepherd souls, He pleads: "Father, forgive them, for they know not what they do."

Blessed Are the Merciful

A person is merciful when he or she feels the sorrow and misery of another as if it were one's own. Disliking misery and unhappiness, the merciful person seeks to dispel the misery of a neighbor just as much as one would if the misery were one's own. That is why, whenever mercy is confronted not only with pain, but also with sin and wrongdoing, it becomes forgiveness that not merely pardons, but even rebuilds into justice, repentance, and love.

Mercy is one of the dominant notes in the preaching of Our Lord. His parables were parables of mercy. Take for example the hundred sheep, the ten pieces of money, and the two sons. Of the hundred sheep, one was lost; of the ten pieces of money, one was lost; of the two sons, one led a life of dissipation.

It is interesting to note that the lost sheep is the one that was sought, and the shepherd, finding it, places it upon his shoulders and brings it into the house rejoicing. But there is no record in the gospels of any such attention being paid to the ninety-nine sheep who were not lost.

When the woman lost a piece of money and found it, she called in her neighbors to rejoice. But there is no record that she ever called in her neighbors to rejoice in the possession of the other nine that were never lost.

One son went into a foreign country and wasted his substance living riotously. And when he came back he was given the fatted calf. But the brother who stayed at home was not so rewarded. All these illustrations Our Lord followed with the simple truth: "There shall be more joy in heaven upon one sinner that doth penance than upon ninety-nine who need not penance."

One day Peter went to Him to inquire just what limitation should be placed upon mercy. And so he asked Our Lord a question about mercy and gave what he thought was rather an extravagant limit: "How often shall my brother offend against me, and I forgive him? till seven times?" And Our Lord answered, "Not till seven times, but till seventy times seven times." And that does not mean four hundred and ninety—that means infinity.

Blessed Are the Clean of Heart

This, of course, is not the beatitude of the world. The world is living today in what might be described as an era of carnality, which glorifies sex, hates restraint, identifies purity with coldness, innocence with ignorance, and turns men and women into Buddhas with their eyes closed, hands folded across their breasts, intently looking inward, thinking only of self.

It is just precisely against such a glorification of sex and such egocentrism that is so characteristic of the flesh that Our Lord reacted in His third Beatitude: "Blessed are the clean of heart."

Blessed Are the Poor in Spirit

Modern society is what might be characterized as acquisitive, for its primary concern is to acquire, to own, to possess; its aristocracy is not one of blood or virtue, but of money; it judges worth not by righteousness but in terms of possessions.

Our Blessed Lord came into the world to destroy this acquisitiveness and this subservience of moral to economic ends by preaching the blessedness of the poor in spirit. It is worth noting immediately that the poor in spirit does not necessarily mean the indigent or those straitened circumstances of life; poor in spirit means interior detachment and as such includes even some who are rich in the world's goods, for detachment can be practiced by the rich just as avarice can be practiced by the poor.

The poor in spirit are those who are so detached from wealth, from social position, and from earthly knowledge that, at the moment the Kingdom of God demands a sacrifice, they are prepared to surrender all.

The Beatitude means then: Blessed are those who are not possessed by their possessions; blessed are they who whether or not they are poor in *fact* are poor in their inmost spirit.

Our Lord not only preached poverty of spirit, He also lived it, and He lived it in such a way as to conquer the three kinds of pride—the pride of what one *has,* which is economic pride; the pride of what one *is,* which is social pride; and the pride of what one *knows,* which is intellectual pride.

Blessed Are They That Hunger and Thirst After Justice

Not only negatively but positively did He preach the necessity of zeal for the justice of the Kingdom of God. His circumcision was a kind of impatience to run His course of justice that led to the garden and the cross; His teaching the doctors in the temple at twelve years of age was an impatience to teach men the sweetness of His Father's ways.

At the beginning of His public life we find Him driving merchants out of the temple, in fulfillment of the prophecy of apostleship: "The zeal of thy house hath eaten me up." Later on, He made use of a dinner invitation, to save the soul of Magdalen and, on a hot day, made use of a common love of cold water to bring the Samaritan woman to a knowledge of everlasting fountains.

He came, He said, "not to destroy souls, but to save"; and, "seeing the multitude, he had compassion on them because they were distressed, and lying as sheep having no shepherd." Then he said to His disciples: "The harvest indeed is great, but the laborers are few. Pray ye therefore the Lord of the harvest, that he send forth laborers into his harvest." His whole mission in life was one of zeal, a hunger and thirst for the justice of God, which He perhaps best expressed in words of fire: "I am come to cast fire on the earth: and what will I but that it be kindled? And I have a baptism wherewith I am to be baptized. And how am I straitened until it be accomplished?" "And other sheep I have that are not of this fold: them also I must bring. And they shall hear my voice, and there shall be one fold and one shepherd."

And now at the end of His life, He yearns still more for justice, as He who called himself the Fountain of Living Waters, and He who was figuratively the Rock that gave forth water as Moses struck it in the desert now lets well from out His Sacred Heart the shepherd's call to all the souls of the world: "I thirst."

It was not a thirst for earthly waters, for the earth and its oceans were His. And when they offered Him vinegar and gall as a sedative for His sufferings, he refused it. It was therefore not a physical, but a spiritual thirst that troubled Him—the thirst for the beatitude of justice—an insatiable thirst for the souls of humans.

Blessed Are the Peacemakers

What is the peace spoken of in this Beatitude? The most perfect definition of peace ever given was that of St. Augustine: *"Peace is the tranquillity of order."* It is not tranquillity alone; rather it is the tranquillity of order in which there is no oppression from without, but rather a subordination of all things to the sovereign good that is God. Therefore the subjection of senses to reason, reason to faith, and the whole person to God as the eternal end and final perfection—that is the basis of peace.

It was just such a tranquillity of order that Our Lord brought to earth as the angels sang at His birth: "Glory to God in the highest, and on earth peace to men of good will." He bade His disciples to have peace with one another. Into whatsoever house they entered, they were first to say: "Peace be to this house."

The very Beatitude we are considering is a blessing on such peacemakers, and His words over Jerusalem a reminder of His sorrow at those who loved not peace: "If thou also hadst known, and that in this thy day, the things that are to thy peace; but now they are hidden from thy eyes."

The night of His arrest in the garden, when Peter drew his sword and cut off the right ear of the servant of the high priest, Our Lord rebuked him, saying, "Put up again the sword into its place, for all that take the sword shall perish with the sword." Touching the ear of the wounded servant, He made it whole.

The next afternoon, He who came to preach peace was put to death in the first world war of man against his Redeemer; but before He died he pronounced the last and final words of peace: "It is finished."

Blessed Are They That Mourn

The world never regards mourning as blessing, but always as a curse. Laughter is the gold it is seeking, and sorrow is the enemy it flees.

It can no more understand the beatitude of mourning than it can understand the Cross. In fact, many modern people steel themselves even against the suffering of another by wearing the mask of indifference, quite unmindful that such a thickening of the spiritual skin, though it may sometimes protect them from sorrow, nevertheless shuts in their own morbidity until it festers and corrupts.

But it must not be thought that the beatitude of Our Lord is either a condemnation of laughter and joy or a glorification of sorrow and tears. Our Lord did not believe in a philosophy of tragedy any more than we do. As a matter of fact, He upbraided the Pharisees because they wore long faces and looked sad when they fasted, and His Apostles summed up His Life and Resurrection in the one word *rejoice.*

The difference between the beatitude of the world, "Laugh and the world laughs with you," and the beatitude of Our Lord, "Blessed are they that mourn," is not that the world brings laughter and Our Lord brings tears. It is not even a choice of having or not having sadness; it is rather a choice of where we shall put it: at the beginning or at the end. In other words, which comes first, laughter or tears?

Shall we place our joys in time or in eternity? for we cannot have them in both. Shall we laugh on earth or laugh in heaven? for we cannot laugh in both. Shall we mourn before we die or after we die? for we cannot do both. We cannot have our reward both in heaven and on earth.

That is why we believe one of the most tragic remarks of Our Lord is what He will say to the worldly at the end of time: "You have already had your reward."

Blessed Are They That Are Persecuted

The eighth beatitude, in the language of St. Thomas Aquinas, "is a confirmation and a declaration of all those that precede. Because from the very fact that a man is confirmed in poverty of spirit, meekness, and the rest, it follows that no persecution will induce him to renounce them. Hence the eighth beatitude corresponds in a way to all the preceding seven."

Archibald MacLeish

1892–1982

Archibald MacLeish, Pulitzer Prize-winning poet, Librarian of Congress, and Assistant Secretary of State near the end of World War II, is remembered not only as an outstanding lyric poet, and an essayist on social and political questions, but as the author of verse plays. *Nobodaddy* was based on the story in Genesis of Adam, Eve, Cain, and Abel. When MacLeish, in his turn toward "the dramatic situation which the condition of self-consciousness in an indifferent universe presents," moved on to the biblical drama of the Book of Job, he confronted even more directly these issues of suffering, human existence, and faith. *J.B.* was performed on Broadway in 1959; the play attracted the attention of theologians as well as theatergoers and critics. MacLeish's play posits human love as compensation for disaster and argued that man's love for God, and God's need of that love, in his battle with the adversarial figure of Satan, is at the center of the biblical narrative. (MacLeish was not the first American poet to take up the theme of good and evil in Job; his contemporary Robert Frost engaged its topics as well, in verse theater.)

In 1955, four years before the first performance of *J.B.*, Archibald MacLeish preached a lay sermon in Farmington, Connecticut, in which he grappled with the meaning of the biblical work. His reading of the Book of Job is informed not only by the consciousness MacLeish brought to its chapters as a poet but by a public servant's memory of the recent events of the twentieth century and the destruction of millions of human beings as innocent and tormented as the steadfast hero of the Old Testament story.

ᖋ

The Book of Job

To preach is to speak with something more than one's own voice—something that only ordination can give, that only the relation of minister to congregation can make possible. I cannot preach here this morning. I can only *say*—say the things possible to me as the kind of human being I am—not perhaps a religious man in the ordinary sense of that term but one who, because of the nature of the art he has followed and because of the character of the time in which he has lived, has had to think much about the things with which religion is concerned. *Whence* and *whither* are questions for the poet as they are questions for the priest: in a dark time, even greater questions, for the priest has answers while the man who writes the poem has only, as Yeats put it, his blind, stupefied heart.

It was a poet's question that brought me to the text I wish to speak of this morning, the most difficult and the most urgent of all poet's questions in a time like this, the question of the belief in life—which is also and inevitably the question of the belief in the meaning, the justice, of the universe—which, in its ultimate terms, is the question of the belief in God.

No man can believe in the imitation of life in art who does not first believe in life itself, and no man can believe in life itself who does not believe that life can be justified. But how can life be justified in a time in which life brings with it such inexplicable sufferings: a time in which millions upon millions of men and women and children are destroyed and mutilated for no crime but the crime of being born in a certain century or of belonging to a certain race or of inhabiting a certain city; a time in which the most shameless and cynical tyranny flourishes, in which the ancient decencies are turned inside out to make masks for cruelty and fraud, in which even the meaning of the holiest words is perverted to deceive men and enslave them? How can we believe in our lives unless we can believe in God, and how can we believe in God unless we can believe in the justice of God, and how can we believe in the justice of God in a world in which the innocent perish in vast meaningless massacres, and brutal and dishonest men foul all the lovely things?

These are questions we in our generation ask ourselves. But they are not new questions. They have been asked before us over thousands of years and by no one more passionately and more eloquently than by that ancient writer—the author of the book of Job. It is of that book I wish to speak— but of that book, not as a fragment of the Bible, but as the great, self-containing poem it actually is.

Most of us who read the book of Job read it for the magnificence of its metaphors, or for the nobility of its language in the great translation in which we know it; but the language and the metaphors are not the poem. The poem is the whole: not the language only but the action, and not alone the action but the meaning to which the action moves, and not the meaning as part of a web of meanings which the Old and New Testaments compose, but the meaning in itself.

It is commonly said, I know—and for reasons which are understandable enough—that the meaning of the book of Job is incomplete and unsatisfactory to any Christian; that the book of Job does no more than pose the tremendous question of man's lot; that we must go on to the teachings of Jesus for an answer to that question. It is understandable that men should say this, for certainly the meaning of the book of Job is a hard meaning and the terms of the dramatic action are brutal terms, terms that the modern mind may well find shocking and even blasphemous. But the fact remains that there *is* a meaning—a meaning proffered by one of the greatest poets who ever wrote—a meaning that directly touches the enormous question which haunts us all in our time as it haunted him in his.

The book begins with the passage which I read you (1:1–12). It is not a passage most of us care to dwell on, or to take in the literal sense and meaning of the words, for it makes God party to the undeserved sufferings of a human being. Consider what is being said in those beginning verses of the first chapter. Job, it is said, was "perfect and upright and one that feared God and eschewed evil." This was God's judgment of Job also, for God describes him in these same words, you will remember, in His conversation with Satan. But notwithstanding his innocence God delivers Job into the hands of Satan, empowering the great Adversary to destroy everything but Job's person—his seven sons, his three daughters, all his people but the five servants who escape from the five massacres and disasters, all his goods and wealth, and, eventually, after the second conversation with Satan, his health also. And all this is done. And done with God's consent. And done furthermore, as God Himself asserts in the second conversation, "without cause." There can be no misunderstanding the intention of the text. The death and destruction are Satan's work, but without God's consent they could not have been accomplished, and God recognizes from the beginning that they are unjustified by any guilt of Job's.

And not only is all this explicitly said: it is also the essential precondition to the dramatic action and to the whole colloquy which follows between Job and his three "comforters." Job's agony results far more from his consciousness of this lack of cause than from the loss of his wealth or even the destruction of his children. The cry for death with which the great debate begins is not a cry for release from life but for the obliteration and canceling out of a condition in which such brutal injustice is possible. "Let the day perish in which I was born," says Job, "and the night in which it was said, There is a man child conceived" (3:3). And it is to this same issue the comforters address their bitter comforts. Eliphaz undertakes to answer the complaint of *injustice* by foreclosing the appeal to justice. Justice, he says, is not for men to think of: "In thoughts from the visions of the night, when deep sleep falleth on men, Fear came upon me . . . a spirit passed before my face; the hair of my flesh stood up . . . an image was before mine eyes, there was silence, and I heard a voice saying, Shall mortal man be more just than God?" (4:13–17). It is not for men to debate justice with the Almighty.

But Job will not be answered in these terms. He will not forgo his deep conviction that some how, some way, his suffering must be justified: "Teach me and I will hold my tongue; and cause me to understand *wherein I have erred"* (6:24). Job's challenge is the challenge of his innocence, and it is of his innocence the comforters speak. If Job insists on discussing the justice of his suffering, says Bildad, he is condemned forthwith because God *is* just, and a man who suffers, therefore, suffers necessarily for cause. "Doth God pervert judgment? Or doth the Almighty pervert justice?" (8:3). But Job, like men before him and men since, rejects the unanswerable logic of this proposition: God destroys the good as well as the evil. "The earth is given into the hand of the wicked; He covereth the faces of the judges thereof; if not, where and who is He?" (9:24). All one needs to do is to look at the world where the dishonest and the brutal flourish—and Job breaks out with that poignant cry our time has made its own: "changes and war are against me" (10:17).

But the comforters are not persuaded. Zophar picks up Bildad's argument and presses it home with the ultimate thrust. Not only are all sufferers presumably guilty: *Job* is guilty. God exacts less than Job's wickedness deserves. Job's very self-justification is proof of his guilt. But Job will not be browbeaten. He knows and fears God as well as his friends, but he respects his own integrity also: "Though He slay me, yet will I trust in Him; but I will maintain my own ways before Him" (13:15).

And thereupon Job turns from the debate with his friends to that greater debate in which we are all inevitably engaged: the debate with God. He demands of God to show him "how many are my iniquities and sins? Make me know my transgression and my sin" (13:23). But God does not answer. "Oh that I knew where I might find Him, that I might come even to His seat! I would order my cause before Him, and fill my mouth with arguments. . . . Behold, I go forward, but He is not there; and backward, but I cannot perceive Him" (23:3, 4, 8).

And so the argument goes on, until at last God answers Job out of the whirlwind and the dust. But answers him how? By showing him the hidden cause? No, by convicting him of insignificance! Where was Job when the world was made—"when the morning stars sang together, and all the sons of God shouted for joy"? Has Job "entered into the treasure of the snow"? Can Job "bind the sweet chains of the Pleiades"? Has Job clothed the neck of the horse with thunder who "saith among the trumpets, Ha, ha; and he smelleth the battle afar off"? Does the hawk fly by Job's wisdom or the eagle?—"where the slain are, there is she" (38–39).

Power by power and glory by glory it piles up, all that unmatchable, rich fountaining and fluency of image and metaphor, heaping strength on strength and beauty on beauty only to culminate in that terrible challenge: "Gird up thy loins now like a man; I will demand of thee, and declare thou unto me. Wilt thou disannul my judgment? Wilt thou condemn me, that thou mayest be righteous? Hast thou an arm like God or canst thou thunder with a voice like Him? Deck thyself now with majesty and excellency; and array thyself with glory and beauty. . . . Then will I also confess unto thee that thine own right hand can save thee" (4:7–14). What can man reply? What does Job reply to that tremendous utterance from the blind wind? "Behold I am vile," he cries, "what shall I answer Thee? I will lay my hand upon my mouth" (40:4).

But what is this poem then? What has happened? What has been shown? Only that Job is less than God in wisdom and in power? It scarcely needed all these words, all this magnificence of words, to make that evident. And no matter how evident, how doubly evident it may be, what answer can the insignificance of Job provide to the great question that has been asked of God?

Well, of one meaning of the poem we can be certain, can we not? To the old poet who wrote this drama thousands of years ago, the injustice of the universe was self-evident. He makes this clear not once but three times. Job, he says, was a perfect and an upright man—that is to say, a man who did not merit punishment, let alone the terrible scourge of disasters with which he was afflicted. Again, God by His own admission was moved to destroy Job "without cause" (2:3). Finally, the comforters, who had argued that Job must have deserved his sufferings, must have been wicked after all, are reproved—angrily reproved—by God at the end: "My wrath is kindled against thee, and against thy two friends," God says to Eliphaz, "for ye have not spoken of me the thing that is right" (42:7).

The conclusion is inevitable: Job's sufferings—and they are clearly meant to be the most dreadful sufferings of which the imagination can conceive, the steepest plunge from fortune to misery—Job's sufferings are unjustified. They are unjustified in any human meaning of the word justice. And yet they are God's work—work that could not have been done without the will of God.

But is this all the poem's meaning? Has the poet of the old visionary time nothing more to say to us than this—that the universe is cruel, that there is no justice, that God may plunge us into misery for no cause and then, at the end, for no cause either, give back to us twofold all that was taken away—all but the lost, all but the dead? (For this, you will remember, happens to Job at the book's end.)

No, surely this is not the only meaning. If it were, men would not have read the book of Job generation after generation, century after century, no matter how magnificent its language. But what other meaning is there? What other meaning can there be? What has the poem to say to us of our real concern: the possibility of our living in this world? If the universe is unjust, if God permits our destruction without cause, how are we to believe in life? And if we cannot believe in life, how are we to live?

This is, for all of us, the crucial question. It was the crucial question for the author of the book of Job also. "Why died I not from the womb?" cries Job; "as a hidden untimely birth *I had not been*" (3:11, 16). What answer to *that* question does the poet find? What answer does he show us in this drama of man's agony?

A deep and, I think, a meaningful answer.

Consider the drama as drama: the play as play. What is the fateful action from which all the rest follows? Is it not God's action in delivering Job, though innocent, into Satan's hands? Without this, Job would not have suffered, the comforters would not have come, the great debate would not have been pursued, God would not have spoken from the whirlwind.

But *why* did God deliver Job into Satan's hands? Why?

For a reason that is made unmistakably plain. Because God had need of the suffering of Job—had need of it for Himself *as God*.

Recall that scene in heaven with which the play begins. Satan has returned from going to and fro in the earth and from walking up and down in it. God, hearing where he has been, asks him to admire Job's uprightness and reverence. Satan replies with that oldest of sneering questions: "Doth Job fear God for nought?" Has God not protected Job and enriched him? Has God not bought Job's love and paid for it? Do you think, cries Satan, Job would still love You if You took it all away? "Put forth Thy hand now and touch all that he hath, and he will curse Thee to Thy face" (1:9ff.).

And God gives His consent.

Why? For proof? To silence Satan? Obviously. But still, why? Clearly because God believes in Job: because God believes it will be demonstrated that Job loves and fears God because He is God and not because Job is prosperous—proved that Job will still love God and fear Him in adversity, in misfortune, in the worst of misfortunes, *in spite of everything.*

Which means? Which gives what meaning to this book?

Which means that in the conflict between God and Satan, in the struggle between good and evil, God stakes His supremacy as God upon man's fortitude and love. Which means, again, that where the nature of man is in question—and it is precisely, you will note, the nature of man that Satan has brought into question with his sneering challenge—where the nature of man is in question, *God has need of man.*

Only Job can prove that Job is capable of the love of God, not as a *quid pro quo* but for the love's sake, for God's sake, in spite of everything—in spite even of injustice, even God's injustice. Only man can prove that man loves God.

If one were to write an argument to go at the head of the book of Job in some private notebook of one's own, it might well be written in these words: Satan, who is the denial of life, who is the kingdom of death, cannot be overcome by God who is his opposite, who is the kingdom of life, except by man's persistence in the love of God in spite of every reason to withhold his love, every suffering.

And if one were then to write an explanation of that argument, the explanation might be this: Man depends on God for all things: God depends on man for one. Without man's love, God does not exist as God, only as creator, and love is the one thing no one, not even God Himself, can command. It is a free gift or it is nothing. And it is most itself, most free, when it is offered in spite of suffering, of injustice, and of death.

And if one were to attempt, finally, to reduce this explanation and this argument to a single sentence which might stand at the end of the book to close it, the sentence might read this way: The justification of the injustice of the universe is not our blind acceptance of God's inexplicable will, nor our trust in God's love—His dark and incomprehensible love—for us, but our human love, notwithstanding anything, for Him.

Acceptance—even Dante's acceptance—of God's will is not enough. Love—love of life, love of the world, love of God, love in spite of everything—is the answer, the only possible answer, to our ancient human cry against injustice.

It is for this reason that God, at the end of the poem, answers Job not in the language of justice but in the language of beauty and power and glory, signifying that it is not because He is just but because He is God that He deserves His creature's adoration.

And it is true. We do not love God because we can believe in Him; we believe in God because we can love Him. It is because we—even we—can love God that we can conceive Him, and it is because we can conceive Him that we can live. To speak of "justice" is to demand something for ourselves, to ask something of life, to require that we be treated according to our dues. But love, as Saint Paul told the Corinthians, does not "seek her own" (1 Cor. 13:5). Love creates. Love creates even God, for how else have we come to Him, any of us, but through love?

Man, the scientists say, is the animal that thinks. They are wrong. Man is the animal that loves. It is in man's love that God exists and triumphs, in man's love that life is beautiful, in man's love that the world's injustice is resolved. To hold together in one thought those terrible opposites of good and evil which struggle in the world is to be capable of life, and only love will hold them so.

Our labor always, like Job's labor, is to learn through suffering to love . . . to love even that which lets us suffer.

Martin Niemöller

1 8 9 2 – 1 9 8 4

O n Christmas Eve, 1944, the German Lutheran clergyman Martin Niemöller first conducted a religious service in Dachau concentration camp. His congregation was eclectic, both in nationality and in religious denomination; the service was the first Niemöller was allowed to hold during his seven and a half years of imprisonment. In his long confinement any contact of "special prisoners" (jailed primarily for political and moral resistance to the Third Reich) with one another had been forbidden. In this example from Niemöller's *Dachau Sermons,* preached in a cell during the last days of the Third Reich, and celebrating the Last Supper and the feast of Maundy Thursday, there is something reminiscent of both the isolation of these prisoners and their solidarity in worship at a time when the gospel, as Niemöller wrote when these texts were published in 1945, "remained alive for us as the power of God . . . and even now our only hope."

Before Niemöller began his theological studies, he was a naval officer in World War I, commander of a German U-boat. During his pastorate in the 1930s in Berlin, he founded the Pastors' Emergency League and combated rising discrimination against Christians of Jewish background. In 1934, Niemöller, proclaiming the resistance of the Confessing Church of Germany (an amalgam of Lutheran and Reformed churches), participated in the Synod of Barmen. In 1937 he was arrested and sent to Dachau. During the postwar period, Niemöller became convinced of the collective guilt of the Germans, and as a controversial pacifist he spoke from the pulpit against the arms race. In the Maundy Thursday sermon, Niemöller evokes a small table of feasting and reconciliation in a world at war. His argument for unity among Christians and his conviction that all strife is diluted in an ecumenical spirit in wartime remains as hard to assess as any universal agreement in the Christian churches as to the true meaning of the sacrament of the Eucharist. What follows is Pastor Niemöller's reading of the symbolism of the paschal meal on the eve of the Crucifixion.

Dachau Sermon: Maundy Thursday, March 29, 1945

For as often as ye eat this bread, and drink this cup, ye do shew the Lord's death till he come.

—1 CORINTHIANS 11:26

On the eve of that Good Friday on which three crosses were erected on Golgotha, our Lord and Savior gathered about himself his more intimate

circle of disciples—the later apostles—for the last Paschal meal, for that
remembrance meal through which God's people of the old covenant
recalled the wonderful rescue from the Egyptian bondage. In accordance
with the customary celebration of the festival, they ate the Paschal lamb,
drank the cup of thanksgiving, and sang together the great hymn of praise.
Now the celebration is finished and the disciples await the evening departure to the usual lodging house outside the city, on the Mount of Olives. But
Jesus makes no move to get ready to leave, but rather joins to the just-
finished Paschal meal a second solemn act. He takes the bread, which is still
lying on the table at which they had eaten, breaks it in pieces, and gives it
to the disciples with the words: "Take, eat: this is my body, which is broken
for you: this do in remembrance of me." (1 Cor. 11:24.) Thereafter he took
the cup, which was still standing before him after the Paschal meal, passed
it to his friends, and said, "This cup is the new testament in my blood: this
do ye, as oft as ye drink of it, in remembrance of me." (1 Cor. 11:25.)

At first, in their astonishment, the Twelve presumably did not know
what was happening. But one thing they could not fail to hear, even in their
first amazement: the Lord spoke here to them about his death. His body is
broken like the bread that he distributes to them; his blood is shed like the
draught of wine that he has given them to drink. His earthly life's work,
hardly begun according to human reckoning, is finished: their Master takes
from them.

According to what the Evangelists have recorded for us, this was not
the first time Jesus spoke to his disciples about his impending death; but we
always read, in connection with the preceding announcements of the coming sufferings, that they did not understand him. Jesus spoke to them in riddles when he said that his death was a divine necessity. They hoped for the
inauguration of the Kingdom of God announced by him, they waited for the
time when their Master would appear before the world as ruler and judge
in order to usher in a new Golden Age. But now such a misunderstanding is
no longer possible: all these dreams are at an end. One of the Twelve goes
forth to betray his Lord, the others will be scattered, and the most loyal of
them will deny that he had anything to do with this man. The whole thing
is a catastrophe, an utter collapse!

Since that evening almost two thousand years have passed, and still
now, and always, the disciples of Jesus gather again on the evening of

Maundy Thursday around his table to partake of the meal to which the Lord invites them. Thereby they think of that hour in which Jesus ordered the disciples to observe this holy command. "This do in remembrance of me." Here one asks naturally—and who among us has never raised this question?—"Fundamentally what is it that gives to this celebration its unparalleled power over the human heart? How does it happen that in spite of all theological disputations and schisms, which have flared up again and again, particularly about this sacrament, the Christian community continues to break the bread and partake of the cup as if all this strife did not concern it at all?"

Yes, my friends, it really does not concern the Christians at all. The Lord Jesus has given us no doctrines about this Holy Supper of his, nor did he wish to give us any such doctrines at all. All doctrines by which we try to assert something about God's activity are subject to the law of aging and changing. What interested mightily the ancient Greeks, in their pious curiosity, namely, the question of how a man could be at the same time the Son of God, involved theological disputations for centuries. They fought about it back and forth with arguments and counterarguments. Today this no longer interests us in the least; not because we have become so much more indifferent about religion, but because we know that this is not a question which is connected with and rooted in the spirit of the New Testament and therefore in our Christian faith. Later periods have racked their brains trying to find out how it is possible that God, for the sake of Jesus, forgives the sins of those who believe in Him. How can He, if He is the holy and just God, place our sins upon another? Nowadays only some very learned theologians are accurately informed about these theories and mental exercises, while the Christian community has long since understood that a miracle cannot be explained, and consequently it is better to abstain from the attempt.

And in regard to the disputed questions about the Holy Supper the situation is not radically different. How can bread and wine be the body and blood of Jesus Christ? The great division in the Reformation Church springs in a considerable measure from the different answers to this question. Luther taught differently from Zwingli in the matter, and the latter differently from Calvin; all of them united only in the rejection of the medieval Roman Catholic doctrine of transubstantiation. At present these theological differences have become so subtle that one must be a philosopher with a better-than-average education in order to recognize them in their variety of types. If our salvation depended upon such a recognition, then the Kingdom of Heaven would be accessible only to learned thinkers—which is obviously contrary to the conception held by Jesus himself, and to his own words.

No, what matters in the Holy Supper is something essentially different, something which the shrewdest cannot conceive with all his shrewdness, but which the most simple-minded can well grasp and comprehend. The Lord Jesus announces in this meal his own death, and thus he draws the veil from the mystery of his life's conclusion. And what he himself said at the time about the significance of his death became for his apostles and then for his church the actual core of the Christian faith and of the Christian message; and it has remained so until this day. When Paul wished to condense the contents of his missionary preaching in a single sentence, he wrote: "I determined not to know any thing [namely, in the field of religion] among you, save Jesus Christ, and him crucified." (1 Cor. 2:2.) And when the Christian Church wishes to give to its faith the shortest and yet the most unmistakable expression, it uses the symbol of the cross. The cross stands over the altars in our churches, greets us on the paths of our homeland, it is the sign of hope on the graves of our beloved. We know only one comfort and one assurance, Jesus Christ the crucified.

The interpretation of his death which the Lord Jesus gives his disciples in the Holy Supper is extremely plain. To understand it there is no need of any philosophy nor of any Biblical learning, but only of an open heart which is ready to see what is here happening, and to hear what is here being said.

The Lord himself breaks the bread, he himself passes the cup: he himself gives up his body and blood. There is therefore no basis to what may have appeared true to a casual bystander, namely, that his life was taken from him against his will. No, he gives it up voluntarily, as a saying of the Lord states in the Gospel of John: "No man taketh it [i.e., my life] from me, but I lay it down of myself." (John 10:18.) But he does not cast it from himself, as may happen in other cases, as something good for nothing, for which one has no further use. He gives the bread and the wine to his disciples to eat and to drink, that they may live thereby. So his death is a gift that should be of advantage to them. Finally, however, there arises from this eating and drinking a new kind of communion, the communion of those to whom the

Lord grants a share in his self-sacrifice—the eucharistic community. This much the action per se, as we see it taking place before our eyes, tells us.

The Lord Christ, however, adds to the action his explaining words. These words are not transmitted identically in the various accounts, but on the whole the meaning is the same. According to these accounts, as Jesus broke and distributed the bread, he said, "Take, eat; this is my body, which is given for you"; and in passing the cup: "Take and drink all of it; this cup is the new testament in my blood, which will be shed for you and for many for the remission of sins." And both times he added as a conclusion, "This do in remembrance of me."

We are therefore told here that the Lord does not withdraw from us by his death, especially not if we accept his gift. On the contrary, here he would become entirely united with us, here he gives himself fully to us, his body and his blood belong to us—"for you." Nay, in this "for you" lies the real and effective mystery of his death on the cross. For it does not merely say that Jesus dies for his own friends, like a soldier for his people and country, or like the saver of a life who snatches another from the flames or from the waves and perishes himself. He says so: "For you for the remission of sins." This is the unparalleled feature of his death, that he dies in our place, the just for the unjust, the holy one for the sinners. And now we stand in his place: freed of all guilt and through him and on his account beloved children of God.

This is the end of the old covenant, in which the relation between God and us was regulated according to the principle of reward and punishment. With the death of Jesus for us, the new covenant, which rests on the forgiveness of sins, has been established, and it removes terror from our own death because another has already allowed our punishment to be executed upon himself. Now the saying is, "Where there is forgiveness of sins, there is also life and bliss."

This interpretation which Jesus himself gives of his death is, as we noted, plain; but in its wonderfulness incomprehensible and in its depth unfathomable: with brain work we get nowhere here. But where a human heart is in distress because it longs for the assurance of a merciful God, where a conscience is afraid under the pressure of guilt, there the message of the cross and death of the Lord Christ becomes tidings of joy: "For you for the remission of sins." This is no human mental invention, he himself has so said it. And he has given us, his congregation, the covenant meal in order that we may not only hear, but also "taste and see that the Lord is good." (Ps. 34:8.)

"This do in remembrance of me." Thus we celebrate with the Christian Church of all times the meal of the Lord in remembrance of his death, and we hear at the same time his voice, which allots to us his death: "For you— for the remission of sins." And we eat of the bread and drink of the cup and listen to the words, "My body given for you, my blood shed for you." This message does not age, does not lose any of its living strength with the passage of time. For in its need for God and in its longing for Him the human heart remains ever the same. And when all the dead are once forgotten, the death of the Lord Jesus Christ will ever be preached and confessed by his church because there flows the source of its life, and the church will continue to gather around his table and confess thereby its crucified Lord in repentance for its transgression, in gratitude for his love, and in the praise of God for his inconceivable loving-kindness, until—yes, until its Lord will come at the end of time, and with him that Kingdom of God in which all patchwork ceases. There we see him as he is, and there we shall be with him forever.

To this great community of those who proclaim the death of their Lord as a message of joy belong this evening also we, who come here to his table. A small company, every one of us torn away from his earthly home and from the circle of his dear ones, all of us robbed of freedom and ever uncertain about what the following day or even the following hour will bring. But, despite all this, we are at home. We eat and drink at the table of our heavenly Father and we may be comforted. There is nothing that could tear us away and separate us from Him, since our Lord and Master gave his life for us and for many, indeed even for both of the friends who have gone away from our circle and whom we remember in our intercession, even for our dear ones far away and out there at the fronts, for whom we are anxious. For them also did the Lord die, and with him they and we are well protected.

> We are people washed up by the stream of time on the earth-isle,
> Full of mishaps and full of heartache, till home brings us the Savior.
> The father-home is ever near, though changeable be fates:
> It is the cross on Golgotha, the home for the homeless!

Amen.

C. L. Franklin

1915–1984

*I*nvariably the liner notes of his daughter Aretha's recordings point out that the musical roots of the Queen of Soul can be found in the African-American Baptist churches of her youth. They don't always remember to mention her father's, the Reverend C. L. Franklin's, own million-copy-selling records of the sermons he preached during the 1950s and 1960s when he was billed as the "Million Dollar Voice." The Reverend Jesse Jackson, whose ordination sermon he also preached, has called him "the most imitated soul preacher in history, a combination of soul and science and substance and sweetness."

He was born in Sunflower County, Mississippi, to a sharecropper family living in a world of segregation, enforced ignorance, and forced labor that has mercifully begun to be revoked over the last half century. Clarence LaVaughn Franklin was expecting to become a sharecropper, too, except that when he was thirteen, "I was standing in the back of our church, with a cap rolled up in my hand, and . . . the late Dr. Benjamin J. Perkins preached on a passage dealing with Thomas, the disciple Thomas, who doubted the resurrection of Jesus. And his sermon was so vivid and clear to me, and so impressive, that from that night forward, I really felt that I was called to preach."

Thereafter, from small Southern towns to Memphis, to Buffalo, and eventually to Detroit, where his famous New Bethel Church had, at the height of his pastorate, a congregation of ten thousand, Franklin became a Baptist preacher par excellence. Radio and guest-preaching tours led to the recording studio and put him in national demand.

As Jeff Todd Titon, who lovingly transcribed them, has written,

"Franklin's sermons flow from a rich African American literary, cultural, and religious tradition. For although he was a learned man and attended both seminary and college, he 'whooped,' or chanted, in an old-fashioned extemporaneous black ministerial mode, without manuscript or notes. Combining oratory with intoned poetry, he reached both head and heart. Imaginatively narrating biblical events, locked with his shouting congregation in a driving, rhythmic embrace, his 'whooping' climaxed each sermon in a musical ecstasy of communal, ritual drama. In so doing, preacher and congregation affirmed the felt presence of the divine and holy, nurturing trust in themselves and God."

He might warm up by saying, "I hope I can get somebody to pray with me tonight, because you know, I'm a *Negro* preacher, and I like to talk to people and have people talk *back* to me." Here is Franklin talking to his congregation—and to us—about Doubting Thomas.

ℭ

Except I Shall See in His Hands the Print of the Nails and Thrust My Hand into His Side

We call your attention to the book of St. John, the twentieth chapter, the twenty-fourth through the twenty-ninth verses. "But Thomas, one of the twelve, called Didymus, was not with them when Jesus came. The other disciples therefore said unto him, We have seen the Lord. But he said unto them, Except I shall see in his hands the print of the nails, and put my finger into the print of the nails, and thrust my hand into his side, I will not believe. And after eight days again his disciples were within, and Thomas with them. Then came Jesus, the doors being shut, and stood in the midst, and said, Peace be unto you. Then said he to Thomas, Reach hither thy hand and thrust it into my side, and be not faithless, but believing. And Thomas answered and said unto him, My Lord and my God. Jesus saith unto him, Thomas, because thou hast seen me, thou hast believed. Blessed are they that have not seen and yet believeth."

Doubting Thomas. Doubting Thomas.

The passage that I have read in your hearing tonight deals with one of the post-Resurrection incidents. If you can call upon your knowledge of history, and upon your powers of imagination, you could picture the hostile world in which these followers of Jesus found themselves. The Jewish hierarchy had put their leader to death. He had been tried and condemned by the Jewish church, by the Roman courts, and he had been nailed to a tree while they looked on. They had seen him drop his head after a terrible experience during the night of the trial, scourging, and crucifixion, that ended on Friday evening about three o'clock [sic]. They heard him say after that terrible night, "It is finished." You know how they must have felt when they had chosen to follow him, when they had accepted him as their Messiah, the anointed of God.

And now the man whom they had called the Son of God, was now dead, and apparently disgraced. And of course you know how they must have felt. Some of them said, "Well, I'm going back to fishing. I'm going back to my old job. I'm going back to my old vocation. It seems that we made a mistake." I believe Peter made the suggestion, and the others followed his lead.

Thomas, who was of the scientific turn of mind, heard some rumors. The women had said that they had seen him, and that he was alive. Others said that they were en route to Emmaus, and he joined them and talked with them and while he talked their hearts burned. Some of the rest of them reported that they had seen him. Lately it was said that in their secret gathering place in Jerusalem to avoid the police and to avoid arrest and embarrassment, that he had come into their meetings.

But Thomas said, "I don't believe it. I don't believe it. Obviously you're being swept by rumors or you're suffering from hallucinations. Nobody has ever died as I saw that man die, and come back again. I was looking at them when they hung him to the tree. I was looking at them when they nailed his hands and his feet. I was looking when the soldier thrust the sword into his side. And I heard him when he dropped his head say, 'It is finished.' And I saw them take him down from the cross and lay him in Joseph's tomb. I know he's dead. Now there's only one way that you can ever tell me anything different, and that is I'll have to see him. And I'm not going to trust that. He is going to have to show me his hands, and let me see the nail prints in his hands. He will have to let me look at his side, and then I will have to examine his side for myself. I must satisfy the sense of seeing and of feeling before I shall be convinced. I don't believe that he's alive."

Now Thomas, called Didymus, which means the twin, has received a great deal of ridicule from the Christian world about his doubting position. But you know, you must give some respect to people who want to know, to people who are not satisfied with hearsay. You must give some respect to people who want to base their faith upon as much knowledge as they can acquire. You see, superstition, rumor and hearsay is not a sufficient foundation for faith. I know that faith transcends knowledge, but you get all the knowledge you can get before you stop. For you see, Thomas was moving on fact. And you see fact can carry you just so far. It was a fact that Jesus was put to death, that he was hanged to a tree. It was a fact that he dropped his head and died, and declared, "It is finished." This was a fact. It was a fact that they took him down and laid him in a tomb. All of this was fact. But that is as far as fact could go. This is the reason that Thomas couldn't go any further: because he was proceeding on the basis of fact. You understand what I'm talking about. His whole operation was based upon empiricism, investigation and what one can find out. But you see, faith—you understand what I mean—goes on beyond the grave. (I don't believe you know what I'm talking about.)

Faith doesn't stop at the grave. Faith didn't stop when he said, "It is finished." Faith didn't stop when they rolled the stone to the tomb. And faith didn't stop when the governor's seal was placed thereon. For you see faith goes beyond what I can see and what I know. I can't prove God. And you don't have to prove God. Somebody said, "If you haven't seen God or you haven't seen heaven," and all that kind of thing. . . . That doesn't mean anything. Say, "Who's been there?" That doesn't mean anything, what you cannot prove. What you cannot see is no argument against its existence. You can't see electricity but God knows it exists. You can't see energy, but take all the energy out of this room tonight and all of us would be dead shortly. Hmm? Many of the forces of the universe, you can't prove them, you can't see them, you can't touch them, but they do exist. They are realities. (I don't believe you know what I'm talking about.)

But Thomas was like many of you that are listening at me tonight. He wanted to base his faith totally upon fact. Totally upon faith, or rather upon fact. But you see faith moves out beyond what I can touch, beyond what I can see, beyond sometimes what I can hear, and even beyond what I can investigate. I don't know where God is, but I believe he liveth. I don't know anything about how he raised his Son. I'm not concerned about whether it was bodily or spiritual. I believe that Jesus liveth tonight. I believe that he is a living reality. He is a transforming influence in this old world of ours. Don't you know all of these people wouldn't have been following him by the thousands and by the millions for twenty centuries if he didn't live? Don't you know all of these people who go to their graves with his name on their lips, saying, "Death cannot make my soul afraid if God be with me there, though I walk through the darkest shades, I'll never yield to fear," if he didn't live tonight? (I don't believe you know what I'm talking about.) The great impact that his name has had upon history would not have changed the world society if he wasn't a living influence. I believe he liveth.

So Thomas wasn't at the meetings. And you know when you fail to meet constantly with that Christian fellowship, you miss so much. You miss so much in inspiration, you miss so much in God-consciousness, you miss so much in soul-enrichment, when you fail to fellowship with that Christian society. (I don't believe you know what I'm talking about.) So Thomas's great mistake was he wasn't there. And when he came in after having given voice to his doubts, he eventually presented himself at one of the services. And while they were no doubt musing and meditating upon God, singing his praises, while they were no doubt talking about the fact of his Resurrection, while they were no doubt talking about their faith in the fact that he was alive . . . , without a door being opened he walked in. And thank God he can walk in here without a door being opened. He can walk in to your life sometime when you unconsciously open the door. The door of your life might be open and you don't know it. He can walk in. While they were in their meeting he walked in, without a door or window being opened. [Whooping:]

And
    when they looked around
       he was standing in their midst.
When
    they looked around

      he was there
        in their presence.
     And it seemed that,
why,
     his address
       was so consoling.
     He knew how
       doubtful some of them were.
And
     he knew how afraid
       some of them had been.
And
     he knew how their faith
       had been tried.
And
     he knew what a terrible ordeal
       they'd gone through.
     And think about how
    consoling
       his address was.
     Listen at him: "Peace be unto you."
O Lord.
     You know when I think about
       the world that we live in,
     when I think about
       how frustrated
       many of us are,
     when I think about how
       neurotic we've become,
     when I think about
       how tension-filled
       many of our lives are,
     when I think about
       how afraid of life
       so many of us are,

why,
   I think about what Jesus said,
      to those fearing
      and doubting disciples.
   "Peace be unto you."
Great God.
   You that are afraid tonight,
great day,
   you that are anxious tonight,
and
   you that don't know how
      to face your problems,
   you ought to hear his word
      coming down through the centuries,
      saying "Peace be unto you."
O Lord.
   Though the storms
      may rage around you,
   though the road
      that you are traveling
      may be rough,
   though the problem that you're faced with
      may be perplexing,
O Lord,
   he'll still say to you,
      "Peace be unto you."
O Lord.
   Listen.
   Did you know what Thomas said
when
   he beheld the reality
      of Jesus Christ?
   You know what Thomas said
      when he saw
      his wounded hands,

when he beheld
    his wounded side?
"My Lord,
    and my God."
Great God.
    And I'm going to close when I tell you this.
O Lord.
    I'm not going to wait
        until I behold
        the wounds in his hands.
O Lord.
    I'm not going to wait
        until I behold the wounds
        in his feet.
    I'm not going to wait
        until I have a chance
        to behold the wounds in his side.
    I'm going
        to acknowledge him as Lord
        right now,
        every day of my life.
O Lord.
    Would you be my guide,
    would you be my real leader,
    would you lead me through the crises of life?
    I've got to stop right here.
O Lord.
    Yes,
    the winds that blow me about,
    yes,
    my faith is tried sometime,
    but I'm going to hold on
        to his unchanging hand.
Yes I am.
    Yes every day,
    every day,

yes every day,
every day of my life,
I'm going to hold on,
in the midst of doubting,
in the midst of the windstorm,
in the midst of failure,
in the midst of frustration,
I'm going to hold on anyhow.
Oh.
O Lord.
Oh yes.
Yes.
For he is my Lord.
and he is my God.

[Speaking:] He is the Lord of my life. He is the Lord of my life. He reigns and he liveth. He liveth. [Singing:]

Maybe you don't believe it,
        but God is real tonight.
        God is real tonight.
Sometimes Satan
        tries to
        make me doubt.
He tells me
        that there are a lot of things that I imagine
        are not so.
He tries to tell me that I'm caught up
        in the grip of
        my traditional upbringing;
        that God is not real.
But if God is not real
who is it
that watch over me every night?
Oh
        who is it

      that calms the storms about me
         if he's not real?
Tell me who is it?
Who is it
that makes me cry
when there ain't nobody hurting me,
that makes a fire burn
         down in my soul?
Who is it?
If it's not the Lord,
         then who is it
         that makes me run sometimes
         when nobody's behind me?
God is real.

Karl Rahner

1904–1984

There is no guarantee that a good theologian will be a good preacher. In fact, given the often hyperabstract and convoluted nature of theological argument—usually presented for fellow theologians rather than for ordinary laymen—it is rather surprising to find a theologian who can also deliver a fine sermon. German theologian Karl Rahner was a good preacher and in fact preached frequently and with consistent focus over his fifty-two years as a priest.

He was born in Swabia in Bavaria and entered the Jesuit order in 1922, a few years after his elder brother, and was ordained in 1932. Rahner studied with the existentialist Martin Heidegger at the University of Freiburg, which may account for the strong philosophical dimension to his writing. He became a professor on the faculty of theology at the University of Innsbruck after the Second World War and was designated a *peritus* at the Second Vatican Council. He was a prolific writer, most commonly of articles (see his twenty-three-volume collection translated into English as *Theological Investigations,* 1961–92).

For Rahner, whose theological writings are dense and difficult, the whole work of theology is given meaning only because of its relation to the Word of God. Moreover, since that Word lives for us and is renewed in us because it is preached and proclaimed to us, his commitment to preaching was at the deepest level of his priesthood. In a sermon he once preached on the feast day of St. Ignatius of Loyola, founder of the Jesuits, he talked about the concept of life as *prolixitas mortis,* a kind of ongoing dying that anticipates a new life after death. In the sermon that follows, he examines our relationship to those who have gone before us into that new and fuller life.

⊂℞

All Saints and All Souls Day

All Saints day and All Souls day are the feasts of *every* saint and of *every* soul who has died and gone home into the eternal love of God. *All* of them and therefore not only those already celebrated by name in the church's feasts throughout the year but also the silent, unknown ones who have departed as if they had never even existed. There are no legends about them; their lives are recorded neither in poetry nor in history, secular or ecclesiastical. Only one person knows anything about these saints, and that is God. He has inscribed their names in the book of life, which is the heart of his eternal love.

But we are supposed to celebrate these saints who are not known to us by name. How can we do this—really do it, with life and zest—if not by lovingly remembering our dead? They may already be forgotten by the world; perhaps their name is not even inscribed on a gravestone. Yet they not only live on with God, but also with us, in our hearts.

Let us then prepare our hearts for these feasts of the dead who live with God. May our hearts be mindful of the dead. Be still, O heart, and let all whom you have loved rise from the grave of your breast. Is there no one among All Saints and All Souls for you to celebrate? Have you ever come in contact with love and meekness, goodness and purity and fidelity in a person? Not even in your mother, so quiet and forgetful of herself? Nor in your patient father? Should you say no, I think you would be contradicting your heart, which has its own experiences. It is not the heart's experience to have met throughout life only darkness and no light, only selfishness and no selfless kindness.

But if you have met faith, hope, and love, kindness and pardon, great courage and fidelity in persons who now are dead—a grain of virtue such as these is worth a mountain of selfishness and vice—then you have met men and women whom your heart may seek with God. Up, then, and celebrate the heart-feast of All Saints, of All Souls—*your* saints, *your* beloved souls! Sorrow and joy, grief and happiness are strangely blended into this feast. Just as they are with the things of eternity. Celebrate an All Saints of peace and loyalty. Of yearning and of faith. Celebrate your dead who are still living.

Today, then, we want to remember before God our dead, all those who once belonged to us and who have departed from us. There are so many of them that we can by no means take them all in at one glance. If our celebration is to greet them all, we must go back in memory over our path through life. When we go about it in this way, from our point of view it is like a procession of persons marching down the street of life.

At each moment, without bidding farewell, someone or other silently withdraws from the procession and, turning aside from the road, is lost in the darkness of the night. This procession becomes smaller and smaller for each one of us, for the new person constantly stepping onto our path through life only seems to be marching along with us. To be sure, many are walking the same street, but only a few walk *together with* each one of us. Strictly speaking, only those who set out together with each one of us are really journeying together with us. Only those who were with us at the very beginning of our journey to God—only those who were and still are really close to our heart.

The others are traveling companions on the same road; they are many, and they are constantly coming and going. We greet each other, and give each other a helping hand, and then, no more. But the real procession of each of our lives is made up of those whom we really love. This procession is always becoming smaller and quieter, until each one of us becomes silent once and for all, turns aside from the road, and passes away without a farewell, never to return.

That is why our heart today is with those who have already departed in just such a way. There are no replacements for them; no other human being could really fill the vacancy left by a loved one when she suddenly and unexpectedly departs and is at our side no longer. In true love no one can replace the beloved, for true love loves the beloved in those depths where each individual is uniquely and irreplaceably herself. That is why each one of those who have passed away have taken the heart with them, if death has trodden through our lives from beginning to end.

If someone has really loved and continues to love, then even before his own death his life is changed into a life with the dead. Could the lover forget her dead? If one has really loved, then her forgetting and the fact that she has ceased weeping are not signs that nothing has really changed, that she is just the same as before. They are, rather, signs that a part of her own heart has really died with the loved one, and is now living with the dead. That is why she can no longer mourn. We live, then, with the dead, with those who have gone before us into the dark night of death, where no one can work any more.

But how are we supposed to be able to live with the dead in the one reality of our mutual love; how are we to celebrate a feast of all the holy dead? Is this possible simply because God is the God of the living and not of the dead, because his word and even the wisdom of this world tells us that these dead still live? Because we loved the dead and still love them, we must be with them always. But are they also with us? Do they belong to this love and to the celebration of this love?

They have departed, they are silent. No word from them reaches our ears; the gentle kindness of their love no longer fills our heart. How quiet the dead are, how *dead* they are! Do they want us to forget them, as we forget a casual acquaintance on a trip, with whom we exchanged a few insignificant words? If life is not taken away from those who depart this life in God's love, but [is] changed into eternal, measureless, superabundant life, why then should it seem to us that they no longer exist? Is the inaccessible light of God into which they have entered so faint that it cannot penetrate to us down here? Does even their love (and not only their bodies) have to abandon us in order to live with God in his light? Does their silence imitate the silence of their God, to whose home they have gone?

That is the way it is. For God is silent just like the dead. For us to celebrate his feasts in our hearts this silent God must certainly be with us, even though he seems so distant and so silent. We certainly must love him, too, as we love our dead, the distant and silent dead, who have entered into the night. Does he not give to our love an intelligible answer when we call him to the feast of the heart, and ask him for a sign that his love exists for us and is present to us? And that is why we cannot lament the silence of the dead, for their silence is only an echo of his silence.

But if we keep silent and meek, if we listen to this silence of God's, then we begin to grasp with a comprehension that exceeds our own power to evoke or even to understand why both God and the dead are so silent. Then it dawns on us that they are near us precisely in our feast of the holy souls. God's silence is the boundless sphere where alone our love can produce its act of faith in his love.

If in our earthly life his love had become so manifest to us that we would know beyond a shadow of a doubt what we really are, namely, God's own beloved, then how could we prove to him the daring courage and fidelity of our love? How could such a fidelity exist at all? How could our love, in the ecstasy of faith, reach out beyond this world into his world and into his heart? He has veiled his love in the stillness of his silence so that our love might reveal itself in faith. He has apparently forsaken us so that we can find him.

For if his presence in our midst were obvious, in our search for him we would find only ourselves. We must, however, go out from ourselves, if we are to find him where he is really himself. Because his love is infinite, it can dwell openly and radiantly only in his own infinity; and because he wants to show us his infinite love, he has hidden it from us in our finiteness, whence he calls out to us. Our faith in him is nothing but the dark road in the night between the deserted house of our life with its puny, dimly lit rooms, and the blinding light of his eternal life. His silence in this world is nothing but the earthly appearance of the eternal word of his love.

Our dead imitate this silence. Thus, through silence, they speak to us clearly. They are nearer to us than through all the audible words of love and closeness. Because they have entered into God's life, they remain hidden from us. Their words of love do not reach our ears because they have blended into one with the joyous word of his boundless love. They live with the boundlessness of God's life and with his love, and that is why their love and their life no longer enter the narrow room of our present life. We live a dying life. That is why we experience nothing of the eternal life of the holy dead, the life that knows no death. But just in this very way they also live for us and with us. For their silence is their loudest cry, because it is the echo of God's silence. It is in unison with God's word that it speaks to us.

Over against the loud cries of our drives, and over against the anxious, hasty protestations with which we mortals assure ourselves of our mutual love, God's word enwraps us and all our noisy words in his life. This is the way he commands us to relinquish all things in the daring act of loving faith, in order to find our eternal homeland in his life.

And it is precisely in this way that the silence of our dead also calls out to us. They live in his life, and that is why they speak his words to us. They speak the word of the God of the true life, the word that is far removed from our dying. The dead are silent because they live, just as our noisy chatter is supposed to make us forget that we are dying. Their silence is the word of their love for us, the real message that they have for us. By this word they are really near to us, provided only that we listen to this soundless word and understand it, and do not drown it out through the noise of everyday life.

It is in this way that they are close to us whose feast we celebrate today in the silent composure of the heart. They are near us together with the silent God, the God of the silent dead, the living God of the living. He calls out to us through his silence, and they, by their silence, summon us into God's life.

Let us therefore be mindful of our dead, our living. Our love for them, our loyalty to them is the proof of our faith in him, the God of everlasting life. Let us not ignore the silence of the dead, the silence that is the most ardent word of their love. This, their most ardent word, accompanies us today and every day, for they have gone away from us in order that their love, having gone into God, may be all the closer to us.

Be mindful of the dead, O heart. They live. Your own life, the life still hidden even to you, they live unveiled in eternal light. Our living who are with the God of life cannot forget us dead. God has granted our living everything, for he has given them himself. But he goes further and also grants them this favor: that their silence will become the most eloquent word of their love for us, the word that will accompany our love home to them, into their life and their light.

If we really celebrate All Saints and All Souls as the feast of faith, of love, of quiet remembering; if our life is and is always becoming more and more a life of the dead who have gone before us in the sign of faith into the dark night of death, where no one can work; then through God's grace our life becomes, more and more, a life of faith in his light during the night of this earthly life. Then we who are dying live with the living who have gone before us into the bright, shining day of life, where no one has to work, because God himself is this day, the fullness of all reality, the God of the living.

Today or tomorrow, when we stand by the graves, or when our heart must seek distant graves, where perhaps not even a cross stands over them any longer; when we pray, "Lord, grant them eternal rest, and may perpetual light shine upon them"; when we quietly look up toward the eternal homeland of all the saints and—from afar and yet so near—greet God's light and his love, our eternal homeland; then all our memories and all our prayers are only the echo of the words of love that the holy living, in the silence of their eternity, softly and gently speak into our heart.

Hidden in the peace of the eternal God, filled with his own bliss, redeemed for eternity, permeated with love for us that can never cease, they, on their feast, utter the prayer of their love for us: "Lord, grant eternal rest to them whom we love—as never before—in your love. Grant it to them who still walk the hard road of pilgrimage, which is nonetheless the road that leads to us and to your eternal light. We, although silent, are now closer to them than ever before, closer than when we were sojourning and struggling along with them on earth. Grant to them, too, Lord, eternal rest, and may your perpetual light shine on them as on us. May it shine upon them now as the light of faith, and then in eternity, as the light of blessed life."

Be mindful of the dead, O heart. Call them into your heart today, listen to their silence, learn from them the one thing necessary: celebrate the feast of your saints. For then the God of all the living will be mindful of us who are dead, and he will one day be our life, too. And there will be one, single, eternal feast of all the saints.

PART X

"Who Will
Go for Us?"

Living Preachers

Billy Graham

1918–

I had run out of sermons in my stockpile and was having to prepare a new one every day. That took up to six or eight hours. Increasingly, I forgot about illustrations and applications, though I knew they were supposed to be necessary to good sermon construction. In some of these later messages, I used mostly Scripture references. I had two or three old Bibles from which I clipped out passages to paste onto my outline. Then, from the platform, I read these as part of my sermon without having had to write them out longhand.[1]

This unorthodox sermon-preparation technique was born of necessity on the stage in the 1949 Los Angeles tent (billed as the "Canvas Cathedral") revival that transformed a callow young preacher from a dairy farm in North Carolina into the avatar of old-time religion, heir to a lineage that stretched from Billy Sunday and Dwight L. Moody to Charles Grandison Finney and the Great Awakening of the 1830s all the way back to George Whitefield and John Wesley, the circuit-riding knight-founders of Methodism and modern mass evangelism.

Graham had planned the usual Youth for Christ campaign, the huge tent was emblazoned "SOMETHING'S HAPPENING INSIDE . . . 6,000 FREE SEATS . . . DYNAMIC PREACHING . . . GLORIOUS MUSIC," and three weeks of leave were set aside from his recently assumed duties as president of North-

---

[1]Billy Graham, *Just as I Am: The Autobiography of Billy Graham* (New York: HarperCollins, 1997; HarperPaperbacks ed., 1998), p. 180.

western Schools, a religious institute in Minneapolis. All was going according to the modest plan when, one night toward the end, the place was suddenly overrun by reporters and photographers enthusiastically recording
every colorful and dramatic moment of the proceedings. The unexpected
spotlight forced an extension of three more weeks and induced record
crowds approaching eleven thousand a day and a media frenzy that cata-
pulted Billy Graham onto a national—and soon international—stage he has
never left.

Among the mysterious reasons it happened at all was the rumor that,
because Billy was preaching anti-Communism, the aging William Randolph
Hearst, owner of two L.A. newspapers, decided to confer precious cover-
age on the campaign with the enigmatic instruction, "Puff Graham." *Time,
Life, Newsweek,* AP, UPI, and all other obedient gentlemen of the press followed suit. America's favorite pulpit star was born. In a career ministry
rivaled only by that of Pope John Paul II for its global reach and immense
magnetism, Billy Graham—friend of presidents from Truman to Clinton,
televangelist extraordinare to five continents—is both an anachronism and
a preacher for our time. His gospel-based conservatism is grounded in the
biblical inerrancy and born-again personal Christianity of his agricultural
youth. It is a message whose power may have waned after the 1925 Scopes
trial in Dayton, Tennessee, but into which Graham has breathed constant,
compelling new life for half a century.

For all the undoubted power of his witness, well displayed in the sermon on the Prodigal Son that follows, delivered on June 16, 1969, more
than one critic has noted the somewhat congealed quality of the Billy Graham cosmos:

> Judgment Day, that instant thunderclap of trumpets in a calm sky,
> Jesus and the angels spilling suddenly out of nowhere in a vast slow
> tumble earthward to end the game; and of course Hell, a smokily glar-
> ing grotto of writhing bodies and wails and gnashing teeth; and
> Heaven, an everlasting sunlit Sabbath morning in Easter pastels with
> pink cumulus clouds and rosy-cheeked choirs.[2]

---

[2]Marshall Frady, *Billy Graham: A Parable of American Righteousness* (Boston: Little, Brown and
Company, 1979), p. 52.

The Prodigal Son

Now tonight, let's turn to the 15th chapter of Luke. I'm not going to read the passage because it's too long, but it is a familiar story that all of us have read and heard since childhood. It is called "The Story of the Prodigal Son." That's what we call it. There are many ways we could term this passage from Luke's Gospel. It could be called "The Story of the Loving Father." It could be called "The Story of the Church Member Without Christ," because that is exactly what the elder brother was.

But tonight I want to dwell on the story of this boy because he was a rebel. He rebelled against his father. And you know what I read the other day? That over two thousand young people who run away from home come to New York every month seeking fame and fortune. They become prey to all the thugs and con men and drug merchants and sex perverts and all the others. Two thousand a month are lured away from their parents to New York City.

This is also a city where young people do a lot of damage. Do you know last year how many school windows were broken in New York? Over 200,000. Do you know how many telephone booths were wrecked in the city of New York last year? Over 300,000. And did you know that these crimes are largely among young people? Now I grant you the older people tell them how to do it, and it is the older people who print the pornography, and it is the older people who produce the motion pictures, and it is the older people who think up all the violence on television, and it is the older people who have handed this world and the mess we're in to our young people.

But young people are striking out at society in every kind of way today. Some of it is violent, some is destructive, some of it is just plain rebellion, and some of it is justified.

This is the story of a young fellow who ran away from home. Now in this passage Jesus tells three little stories. Jesus always used stories to illustrate spiritual truths. They are called parables in the Bible. He told a story of a lost sheep. He told a story of a lost coin. He told a story of this lost son, and in all three stories he is picturing a loving father searching for that which is lost, and that Father is God. You see God is searching for you tonight. God loves you. He is searching for you, and the search takes Him all the way to the Cross where He gives His Son for you. That is how much God loves you.

But it is also a story of how we are lost from God. The Bible teaches that we are like the lost sheep or the lost coin or the lost boy. We are away from God. We have rebelled against God. We have run away from God, but God loves us. He wants us back, and He is willing to go to any length to get us back. He won't compromise in telling us how to get back. Some people try to come other ways. He said, "There is only one way back and that's through my Son, Jesus Christ. If you are willing to come that way, I will receive you and I will forgive you." And that's the story of this boy. One day he goes to his father and says: "Dad, you know I am tired of living out here in the country—all the discipline and the hard work—and I am eighteen years of age. I would like to have my inheritance now and I want to go out to 'New York,' because I am going to make it big up there." He had read about "Broadway" and he had heard all about the bright lights. He had heard about all the different things that happened there, and he decided he would like to go.

And his father said, "Son, I don't advise it, but if you are determined to go, go ahead." So he starts out for the big city.

You know this weekend one of the people who made the news all across the country was a brilliant young member of the senior class at Wellesley. She expressed how young people are feeling lost today. She described how young people are exploring a world that none of us understand, and are searching for more immediate and ecstatic and penetrating modes of living. And what she was saying was this: young people are lost, confused and frustrated and are searching for a way back.

And this is what Jesus Himself said. He said, "The Son of Man is come to seek and save that which is lost."

Well, this young fellow came from an affluent home. They had a great deal of love in the home, a great deal of discipline in the home, and there was faith in God. I imagine his father gathered the family together every day for prayer and Bible reading, and the boy said, "Oh, I don't want to talk about God. I don't want religion. I can't wait to get away from home."

How many young people are like that here tonight?

Or, maybe he had to go to church. And he said, "I don't want to go to church. I can't wait until I can get away and get to the university and get to college, and go to town—get somewhere so I don't have to go to church."

So he rebelled against his father, and rebellion became a way of life for him.

Now it is perfectly normal for a young fellow to pull away from his father. The Bible says, "Therefore shall a man leave his father and mother and cleave unto his wife and they shall be one flesh." After you are married you are in for trouble if you start living with your parents and depending on your parents. Live with your wife; be on your own; establish your own friends. But here was a young man in his teens, not married, and the reason he was leaving home was because he didn't like the discipline at home. He wanted to go out and have a good time. Now if he wanted to go out and work and get a job, that was one thing, but that wasn't what he wanted. He wanted to "goof off." He didn't want to go to school any more. He didn't want to get up and milk the cows on the farm any more. He wanted to go out and have a good time. It was to please self.

You know down here on Times Square—I've walked down there a couple of times, and one of those theaters down there has a big marquee that says, "Unsatisfied." And then you know the pop song that the Rolling Stones made so famous, "I Can't Get No Satisfaction"?

Well, this young fellow was going out trying to find fulfillment and satisfaction and happiness, and he thought it lay where all the bright lights and the music and the night clubs and all the rest were. He said, "I am going to have a real ball."

I heard about a girl the other day. She was wooed by a boy with promises of marriage. She became pregnant. He left her alone. Her father, mother and family suffered shame and disgrace because of a boy's selfishness, and that is the very essence of sin—selfishness. That is what sin is all about—self. I want to satisfy self.

I was interviewed on television by a group of students this past week, and one of them said, "What is wrong with being aroused sexually?" He said, "I go out and buy my sex. What's wrong with that?" Well, the thing that is wrong with it is that the ingredient that sex was made for is not there—love within marriage. Some go out and buy it like shopping in a supermarket—like a steak, like a lunch—with no love, no relationship.

The Bible goes further. It says it is wrong outside of marriage.

But you see this boy was already wandering away from home even while he was at home. He was thinking about it. We don't wander away all at once. Like sheep, we wander gradually. The Bible says, "All we like sheep have gone astray." And so this young fellow went, and when he got to town he was like the fellow I read about in London, England, in one of the British newspapers, who had a home in the country and a home in town. He said, "When I am in the country, I want to be in the city, and when I am in the city, I want to be in the country." The problem was not where he was; the problem was his own heart. Going to town is not going to meet your needs. Going to the country is not going to meet your needs.

I talked to a young person day before yesterday, and he said, "Boy, I'd like to get out of this rat race in this city and get out to the country and listen to the birds and see the grass." Well, he'd be out there about three days and he'd be wanting to hear the honking of the taxicabs and hear all the screaming of the sirens.

You see it is a heart problem we have. We want fulfillment in our lives. We want a peace and a joy and a happiness that we don't find anywhere in life. It is just not found apart from God. You can't find it just anywhere.

And during this past week I have been very interested in reading some of the addresses being given by valedictorians and professors and famous people at the various universities and colleges. Nearly all of them were pessimistic. Every one of them said that young people were looking for something they can't find, and the youth themselves, I thought, brought the greatest message. They said, "We are living in a lousy, messed up world. We feel lousy ourselves. We don't know the answer." And it was very pessimistic, this commencement season across the country. And one young fellow got up and told them. He said, "This university is standing now, but we're going to be back. We're going to be back this fall and we're going to burn it down." That's how he felt.

I talked to a fellow the other day right here in New York City. He said, "Yes, we're going to burn the town down." I said, "What are you going to build in its place?" He said, "Oh, we don't have any plans for that, but anything is better than what we've got now. We are going to tear it down."

Well, I agree there are a lot of things wrong. A lot of things need straightening out, but I don't believe the way to do it is to tear it down and burn it up. Let's try to use the democratic processes and straighten it out because I'm not so sure that some of the people I've seen marching around saying they are going to change it all would do any better than the people who are running it now. They don't seem to have any ideas—any constructive ideas.

But you see, this fellow went off to town, and when he got there he had his pockets full of money. Well, anyone who has any money has a crowd around him. You can make friends quickly if you've got money. I would hate to be a wealthy man because I would never know who my friends were. Everybody is after your money. When your money is gone, your friends are gone. Some friends are freeloaders. His friends were. He had a lot of friends around him.

Did you read the other day in the paper that in the Detroit Zoo they lost their prize ostrich? I think her name was Susie, and they performed an autopsy on Susie and found $3.85 in pennies, dimes and quarters inside that beautiful bird. That bird was killed by money.

This fellow had a lot of money—went off to town, and got a lot of friends around him. The Bible says there is pleasure in sin. He started doing the things that he learned from his city cousins. He learned a little bit about dope. He took some "trips." At first it was just a lot of fun, a lot of kicks. It wasn't long until he began to be hooked. He started taking a few sips of alcohol and it wasn't long before he had to have it before lunch. He began to fool around with a girl. It wasn't long before he was in trouble—had to move to the other side of town. All kinds of trouble plagued him.

You see the devil is fishing with bait. He comes along and whispers in your ear and tells you that it is greener on the other side of the fence. Everything is better over there. You just rebel against your parents, rebel against God, rebel against religion, and go out here on your own and you think it's going to be better. But the devil doesn't tell you that he's got a hook in you. Fools make a mockery of sin. The Bible says, "Be sure your sin will find you out." The Bible says, "There is pleasure in sin for a season." You see, for a short time you can have a good time, but it is very short. It disappears. It becomes empty. You become disillusioned! Disenchanted!

I was in a European country last summer, and one of the top young people told me—he said, "You know, we've had this permissive society now for a generation." And he said, "Anything goes and we are filled up to here with it. We are sick of it. Let's take a walk down through the streets of Stockholm." He said, "Do you see much laughter, much joy, much happiness?" There were throngs of young people, but there was something missing. They looked bored. They had one of the highest suicide rates among the young people in the world. Why? Because all of this permissiveness without discipline doesn't bring happiness. Happiness and peace and joy are found in God, in a relationship with Jesus Christ, and in a disciplined life.

The Bible says, "Sin when it is finished bringeth forth death."

And the Bible says that this young fellow began to be in want. It wasn't long before his money was gone; he spent it all. And when his money left him, his friends left him.

I read the other day in the *Daily News*—I think they called it "The Prodigal Daughter." She was nineteen years of age, she had a steady boyfriend to whom she was engaged until one day she stepped out on him. She was unfaithful to him, and listen to what she says as quoted:

"I got into trouble with a guy I don't even like because I went to a drug and booze party. I completely lost control of myself, and I didn't even know what happened except that the guy whose baby I am going to have disappeared after he heard of my condition. I brought shame to my family and friends, and now I cry myself to sleep at night. I feel like I am falling apart. I haven't gone out of the house since it happened."

She began to be in want. She went to a party to have a big time, but there came a moment when sin paid its wages. And it always does. You see you can't commit a single sin without paying for it. You may not pay for it immediately. You may not pay for it as quickly as this girl, but you're going to pay for it.

The Bible says, "Whatsoever a man soweth that shall he also reap."

This young man began to be in want.

There is a film in New York for "Adults Only," and it is entitled, "I Want."

The Bible says, "The Lord is my shepherd, I shall not want."

But you see, the Lord was not the shepherd of this boy. He began to be in want. His body began to be in want. Is your body in want tonight for bigger kicks, more high-powered drugs, more sex deviation to satisfy—trying to stay awake at night thinking up things you can do for kicks? Is your mind in want?

The Bible says our minds have been affected by sin and the more we learn, the less truth we know many times—"ever learning but never able to come to a knowledge of truth," because, you see, God is Truth, Christ is Truth, and if you don't know Christ, you don't have the foundation of truth.

And, so many of our scientists today—see how many breakthroughs we have. They are beginning to see new areas of knowledge they didn't know existed a few years ago. Knowledge is now doubling every ten years so that no scientist can know it all. They can only specialize in one small field, and a scientist feels frustrated and hemmed in.

Dr. Elmer Engstrom, who spoke to you a moment ago, Chairman of this Crusade, is a great scientist, and he would tell you that scientists feel frustrated because they have to specialize now in little fields, and they cannot have the whole range of knowledge they once had.

And you see, the spirit began to be in want. He rebelled against God. The human soul is so large the world cannot satisfy it. "What shall it profit a man if he gain the whole world and lose his own soul."

And then something interesting happened. He became a slave. He had to find employment, but a depression had come, and he couldn't get a job. Finally, the only job he could get was to go out and feed the hogs. And so Jesus said he went out and began to feed the swine. And then he became so hungry that he began to eat with the hogs. It wasn't long before he looked like a hog. He smelled like a hog. He grunted like a hog. Down in the pig-pen with the hogs—a boy who had come from a fine home—gone to have a big time in the big city. How many in New York are like that tonight? Or any of the other great cities of America? In rebellion, going into all kinds of sin, but becoming slaves of sin. Jesus said, "Whoever committeth sin is the slave of sin."

He had walked out on his father and the love and the discipline of his father, to come under the bondage of a stranger. What an exchange! "What shall a man give in exchange for his soul?"

You know Prince Philip was speaking a few days ago at Edinburgh, and he said something I like. He got pretty tough with some students. He said, "Shut up and grow up." He said, "Freedom is not license. You can destroy freedom as successfully by making a mockery of it as you can by retraction." Hurray for Prince Philip! Maybe he will become an evangelist yet.

The Bible says we cannot be neutral. Lots of people try to be neutral.

They say, "Well, I'm not for God, I'm not against Him. I just don't take a stand." But God says you have to take a stand. You have to choose—you have to choose which road of life you are going to go—a broad road or a narrow road. The narrow Road leads to heaven, the broad road leads to hell, and you must make the choice.

And so this young fellow got to thinking one day, and it's a good thing when you start to think about yourself. He began to think, and the Spirit of God began to speak to him, and he began to think about his father back there on the farm. He thought to himself, "What am I doing here in these rags, in this dirt, in this filth, eating with hogs when my father has a beautiful farm back there with many servants and many cattle, and I could go be there and be a servant of his. What a fool I've made of myself."

You know the Bible teaches that sin is a form of insanity? The Bible says if our Gospel is hid or veiled, the veil must be in the minds of those who have spiritually died. The spirit of this world has blinded the minds of those who do not believe and who prevent the light of the glorious Gospel of Christ, the image of God, from shining in there. Notice, "The spirit of this world." There is an evil spirit in our world that blinds us to the reality of what God can do. It blinds us to our own condition. Then the Holy Spirit comes along and convinces us and disturbs us of our sins, and we sit and think about it and we are disturbed and unhappy about our condition. We don't know where to escape. We don't know which way to go. But this young fellow decided to do the right thing. He decided to get up and go back. He said, "I have sinned against heaven." He didn't just say, "I have sinned against my father." He said, "I have sinned against God." That's your problem. Your problem is not a family relationship. Your problem is not really a race problem. Your problem is a problem with God. You get the problem with God straightened out, and you will have a new perspective on how to straighten out some of the other problems. That's the real problem. The real hangup in your life is what to do about God, what to do about Christ. Let Him come and change and transform your life and see the fulfillment and the power and the strength you will have.

This young fellow reflected; then he made a resolution. He said, "I will arise and go to my father."

Sixteen thousand young people in Miami the other day arose and demonstrated for decency. Thousands of people followed an Olympic track star down the streets of Toronto the other day, to witness for Christ. They called it "A mile for morals march." When are we going to wake up? When are the young people in this country who believe in God finally going to start carrying their flag? Maybe we are going to see a great tide turned, but we will never turn unless we are willing to make Christ the very heart and the very center of our lives. There is nothing else in the arena of American philosophy and thought today except Christ. It is either Christ or it is chaos. Which is it going to be?

The Beatles' latest controversial record is called, "Oh, Christ, It Ain't Easy," and it's not easy to follow Christ. It is not easy to be a Christian. It's not easy to live in New York or any of our other great metropolitan areas and live the disciplined life for Jesus Christ. It's not easy for a young person to resist the temptations of this hour.

Jesus said, "Sit down and count the cost. If you want something easy, then go somewhere else. I'm not the man; I'm not the one." He said, "Count the cost." He said, "It's going to mean death to your self—your own self-interests, your own self-pride." He said, "It's going to mean a cross. You may have to be crucified." He meant that not only figuratively; He also meant it literally. It is going to have to mean less of you and your desires and your ambitions, and Christ is going to have to be first, and He'll test you; He'll take you to many Crosses, and He will see if you are willing to go there without flinching. That is what it will cost to follow Christ.

This fellow said, "I will arise and go."

He started back home, and while he was a long way off, his father was watching for him. Now notice, this is a picture of God. Jesus is telling a story to illustrate a spiritual truth. Here is a picture of God watching for you all the time. He sees you coming down the road, and the son is filled with shame, and dirt, and filth, and sin, and rebellion. Was his father apathetic to his condition? Was his father indifferent? No. The Bible says that he was watching, waiting for his son to return, hoping and praying he would return. And when he saw him, he ran down the road and threw his arms around him and the son blurted out in tears, "Father, I have sinned against you. I am sorry. I have come home to be a servant."

But the father said, "Nothing doing." He said, "Bring the ring and put it on his finger, the ring of the authority of sonship. Give him a bath and put on the finest clothes, and then kill the fatted calf. We are going to have a barbecue, we're going to have a party that will be the greatest party we ever had. My son that was lost has been found. My son has returned." The Bible says, "There is rejoicing in heaven over one sinner that repents." That is why Madison Square Garden is worth all the expense and all the trouble and all the work if just one person comes to Christ. If you knew the value of one soul, if you knew it made heaven rejoice over one person returning to the Father, you would receive Christ. You would return to the Father. You say, "But Billy, you don't know my sins. You don't know how rebellious my heart has been. You don't know how many lies I've told, how many immoralities I've committed, how many drugs I've taken. You don't know all I've done. I couldn't possibly come."

You are the kind of person He is really looking for. He receives you tonight. Jesus receives sinful men. That's why He died. That's why He rose again—to receive you.

But then out in the field there was his brother. He hadn't seen his younger brother for years. He was working out in the fields and he heard all the shouting and all the commotion, and he said, "What's going on?" One of the servants said, "Your brother has returned." He said, "That scoundrel? You mean that reprobate, that sinner has returned and he expects us to welcome him?"

You see this fellow had been in his father's home all along, but his loyalty wasn't really to his father. His loyalty was to his own selfish interests. And it is possible to be in the church and be lost. It is possible to be in the church and be without a personal relationship with Jesus Christ. And there is many an elder brother here tonight. You are a member of the church, you haven't yet left home, but even while you are at home, in the church, your heart is not right with God. You need to repent of your sins and receive Christ as your Lord and as your Savior.

Lincoln—before he was killed—was asked how he would treat the rebellious Southerners, and he answered, "As if they had never been away." That is how God will treat you if you receive Christ tonight—as if you had never been away. He forgives all the past. He writes your name in His Book. You have the assurance that you are going to heaven. Now it is complicated, and it is hard to live the Christian life. I don't want to fool you. I don't want you to come under false colors. It is not easy to be a Christian. It means reading your Bible daily, it means spending time in prayer, and it means persecution.

"All that will live godly in Christ Jesus shall suffer persecution," the Bible says.

We are to live disciplined lives, under the Lordship of Christ. That is not easy, but let me tell you something. The Holy Spirit comes to live in your heart to help you live the Christian life, and then He begins to live through you and in you. It is no longer you living. It is Christ living in you, and it becomes a life of joy. Problems? Yes. Difficulties? Yes. But a life of joy and peace and forgiveness. He can change your life tonight.

There is a man here in this audience who I saw here a moment ago. Maybe you saw me put my arm around him when I came into the Garden. His name is Jim Vaus. Jim does one of the great social jobs here in New York City. Twenty years ago this year, Jim wandered into a tent where we were holding a meeting in Los Angeles. Jim—he wouldn't mind me saying this—was Mickey Cohen's wire tapper, had been written up as one of the great criminals of the West Coast. That night Jim found Christ. He and Alice and their children are here tonight, they love the Lord with all their heart, and Jim speaks all over the world. Thousands of people have found Christ under his ministry. What Christ has done for Jim Vaus He can do for you tonight if you put your faith and your confidence in Him. I am going to ask you to do it tonight. You ask, "What do I have to do, Billy?"

I am going to ask you to get up and come.

John Paul II
(Karol Wojtyla)

1920–

*T*he first non-Italian Pope since the sixteenth century, John Paul II was not crowned with the traditional papal tiara but instead was invested as "Universal Pastor of the Church" in 1978. Karol Wojtyla was born in Wadowic, Poland, the grandson of a master tailor and a refinisher of carriages. During the years before World War II, he was a student in the gymnasium and later the University of Krakow, a city of medieval architecture and intense Catholic piety, and was immersed in the study of literature, philosophy, and classical languages. A poet and scholar whose verses have been published as work of real distinction, he was active in the clandestine theater of the German occupation, worked as a stonecutter, and began his studies for the priesthood in an underground seminary.

Karol Wojtyla's biography as Pontiff is no more conventional, championing the rights of the Church in Poland under Soviet domination and serving in his papacy as a world traveler who has criticized the defects and excesses of both Communism and capitalism. His pastoral visits outside Italy have been extensive, leading him to remark on a visit to Poland, "It is not possible to understand the history of the Polish nation without Christ," and to take highly controversial positions on family planning and capital punishment in areas of moral as well as geographical instability. In 1981 a Turkish terrorist made an attempt on his life; during his hospitalization he recited the Angelus, requesting his listeners to "Pray for the brother who shot me, whom I have sincerely forgiven." He met his would-be assassin later in the year on a visit to the Redibbia prison.

John Paul II's encyclicals, meditative homilies, and books are as numerous in quantity as the miles of his global travels, dealing with the power of mercy in human life, the fallacies of Marxism and materialism, and the destructive effects of rivalries between the superpowers. While taking difficult and frequently divisive positions, as a religious conservative in the seismic territory of the post–Vatican II Roman Catholic Church, he has constantly emphasized the role of the Virgin Mary as a source of Christian unity.

ᴄᴇ

Homily at Lourdes
August 15, 1983

A great sign appeared in the sky, a woman clothed with the sun.

—REVELATION 12:1

We have come on pilgrimage toward this Sign.

It is the solemnity of the Assumption into heaven: now the Sign attains its fullness. A woman is clothed with the sun of the inscrutable Divinity, the sun of the impenetrable Trinity. "Full of grace": she is filled with the Father, the Son and the Holy Spirit who give themselves to her as one God—The God of creation and of revelation, the God of the Covenant and of the Redemption, the God of the beginning and of the end. The Alpha and the Omega. The God of Truth. The God of Love. The God of Grace. The God of Holiness.

A woman clothed in the sun.

Today we are making a pilgrimage to this Sign. It is the Sign of the Assumption into heaven, which occurs above the earth and, at the same time, rises from the earth in which the mystery of the Immaculate Conception was implanted. Today these two mysteries come together: the Assumption into heaven and the Immaculate Conception. And today, they are shown to be complementary.

Today, for the feast of the Assumption into heaven, we come in pilgrimage to Lourdes where Mary told Bernadette: "I am the Immaculate Conception."

We have come here because of the extraordinary Jubilee marking the year of the Redemption. We want to fulfill this Jubilee close to Mary.

Lourdes is the best place for such proximity.

Here, once, the "Beautiful Lady" spoke to a simple young girl of Lourdes, Bernadette Soubirous, reciting the Rosary with her and entrusting various messages to her. In making this pilgrimage to Lourdes, we want to experience once again this extraordinary nearness which has never ceased here, but has rather grown stronger.

This proximity to Mary is like the soul of this sanctuary.

We come on pilgrimage to Lourdes to be close to Mary.

We come on pilgrimage to Lourdes to get close to the mystery of the Redemption.

No one is more deeply involved in the mystery of the Redemption than Mary. And no one is in a better position to bring this mystery home to us. She is at the very heart of the mystery. We pray that the very heart of this mystery will beat more strongly in all of us during this extraordinary Jubilee Year.

That is why we have come here.

We find ourselves in Lourdes on the solemnity of the Assumption of Mary into heaven, when the Church proclaims the glory of her definitive birth in heaven. We want to share in this glory especially through the liturgy.

At the same time, we want to honor, through the glory of her birth in heaven, the blessed moment . . . of her birth on earth. The Year of the Redemption 1983 turn our hearts and minds to this blessed moment.

But first, the birth in heaven: the Assumption into heaven. The liturgy, so to speak, shows us the Assumption of Mary into heaven under three aspects. The first aspect is the Visitation, in the house of Zechariah.

Elizabeth said: "Blest are you among women and blest is the fruit of your womb . . . Blest is she who trusted that the Lord's words to her would be fulfilled." (Luke 1:42, 45.)

Mary believed the words spoken to her on behalf of the Lord. And Mary received the Word who took flesh in her and who is the fruit of her womb.

The Redemption of the world is based on the faith of Mary. It was linked to her *fiat* at the moment of the Annunciation. But it started to become a reality because "the Word became flesh and made his dwelling among us." (John 1:14.)

At the time of the Visitation, on the threshold of the house of Zechariah and Elizabeth, Mary makes a pronouncement concerning the beginning of the mystery of the Redemption when she says: "God who is mighty has done great things for me, holy is his name." (Luke 1:49.)

This statement taken from the context of the Visitation is placed through today's liturgy in the context of the Assumption. The entire Magnificat spoken at the time of the Visitation becomes, in today's liturgy, the hymn of the Assumption of Mary into heaven.

The Virgin of Nazareth uttered these words when, with her help, the Son of God was to be born on earth. With what stronger voice must she not have uttered them again, when, with the help of her Son, she was herself to be borne into heaven!

The liturgy of this solemn feast reveals the second aspect of the Assumption in the words of Saint Paul in his letter to the Corinthians.

The Assumption of the Mother of Christ into heaven is part of the victory over death, that victory which originates in the Resurrection of Christ: "Christ is now raised from the dead, the first fruits of those who have fallen asleep." (1 Cor. 15:20.)

Death is the portion of man because of original sin: "In Adam all die." (1 Cor. 15:22.)

The Redemption achieved by Christ transformed this inheritance: "In Christ all will come to life again, but each one in proper order: Christ the first fruits and then . . . all those who belong to him." (1 Cor. 15:22–23.)

And who belongs to Christ more than his Mother? Who was redeemed by him more than she was? Who co-operated in the Redemption more closely than she did by her *fiat* at the Annunciation and by her *fiat* at the foot of the Cross?

Thus, it is at the very heart of the Redemption achieved through the Cross on Calvary, it is in the very power of the Redemption revealed by the Resurrection, that the victory over death which the Mother of the Redeemer experienced, that is, her Assumption into heaven, finds its origin.

Such is the second aspect of the Assumption revealed by today's liturgy.

The third aspect is expressed in the words of the responsorial psalm, through the poetic language found there: the daughter of the king, clothed in rich garments, comes in to take her place by the throne of the king.

"Your throne, O God, stands forever and ever; a tempered rod is your royal sceptre." (Ps. 45:7.)

The Kingdom of God, which began with creation but was weakened in the heart of man by sin, is renewed in the Redemption.

Mary, Mother of the Redeemer, is the first to share in this reign of glory and union with God in eternity.

Her birth in heaven is the definitive beginning of the glory which the sons and daughters of this earth must attain in God himself in virtue of Christ's Redemption.

In fact, the Redemption is the basis for the transformation of the history of the universe into the Kingdom of God.

Mary is the first of those who were redeemed. In her also has begun the transformation of the history of the universe into the Kingdom of God.

That is what the mystery of her Assumption into heaven reveals: her birth in heaven with her body and soul.

In the Assumption of the Mother of God into heaven, her birth in Heaven, we want to honor the blessed moment of her birth on earth.

Many ask themselves: When was she born? When did she see the light of day? This question is being asked now especially as we approach the second millennium of the birth of Christ. The birth of the Mother obviously had to come before the birth of her Son. So would it not be appropriate to celebrate first the second millennium of the birth of Mary?

The Church has recourse to history and historical dates in order to celebrate anniversaries and jubilees (taking into account the precision supplied by science). All the same, the true rhythm of anniversaries and jubilees is set by the history of salvation. So we want especially to situate in time the events related to our salvation and not only to note with historical precision the moment of these events.

In this sense, we agree that this year's Jubilee of the Redemption relates to the events of Calvary 1950 years ago, that is, to the death and resurrection of Christ. But all the attention of the Church is directed primarily to the salvific event (besides consideration of the date) and not to the historical date alone.

At the same time, we constantly recall that this year's extraordinary Jubilee is preparing the Church for the great Jubilee of the second millennium (the year 2000). In this way, our Year of Redemption also takes on the form of the Advent: it leads [us] to anticipate the jubilee of the coming of the Lord.

But Advent is especially the time of Mary. It is in her alone that the expectation of the entire human race for the coming of Christ reaches its highest point. She brings this expectation to its fullness: the fullness of Advent.

With this year's Jubilee of the Redemption, we want to enter into this Advent. We want to share in the expectation of Mary, the Virgin of Nazareth. In the jubilee of this salvific event which is also like an Advent, we want to include also her own coming, her own birth on earth.

Yes, the birth of Mary is the beginning of the salvific Advent.

And that is why we make this pilgrimage to Lourdes: not only to honor the birth of Mary in heaven through the solemn feast of the Assumption, but also to honor the blessed moment of her birth on earth.

We come on pilgrimage to Lourdes where Mary, "the Beautiful Lady," said to Bernadette: "I am the Immaculate Conception."

With these words, she explained the mystery of her birth on earth as a salvific event very closely linked with the Redemption—and to Advent.

Beautiful Lady! O Woman clothed with the sun! Accept our pilgrimage in this Advent year of the Jubilee of the Redemption. Help us, through the light of this Jubilee, to penetrate your mystery: the mystery of the Virgin Mother—the mystery of the Queen Servant—the mystery of a Woman so powerful who yet pleads.

Help us to discover always more fully, in this mystery, Christ, the Redeemer of the world, the Redeemer of mankind.

You are clothed with the sun of the inscrutable Divinity, the sun of the impenetrable Trinity. "Full of grace" to the extent of the Assumption into heaven!

And at the same time . . . for us who live here on earth, for us poor sons of Eve in exile, you are clothed with the sun of Christ since Bethlehem and Nazareth, since Jerusalem and Calvary. You are clothed with the sun of the Redemption of man and of the World by the Cross and the Resurrection of your Son.

Make this sun ever shine for us here on earth!

Make it never grow dark in the souls of mankind!

Make it light the earthly ways of the Church of which you are the leading figure!

And may the Church, casting its look on you, Mother of the Redeemer, always learn herself to be a mother!

Behold, here is what we read in the Book of Revelation: "The dragon stood before the woman about to give birth, ready to devour her child when it should be born." (Rev. 12:4.)

O Mother, you who, by your Assumption into heaven, have experienced complete victory over death of soul and body, protect your sons and daughters on earth from death of the soul! O Mother of the Church!

For humanity which is fascinated by what is temporal, and at a time when the domination of the world masks the perspective of man's eternal destiny in God, be yourself a witness to God!

You, his Mother! Who can resist the evidence of a mother?

You who were born for the toils of this world: conceived in an immaculate way!

You who were born for the glory of heaven! Raised to heaven!

You who are clothed with the sun of unfathomable Divinity, the sun of the impenetrable Trinity, filled with the Father, the Son and the Holy Spirit!

You to whom the Trinity gives itself as one God, the God of Creation and of revelation. The God of the Covenant and of the Redemption. The God of the beginning and the end. The Alpha and the Omega. The God of Truth. The God of Love. The God of Grace. The God of Holiness. The God who is above everything and who encompasses everything. The God who is "all in all."

You who are clothed with the sun! Our Sister! Our Mother! Be the witness of God! . . .

—before the world of the millennium drawing to a close.

—before us, children of Eve in exile, be the witness to God! Amen.

Robert Runcie

1921–

In 1979, Robert Runcie was elected Archbishop of Canterbury. There had been a continuous line of 101 archbishops before him, stretching back to the seventh century. (For comparison, there have been some 265 popes—and antipopes—since St. Peter.) The first Archbishop of Canterbury, appointed in 601, was St. Augustine, an Italian monk (not to be confused with his fifth-century namesake from Hippo in North Africa). He had arrived in Kent in 597 on a mission organized by Pope Gregory the Great to convert the Anglo-Saxons. Though Scotland had earlier been Christianized by Irish monks, much work remained to be done in the southern part of the island. By its preeminence, the see of Canterbury carried the title for its bishop of Primate of All England. Among Runcie's illustrious predecessors were Thomas à Becket, whose martyrdom in 1170 made Canterbury Cathedral a popular medieval pilgrim destination, Thomas Cranmer, Hugh Latimer, William Laud, and John Tillotson.

The duties of the Archbishop are numerous. Because of his connection to the Crown through the Church of England, he lives in Lambeth Palace in London, rather than full time in Canterbury itself. As chief cleric of the realm, he is the spiritual director of more than sixty million members of the Anglican Communion, in addition to presiding over the great liturgical feast days and various royal events. Runcie's term of office (he retired in 1991) also witnessed the Falklands War and the painful and protracted kidnapping of his aide, Terry Waite, in Lebanon.

Though Runcie had seen his share of death and tragedy when he was a young officer in the Scots Guards in France in World War II, he must have had to summon up all his inner resources to preach a sermon in Canterbury Cathedral to a nation mourning the aftermath of the Zeebrugge ferry disaster.

The loss of so many at sea when the Belgian ferry capsized in April 1987 inevitably summons up thoughts about the seeming cheapness of life and, for the faithful, challenges their understanding of God's role in Providence. As the Archbishop put it in the sermon that follows, "Faith is not hoping the worst won't happen. It's knowing there is no tragedy which cannot be redeemed."

❧

Zeebrugge Ferry Disaster

Where there is sorrow there is holy ground. The preacher must tread sensitively. It is tempting to leave it to music, readings and prayers to match the varied moods of those who mourn. But our service today would not be complete without an attempt to put into words of a direct and personal character the sympathies of a nation, and to articulate the faith for which this cathedral has stood over the centuries of our island story.

First we want to express our solidarity with the families and friends of those who died in this disaster. For them the tragedy was so sudden—the loss so unexpected. To those who carry this burden of pain we offer our deepest sympathy. And no sympathy will, I know, be so heartfelt as the sympathy of those who shared the horrors of that night but came through unhurt, and with their families and friends unharmed.

Not even the firmest faith is enough to insulate us from the pain of loss and grief, or from that sense that, with the death of someone dear to us, our own life has lost its meaning. *Time* must help. It is said that you must survive in grief through the course of a full year before life begins to knit together again, and threads of purpose begin to appear. Those of us who have friends who are in sorrow must give them time, and with it the chance to speak of their sadness. We must not only be ready to offer our words of comfort— we must also be ready to listen patiently to their words of grief. There are moments, of course, when we are so overwhelmed that we can say nothing. There is no reason to be alarmed at that. The better part of mourning, better even than patience, is *silence*—silence which touches the edges of the grief which others must endure. Patience and silence and time—and standing beside us through all is God.

To some who mourn, the question is bound to arise, inevitably, bitterly perhaps: *Why* should this happen? *Why* should a good God let it happen? I do not believe that they will be easily satisfied by argument or explanation. In suffering and bereavement we know that no theoretical answer will do. Hearts cry out not for answers but for friends who will share suffering with us. The stilted, agonized-over lines in a letter; the tongue-tied neighbor who is content just to sit with us—these are the things which count.

In this disaster it has been the practical, down-to-earth support given by so many doctors and nurses, rescue-workers, company officials, police and clergy which has struck us all. Even in the darkest moments at Zeebrugge there were rays of light—light in the instinctive co-operation of helpers from our neighbor nations; light in the gallant rescue work of divers, helicopter crews, harbor workers; light in the extraordinary courage of sailors and passengers who risked and sometimes lost their own lives to save others. Some of this light has already become legend. I think of the seaman who found that his diving gear was obstructing his search. So he discarded it, and stayed down in the dark until he found three lorry drivers, trapped alive in an air pocket. I think of the passenger with spinal injuries carrying his baby daughter to safety in his teeth. I think of the four men trapped in lower decks taking turns to hold above water the head of an elderly woman. I think of the man who acted as a bridge to allow others to crawl across, and the grandmother who tried to save someone in a falling wheelchair.

These are but a few examples of human heroism which this disaster encouraged and inspired. There are many, many others, and some will never be known. Our whole nation joins today with those who were rescued at Zeebrugge in admiration and gratitude for all who saved life at sea, or brought kindness and comfort on land. We owe a special debt to our friends in Belgium—the total commitment and excellence of their rescue and hospital services figure in every account I have heard or read. As so often in the past, tragedy at sea has displayed the human qualities of courage and generosity in all their splendor.

In the last century a terrible earthquake struck Italy. An eyewitness described "the wreckage and ruin, the apparently blind and stupid carnage inflicted by sheer physical forces." In the midst of it moved a man carrying two small children: "Wherever he went he seemed to bring order, hope and faith in that confusion and despair." The eyewitness said that he made them feel "that somehow love was at the heart of all things."

Someone who in the midst of things at Zeebrugge said later: "Tragedy does not take away love: it increases it. Perhaps we are more loving people, more sensitive, more concerned for each other because of that moment of grief which overthrew our ideas of what things matter, and opened our eyes again to the importance of our common humanity."

It is in the selfless heroism of so many at Zeebrugge that we can see God's love at work. For the God and Father of our Lord Jesus Christ is not a God who stands outside us, and sends disaster. He is not even a God who offers comfort from a distance. He is Immanuel, God with us, the God who in Christ crucified plunges into the darkness of human sorrow and suffering, to stand alongside us, even in death.

Christian faith does not mean believing in impossible things. It means trusting that Christ's promises never fail. "Though a man die, yet shall he live." Faith is not hoping the worst won't happen. It is knowing there is no tragedy which cannot be redeemed.

These things we shall remember again on Good Friday. On Saturday, on the night before Easter Day, we shall light the Easter fire in Canterbury. A large single candle is lit from it and carried into the Cathedral. With the shadows of the vast vaulted roof above us, it seems such a little, vulnerable thing—and yet it is there, making its way through the darkness, and, as other candles are lit from it, a pool of light and hope begins to spread. Such is our faith and hope in the risen Christ. Not a hope which ignores the shadows of suffering and death, but a hope strong and secure in the assurance that love is "at the heart of all things," that the eternal God is our refuge, and underneath are the everlasting arms in which are held those who have died, as well as those who mourn their loss.

Those who died at Zeebrugge did not die deserted by God, abandoned by him in an alien element, far away from his care and love. Though for a few who died their graves should be the sea bed, nevertheless they are as truly in God's loving hands as if their bodies lay in the most gracious of country churchyards. There also his right hand shall hold them in death as in life. That is the faith of the Bible.

There is no more beautiful expression of this faith than some words of the poet who wrote the book in the Bible called "The Song of Songs." I hope those of you who have suffered loss may be able to take these words home with you, and keep them close to your troubled minds and grieving hearts. The words are these: "Many waters cannot quench love, neither can the depths drown it." (Cant. 8:7.) Many waters have not quenched your love for those who died. How much less shall the waters quench God's love for them, the God who gave them power to live and be yours—and who gave you the power to love them.

In the words of St. Paul to companions physically and emotionally distressed,

> In all these things we are more than conquerors through him who loved us. For I am sure that neither death, nor life, nor things present, nor things to come, nor height, nor depth, nor anything else in all creation, can separate us from the love of God in Christ Jesus our Lord. (Rom. 8:37ff.)

To that love we commend all those who died at Zeebrugge. To that love we pray for all those who mourn them. Amen.

William Sloane Coffin, Jr.

1924–

When he left Yale Divinity School for his first assignment, Coffin was already in his early thirties. The reason for his late start as a minister was not his family. After all, his uncle, Henry Sloane Coffin, had been the president of New York's Union Theological Seminary. But the comfortable, predictable life forecast for this young, well-to-do scion of a wealthy, philanthropic father was altered when the latter suddenly died of a heart attack in 1933. Before long, mother and children began a series of moves, first to Carmel, California, and then to Europe. Coffin's ambition to be a concert pianist enabled him to study with Nadia Boulanger in Paris. Later, in Geneva, he met the great Polish pianist Ignace Paderewski.

Once the war broke out, he returned to school at Phillips Academy, Andover, graduating like so many of his peers into a military uniform. His European experience and linguistic skills gained him officer rank in intelligence work. In 1947 he finally left the army and picked up his college education at Yale, where his father and grandfather had gone before him. After graduation, though he tried unsuccessfully to enter the CIA, he began studies at Union, under the charge of such professors as Reinhold Niebuhr and Paul Tillich, only to interrupt them after a second, successful effort to join the CIA resulted in further intelligence work in Europe.

Back on the ministerial career track, he married the daughter of another famous pianist, Arthur Rubinstein, who wasn't sure he wanted "a Billy Graham" for a son-in-law. Coffin said he wasn't sure he wanted "a Liberace" for a father-in-law. There followed a succession of school chaplaincies, with Yale University as the culmination. In his years at Yale, a thirst for social justice began to show itself in Coffin by his dramatic efforts to engage, first, the evil of segregation by becoming a Freedom Rider, testing the right of blacks to equal interstate travel; next, the Vietnam War, by mobilizing the nation's clergy against the war, by his arrest and trial for encouraging resistance to the draft, and finally by going with a committee to Hanoi, at the request of the North Vietnamese government, to accept the release of three U.S. POWs.

After seventeen years in a university pulpit, Coffin left Yale in 1975 and eventually returned to New York, where he became pastor of the Riverside Church. It was there on January 23, 1983, that the sad task befell him of having to preach a eulogy for his own son, Alex, twenty-four, who had died the week before at the wheel in an automobile accident.

The eulogy as a form of public speech, of course, long precedes Christianity. The tradition, however, was certainly one well known to the Church Fathers, who adapted it to their funeral sermons and made it—as did rabbis in the Jewish tradition—a notable part of liturgies over the centuries. Coffin's brave and beautiful words, and his refusal to permit grief to challenge God's unconditional love, are memorable indeed.

Alex's Death

I will bless the Lord at all times:
his praise shall continually be in my mouth.
My soul shall make her boast in the Lord:
The humble shall hear thereof, and be glad.
O Magnify the Lord with me,
and let us exalt his name together.

I sought the Lord, and he heard me,
and delivered me from all my fears.
They looked unto him, and were lightened:
and their faces were not ashamed.
This poor man cried, and the Lord heard him,
and saved him out of all his troubles.

The angel of the Lord encampeth
round about them that fear him, and delivereth them.
O taste and see that the Lord is good:
blessed is the man that trusteth in him.
O fear the Lord, ye his saints:
for there is no want to them that fear him.
The young lions do lack, and suffer hunger:
but they that seek the Lord shall not want any good thing.

—PSALM 34:1–9

For I am persuaded that neither death, nor life, nor angels, nor principalities, nor powers, nor things present, nor things to come, Nor
height, nor depth, nor any other creature, shall be able to separate
us from the love of God, which is in Christ Jesus our Lord.

—ROMANS 8:38–39

As almost all of you know, a week ago last Monday night, driving in a terrible storm, my son Alexander—who to his friends was a real day-brightener, and to his family "fair as a star when only one is shining in the sky"—my twenty-four-year-old Alexander, who enjoyed beating his old man at every game and in every race, beat his father to the grave.

Among the healing flood of letters that followed his death was one carrying this wonderful quote from the end of Hemingway's *Farewell to Arms:* "The world breaks everyone, then some become strong at the broken places." My own broken heart is mending, and largely thanks to so many of you, my dear parishioners; for if in the last week I have relearned one lesson, it is that love not only begets love, it transmits strength.

Because so many of you have cared so deeply and because obviously I've been able to think of little else, I want this morning to talk of Alex's death, I hope in a way helpful to all.

When a person dies, there are many things that can be said, and there is at least one thing that should never be said. The night after Alex died I was sitting in the living room of my sister's house outside Boston, when the front door opened and in came a nice-looking middle-aged woman, carrying about eighteen quiches. When she saw me she shook her head, then headed for the kitchen, saying sadly over her shoulder, "I just don't understand the will of God." Instantly I was up and in hot pursuit, swarming all over her. "I'll say you don't, lady!" I said. (I knew the anger would do me good, and the instruction to her was long overdue.) I continued, "Do you think it was the will of God that Alex never fixed that lousy windshield wiper of his, that he was probably driving too fast in such a storm, that he probably had had a couple of 'frosties' too many? Do you think it is God's will that there are no streetlights along that stretch of road, and no guard rail separating the road and Boston Harbor?"

For some reason, nothing so infuriates me as the incapacity of seemingly intelligent people to get it through their head that God doesn't go around this world with his finger on triggers, his fist around knives, his hands on steering wheels. God is dead set against all unnatural deaths. And Christ spent an inordinate amount of time delivering people from paralysis, insanity, leprosy, and muteness. Which is not to say that there are no nature-caused deaths (I can think of many right here in this parish in the five years I've been here), deaths that are untimely and slow and pain-ridden, which for that reason raise unanswerable questions, and even the specter of a Cosmic Sadist—yes, even an Eternal Vivesector. But violent deaths, such as the one Alex died—to understand those is a piece of cake. As his younger brother put it simply, standing at the head of the casket at the Boston funeral, "You blew it, buddy. You blew it." The one thing that should never be said when someone dies is, "It is the will of God." Never do we know enough to say that. My own consolation lies in knowing that it was *not* the will of God that Alex die; that when the waves closed over the sinking car, God's heart was the first of all our hearts to break.

I mentioned the healing flood of letters. Some of the very best, and easily the worst, came from fellow reverends, a few of whom proved they knew their Bibles better than the human condition. I know all the "right" Biblical passages, including "Blessed are those who mourn," and my faith is no house of cards; these passages are true, I know. But the point is this: While the words of the Bible are true, grief renders them unreal. The reality of grief is the absence of God—"My God, my God, why hast thou forsaken me?" The reality of grief is the solitude of pain, the feeling that your heart's in pieces, your mind's a blank, that "there is no joy the world can give like that it takes away" (Lord Byron).

That's why immediately after such a tragedy people must come to your rescue, people who only want to hold your hand, not to quote anybody or even say anything, people who simply bring food and flowers—the basics of beauty and life—people who sign letters simply, "Your broken-hearted sister." In other words, in my intense grief I felt some of my fellow reverends—not many, and none of you, thank God—were using comforting words of Scripture for self-protection, to pretty up a situation whose bleakness they simply couldn't face. But like God Herself, Scripture is not around for anyone's protection, just for everyone's unending support.

And that's what hundreds of you understood so beautifully. You gave me what God gives all of us—minimum protection, maximum support. I swear to you, I wouldn't be standing here were I not upheld.

After the death of his wife, C. S. Lewis wrote, "They say, 'the coward dies many times'; so does the beloved. Didn't the eagle find a fresh liver to tear in Prometheus every time it dined?"

When parents die, as did my mother last month, they take with them a large portion of the past. But when children die, they take away the future as well. That is what makes the valley of the shadow of death seem so incredibly dark and unending. In a prideful way it would be easier to walk the valley alone, nobly, head high, instead of—as we must—marching as the latest recruit in the world's army of the bereaved.

Still there is much by way of consolation. Because there are no ranking unanswered questions, and because Alex and I simply adored each other, the wound for me is deep, but clean. I know how lucky I am! I also know that this day-brightener of a son wouldn't wish to be held close by grief (nor, for that matter, would any but the meanest of our beloved departed), and that, interestingly enough, when I mourn Alex least I see him best.

Another consolation, of course, will be the learning—which better be good, given the price. But it's a fact: few of us are naturally profound; we have to be forced down. So while trite, it's true:

> I walked a mile with Pleasure,
>   She chattered all the way;
> But left me none the wiser
>   For all she had to say.
>
> I walked a mile with Sorrow
>   And ne'er a word said she;
> But oh, the things I learned from her
>   When sorrow walked with me.
>
>   —ROBERT BROWNING HAMILTON

Or, in Emily Dickinson's verse,

> By a departing light
> We see acuter quite
> Than by a wick that stays.
> There's something in the flight
> That clarifies the sight
> And decks the rays.

And of course I know, even when pain is deep, that God is good. "My God, my God, why hast thou forsaken me?" Yes, but at least, "My God, my

God"; and the psalm only begins that way, it doesn't end that way. As the grief that once seemed unbearable begins to turn now to bearable sorrow, the truths in the "right" Biblical passages are beginning, once again, to take hold: "Cast thy burden upon the Lord and He shall strengthen thee"; "Weeping may endure for a night, but joy cometh in the morning"; "Lord, by thy favor thou hast made my mountain to stand strong"; "For thou hast delivered my soul from death, mine eyes from tears, and my feet from falling." "In this world ye shall have tribulation, but be of good cheer, I have overcome the world." "The light shines in the darkness, and the darkness has not overcome it."

And finally I know that when Alex beat me to the grave, the finish line was not Boston Harbor in the middle of the night. If a week ago last Monday a lamp went out, it was because, for him at least, the Dawn had come.

So I shall—so let us all—seek consolation in that love which never dies, and find peace in the dazzling grace that always is.

Frederick Buechner

1926–

Buechner's first novel, *A Long Day's Dying*, appeared two years after his graduation from Princeton University; he had previously served in the army during World War II. By the time he had published his third novel, *The Return of Ansel Gibbs*, Buechner had been ordained a minister of the United Presbyterian Church, and favorable reviews of his novels noted the combination of a writer's imagination and insight with a sense of Christian mission. Buechner himself explained that writing "is a kind of ministry," and that "as a preacher" he was trying to use both tasks to explore ". . . what I believe life is all about, to get people to stop and listen a little to the mystery of their own lives. The process of telling a story is something like religion if only in the sense of suggesting that life itself has a plot and leads to a conclusion that makes some kind of sense."

Frederick Buechner's novels deal, then, with theology and narrative, and the ability to find the sacred nearly everywhere in the re-creation of the human heart. As a Christian writer and minister in the pulpit he has composed fiction, meditative pieces, and sermons which are refulgent with the deep promise and endless possibility of life open to God's grace. But his use of "story" on the page and in the pulpit is never a facile use of the allegorical; rather, he achieves a difficult and human rendering of everyman's spiritual autobiography. In this piece from his late 1960s collection, *The Hungering Dark,* Buechner gives a chapter from his Protestant pilgrimage to the Vatican at the end of a turbulent decade in which the notion of the death of God became the cover for a celebrated issue of *Time* magazine. But Buechner's imagination has discovered nonetheless a different kind of hope for the Second Coming alluded to in the biblical texts he has chosen, in a world on fire with anxiety, disbelief, and a hunger for a return of the Divine.

The Hungering Dark

O that thou wouldst rend the heavens and come down,
    that the mountains might quake at thy presence—
as when fire kindles brushwood
    and the fire causes water to boil—
to make thy name known to thy adversaries,
    and that the nations might tremble at thy presence!...
There is no one that calls upon thy name,
    that bestirs himself to take hold of thee;
for thou hast hid thy face from us,
    and hast delivered us into the hand of our iniquities.

—ISAIAH 64:1–2, 7

And there will be signs in sun and moon and stars, and upon the earth distress of nations in perplexity at the roaring of the sea and

the waves, men fainting with fear and with foreboding of what is
coming on the world; for the powers of the heavens will be shaken.
And then they will see the Son of man coming in a cloud with
power and great glory. Now when these things begin to take
place, look up and raise your hands, because your redemption is
drawing near.

—LUKE 21:25—28

About twenty years ago I was in Rome at Christmastime, and on
Christmas Eve I went to St. Peter's to see the Pope celebrate mass. It happened also to be the end of Holy Year, and there were thousands of pilgrims
from all over Europe who started arriving hours ahead of when the mass
was supposed to begin so that they would be sure to find a good place to
watch from, and it was not long before the whole enormous church was
filled. I am sure that we did not look like a particularly religious crowd. We
were milling around, thousands of us, elbowing each other out of the way
to get as near as possible to the papal altar with its huge canopy of gilded
bronze and to the aisle that was roped off for the Pope to come down. Some
had brought food to sustain them through the long wait, and every once in
a while singing would break out like brush fire—"Adeste Fidelis" and
"Heilige Nacht." I remember especially because everybody seemed to know
the Latin words to one and the German words to the other—and the
singing would billow up into the great Michelangelo dome and then fade
away until somebody somewhere started it up again. Whatever sense anybody might have had of its being a holy time and a holy place was swallowed
up by the sheer spectacle of it—the countless voices and candles, and the
marble faces of saints and apostles, and the hiss and shuffle of feet on the
acres of mosaic.

Then finally, after several hours of waiting, there was suddenly a hush,
and way off in the flickering distance I could see that the Swiss Guard had
entered with the golden throne on their shoulders, and the crowds pressed
in toward the aisle, and in a burst of cheering the procession began to work
its slow way forward.

What I remember most clearly, of course, is the Pope himself, Pius XII
as he was then. In all that Renaissance of splendor with the Swiss Guard in
their scarlet and gold, the pope himself was vested in plainest white with

only a white skullcap on the back of his head. I can see his face as he was carried by me on his throne—that lean, ascetic face, gray-skinned, with the high-bridged beak of a nose, his glasses glittering in the candlelight. And as he passed by me he was leaning slightly forward and peering into the crowd with extraordinary intensity.

Through the thick lenses of his glasses his eyes were larger than life, and he peered into my face and into all the faces around me and behind me with a look so keen and so charged that I could not escape the feeling that he must be looking for someone in particular. He was not a potentate nodding and smiling to acknowledge the enthusiasm of the multitudes. He was a man whose face seemed gray with waiting, whose eyes seemed huge and exhausted with searching, for someone, some *one,* who he thought might be there that night or any night, anywhere, but whom he had never found, and yet he kept looking. Face after face he searched for the face that he knew he would know—was it this one? was it this one? or this one?—and then he passed on out of my sight. It was a powerful moment for me, a moment that many other things have crystallized about since, and I have felt that I knew whom he was looking for. I felt that anyone else who was really watching must also have known.

And the cry of Isaiah, "O that thou wouldst rend the heavens and come down, that the mountains would quake at thy presence . . . that the nations might tremble at thy presence! . . . There is no one that calls upon thy name, that bestirs himself to take hold of thee; for thou hast hid thy face from us, and hast delivered us into the hand of our iniquities."

In one sense, of course, the face was not hidden, and as the old Pope surely knew, the one he was looking for so hard was at that very moment crouched in some doorway against the night or leading home some raging Roman drunk or waiting for the mass to be over so he could come in with his pail and his mop to start cleaning up that holy mess. The old Pope surely knew that the one he was looking for was all around him there in St. Peter's. The face that he was looking for was visible, however dimly, in the faces of all of us who had come there that night mostly, perhaps, because it was the biggest show in Rome just then and did not cost a cent but also because we were looking for the same one he was looking for, even though, as Isaiah said, there were few of us with wit enough to call upon his name. The one we were looking for was there then as he is here now because he haunts the world, and as the years have gone by since that Christmas Eve, I think he has come to haunt us more and more until there is scarcely a place any longer where, recognized or unrecognized, his ghost has not been seen. It may well be a post-Christian age that we are living in, but I cannot think of an age that in its own way has looked with more wistfulness and fervor toward the ghost at least of Christ.

God knows we are a long way from the brotherhood of man, and any theory that little by little we are approaching the brotherhood of man has to reckon that it was out of the Germany of Goethe and Brahms and Tillich that Dachau and Belsen came and that it is out of our own culture that the weapons of doom have come and the burning children. Yet more and more, I think, although we continue to destroy each other, we find it harder to hate each other.

Maybe it is because we have seen too much, literally *seen* too much, with all the ugliness and pain of our destroying flickering away on the blue screens across the land—the bombings and the riots, the nightmare in Dallas, the funeral in Atlanta. Maybe it is because having no cause holy enough to die for means also having no cause holy enough to hate for. But also I think that is because as men we have tried it so long our own grim way that maybe we are readier than we have ever been before to try it the way that is Christ's—whether we call upon his name or not.

Out there beyond this world there are more worlds and beyond them more worlds still, and maybe on none of them is there anything that we would call life, only barrenness, emptiness, silence. But here in this world there is life, we are life, and we begin to see, I think, that negatively, maybe nothing is worth the crippling and grieving of life. We begin to see that, positively, maybe everything glad and human and true and with any beauty in it depends on cherishing life, on breathing more life into this life that we are. However uncertainly and ambiguously, something at least in the world seems to be moving that way. I cannot believe that it is just fear of the bomb that has kept us as long as this from a third world war, or that it is just prudence and political pressure that slowly and painfully move the races and the nations to where they can at least begin to hear all the guilt and fear that have kept them apart for so long. I cannot believe that it is just a fad that young men in beards and sandals refuse in the name of love to bear arms or that it is entirely a joke that, with Allen Ginsberg and Humphrey Bogart,

Jesus of Nazareth is postered on undergraduate walls. Call it what you will, I believe that something is stirring in the hearts of men to which the very turbulence of our times bears witness. It is as if the moral and spiritual struggle that has always gone on privately in the consciences of the conscientious has exploded into the open with force enough to shake history itself no less than our private inner histories.

Maybe it will shake us to pieces, maybe it has come too late, but at least I believe that there are many in the world who have learned what I for one simply did not know twenty years ago in Rome: that wherever you look beneath another's face to his deepest needs to be known and healed, you have seen the Christ in him; that wherever you have looked to the deepest needs beneath your own face—among them the need to know and to heal—you have seen the Christ in yourself. And if this is what we have seen, then we have seen much, and if this is what the old Pope found as he was carried through the shadow and shimmer of his church, then he found much. Except that I have the feeling that he was looking for more, that in the teeming mystery of that place he was looking not just for the Christ in men but for the Christ himself, the one who promised that the son of man would come again in a cloud with power and great glory.

"There will be signs in sun and moon and stars," he said, "and upon the earth distress of nations in perplexity at the roaring of the sea and the waves, men fainting with fear and with foreboding," and then, at just such a time, we are tempted to say, as our own time, "look up and raise your heads," he said, "because your redemption is drawing near." And the words of Jesus are mild compared with the words of a later generation. The Son of Man with face and hair as white as snow and eyes of fire, the two-edged sword issuing from his mouth. The last great battle with the armies of heaven arrayed in white linen, and the beast thrown into the lake of fire so that the judgment can take place and the thousand years of peace. Then the heavenly city, Jerusalem, coming down out of heaven like a bride adorned for her husband, and the great voice saying "Behold. . . ." The New Testament ends, of course, with the words, "Come Lord Jesus," come again, come back and inaugurate these mighty works, and I always remember a sign that I used to pass by in Spanish-speaking East Harlem that said simply, "Pronto viene, Jesus Cristo."

Surely there is no part of New Testament faith more alien to our age than this doctrine of a second coming, this dream of holiness returning in majesty to a world where for centuries holiness has shone no brighter than in the lines of a certain kind of suffering on faces like yours and mine. Partly, I suppose, it is alien because of the grotesque, Hebraic images it is clothed in. Partly too, I suppose, it is alien to us because we have come to associate it so closely with the lunatic fringe—the millennial sects climbing to the tops of hills in their white robes to wait for the end of the world that never comes, knocking at the backdoor to hand out their tracts and ask if we have been washed in the blood of the lamb.

But beneath the language that they are written in and the cranks that they have produced, if cranks they are, I suspect that what our age finds most alien in these prophecies of a second coming, a final judgment and redemption of the world, is their passionate hopefulness. "Faith, hope, love," Paul wrote, "these three—and the greatest of these is love," and yes, love. We understand at last something about love. Even as nations we have come to understand at last something about love, at least as a practical necessity, a final expedient, if nothing else. We understand a little that if we do not feed the hungry and clothe the naked of the world, if as nations, as races, we do not join forces against war and disease and poverty in something that looks at least like love, then the world is doomed. God knows we are not very good at it, and we may still blow ourselves sky high before we are through, but at least maybe we have begun as a civilization to see what it is all about. And just because we have seen it, if only through a glass, darkly, just because maybe love is not so hard to sell the world as once it was, perhaps Paul would have written for us: "Love, yes, of course, love. But for you and your time, the greatest of these is hope because now it is hope that is hardest and rarest among men."

We have our hopes of course. This election year especially, jaded as you get after a while, the hope that out of all these faces that we come to know like the faces of importunate friends there will emerge a face to trust. The hope that if the lives of a Gandhi, a Martin Luther King, cannot transform our hearts, then maybe at least their deaths will break our hearts, break them enough to let a little of their humanity in. The hope that even if real peace does not come to the world, at least the worst of the killing will

stop. The hope that as individuals, that you as you and me as me, will somehow win at least a stalemate against the inertias, the lusts, the muffled cru-
elties and deceits that we do battle with, all of us, all the time. The hope that
by some chance today I will see a friend, that by some grace today I will be
a friend. These familiar old hopes. No one of them is enough to get us out
of bed in the morning but maybe together they are, must be, because we do
get out of bed in the morning, we survive the night.

There is a Hebrew word for hope, *gāwāh,* whose root means to twist,
to twine, and it is a word that seems to fit our brand of hoping well. The
possibility that this good thing will happen and that that bad thing will not
happen, a hundred little strands of hope that we twist together to make a
cable of hope strong enough to pull ourselves along through our lives with.
But we hope so much only for what it is reasonable to hope for out of the
various human possibilities before us that even if we were to play a child's
game and ask what do we hope for most in all the world, I suspect that our
most extravagant answers would not be very extravagant. And this is the
way of prudence certainly because to hope for more than the possible is to
risk becoming the ones who wait, helpless and irrelevant in their white
robes, for a deliverence that never comes. To hope for more than the possible is a kind of madness.

For people like us, the reasonably thoughtful, reasonably reasonable
and realistic people like us, this apocalyptic hope for the more than possible
is too hopeful. We cannot hope such a fantastic hope any more, at least not
quite, not often. It is dead for us, and we have tried to fill the empty place
it left with smaller, saner hopes that the worst possibilities will never happen and that a few of the better possibilities will never happen and that a
few of the better possibilities may happen yet. And all these hopes twisted
together do make hope enough to live by, hope enough to see a little way
into the darkness by. But the empty place where the great hope used to be
is mostly empty still, and the darkness hungers still for the great light that
has gone out, the crazy dream of holiness coming down out of heaven like
a bride adorned for us.

We cannot hope that hope any more because it is too fantastic for us,
but maybe if in some dim, vestigial way we are Christians enough still to
believe in mystery, maybe if beneath all our sad wisdom there is some little

gibbering of madness left, then maybe we are called to be in some measure fantastic ourselves, to say at least maybe to the possibility of the impossible. When Jesus says that even as the world writhes in what may well be its final agony, we must raise our heads and look up because our redemption is near, maybe we are called upon to say not yes, because yes is too much for us, but to say maybe, maybe, because maybe is the most that hope can ever say. Maybe it will come, come again, come pronto. Pronto viene, Jesus Cristo.

Where do they come from, the Christs, the Buddhas? The villians we can always explain by the tragic conditions that produced them—the Hitlers, the Oswalds—but the births of the holy ones are in a way always miraculous births, and when they come, they move like strangers through the world. History does not produce holiness, I think. Saints do not evolve. If we cannot believe in God as a noun, maybe we can still believe in God as a verb. And the verb that God is, is transitive, it takes an object, and the object of the verb that God is, is the world. To love, to judge, to heal, to give Christs to. The world. The thousand thousand worlds.

Certainly a Christian must speak to the world in the language of the world. He must make the noblest causes of the world his causes and fight for justice and peace with the world's weapons—with Xerox machines and demonstrations and social action. He must reach out in something like love to what he can see of Christ in every man. But I think he must also be willing to be fantastic, or fantastic in other ways too, because at its heart religious faith is fantastic. Because Christ himself was fantastic with his hair every whichway and smelling of fish and looking probably a lot more like Groucho Marx than like Billy Budd as he stood there with his ugly death already thick as flies about him and said to raise our heads, raise our heads for Christ's sake, because our redemption is near.

Maybe holiness will come again. Maybe not as the Son of Man with eyes of fire and a two-edged sword in his mouth, but as a child who had maybe already been born into our world and beneath whose face the face of Christ is at this moment starting to burn through like the moon through clouds. Or if even that is too supernatural for us, maybe it will come in majesty from some other world because we have begun to take seriously the fantastic thought that maybe we are not alone in the universe.

Who knows what will happen? Except that in a world without God, in a way we do know. In a world without God we know at least that the thing that will happen will be a human thing, a thing no better and no worse than the most that humanity itself can be. But in a world with God, we can never know what will happen—maybe that is the most that the second coming can mean for our time—because the thing that happens then is God's thing, and that is to say a new and unimaginable and holy thing that humanity can guess at only in its wildest dreams. In a world with God, we come together in a church to celebrate, among other things, a mystery and to learn from, among other things, our ancient and discredited dreams.

It is madness to hope such a hope in our grim and sober times, madness to peer beyond the possibilities of history for the impossibilities of God. And there was madness among other things in the face of the old Pope that gaudy night with Hitler's Jews on his conscience maybe and whatever he died of already on its way to killing him. There was anxiety in his face, if I read it right, and weariness, and longing, longing. And to this extent his face was like your face and my face, and I would have had no cause to remember it so long. But there was also madness in that old man's face, I think. Like a monkey, his eyes were too big, too alive, too human for his face. And it is the madness that has haunted me through the years. Madness because I suspect that he hoped that Christ himself had come back that night as more than just the deepest humanness of every man's humanity, that Impossibility itself stood there resplendent in that impossible place.

He was not there, he had not come back, and as far as I know he has not come back yet. It is fantastic, of course, to think that he might, but that should not bother too much the likes of us. It is fantastic enough just that preachers should stand up in their black gowns making fools of themselves when they could be home reading the papers where only their children need know they are fools. It is fantastic that people should listen to them. It is fantastic that in a world like ours there should be something in us still that says at least maybe, maybe, to the fantastic possibility of God at all.

So in Christ's name, I commend this madness and this fantastic hope that the future belongs to God no less than the past, that in some way we cannot imagine holiness will return to our world. I know of no time when the world has been riper for its return, when the dark has been hungrier. Thy kingdom come . . . we do show forth the Lord's death till he come . . . and maybe the very madness of our hoping will give him the crazy, golden wings he needs to come on. I pray that he will come again and that you will make it your prayer. We need him, God knows.

"He who testifies to these things says, 'Surely I am coming soon.' Amen, Come, Lord Jesus!" [RSV.]

Lord Jesus Christ,

Help us not to fall in love with the night that covers us but through the darkness to watch for you as well as to work for you; to dream and hunger in the dark for the light of you. Help us to know that the madness of God is saner than men and that nothing that God has wrought in this world was ever possible.

Give us back the great hope again that the future is yours, that not even the world can hide you from us forever, that at the end the One who came will come back in power to work joy in us stronger even than death. Amen.

Jean-Marie Lustiger

1926–

It might seem at first a great anomaly that a Jewish convert to Christianity should preach a homily on the meaning the life of a young, cloistered nineteenth-century nun might have for this most violent of centuries, our own. On another plane, what we see is the cardinal Archbishop of Paris quite appropriately celebrating the September 25 feast day of one of its greatest modern saints, Thérèse of Lisieux. For an explanation, a closer look at the preacher and his topic is called for.

Jean-Marie Lustiger's parents were Eastern European Jewish immigrants to France. They did not practice their religion but nonetheless retained their identity as Jews, running a shop in Paris. As a child of ten, Aaron (his given name) got hold of a Protestant Bible and read it through, Old and New Testaments. He became interested in Jesus as well as in the long and difficult history of the covenant God made with Abraham and his descendants. As a schoolboy in Paris he was identified as a Jew and suffered verbal and physical punishment for it. (Astonishingly, his parents in the summers of 1937 and 1938 sent him to Germany to live with German families to learn the language, one such family being Nazi Party members.)

When the Second World War broke out, he was sent out of harm's way to Orléans. There, after making repeated petitions to his parents, he was given permission to be baptized a Christian. Under Nazi occupation, his father went ahead to the unoccupied part of the country to prepare to reunite with his wife and son. However, Lustiger's mother was arrested and interned by the French police and turned over to the Nazis for transport to Auschwitz and death. He did manage to survive the war with his father in Vichy France, engaging in modest efforts to help the Resistance movement. After the war he entered the seminary and in 1954 was ordained a Roman Catholic priest. Following more than a decade as a university chaplain in Paris and then a period as a parish priest near Boulogne, he was, to his surprise, made, first, bishop of Orléans by Pope John Paul II, and later, Archbishop of Paris, the central diocese of France.

He has described his becoming a Christian as a "crystallization rather than a conversion" and, while fully cognizant of the reproach he may represent to many fellow Jews, nonetheless also believes he has never ceased being a Jew himself. In a complex sense, he says what Walt Whitman said: "Do I contradict myself? Very well, then, I contradict myself." For Lustiger, the potential of simultaneous salvation for Jews and Christians is real; moreover, their inextricably entwined histories foretell their inextricably intertwined fates.

All this would have been understood by Thérèse of Lisieux (1873–1897), whose short life was ended by tuberculosis at twenty-four in a Carmelite convent. She was asked by the prioress, Mother Agnes (who was her older sister, Pauline), to write down her childhood memories, and her journal and other writings were published within a year of her death as the widely popular *Story of a Soul,* since translated into dozens of languages.

It is as profound a work of spirituality as any Church Father ever composed, and indeed Thérèse has recently been honored with the title Doctor of the Church. In one document among her papers, she wrote, "In order to live in one single act of perfect Love, I OFFER MYSELF AS A VICTIM OF HOLOCAUST TO YOUR MERCIFUL LOVE, asking You to consume me incessantly, allowing the waves of *infinite tenderness* shut up within You to overflow into my soul, and that thus I may become a *martyr* of Your *Love,* O my God!"

In emptying herself so God might fill her with His grace, it is not too anomalous a thought to imagine Thérèse, mystic that she was, hoping to offer herself not just then but continuously in some way for us, now. Cardinal Lustiger would appear to understand this.

The Greatest Saint of Modern Times

Prophecy of Youth, Sign of Hope

The first and overwhelming reality in the life of Saint Thérèse is her youth. Twenty-four years old! And, as she herself said, she walked the road of a giant.

Do you remember, you of the older generations, the years of Saint Thérèse's life and those that followed: you heard about them from your parents and grandparents. What happened to youth in this century? What did it do in our country, in the other countries of the West, in the whole world? If some among you were eighteen years old during the terrible years of World War I, you know and remember the conditions of life of the young, the children, when this world in which we live was erected in its pride, ambition, and conceit. The young were turned into fanatics, torn away from their very selves to serve lost causes. And now, what are we doing with our youth? It is presented to us as the chimera of humankind, as the dream of life. Youth is used as an argument in advertising . . . The result is already visible: the youth that goes before us has left us and has nothing; we do not understand it and it does not understand us; we have lost it and it is lost. Youth, victim of the ambitions, errors, and delusions of our century which is so rich in beauty and hope! Youth which does not exist outside of the rest of humankind and belongs to no one. Each one of us, at one point in his or her life had youth to himself or herself; we too have been young!

Thérèse was twenty-four years old when she reached the end of her giant road. This young girl, sick in her body and wounded in her sensitivity, fighting alone against herself and against all she foresaw, was at the dawn of this tremendous and terrible century, the hope of life, of tenderness, of pardon, and goodness that youth brings when it is totally given to God, for God. In a little Norman girl, locked up in the obscurity of a Carmelite convent, many men and women of all walks of life found a sign of hope.

God wanted to use this weakness of Thérèse, sign of the youth which was going to be the victim of our civilization, to make of her the stake and guarantee of the salvation he offers to us. The sufferings and trials of Thérèse were, ahead of time, the very ones that were going to befall the youth of this century. But far from being a sign of loss, the youth of Saint Thérèse was an open door to salvation. Far from being an absurd destruction, it was an offering of liberating love. Far from being a slaughter (like the great war), it was the free sacrifice of a freedom enabling human persons to become free in a love giving love. It shows us in her obscurity, in her humility, in this unknown life, the daring that can be ours and the hope that God wants to put in us. This particular youth invites us to recognize that we are born from God, children of God; it gives us back hope.

Young people, when you look at Saint Thérèse; when you see the very young face of Saint Thérèse whose photographs, thank God, we have kept; when you look at her smile, I would like you to recognize someone who is of your age, one of you, almost an elder sister. See what she did: you can do it. You are not separated from us: you are our hope because God gives you, young people, a daring that might be missing in us, an intensity of love we need. You have received life: your responsibility is to give to the world the hope of life. Young people, you think that you are rejected, despised, unknown, you think that we do not trust you. God trusts you, you are children of God and your youth is a grace. You think that you came into a world where there is nothing to do because all is kept away from you: work, studies. . . . Look at Saint Thérèse: in the secret of a humble life, hidden from all, she opened the door of love, forgiveness, and freedom. Your youth is a gift from God: accept it joyfully, give it generously, do not waste it, make it a source of love and daring. God is asking this of you, you who are ceaselessly given to the church as the sign of new birth from above.

Thérèse, at the beginning of this century, was already showing that we have to be reconciled with ourselves in this incredible and daring figure of God's youth when he gives birth to his children.

Prophecy of Holiness, Our Vocation

The life of Saint Thérèse prophesies another truth. She seems to me to be essential for the time in which we live. George Bernanos was right to say that Thérèse is "the greatest saint of modern times." In the secret of her cloister, not knowing and unable ever to know in this world how her poor words, written in a child's notebook, would echo through the whole world, Thérèse wants to convince us—in a way which is all the more eloquent that her voice is so weak, so frail, the voice of a poor little girl—that holiness is possible for all, is the vocation of all; that love is meant for all because God loves us all. All of us are begotten, brought to life as children of God, in the grace of baptism, by the Father in heaven who loves us, God whose fatherhood is higher, purer, greater, broader, than any paternity in this world.

If you are fathers and mothers and love your children, you know that you love all of them, that you want to love all of them, even the weakest, and especially the sick ones, even the hothead and especially the one who fails. When your children cry, fail, are sick, or believe themselves lost, if you are really fathers and mothers, you love them, you try to help them, to reassure them, to give them back strength and hope. If you are really a father and a mother, you do not choose among your children. Even the one who tells you: "I want to leave you." Even the one who tells you: "I don't understand you." You love him or her, you cannot help but loving and forgiving. You must love all of them with the same love, and even with a greater love for the one who seems to you the most lost, desperate, and wounded.

Our holiness, the holiness of the Christian people, is to be born from God, to become children of God. In these incredible words we perceive what it means that God loves us. God does not tell us: "If you do this, if you do that, I will love you." God does not tell us: "On condition that you behave in such a way, I will love you." God tells us: "I love you; I make of you my

child in my Son, and because I love you, you can act as a son or a daughter
of God." God tells us: "I love you and I know your wound, I know your
weakness, I know your sin. Do not fear. Because I love you, you can love me
in spite of your sin, in spite of your wound, in spite of your weakness, with
your sin, your wound, your weakness. Because I love you and you are a child
of God, I will carry your sin, your wound, your weakness. Because you are
my son and my daughter and I give you life to make you like my eternal Son,
Jesus Christ, through the Holy Spirit that I put in you, I am going to forgive
your sin, heal your wound and give you the strength to overcome your
weakness." And holiness is made for the little ones, that is, for those who
accept to be carried in God's arms. They discover in the love God shows
them who they are: sons and daughters of God. Holiness is first of all to be
forgiven sinners, wounded people that God wants to heal, weak people to
whom God gives the strength to love. Holiness is what is given to sinners:
Thérèse understood this, she wanted to sit at the table of sinners, she did
not try to be brave. Yet she had the daring to say that she knew she was a
saint, a very small saint.

Brothers and sisters, I would like each of you and all the Christian
people to be able to say humbly, poorly, and even contritely: "I too am a
saint." Why? Because God gives you his love. Because when you confess your
sins in the secret of God and you receive from the priest who heard you the
pardon and mercy given to the church, you are filled with the holiness of
God and thus you allow the love of God to be the heart of the world, the
heart of the church. Thus you enter into the will of our Father in heaven
who wants to give life to the world through our lives. The saints we are destined to become are those who enable the world to live and who save it.
Today the fabulous ambitions of human beings fascinate us and, at the same
time, terrify us, for we see quite well that their accumulations of power can
quickly turn into calamity, that the best can bring the worst, that the most
beautiful achievements can bring about our perdition, that the most
tremendous and remarkable improvements can destroy what is most precious in us: our dignity as children of God created in the image of the
Father, made like the Son, and made into temples of the Spirit. Our dignity
as human beings, our freedom, our capacity to love and to pardon, all this,
we ourselves run the risk of putting in chains and annihilating. This is not an
illusory threat but a sad reality in many countries and in many ways! And

now we live in fear, bitterness, guilt, and despair during these last years of the twentieth century which started under the sign of insane hope.

Thérèse, the little girl, when showing us the way of the holiness that is meant for us, exorcises despair before it comes, chases fear away before it comes, opens the path on which we must bravely advance. We must be saints. We can be saints. Not as we imagine saints to be, but as God enables us to become. Holiness is meant for all; holiness is possible for all: it is to be begotten by God, to be carried in his all powerful love—wounded, sinners, weak—to be healed, forgiven, strengthened.

Prophecy of the Relevance of Redemption, Invisible Force of Love

Prophecy of youth, prophecy of holiness, Thérèse says even more. She lives ignored by all in this house of Lisieux. No one knows her beyond her family circle. Her life is secluded: the garden is small; she has a short life; she does not know many things; she lives without radio or television, without newspapers. She is locked up in a world which, to the young people of today, might seem narrow and limited. Yet the life, the love, the daring of a young girl who was so isolated are at the service of the salvation of the entire world. She offers her life, her prayer, her suffering for famous men and women who are losing themselves, for the universal mission. What this little Carmelite experiences alone and in secret has an incredible weight on the scales of history, greater than that of so many economic, industrial, political forces, greater than that of so many intelligences and powers which created entire cities and destroyed human generations, built splendid things and heaped up disasters. Here is the secret that we carry in our heart, with all our faith, with the whole church: the secret of the meaning of our life.

We often have the impression that our life has no great significance, that it is a little speck of dust lost in a great whirlwind. Often we have the feeling that we can do nothing or almost nothing vital for ourselves, our relatives, parents, family, friends, those we love, but also and even more for the whole world. Most of the time we think that we do not have true freedom of choice or action. We think that the powerful of the world—heads of state, scientists, important people—can act, can really influence events, while we, ordinary folk, nobody listens to us, nobody hears or barely so! I meet important people: they ask me questions, they ask themselves questions. They too, like you, have the impression that they cannot do much. In the face of difficult and tragic situations they think: "We must do our duty, act for the good of all." But they are not sure of anything, they don't know what will happen. While they seem to us to be able to settle problems, they imagine that they have no grasp of anything and that reality escapes them as much as it does us.

To look closely at the course of events, we might believe that we are aboard a mad ship, without a pilot, and whose helm does not respond anymore. If one does not look too much at what is happening outside, one can feel secure as long as the ship is afloat and moving; but let a gale come and we do not know what to do and what to hang on to. Now we Christians—Thérèse reminds us of this—are hanging on to the helm. The force that moves the world is the love of God that Christ gives us and reveals to us in its immensity. A frail and unknown young girl of twenty-four can, from her convent, influence the destiny of the world through the secret power of her love.

Each one of our lives is useful. You may be poor, sick, old, ignored, lost, despised, but in Christ you have the great power of those God loves. God unites us to his Son to manifest the strength of his love. God who gave his Son to save us placed him in our hands, as he gives us the eucharistic body. He wants to associate us to this work, this task of redemption in which each one of us and each moment of our life matters. What matters is not what the newspapers print or what people see, it is the invisible and all powerful love which, little by little, builds the Kingdom of God until the day when he will wipe away all the tears from our eyes. He comes to dwell among us to make us like him, to save us and make us live, to share with us the joy of God, to make us discover the joy of being human and of accepting ourselves for he restores us to our true dignity as kings of creation, as beloved children of God. He gives us the joy of loving one another and of living in the communion of God, the very joy of Redemption in this paradoxical love of which the crucified is the sign: lost man, hanging on the cross, who by the power of the Resurrection is now a hope for all humankind.

Thérèse prophesies youth, Thérèse prophesies the holiness given to us all by the pardon that we, sinners, receive. Thérèse prophesies the incredible relevance of the Redemption in which we too participate and act in Christ.

Thérèse, this giant, "the greatest saint of modern times" because she is only a very ordinary young girl, hidden in the obscurity of a Carmelite convent in Normandy. Thérèse, little Thérèse, a real heroine because she is nothing but the sign of the power of love that God has for us all.

Thérèse, our little sister. What he did for her, God is doing for us too.

Desmond Tutu

1931–

On arriving home in Johannesburg after learning he had been awarded the 1984 Nobel Peace Prize, Desmond Tutu spoke to his people, still living under the hated laws of apartheid:

This award is for you—Mothers, who sit near railway stations trying to eke out an existence, selling potatoes, selling meali, selling pigs' trotters.

This award is for you—Fathers, sitting in a single-sex hostel, separated from your children for eleven months of the year.

This award is for you—Mothers in the squatter camps, whose shelters are destroyed callously every day and who have to sit on soaking mattresses in the winter rain holding whimpering babies and whose crime in this country is that you want to be with your husbands.

This award is for you—three and a half million of our people who have been uprooted and dumped as if they were rubbish. The world says we recognize you, we recognize that you are people who love peace.

For most of his life Tutu has chosen to be the thin end of the wedge in his efforts to represent and better such people.

Tutu was not ordained an Anglican priest until he was thirty years old, married, and the father of five children. His first career choice had been to follow his father's example by training to be a teacher, with the eventual prospect of becoming a headmaster. Tutu's father, Zachariah, ran the Methodist Primary School in Klerksdorp in the western Transvaal, where Desmond was born.

However, the racial legislation enacted after the repressive National Party took power in South Africa in 1948 soon put an end to those hopes by restricting the education permitted to blacks in ways that would ensure their future subservience. Whites were at the apex of opportunity and status; next, those of mixed race were distinguished from blacks; and at the bottom, blacks placed apart from all others. By such means blacks were also forced to live either in tribal regions with the poorest land and resources or in restricted areas near cities where they provided cheap day labor for whites (e.g., the well-known Soweto, short for South Western Townships). Movement of blacks required them always to carry a passbook, to be produced on demand for security officers at any time.

Tutu's remarkable rise to visibility and authority with the anti-apartheid movement and simultaneously within the Anglican Church resulted from a number of factors: his quick intelligence, his irresistible joy-fulness and inclusive manner, his fearlessness in the face of physical danger, his powerful eloquence—especially as a preacher—and his always seeming to others to be exactly the right South African black appointee to break the color line in a series of increasingly important Church offices, climaxing in 1986 when he was installed as Archbishop of Cape Town.

The past decade has seen the collapse of apartheid under international and internal pressures. In 1982, Bishop Tutu had promised to burn his Bible if he was wrong about its inevitable demise. Now, retired, his lifelong activism has once again placed him at the center of South Africa's future as chairman of the South African Truth and Reconciliation Commission. Perhaps the measure of his thirst for justice might be taken from the funeral sermon he preached in 1977 for Steve Biko, the most notable of many black political martyrs, who died at the vicious hands of his jailers. He told his audience to pray for the whites who killed him. He has often said that "a person is a person through other persons." He knows that we must lift up others before we can be lifted up, too.

What Jesus Means to Me

One day at a party in England for some reason we were expected to pay for our tea. I offered to buy a cup for an acquaintance. Now he could have said, "No, thank you." You could have knocked me down with a feather when he replied, "No, I won't be subsidized!" Well, I never! I suppose it was an understandable attitude. You want to pay your own way and not sponge on others. But it is an attitude that many have seemed to carry over into our relationship with God—our refusal to be subsidized even by Him. It all seems very much from the prevailing achievement ethic which permeates our very existence. It is drummed into our heads, from our most impressionable days, that you must succeed. At school you must not just do well, no, you must grind the opposition into the dust. We get so worked up that our children can become nervous wrecks as they are egged on to greater efforts by competitive parents. Our culture has it that ulcers have become status symbols. It has got to the stage where the worst sin in our society is to have failed. We don't mind how a person succeeds, or even at what he excels, so long as he succeeds. Then they become superstars. Success is something we *achieve,* it crowns *our* effort and says we have arrived. It serves to massage our ego and says we amount to something, the world testifies to that. Of course this rampant competitiveness takes its toll. We are hagridden by anxiety lest we fail. We worry that we may be inadequate (and often we are—we are like the chap who went to the psychiatrist and said, "Doctor, I think I have an inferiority complex" and the doctor said, "No, you don't have an inferiority complex. You are inferior"). All of us have some inadequacy or other. We prove our maturity by how we deal with that fact. Most of us pretend we aren't inferior and throw our weight around to prove that we count. We work ourselves into a frazzle in order to succeed, in order to be accepted, and we can't understand that we should certainly not carry this attitude over to our relationship with God.

What a tremendous relief it should be, and has been to many, to discover that we don't need to prove ourselves to God. We don't have to do anything at all, to be acceptable to Him. That is what Jesus came to say, and for that He got killed. He came to say, "Hey, you don't have to earn God's love. It is not a matter for human achievement. You exist because God loves you already. You are a child of divine love." The Pharisees, the religious leaders of His day—the bishops and presidents and moderators—they couldn't buy that. Jesus tried to tell them all sorts of stories to prove this point, like the one about the laborers in the vineyard, who were hired in batches at different times of the day. With all but the very last lot the owner of the vineyard came to an agreement about the wages. The last lot worked for no time at all and yet they were paid a full day's wage—God's love and compassion are given freely and without measure, they are not earned. They are totally unmerited and gracious. The religious leaders thought Jesus was proclaiming a thoroughly disreputable God with very low standards—any Tom, Dick and Harry, Mary and Jane would soon be jostling with the prim and proper ones. Stupendously that was true; no, just part of the truth. Jesus was saying that the unlikely ones, those despised ones, the sinners, the prostitutes, the tax collectors, would in fact precede the prim and proper ones into the Kingdom of God. That really set the cat among some ecclesiastical pigeons, I can tell you.

He really scandalized them. He ate with the riffraff and the scum—those were the ones with whom He hobnobbed, because He had come to seek and to find the lost, and as a physician He was needed by those who were sick, not the whole (or those who thought they were whole and righteous). He told the story of the Pharisee and the publican who went to pray. The one boasted to God that he was thankful he was not like other men, especially that publican over there; whereas the publican hardly dared lift his eyes to heaven.

He knew his need, his utter unworthiness, and so he was acceptable to God and received God's gift because he was empty of self.

The Good News is that God loves me long before I could have done anything to deserve it. He is like the father of the prodigal son, waiting anxiously for the return of his wayward son, and when he sees this feckless creature appearing on the horizon, he rushes out to meet him, embrace and kiss him, not recriminating, but asking that the fatted calf be slaughtered, a ring be placed on his finger, and the best robe be put on him; and they must rejoice in a party to celebrate because this lost one has been found, this dead one has come to life again. God is like the good shepherd who goes out looking for the lost sheep. We are misled by the religious pictures which depict Jesus as the good shepherd carrying a cuddly white lamb on His shoulder. A lamb will hardly stray from its mother. It is the troublesome, obstreperous sheep which is likely to go astray, going through the fence, having its wool torn and probably ending up in a ditch of dirty water. It is this dirty, smelling, riotous creature which the Good Shepherd goes after, leaving the good, well-behaved ninety-nine sheep in the wilderness, and when He finds it, why, He carries it on His shoulder and calls His friends to celebrate with Him.

That is tremendous stuff—that is the Good News. Whilst we were yet sinners, says St. Paul, Christ died for us. God did not wait until we were die-able, for He could have waited until the cows came home. No, whilst we were God's enemies He accepted us. God loves us, says Jesus, not because we are lovable, but we are lovable because God loves us. That has liberated me to give me the assurance of the child in his father's home. I am loved. That is the most important fact about me and nothing, absolutely nothing, can change that fact. All I do now is an expression of my gratitude for what God has already done for me in Christ Jesus, my Lord and Savior. Of course, only those who have never loved will say there will be a lowering of standards. When a chap is in love, he will go out in all kinds of weather to keep an appointment with his beloved. Love can be demanding, in fact more demanding than law. It has its own imperatives—think of a mother sitting by a bedside of a sick child through the night, impelled only by love. Nothing is too much trouble for love.

Jesus Attests My Infinite Value as a Child of God

In Jeremiah 1:4 we find a strange statement. You could almost say God didn't know much about human biology. But what was He saying to Jeremiah? He wanted to assure him that His call to be a prophet was no divine afterthought, that it was part of God's plan from all eternity. It says that each one of us is part of the divine plan and as such totally irreplaceable and unique. We might some of us look like accidents but we are not accidents for God. No one, not even my identical twin, can love God in exactly the way that I can love God. We are each unique originals not carbon copies. On my birthday my wife gave me a card showing a Darby and Joan couple. On the outside it said, "We have a beautiful and unique relationship," and inside it said, "I am beautiful and you are certainly unique." But have you seen a symphony orchestra? They are all dolled up and beautiful with their magnificent instruments, cellos, violins, etc. Sometimes, dolled up as the rest, there is a chap at the back carrying a triangle. Now and again the conductor will point to him and he will play "ting." That might seem so insignificant, but in the conception of the composer something irreplaceable would be lost to the total beauty of the symphony if that "ting" did not happen. In the praise ascending to God's throne something totally irreplaceable of your unique way of loving God would be missing. We are each, says Jesus, of unique and inestimable value, so that while He is rushing to the house of Jairus to be with his dying daughter, Jesus must needs stop to attend to the woman with a hemorrhage, or He will speak directly in a crowd to one person, as He did to Zacchaeus. You know something—we are each a temple, a tabernacle, a sanctuary of the Holy Spirit, of Jesus, of God. Yes, you are a God-carrier. God dwells in you He dwells in me, that is why it is such a blasphemy for God's children to be treated as if they were things, uprooted from their homes and dumped in arid resettlement camps. Jesus says that to do something to those He called the least of His brethren is to do it unto Him. My value is intrinsic—i.e., it is constitutive of me as a human being created in the image of God. I am God's viceroy on earth, you are God's viceroy. *Magtig,* if only we could believe this of ourselves then we would behave so differently to our usual conduct. Those who are victims of injustice and oppression would not have to suffer from a slave mentality by which they despised themselves and went about apologizing for their existence. They would know that they matter to God, and nothing anybody did to them could change that fundamental fact about themselves. And those who are privileged would realize that they matter too. They have an intrinsic and inalienable value and so don't need to amass material possessions so obsessionally as if to say "That is what I am worth—that is who I am"; nor would they have to behave like a bully—his behavior is really a cry for help, for recognition. They would then have to stop throwing their weight around. God, please help us to know that we matter, that we are creatures of your love, from all eternity, for you chose us in Christ even before the foundation of the world. What bliss, what ecstasy! If we really could believe that, the world would be revolutionized.

Jesus Is the Affirming One

Often we think of religion as life-denying—as a series of "Don't this and don't the other," as a spoilsport wet-blanket, stopping us from doing the things we most enjoy doing or letting us do them, but with a guilty conscience. There are religious pictures which were popular, certainly in the townships, which showed two sets of people. One set was carrying palm branches and the people were dressed in white, walking in solemn procession towards a great light with hardly a smile on anyone's face. The other group showed people who were having fun, dancing, playing guitars, and cards, and they were all being pitchforked into a red-hot fire by the Devil (who was black) and his angels, who were obviously enjoying themselves.

Let me tell you straight away that that is a travesty of what religion is all about—certainly the religion of Jesus. Jesus was splendidly life-affirming. How else can you explain His concern to heal the sick, to feed the hungry, etc., when He could have said, "Let's pray about it, and it will all be okay upstairs when you die"? He forgave sins, to relieve God's children of all that was unnecessarily burdensome. And He celebrated life and the good things that His Father had created. He rejoiced in the lilies of the field and the birds of the air. He knew that it was all created good, very good according to Genesis. He was often depicted attending dinner parties and weddings, and had provided wine once at a wedding when supplies had run out. He was accused in fact of being a wine-bibber and a friend of sinners. He declared by this open and welcoming attitude to life, that all life, secular and sacred, material and spiritual, belonged to God, came from God and would return to God. Many religious people think that long sulky faces somehow are related to holiness—they often look as though they have taken an unexpected dose of castor oil and find it hard to laugh in church, being somewhat sheepish when they do. And yet Jesus was funny when He described the chap who is concerned to remove a speck of dust from his brother's eye while a huge beam was sticking out of his own. Jesus was poking fun at this chap and his audience would roar with laughter. You often hear people say that the sin Adam and Eve committed must have been related to sex. What utter nonsense! If God said they should be fruitful and multiply, do those people think He expected them to do so by looking into each other's eyes? He, Jesus, celebrated life and He declares all wholesome things good—we are meant to enjoy good food, glorious music, beautiful girls and lovely men, attractive scenery, noble literature, refreshing recreation—they are part of what life is about. Jesus leads us into all truth through His spirit, and therefore as a Christian I glory in the tremendous discoveries of science, I do not see science as a rival or enemy of religion. All truth is of God and can never be self-contradictory. We don't have a God who rules only over the areas of human ignorance, so that as the frontiers of knowledge extend His domain keeps diminishing. No, ours is not a God of the gaps. We say, as we marvel at the discoveries and inventions of science, if man is so wonderful, how much more wonderful must God the creator be. Christians must glory in the strides of human knowledge. Our God does not reign over puny, guilt-ridden, obsequious creatures. He reigns over human beings at their best and most noble, and seeks to help us attain a mature humanity measured by nothing less than the perfect humanity of Christ Himself, the man for others, always a spendthrift for others, ready to suffer the vulnerability of love, willing to be taken advantage of, ready to serve and not be served, to tie a towel round His waist and to wash the disciples' feet. There can be no greater love—because it is only in giving that we receive, it is only in dying that we shall rise to eternal life.

This Jesus affirms me and says I matter, so I can have a proper self-assurance. You know how we all blossom in the presence of one who sees the good in us and who can coax the best out of us. And we know just how we wilt in the company of the person who is forever finding fault with us. We are sure to break that special cup of the lady who is always fussy about her precious heirlooms. We become all thumbs in her presence. Just note how Jesus was able to get a prostitute like Mary Magdalene to become one of the greatest saints. He mentioned the quality in her which nobody else had noticed—her great capacity to love; and from selling her body she became one of His most loyal followers. Or His treatment of Peter after the resurrection—Peter who had indicated that he would follow Jesus even to death, and then at the precise moment when Jesus needed him most had denied Him three times. Can you imagine what a roasting I would have given to a friend who had left me so badly in the lurch? I would have fairly excoriated him. But Jesus, what does he do? He asks Peter three times whether he loves Him, so that Peter can assert three times that he does, canceling out the threefold denials. And then Jesus gives this fickle, unpredictable Peter a demanding task—He calls him at another point "rock," this most unrocklike creature.

At the Lambeth Conference we had the privilege of listening to some outstanding devotional addresses, some of the best being by Anthony Bloom, the Orthodox master of the spiritual life. He told us at one point the story of a simple Russian country priest who was confronted by an eminent scientist. This chap trotted out apparently devastating arguments against the existence of God and declared, "I don't believe in God." The unlettered priest retorted quickly, "Oh, it doesn't matter—God believes in you." That is what Jesus says to me—God believes in you. St. Paul never ceased to marvel at the Good News of God's unmerited love for us. He described some of what God had done for us—that in baptism we had died and been buried with Christ, that we had risen to a new life of righteousness with Him. Not only that, but that we had already ascended with Christ and staggeringly, unbelievably, we were already reigning with Jesus at the right hand of the Father. Can you believe that—you and I are, despite all appearances to the contrary, princes and princesses together with Christ.

You know, students sometimes don't know the answers to exam questions (not you here!) and they produce those gems called howlers. Once in a scripture exam the students were asked, "What did John the Baptist say to Jesus when He came to be baptized?" Well this chap (I don't think it was a chappess) did not know the answer but was going to give a shot at it, and wrote, "John the Baptist said to Jesus 'Remember you are the Son of God and behave like one!' "

Well, remember you are princes and princesses, God's loved ones— behave like one.

University of Natal, Durban
6 and 7 August 1981

Peter J. Gomes

1942–

The university sermon has been a staple of preaching as long as there have been universities. The medieval masters of theology in Paris, Bologna, Oxford—all had clerical status and deemed priestly preaching an integral part of their vocations as teachers and interpreters of holy truth. In every century since, sermons momentous—as well as sermons needlessly pedantic—have been delivered from the university pulpit: Thomas Aquinas at Paris, Isaac Barrow at Cambridge, Ralph Waldo Emerson at Harvard, John Henry Newman at Oxford, Karl Barth at the University of Basel, to name only a few here present in this volume.

All good preachers look to their predecessors with admiration and for inspiration. It is no surprise that one model for a modern preacher like the Reverend Professor Peter Gomes of Harvard University's Memorial Church would be John Henry Newman. The latter's title for his collected preachings was *Plain and Parochial Sermons*. Gomes particularly admires the plain part of Newman's preaching because, by drawing less attention to the preacher, it serves to draw more attention to the Word of God. Gomes, a Baptist with Episcopal leanings and Newman an Anglican drawn to Roman Catholicism, would seem to have much in common.

The audience for campus worship to whom Gomes directs his words is deemed by him as largely untrained in (a) church history, (b) theology, or even (c) the actual experience of listening to thoughtful preaching. Yet far from seeing these circumstances as glum and discouraging, he detects instead a great opportunity to bring about a fundamental change of heart in his auditors. The proof of his Harvard pudding is in his growing national status in America as a preacher for our times—witty, empathetic, grounded, and able to provide solid theology in palatable form.

Gomes was born in Boston but raised in the aboriginal New England town of Plymouth, Massachusetts. His mother was a strong churchgoer and musician, so his childhood Sundays passed in Plymouth churches at the morning service of the mostly white First Baptist and the evening service of the Bethel A.M.E. He attempted his first sermon at the age of twelve, but, uncertain of the call, did not begin formal religious training until attending Harvard Divinity School at about age twenty-three.

He playfully refers to himself as an "Afro-Saxon," but in truth he does represent a complex fusion of the best of mainline American Protestantism and, in his person, a special brand of pluralism. Here is his own explanation: "A lot of black preaching is 'tornado' preaching. It relies on vivid word-painting, repetition, and rhythmic alliteration—the click-and-clack phrases that sound like jazz. [Then there is] 'clock preaching' [which he associates with the best English sermons.] It has the precise, elegant form of a clock, . . . I love the splendor of the tickery."

In recent years Reverend Gomes has resumed an encouraging tradition—publishing periodic volumes of his sermons—in his case, annual books that select highlights from the overlapping liturgical and academic calendars. In their pages he can be seen in his pulpit comforting the afflicted and afflicting the comfortable—but always alert to the spiritual movement of his congregation. The example that follows is a short—and plain—look at the concept of Christian hope.

The Invisible Reality of Hope

The Fourth Sunday in Lent
Refreshment Sunday
(March 17, 1996)

Now hope that is seen is not hope. For who hopes for what he sees?

ROMANS 8:24

My sermon this morning takes an unusual form: it is in two parts, with the first consisting of these brief comments on the lesson we have just heard from St. Paul's epistle to the Romans, and the second in the form of the motet which we will hear after the offertory. It too is a commentary on St. Paul's epistle to the Romans, and it has the advantage of having been written by the "fifth evangelist," Johann Sebastian Bach. Martin Luther once wrote that he loved music next to God, and that no one who did not love music could know God, which was a creative thought from that dreary old German bore. It was Luther's great misfortune in his life never to have heard Bach: it is our great good fortune on this morning of "Refreshment" to hear in all its glory the gospel according to Bach, in the motet *Jesu, Meine Freude, BVW 227.*

What holds the sermon and the motet together is the great theme of the Christian hope which is at the heart of Paul's epistle. Hope, not optimism, is what Paul is all about here in Romans, and what we are about. This hope is not mere wishful thinking and an aversion to unpleasant facts, for Paul is not interested in some cheap therapeutic notion of mind over matter.

Hope, for Paul, is the result, the consequence, the product, if you will, of an incontestable fact, and that fact is that we live at the level of the spirit and not merely of the flesh. We *exist* at the level of the flesh and in the realm of the material—look around you—but a life, as opposed to merely a living, is lived by the Christian at the level of the spirit. That is what it means to take on a life in the spirit of Christianity, and it is hard because it means that we cannot be seduced by the appearances of reality that would over-whelm us by their delights and pleasures, and we are not to be intimidated by the terrors and troubles of this life. You and I are seduced and intimidated every day in every way.

Remember Madonna, not the blessed Virgin but the professional non-virgin and alleged singer, whose anthem for the greedy nineteen-eighties was *I'm just a material girl in a material world?* Even in our search to acquire, like Midas, the things we acquire are deadly and unspiritual, and even the dimmest of us recognizes the poverty of spirit in a world dominated by the tyranny of "things"; when you have it all and find that you have nothing at all. Remember the conversation after the funeral of Aristotle Onassis, the richest man in the world, when people asked, "How much did he leave?" The answer came back, "Everything." Things dominate the world, things domi-nate the age, things dominate the University. Remember, don't be seduced. The Christian hope of which St. Paul speaks tells us not to be seduced into a false sense of security by the tyranny of things.

By that same hope, we are not to be intimidated by the terrors and troubles of this life. I saw only yesterday in an antique shop in Boston a silken pillow presented to a newborn child in the early days of the nine-teenth century, and in embroidery was written, "Welcome, little stranger, to this world of care." Now you wouldn't find that a fashionable sentiment in natal fashion today, but growing up modern is to find that this world is filled with the means to cut us down to size and to intimidate and inhibit us at every turn. When we discover that war is the rule and peace the excep-tion, that virtue is in short supply and intelligence even more so, that Thomas Hobbes has more to offer about the nature of human existence than Kahlil Gibran, then, if we are not careful, we are driven to drink, to drugs, to depression, and to despair; and in order to "get along," as Sam Rayburn used to say, we "go along." The English weatherpeople have it right when they say that "there may be sunspots," when with the same climate configu-ration our weatherpeople say that "there may be showers."

None of this is news, none of this is new, and this dilemma is not new: there has always been enough mendacity and mediocrity to go around. This is the substance of the material world: this is what St. Paul means by the word "flesh."

The spirit, however, is another matter, another realm not opposite to "reality" as we define it but the only reality that there really is. In a world of facts that are fictions and fictions that resemble facts, Christians live by an invisible reality that overcomes seduction and intimidation. To live in such a world as this as a Christian is to affirm that this world alone cannot and must not define by itself who you are. If you let the world define you, you are dead, and that is all there is to it. If you let the spirit define you, you have a life that even death itself cannot intimidate or extinguish. To live in a visible world by the invisible reality of hope is the most revolutionary and life-giving existence possible, and you do not have to die to live such a life. That is what St. Paul is saying in Romans, and it is the essence of that conviction that Bach captures in his motet. Listen with particularly keen hearts to the chorales, for what you may have missed in Paul, or what you may have missed in me, you will find there. "Hope means expectancy when things are hopeless," wrote G. K. Chesterton; and since things are always and ultimately hopeless, hope is all that the Christian has and all that the Christian requires.

Let me close with an illustration that you may find peculiar. In Plymouth, my home, there stands a splendid eighteenth-century house on North Street, the Edward Winslow House, built in 1744 in England and taken apart in England, its parts numbered, and shipped across the Atlantic to be re-erected in Plymouth—which probably qualifies it as America's oldest prefabricated house. It has many features, but its most splendid one and the one which appealed to me even as a young boy, is a double-wing staircase in the front hall that flies as if by magic up the center of the house, with no pillars, no walls, and no braces to support it. It looks like a glorious bird, and the guides in the house point out this quite remarkable architectural feature, and ask the visitor, "Do you know what this type of staircase is called?" No one really does, so they pause, then give this delicious answer, a lovely one, I think: "This staircase is called a *vagrant* staircase, because it is sustained by no visible means of support."

Christians are vagrants sustained by no visible means of support but only by the invisible reality of hope, and for that we thank God.

Let us pray:

We thank Thee, O God, for the invisible lifeline that sustains us amid the temptations and trials and anxieties of this life. Let us affirm that hope which is Thy gift to us through Jesus Christ our Lord. Amen.

Acknowledgments and Sources

Acknowledgments

The greatest source of encouragement for us to complete this project was the positive reaction it evoked whenever the subject came up. The recollections so many people shared with us of good preaching remembered from their own past made the yoke of hunting down and the burden of gathering these sermons light indeed. This book came together largely from the resources of the Burke Library at Union Theological Seminary and the libraries of Columbia University, the Quinn Library of Fordham University, Jewish Theological Seminary, and the Osborne Collection of Yale University Library.

Many individuals provided generous help and advice to get the project done: Seth Kasden, Milton Gatch, and the always friendly staff of the Burke Library at Union Theological Seminary, as well as many who offered support, interest, enthusiasm, and sometimes all three: Rev. Peter Bannan, Marybeth Berlemann, Rev. Msgr. Myles M. Bourke, the late Rev. Raymond Brown, Rev. Joan Brown Campbell, Loretta Chan, Fred Courtright, Roger Deakins, Mark Ellingsen, David C. Ford, Harold Grabau, Allan S. Halpern, Dr. Susan Karen Hedahl, Francine Klagsbrun, Richard Lischer, Phillip Lopate, Laurie Mahler, George M. Marsden, Ada Muellner, Marygrace Peters, OP, Rev. Msgr. John Quinn, Don Reynolds, Rev. John E. Rotelle, O.S.A., John Rousmaniere, Samara Rubenstein, Raymond P. Scheindlin, Gilbert Sewall, Bruce E. Shields, David R. Slavitt, Rev. Gerard Sloyan, James Tetreault, Trish Todd, Mark Valeri, Susan B. Varenne, Elizabeth Walter, Michael Washburn, Will Alexander Washburn, William H. Willimon, and Linda Young.

Special thanks are due to our literary agent, Joe Spieler, whose steady hand steered the project through weather occasionally foul and occasionally becalmed; to our publisher, Eric Major, an Englishman possessed of two admirable gifts—patience and excellent taste in preachers and preaching; and finally, from John Thorton, to Katharine Thornton, a wife whose encouragement and forbearance I have drawn on in prodigal fashion. I hope she will see this book as a down payment on a debt quite impossible to repay; and from Katharine Washburn to Michael and Will Washburn for manuscript and the fetching and return of library books.

Sources

I. THE APOSTOLIC ERA

Jesus of Nazareth. "The Sermon on the Mount," from *The Holy Bible* . . . *King James Version, 1611,* Matthew 5:3–8:1. New York: American Bible Society, n.d.

St. Peter. "The Pentecost Sermon," from *The Holy Bible . . . King James Version, 1611,* Acts 2:14b–39. New York: American Bible Society, n.d.

St. Paul. "At Antioch and Athens," from *The Holy Bible . . . King James Version, 1611,* Acts 13:16–41, 17:22–31. New York: American Bible Society, n.d.

Clement of Rome. "Christ and the Church," from *Great Sermons of the World,* pp. 25–35. Edited by Rev. Clarence Edward McCartney, D.D. Boston: Stratford Company, 1926.

II. THE CHURCH FATHERS

Origen. "Exodus Homily 3," from *Origen: Homilies on Genesis and Exodus,* pp. 248–59. Translated by Ronald E. Heine. Copyright © 1982 by Catholic University of America Press, Inc. Reprinted with the permission of the publishers.

St. John Chrysostom. "Homily 20," from *Saint Chrysostom: Homilies on Galatians . . . and Philemon,* Vol. XIII of A Select Library of the Nicene and Post-Nicene Fathers of the Christian Church, 14 vols. Edited by Philip Schaff. Grand Rapids, Mich.: Wm. B. Eerdmans, 1978–79, pp. 143, 144, 145–46, 148, 151, 152.

St. Basil The Great. "Homily 7: On the Creation of Crawling Creatures," from *Saint Basil: Exegetic Homilies,* pp. 105–16. Translated by Sister Agnes Clare Way. Copyright © 1963 by Catholic University of America Press, Inc. Reprinted with the permission of the publishers.

St. Ambrose. "On the First Day of Creation," from *Saint Ambrose: Hexameron, Paradise, and Cain and Abel,* pp. 3–16. Translated by John J. Savage. Copyright © 1961 and renewed 1980 by Fathers of the Church, Inc. Reprinted with the permission of Catholic University of America Press, Inc.

St. Augustine of Hippo. "To the Newly Baptized—on the Eucharist," from *Selected Easter Sermons of Saint Augustine,* pp. 109–11. Edited by Philip T. Weller. Copyright © 1959. Reprinted with the permission of Crossroad Publishing Company.

"On Charity" ("Sermon 350: On Charity"), from *The Works of Saint Augustine: Sermons,* Vol. 10, pp. 107–9. Translation and notes by Edmund Hill. Copyright © 1995 by Augustinian Heritage Institute. Reprinted with the permission of New City Press. All rights reserved.

St. Gregory the Great. "Homily 25," from *Forty Gospel Homilies,* pp. 187–99. Translated by Dom David Hurst. Copyright © 1990 by Cistercian Publications, Inc. Reprinted with the permission of the publishers.

III. THE MEDIEVAL PULPIT

St. Patrick. "A Slave in Ireland," from *Celtic Fire: The Passionate Religious Vision of Ancient Britain and Ireland,* pp. 28–35. Edited by Robert van de Weyer. Copyright © 1990 by Robert van de Weyer. Reprinted with the permission of Doubleday, a division of Random House, Inc., and Darton, Longman, & Todd, Ltd.

Caesarius of Arles. "On the Beginning of Lent," from *Saint Caesarius of Arles: Sermons,* Vol. 3, pp. 41–44. Translated by Sister Mary Magdalene Mueller. Washington, D.C.: Fathers of the Church, 1956. Copyright © 1956 by Fathers of the Church, Inc., and renewed 1984 by Sister M. Magdalene Mueller. Reprinted with the permission of Catholic University of America Press, Inc.

The Venerable Bede. "The Meeting of Mercy and Justice," from *Great Sermons of the World,* pp. 61–65. Edited by Rev. Clarence Edward McCartney, D.D. Boston: Stratford Company, 1926.

Anonymous. "Homily 2: The End of the World," from *The Vercelli Book Homilies: Translations from the Anglo-Saxon,* pp. 27–30. Translated by James Schonewise. Copyright © 1991 by University Press of America, Inc. Reprinted with the permission of the publishers.

St. Bernard of Clairvaux. "Various Meanings of the Kiss," from *Bernard of Clairvaux: Selected Works*, pp. 8–15. Translated by G. R. Evans. Copyright © 1987 by Gillian R. Evans. Reprinted with the permission of Paulist Press.

Hildegard of Bingen. "Vision Seven: The Devil," from *Hildegard of Bingen*, pp. 293–303. Translated by Columba Hart and Jane Bishop. Copyright © 1991 by the Abbey of Regina Laudis: Benedictine Congregation Regina Laudis of the Strict Observance, Inc. Reprinted with the permission of Paulist Press.

St. Francis of Assisi. "St. Francis Preaches to the Birds," from *The Little Flowers of St. Francis*, pp. 28–30. Translated by T. W. Arnold. London: J. M. Dent, 1904.

St. Thomas Aquinas. "On the Apostles' Creed," from *The Sermon-Conferences of St. Thomas Aquinas on the Apostles' Creed*, pp. 79, 81, 83, 85, 153, 155, 157, 159. Edited and translated by Nicholas Ayo. Copyright © 1988 by University of Notre Dame Press. Reprinted with the permission of the publishers.

Meister Johannes Eckhart. "The Feast of the Holy Trinity," from *Meister Eckhart: Teacher and Preacher*, pp. 207–11. Edited and translated by Bernard McGinn. Copyright © 1986 by Bernard McGinn. Reprinted with the permission of Paulist Press.

Thomas à Kempis. "Taking up the Cross," from *Great Sermons of the World*, pp. 69–76. Edited by Rev. Clarence Edward McCartney, D.D. Boston: Stratford Company, 1926.

Jacob Anatoli. "On Proverbs" ("A Homily on Education"), from *Jewish Preaching, 1200–1800: An Anthology*, pp. 113–23. Edited by Marc Saperstein. Copyright © 1989 by Yale University Press.

IV. REBIRTH, REFORM, AND COUNTER REFORM

St. John Fisher. "Dependence upon Divine Mercy," from *English Prose: Selections*, Vol. I, *Fourteenth to Sixteenth Century*, pp. 143–45. Edited by Henry Craik. New York and London: Macmillan, 1916.

Martin Luther. "Sermon on the Raising of Lazarus," from *Luther's Works*, Vol. 51, *Sermons*, I, pp. 44–49. Edited and translated by John Doberstein. Copyright © 1959 by Fortress Press. Reprinted with the permission of Augsburg Fortress Press.

Hugh Latimer. "Sermon of the Plow," from *In God's Name: Examples of Preaching in England from the Act of Supremacy to the Act of Uniformity, 1534–1662*, pp. 12–13. Edited by John Chandos. Indianapolis, Ind. Bobbs-Merrill Company, 1971.

"Duties and Respect of Judges," from *English Prose: Selections*, Vol. I, *Fourteenth to Sixteenth Century*, pp. 229–32. Edited by Henry Craik. New York and London: Macmillan, 1916. (Reprint, New York: AMS Press, n.d.)

John Calvin. "I Know My Redeemer Lives" ("Sermon 8: I Know My Redeemer Lives"), from *Sermons from Job*, pp. 105–19. Selected and translated by Leroy Nixon. Copyright 1952 and renewed © 1980 by Wm. B. Eerdmans Publishing Company. Reprinted with the permission of the publishers.

John Knox. "O Lord Our God, Other Lords Besides Thee Have Ruled Us," from *The Works of John Knox*, Vol. 6, pp. 233–39. Edited by David Laing. Edinburgh, Scotland, Bannatyne Club, 1864. (Reprint, New York: AMS Press, 1966.)

V. THE SEVENTEENTH CENTURY

Lancelot Andrewes. "A Cold Coming," from *In God's Name: Examples of Preaching in England from the Act of Supremacy to the Act of Uniformity, 1534–1662*, pp. 229–31. Edited by John Chandos. Indianapolis: Bobbs-Merrill Company, 1971.

John Donne. "Death's Duel," from *The Sermons of John Donne*, pp. 261–83. Edited by Theodore A. Gill. New York: Living Age Books (Meridian Books), 1958.

William Perkins. "The Good Witch Must Also Die," from *In God's Name: Examples of Preaching in England from the Act of Supremacy to the Act of Uniformity, 1534–1662*, pp. 132–35. Edited by John Chandos. Indianapolis, Ind.: Bobbs-Merrill Company, 1971.

Thomas Grantham. "A Wife Mistaken, or a Wife and No Wife," from *In God's Name: Examples of Preaching in England from the Act of Supremacy to the Act of Uniformity, 1534–1662*, pp. 377–83. Edited by John Chandos. Indianapolis, Ind.: Bobbs-Merrill Company, 1971.

Jeremy Taylor. "Lust for Revenge," from *In God's Name: Examples of Preaching in England from the Act of Supremacy to the Act of Uniformity, 1534–1662*, pp. 486–88. Edited by John Chandos. Indianapolis, Ind.: Bobbs-Merrill Company, 1971.

William Laud. "The Last Words of the Archbishop of Canterbury," from *In God's Name: Examples of Preaching in England from the Act of Supremacy to the Act of Uniformity, 1534–1662,* pp. 415–19. Edited by John Chandos. Indianapolis, Ind.: Bobbs-Merrill Company, 1971.

John Bunyan. "Mr. Bunyan's Last Sermon," from *The Works of That Eminent Servant of Christ, John Bunyan, Minister of the Gospel,* Vol. I, pp. 281–83. Philadelphia, 1870.

Isaac Barrow. "Of Submission to the Divine Will," from *Selected English Sermons: Sixteenth to Nineteenth Centuries,* pp. 167–84. Edited by Hensley Henson. London: Oxford University Press, 1939.

Jacques Bénigne Bossuet. "Funeral Oration for Louis Bourbon, Prince of Condé," from *Great Sermons of the World,* pp. 109–25. Edited by Rev. Clarence Edward McCartney, D.D. Boston: Stratford Company, 1926.

Saul Levi Morteira. "Second Farar Eulogy: 'The Tsaddiq Is Lost,' " from *"Your Voice Like a Ram's Horn": Themes and Texts in Traditional Jewish Preaching,* pp. 387–98. Edited by Marc Saperstein. Reprinted with the permission of Hebrew Union College Press, Cincinnati, Ohio, 1996.

VI. COLONIAL AMERICA

John Winthrop. "A Model of Christian Charity," from *Winthrop Papers,* Vol. II, 1623–1630, pp. 282–95. Boston: Massachusetts Historical Society, 1931.

Cotton Mather. "Thanksgiving," from *The Wonderful Works of God Commemorated . . . a Thanksgiving Sermon.* Boston, 1690.

Jonathan Edwards. "Sinners in the Hands of an Angry God," from *Jonathan Edwards: Basic Writings,* pp. 150–67. Edited by Ola Elizabeth Winslow. New York: New American Library, (Meridian Books), 1966.

VII. EIGHTEENTH-CENTURY ENGLAND AND EUROPE

John Tillotson. "Against Evil-Speaking," from *The Golden Book of Tillotson: Selections from the Writings of the Rev. John Tillotson, D.D., Archbishop of Canterbury,* pp. 46–58. Edited by James Moffatt. London: Hodder and Stoughton, 1926.

Jonathan Swift. "Upon Sleeping in Church," from *Irish Tracts, 1720–1723, and*

Sermons, pp. 210–18. Edited by Louis Landa. Oxford: Basil Blackwell, 1948.

Laurence Sterne. "The Prodigal Son," from *The English Sermon,* 3 vols., Vol. III: 1750–1850, pp. 80–86. Edited by Robert Nye. Cheadle Hulme, England: Carcanet, 1976.

Samuel Johnson. "All Is Vanity," from *The Yale Edition of the Works of Samuel Johnson,* Vol. XIV, pp. 127–36. Edited by Jean Hagstrum and James Gray. New Haven, Conn., and New York: Yale University Press, 1978.

John Wesley. "The Great Assize," from *Great Sermons of the World,* pp. 191–207. Edited by Rev. Clarence Edward McCartney, D.D. Boston: Stratford Company, 1926.

Charles Wesley. "Awake, Thou That Sleepest," a sermon preached on Sunday, April 4, 1742, before the Oxford University community, London, 1742.

Rabbi Nachman of Bratislava. "The Lost Princess," from Meyer Levin's *Classic Hassidic Tales,* pp. 190–97. New York: Penguin, 1975. First published as *The Golden Mountain* (1932). Copyright 1932, © 1975 by Meyer Levin. Reprinted with the permission of the author's estate and its agents, Scott Meredith Literary Agency, L.P.

Ezekiel Landau. "Eulogy for Empress Maria Theresa," from *"Your Voice Like a Ram's Horn": Themes and Texts in Traditional Jewish Preaching,* pp. 455–68. Edited by Marc Saperstein. Reprinted with the permission of Hebrew Union College Press, Cincinnati, Ohio, 1996.

VIII. THE NINETEENTH CENTURY

Isaac Meier Rothenberg of Ger. "On the Eve of the Day of Atonement" ("A Sermon"), from Martin Buber's *Tales of the Hasidim,* Book 2: *The Later Masters,* pp. 306–7. Translated by Olga Marx. Copyright 1947, 1975 by Schocken Books. Reprinted with the permission of Schocken Books, published by Pantheon Books, a division of Random House, Inc.

St. Jean Baptiste Marie Vianney (The Curé of Ars). "Beware If You Have No Temptations," from *The Sermons of the Curé of Ars,* pp. 94–100. Translated by Una Morrissy. Copyright © 1960 by Henry Regnery Company. Reprinted with the permission of the publishers.

Theodore Parker. "A Sermon of Slavery," from *Sermons in American History: Selected Issues in the American Pulpit, 1630–1967,* pp. 208–18. Edited by DeWitte Holland. Nashville, Tenn.: Abingdon Press, 1971.

Charles Grandison Finney. "Stewardship," from *Great Sermons of the World*, pp. 381–95. Edited by Rev. Clarence Edward McCartney, D.D. Boston: Stratford Company, 1926.

Ralph Waldo Emerson. " 'Pray Without Ceasing,' " from *The Complete Sermons of Ralph Waldo Emerson*, Vol. 1, pp. 55–62. Edited by Albert J. von Frank. Columbia, Mo.: University of Missouri Press, 1989.

Henry Ward Beecher. "Spared!" from *Great Sermons of the World*, pp. 497–510. Edited by Rev. Clarence Edward McCartney, D.D. Boston: Stratford Company, 1926.

Gerard Manley Hopkins. "And Joseph and His Mother Marveled," from *The Sermons and Devotional Writings of Gerard Manley Hopkins*, pp. 34–38. Edited by Christopher Devlin, S.J. London: Oxford University Press, 1959.

John Henry Newman. "The Powers of Nature," from *Selected Sermons*, pp. 146–51. Edited by Ian Ker. New York: Paulist Press, 1994.

"Holiness Necessary for Future Blessedness," from *Parochial and Plain Sermons*, pp. 5–13. San Francisco: Ignatius Press, 1997.

John J. Jasper. "De Sun Do Move," from *The Book of Negro Folklore*, pp. 225–33. Edited by Langston Hughes and Arna Bontemps. New York: Dodd, Mead, & Co., 1958.

Phillips Brooks. "The Fire and the Calf," from *The Protestant Pulpit: An Anthology of Master Sermons from the Reformation to Our Own Day*, pp. 129–37. Edited by Andrew Watterson Blackwood. New York and Nashville, Tenn.: Abingdon Press, 1947.

Dwight Lyman Moody. "Come," from *The Best of D. L. Moody*, pp. 163–77. Edited by Wilbur Smith. Chicago: Moody Press, 1971.

Sabine Baring-Gould. "Perseverance," from *Sermons to Children*, pp. 50–60. London, 1882.

William Jennings Bryan. "God and Evolution," from *Sermons in American History: Selected Issues in the American Pulpit, 1630–1967*, pp. 262–70. Edited by DeWitte Holland. Nashville, Tenn.: Abingdon Press, 1971.

IX. THE TWENTIETH CENTURY

Billy Sunday. "Heaven," from *The Protestant Pulpit: An Anthology of Master Sermons from the Reformation to Our Own Day*, pp. 144–46. Edited by Andrew Watterson Blackwood. New York and Nashville, Tenn.: Abingdon Press, 1947.

Dietrich Bonhoeffer. "The Judas Sermon," from *Dietrich Bonhoeffer: Selected Writings*, pp. 77–81. Edited by Edwin Robertson. Copyright © 1995. Reprinted with the permission of HarperCollins Publishers, Ltd.

Ronald Knox. "The Creed in Slow Motion," from *The Creed in Slow Motion*, pp. 142–160. New York: Sheed and Ward, 1949. Copyright 1949 by Sheed & Ward, Inc. Reprinted with the permission of A. P. Watt, Ltd., on behalf of the Earl of Oxford and Asquith.

C. S. Lewis. "Membership," from *The Weight of Glory*, pp. 119–131. Copyright © 1975, 1980 by the Trustees of the Estate of C. S. Lewis. Reprinted with the permission of HarperCollins Publishers, Ltd.

Paul Tillich. "Loneliness and Solitude," from *The Eternal Now*, pp. 15–25. Copyright © 1963 by Paul Tillich, renewed 1991 by Mutie Tillich Rarris. Reprinted with the permission of Scribner's, a division of Simon & Schuster.

Karl Barth. "Saved by Grace," from *Deliverance to the Captives*, pp. 35–42. Copyright © 1961 by SCM Press, Ltd. Reprinted by permission of HarperCollins Publishers, Inc.

Martin Luther King, Jr. "The Dimensions of a Complete Life," from *The Measure of a Man*, pp. 35–56. Philadelphia: Fortress Press, 1988. Copyright © 1959 by Martin Luther King, Jr., renewed 1987 by the Estate of Martin Luther King, Jr. Reprinted with the permission of Writer's House, Inc., on behalf of the proprietors.

Harry Emerson Fosdick. "The Church Must Go Beyond Modernism," from *Successful Christian Living: Sermons on Christianity Today*. Copyright © 1937 by Harry Emerson Fosdick. Reprinted with the permission of HarperCollins Publishers, Inc.

Reinhold Niebuhr. "The Wheat and the Tares," from *Justice and Mercy*. Edited by Ursula M. Niebuhr. Copyright © 1974 by Ursula M. Niebuhr. Reprinted with the permission of the Estates of Reinhold Niebuhr and Ursula Niebuhr.

Harry Wolfson. "The Professed Atheist and the Verbal Theist," from *Religious Philosophy: A Group of Essays*, pp. 270–71. Originally published in the *Harvard Divinity School Bulletin*, 20 (1954–1955). Copyright © 1955 by the President and Fellows of Harvard College. Reprinted with the permission of *Harvard Divinity School Bulletin*. All rights reserved.

Rudolf Bultmann. "This World and the Beyond," from *This World and Beyond:*

Marburg Sermons, pp. 238–48. Copyright © 1960 by Rudolf Bultmann. Reprinted with the permission of Prentice-Hall, Inc., Upper Saddle River, N.J.

Fulton J. Sheen. "The Beatitudes," from *The Electronic Christian: 105 Readings from Fulton J. Sheen,* pp. 33–41. Copyright © 1979. Reprinted with the permission of Simon & Schuster.

Archibald MacLeish. "The Book of Job" ("God Has Need of Man"), from *The Dimensions of Job: A Study and Selected Readings,* pp. 278–86. Edited by Nahum N. Glatzer. New York: Schocken Books, 1969. Copyright © by the Estate of Archibald MacLeish. Reprinted with the permission of the Estate.

Martin Niemöller. "Dachau Sermon: Maundy Thursday, March 29, 1945," from *Dachau Sermons,* pp. 67–79. Translated by Robert H. Pfeiffer. Copyright © 1946 by Harper and Bros. Reprinted with the permission of HarperCollins Publishers, Inc.

C. L. Franklin. "Except I Shall See in His Hands the Print of the Nails and Thrust My Hand into His Side," from *Give Me This Mountain: Life Story and Selected Sermons,* pp. 138–44. Edited by Jeff Todd Titon. Copyright © 1989 by the Board of Trustees of the University of Illinois. Reprinted with the permission of the University of Illinois Press.

Karl Rahner. "All Saints and All Souls Day," from *The Great Church Year: The Best of Karl Rahner's Homilies, Sermons and Meditations,* pp. 366–71. Edited by Albert Raffelt; translation edited by Harvey D. Egan, S.J. Originally published in *The Eternal Year.* Translated by John Shea, S.S. Copyright © 1964. Reprinted with the permission of Crossroad Publishing Company, Inc.

X. LIVING PREACHERS

Billy Graham. "The Prodigal Son," from *The Challenge: Sermons from Madison Square Garden,* pp. 53–69. Reprinted with the permission of the Graham Family Trust.

John Paul II. "Homily at Lourdes," from *Pope John Paul II: Mother of the Church,* pp. 124–30. Edited by Seamus O'Byrne. Cork, Ireland: Mercier Press, 1987. Reprinted with the permission of Fr. Seamus O'Byrne.

Robert Runcie. "Zeebrugge Ferry Disaster," from *One Light for One World,* pp. 77–80. Compiled and arranged by Margaret Pauley. London: SPCK, 1988. Reprinted with the permission of the author.

William Sloane Coffin, Jr. "Alex's Death," from *Sermons from Riverside* (January 23, 1983). Reprinted with the permission of the author.

Frederick Buechner. "The Hungering Dark," from *The Hungering Dark,* pp. 20–29. Copyright © 1969 by Seabury Press. Reprinted with the permission of Crossroad Publishing Company, Inc.

Jean-Marie Lustiger. "The Greatest Saint of Modern Times," from *Dare to Believe: Addresses, Sermons, Interviews, 1981–1984,* pp. 235–41. Translated by Nelly Marans and Maurice Couve de Murville. Copyright © 1986 by Crossroad Publishing. Reprinted with the permission of Crossroad Publishing Company, Inc.

Desmond Tutu. "What Jesus Means to Me," from *Hope and Suffering: Sermons and Speeches,* pp. 136–45. Grand Rapids, Mich.: Wm. B. Eerdmans Publishing Company, 1984. Copyright © 1983 by Desmond Mpilo Tutu. Reprinted by permission of The Right Reverend Desmond Mpilo Tutu.

Peter J. Gomes. "The Invisible Reality of Hope," from *More Sundays at Harvard: Sermons for an Academic Year, 1995–1996,* pp. 101–3. Cambridge, Mass.: Memorial Church, Harvard University. Copyright © 1996 by the President and Fellows of Harvard College. Reprinted by permission.

Bibliography

Just as this book is not meant to be in any way a definitive collection of the world's greatest sermons, so its bibliography is a reflection of the varied sampling of materials its editors found interesting as they went about their researches. It offers leads and openings for the interested reader to pursue his or her own researches into what Edward Charles Dargan (see below) called "the practically infinite quantity of published sermons" and, we can add, the equally practically infinite number of works about preachers, preaching, and the historical background thereof.

Ahlstrom, Sidney E. *A Religious History of the American People.* New Haven, Conn.: Yale University Press, 1972.

Anderson, Gerald H., ed. *Sermons to Men of Other Faiths and Traditions.* Nashville, Tenn.: Abingdon Press, 1966.

Augustine, Saint. *On Christian Teaching.* Translated by R.P.H. Green. New York: Oxford University Press, 1997.

————. *The Works of Saint Augustine, A Translation for the 21st Century.* Gen. ed., John E. Rotelle, trans. by Edmund Hill. Part III: *Homilies,* 10 vols. (of 17 announced). Hyde Park, N.Y.: New City Press, 1990–. An ambitious and worthy project under the auspices of the Augustinian Heritage Institute.

Bainton, Roland H. *Christendom: A Short History of Christianity and Its Impact on Western Civilization.* 2 vols. New York: Harper & Row, 1966. First published in 1964.

————. *Erasmus of Christendom.* New York: Scribner's, 1969.

————. *Here I Stand: A Life of Martin Luther.* Nashville, Tenn.: Abingdon Press, 1978. First published in 1950.

————. *The Reformation of the Sixteenth Century*. Enl. ed. Boston: Beacon Press, 1985. First published in 1952.

Baring-Gould, S. *Post-Mediæval Preachers: Some Account of the Most Celebrated Preachers of the 15th, 16th, & 17th Centuries; with Outlines of Their Sermons, and Specimens of Their Style*. London, 1865.

————. *Sermons to Children*. 3rd ed. London, 1882. A most charming Victorian work.

Barstow, Lewis O. *Representative Modern Preachers*. New York: Macmillan, 1904.

Barth, Karl. *Call for God*. New York: Harper & Row, 1967.

————. *Deliverance to the Captives*. New York: Harper and Bros., 1961.

————. *Homiletics*. Trans. by Geoffrey W. Bromiley and Donald E. Daniels. Louisville, Ky.: Westminster/John Knox Press, 1991.

————. *A Karl Barth Reader*. Rolf Joachim Erler et al., eds. Grand Rapids, Mich.: Wm. B. Eerdmans, 1986.

Baxter, Batsell Barrett. *The Heart of the Yale Lectures*. New York: Macmillan, 1947. An effort to distill the essence of the annual Lyman Beecher Lectureship on Preaching given at Yale University since 1872 and inaugurated by Beecher's son, Henry Ward Beecher, who gave the first three series, 1872–74.

Bayley, Peter. *French Pulpit Oratory, 1598–1650*. Cambridge, England: Cambridge University Press, 1980.

Bennett, R. F. *The Early Dominicans: Studies in 13th Century Dominican History*. New York: Russell and Russell, 1971.

Bernard of Clairvaux, St. *Bernard of Clairvaux: Selected Works*. Trans. by G. R. Evans, Intro. by Jean Leclercq. New York: Paulist Press, 1987.

Blackwood, Andrew Watterson, ed. *The Protestant Pulpit: An Anthology of Master Sermons from the Reformation to Our Own Day*. Nashville, Tenn.: Abingdon-Cokesbury Press, 1947.

Blench, J. W. *Preaching in England in the Late Fifteenth and Sixteenth Centuries: A Study of English Sermons, 1450–c. 1600*. New York: Barnes & Noble, 1964.

Bokenkotter, Thomas. *A Concise History of the Catholic Church*. Rev. ed. New York: Doubleday Image Books, 1978.

Brastow, Lewis O. *Representative Modern Preachers*. London: Macmillan, 1904.

Brilioth, Yngve. *A Brief History of Preaching*. Trans. by Karl E. Mattson.

Philadelphia: Fortress Press, 1965. (First ed. in Swedish, 1945.) Though a half century old, this comprehensive account of the subject holds up remarkably well and is perhaps the best short introduction to it.

Brooks, Phillips. *On Preaching.* London: S.P.C.K., 1964. Originally given in 1877 as the annual Lyman Beecher Lectureship on Preaching at Yale University.

———. *Selected Sermons.* Edited by William Scarlett. New York: E. P. Dutton, 1950.

Brown, Peter. *Augustine of Hippo: A Biography.* Berkeley and Los Angeles: University of California Press, 1967.

Brown, Raymond E. *An Introduction to the New Testament.* New York: Doubleday, 1997.

Brown, Robert McAfee, ed. *The Essential Reinhold Niebuhr: Selected Essays and Addresses.* New Haven, Conn.: Yale University Press, 1986.

Buechner, Frederick. *The Hungering Dark.* New York: Seabury Press, 1969.

———. *The Magnificent Defeat.* New York: Seabury Press, 1988.

Bultmann, Rudolf. *This World and Beyond: The Marburg Sermons.* Trans. by H. Knight. New York: Scribner's, 1960.

Caesarius of Arles, Saint. *Sermons.* Trans. by Mary Magdalene Mueller. Washington, D.C.: Catholic University of America Press, 1956.

Calvin, John. *Sermons from Job.* Selected and trans. by Leroy Nixon. Grand Rapids, Mich.: Wm. B. Eerdmans, 1952.

Carroll, Thomas, K. *Preaching the Word.* Vol. 11, Message of the Fathers of the Church series, Thomas Halton, gen. ed. Wilmington, Del.: Michael Glazier, 1984.

Chadwick, Henry. *Augustine.* Oxford, England: Oxford University Press, 1986; reissued, 1996.

———. *The Early Church.* London: Penguin Books, 1990. First published in 1964.

Chadwick, Owen. *From Bossuet to Newman.* 2nd ed. New York: Cambridge University Press, 1987.

———. *The Reformation.* London: Penguin, 1990. First published in 1964.

———. *The Secularization of the European Mind in the Nineteenth Century.* Cambridge: Cambridge University Press, Canto ed., 1990. First published in 1975.

———. *Western Asceticism.* Library of Christian Classics, Ichthus ed. Philadelphia: Westminster Press, 1958.

Chandos, John, ed. *In God's Name: Examples of Preaching in England from the Act of Supremacy to the Act of Uniformity, 1534–1662.* Indianapolis, Ind.: Bobbs-Merrill Company, 1971.

Chaunu, P., ed. *The Reformation.* New York: St. Martin's Press, 1990.

Chesterton, G. K. *St. Francis of Assisi.* New York: Doubleday Image Books, 1956. First published in 1924.

————. *Saint Thomas Aquinas.* New York: Doubleday Image Books, 1966. First published in 1933.

Coffin, William Sloane, Jr. *The Courage to Love.* San Francisco: Harper & Row, 1984.

————. *Once to Every Man: A Memoir.* New York: Atheneum, 1977.

————. *Sermons from Riverside,* November 6, 1977–November 29, 1987. New York: Riverside Church, 1977–1987.

Cole, Penny J. *The Preaching of the Crusades to the Holy Land, 1095–1270.* Cambridge, Mass.: Medieval Academy of America, 1991.

Conway, James S. "Protestantism and the Holocaust," article in *The Yale University Encyclopedia of the Holocaust.* New Haven, Conn.: Yale University Press, forthcoming in 2000.

Cox, J. Charles. *Pulpits, Lecterns, & Organs in English Churches.* London: Oxford University Press, 1915.

Cox, James W., ed. *Best Sermons 7.* San Francisco: HarperSanFrancisco, 1994. The last vol. in a series devoted to annual compilations of excellent American preaching.

————. *Preaching: A Comprehensive Approach to the Design and Delivery of Sermons.* San Francisco: Harper & Row, 1985.

————. *The Twentieth-Century Pulpit.* Nashville, Tenn.: Abingdon Press, 1978.

Cragg, Gerald R. *The Church and the Age of Reason, 1648–1789.* London: Penguin, 1990. First published in 1960.

Crocker, Lionel, ed. *Harry Emerson Fosdick's Art of Preaching.* Springfield, Ill.: Charles C. Thomas, 1971.

Dargan, Edwin Charles. *A History of Preaching.* Vol. I: *From the Apostolic Fathers to the Great Reformers, A.D. 70–1572;* Vol. II: *From the Close of the Reformation Period to the End of the Nineteenth Century, 1572–1900.* Grand Rapids, Mich.: Baker Book House, 1954. (Originally 2 vols.; reprinted as 2 vols. in 1; see also Turnbull, below.) Dargan (1852–1930) was Professor of

Homiletics at Southern Baptist Theological Seminary in Louisville, Kentucky.

Davies, Alfred T., ed. *The Pulpit Speaks on Race*. Nashville, Tenn.: Abingdon Press, 1965.

Davis, Gerald L. *I Got the Word in Me and I Can Sing It, You Know: A Study of the Performed African-American Sermon*. Philadelphia: University of Pennsylvania Press, 1985.

Demaray, Donald E. *Pulpit Giants: What Made Them Great*. Chicago: Moody Press, 1973.

Dick, Oliver Lawson, ed. *Aubrey's Brief Lives*. London: Mandarin, 1992. 1st ed., 1949. John Aubrey (1625–1697) compiled dozens of vols. of life sketches of his contemporaries, including many notable clergymen, most of which were not transcribed for publication until the late nineteenth century.

Dickens, A. G. *The Counter Reformation*. New York: Harcourt, Brace & World, 1969.

Dix, Gregory. *The Shape of the Liturgy*. 2nd ed. Westminster, England: Dacre Press, 1945.

Dodd, C. H. *The Apostolic Preaching and Its Development. Three Lectures*. New York: Harper and Bros., 1936.

Duffy, Eamon. *The Stripping of the Altars: Traditional Religion in England, c. 1400–c. 1580*. New Haven, Conn.: Yale University Press, 1992.

Dunelm, Herbert, ed. *Selected English Sermons: Sixteenth to Nineteenth Centuries*. London: Oxford University Press, 1939.

Dunn, Richard S., and Laetitia Yeandle, eds. *The Journal of John Winthrop, 1630–1649*. Abr. ed. Cambridge, Mass.: Belknap Press of Harvard University Press, 1996.

Eckhart, Meister. *The Best of Meister Eckhart*. Edited by Halcyon Backhouse. New York: Crossroad, 1992.

Eisenstein, Elizabeth L. *The Printing Revolution in Early Modern Europe*. Cambridge: Cambridge University Press, Canto ed., 1993. First published in 1983.

Emerson, Ralph Waldo. *The Complete Sermons of Ralph Waldo Emerson*. 4 vols. Vol. 1, edited by Albert J. von Frank. Columbia, Mo.: University of Missouri Press, 1989.

Endo, Shusako. *A Life of Jesus.* Trans. by Richard A. Schuchert, S.J. New York: Paulist Press, 1978. First published in Japanese in 1973.

Englebert, Omer. *St. Francis of Assisi: A Biography.* 2nd Eng. ed., rev. Ann Arbor, Mich.: Servant Books, 1979. First published in 1965.

Fant, Clyde E., and William M. Pinson, eds. *20 Centuries of Great Preaching: An Encyclopedia of Preaching.* 20 vols. Waco, Texas: Word Books, 1971. Contains many standard examples of historical preaching and biographical sketches of respective preachers.

Farmer, David Albert, and Edwina Hunter, eds., *And Blessed Is She: Sermons by Women.* New York: Harper & Row, 1990.

Fox, Richard. *Reinhold Niebuhr: A Biography.* New York: Pantheon Books, 1986.

Franklin, C. L. *Give Me This Mountain: Life History and Selected Sermons.* Edited by Jeff Todd Titon. Urbana, Ill.: University of Illinois Press, 1989.

Frazier, E. Franklin. *The Negro Church in America.* New York: Schocken Books, 1964.

Gamble, Harry Y. *Books and Readers in the Early Church: A History of Early Christian Texts.* New Haven, Conn.: Yale University Press, 1995.

Gaustad, Edwin Scott. *A Religious History of America.* New, rev. ed. San Francisco: HarperSanFrancisco, 1990. First published in 1966.

Graham, Billy. *Just as I Am: The Autobiography of Billy Graham.* New York: HarperPaperbacks, 1998. First published in 1997.

Gregory the Great. *Forty Gospel Homilies.* Trans. by Dom David Hurst. Kalamazoo, Mich.: Cistercian Publications, 1990.

Hambrick-Stowe, Charles E. *The Practice of Piety: Puritan Devotional Discipline in Seventeenth Century New England.* Chapel Hill, N.C.: University of North Carolina Press, 1982.

Herbermann, Charles G., et al., eds. "Homily" and "Homiletics," Vol. 7, *The Catholic Encyclopedia.* 15 vols. New York: Robert Appleton, 1910.

Hexter, J. H. *The Judaeo-Christian Tradition.* 2nd ed. New Haven, Conn.: Yale University Press, 1995. First published in 1966.

Hibbs, Ben, ed. *White House Sermons.* Intro. by President Richard Nixon. New York: Harper & Row, 1972.

Hill, Christopher. *The English Bible and the Seventeenth-Century Revolution.* London: Penguin, 1994. First published in 1993.

————. *The World Turned Upside Down: Radical Ideas During the English Revolution*. London: Penguin, 1991. First published in 1972.

Hillerbrand, Hans J., ed. "Preaching and Sermons," Vol. 3, *The Oxford Encyclopedia of the Reformation*. 4 vols. New York: Oxford University Press, 1996.

Hirsch, Rudolf. *Printing, Selling, and Reading, 1450–1550*. Wiesbaden, Germany: Harrassowitz, 1967.

Holland, DeWitte T. *The Preaching Tradition: A Brief History*. Nashville, Tenn.: Abingdon Press, 1980.

————, ed. *Sermons in American History: Selected Issues in the American Pulpit, 1630–1967*. Nashville, Tenn.: Abingdon Press, 1971.

Hubbard, Dolan. *The Sermon and the African American Literary Imagination*. Columbia, Mo.: University of Missouri Press, 1994.

Hudson, Winthrop S. *Religion in America: An Historical Account of the Development of American Religious Life*. 3rd ed. New York: Scribner's, 1981. First published in 1965.

Hughes, Langston, and Arna Bontemps, eds. *The Book of Negro Folklore*. New York: Dodd, Mead, & Co., 1958.

Hunter, David G., ed. *Preaching in the Patristic Age: Studies in Honor of Walter J. Burghardt, S.J.* New York: Paulist Press, 1989.

Jeffrey, David Lyle, ed. *English Spirituality in the Age of Wesley*. Grand Rapids, Mich.: Wm. B. Eerdmans, 1987.

John, Abbot of Ford. *Sermons on the Final Verses of the Song of Songs*. 7 vols. Trans. by Wendy Mary Beckett, Intro. by Hilary Costello. Kalamazoo, Mich.: Cistercian Publications, 1977–84. If you wondered what Sister Wendy was up to before her art appreciation period . . .

John Chrysostom, St. *Chrysostom and His Message: A Selection from the Sermons of St. John Chrysostom of Antioch and Constantinople*. London: United Society for Christian Literature, 1962.

Jungmann, Joseph A. *The Mass of the Roman Rite: Its Origins and Development*. New York: Benziger Brothers, 1951.

Kempis, Thomas à. *The Imitation of Christ. From the First Edition of an English Translation Made c. 1530 by Richard Whitford*. Edited by Edward J. Klein. New York: Harper and Bros., 1941.

Ker, Ian. *John Henry Newman: A Biography*. New York: Oxford University Press, 1988.

Kerr, Hugh T., and John M. Mulder, eds. *Famous Conversions: The Christian Experience.* Grand Rapids, Mich.: Wm. B. Eerdmans, 1994.

Kienzle, Beverly Mayne, and Pamela J. Walker, eds. *Women Preachers and Prophets Through Two Millennia of Christianity.* Berkeley and Los Angeles: University of California Press, 1998.

Klingshirn, William E. *Caesarius of Arles: Life, Testament, Letters.* Vol. 19, Translated Texts for Historians. Liverpool, England: Liverpool University Press, 1994.

Larsen, David L. *The Company of the Preachers: A History of Biblical Preaching from the Old Testament to the Modern Era.* Grand Rapids, Mich.: Kregel Publications, 1998. The most recent attempt at a comprehensive account of preaching.

Latimer, Hugh. *Selected Sermons of Hugh Latimer.* Alan Chester, ed. Charlottesville, Va.: University of Virginia Press, 1968.

Laurence, William B. "The History of Preaching in America," Vol. 1, *Encyclopedia of the American Religious Experience.* 3 vols. Edited by Charles H. Lippy and Peter W. Williams. New York: Scribner's, 1988.

Leclercq, J., F. Vandenbroucke, and L. Bouyer. *The Spirituality of the Middle Ages.* London: Burns & Oates, 1968.

Lesnick, Daniel. *Preaching in Medieval Florence: The Social World of Franciscan and Dominican Spirituality.* Athens, Ga.: University of Georgia Press, 1989.

Lischer, Richard. *The Preacher King: Martin Luther King, Jr., and the Word That Moved America.* New York: Oxford University Press, 1995.

Littell, Franklin H., ed. *Sermons to Intellectuals from Three Continents.* New York: Macmillan, 1963.

Lustiger, Jean-Marie. *The Mass.* Trans. by Rebecca Howell Balinski. San Francisco: Harper & Row, 1987.

McCartney, Clarence Edward, ed. *Great Sermons of the World.* Boston: Stratford Company, 1926.

McGinn, Bernard, gen. ed. *The Classics of Western Spirituality, A Library of the Great Spiritual Masters.* New York: Paulist Press, 1978. A successful ongoing series—now nearly a hundred volumes long—that makes readily available a wide variety of selected source materials, including many examples of sermons.

MacLure, Millar. *The Paul's Cross Sermons, 1534–1642.* Toronto: University of

Toronto Press, 1958. A very entertaining and well-researched account of one of English Christendom's most important listening posts during the period of the Reformation.

McLynn, Neil B. *Ambrose of Milan: Church and Court in a Christian Capital.* Vol. XXII, The Transformation of the Classical Heritage series, Peter Brown, gen. ed. Berkeley and Los Angeles: University of California Press, 1994.

McManners, John, ed. *The Oxford Illustrated History of Christianity.* New York: Oxford University Press, 1990.

MacMullen, Ramsay. *Paganism in the Roman Empire.* New Haven, Conn.: Yale University Press, 1981.

Marnell, William H. *Light from the West.* New York: Seabury Press, 1978.

Marty, Martin E. *Pilgrims in Their Own Land: 500 Years of Religion in America.* New York: Penguin, 1985. First published in 1984.

————. *A Short History of Christianity.* Philadelphia: Fortress Press, 1980. First published in 1959.

Matarosso, Pauline, ed. and trans. *The Cistercian World: Monastic Writings of the Twelfth Century.* London: Penguin, 1993.

Maycock, A. L. *The Inquisition from Its Establishment to the Great Schism: An Introductory Study.* Introduction by Father Ronald Knox. New York: Harper and Bros., 1927.

Moody, Dwight L. *The Best of D. L. Moody: Sixteen Sermons by the Great Evangelist.* Wilbur M. Smith, ed. Chicago: Moody Press, 1971.

Moore, George Foot. *Judaism in the First Centuries of the Christian Era: The Age of the Tannaim.* 2 vols. New York: Schocken Books, 1971. First published in 1930.

Moore, R. Laurance. *Selling God: American Religion in the Marketplace of Culture.* New York: Oxford University Press, 1995.

Moorman, John. *A History of the Franciscan Order from Its Origins to the Year 1517.* Oxford: Clarendon Press, 1968.

Newman, John Henry. *Parochial and Plain Sermons.* 8 vols. in 1. San Francisco: Ignatius Press, 1997. Highly recommended.

Newton, Joseph Fort, ed. *If I Had Only One Sermon to Prepare.* New York: Harper and Bros., 1932. A number of well-known preachers of the day, including a young Fulton J. Sheen, talk about how they get a sermon ready for delivery.

Niebuhr, Reinhold. *The Irony of American History.* New York: Scribner's, 1952.

―――. *The Essential Reinhold Niebuhr: Selected Essays and Addresses.* Edited by Robert McAfee Brown. New Haven, Conn.: Yale University Press, 1986.

Nye, Robert. *The English Sermon.* Vol. III: 1750–1850. Cheadle Hulme, England: Carcanet, 1976.

Old, Hughes Oliphant. *The Reading and Preaching of the Scriptures in the Worship of the Christian Church.* Vol. 1, *The Biblical Period;* Vol. 2, *The Patristic Age.* Grand Rapids, Mich.: Wm. B. Eerdmans, 1998.

Olin, John C. *The Catholic Reformation: Savonarola to Ignatius Loyola, Reform in the Church, 1495–1540.* New York: Harper & Row, 1969.

O'Malley, John W. *The First Jesuits.* Cambridge, Mass.: Harvard University Press, 1993.

Osmond, Percy Herbert. *Isaac Barrow, His Life and Times.* London: S.P.C.K., 1944.

Owst, G. R. *Preaching in Medieval England: An Introduction to Sermon Manuscripts of the Period, c. 1350–1450.* Cambridge, England: Cambridge University Press, 1926.

Ozment, Steven. *The Age of Reform, 1250–1550: An Intellectual and Religious History of Late Medieval and Reformation Europe.* New Haven, Conn.: Yale University Press, 1980.

―――. *Protestants: The Birth of a Revolution.* New York: Doubleday Image Books, 1993.

Pennington, M. Basil. *Monastery: Prayer, Work, Community.* San Francisco: Harper & Row, 1983.

Petry, Ray C. *No Uncertain Sound: Sermons That Shaped the Pulpit Tradition.* Philadelphia: Westminster, 1948.

Rahner, Karl. *The Great Church Year: The Best of Karl Rahner's Homilies, Sermons, and Meditations.* New York: Crossroad, 1994. First published in German in 1987.

Ramsey, Boniface. *Ambrose.* New York: Routledge, 1997.

―――. *Beginning to Read the Fathers.* New York: Paulist Press, 1985.

Rosenberg, Bruce A. *Can These Bones Live? The Art of the American Folk Preacher.* Rev. ed. Urbana, Ill.: University of Illinois Press, 1988. First published in 1970.

Roth, Cecil. *A Short History of the Jewish People.* Rev. and enl. illus. ed. Hartford, Conn.: Hartmore House, 1969. First published in 1936.

Runciman, Steven. *The First Crusade.* Cambridge, England: Cambridge University Press, 1980. First published as Vol. 1 of *The History of the Crusades,* 1951.

Saperstein, Marc, ed. *Jewish Preaching, 1200–1800: An Anthology.* New Haven, Conn.: Yale University Press, 1989.

Schleiermacher, Friedrich. *Servant of the Lord: Selected Sermons of Friedrich Schleiermacher.* Philadelphia: Augsburg Fortress Press, 1987.

Seaver, Paul S. *The Puritan Lectureships: The Politics of Religious Dissent, 1560–1662.* Stanford, Calif.: Stanford University Press, 1970.

Simon, Irène. *Three Restoration Divines: Barrow, South, Tillotson. Selected Sermons.* 2 vols., fasc. 181, 213. Liège, Belgium: *Bibliothèque de la Faculté de philosophie et lettres de l'Université de Liège,* 1967–.

Sisson, C. H. *The English Sermon.* Vol. II: 1650–1750. Cheadle Hulme, England: Carcanet, 1976.

Smith, Joseph. *Joseph Smith: Selected Sermons and Writings.* Edited by Robert L. Millet. New York: Paulist Press, 1989.

Southern, R. W. *Western Society and the Church in the Middle Ages.* London: Penguin, 1990. First published in 1970.

Swift, Jonathan, *Irish Tracts and Sermons.* Edited by Louis A. Landa (1948).

Tauler, Johannes. *Johannes Tauler: Sermons.* Trans. by Maria Shrady, Intro. by Josef Schmidt. New York: Paulist Press, 1985.

Taylor, Larissa. *Soldiers of Christ: Preaching in Late Medieval and Reformation France.* New York: Oxford University Press, 1992.

Thomas Aquinas, Saint. *The Sermon Conferences of St. Thomas Aquinas on the Apostles' Creed.* South Bend, Ind.: Notre Dame Press, 1988.

Tillich, Hannah. *From Time to Time.* New York: Stein and Day, 1973. A memoir.

Tillich, Paul. *The New Being.* New York: Scribner's, 1955.

Tillotson, John. *The Golden Book of Tillotson: Selections from the Writings of the Rev. John Tillotson, D.D.* Edited by James Moffatt. London: Hodder and Stoughton, 1926.

Turnbull, Ralph G. *A History of Preaching. Volume III: From the Close of the Nineteenth Century to the Middle of the Twentieth Century (Continuing the Work of*

Volumes I and II by Edwin C. Dargan). Grand Rapids, Mich.: Baker Book House, 1974. (See Dargan above.)

Tyson, John R., ed. *Charles Wesley: A Reader.* New York: Oxford University Press, 1989.

Ugolino di Monte Santa Maria. *The Little Flowers of St. Francis of Assisi.* Trans. by W. Heywood, New York: Vintage Books, 1998. Adapted from a translation first published in 1906.

Washington, James Melvin, ed. *Conversations with God: Two Centuries of Prayers by African Americans.* New York: HarperCollins, 1994.

White, R.E.O. *A Guide to Preaching: A Practical Primer of Homiletics.* London: Pickering & Inglis, 1973.

Williams, William Carlos. *In the American Grain: Essays.* New York: New Directions, 1956.

Willimon, William H., and Richard Lischer, eds. *The Encyclopedia of Preaching.* Louisville, Ky.: Westminster/John Knox Press, 1995. An excellent recent source on a comprehensive variety of historical, biographical, and thematic topics.

Wilson, A. N. *C. S. Lewis: A Biography.* New York: W. W. Norton, 1990.

————. *Paul: The Mind of the Apostle.* New York: W. W. Norton, 1997.

Wyclif, John. *Selected English Works of John Wyclif.* Edited by Thomas Arnold. Vol. 1: *The Sermons of the Gospels for Sundays and Festivals.* Oxford, England: Clarendon Press, 1869.

Zarnecki, George. *The Monastic Achievement.* New York: McGraw-Hill, 1972.

Zawant, Anscar. *The History of Franciscan Preaching and of Franciscan Preachers (1209–1927).* New York: Wagner, 1948.

Zwingli, Ulrich. *Selections.* Trans. by H. Wayne Pipkin. Allison Park, Pa.: Pickwick Publications, 1984.

Index of Preachers

Index of Themes

Sermon main topics are indicated by **bold numerals.** Sermons on specific biblical passages can be found under the main heading Scripture passages, sermons on. Sermons by specific preachers can be found in the Index of Preachers (p. 805). The historical introductions were not indexed.